THE RORSCHACH®

volume

2

{ Advanced Interpretation }

3rd
edition

THE RORSCHACH®

{ A Comprehensive System }

JOHN E. EXNER JR.   PHILIP ERDBERG

WILEY

John Wiley & Sons, Inc.

Contents

Table of Tables   ix

Preface   xiii

PART ONE   GENERAL INTRODUCTION   1

1 | Recent Developments and Interpretive Strategies   3

2 | Rorschach Assessment: A Consultation Model   19

PART TWO   USING THE RORSCHACH IN CLINICAL CONSULTATION AND TREATMENT PLANNING   27

3 | An Issue of Stress Management   29

4 | An Issue of Depression and Suicide Risk   55

5 | An Issue of Panic Attacks   81

6 | An Issue of Delusional Thinking   101

7 | An Issue of Dissociation   123

8 | An Issue of Anxiety and Sleep Problems   149

9 | Issues Regarding an Acute Psychotic Episode   169

10 | An Evaluation Related to Substance Abuse   191

11 | An Issue of Motivation for Substance Abuse Treatment   215

12 | An Issue of Impulse Control   237

13 | Problems with Interpersonal Relations   257

PART THREE   USING THE RORSCHACH IN FORENSIC CONSULTATION   279

14 | An Issue of Danger to the Self or Others   281

15 | Issues of Sanity and Competency   303

16 | Pain Problems in Personal Injury Litigation   323

PART FOUR   USING THE RORSCHACH WITH CHILDREN AND ADOLESCENTS   345

17 | An Issue of Deteriorating Academic Performance   347

18 | A Problem with Aggressiveness   367

19 | Drug Overdose in an Adolescent   389

PART FIVE   THE RORSCHACH AND ISSUES OF IMPRESSION MANAGEMENT   413

20 | Issues of Malingering   415

21 | Simulation of Good Adjustment   441

PART SIX   SOME NEW NONPATIENT DATA   465

22 | Progress in Building a New Nonpatient Sample   467

23 | Frequency Data by Card and Location   479

Author Index   547

Subject Index   553

Table of Tables

Table 1.1	Steps Used to Assign Good (GHR) or Poor (PHR) Designations to Human Representational Responses	6
Table 1.2	Interpretive Search Strategies Based on Key Variables	10
Table 1.3	Search Strategies Based on Tertiary Variables	11
Table 1.4	Order for Reviewing Variables within Each Cluster	16
Table 21.1	Some Frequency Data for 25 Nonpatient Male–Female Pairs Involved in Custody Litigation	443
Table 22.1	Descriptive Statistics for 450 Nonpatient Adults	471
Table 22.2	Demography Data and Frequencies for 36 Variables for 450 Nonpatient Adults	473
Table 22.3	A Comparison of Data for 17 Variables from the 2001 Sample of 600 Nonpatients and 450 Nonpatients from the Current Project	474
Table 23.1	Frequencies for Location Selections by Card for 450 Nonpatients	482
Table 23.2	Frequencies for Location Selections by Card for 1050 Nonpatients	483
Table 23.3	Frequencies and Percentages for DQ Codes by Card for 450 Nonpatients	484
Table 23.4	Frequencies and Percentages for DQ Codes by Card for 1050 Nonpatients	485
Table 23.5	Frequencies and Percentages for Form Quality Codes for 450 Nonpatients	486
Table 23.6	Frequencies and Percentages for Form Quality Codes for 1050 Nonpatients	487
Table 23.7	Card I Frequencies for DQ, FQ, and Blends for 450 Nonpatients (R = 1090)	488
Table 23.8	Card I Frequencies for DQ, FQ, and Blends for 1050 Nonpatients (R = 2437)	488
Table 23.9	Card II Frequencies for DQ, FQ, and Blends for 450 Nonpatients (R = 1070)	489

Table 23.10   Card II Frequencies for DQ, FQ, and Blends for 1050
Nonpatients (R = 2344)   489

Table 23.11   Card III Frequencies for DQ, FQ, and Blends for 450
Nonpatients (R = 927)   490

Table 23.12   Card III Frequencies for DQ, FQ, and Blends for 1050
Nonpatients (R = 1998)   490

Table 23.13   Card IV Frequencies for DQ, FQ, and Blends for 450
Nonpatients (R = 877)   491

Table 23.14   Card IV Frequencies for DQ, FQ, and Blends for 1050
Nonpatients (R = 1948)   491

Table 23.15   Card V Frequencies for DQ, FQ, and Blends for 450
Nonpatients (R = 803)   492

Table 23.16   Card V Frequencies for DQ, FQ, and Blends for 1050
Nonpatients (R = 1859)   492

Table 23.17   Card VI Frequencies for DQ, FQ, and Blends for 450
Nonpatients (R = 891)   493

Table 23.18   Card VI Frequencies for DQ, FQ, and Blends for 1050
Nonpatients (R = 2077)   493

Table 23.19   Card VII Frequencies for DQ, FQ, and Blends for 450
Nonpatients (R = 934)   494

Table 23.20   Card VII Frequencies for DQ, FQ, and Blends for 1050
Nonpatients (R = 2093)   494

Table 23.21   Card VIII Frequencies for DQ, FQ, and Blends for 450
Nonpatients (R = 1073)   495

Table 23.22   Card VIII Frequencies for DQ, FQ, and Blends for 1050
Nonpatients (R = 2495)   495

Table 23.23   Card IX Frequencies for DQ, FQ, and Blends for 450
Nonpatients (R = 1086)   496

Table 23.24   Card IX Frequencies for DQ, FQ, and Blends for 1050
Nonpatients (R = 2464)   496

Table 23.25   Card X Frequencies for DQ, FQ, and Blends for 450
Nonpatients (R = 1761)   497

Table 23.26   Card X Frequencies for DQ, FQ, and Blends for 1050
Nonpatients (R = 4327)   497

Table 23.27   Frequencies and Percentages for Determinant Codes for 450 Nonpatients   499

Table 23.28   Frequencies and Percentages for Determinant Codes for 1050 Nonpatients   500

Table 23.29   Card I Determinant Frequencies for 450 Nonpatients (R = 1090)   502

Table 23.30   Card I Determinant Frequencies for 1050 Nonpatients (R = 2437)   503

Table 23.31   Card II Determinant Frequencies for 450 Nonpatients (R = 1070)   504

Table 23.32   Card II Determinant Frequencies for 1050 Nonpatients (R = 2344)   505

Table 23.33   Card III Determinant Frequencies for 450 Nonpatients (R = 927)   506

Table 23.34   Card III Determinant Frequencies for 1050 Nonpatients (R = 1998)   507

Table 23.35   Card IV Determinant Frequencies for 450 Nonpatients (R = 877)   508

Table 23.36   Card IV Determinant Frequencies for 1050 Nonpatients (R = 1948)   509

Table 23.37   Card V Determinant Frequencies for 450 Nonpatients (R = 803)   510

Table 23.38   Card V Determinant Frequencies for 1050 Nonpatients (R = 1859)   511

Table 23.39   Card VI Determinant Frequencies for 450 Nonpatients (R = 891)   512

Table 23.40   Card VI Determinant Frequencies for 1050 Nonpatients (R = 2077)   513

Table 23.41   Card VII Determinant Frequencies for 450 Nonpatients (R = 934)   514

Table 23.42   Card VII Determinant Frequencies for 1050 Nonpatients (R = 2093)   515

Table 23.43   Card VIII Determinant Frequencies for 450 Nonpatients (R = 1073)   516

Table 23.44   Card VIII Determinant Frequencies for 1050 Nonpatients (R = 2495)   517

Table 23.45   Card IX Determinant Frequencies for 450 Nonpatients (R = 1086)   518

Table 23.46   Card IX Determinant Frequencies for 1050 Nonpatients (R = 2464)   519

Table 23.47   Card X Determinant Frequencies for 450 Nonpatients (R = 1761)   520

Table 23.48   Card X Determinant Frequencies for 1050 Nonpatients (R = 4327)   521

Table 23.49   Frequencies for Content Selections by Card for 450 Nonpatients   522

Table 23.50   Frequencies for Content Selections by Card for 1050 Nonpatients   522

Table 23.51   Card I Content Frequencies for 450 Nonpatients (R = 1090)   524

Table 23.52   Card I Content Frequencies for 1050 Nonpatients (R = 2437)   525

Table 23.53   Card II Content Frequencies for 450 Nonpatients (R = 1070)   526

Table 23.54   Card II Content Frequencies for 1050 Nonpatients (R = 2344)   527

Table 23.55   Card III Content Frequencies for 450 Nonpatients (R = 927)   528

Table 23.56   Card III Content Frequencies for 1050 Nonpatients (R = 1998)   529

Table 23.57   Card IV Content Frequencies for 450 Nonpatients (R = 877)   530

Table 23.58   Card IV Content Frequencies for 1050 Nonpatients (R = 1948)   531

Table 23.59   Card V Content Frequencies for 450 Nonpatients (R = 803)   532

Table 23.60   Card V Content Frequencies for 1050 Nonpatients (R = 1859)   533

Table 23.61   Card VI Content Frequencies for 450 Nonpatients (R = 891)   534

Table 23.62   Card VI Content Frequencies for 1050 Nonpatients (R = 2077)   535

Table 23.63   Card VII Content Frequencies for 450 Nonpatients (R = 934)   536

Table 23.64   Card VII Content Frequencies for 1050 Nonpatients (R = 2093)   537

Table 23.65   Card VIII Content Frequencies for 450 Nonpatients (R = 1073)   538

Table 23.66   Card VIII Content Frequencies for 1050 Nonpatients (R = 2495)   539

Table 23.67   Card IX Content Frequencies for 450 Nonpatients (R = 1086)   540

Table 23.68   Card IX Content Frequencies for 1050 Nonpatients (R = 2464)   541

Table 23.69   Card X Content Frequencies for 450 Nonpatients (R = 1761)   542

Table 23.70   Card X Content Frequencies for 1050 Nonpatients (R = 4327)   543

Preface

A Preface is supposed to introduce a work by offering some hints about what it contains. There seems to be no useful purpose in attempting to do that here because the subtitle *Advanced Interpretation* should suffice, but it may be worthwhile to offer some explanation about why this volume exists. Although it is called *Volume 2,* it is really the ninth volume in the *Comprehensive System* series. Thirty-five years have passed since the decision was made to integrate the empirically defensible components of five major Rorschach Systems into a single, standardized approach to Rorschach's Test. It was decided to call the new approach *A Comprehensive System* because the effort involved the integration of elements from each of the five Systems that had evolved between the mid-1930s and the mid-1950s. The first edition of *Volume 2,* released in 1978, was simply an extension of the first edition of *Volume 1.* It was necessary because *Volume 1* was incomplete, although I did not realize how incomplete when the manuscript for it was finished in late 1973.

The original decision to create the *Comprehensive System* was not reached quickly or easily. Although the actual decision to do it occurred about 35 years ago, the seed for the idea existed well before then. It was more than 50 years ago that I first laid hands on a set of Rorschach blots. I remember it vividly because I was awestruck at the prospect of being permitted into the inner sanctum of clinical psychology. During the next two years, I became even more excited about the test as I served as a summer intern, first with Samuel Beck and then with Bruno Klopfer. There were no limits to my admiration for the seemingly magical ways that they culled information about people from no more than a handful of Rorschach answers. They became two of my professional models, not just because of the wonders they could perform with the Rorschach, but because they were also extraordinarily sensitive about people. At that time, I had no idea about my own future with the test, but I did sense that something was wrong in the world of the Rorschach. This was because of the considerable animosity that Beck and Klopfer conveyed toward each other and because of the markedly different approaches that they used when addressing the data and substance of the test. I was truly baffled when I learned that they had not communicated with each other after 1939. As I studied their disagreements during the middle to late 1950s, my awareness of the need for a standard approach to the Rorschach probably began to develop.

It clearly existed in 1960 when I approached Beck and Klopfer with the grandiose notion of enticing them to permit me to serve in the role of a monitor as they discussed and possibly resolved some of their many differences. They were both kind but firm in their refusals, and the idea might have died then had not Beck added the suggestion that I should write a paper describing the differences between him and Klopfer. When Klopfer cautiously endorsed the notion of comparing his and Beck's work, the seed took on new dimensions.

When I began the comparative analysis in 1961, I envisioned a reasonably long article that would contrast the two approaches, but I found it difficult to write about Klopfer without also mentioning the contributions that Zygmunt Piotrowski had made to Klopfer's approach. Consequently, I began corresponding and meeting with Piotrowski to try to understand why he had broken away from the Klopfer group and ultimately created his own approach to the test. I was also very aware of the contributions of David Rapaport and Roy Schafer and had passing familiarity with some of the work of Marguerite Hertz. Thus, by late 1962, an obvious logical conclusion surfaced. The project should be expanded to compare the work of all five approaches rather than focus exclusively on Beck and Klopfer.

During the next six years, I devoted as much of my free time as possible to the project, which I found very knotty because each of the *Systematizers* often used the same concepts or scoring symbols but with different definitions and/or interpretations. Although it was a laborious task, there were two rewards that more than offset the effort. First, I found myself with a vast bank of knowledge concerning the development and use of the test. Second, and more important, were the delightful personal relationships that I formed with these Rorschach legends. Rapaport died while I was early into the project, so much of his personal input was not to be, but Beck, Hertz, Klopfer, and Piotrowski gave generously to the effort and there is no way to acknowledge the warmth and support that each devoted to the project. Not only were they eager to clarify their own positions, but they also shared many personal and private bits of history to aid in helping me gain a more complete understanding of their work with the test.

As more and more information accumulated, it became easy to understand how many criticisms of the test had originated and how some were clearly justified. When the manuscript, published as *The Rorschach Systems* by Grune & Stratton in 1969, was finished, I arranged for it to be sent to Beck, Hertz, Klopfer, Piotrowski, and Schafer, mainly to ensure that there was no historically incorrect material and to receive some assurance that I had presented their positions fairly and objectively. Klopfer was the first to respond. He was complimentary, suggesting one or two minor changes, but he also expressed some disappointment about the fact that I had drawn no conclusions about the respective merits of the *Systems*. Two days later I met with Beck and heard almost the same commentary, including his sense of disappointment that I had drawn no conclusions.

A few weeks later, the seed of the original idea began to emerge again. I visited Klopfer, and with his usual marvelous sensitivity, he brought up the issue of our mutual disappointment about the lack of conclusions in the book. He said, "but maybe you should look further." On returning to my office a few days later, I found a letter from Beck. In it, he asked if I had any plans to investigate the various *Systems* further in an effort to arrive at the "missing conclusions." Not long thereafter, Piotrowski offered access to his files if I decided to pursue the issue of the missing conclusions further, and Hertz, in her customarily charming manner added to the challenge with the contention that any thorough research concerning the different *Systems* would show that they all reach the same conclusions.

The friendly and sincere encouragement from these Rorschach Godfathers (and Godmother) could not be ignored, and in 1968 the *Rorschach Research Foundation,* which quickly became known as *Rorschach Workshops,* was created. Its purpose was not to integrate, but to find the missing conclusions. Which *System* had the greatest empricial sturdiness? Which *System* had the greatest clinical efficacy? Those were the questions that nourished the seed and caused it to finally sprout. Nearly three years of considerable research ensued, and by late 1970, the results of those early investigations highlighted three inescapable conclusions. First, there were *five* Rorschach tests that were extremely diverse. Second, although each included some highly valuable components, each was also marked by serious liabilities. None was uniformly superior to the others. One might be superior in one area, yet inferior in several other areas. Third, the professional Rorschach community seemed prone to ignore the vast intersystem differences and lay praise or criticism on *The Rorschach* as if only one test existed. Thus, the seed finally blossomed into a decision. Integration of the best of each approach was not only wise, but necessary if the integrity of Rorschach's Test was to be established.

Before the final decision was made, during a two-week period I met with Klopfer, Piotrowski, Beck, and Hertz, in that order. I prefaced my visits with a written communication concerning our findings and included a description of my intentions. Bruno Klopfer was in ill health and we spoke only briefly during a luncheon lovingly prepared by his wife Erna. His words were, "work as you will to find the truth." He died less than a year later, and I have always regretted that I could not share my conclusions with him. Zygmunt Piotrowski was quite enthusiastic and optimistic about the notion of a *Comprehensive System*. He continued to offer suggestions and hypotheses for testing during the first 10 years of our work at *Rorschach Workshops*. Sam Beck was also quite favorable about the project, seemingly delighted that it would provoke a new wave of Rorschach research. Marguerite Hertz, even though skeptical at first, probably offered the greatest emotional support for an integrated approach. After reviewing the findings of our research concerning the *Systems,* she acknowledged that personalities probably played a much more important role in the test development than should have been the case and in her warm but straightforward manner said, "if you can make it better, do the best you can."

Hertz' advice has been a guideline for the development of the *Comprehensive System*. At the onset, I naively assumed that all of the pieces to the puzzle were already in place and the task would be to select those pieces that fit neatly together to make the complete test. It was the product of that selection process that constituted most of the original *Volume 1*. But even as the manuscript was completed, many gaps in information remained obvious. Data for nonpatients were sparse, the new approach contained no special scores, something was not quite right with the form quality definitions, and components of the developmental quality distributions overlapped. And so the research effort continued, provoking additions and changes and the first edition of *Volume 2* was a natural byproduct of the work.

But *Volume 2* also became outdated as new findings accumulated as a result of the efforts of a small army of dedicated and enthusiastic project directors, workshop assistants, and field examiners. Their numbers varied from year to year, ranging from as few as a dozen when the first pieces of the *System* were put into place to nearly 100 during the span of years from 1977 to 1981. Although most all worked on a part time underpaid basis, their productivity exceeded anything that might have been expected. By 1982, the raw data input had far outdistanced data analyses. After the completion of many studies concerning children, including the collection of nearly 2000 records from nonpatient youngsters, *Volume 3* in the series about the *System* was released. Shortly thereafter, the number of data collection projects was scaled back and the focus shifted to a more careful and systematic culling through the large numbers of records that had accumulated from dozens of groups since 1971.

Changes and additions in the *System* have occurred frequently, requiring major revisions of *Volume 1* in 1986, 1993, and 2003. Those changes and additions have had a direct impact on the concepts, strategies, and procedures that are involved as the data of the test are interpreted and findings are integrated. Thus, a second edition of *Volume 2,* focusing mainly on interpretation, was released in 1991 and is updated once again in this book. The bulk of this new work involves the presentation of 21 cases. In an effort to broaden the interpretive basis for each case, a brief literature review of findings relevant to issues raised in the various referrals has also been included prior to the test interpretation, together with a general formulation of the issues concerning the case.

Each case has been selected to illustrate how various findings are woven together to describe the individual. At times, some of the interpretative hypotheses or concepts that are derived from single data points may seem concretely redundant or mechanistic but, as the findings unfold, the results illustrate how the interpretation builds from a series of relatively simplistic postulates into a meaningful and valid idiographic description of the individual. In turn, that psychological picture is used to address issues that are relevant for that person.

Hopefully, this work demonstrates how to use this remarkable test to highlight the unique features of the individual while weighing their assets and liabilities realistically. Experienced Rorschachers are well aware that interpretation is a slow process that requires much attention to detail. It is difficult because of the constant struggle to translate and weave together interpretive findings into statements that are meaningful and not concrete or overgeneralized. Interpretation can also be frustrating because, at times, the data are incomplete and only serve to raise questions that must be addressed from other sources.

Because this work focuses on interpretation, some new data concerning nonpatient response rates have been included in the last two chapters. Chapter 22 represents a progress report concerning a project that began in 1999 designed to collect a new nonpatient sample. While the project is still ongoing, the number of new records (450) has reached a level that permits some meaningful analyses, including comparisons of data from the new sample with those published previously regarding the sample of 600 nonpatients. Chapter 23 consists mainly of a large number of tables containing frequency and proportional data, by card and location areas, for the various components of responses given by nonpatients (location selections, *DQ*, *FQ*, determinants, blends, and contents). One set of tables provides these data for the new sample of 450 nonpatients and a second set of tables includes similar data for the samples of 450 and 600 nonpatients when they are combined. These data sets provide considerable information about the distal features of the 10 figures and especially about some of the critical stimulus bits that appear to be present in each of the 10 fields.

ACKNOWLEGMENTS

Far too many people to list here have been involved in the research effort at *Rorschach Workshops* during the past decade. I hope that they know of my appreciation and affection. The 29 examiners who have participated thus far in the collection of new nonpatient records deserve a very special thanks for their efforts. They have been remarkably dedicated and often very creative in their abilities to recruit subjects and contend with the complexities involved with this arduous project.

Finally, in the *Preface* to the 1978 *Volume 2* I noted, "the test itself continues to pose many mysteries and there is no end in sight to the continuing research needs." Although some of those mysteries have been resolved and many researchers have invested much time and effort studying various aspects of the test, the statement continues to remain true today. To those who will continue to seek out new knowledge about the test and its utility, I again offer a paraphrase of the advice that Klopfer and Hertz gave to me long ago, and that has meant very much to me—go and seek out the truth as best you can and never settle for the pedestrian way.

JOHN E. EXNER JR.

Asheville, North Carolina
April 2005

PART ONE
General Introduction

CHAPTER 1

Recent Developments and Interpretive Strategies

The *Comprehensive System* began to take shape in late 1971. The cumulative findings from a series of studies done between 1967 and 1970 had revealed that, although each of the five markedly different Rorschach systems (Beck, Hertz, Klopfer, Piotrowski, and Rapaport-Schafer) had considerable merit, each also contained features that could not be supported empirically. Consequently, a plan was formulated to integrate the empirically defensible features from each of those approaches into a format that could stand the test of scientific scrutiny and from which research regarding various issues of reliability and validity could proceed.

The first *Comprehensive System* manuscript was completed in late 1973 and published in 1974. It soon became clear, however, that the task was far from complete; what had looked like a fairly straightforward series of decisions in 1973 began to seem more like a never-ending project by 1977. Research completed from 1973 to 1977 suggested that some of the 1973 decisions needed to be revised or expanded, and although many newly completed studies offered clarification and elaboration, they also highlighted areas where further investigation was needed. The first edition of *Volume 2* was completed in late 1977 and published in 1978. It contained an update of research developments, expanded reference data, and some 21 cases illustrating the Rorschach's use with children, adolescents, and adults in a variety of clinical and forensic settings.

Over the next quarter century, the same sequence has repeated itself, now for the third time. A major revision of *Volume 1* was published in 1986, followed in 1990 by the second edition of *Volume 2*. Further revisions of *Volume 1* were released in 1993 and 2003, and this new work is the third edition of *Volume 2*. Like its predecessors, it provides an update: features that have been added to the *Comprehensive System* over the past few years, some new nonpatient reference data, and an extensive series of newly developed tables that detail the frequencies and some proportional data for developmental and form quality, blends, determinants, and contents for every location on every card. And like its predecessors, it contains a wide-ranging series of cases. They attempt to illustrate how the consolidation of accumulated research and experience that now defines the *Comprehensive System* allows empirically anchored personality descriptions that are of practical value in the clinical and forensic settings where assessment psychologists work. The second edition of *Volume 2* introduced the cluster approach, and this new work expands on that strategy for organizing the increasing amount of structural and content data that is available for interpretation. It also introduces a model for providing consultation, presented in Chapter 2, that describes two preliminary steps that can help focus the interpretation. The first involves formulating the case in terms of specific referral questions. The second involves a review of the relevant research literature as a way of directing the psychologist's attention to Rorschach data specifically pertinent for responding to those questions.

Some new features have been added to the *Comprehensive System* in the past few years, and this chapter begins with a description of these developments and their interpretive implications. It concludes with an updated summary of the cluster approach to organizing Rorschach data.

NEW VARIABLES AND INDICES

XA% and *WDA%*

The Extended Form Appropriate (*XA%*) is calculated as the sum of all +, *o,* and *u* responses divided by the total number of responses (*R*). The feature that all +, *o,* and *u* responses share is that they identify objects with characteristics that are appropriate for the chosen locations. The *XA%* provides information about the *source* of a person's data, that is, the proportion of responses guided by a reasonable use of the distal features of the blot. The coding for between 70% and 75% of +, *o,* or *u* responses reflects the fact that the shape of the object reported is generally commensurate with the contours of the location area selected, such as a butterfly to the whole of Card I, two people to the *D9* areas of Card III, or a totem pole to the *D3* area of Card VI. For the remaining 25% to 30% of +, *o,* or *u* answers, the coding indicates that other distal features of the location area such as color are consistent with the object reported, and there is *no significant distortion or disregard* of the form features of the location area selected. Many, but not necessarily all of these responses, will also be coded as *DQv,* such as blood to the *D3* area of Card II, clouds to the whole of Card VII, water to the *D5* area of Card VIII, or an island to the *D1* area of Card X.

The *WDA%,* which includes +, *o,* or *u* responses given to *W* or *D* locations, provides an even more precise measure, evaluating the appropriate use of blot features only for those locations whose relatively obvious distal features should increase the likelihood of readily identifiable choices. The *XA%* and *WDA%* can be contrasted with the *X−%,* the proportion of responses that show either partial or complete disregard for the external stimulus field and whose source increasingly is the person's internal psychology.

Whereas the *XA%* and *WDA%* are variables that represent a broad overview of the extent to which the distal features of the figures have been used appropriately in formulating answers, the *X+%* deals with a more specific issue. It is calculated using only + and *o* responses divided by *R*. Because + and *o* answers are defined as objects reported to *W* or *D* locations in at least 190 (2%) of the 9,500 protocols that comprised the sample used to develop the Form Quality Table or by at least two-thirds of the 50 or more individuals who used a particular *Dd* area, the *X+%* can be viewed as representing the extent to which the distal features of the figure have been identified in ways that are similar to those reported by a relatively substantial percentage of other people. As such, it is a measure of *conventionality.* A useful contrast here is with the *Xu%.* It is the proportion of answers in which the use of the distal features of the figure is appropriate, but the specific object(s) reported appear with a very low frequency in a large group of protocols and, as such, represent the more idiosyncratic and unconventional answers in a person's protocol.

Perceptual-Thinking Index (PTI)

The Perceptual-Thinking Index (PTI) replaces the Schizophrenia Index (SCZI) and brings both psychometric and conceptual improvements. The PTI is a nine variable index with five criterion tests as follows:

1. $XA\% < .70$ and $WDA\% < .75$
2. $X-\% > .29$
3. $LVL2 > 2$ and $FAB2 > 0$
4. $R < 17$ and $WSUM6 > 12$ OR $R > 16$ and $WSUM6 > 17$ (Adjust for age 13 and younger: If $R > 16$: 5 to 7 = 20; 8 to 10 = 19; 11 to 13 = 18 and if $R < 17$: 5 to 7 = 16; 8 to 10 = 15; 11 to 13 = 14)
5. $M- > 1$ OR $X-\% > .40$

The PTI substitutes $XA\%$ and $WDA\%$ for the $X+\%$ and $FQ-$ variables used in the SCZI and also includes some age and protocol length adjustments for the cognitive slippage special scores ($WSUM6$). These changes have considerably reduced the relatively high false positive rate that had characterized the SCZI, particularly with younger persons.

One study (Smith, Baity, Knowles, & Hilsenroth, 2001) investigated the PTI with 42 inpatient children and adolescents in a private psychiatric hospital specializing in acute short-term treatment. Using a >2 cutoff for the five-item PTI, the authors found that patients with higher PTI scores had significantly higher findings on measures of atypicality, reality distortion, hallucinations and delusions, feelings of alienation, and social withdrawal derived either from a parent rating scale (Basic Assessment System for Children—Parent Report Form [BASC-PRF]; Reynolds & Kamphaus, 1992) or from a self-report measure (Personality Inventory for Youth [PIY]; Lachar & Gruber, 1995). The authors conclude that ". . . the PTI may be a more pure measure of thought disturbance in children and adolescents than the SCZI" and that it ". . . may be assessing a more severe thought disturbance that not only has characteristics of cognitive slippage but may be marked by behavioral disturbance as well" (p. 458).

Ritsher (2004) studied 180 Russian adult psychiatric patients with clinically significant psychiatric impairment. Using a cutpoint of >2, the PTI had a correct classification rate of 48% in discriminating patients diagnosed with schizophrenia from those diagnosed with depression. The false positive rate was quite low (3%).

From a conceptual standpoint, the change in name from "Schizophrenia Index" to "Perceptual-Thinking Index" emphasizes that the function of the PTI is not a diagnostic one. Rather, it is designed to indicate potential difficulties in two important areas of psychological function: reality testing and ideational clarity. As such, there is no longer a critical cutoff value for the PTI. It is a dimensional scale, with higher values that include both perceptual and ideational components directing the psychologist's attention to these critical areas.

GHR:PHR

The good to poor human representation (GHR:PHR) variable had its roots in a review of the Rorschach literature on interpersonal function done by Perry and Viglione (1991). Using a group of relevant *Comprehensive System* variables, they created an algorithm that could classify human responses into one of two categories: positive/intact or negative/problematic. The algorithm demonstrated substantial criterion validity in discriminating individuals with well functioning relationships from those with less effective interpersonal histories (e.g., Burns & Viglione, 1996).

A study by Viglione, Perry, Jansak, Meyer, and Exner (2003) modified the algorithm. It focuses on responses that contain any human content coding [*H, (H), Hd, (Hd), Hx*], responses with the determinant *M*, or *FM* responses that contain either the COP or *AG* special scores, and categorizes

Table 1.1   Steps Used to Assign Good *(GHR)* or Poor *(PHR)* Designations to Human Representational Responses.

1. Score *GHR* for answers containing a Pure *H* coding that also *have all* of the following:
   (a) Form Quality of *FQ+, FQo,* or *FQu.*
   (b) No cognitive special scores except *DV.*
   (c) No special scores of *AG* or *MOR.*
2. Score *PHR* for answers that have either:
   (a) *FQ* minus or *FQ*none (No Form), or
   (b) *FQ+, FQo,* or *FQu* and have an *ALOG, CONTAM,* or *any* Level 2 cognitive special score.
3. Score *GHR* for any remaining human representational answers that have the special score *COP, but do not* have the special score *AG.*
4. Score *PHR* for any remaining human representational answers that have either:
   (a) The special scores *FABCOM* or *MOR.*
   (b) The content score *An.*
5. Score *GHR* for any remaining human representational answers to Cards III, IV, VII, and IX that are coded Popular.
6. Score *PHR* for any remaining human representional answers that have any of the following:
   (a) The special scores *AG, INCOM,* or *DR.*
   (b) An *Hd* coding [<u>not</u> *(Hd)* coding].
7. Score *GHR* for all remaining human representational answers.

them as good or poor human representations (*GHR* or *PHR*) using the steps in the algorithm that are shown in Table 1.1.

An examination of steps 2, 4, and 6 of the algorithm highlights the aspects of interpersonal function that are associated with poor human representation codings. They include distortion, cognitive slippage, and a variety of aggressive, morbid, and somatic content. Conversely, steps 1, 3, and 5 demonstrate the accurate, logical, and intact features that define good human representation codings.

When a protocol contains at least three human representation answers, the relation of good to poor codings (GHR:PHR) allows a broad-based description of the effectiveness of a person's interpersonal function. If *GHR* is greater than *PHR,* it is likely that the individual handles interpersonal situations adequately and will be viewed by others in a relatively positive light. Alternatively, if *PHR* is equal to or greater than *GHR,* it is likely that the person's interpersonal function is less adaptive and that others will view him or her less favorably.

ORGANIZING RORSCHACH DATA BY CLUSTERS

Any interpretation of a Rorschach protocol must include careful consideration of all the data, but the steps through which the interpretation proceeds will not always be the same. The test data fall into three general groupings: the *Structural Summary,* the *Sequence of Scores,* and the *Verbalizations.* It is unfortunate but true that these three data sources vary considerably with regard to the breadth and sturdiness of the empirical foundations on which their interpretation rests. When each is scrutinized in the context of psychometric reality, it is the *Structural Summary* that typically constitutes the "hard data" of the Rorschach.

Although it is reasonable to expect that the structural data offer the greatest utility in forming interpretive hypotheses, those hypotheses can sometimes be too general, too narrow, or even misleading. Therefore, it is critically important that the other data groups are reviewed intelligently in the context of findings from the structural data. The Sequence of Scores often provides information that clarifies or expands postulates developed from the structural data, and in some instances unusual sequencing effects may give rise to new hypotheses. Similarly, while new hypotheses developed from the Verbalizations must be regarded with the utmost caution, the astute interpreter should be able to cull considerable information from the verbal material. Most postulates generated from verbal material are likely to have the greatest validity when derived from a composite of responses that are homogeneous for content or verbiage.

The interpretation should proceed cluster by cluster until all of the data have been exhausted. Although the first steps in addressing a cluster focus on the structural data, this does not mean that the Sequence of Scores and/or the verbal material are ignored until all possible hypotheses have been developed from the structural variables. On the contrary, issues will usually arise during the review of those variables that necessitate turning to the sequence and/or the verbal material before continuing with other structural variables.

This flexibility—moving from one data set to another—is crucial for a sophisticated interpretation of the test. This is because structural data on its own can be misused. It is not uncommon for the novice interpreter to draw premature conclusions from the value for a single variable. Such errors usually come from a faulty conception of test findings that disregards the fact that only a very few variables are independent of all other variables. Even more experienced interpreters can err by assuming that once the data for the structural variables in a cluster relating to a feature or function have been reviewed, no additional input is necessary and/or possible. Either of these errors promotes a concrete and simplistic use of the test that flirts with disaster and inevitably ignores a wealth of information that is available concerning the person's organization and functioning.

It is easy to understand how some errors in interpretive logic occur. Relatively large numbers of studies concerning each variable do encourage the notion that each has some discrete meaning. These studies tend to promote the idea that variables can be interpreted in isolation. Unfortunately, if such an approach is used, the result is a concrete and disconnected picture that at best fails to capture the organization of the person and at worst presents misleading or distorted conclusions. Even the discriminant functions, intercorrelational, and factorial studies that demonstrate that variables fall into clusters tend to convey the notion that each cluster of variables is somehow discrete and should be interpreted as such. Unfortunately, such an interpretive routine only serves to create a fragmented portrait of the person. Interpretation should evolve conceptually. Each finding should be integrated with other findings so that, ultimately, hypotheses and/or conclusions come from the totality of available information. In turn, these hypotheses and conclusions are synthesized logically with a careful view of the relationships between the numerous psychological features of the person. Any valid record contains some data that provides information about ideation, cognitive mediation, information processing, emotion, coping preferences and response styles, capacity for control, self-perception, and interpersonal perception. Most protocols will also include some information about routine defensive strategies. Thus, the challenge for the interpreter is twofold: first, to search methodically through all of the data concerning each component; second, to weave together the resulting yield in a manner that describes the total person.

VARYING STRATEGIES FOR INTERPRETATION

Once a protocol has been judged to be interpretively valid, a decision is required concerning the interpretive routine to be followed. The order in which each data cluster is evaluated varies from record to record, but it should never be random. The decision concerning the search order is not as simple as once seemed the case. During an earlier phase of development of the *Comprehensive System* (Exner, 1978), all interpretive routines began with a review of the data for four variables (*EB, EA, eb,* and *es*) that were called the Four Square. The rule of beginning with the Four Square was based on the logic that those four variables constituted the basic source of information regarding the core personality features of coping style and capacity for control. As such, that information would form a nucleus from which the interpretive routine would unfold naturally as each finding raised new issues to be addressed.

The practice of beginning the interpretation with the Four Square worked well for many records, but there were also many protocols in which hypotheses formed early in the interpretation required modification or, in some instances, abandonment as findings from other test data unfolded. This unexpected need to backtrack and reorganize hypotheses posed problems for the interpreter. It often required a change in set and a reintegration of findings, and it sometimes created confusion about how best to weigh findings in the total picture. Any of these challenges, if not properly addressed, risked sacrificing the richness of the interpretive yield.

In studying many protocols in which hypotheses generated from the data of the Four Square required modification, it became apparent that the recommended tactic for beginning interpretation had failed to appreciate two facts that had become much more apparent as research findings continued to unfold. First, while the *EB* does provide information regarding coping preferences, there are other stylistic features of the personality that can supercede that preference or have a more dominating impact on decisions and/or behaviors. Second, in some cases, the data of the Four Square may present a less accurate picture because other psychological features, usually pathological ones, have substantially altered the person's organization and/or functioning.

This problem was addressed by using a pool of 300 nonschizophrenic patient protocols. One hundred fifty records contained hypotheses developed from the Four Square that subsequently had to be modified or rejected because of other test data. In the remaining 150 records, used as a control group, hypotheses generated from the Four Square remained viable throughout the interpretive search. Frequency data for each of 241 computer-generated interpretive statements were tallied for the 300 records.

The records were then sorted into seven groups (controls or situational stress, affect, ideation, mediation, processing, self-perception, interpersonal perception), based on which cluster of variables yielded the largest number of statements for the record. One hundred forty-three of the 150 control group records sorted rather neatly into three groups (controls or stress, $N = 69$; ideation, $N = 36$; and affect $N = 38$). Interestingly, these three groupings drew extensively on the data of the Four Square. Five of the remaining seven protocols were sorted into the mediation group, one into self-perception, and one into processing. The sort of the 150 target group records was much more diverse (controls or stress, $N = 33$; ideation, $N = 21$; mediation, $N = 27$; processing, $N = 13$; affect, $N = 22$; self-perception, $N = 25$; interpersonal perception, $N = 9$).

A search program was then applied to determine if there were homogeneous data sets within each group that would differentiate it from the other groups. The results were very striking but not unexpected. For example, records sorted into the ideation group contained either an introversive

EB or evidence of markedly strange thinking. Records sorted into the controls or stress group contained a D Score lower than the Adjusted D Score, a minus Adjusted D Score, or a very low *EA*. Records sorted into the self-perception group all contained reflection responses, whereas those sorted into the processing group all had *Lambda* values of 1.0 or more, and so on.

The results of this search yielded 10 Key Variables which, when set in an order of dominance or priority, actually predicted the results of the sort for 282 of the 300 records. In other words, if a record contained only one positive Key Variable, it could be used to predict the cluster from which the largest number of statements would be generated. If a record contained two or more positive Key Variables, one had clear precedence in determining the sort and also could be used as a predictor. The 10 Key Variables, in their order of dominance, were: (1) Depression Index greater than 5, (2) D Score less than Adjusted D Score, (3) CDI positive, (4) Adjusted D Score in the minus range, (5) *Lambda* greater than .99, (6) at least one reflection answer, (7) *EB* introversive, (8) *EB* extratensive, (9) passive movement greater than active movement by more than one point, and (10) HVI positive.

The consistency for each of the groups provoked two additional sorts, again using the number of statements from each cluster as the basis for the differentiation. The results of the second and third sorts proved to be quite uniform and predictable from the first sort. For instance, if a record had been placed in the ideation group in the first sort, the second and third sorts almost always identified mediation and processing as yielding the next largest number of statements. Conversely, if a record initially had been sorted into the affect group, the clusters concerning self-perception and interpersonal perception invariably yielded the next largest number of statements.

In effect, the presence of a given Key Variable predicted which combination of two or three clusters of data would yield the largest number of statements from the pool of 241 statements. Stated differently, the Key Variables permitted the identification of the data sources that would contribute the most substantial information about the person's core psychological features. Generally, these are features that deserve considerable emphasis in forming a personality description. They are dominant elements of personality structure that have a major impact on psychological organization, exerting a significant influence on the way other features are expressed.

SELECTING THE INTERPRETIVE STRATEGY

The findings about Key Variables reaffirmed the notion that the interpretive search for all protocols should not follow the same sequence. It became clear that unique search strategies could be developed that allowed the interpretive routine to flow systematically, avoiding backtracking and reorganization of hypotheses. In such a format, the first data elements that are evaluated provide information concerning the predominant aspects of personality structure and/or response style. Thus, the decision about which cluster of data to use as the starting point is important, because its yield provides a context for the entire network of descriptive statements that will ultimately be generated. In turn, the first cluster selected typically provides direction for the order in which the remaining clusters are reviewed.

The details of the search strategy have evolved over the years, and the current sequence shown in Table 1.2 includes 12 Key Variables that can be divided conceptually into two groups. Six of the variables (PTI > 3, DEPI > 5, D Score < Adjusted D Score, CDI > 3, and Adjusted D Score < 0) focus on the presence of potentially disorganizing psychopathology. The remaining six variables

Table 1.2   Interpretive Search Strategies Based on Key Variables.

Positive Variable	Typical Cluster Search Routine
PTI > 3	Processing > Mediation > Ideation > Controls > Affect > Self Perception > Interpersonal Perception
DEPI > 5 and CDI > 3	Interpersonal Perception > Self Perception > Controls > Affect > Processing > Mediation > Ideation
DEPI > 5	Affect > Controls > Self Perception > Interpersonal Perception > Processing > Mediation > Ideation
D < ADJ D	Controls > Situation Stress > (The remaining search routine should be that identified for the next positive key variable or the list of tertiary variables)
CDI > 3	Controls > Interpersonal Perception > Self Perception > Affect > Processing > Mediation > Ideation
ADJ D is	Controls > (The remaining search routine should be that identified for Minus the next positive key variable or the list of tertiary variables)
Lambda > 0.99	Processing > Mediation > Ideation > Controls > Affect > Self Perception > Interpersonal Perception
FR+RF > 0	Self Perception > Interpersonal Perception > Controls (The remaining search routine should be selected from that identified for the next positive key variable or the list of tertiary variables)
EB is Introversive	Ideation > Processing > Mediation > Controls > Affect >Self Perception > Interpersonal Perception
EB is Extratensive	Affect > Self Perception > Interpersonal Perception > Controls Extratensive > Processing > Mediation > Ideation
p > a+1	Ideation > Processing > Mediation > Controls > Self Perception > Interpersonal Perception > Affect
HVI Positive	Ideation > Processing > Mediation > Controls > Self Perception >Interpersonal Perception > Affect

(*Lambda* > .99, *FR+RF* > 0, *EB* introversive, *EB* extratensive, $p > a+1$, and HVI positive) describe entrenched personality styles, any of which can form the cornerstone of organization and functioning.

The Key Variables shown in Table 1.2 are listed in order of interpretive priority. In other words, the first positive Key Variable defines the sequence in which clusters are interpreted. Most of the sequences are straightforward, but in some cases the entire routine cannot be defined by simply using the first positive Key Variable. In that situation, subsequent Key Variables or Tertiary Variables must also be used to establish the complete routine. These sequences provide a path that allows each new finding to follow from those already developed.

The search sequences shown in Table 1.2 have been developed both empirically and logically. They are empirical in the sense that the first two or three clusters reviewed are likely to yield the greatest amount of information about the core features of the individual's personality. They are logical in the sense that the sequence is designed so that each new finding merges neatly with those that precede it. It is important to note that the 12 search strategies are not entirely discrete. Three of the clusters—ideation, mediation, and processing—are always analyzed together because they describe different aspects of cognitive functioning. Likewise, the clusters pertaining to self-perception and interpersonal perception are always interpreted in tandem because of their interrelationship.

Table 1.3   Search Strategies Based on Tertiary Variables.

Positive Variable	Typical Cluster Search Routine
OBS Positive	Processing > Mediation > Ideation > Controls > Affect > Self Perception > Interpersonal Perception
DEPI = 5	Affect > Controls > Self Perception > Interpersonal Perception > Processing > Mediation > Ideation
EA > 12	Controls > Ideation > Processing > Mediation > Affect > Self Perception > Interpersonal Perception
M – > O or Mp > Ma or Sum6 Sp Sc > 5	Ideation > Mediation > Processing > Controls > Affect > Self Perception > Interpersonal Perception
Sum Shad > FM+m or CF+C > FC+1 or Afr < 0.46	Affect > Controls > Self Perception > Interpersonal Perception > Processing > Mediation > Ideation
X-% > 20% or Zd > +3.0 or < – 3.0	Processing > Mediation > Ideation > Controls > Affect > Self Perception > Interpersonal Perception
3r+(2)/R < .33	Self Perception > Interpersonal Perception > Affect > Controls > Processing > Mediation > Ideation
MOR > 2 or AG > 2	Self Perception > Interpersonal Perception > Controls > Ideation > Processing > Mediation > Affect
T = 0 or > 1	Self Perception > Interpersonal Perception > Affect > Controls > Processing > Mediation > Ideation

Although the search sequences dictated by each Key Variable nearly always define the most logical path for moving through Rorschach data, there are exceptions. As an example, Case 17 (Chapter 19) presents a situation in which findings early in the interpretive sequence suggested that the individual's reality testing and thinking difficulties had a significant affective component. Consequently, it seemed appropriate to alter the initial search strategy, which had listed affect as the last cluster to be analyzed.

If the protocol does not contain any positive Key Variables, a starting point can be identified from positive findings among the Tertiary Variables listed in Table 1.3. These variables typically point to the cluster that is likely to have the greatest yield, but they have less predictive power than the Key Variables for identifying the subsequent clusters that will contribute the most useful supplementary information.

A REVIEW OF THE VARIABLES THAT GUIDE SEARCH SEQUENCES

As noted previously, the purpose of the search sequences is to direct the psychologist's attention to those aspects of the data likely to produce the greatest interpretive yield. For that reason, if the person is 15 or older, the Suicide Constellation is always reviewed before moving to the search sequence identified by the first positive Key Variable. A review of the variables that dictate these search sequences highlights their importance in suggesting, for each individual, the organizing principle that allows an integrated description of his or her personality.

The Suicide Constellation

The Suicide Constellation (S-CON) should always be reviewed *before* beginning the interpretive routine if the patient is age 15 or older. Technically, it is not a cluster but rather an array of variables from several clusters which, as a collective, has an actuarial usefulness in identifying individuals with features similar to those who have effected their own death. Some groupings of items in the S-CON have a conceptual similarity, but the empirically developed listing as a whole does not.

The preliminary research on the S-CON (Exner, Martin, & Mason, 1984; Exner & Wylie, 1977) suggested that if the value for the S-CON is eight or more it should be concluded that the person does have features similar to those found in people who have committed suicide within a relatively short period of time after taking the Rorschach. A study by Fowler, Piers, Hilsenroth, Holdwick, and Padawer (2001) provides some justification for concern if seven or more of the S-CON variables are present. Using detailed medical record documentation extending up to 60 days after Rorschach administration, the authors classified the self-destructive behavior of a predominantly female inpatient sample into three categories: nonsuicidal, parasuicidal, and near-lethal. They found that an S-CON score of seven or more discriminated those patients who later made near-lethal suicide attempts from the other two groups. The S-CON cutoff of seven or more identified 81% of the patients who made near-lethal suicide attempts and 78% who did not, achieving an overall correct classification rate of 79%.

S-CON values less than seven or eight should not be automatically interpreted to mean that no self-destructive preoccupation exists. The false negative rate for this constellation ranges up to approximately 25%, and a review of all available history, interview, and test data is always indicated when evaluating self-destructive potential.

Perceptual-Thinking Index

As noted earlier, the Perceptual-Thinking Index (PTI) is not a diagnostic index but rather an indicator of the kinds of difficulties in perceptual accuracy and thinking that can have a pervasive impact throughout an individual's personality structure. PTI scores of four or five signal difficulties in both perceptual accuracy and thinking and suggest that findings from the Processing, Mediation, and Ideation clusters will play an important part in describing virtually every aspect of the individual's function.

Depression Index

Because the variables in the Depression Index (DEPI) are typically not directly related to observable behavior, Meyer and Archer (2001) concluded that ". . . psychologists should not use the DEPI on its own to diagnose a major depressive disorder from the *Diagnostic and Statistical Manual of Mental Disorders*" (p. 499). Instead, the DEPI serves to identify individuals who may be emotionally distraught, cognitively pessimistic, lethargic, or self-defeating.

Coping Deficit Index

A Coping Deficit Index (CDI) of four or five is a significant finding. Seven of the 11 variables in the CDI relate to interpersonal needs or deficits, while two of the remaining four variables seem to signal emotional avoidance or impoverishment. The other two variables indicate either poor control capacity or limited coping resources. Thus, anyone with a value of 4 or more on the CDI is predisposed to functional disorganization, especially in unusual stress situations or those in which there are expectations for social/interpersonal effectiveness.

Two treatment outcome studies (Exner & Andronikof-Sanglade, 1992; Weiner & Exner, 1991) indicate that relatively extensive (8 to 14 months) of mental health intervention has the potential for lowering the CDI. Briefer interventions (2 to 3 months) demonstrated little effect on this variable.

Adjusted D Score Is Greater Than D Score

If the Adjusted D Score (Adj D) is greater than the D Score, the elevations on *m* and/or *SumY* that created this difference signal the presence of situationally related stress. As the difference between D and Adj D become greater, it is increasingly likely that the impact of the stress will interfere with the person's customary task-oriented behavior. If the value for *m* is more than three times *SumY,* the stress is likely to have a more substantial effect on the person's attention and concentration. Conversely, if *SumY* is more than three times *m,* the stress is likely to manifest with rather diffuse experiences of anxiety, tension, and helplessness.

Adjusted D Score

If the Adjusted D Score (Adj D) falls in the minus range, particularly as it moves toward −2 or below, it suggests potential problems in the effectiveness of the person's ongoing psychological function. These day-to-day problems often result from developmental difficulties that have produced a less mature form of personality organization than might be expected. Alternatively, an Adj D score in the minus range may indicate some psychological disintegration caused by a chronic stimulus overload state. In either event it suggests problems in both ideational and affective control that can set the stage for impulsive behavior.

The Key Variable finding of Adj D in the minus range does not predict well which clusters beyond Controls will offer the most salient information. For this reason, the decision concerning the remainder of the interpretive search must be based on a subsequent positive Key or Tertiary Variable.

Lambda

The finding that *Lambda* has a value of 1.0 or greater signals the presence of an *avoidant* response style, oriented toward reducing stimulus situations to their most easily managed level. This typically involves a narrowing or simplification of the stimulus field by ignoring its complex or ambiguous aspects. At best, this style may allow some sense of control by reducing the possibility of overload, and it is associated, for example, with schizophrenics who are able to avoid rehospitalization for longer periods (Exner & Murillo, 1977). But if the situation is intrinsically complex or ambiguous, avoiding some of its relevant elements can increase the likelihood of ineffective responses.

The behavior of individuals who have an *avoidant* style often conveys the impression that the simplification occurs at the input level. But this explanation does not seem viable in light of the fact that, as a group, high *Lambda* individuals do not show unusual distributions for *Zf* or *DQv,* and their frequency of underincorporation is only very slightly greater than individuals with *Lambda* findings below 1.0. A more logical explanation posits that the simplification is a defensive process through which some significant elements of the field are viewed as having little importance when judged against the person's needs and the perceived demands of the situation. As such, those elements receive little or no attention in the formulation of responses.

Because a *Lambda* value of 1.0 or higher describes a pervasive response style, it is important to consider how it relates to the *EB,* which also provides data about preferred problem-solving approaches. High *Lambda* values tend to lower the complexity with which problems are engaged. As an example, the extratensive individual usually tests possible solutions through trial and error and then carefully differentiates the emotional feedback that different solutions engender. However, the *avoidant extratensive* does not take the time to differentiate this complex emotional feedback carefully, and the resulting behavior may be less effective and seemingly impulsive. Analogously, introversive individuals typically "think through" the costs and benefits of a variety of solutions quite carefully. However, the *avoidant introversive* may short-circuit this time-consuming process, arriving at simplistic solutions that are less likely to be adaptive. The *avoidant ambitent,* with no secondary extratensive or introversive orientation, is likely to manifest less and less effective behavior as the complexity of demands increases.

Reflection Responses

The presence of one or more reflection answers triggers an interpretive routine that differs from those previously outlined, shifting the focus to self-concept and interpersonal issues. The reflection response is an important finding that, in adults, relates to a stable core characteristic of personality. It signifies the presence of a marked tendency to overvalue one's personal worth. Although not uncommon among younger children, these responses are not expected in the records of older adolescents or adults. If they do occur, it is very likely that the person will be strongly influenced by the need to support and defend this feature, and this drive will have a marked impact on many psychological operations.

In addition, the inflated sense of self cannot help but have a direct effect on the person's interpersonal world. To the extent that he or she is able to obtain reassurance and support from others, the likelihood of pathology decreases. But failure to receive affirmation can lead to elaborate defensive operations that include externalization of blame, rationalization, and denial.

Introversive or Extratensive Style

If the scan of Key Variables to this point does not define the interpretive routine, a review of the *EB* frequently will provide that identification. The presence of either of the predominant coping styles, introversive or extratensive, offers clear direction to the sequence of clusters that will provide the greatest interpretive yield.

The search of an introversive record begins with the cluster of variables concerning ideation and continues through the other clusters in the cognitive triad, processing and mediation. As already noted, the introversive style involves a preference for delay and thinking through alternatives before deciding on a response. The cognitive triad data will typically provide important information concerning the efficiency and effectiveness of that style. The routine continues through the clusters regarding controls and affects and ends with a review of data about self-perception and interpersonal perception.

If the *EB* indicates an extratensive style, the initial focus of the interpretive routine is quite different. It begins with the cluster concerning affect, as this style is one in which feelings play an important role in making decisions. Extratensives solve problems by evaluating their emotional reactions as they try out a variety of solutions. Needless to say, the appropriate modulation of emotional discharge is often quite important to the integrity of the style.

p Is Greater Than *a*+1 or the Hypervigilance Index Is Positive

If either of the remaining two Key Variables provides the basis for selecting the search strategy, an interpretive routine that emphasizes ideation will produce the most useful initial data. If *p* exceeds *a* by a value of more than one, it suggests that passivity is an integral psychological style that plays out in much of the person's thinking and behavior. The passive style usually serves any one of or a combination of several objectives. It can provide a convenient way to avoid complexity and responsibility, manifest a subtle aggressiveness, or perpetuate dependency. A positive HVI also points to a basic personality style. Individuals with this finding tend to be ill at ease in a world in which they see themselves as vulnerable. As a consequence they maintain a state of hyperalertness that is costly in two respects. First, a considerable energy commitment is required to sustain this level of anticipatory guardedness. Second, the orientation that gives rise to this hypervigilant apprehensiveness involves a more cautious or guarded set concerning others, which in turn can have a marked impact on interpersonal relationships. People who are hypervigilant are usually less trusting of others and preoccupied with matters of personal space.

The Within Cluster Analyses

As noted earlier, each Rorschach element, whether structural data, sequencing effects, or verbal material, ultimately contributes to the interpretation and *none* can be neglected. Each Rorschach protocol is unique in its total configuration, different from all other Rorschachs and illustrative of the idiography of the person who gave it. Thus, the process of interpretation involves a step-by-step sequence in which each new element is reviewed in the context of *all* previously examined data. It requires inductive and deductive reasoning. At almost every step, whether across clusters or within a cluster, hypotheses are developed that must be tested to the extent possible and confirmed, modified, or rejected. Much of this occurs during the within cluster analyses.

Once the interpretive search through a cluster begins, all of the data for the cluster is reviewed *before* turning to another cluster. This is to ensure that the postulates and/or conclusions that are developed about the feature being studied are as unambiguous and complete as possible and above all, that misleading sets or premature conclusions about the subject are not created. Clusters vary considerably in the breadth and/or depth of information concerning organization and functioning that they may provide. As a consequence, the specificity of propositions and conclusions that are derived also varies.

For example, there are only five variables that relate directly to issues of control and stress tolerance (the D Scores, *EA, es* and the CDI). Sometimes, the findings from this cluster will be quite specific, but in the majority of cases the yield will be little more than a general statement regarding the availability of resources and the capacity for control. On the other hand, seven structural variables [3r+(2)/R, *Fr+rF, FD, SumV,* MOR, *An+Xy, H:(H)+Hd+(Hd)*] plus a potentially sizable number of responses (any containing movement, MOR, or minus form quality) offer information about self-perception and thus, the yield of information concerning this feature often allows a highly idiographic description. This does not mean that the number of

Table 1.4 Order for Reviewing Variables within Each Cluster.

Control and Stress Tolerance
Step 1. Adjusted D Score and CDI
Step 2. EA
Step 3. EB and Lambda
Step 4. es and Adj es
Step 5. eb

Situation Related Stress
Step 1. D Score in relation to es and Adj es
Step 2. Difference between D & Adj D Scores
Step 3. m & Y
Step 4. T, V, 3r+(2)/R in relation to History
Step 5. D Score (re Pure C, M−, M no form)
Step 6. Blends
Step 7. Color-Shading & Shading Blends

Affective Features
Step 1. DEPI & CDI
Step 2. EB & Lambda
Step 3. EBPer
Step 4. Right Side eb & variables related to it
Step 5. SumC':WSumC
Step 6. Affective Ratio
Step 7. Intellectualization Index
Step 8. Color Projection
Step 9. FC:CF+C
Step 10. Pure C
Step 11. Space responses
Step 12. Blends (Lambda & EB)
Step 13. m & Y blends
Step 14. Blend complexity
Step 15. Color-shading blends
Step 16. Shading blends

Information Processing
Prerequsites (L,EB,OBS,HVI)
Step 1. Zf
Step 2. W:D:Dd
Step 3. Location Sequencing
Step 4. W:M
Step 5. Zd
Step 6. PSV
Step 7. DQ
Step 8. DQ Sequencing

Mediation
Prerequisites (R,OBS,L)
Step 1. XA% & WDA%
Step 2. FQnone
Step 3. X−%, FQ− frequency, S− frequency
    a. Homogeneity issues
    b. Minus distortion levels
Step 4. Populars
Step 5. FQ+ frequency
Step 6. X+% & Xu%

Ideation
Step 1. EB & Lambda
Step 2. EBPer
Step 3. a:p
Step 4. HVI, OBS, MOR
Step 5. Left side eb
Step 6. Ma:Mp
Step 7. Intellectualization Index
Step 8. Sum6 & WSum6
Step 9. Quality 6 Spec Scores
Step 10. M Form Quality
Step 11. Quality of M responses

Self Perception
Step 1. OBS & HVI
Step 2. Reflections
Step 3. Egocentricity Index
Step 4. FD and Vista (in relation to History)
Step 5. An+Xy
Step 6. Sum MOR
Step 7. H:(H)+Hd+(Hd) & Review codings for
         Human Content responses
Step 8. Search for projections in:
    a. Minus responses
    b. MOR responses
    c. M & Human Content responses
    d. FM & m responses
    e. Embellishments in other responses

Interpersonal Perception
Step 1. CDI
Step 2. HVI
Step 3. a:p Ratio
Step 4. Food responses
Step 5. Sum T
Step 6. Sum Human Contents & Sum Pure H
Step 7. GHR:PHR
Step 8. COP & AG frequencies & codings
Step 9. PER
Step 10. Isolation Index
Step 11. Contents of M & FM responses with pairs

variables in a cluster is directly related to interpretive specificity. On the contrary, the accumulated findings from variables within a cluster dictate where the resulting information falls on the general to specific continuum.

The within cluster analysis *always* begins with a review of the structural variables in the cluster because they are empirically derived. Table 1.4 on page 16 presents the sequence for reviewing variables within each cluster. Although the propositions generated from them are often more general, their validity is less subject to challenge, and typically they lead to the formation of hypotheses that give focus to the remainder of the cluster search.

SUMMARY

The importance of careful planning for the interpretive strategy used in approaching a protocol cannot be overestimated in relation to the *Comprehensive System.* An enormous number of variables are involved, and they should not be addressed in a random or haphazard manner. To do so risks the possibility of inadvertently neglecting important findings or failing to integrate data appropriately. Each person is a very complex entity, different from all other people. Similarly, each Rorschach is complex and different from all others. If the data of the Rorschach are addressed in a systematic and intelligent manner, the person's uniqueness will emerge as the interpretation evolves.

REFERENCES

Burns, B., & Viglione, D. (1996). The Rorschach human experience variable, interpersonal relatedness, and object representation in nonpatients. *Psychological Assessment, 8*(1), 92–99.

Exner, J. E. (1978). *The Rorschach: A comprehensive system: Vol. 2. Current research and advanced interpretation.* New York: Wiley.

Exner, J. E., & Andronikof-Sanglade, A. (1992). Rorschach changes following brief and short-term therapy. *Journal of Personality Assessment, 59*(1), 59–71.

Exner, J. E., Martin, L. S., & Mason, B. (1984). A review of the Rorschach suicide constellation. Paper presented at the 11th International Congress of Rorschach and Projective Techniques, Barcelona, Spain.

Exner, J. E., & Murillo, L. G. (1977). A long-term follow-up of schizophrenics treated with regressive ECT. *Diseases of the Nervous System, 38,* 162–168.

Exner, J. E., & Wylie, J. (1977). Some Rorschach data concerning suicide. *Journal of Personality Assessment, 41*(4), 339–348.

Fowler, J. C., Piers, C., Hilsenroth, M. J., Holdwick, D. J., & Padawer, J. R. (2001). The Rorschach Suicide Constellation: Assessing various degrees of lethality. *Journal of Personality Assessment, 76*(2), 333–351.

Lachar, D., & Gruber, C. P. (1995). *Personality Inventory for Youth: Technical guide.* Los Angeles: Western Psychological Services.

Meyer, G. J., & Archer, R. P. (2001). The hard science of Rorschach research: What do we know and where do we go? *Psychological Assessment, 13*(4), 486–502.

Perry, W., & Viglione, D. (1991). The Ego Impairment Index as a predictor of outcome in melancholic depressed patients treated with tricyclic antidepressants. *Journal of Personality Assessment, 56*(3), 487–501.

Reynolds, C. R., & Kamphaus, R. W. (1992). *Behavior assessment system for children.* Circle Pines, MN: American Guidance Service.

Ritsher, J. B. (2004). Association of Rorschach and MMPI psychosis indicators and schizophrenia spectrum diagnoses in a Russian clinical sample. *Journal of Personality Assessment, 83*(1), 46–63.

Smith, S. R., Baity, M. R., Knowles, E. S., & Hilsenroth, M. J. (2001). Assessment of disordered thinking in children and adolescents: The Rorschach Perceptual-Thinking Index. *Journal of Personality Assessment, 77*(3), 447–463.

Viglione, D., Perry, W., Jansak, D., Meyer, G. J., & Exner, J. E. (2003). Modifying the Rorschach Human Experience Variable to create the Human Representational Variable. *Journal of Personality Assessment, 81*(1), 64–73.

Weiner, I. B., & Exner, J. E. (1991). Rorschach changes in long-term and short-term psychotherapy. *Journal of Personality Assessment, 56*(3), 453–465.

CHAPTER 2

Rorschach Assessment: A Consultation Model

Hermann Rorschach initially conceived his "experiment" as a way of describing perception, reality testing, and, indirectly, problem-solving capacity. As his investigation unfolded, he began to realize that its findings could be translated into descriptions about how individuals handle the moderately ambiguous and/or complex perceptual-cognitive demands they face in everyday life.

Rorschach held that the instrument's ability to describe real-world function began with careful coding of the person's solutions to the "What might this be?" question that defines the task. He emphasized the structural aspects of those solutions, writing that "In scoring the answers given by [the] subject, the content is considered last. It is more important to study the *function* of perception and apperception. The experiment depends primarily on the pattern" (1942/1981, p. 19). "Pattern" was the translation of the German *"formale."* An equally good translation would have been "structure," because Rorschach was referring to elements such as determinants and location.

Rorschach hoped that empirical studies could link these structural elements to increasingly detailed descriptions of real-world behavior. It was a hope that has resonated for hundreds of researchers during the decades since the test's introduction. The PsycINFO (American Psychological Association, 2004) database contains more than 7,300 Rorschach citations, and they provide a rich resource for the psychologist responding to the referral questions that constitute the day-to-day reality of assessment practice.

Although earlier researchers (e.g., Rybakow, 1910; Whipple, 1910) had used inkblots to study imagination, Rorschach's emphasis on structure opened a uniquely different set of possibilities. His breakthrough idea was that documenting the strategies people use to formulate inkblot responses could allow descriptions of how they are likely to handle real-world situations. One of the Rorschach systematizers, Zygmunt Piotrowski (1957), summarized it well: "Rorschach's genius consisted in discovering that very significant traits can be deduced from the formal aspects of the blots, and in indicating what trait is revealed by what formal aspect" (p. 3).

Another of the systematizers, Samuel Beck (1976), who had worked as a newspaper reporter, took a more graphic approach to describing the relationship between Rorschach structure and real-world behavior. He related accurate form quality (*F+* in his system) to ". . . the solid stuff of everyday life, what we must understand accurately if we are to get along as social beings; in instances, as say, in judging the speed of an oncoming automobile before crossing a street, with consequences regarding whether we will stay alive" (p. 6).

Bruno Klopfer (Klopfer, Ainsworth, Klopfer, & Holt, 1954) also viewed the Rorschach as a problem-solving task whose structural findings linked to real-world function, noting that "The assumption is that, on the basis of this limited sample of behavior, it will be possible to predict other kinds of behavior on the part of the subject in other situations" (p. 3).

Klopfer went on to describe another kind of data the test can offer: "As a projective technique, the Rorschach has the further characteristic of providing a relatively ambiguous stimulus situation which will enable the subject to optimally reveal his individuality of functioning" (1954, p. 3). David Rapaport had also suggested viewing the Rorschach as a multifaceted data source when he wrote, ". . . one can learn more about the subject sometimes by looking at a response from the point of view of its perceptual organization, and at other times by looking at it from the point of view of the associative process that brought it forth" (Rapaport, Gill, & Schafer, 1968, p. 274).

The accumulated research literature has provided substantial backing for the way Rorschach and the early systematizers conceptualized the instrument's yield. The Rorschach is a multifaceted data source whose structural and content findings have been linked, with greater or lesser empirical support, to a spectrum of observable behaviors and internal states. It is at its best in describing the person as he or she is now in terms of the broad areas described in Chapter 1: coping strategies and controls, affect, interpersonal function, self-concept, and information processing. Because many Rorschach elements are stable over time, it also allows some speculation about past and future function.

Although the Rorschach can provide descriptions of attributes that are relevant for diagnostic decisions—reality testing would be an example—it is not a diagnostic test. The Rorschach's goal is to describe how the various aspects of an individual coalesce to form his or her unique personality, and that is a different destination than the diagnostic one. The *Diagnostic and Statistical Manual of Mental Disorders* (*DSM-IV-TR;* American Psychiatric Association, 2000) articulates this distinction succinctly: "A common misperception is that a classification of mental disorders classifies people, when actually what are being classified are disorders that people have" (p. xxxi). The Rorschach describes the day-to-day function of an individual; a structured diagnostic interview like the *Structured Clinical Interview for DSM-IV Axis I Disorders* (SCID-I; First, Spitzer, Gibbon, & Williams, 1997) determines whether someone has the observable features necessary for a *DSM* diagnosis.

Very frequently it is a description of the relevant aspects of day-to-day function, not a diagnostic categorization, that best serves the professional whose job it is to provide services for or make decisions about an individual referred for assessment. That is where the Rorschach can be most helpful. The cases in this book come from a spectrum of referring professionals: physicians, psychotherapists, attorneys, judges, program managers, teachers, and guidance counselors. Although these professionals come from a variety of disciplines, at the most basic level their jobs are very similar. Each must plan an intervention or make a decision about the person he or she has referred. Each of these professionals must act, and psychological assessment is useful to the extent that it provides consultation that informs their decisions and interventions. A few examples will serve to illustrate this process.

Rubin and Arceneaux (2001) provided treatment for a 67-year-old woman whose long-standing depression had been resistant to extensive intervention over nearly five decades. Although her work history as a legal assistant had been quite stable, unfamiliar or ambiguous tasks were difficult for her and her interpersonal life had been characterized by ineptness and conflict. A treatment regimen that included psychotherapy and a combination of antidepressant and antianxiety medications was ineffective against her intractable depression, anxiety, and interpersonal difficulties. Rorschach assessment suggested problems with reality testing and cognitive slippage, and a trial of a low-dose atypical antipsychotic (risperidone) was instituted. Within a month, the patient reported a difference that she described as, "kind of like putting glasses on my mind, things are clearer and they make more sense." She noted that "for the first time in my life, I feel good" (p. 404).

Rubin and Arceneaux (2001) speculate that there may be a subset of subtle psychotic disorders that do not manifest the overt symptoms necessary for a *DSM-IV* diagnosis of Schizophrenia, Psychosis NOS, or Major Depression with Psychotic Features. They note that ". . . the Rorschach was an effective tool in the identification of this disorder, while other assessment tools (e.g., SCL-90, MMPI-2), including clinical interview, failed" (p. 404).

Mortimer and Smith (1983) point out that psychotherapists frequently must decide how best to understand the material a patient presents during a session. They describe a case of a woman readmitted to inpatient treatment for a psychotic break after 3 years of increasingly capable and autonomous function. Psychological assessment suggested significant organizing difficulties that set limits on her ability to handle complex tasks, especially when doing more than one thing at a time. As her initial success had pushed her to undertake more and more activities, her confusion and the resulting depression about her failures had once again become overwhelming for her.

Mortimer and Smith (1983) note that the assessing psychologist's consultation provided a focus for listening to the patient: "The psychotherapist, who had been hearing the material presented in the therapy hours as representing a fear of individuation, took a new direction from the test report. He began hearing the content of therapy hours in terms of the patient's response to cognitive limitations" (p. 135). This new focus allowed the therapeutic work to emphasize ways of preventing the sort of overload that could lead to decompensation. These included early identification of potentially stressful situations, schedule planning and simplification, and an ability to view her organizational difficulties not as pervasive inadequacy but rather as a specific deficit for which compensatory strategies were available.

Stewart and Golding (1985) describe the use of psychological assessment in a general hospital consultation-liaison service. As an example, they present a case of a 45-year-old man for whom extensive medical assessment could find no cause for the unremitting and unusual pain he described as "like a rock" in his chest. Although the patient was rather guarded, a clinical interview did not indicate any depressive content or vegetative signs. Rorschach and TAT findings were suggestive of significant depression in the absence of reality testing difficulties or cognitive slippage, and ". . . the consultant proposed a program calling for psychotherapy and antidepressant medication. Neuroleptics were not prescribed. Previously denied losses had more impact than he had realized" (p. 153).

A CONSULTATION MODEL FOR PSYCHOLOGICAL ASSESSMENT

These examples illustrate a basic premise about psychological assessment: It is useful to the extent that it produces consultation that enhances the referring professional's ability to make accurate decisions and provide effective interventions. This premise leads to a consultation-oriented model for psychological assessment that includes the following four steps:

1. *Case formulation:* This involves a summary of the person's history and the circumstances that resulted in the current referral. It also includes identification of all the individuals for whom consultation will be provided and articulation of the decisions or intervention plans they have under consideration.

2. *Literature review:* This step reviews literature both about the referral question (e.g., depression, competence to stand trial) and the instruments relevant for addressing that question. It results in

a decision about the most appropriate psychological assessment battery for responding to the referral.

3. *Psychological assessment:* This step begins with helping the referring professional describe the assessment and its purpose to the person being referred. It also includes a decision about how feedback will be provided.

4. *Consultation:* Once the assessment is completed, this step involves integrating the findings into a consultation that responds specifically to the referral questions and places them in the broader context of overall personality function within the person's environment.

Although the specifics of each case will differ, this general model is appropriate for the vast majority of situations that involve psychological assessment. It will be useful to discuss each of its steps in some detail.

Case Formulation

A thorough review of the person's history alerts the assessing psychologist to significant issues that may not have been mentioned in the referral questions. As an example, an extensive history of drug abuse often points to the need for cognitive assessment, even if that was not among the reasons for the referral. Previous medical or mental health contacts may have involved assessment or treatment, and a review of those records may raise other questions and provide helpful comparisons with current findings.

It is often the case that more than one person is interested in the findings that come from psychological assessment. In the case of a child referred because of school difficulties, for example, it is likely that the findings will be of interest to the child's parents, teachers, guidance counselors, and school administrators. And it is virtually always appropriate to assume that the person being assessed—whether a child or an adult—will be among those most interested in the results.

Once all the relevant individuals have been identified, it is important to articulate the questions they would like the assessment to address. For referring professionals, these questions are often best conceptualized in terms of the decisions they must make, interventions they are planning, or problems with interventions they are currently providing.

Literature Review

The increasing availability of extensive online databases makes it possible for assessment psychologists in a variety of settings to review the literature relevant for the referral questions they encounter. These reviews typically involve two approaches. The first targets the question or syndrome, and the second targets how psychological assessment addresses that question or syndrome. The results place the referral question in perspective and allow a decision about the battery of assessment instruments that can provide the most comprehensive consultation possible.

It is important to note that comprehensive assessment typically involves the use of multiple methods. In an extensive review of major issues in psychological assessment, Meyer and his colleagues (Meyer et al., 2001) write that "Just as optimal research recognizes that any method of measurement and any single operational definition of a construct are incomplete, optimal clinical assessment should recognize that the same constraints exist when measuring phenomena in the life of a single person." They go on to note that "The data indicate that even though it may be less expensive at the outset, a single clinician using a single method (e.g., interview) to obtain information from a patient will develop an incomplete or biased understanding of that patient," and they conclude that "The evidence indicates that clinicians who use a single method to obtain patient information regularly draw faulty conclusions" (p. 150).

The literature review helps identify the various assessment instruments relevant for a broad-based, multimethod response to the referral questions. Such a review is the appropriate way to deal with the issue of validity. The question of whether any psychological test instrument is "valid" in general cannot be answered. As Meyer and Archer (2001) note: ". . . validity is conditional. It varies as a function of the predictor and the criterion" (p. 492). The literature review helps identify a battery of instruments with elements (predictors) that have been empirically linked to the referral question (criterion) under consideration.

Because this book is about Rorschach interpretation, the literature reviews for the various cases emphasize empirical studies that relate the Rorschach to the specific referral question each case presents. However, the assumption is that the Rorschach would typically be part of a multimethod approach and that its yield could range from very specific to quite general, depending on the referral question. A few examples will illustrate the continuum of specificity with which Rorschach findings address referral questions.

Fowler, Piers, Hilsenroth, Holdwick, and Padawer (2001) followed psychiatric inpatients for up to 60 days after Rorschach administration in order to investigate the relation of the Suicide Constellation (S-CON) with chart-documented self-destructive behaviors. They found that total S-CON scores were significantly correlated with serious overdose attempts and emergency transfers to a medical facility but not with superficial wrist cutting incidents. The authors concluded that ". . . the total S-CON score is associated with ecologically valid, real-world behaviors of serious suicide attempts, rather than assessing general impulsivity or self-destructive trends" (p. 347).

Literature reviews sometimes allow comparisons of different instruments in relation to the specificity with which they can respond to referral questions. For instance, a study by Blais, Hilsenroth, Castlebury, Fowler, and Baity (2001) found that the Rorschach was the best predictor of the total number of *DSM-IV* histrionic personality disorder criteria, while the MMPI-2 was the best predictor of antisocial criteria. And the literature does not always provide specific empirical support for the use of an instrument in response to a referral question. As an example, although Rorschach findings might be of adjunctive help in consulting with an attorney about a client's competence to stand trial, there is nothing in the literature that supports its use as the primary instrument for addressing that question.

Psychological Assessment

An often-overlooked aspect of the assessment process involves teaching professionals how to prepare the individuals they refer. At best, this preparation should involve two elements: an explanation of the reasons for requesting psychological assessment and a description of how the results will be communicated. There are a variety of ways in which these two functions can be accomplished.

Fischer (1994), Finn (e.g., Finn & Tonsager, 1997), and Engelman and Frankel (2002) have all suggested collaborative approaches in which client and therapist work together to develop a set of questions for assessment. Feedback is then given either as the assessment progresses or during a joint session with client and therapist.

Another approach might involve the referring professional explaining the reason for the assessment and how the feedback will be accomplished. As an example, a high school guidance counselor might describe the process to a student in the following way: "I've arranged for you to see Dr. Smith to help us understand why you're running into difficulty finishing some of your work on time. She'll do some tests and then she'll write a report that I'll go over with you as a way of getting us started figuring things out."

Whatever the format, a thoughtful introduction by the referring professional facilitates psychological assessment. If the individual understands the reason for the referral and how the results will be used, the psychologist can confirm those details at the first meeting and then move easily into administering the appropriate tests.

Consultation

Integrating assessment findings in order to provide a comprehensive response to the referral questions is the goal of effective consultation. As noted previously, the format in which the consultation occurs can vary, ranging from a written report to a case conference presentation to a discussion with the referring professional to a joint feedback session. Throughout these different formats, there are some approaches that can be helpful and some caveats to keep in mind when presenting assessment findings.

It is often useful to place assessment findings in the context of the person's past and future (Caldwell, 2001). As an example, after describing the simplifying and affect-avoiding style that characterizes a current finding of *Lambda* = 1.33 and *Afr* = .38, the psychologist might speculate that the chaotic family in which the patient grew up made the development of that style quite adaptive. The psychologist could then suggest that the style might be detrimental in vocational and interpersonal situations requiring comfort with complexity and emotion, and if the patient and therapist see that as a potential problem, there are a range of relevant intervention options.

It is always important to remember that psychological assessment occurs within a broader context and that sometimes individual personality issues do not account for the most relevant part of the variance for making predictions. As an example, Exner and Murillo (1975) followed 148 patients for a year after their discharge from a private psychiatric hospital. Seven to nine weeks after discharge each patient was interviewed and rated on the Inpatient Multidimensional Psychiatric Scale (IMPS; Lorr et al., 1966), a measure that includes 10 factorially derived pathology scores. Additionally, the patients and their closest available significant other both completed the Katz Adjustment Scales (KAS; Katz & Lyerly, 1963).

Exner and Murillo (1975) found that level of pathology as measured by the IMPS did not differentiate patients who relapsed during the year from those who did not. Difference scores calculated by comparing the patients' ratings with those of their significant others on two of the KAS scales (socially expected behaviors and free-time activities) identified approximately 90% of the patient relapses. False positive rates were relatively low, ranging from 15% for schizophrenic patients for whom the significant other reported frequent contact to 25% for nonschizophrenic patients. The findings suggest that individual psychopathology may play a less important role in the prediction of posthospitalization relapse than does interpersonal environment variables.

It is also helpful for the assessment psychologist to be knowledgeable about the interpersonal context in which interventions occur. A study by Bihlar and Carlsson (2000) explored the relationship between patients' problems as indicated by psychological assessment and therapists' goals.

They compared Rorschach findings with the initial treatment plans developed independently for 130 outpatients by 84 treating psychotherapists. The authors found that there was significantly lower agreement between therapist-identified treatment targets and problems identified by the Rorschach for patients with *Lambda* > .99, Isolation Index > .24, *AG+COP*< 3, *Fr+rF* > 0, Populars < 4, *Sum6* > 6 and *WSum6* > 17, *M−* > 1, and Intellectualization Index > 5. For those patients, the authors suggest that ". . . the Rorschach may provide information about aspects of patients' psychological functioning which they are not able to communicate or which are not paid attention to by the therapists" (p. 196). These findings are important in planning how to present assessment findings. If a patient's Rorschach contains some of these features, the consultation may introduce information that will be surprising for the referring therapist and that may not correspond with his or her initial impression of the patient.

SUMMARY

A major function of psychological assessment is to provide consultation to professionals who must make decisions or plan interventions for the individuals they refer. A four-step model describes the sequence in which this consultation occurs: (1) a formulation of the case that allows articulation of the referral questions and identification of everyone for whom the consultation will be provided, (2) a literature review about the referral issues and the empirically anchored assessment approaches that can address them, (3) an explanation to the person being referred about the reasons for the assessment and a decision about how the results will be communicated, and (4) a consultation that addresses the referral questions and places them in the broader context of the person's environment and overall function.

The remainder of this book is divided into five sections. The first four include the presentation of cases that illustrate the consultation model in a variety of settings and with a variety of individuals. Each begins with a review of the person's history and a description of the questions that occasioned a referral for psychological assessment. A review of the relevant literature comes next. These reviews are not meant to be exhaustive, but rather to survey the empirical foundations available for responding to the specific issues each case presents. The search strategies described in Chapter 1 then guide a systematic approach to Rorschach interpretation and allow the findings to be integrated into a comprehensive consultation.

The final section of this book focuses on new nonpatient data, contrasting findings from a new sample with those published previously for use with the *Comprehensive System*. This section also includes frequency and proportional data concerning responses to each card, plus frequency data for responses to each card by location area. These data are discussed in the context of card difficulty and the relative potency of the distal features of various areas of the 10 figures.

REFERENCES

American Psychiatric Association. (2000). *Diagnostic and statistical manual of mental disorders* (4th ed., text rev.). Washington, DC: Author.

American Psychological Association. (2004). *PsycINFO*. Washington, DC: Author.

Beck, S. J. (1976). *The Rorschach Test exemplified in classics of drama and fiction*. New York: Stratton.

Bihlar, B., & Carlsson, A. M. (2000). An exploratory study of agreement between therapists' goals and patients' problems revealed by the Rorschach. *Psychotherapy Research, 10*(2), 196–214.

Blais, M. A., Hilsenroth, M. J., Castlebury, F., Fowler, J. C., & Baity, M. R. (2001). Predicting *DSM-IV* Cluster B personality disorder criteria from MMPI-2 and Rorschach data: A test of incremental validity. *Journal of Personality Assessment, 76*(1), 150–168.

Caldwell, A. B. (2001). What do the MMPI scales fundamentally measure? Some hypotheses. *Journal of Personality Assessment, 76*(1), 1–17.

Engelman, D. H., & Frankel, S. A. (2002). The three person field: Collaborative consultation to psychotherapy. *Humanistic Psychologist, 30*, 49–62.

Exner, J. E., & Murillo, L. (1975). Early prediction of post-hospitalization relapse. *Journal of Psychiatric Research, 12*, 231–237.

Finn, S. E., & Tonsager, M. E. (1997). Information gathering and therapeutic models of assessment: Complementary paradigms. *Psychological Assessment, 9*, 374–385.

First, M. B., Spitzer, R. L., Gibbon, M., & Williams, J. B. (1997). *Structured Clinical Interview for* DSM-IV *Axis I Disorders (SCID-I)*. Washington, DC: American Psychiatric Publishing.

Fischer, C. T. (1994). *Individualizing psychological assessment*. Mahwah, NJ: Erlbaum.

Fowler, J. C., Piers, C., Hilsenroth, M. J., Holdwick, D. J., & Padawer, J. R. (2001). The Rorschach suicide constellation: Assessing various degrees of lethality. *Journal of Personality Assessment, 76*(2), 333–351.

Katz, M., & Lyerly, S. (1963). Methods for measuring adjustment and social behavior in the community. *Psychological Reports, 13*, 503.

Klopfer, B., Ainsworth, M. D., Klopfer, W. G., & Holt, R. R. (1954). *Developments in the Rorschach technique: Vol. I. Technique and theory*. New York: Harcourt, Brace, & World.

Lorr, M., McNair, D., & Klett, C. J. (1966). *Inpatient Multidimensional Psychiatric Scale*. Palo Alto, CA: Consulting Psychologists Press.

Meyer, G. J., & Archer, R. P. (2001). The hard science of Rorschach research: What do we know and where do we go? *Psychological Assessment, 13*(4), 486–502.

Meyer, G. J., Finn, S. E., Eyde, L., Kay, G. G., Moreland, K. L., Dies, R. R., et al. (2001). Psychological testing and psycholological assessment: A review of evidence and issues. *American Psychologist, 56*, 128–165.

Mortimer, R. L., & Smith, W. H. (1983). The use of the psychological test report in setting the focus of psychotherapy. *Journal of Personality Assessment, 47*(2), 134–138.

Piotrowski, Z. A. (1957). *Perceptanalysis: A fundamentally reworked, expanded, and systematized Rorschach method*. New York: Macmillan.

Rapaport, D., Gill, M., & Schafer, R. (1968). *Diagnostic psychological testing* (rev. ed.). New York: International Universities Press.

Rorschach, H. (1981). *Psychodiagnostics* (9th ed.). Berne: Hans Huber. (Original work published 1942)

Rubin, N. I., & Arceneaux, J. M. (2001). Intractable depression or psychosis. *Acta Psychiatrica Scandinavica, 104*(5), 402–405.

Rybakow, T. (1910). *Atlas for experimental research on personality*. Moscow: University of Moscow.

Stewart, T. D., & Golding, E. R. (1985). Use of projective testing on a consultation-liaison service. *Psychotherapy and Psychosomatics, 43*(3), 151–155.

Whipple, G. M. (1910). *Manual of mental and physical tests*. Baltimore: Warwick and York.

PART TWO

Using the Rorschach in Clinical Consultation and Treatment Planning

CHAPTER 3

An Issue of Stress Management

This 23-year-old woman was evaluated at a private mental health clinic on the recommendation of her physician, who has been treating her for a spastic colon problem for approximately seven months. He suggested that the condition probably relates to difficulties that she has in dealing with stress and suggested that treatment for stress management could be beneficial. The therapist who will be providing treatment has requested psychological assessment to aid in planning.

The patient is the second of two children. Her sister, age 25, is a college graduate and has been married for three years. Her father, age 50, is an executive for a manufacturing firm and her mother, age 48, is a housewife. She and her sister are very close. Although they live in different states, they talk frequently by phone, especially during the past 18 months since the sister gave birth to twin girls. She says that the calls to her sister are a very important part of her life and "usually keep me on an even keel."

She graduated in the top 20% of her high school class at age 18 and entered college with the intention of majoring in elementary education. By the end of her sophomore year, she felt disillusioned about the prospect of teaching and decided to drop out of school for at least two years to explore her interests further through work. She obtained a position as a paralegal and has found the work to be quite interesting. Currently, she is weighing the possibility of returning to school and completing prelaw requirements and then applying to law school. She reports that her work is rewarding, but her personal life has been far less so. Since being employed, she has maintained her own apartment and approximately two years ago agreed to a "live in" arrangement with a man (student) she had been dating regularly. That relationship ended after only four months: "I couldn't believe I misjudged him so much. He was always demanding and never helped out. After a while I felt like I was his maid, and even though I knew that, it took me almost a month before I mustered the courage to throw him out."

During the next year, she dated frequently. She describes numerous sexual liaisons during that time, stating, "That was pretty stupid too because I really could have gotten myself in trouble." About a year ago, she began dating a 37-year-old man who was separated and who told her that he was to be divorced. He moved in with her during the third month of their relationship and remained as a "live-in" for nearly three months. Their relationship terminated when he admitted to her that he was also visiting his wife and they would likely reconcile.

She says that during the past six months "My life has been a mess." She finds herself distracted at work, and reports sleep difficulties and frequent, considerable pain. She complains that, although she has several acquaintances, the only person she can really share her distress with is her

29

sister. She seems to recognize the need for intervention, saying, "I'll do anything I have to, to straighten myself out." The referring therapist asks about her personality structure and the extent to which she is amenable to an uncovering model of treatment versus a more simple present-oriented stress-management approach. The therapist also asks about the advisability of supplementing individual psychotherapy with a group model.

CASE FORMULATION AND RELEVANT LITERATURE

This request raises a number of questions about which the assessing psychologist can provide consultation. The initial referral into mental health channels came from a treating physician who suspected that some of the patient's painful gastrointestinal symptoms and sleep problems were stress related. She reports concentration difficulties in a work situation that she has typically found interesting. And after two failed relationships, she is concerned about the accuracy of her judgment and her potential for impulsive interpersonal behavior. An initial review of the relevant Rorschach literature on anxiety and stress, somatic problems, and interpersonal competence provides focus as the psychologist works through the data, formulates hypotheses, and responds to the referring therapist's questions.

Assessment of Anxiety and Stress

Current stress and chronic anxiety are among the most common mental health presenting problems. Treaters frequently request consultation about these issues, and their assessment has been an important part of Rorschach interpretation throughout the test's history. A review of this literature highlights many of the complexities the clinician encounters in assessing anxiety and stress. A decision about whether the anxiety is primarily situational or whether it represents a more chronic personality trait has significant intervention implications. Whether the individual feels that the stressors are out of his or her control is important for treatment planning as well. Both of these questions have figured heavily in the Rorschach research literature on anxiety and stress.

The *Comprehensive System* structural variables that have emerged as most important in assessing stress and anxiety are diffuse shading (*FY, YF,* and *Y*), inanimate movement (*m*), and the components of the D Score and Adjusted D Score (Adj D). From a content standpoint, probably the most systematic approach to the analysis of anxiety was formulated by Elizur (1949). A brief review of both the structural and content approaches is useful for the psychologist in responding to this referral question.

The possibility that percepts containing light-dark shading variations could be associated with anxiety can be traced back to Rorschach's posthumously published paper (Rorschach, 1942; Rorschach & Oberholzer, 1923). He suggested that the use of "light and shadow" may be associated with affective flexibility but may also ". . . indicate a timid, cautious and hampered sort of adaptability" (p. 195). More than a decade later, Binder (1937) suggested that shading responses reflect an ". . . anxious, cautious, painfully conscientious form of adaptation to the environment" (p. 40).

Among the early Rorschach systematizers, Beck (1945) viewed diffuse shading responses as uniquely suggestive of a helpless inability to act. Rapaport, Gill, and Schafer (1946) saw these responses as associated with levels of anxiety that could compel behavior, while Klopfer (Klopfer, Ainsworth, Klopfer, & Holt, 1954) suggested they indicated anxiety of a more free-floating nature. Piotrowski (1957) viewed inanimate movement as suggestive of general frustration and tension. The current literature tends to support a differentiation in which inanimate movement responses are associated with the general experience of external stress, while diffuse shading is more specifically suggestive of a sense of helplessness in situations the individual views as out of his or her control.

Rozensky, Tovian, Stiles, Fridkin, and Holland (1987) randomly assigned 50 undergraduates either to a learned-helplessness condition or to a control condition and then compared their Rorschach findings. Participants in the learned-helplessness condition received negative feedback ("that's the wrong answer") that was noncontingent on the accuracy of their solutions to a complex problem-solving task. Control participants received accurate feedback as they worked through the task. The researchers found that the right-side eb (the sum of diffuse shading, texture, vista, and achromatic color) for the learned-helplessness group was significantly higher, with achromatic color (FC') and diffuse shading (FY and YF) variables accounting for the difference.

McCown, Fink, Galina, and Johnson (1992) also looked at the differential effects of controllable versus uncontrollable stress with a design in which 75 male undergraduates were subjected to three minutes of stress-inducing noise and then asked to solve 10 anagrams whose difficulty ranged from easy to unsolvable. Participants were then randomly assigned to three groups. Those in the first group were told that they would be asked to do an additional anagram task but with no more aversive events (no stress group). Those in the second group (controllable stress group) were told that their results on the second anagram task would determine whether they would receive additional stressful noise and moderate electric shock. Those in the third group (uncontrollable stress group) were told that they would receive additional stressful noise and moderate electric shock regardless of how well they did on the anagram task. Participants were then administered a Rorschach and debriefed.

McCown et al. (1992) found that both the controllable and uncontrollable stress groups differed significantly from the no stress group but not from each other in elevations on inanimate movement (m). They also found that the uncontrollable stress group had significantly more diffuse shading (FY, YF, Y) responses than either the no stress or the controllable stress group. The authors noted that the neuroscience literature has identified neurochemical responses uniquely associated with uncontrollable stress. They tentatively hypothesized that Rorschach diffuse shading responses may be specifically associated with the experience of uncontrollable stress whereas inanimate movement responses may reflect stress in general.

Concurrent validity studies that have evaluated participants during real-life stress add to our understanding of diffuse shading and inanimate movement. Berger (1953) tested 40 tuberculosis patients on the day of their first hospital or sanatorium admission and again 6 weeks later. They showed a significant decrease in diffuse shading over the 6-week period in comparison with a matched control group of patients who had already been in the hospital or sanatorium for at least 6 continuous months at the time of the first testing.

Shalit (1965) administered the Rorschach to 20 young male sailors on board a relatively small ship during a severe storm. He compared his findings with those from about a year earlier, done at the time of their joining the Israeli Navy. He found significant increases in inanimate movement for the storm condition Rorschachs.

These studies suggest that, although the diffuse shading variable ($FY, YF,$ and Y) may be specifically sensitive to the experience of noncontrollable stress while inanimate movement (m) is a more generalized stress indicator, both are state variables that shift over time with changes in an individual's anxiety level. The differentiation of state versus trait anxiety has been an important one in the Rorschach assessment literature.

A 1972 review by Auerbach and Spielberger defined state anxiety as ". . . a transitory emotional reaction that is characterized by feelings of tension and apprehension, and heightened activity of the autonomic nervous system." They defined trait anxiety as ". . . relatively stable individual differences in anxiety proneness" with a disposition to ". . . perceive a wide range of stimulus conditions as dangerous and threatening . . ." (p. 315).

Auerbach and Spielberger (1972) concluded that diffuse shading appears to reflect state anxiety, noting that its test-retest instability demonstrated its sensitivity to situational factors. They also reviewed Elizur's (1949) system for coding Rorschach anxiety and hostility content, which he called the Rorschach Content Test (RCT). In this system, anxiety is coded for answers containing explicit or implicit expression of anxious emotions, such as fear or horror; answers whose content has a fearful connotation, such as snakes or witches; and answers with a clearly symbolic anxious quality, such as a storm cloud foreboding disaster. Auerbach and Spielberger suggested that the RCT is probably more closely associated with trait anxiety, although it may be a confounded measure of both state and trait components.

A study by Aron (1982) provided additional support for the position that content approaches to anxiety assessment provide a more chronic measure of stress. He studied 56 male and female undergraduates selected for their extreme (upper and lower quartile) scores on a measure of the frequency and intensity of negative stressful life events over the past year. Participants in the upper quartile were significantly higher on the RCT anxiety score. Aron concluded that "The experience of accumulated, unhappy, stressful events does become manifest in Rorschach thematic content" (p. 584).

Exner (2003) dealt with the state versus trait issue in assessing stress tolerance by creating two summary variables, the D Score and the Adjusted D Score (Adj D). Both are standardized difference scores that provide a measure of the relationship between an individual's coping resources and the amount of internal and external demand he or she is experiencing. The Adj D adjusts for the fact that two of its component variables, m and $SumY$, have low test-retest reliabilities (.26 and .31 at 1 year, respectively). It does this by eliminating all but normative levels of those two variables. Adj D thus provides a more trait-level measure of stress tolerance. The D Score, which includes the individual's current findings for m and $SumY$, furnishes information about available resources specifically at the time of the evaluation.

Scores of 0 or those in the positive range suggest that the individual has sufficient, although not necessarily adaptive, resources. Scores in the negative range suggest that the person feels under more demand currently (D Score) and/or chronically (Adj D) than can be handled with available coping strategies.

Examination of the reasons for minus range D Score and Adj D findings can provide specific hypotheses about the nature of the stress (Exner, 2003, pp. 247–255). Elevations on animal movement determinants (FM) are associated with unmet drive states; elevations on texture ($SumT$) with interpersonal neediness; elevations on vista ($SumV$) with the painful experience of introspection focusing on perceived negative aspects of the self; and elevations on achromatic color ($SumC'$) with a tendency to internalize affect. As previously noted, elevations on inanimate movement (m) may be associated with a general sense of being under stress, while elevations on diffuse shading ($SumY$) may be more specifically related to stress that is experienced as out of the person's control.

A study by Greenway and Milne (2001) provides informative data about the relationship of the D Score and the Adj D. Using a measure of 129 male and female nonpatients' opinions about their ability to control internal states and minimize the emotional effects of negative events, the authors found that participants with D = 0 and Adj D = 0 were more likely to believe that effective control strategies were available. Individuals with D < Adj D were less likely to feel that such strategies were possible, regardless of the absolute values of D and Adj D. These findings suggest that the D < Adj D condition may be particularly problematical, creating an overload situation in which individuals ". . . tend to lose contact with beliefs about how they might maintain control of stressful situations" (p. 143).

In summary, when issues of anxiety and stress make up part of the referral question, there is a cluster of Rorschach variables that can help in bringing clearer definition to the problem. The relationship of *m* to *SumY* and the D Score to Adj D may provide information about the extent to which the person sees current stress as controllable. Examination of which determinants are elevated to produce minus range D and Adj D findings can suggest specific hypotheses about the chronicity and nature of the stress. Content analysis may be of utility in identifying the individual's view of the world as chronically anxiety provoking.

Assessment of Somatic Problems

Rorschach assessment can be of substantial value when somatic issues play a part in the referral question. In the current case, this young woman's physician has been treating her for a spastic colon problem for 7 months and questions whether emotional factors account for some of her gastrointestinal difficulties. A review of the relevant literature provides additional focus to this aspect of the referral.

Rapaport, Gill, and Schafer (1946) suggested that Rorschach anatomy content was associated with bodily preoccupation. A 1984 study by Ihanus compared four groups of psychosomatic patients with nonpatients and found a significantly higher percentage of anatomy content in colostomy patients (17.5%) than in the nonpatients (6.2%).

Bash (1986, 1995) suggested that, although there is no unique Rorschach profile associated with psychosomatic diseases, many individuals with these syndromes are characterized by constricted records that include low *R, M,* and *EA.* Leavitt and Garron (1982) compared organic and functional low-back-pain patients and found lower *SumC* and higher frequency of pure form (*F*) percepts in the functional group. Krall, Szajnberg, Hyams, Treem, and Davis (1995) tested 15 children between ages 5 and 15 who had recently been diagnosed with inflammatory bowel disease. Although there was no suggestion of severe psychopathology, their Rorschachs were characterized by low *Affective Ratio,* high *Lambda,* and low *R.*

These findings of a cluster of Rorschach variables associated with cognitive and affective constrictedness are consistent with a group of studies that have investigated the relationship between alexithymia and psychosomatic illness. Alexithymia (Sifneos, 1973; Taylor, Bagby, & Parker, 1997) is a syndrome characterized by difficulty identifying and communicating emotions, confusion between emotional and somatic sensations, and inability to move beyond concrete, present-oriented cognitive operations.

Acklin and Alexander (1988) proposed that alexithymic individuals would evidence these difficulties with a cluster of Rorschach constriction variables that included low *R,* low *M,* low *WsumC* and specifically low *FC,* low frequency of blends, high *Lambda,* and low *EA.* They tested groups of psychosomatic patients with low back pain, gastrointestinal, dermatological, and migraine headache complaints and found that all groups differed significantly from nonpatients on the seven hypothesized Rorschach alexithymia variables. There were also significant between-group differences among the psychosomatic patients, with the gastrointestinal group more likely to be introversive, affectively and cognitively controlled and cautious, and positive on the Depression Index.

A more recent study (Porcelli & Meyer, 2002) tested 92 outpatients with both endoscopic and histologic diagnoses of inflammatory bowel disease. These patients varied in their degree of alexithymia, with 32 identified as alexithymic, 15 as indeterminate-alexithymic, and 45 as nonalexithymic on the basis of two administrations of the Toronto Alexithymia Scale (Bagby, Parker, & Taylor, 1994) over a 6-month interval. The authors created six sets of Rorschach variables conceptually linked to the problems with fantasy, affect, adaptive function, cognition, social adaptation, and embellishment of perception that are characteristic of alexithymia.

Porcelli and Meyer (2002) found that 24 of the 27 Rorschach variables they hypothesized to be conceptually associated with various aspects of alexithymia were significant in the expected direction. Notably, the alexithymic individuals with inflammatory bowel disease were significantly higher in their proportion of pure form (*F*) percepts and significantly lower in their percentage of blends. They perseverated more, gave more very conventional responses (Populars), scored higher on the Coping Deficit Index (CDI), and were markedly more likely to have records with no texture determinants (91% as compared with 20% for the nonalexithymic group). The authors suggest that their findings highlight lack of complexity, social conformity, and deficient adaptive resources as the core components of alexithymia, with the emotional features more peripheral.

In summary, when questions concerning the etiology of somatic complaints are part of the referral question, it is often useful to evaluate the Rorschach's level of complexity. As constrictedness and the alexithymia that often accompanies it increase, a more structured and skill-oriented therapeutic approach that emphasizes stress management and effective coping becomes increasingly indicated (Acklin & Alexander, 1988).

Assessment of Interpersonal Competence

There is a substantial literature supporting the Rorschach's utility in describing a person's understanding of people and interpersonal relationships (Blatt & Lerner, 1983; Mayman, 1967; Stricker & Healy, 1990). In the current case, this young woman expresses concerns about her interpersonal judgment and her ability to sustain satisfying relationships. A review of relevant Rorschach variables can provide direction for the psychologist in consulting about this part of the referral question.

Based on a review of the extensive Rorschach literature which had accumulated on interpersonal function, Perry and Viglione (1991) incorporated a group of relevant *Comprehensive System* variables into an algorithm which could classify human responses into one of two categories: positive/intact or negative/problematic. The positive/intact percepts were characterized by accuracy, conventionality, and logic; the negative/problematic answers involved distortion, damage, aggression, and confusion. The algorithm demonstrated impressive criterion validity in its ability to discriminate individuals with strong and stable relationships from individuals with less effective interpersonal styles (e.g., Burns & Viglione, 1996).

In 2003, Viglione, Perry, Jansak, Meyer, and Exner, using a rational empirical approach, modified the algorithm to create the Human Representational Variable (HRV), which classifies responses as Good Human Representation (*GHR*) or Poor Human Representation (*PHR*) and allows a direct comparison of the two (the GHR:PHR ratio). The authors' description serves as a foundation for interpretation: *GHR* responses are positive perceptions or representations of self, other, and relationships manifested in accurate, realistic, logical, intact human responses and benign or cooperative interactions. *PHR* are negative or problematic perceptions or representations as manifested in distorted, unrealistic, damaged, confused, illogical, aggressive, or malevolent representations or perceptions (p. 71).

The GHR:PHR ratio provides useful data for assessing interpersonal competence. Combining it with Interpersonal Cluster and Coping Deficit Index (CDI) variables, content analysis, interview and collateral information, and data from other tests allows the psychologist to develop a more fine-grained picture and provide comprehensive consultation about an individual's interpersonal function (Viglione et al., 2003).

Case 1. A 23-Year-Old Female.

Card	Response	Inquiry
I	1. Oh my, sk of wild animal, I'll say a wolf, his face, he's angry	**E:** (Rpts Ss resp) **S:** Well its lik he's growlg, the way his mouth seems curled up. The eyes r here, cheeks, ears, the eyes are downward. He certainly does look angry
		E: If u look longr I thk u'll find st else **S:** Do u hav to look for st else? **E:** Try, everyone can find more than 1
	<2. A donkey, he's reflected dwn here	**E:** (Rpts Ss resp) **S:** Ths is the water line (midline), & I guess ther r som rocks tht he's standg on, the back legs, front legs, ears up, & dwn here its all being reflected
II	3. A face of sm one who's been hurt	**E:** (Rpts Ss resp) **S:** I don't lik this one, a man's face, but he's been hurt cuz there's bld on his chin, on his beard, he's got a very bushy beard but ths is bld & there's bld on his head, c the red up here, & his mouth (DS5) is open, lik he's in pain **E:** U said his beard is very bushy? **S:** It looks dark & thick, bushy, I used to go w a guy who had one
	<4. It's better ths way, it ll a rabbit lik he's slidg on the ice lik in the movie, a, Bambi, Thumper thts his name	**E:** (Rpts Ss resp) **S:** Here's his nose & tail & this white is the ice tht he's slidg on, & u get his reflection in the ice, c all dwn here (outlines), don't count any of the red tho
III	5. Two dancers, dancg tog, lik at a disco	**E:** (Rpts Ss resp) **S:** Here & here (D9) their heads, neck, either a lapel of a jacket or blouse stickg out, their arms & legs, thyr leang in toward e.o., thy both hav hi heeled shoes
	6. Or 2 waiters cleaning off a table	**E:** (Rpts Ss resp) **S:** Same bodies, dressed in black with white white aprons here, thyr bending ovr ths table lik thyr cleang it off
IV	7. Lik a squirrel, lik lookg up at him, lik he's standg here & u can c up at him, his tail &, big feet	**E:** (Rpts Ss resp) **S:** His head, tail, stomach, lik he's squatting lik squirrels do & u can c him from the undrside lik, the liter coloring shows off his fur & it gives the perspective that his feet r upward **E:** I'm not sure why that ll fur **S:** The way the lines r like textured (rubs)
	8. Or 2 ducks peeking out of a bush in opposite directions	**E:** (Rpts Ss resp) **S:** Black & white ducks' heads, thr lookg out in opposite directions **E:** And the bush? **S:** Here, the diff shades of darkness mak it look thick, rounded lik a bush & thyr hiding in it, j peeking out
V	9. A flying insect if u don't count thes end parts	**E:** (Rpts Ss resp) **S:** It has antenna, wings & a tail, mayb a moth cuz its all grey, yes a moth, it's flittg around the way moths do

Card	Response	Inquiry
	10. Or a woman in a show, she has on a long trailg costume	**E:** (Rpts Ss resp) **S:** Her legs, she has a headdress on, her arms upraised, lik a showgirl in a Las Vegas show her costume is flowing downward as she walks, lik it is big plumes, u c her from the back **E:** I'm not sur about the plumes **S:** Thyr j big lik 1 of thos show costumes when u walk it all trails out onto th floor
VI	11. An eagle sittg on a rock, he's stretchg his wgs	**E:** (Rpts Ss resp) **S:** He's up here (D3), his head, his wings r stretched out, ths is the rock
	12. Ths part cb an Indian robe or blanket, a big fur one	**E:** (Rpts Ss resp) **S:** This part (outlines D1), it's j a big chunk of fur, lik an Indian robe or blanket, it really doesn't hav much of a shape, j a fur robe (rubs area), u can almost feel it
VII	13. A littl girl primping in the mirror, she's squatting on a cushion	**E:** (Rpts Ss resp) **S:** U can't c her legs, thyr prob folded undr her. Here's her head, c th nose & chin, she has a ponytail, this is th cushion, she has a big bow or st out here (Dd21)
		S: Can I turn it upside-down? **E:** If u want to
	v14. It ll a lamp w shadows arnd it	**E:** (Rpts Ss resp) **S:** Here's the shade, it has a wide base, lik a box, & all of this (blot) is the shadows around it, it's just grey, lik when u go out of the light its darker, just diff greys
VIII	15. It ll the seal of a flag, lik a state seal for the flag	**E:** (Rpts Ss resp) **S:** It has 2 A's on either side, lik bears, & it's symmetrical, lik a crest for wildlife or st. There's a peak at the top lik a mtn, & the blue rectangular parts in the middl cld repres water & the orange part at the bottom repres rocks
IX	16. An exotic orange & white flower w large green leaves in a red pot	**E:** (Rpts Ss resp) **S:** The flower is the top & cntr, it has white petals in the cntr & orange petals up here (points), here is the stem going up thru the cntr & thes big green leaves & the pot is down here, ths red, u don't c all of the pot, j the top of it
X	17. This part ll two pixies, their heads, thy hav nitecaps on, lookg at e.o.	**E:** (Rpts Ss resp) **S:** Here at th top of th pink, j th two heads lik not real but lik pixies in a fairytale, thy hav pointed caps on, c the nose & chin & here is th peak of th cap
	18. This littl part ll the headset for a Walkman, I use 1 when I jog	**E:** (Rpts Ss resp) **S:** Right here, the earpieces & ths is the part tht connects them
	v19. Ths way part of it ll 2 pink flowers, very pretty, thy both come from the same stem	**E:** (Rpts Ss resp) **S:** Ths (D11) is the stem, u can't c all of it & the pink r the flowers, large ones, actually, thyr almost identical, very pretty, I don't thk I've ever seen ones lik these

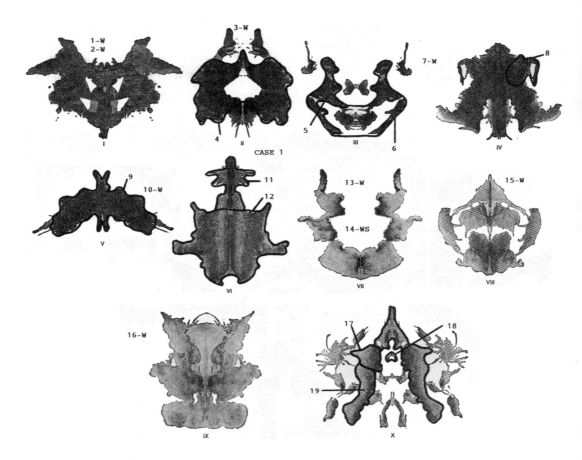

Case 1. Sequence of Scores.

Card	No.	Loc.	No.	Determinant(s)	(2)	Content(s)	Pop	Z	Special Scores
I	1	WSo	1	FMao		Ad		3.5	AG,PHR
	2	W+	1	FMp.Fro		A,Na		4.0	
II	3	WS+	1	CF.FT.Mp–		Hd,Bl		4.5	MOR,PER,PHR
	4	DS+	6	FMp.Fro		(A),Na		4.5	
III	5	D+	9	Ma+	2	H,Cg	P	4.0	COP,GHR
	6	DS+	1	Ma.FC'o	2	H,Cg,Hh	P	4.5	COP,GHR
IV	7	Wo	1	FD.FMp.FTu		A		2.0	
	8	DdS+	99	FMp.FC'.FV–	2	Ad,Bt		5.0	
V	9	Ddo	99	FMa.FC'o		A			
	10	W+	1	Ma.mpo		H,Cg		2.5	GHR
VI	11	D+	8	FMpo		A,Ls		2.5	
	12	Dv	1	TFo		Ad	P		
VII	13	W+	1	Mp.Fr+		H,Hh,Cg	P	2.5	GHR
	14	WS+	1	FYo		Hh,Na		4.0	
VIII	15	Wo	1	FC+	2	Art,A,Na	P	4.5	
IX	16	WS+	1	CF.C'F+		Bt,Hh		5.5	
X	17	Dd+	99	Mpo	2	(Hd),Cg		4.5	GHR
	18	Do	3	Fu		Sc			PER
	19	Ddo	21	CFo		Bt			

Case 1. Structural Summary.

Location Features	Determinants Blends	Single	Contents	S-Constellation
				NO . . .FV+VF+V+FD>2
			H = 4	YES . .Col-Shd Bl>0
		M = 2	(H) = 0	YES . . Ego<.31,>.44
Zf = 15	FM.Fr	FM = 2	Hd = 1	NO . . .MOR > 3
ZSum = 58.0	CF.FT.M	m = 0	(Hd) = 1	YES . .Zd > +− 3.5
ZEst = 49.0	FM.Fr	FC = 1	Hx = 0	YES . .es > EA
	M.FC′	CF = 1	A = 5	YES . .CF+C > FC
W = 9	FD.FM.FT	C = 0	(A) = 1	NO . . .X+% < .70
D = 6	FM.FC′.FV	Cn = 0	Ad = 3	YES . .S > 3
W+D = 15	FM.FC′	FC′ = 0	(Ad) = 0	NO . . .P < 3 or > 8
Dd = 4	M.m	C′F = 0	An = 0	NO . . .Pure H < 2
S = 7	M.Fr	C′ = 0	Art = 1	NO . . .R < 17
	CF.C′F	FT = 0	Ay = 0	6 . . . .TOTAL

DQ			Single	Contents	Special Scores
			TF = 1	Bl = 1		Lv1	Lv2
+ = 12			T = 0	Bt = 3			
o = 6			FV = 0	Cg = 5	DV = 0x1	0x2
v/+ = 0			VF = 0	Cl = 0	INC = 0x2	0x4
v = 1			V = 0	Ex = 0	DR = 0x3	0x6
			FY = 1	Fd = 0	FAB = 0x4	0x7
			YF = 0	Fi = 0	ALOG = 0x5	
			Y = 0	Ge = 0	CON = 0x7	
Form Quality			Fr = 0	Hh = 4	Raw Sum6 = 0	
			rF = 0	Ls = 1	Wgtd Sum6 = 0	

	FQx	MQual	W+D	Single	Contents		
				FD = 0	Na = 4		
+ = 4	= 2	= 4	F = 1	Sc = 1	AB = 0	GHR = 5
o =11	= 3	= 8		Sx = 0	AG = 1	PHR = 2
u = 2	= 0	= 2		Xy = 0	COP = 2	MOR = 1
− = 2	= 1	= 1		Id = 0	CP = 0	PER = 2
none = 0	= 0	= 0				PSV = 0
			(2) = 5			

Ratios, Percentages, and Derivations

R = 19	L = 0.06		FC:CF+C = 1:3	COP = 2 AG = 1	
			Pure C = 0	GHR:PHR = 5:2	
EB = 6:3.5	EA = 9.5	EBPer = 1.7	SumC′:WSumC = 4:3.5	a:p = 5:9	
eb = 8:9	es = 17	D = −2	Afr = 0.36	Food = 0	
	Adj es = 17	Adj D = −2	S = 7	SumT = 3	
			Blends:R = 10:19	Hum Con = 6	
FM = 7	SumC′ = 4	SumT = 3	CP = 0	Pure H = 4	
m = 1	SumV = 1	SumY = 1		PER = 2	
				Iso Indx = 0.63	

a:p = 5:9	Sum6 = 0	XA% = 0.89	Zf = 15.0	3r+(2)/R = 0.74	
Ma:Mp = 3:3	Lv2 = 0	WDA% = 0.93	W:D:Dd = 9:6:4	Fr+rF = 3	
2AB+Art+Ay = 1	WSum6 = 0	X−% = 0.11	W:M = 9:6	SumV = 1	
MOR = 1	M− = 1	S− = 2	Zd = +9.0	FD = 1	
	Mnone = 0	P = 5	PSV = 0	An+Xy = 0	
		X+% = 0.79	DQ+ = 12	MOR = 1	
		Xu% = 0.11	DQv = 1	H:(H)Hd(Hd) = 4:2	

PTI = 0	DEPI = 5*	CDI = 4*	S-CON = 6	HVI = No	OBS = YES

S-CON AND KEY VARIABLE

In this case, the S-CON value of 6 is not positive. The first positive Key variable is the CDI value of 4, indicating that it seems best to begin the interpretation with a review of the data concerning controls. It will be followed by an evaluation of the data regarding interpersonal perception, self-perception, affect, and ending with a review of findings from the clusters in the cognitive triad: processing, mediation, and ideation.

CONTROLS

Case 1.   Control-Related Variables for a 23-Year-Old Female.

EB = 6:3.5	EA = 9.5		D = -2	CDI = 4
eb = 8:9	es = 17	Adj es = 17	AdjD = -2	L = 0.06
FM = 7 m = 1	SumC' = 4	SumT = 3	SumV = 1	SumY = 1

The Adj D Score (−2) and the CDI (4) both signal the likelihood of difficulties with controls and stress tolerance. The positive CDI indicates that her personality organization may be somewhat less mature than expected for a young adult, especially one who, according to the history, is likely to be above average intellectually. Immaturity can easily breed problems in coping with the requirements of everyday living, but even if the CDI were not positive, the Adj D value of −2 strongly suggests that she is highly vulnerable to disorganization and loss of control under stress. There is no reason to question the integrity of the Adj D Score. The *EA* (8.5) is well into the average range for adults and the *EB* (6:3.5) contains no zero values.

The low Adj D is caused by an extremely high Adj *es* value (17). It indicates some unusual psychological complexity, and the presence of considerable internal aggravation. The atypical elevation in the Adj *es* is caused by unexpectedly high values for three variables, *FM, SumC'*, and *SumT*. The higher than usual value for *FM* (7) suggests that she is experiencing more seemingly random or disconnected patterns of thinking, apparently because of unmet needs. This probably relates to the elevation for *SumT* (3), which signals a marked sense of loss and/or loneliness. Possibly most important is the value for *SumC'* (4), which implies that she is prone to internalize many feelings that could be dealt with much more effectively if they were externalized. This sort of internalization often leads to experiences of subjective discomfort, such as anxiety, sadness, tension, that can easily contribute to somatic disruption. The fact that the right side value of the *eb* (8:9) is higher strongly implies the presence of considerable affective distress.

None of these findings are unexpected in light of the report about her rather chaotic social life, but they do emphasize her limited capacity for control and her potential for considerably more disarray, especially in unstructured or ambiguous situations that may seem stressful to her. The findings also suggest that the data concerning affect may be quite important when sorting through potential treatment objectives.

INTERPERSONAL PERCEPTION

Case 1.   Interpersonal Perception Data for a 23-Year-Old Female.

R	= 19	CDI	= 4	HVI	= No	**COP & AG Responses**
a:p	= 5:9	SumT	= 3	Fd	= 0	I 1. WSo FMa Ad 3.5 AG,PHR
		[eb	= 8:9]			II 5. D+ Ma+ 2 H,Cg P 4.0 COP,GHR
Sum Human Contents = 6				H	= 4	II 6. DS+ Ma.FC'o 2 H,Cg,Hh P 4.5 COP,GHR
[Style = Introversive]						
GHR:PHR = 5:2						
COP = 2		AG	= 1	PER	= 2	
Isolation Indx = 0.63						

The positive CDI indicates that she is probably lacking in some of the social skills that are important to create and sustain mature interpersonal relations. The $a:p$ ratio (5:9) signifies that she usually prefers to adopt a more passive role when interacting with others. It suggests that she prefers to avoid decision making and responsibility. However, it is important to note that passivity can also be a tactic by which others are manipulated. The *SumT* (3) was identified earlier in the data regarding controls. It denotes a reasonably strong sense of longing and/or loneliness. It is not surprising in light of her history of broken relationships, which probably represent failures that add to her interpersonal confusion.

The six human content responses, four of which are Pure *H,* are not unusual for an introversive person. Collectively, they suggest that she is interested in others and her perceptions of people tend to be reality based. Usually, such an interest in and perception of people breeds regular interpersonal activities, and the GHR:PHR ratio (5:2) intimates that her interpersonal behaviors usually will be adaptive. However, her marked passivity may compromise some of that adaptiveness. It is possible that some of her behaviors are perceived less favorably when she interacts passively with people, especially those she depends on for gratification and decision making.

Nonetheless, the findings concerning Pure *H* and *GHR* imply that she seems very open to interpersonal exchanges and usually expects them to be positive. This postulate seems to be supported by the presence of the two COP and one *AG* answer. However, it is also worth noting that two of those three answers (one COP and the *AG* answer) also contain *S.* This hints at the possibility that a subtle but persistent resentment may have developed because people have not lived up to her expectations about interpersonal relations. In addition, the presence of two PER answers implies that she is prone to be defensive in interpersonal situations and often will rely on displays of her knowledge as a way of reassuring herself and avoiding or contending with challenges from others.

The Isolation Index is very high (.63) and implies that her social existence is superficial and impoverished even though she is interested in others. This coincides with her history of failed relationships and her report that, although she has several acquaintances, the only person she can discuss her problems with is her sister, with whom she communicates mostly by phone.

Her protocol contains two *M* and two *FM* responses that include pairs, and three of the four (responses 6, 8, and 17) are marked by passivity or subservience. They convey a sense of reluctance or superficiality and tend to support the notion that she is disposed to more social isolation than is obvious to the casual observer.

Overall, the findings highlight some serious social difficulties. Although interested in people and apparently longing for closeness, it is very likely that she lacks the interpersonal skills that might lead to the development of deep, enduring relations. Her tendency to assume a passive role with others is likely to be a major liability for her. Nonetheless, the fact that she seems very aware that her social life is "a mess" may prove to be an important asset in planning treatment for her.

SELF-PERCEPTION

Case 1.   Self-Perception Related Data for a 23-Year-Old Female.

R	= 19	OBS	= Yes	HVI = No	**Human Content Responses**
					II 3. WS+ CF.FT.Mp– Hd,Bl 4.5 MOR,PER,PHR
Fr+rF	= 3	3r+(2)/R	= 0.74		III 5. D+ Ma+ 2 H,Cg P 4.0 COP,GHR
					III 6. DS+ Ma.FC'o 2 H,Cg,Hh P 4.5 COP,GHR
FD	= 1	SumV	= 1		V 10. W+ Ma.mpo 2 H,Cg 2.5 GHR
					VII 13. W+ Mp.Fr+ H,Hh.Cg P 2.5 GHR
An+Xy	= 0	MOR	= 1		X 17. Dd+ Mpo 2 (Hd),Cg 4.5 GHR
H:(H)+Hd+(Hd) = 4:2					
[EB = 6:3.5]					

She is positive on the Obsessive Style Index, suggesting that she may have concerns about her capabilities and has developed an orientation toward perfectionism. Often, people with this feature tend to feel less secure about themselves than they prefer. Her protocol also contains three reflection answers, indicating that she is unusually self-centered and has a narcissistic-like sense of personal worth. Her considerable self-involvement is also denoted by her extremely high Egocentricity Index (.74). These features are very influential in her decisions and behaviors, and can easily cause difficulties for her in creating mature relations with others. Her considerable self-centeredness also increases the likelihood that she externalizes blame and/or denies the existence of unwanted stresses.

An inordinately high self-regard is not very common among obsessive people because they usually tend to be insecure about themselves. In this instance, it seems possible that her concerns for correctness could be a logical tactic to validate her sense of high regard. Assuming this is true, it increases the likelihood that she will rationalize blame for any negative events that mark her life. On the other hand, her proneness to rationalize may not be working well for her. She has an *FD* response plus a vista answer. The latter could relate to a sense of guilt or remorse concerning her most recent relationship, but it may also signify a broader struggle that she is having to reconcile her failed relationships with her high self-regard. If so, she is probably focusing on features of herself that she has gradually come to regard as liabilities. This sort of introspection could relate to a painful and confusing conflict about personal worth and could have some relation to her presenting somatic symptoms.

As noted when studying the interpersonal data, her protocol contains six human content answers, including four Pure *H*, which is not unexpected for an introversive person. All six answers contain *M*, and four are blended answers. The majority of the six answers have positive features, such as *W* or *D* locations, *M* and *H*, but they also include several negative features. None of the additional determinants in the four blended answers are very positive (*CF, FT, FC,' mp,* and *Fr*).

Two of the six human content answers include *S,* and one is an *FQ–*. It is an *Hd* response with a MOR special score. Collectively, the codings for these six answers convey the notion that she may be uncomfortable about her self-image. This seems quite important in light of her inflated sense of self-value.

The search for projected material yields some very important findings. There are two minus answers. The first (Card II, response 3) "a face of someone who's been hurt," is a good illustration of a dramatic projection. Interestingly, she identifies the "someone" as a man in the inquiry, possibly to avoid a more direct association with herself, but the substance of the inquiry coincides well with the history that she gives about her relationships: "he's been hurt . . . there's blood on his chin, on his beard, he's got a very bushy beard but this is blood and . . . on his head . . . he's in pain." The beard is described as texture, probably relating to her sense of loss and/or loneliness. It is a MOR response that conveys both the pain that she feels and the pessimistic attitude that she probably harbors about her situation. The second minus (Card IV, response 8) "ducks peeking out of a bush in opposite directions," is less dramatic but intriguing because of the manner in which an otherwise ordinary response is made into a minus answer. It involves the *D4* area, which taken alone as a long necked bird is *FQo*. But she goes beyond the basic distal properties by extending the answer to include a greater portion of the internal blot (*Dd22*) to create a bush and also incorporates the white area encompassed by *D4* to identify "a black and white" duck head. The bush is protective and the ducks are "peeking out . . . in opposite directions." It is a timid, withdrawn sort of response that includes space and vista, and may denote both alienation and remorse. Collectively, these two minus answers seem to convey much about the basic situation that has led to her referral.

The first of her six human content responses (Card II) has already been studied. The next two are both given to Card III. Response 5 is "two dancers, dancing together, like at a disco." It is a positive answer, which she elaborates by saying, "a lapel of a jacket or blouse sticking out . . . they both have high heels." Her next answer, using essentially the same *D1* area but adding space, is "or two waiters cleaning off a table . . . dressed in black with white aprons." In the first, the figures are engaged in a positive activity, whereas in the second they are engaged in a subservient activity. The *S* included in the second answer implies a sense of negativism about being subservient. The fourth human response, given to Card V, appears related to her narcissistic-like features, "a woman in a show . . . like a showgirl in a Las Vegas show, her costume is flowing downward as she walks . . . you see her from the back." It is an exhibitionistic response but, interestingly, the figure is only seen from the back. Typically, this signifies defensiveness and possibly relates to an earlier postulate that she may be struggling with her inflated sense of worth versus a preoccupation with features that she regards as liabilities. The fifth response, to Card VII, is her third reflection answer, "a little girl primping in the mirror." It is clearly a self-centered answer. The last human content response, an (*Hd*) answer, was given to Card X, "two pixies . . . they have nightcaps on, looking at each other . . . like pixies in a fairytale." Although pixies are small, they are also supposed to have magic powers.

This collection of answers, half of which are passive, conveys two distinctly different impressions of her self-image. One is quite negative, involving hurt, pain, and subservience, while the second presents a tendency to self glorify. Interestingly, the latter, illustrated mainly from the last three *M* responses, relies on fantasy presentations (showgirl, primping, and pixies).

There are seven *FM* and one *m* answers. The *m* determinant is included in her Card V showgirl answer, "her costume is flowing down as she walks . . . it trails out onto the floor." It has no obvious meaning, but does serve to enhance the concealment noted earlier. The seven *FM* responses were given in the first 11 answers. Five include blends and three contain *S,* a composite that should be rich with projected material. The first two were given to Card I. The first is "a wild animal . . . his face . . . he's angry . . . he's growling . . . he certainly does look angry." This may represent her reaction to being evaluated, but it also may denote a more chronic disposition. The second answer is her first reflection and is a passive response, "a donkey, he's reflected down here . . . some rocks that he's standing on . . . its all being reflected." Donkeys are sometimes known for stubbornness, but possibly more important is that she resorts to self-involvement (reflection) after conveying anger.

Her third *FM* appears as response 4 to Card II. It is the first time she has turned the card, and she follows the hurt-face answer with, "It's better this way, a rabbit like he's skidding on the ice like in the movie . . . you get his reflection in the ice." Like the pixie answer, it is a fantasy response and, like the Card I sequence, she resorts to self-involvement after an answer involving negative affect. The next two *FM*'s were given to Card IV. The first, response 7, is dimensional, passive, and the second of three texture answers, "like a squirrel . . . looking up at him like he's standing there . . . the lighter color shows off his fur." Squirrels are small animals, often victimized by predators. The next *FM,* ducks peeking out of a bush, has already been reviewed. It is also passive.

The sixth *FM* is the first response to Card V, "a flying insect . . . a moth, it's flitting around the way moths do." Moths are not very desirable, and flitting involves rapid movement that sometimes appears aimless. Possibly she feels less desirable than she would prefer and may wonder if her own actions are aimless to that end. The final *FM,* Card VI, response 11, is, "an eagle sitting on a rock, he's stretching his wings." Eagles are powerful birds and often a symbol of status. However, this response is also passive, the eagle is sitting and stretching.

One of the most striking features of the *FM* and *m* answers is passivity, which is coded for six of these eight determinants. Three of her six *M* responses were also passive and the composite strongly suggests that passivity is one of her basic characteristics. Some people are passive because they are fearful of accepting responsibility for decisions, but some use passivity to manipulate others into action. Two of her animals, the angry wolf and the eagle, are predators. The others, a donkey, a rabbit, a squirrel, ducks, and a moth are more timid and often victims. This inconsistency raises a question about whether she may be inconsistent in the role that she attempts to portray.

The remaining six answers were given to the last four cards. The first, response 12, is "an Indian robe or blanket, a big fur one . . . a big chunk of fur." Although Popular, the inquiry verbiage is significant because of the tactile emphasis, "you can almost feel it." A robe or blanket is a protective covering, a source of security, which she seems to lack at the moment. The next is her second answer to Card VII, "a lamp with shadows around it." In some ways it may reflect her impressions about her own world: she is the light, but everything around her is dark and unclear. The third of these six answers is the only response to Card VIII, "the seal of a flag, like a state seal . . . like a crest for wildlife or something." It is a status response. The fourth, given to Card IX, is also special, "an exotic orange and white flower." It is not a plain flower but an exotic flower, implying special charm or beauty. The fifth, the second answer to Card X is a headset, "I have one I use when I jog." Headsets control what is heard. The sixth is her last response, "two pink flowers, very pretty, they both come from the same stem . . . I thought the stem should be longer." It is a positive answer but interesting because of her emphasis on the stem which, of course, holds up the flower.

These six answers are all positive and give greater emphasis to desirable features, status, and special characteristics. One, the robe or blanket, suggests a need for protection and a second, the lamp, appears to suggest some lack of clarity about the world around her. The headset response is intriguing because it represents a source of control about what she hears.

Overall, the projected material in her answers appears to contain two contradictory themes. One is negative and involves hurt, pain, anger, and feelings of threat. The second portrays her self-centeredness and is marked by positive and sometimes exhibitionistic features. These conflicting themes suggest that she often finds herself struggling with her inflated sense of worth versus a preoccupation with features and experiences that she regards as negative. It seems likely that she resorts to a fantasy based form of self-involvement as a "safe harbor" where she takes refuge when she experiences negative feelings or external threats. She also gives the impression of being very passive, a feature that she may employ to avoid responsibility and probably also to manipulate others into action on her behalf. She is quite concerned with status and may become upset anytime her integrity is threatened or demeaned.

AFFECT

Case 1.   Affect-Related Data for a 23-Year-Old Female.

EB	= 6:3.5			EBPer	= 1.7	**Blends**	
eb	= 8:9	L	= 0.06	FC:CF+C	= 1:3	M.FC′	= 1
DEPI	= 5	CDI	= 4	Pure C	= 0	M.m	= 1
						M.Fr	= 1
SumC′ = 4	SumT = 3			SumC′:WSumC	= 4:3.5	CF.FT.M	= 1
SumV = 1	SumY = 1			Afr	= 0.36	CF.C′F	= 1
						FM.FC′.FV	= 1
Intellect	= 1	CP	= 0	S = 7 (S to I,II,III	= 4)	FM.FC′	= 1
Blends:R	= 10:19			Col-Shad Bl	= 2	FM.Fr	= 1
m + y Bl	= 1			Shading Bl	= 1	FD.FM.FT	= 1

A DEPI value of 5 usually suggests that a person has a broad-based potential for frequent experiences of affective disruption. However, when the CDI is also positive, as is the case here (4), it implies that emotional problems are likely to be more directly related to difficulties in social adjustment.

The *EB* (6:3.5) reveals that she is an introversive person. She prefers to delay decisions until she has considered all apparent alternatives, and she avoids being overly influenced by emotion. At the same time, the *EBPer* (1.7) offers no indication that she is inflexible in this approach to making decisions. It suggests that, at times, she may engage in a more intuitive, trial-and-error approach to reach a decision when the circumstances of a situation appear to warrant that tactic.

The right side value of the *eb* (9) is greater than the left side value, indicating the presence of substantial internal aggravation or distress. This sort of aggravation can manifest in any of several forms. It may display in ways that are rather obvious, as in sadness, depression, or anxiety. On the other hand, it may manifest in less obvious ways, as tension, apprehensiveness, or various physical anomalies such as insomnia, lethargy, and so on. In this case, it probably relates to her treatment-resistant colon problem.

The unusual elevation in the right side *eb* is due to the presence of three texture responses, an unexpected vista answer, and four achromatic color responses. The texture answers signify strong feelings of loneliness or neediness and are not surprising in light of her interpersonal history. She reports being deceived, manipulated, and abandoned. The vista response was studied earlier in relation to self-perception. Apparently she is somewhat ruminative about personal characteristics that she perceives as negative or disquieting, and this also leads to unwanted feelings. The achromatic color answers are less easily explained. They suggest a marked tendency to inhibit the release of feelings, especially negative feelings, holding them in to suppress their impact. Everyone does this from time to time, but in this instance it is clearly excessive. The *SumC′:WSumC* ratio (4:3.5) is not expected to have a higher left side value. When this occurs, it implies a persistent tendency to inhibit emotional expressions excessively.

The reasons for excessive inhibition of affect vary. Some people do not trust their controls. Others are confused easily by their feelings and prefer to avoid them, and some feel insecure about sharing feelings with others. Any, or all, of these causes may be applicable here. Her *Afr* (.36) is quite low, indicating that she is inclined to avoid emotional stimuli. People with very low *Afr* values usually are uncomfortable dealing with emotion, and quite often are socially constrained. The *FC:CF+C* ratio (1:3) indicates that she often is less stringent about modulating displays of emotion, and her feelings are likely to be obvious and can be rather intense. Such lack of restraint is found among many people and usually is not a liability. However, it is less common among introversive persons, especially those who have very low *Afr*'s. Moreover, if a person has problems with controls and/or limited social skills, displays of intense feelings can sometimes be inappropriate for the situation and tend to keep others at a distance. Thus, her inclination to inhibit the excessive expression of emotion seems to be a tactic to avoid loss of control and also to conceal her feelings from others.

Findings for another variable also seem to emphasize how important it is for her to inhibit or conceal feelings. Her record of 19 answers includes *seven* space responses. When the number of *S*'s is four or more, and they are spread through the protocol, it is reasonable to assume that the person harbors considerable anger. Obviously, some of this may relate to her failed relationships, but a trait-like feature of this magnitude is likely to be generalized. It is doubtful that it manifests openly. It is much more likely to manifest in ways that are subtle and indirect and, because she inhibits the release of feelings so routinely, it seems probable that she simply smolders inside. When considered in light of her passivity, it seems possible that many of her relations are marked by a sort of inadvertent passive aggressiveness that creates the potential of turning others away from her.

She is a very complex person. The protocol contains 10 blended responses, only one of which seems situationally related (*M.m*). Three of the remaining nine blends contain three determinants, and six of the nine include determinants that contribute to the elevated right side *eb*. Two of the six are Color-Shading blends (*CF.TF.M* and *CF.C′F*), indicating confusion about feelings, and one is a shading blend (*FM.FC′.FV*) which signals the presence of considerable pain.

Clearly, she seems to be in a great deal of emotional turmoil that contributes to and compounds her control problems. Some of this turmoil may relate to her seeming confusion about her inflated sense of self, but much of it is likely the result of a more general kind of social immaturity that sets the stage for repeated interpersonal failures and the emotional distresses that accompany them. Unfortunately, she does not seem to know how to handle her feelings, preferring to avoid, deny, or inhibit them. This important feature should be given close consideration when planning treatment.

PROCESSING

Case 1.   Processing Variables for a 23-Year-Old Female.

EB = 6:3.5	Zf = 15	Zd = +9.0	DQ+ = 12
L = 0.06	W:D:Dd = 9:6:4	PSV = 0	DQv/+ = 0
HVI = NO	W:M = 9:6		DQv = 1
OBS = YES			

Location & DQ Sequencing

I: WSo.W+	VI: D+.Dv
II: WS+.DS+	VII: W+.WS+
III: D+.DS+	VIII: Wo
IV: Wo.DdS+	IX: WS+
V: Ddo.W+	X: Dd+.Do.Ddo

The *Zf* of 15, the *W:D:Dd* ratio of 9:6:4, and the *W:M* ratio of 9:6 all suggest that she exerts considerable effort when processing new information. This is consistent with her obsessive style, as is the presence of four *Dd* answers. Her location and *DQ* sequencing is generally regular through the first seven cards, to which she gives two answers each, and at least one of the two involves a synthesis (*DQ+*). Less effort was put forth on cards VIII and IX by giving only one answer, although both are *W* responses. Card X may have been the most troublesome for her. She did deliver three answers, but two of the three are *Dd* locations. Nonetheless, the effort is commendable.

The *Zd* value of +9.0 indicates that she re-scans a great deal. Overincorporation usually relates to a desire to avoid being careless and this motivates the investment of extra effort. It can be an asset because it insures that all cues have been considered, but it can also breed some vacillation in making decisions. In this case, the quality of her processing effort seems quite good. Twelve of her 19 answers are synthesized, which is a bit more than expected of the typical introversive person. In part, this contributes to her overall complexity and probably typifies her obsessive style. She wants to do the right thing and works hard to accomplish that objective. Interestingly, 10 of the 12 synthesis answers occur to the first seven cards. This probably illustrates the negative impact of emotional stimuli on her cognitive operations. It is not disorganizing, but it does cause her to become more conservative.

In effect, there are no significant liabilities noted from the processing data. In fact, the effort and quality of her processing should be a clear asset to intervention.

MEDIATION

Case 1.   Mediation Variables for a 23-Year-Old Female.

R = 19		L = 0.06		OBS = Pos	**Minus & NoForm Features**
FQx+	= 4		XA%	= .89	II 3. WS+ CF.FT.Mp– Hd,Bl 4.5 MOR,PER,PHR
FQxo	= 11		WDA%	= .93	IV 8. DdS+ FMp.FC'.FV– Ad,Bt 5.0
FQxu	= 2		X–%	= .11	
FQx–	= 2		S–	= 2	
FQxnone	= 0				
(W+D	= 15)		P	= 5	
WD+	= 4		X+%	= .79	
WDo	= 8		Xu%	= .11	
WDu	= 2				
WD–	= 1				
WDnone	= 0				

The *XA%* (.89) is at the upper end of the expected range, and the *WDA%* is slightly higher (.93). They indicate that her translations of new inputs are usually appropriate for the situation. The *X–% of .11* is unremarkable. However, it is important to note that both of her minus answers involve locations in which *S* is included. The likelihood of considerable anger was noted during the review of data concerning affect. The finding here suggests that at times those negative feelings may override the perfectionist tendency indicated by the positive OBS and cause distortions in reality to occur.

In this instance, both minus answers include the use of gray-black features. One is a Color-Shading blend and the second is a Shading blend and, as a composite, they seem to indicate that her negative feelings, especially her anger, have the potential to impair her reality testing. However, neither of the minus answers (II 3. A face of someone who's been hurt; IV 8. Two ducks peeking out of a bush in opposite directions) are extreme distortions of the stimulus field. In fact, the Card IV minus would have been coded ordinary had not her striving for perfectionism caused her to extend the area involved to create nonexistent contours. Thus, when impairment occurs, it tends to be modest.

It is probably more surprising that her record contains only five Popular answers, two of which are on Card III, and one each on Cards VI, VII, and VIII. Although five *P* is in the expected range, persons who have obsessive features usually give more. This finding suggests that she is not slavishly bound to perfectionism even though she did give four *FQ+* responses. Her *X+%* of .79 and the *Xu%* of .11 are well within acceptable limits, and neither imply an excessive commitment to convention or a noticeable disregard for it. Overall, there are no significant mediational problems, and this should bode well for intervention.

IDEATION

Case 1.   Ideation Variables for a 23-Year-Old Female.

L	= 0.06	OBS	= Pos	HVI	= No		Critical Special Scores			
							DV	= 0	DV2	= 0
EB	= 6:3.5	EBPer	= 1.7	a:p	= 5:9		INC	= 0	INC2	= 0
				Ma:Mp	= 3:3		DR	= 0	DR2	= 0
eb	= 8:9	[FM = 7 m = 1]					FAB	= 0	FAB2	= 0
				M–	= 1		ALOG	= 0	CON	= 0
Intell Indx	= 1	MOR	= 1	Mnone	= 0	Sum6 = 0	WSum6	= 0		
								(R = 19)		

M Response Features

II   3. WS+ CF.FT.Mp– Hd,Bl 4.5 MOR,PER,PHR
III   5. D+ Ma+ 2 H,Cg P 4.0 COP, GHR
III   6. DS+ Ma.FC'o 2 H,Cg,Hh P 4.5 COP,GHR
V 10. W+ Ma.mpo H,Cg 2.5 GHR
VII 13. W+ Mp.Fr+ H,Hh,Cg P 2.5 GHR
X 17. Dd+ Mpo 2 (Hd),Cg 4.5 GHR

As has been noted, the *EB* (6:3.5) indicates that she is an ideational person. She relies mainly on her own conceptual thinking and is prone to trust internal evaluations more than external feedback. She likes to think things through and strives to be precise in her logic. The *EBPer* of 1.7 suggests that she is not inflexible in this approach to decision making and she is likely to employ a more intuitive or trial-and-error approach when the situation obviously favors such tactics.

The values in the $a:p$ ratio are not markedly disparate and add no information about her thinking. The positive OBS is worth noting again because it emphasizes the complexity of her conceptual thinking as she strives to be precise. The substantial left side eb value (8), noted briefly in the review of data about controls, warrants additional consideration here. It includes seven FM and one m, and because it consists almost entirely of FM, there is an implication that needs states are causing an unusual level of peripheral mental activity. This is a natural phenomenon that serves an alerting functioning, but when the intrusions of peripheral thought into the focus of attention become very frequent, disruptions to directed conceptual thinking occur easily. Her report that she is frequently distracted at work is not surprising, and the frequency of intrusions into her directed thinking probably adds considerably to her discomfort.

The $Ma:Mp$ ratio and the Intellectualization Index are unremarkable, and the fact that the protocol contains none of the six critical special scores is somewhat unexpected and a very positive finding. Usually when considerable distress occurs, it also impacts the clarity of thinking. That does not seem to be the case here. There is one $M-$ in the record. It has already been reviewed and represents some disarray in thought prompted by her pain and anger, but the disarray is not substantial. The quality of her other M responses is rather sophisticated and creative.

Overall, she seems to be reasonably consistent in her approach to making decisions and her thinking seems clear, even though there may be some difficulties in attention or concentration from time to time. This is clearly an asset for her and should contribute positively to various forms of intervention.

SUMMARY

This young woman is in a great deal of turmoil. She is burdened by many unfulfilled needs and very discomforting emotions, neither of which she seems able to contend with easily. Collectively, they create a psychological overload that seriously jeopardizes her capacity for control and her ability to contend with stresses. In this circumstance, she is highly vulnerable to episodes of impulsiveness that can manifest in her thinking or her behaviors. The overload also breeds the potential for frequent episodes of emotional disarray that can manifest as sadness or depression, or less directly in the form of tension, anxiety, or the onset of physical symptoms.

This condition appears to have developed gradually, and apparently has been facilitated by the fact that she seems to lack many of the social skills necessary to create mature interpersonal relationships. Social immaturity can easily lead to problems in everyday relationships, the effects of which tend to accumulate and create many of the negative feelings that she experiences. The situation is made more complex by the fact that she is a very self-centered person who is likely to blame others for her own failures. The composite of self-centeredness and defensiveness increases the likelihood of interpersonal failure and the bad feelings that result. The cumulative effect is a marked sense of loneliness and the gradual development of considerable anger. She has become confused about emotions and tries hard to avoid or conceal her feelings whenever possible.

Apparently, her unrewarding experiences, both personal and interpersonal, have caused her to begin ruminating about personal characteristics that she judges negatively. This adds to the experience of unwanted feelings and also serves to challenge the high regard she has attributed to herself. It is a conflict that she is not able to contend with and probably is a major factor in the evolution of her tendency to hold in feelings that she might prefer to express more openly.

Moreover, she seems to have developed the notion that a passive role is the best way to deal with others. Passivity is a convenient way to avoid responsibility, limit the sharing of feelings, and rely mainly on others to take action to meet one's needs. On the other hand, it creates a vulnerability to being manipulated or even rejected by others when carried to an extreme. This may be the case here and, when it occurs, it is an insult that can easily provoke anger, especially for a person who holds herself in very high regard. Thus, while she is very interested in people and seems to anticipate rewarding relationships, the mixture of her excessive self-involvement, passivity, confusion about feelings, and tendency to inhibit or suppress the expression of feelings creates a substantial probability that relationships will not endure.

On a more positive note, she seems to be an intelligent person who works very hard to process new information. In fact, she is a perfectionist and this contributes to her psychological complexity, which is considerable. Her overall reality testing is commendable and seems vulnerable to impairment only in those situations when her emotions, especially her anger, become very intense. Ordinarily, however, her thinking is clear and not marked by unusual preoccupations. She is an ideational person who prefers to delay decisions until she can consider alternatives, but she is not inflexible in this approach. The greatest handicap that may exist to the effectiveness of her ideational style is the presence of considerable peripheral or subconscious thought, generally related to her unmet needs. It tends to interrupt her directed patterns of thinking more often than is customary for most adults and is probably creating some of the distractions at work that she reports.

RECOMMENDATIONS

Her physician has suggested that the recurring problem with her colon may be related to difficulties dealing with stress, and the therapist asks if she is amenable to uncovering treatment versus a less complex stress-management approach. A question is also raised about supplementing psychotherapy with a group model. In providing consultation, it will be important to address the colon-stress postulate before discussing treatment options and recommendations.

There probably is a relation between stress and her colon problem, especially because she is in considerable overload at this time and vulnerable to being overwhelmed by stress. However, the more basic problem is twofold. It is both emotional and interpersonal and these two components are interrelated. Each is a source of stress, and each contributes to the overload that she is experiencing. Thus, rather than formulating a treatment plan that focuses generally on dealing with stress, intervention should be targeted more specifically on emotional and social issues.

This raises the question of whether an uncovering model of treatment would be the best way to address these issues, at least early in the intervention process. Usually, the development of effective social skills proceeds more rapidly when the therapist assumes an active and sometimes directive role. This may be important to do because of her passivity. Typically, this approach concentrates on matters of interpersonal exchange and the range of options that exist in various situations. It usually does not entail long-term intervention and the process of "uncovering" tends to be more peripheral, but in this case two other elements can impede the process. They are her emotional problems, especially her anger and tendency to suppress feelings, and her marked passivity.

The emotional issues are not necessarily a direct by-product of ineffective social skills, and this may also be true of her passivity. While each does have some relation to her interpersonal world, they also have a direct relation to her exquisite self-centeredness and the struggle that she seems to be having about maintaining her high self-value. Self-centeredness is not an issue that can be approached early or easily in almost any intervention model. Most self-centered clients find this to be a very threatening topic, and if addressed casually or too early can lead to premature termination. Thus, while some of her emotional issues and her passivity can be approached in either a cognitive or a dynamic model, the strategy should avoid any direct challenges to issues of personal worth until a very firm therapeutic relationship has been established.

Finally, the use of a group model as a supplement is probably not warranted, at least as an early part of the intervention. It could be useful in developing effective social skills, but it also carries the risk of challenges to her integrity. Such challenges could easily exacerbate her tendencies to rationalize and become more passive. The possibility of group participation might be revisited after substantial gains have been made regarding social skills and some of her emotional issues, but at the moment it seems to be contraindicated.

EPILOGUE

Follow-up information concerning this woman was made available by the therapist after 11 months of intervention, which involved 67 individual sessions. She was seen once per week during the first and third weeks of each month and twice per week during the second and fourth weeks of the month. During the third month of treatment, the therapist raised the possibility of participation in group psychotherapy, but she declined.

The therapist reports that, during the first 6 months of treatment, major focus was on social interactions with considerable attention to her relationship with men plus the development of closer relationships with female acquaintances. The therapist believes that considerable progress has been made in both of these areas. She communicates with her sister much less frequently and has established at least two close friendships with other women on whom she tends to rely for advice. She dates regularly, but has not become overly involved and appears to exercise much better judgment with regard to sexual activity.

The therapist also notes that she seems much more at ease about making decisions, although her perfectionist strivings are still very obvious. Episodes of the spastic colon diminished very substantially after the fourth month of treatment and have occurred only twice since that time. She has begun taking prelaw courses in night school, but the therapist questions whether this might be some self-imposed form of control rather than a manifestation of more sincere motivation. The therapist also notes that she often continues to avoid direct confrontations with her feelings and deals with emotions on a superficial level. Although this seems to occur less frequently than during the early months of treatment, the therapist is concerned that it remains a significant liability. In the context of these latter issues, the therapist has requested a second psychological assessment to evaluate progress, address the issue of her emotional defensiveness, and provide some guidance concerning future intervention tactics and targets.

REFERENCES

Acklin, M. W., & Alexander, G. (1988). Alexithymia and somatization: A Rorschach study of four psychosomatic groups. *Journal of Nervous and Mental Diseases, 176*(6), 343–350.

Aron, L. (1982). Stressful life events and Rorschach content. *Journal of Personality Assessment, 46*(6), 582–585.

Auerbach, S. N., & Spielberger, C. D. (1972). The assessment of state and trait anxiety with the Rorschach Test. *Journal of Personality Assessment, 36*(4), 314–335.

Bagby, R. M., Parker, J. D., & Taylor, G. J. (1994). The twenty-item Toronto Alexithymia Scale: II. convergent, discriminant, and concurrent validity. *Journal of Psychosomatic Research, 38*, 33–40.

Bash, K. W. (1986). Psychosomatic diseases and the Rorschach test. *Journal of Personality Assessment, 50*(3), 350–357.

Bash, K. W. (1995). Psychosomatic diseases and the Rorschach Test. *Rorschachiana XX: Yearbook of the International Rorschach Society,* 16–26.

Beck, S. J. (1945). *Rorschach's test: Vol. II. A variety of personality pictures.* New York: Grune and Stratton.

Berger, D. (1953). The Rorschach as a measure of real-life stress. *Journal of Consulting Psychology, 17,* 355–358.

Binder, H. (1937). The "light-dark" interpretations in Rorschach's experiment. *Rorschach Research Exchange, 2*(2), 37–42.

Blatt, S. J., & Lerner, H. (1983). The psychological assessment of object representation. *Journal of Personality Assessment, 47*(1), 7–28.

Burns, B., & Viglione, D. J. (1996). The Rorschach Human Experience Variable, interpersonal relatedness, and object representation in nonpatients. *Psychological Assessment, 8*(1), 92.

Elizur, A. (1949). Content analysis of the Rorschach with regard to anxiety and hostility. *Rorschach Research Exchange, 13,* 247–284.

Exner, J. E. (2003). *The Rorschach: A comprehensive system: Vol. 1. Basic foundations* (4th ed.). New York: Wiley.

Greenway, P., & Milne, L. C. (2001). Rorschach tolerance and control of stress measures, D and Adj D: Beliefs about how well subjective states and reactions can be controlled. *European Journal of Psychological Assessment, 17*(2), 137–144.

Ihanus, J. (1984). Anatomical Rorschach responses of gravely psychosomatic patients. *Perceptual and Motor Skills, 59*(1), 337–338.

Klopfer, B., Ainsworth, M. D., Klopfer, W. G., & Holt, R. R. (1954). *Developments in the Rorschach technique: Vol. I. Technique and theory.* Yonkers-on-Hudson, NY: World Books Co.

Krall, V., Szajnberg, N. M., Hyams, J. S., Treem, W. P., & Davis, P. (1995). Projective personality tests of children with inflammatory bowel disease. *Perceptual and Motor Skills, 80*(3), 1341–1342.

Leavitt, F., & Garron, D. C. (1982). Rorschach and pain characteristics of patients with low back pain and "conversion V" MMPI profiles. *Journal of Personality Assessment, 46*(1), 18–25.

Mayman, M. (1967). Object-representations and object-relationships in Rorschach responses. *Journal of Projective Techniques and Personality Assessment, 31*(4), 17–24.

McCown, W., Fink, A. D., Galina, H., & Johnson, J. (1992). Effects of laboratory-induced controllable and uncontrollable stress on Rorschach variables *m* and *Y*. *Journal of Personality Assessment, 59*(3), 564–573.

Perry, W., & Viglione, D. J. (1991). The Ego Impairment Index as a predictor of outcome in melancholic depressed patients treated with tricyclic antidepressants. *Journal of Personality Assessment, 56*(3), 487–501.

Piotrowski, Z. A. (1957). *Perceptanalysis.* New York: Macmillan.

Porcelli, P., & Meyer, G. J. (2002). Construct validity of Rorschach variables for alexithymia. *Psychosomatics: Journal of Consultation Liaison Psychiatry, 45*(5), 360–369.

Rapaport, D., Gill, M., & Schafer, R. (1946). *Diagnostic psychological testing: The theory, statistical evaluation, and diagnostic application of a battery of tests: Vol. II.* Chicago: Year Book.

Rorschach, H. (1942). *Psychodiagnostics.* Bern: Hans Huber.

Rorschach, H., & Oberholzer, E. (1923). The application of the form interpretation test to psychoanalysis. *Zeitschrift fur die gesamte Neurologie und Psychiatrie, 87,* 240–274.

Rozensky, R. H., Tovian, S. M., Stiles, P. G., Fridkin, K., & Holland, M. (1987). Effects of learned helplessness on Rorschach responses. *Psychological Reports, 60*(3), 1011–1016.

Shalit, B. (1965). Effects of environmental stimulation on the, M., FM, and m responses in the Rorschach. *Journal of Projective Techniques and Personality Assessment, 29*(2), 228–231.

Sifneos, P. E. (1973). The prevalence of alexithymic characteristics in psychosomatic patients. *Psychotherapy and Psychosomatics, 22,* 255–262.

Stricker, G., & Healey, B. J. (1990). Projective assessment of object relations: A review of the empirical literature. *Psychological Assessment, 2*(3), 219–230.

Taylor, G. J., Bagby, R. M., & Parker, J. D. (1997). *Disorders of affect regulation.* New York, Cambridge University Press.

Viglione, D. J., Perry, W., Jansak, D., Meyer, G., & Exner, J. E. (2003). Modifying the Rorschach human experience variable to create the human representational variable. *Journal of Personality Assessment, 81*(1), 64–73.

CHAPTER 4

An Issue of Depression and Suicide Risk

CASE 2

This 36-year-old woman was evaluated four days after being voluntarily admitted to a private psychiatric facility. The admission was arranged by her psychiatrist, who had been treating her for depression during the preceding 5 weeks. Treatment, which consisted of weekly visits plus antidepressant medication, began about 3 weeks after the divorce from her third marriage was finalized. She reported that her depression had been building for several months. Hospitalization occurred after the sixth outpatient session, during which she ruminated at length about death, stating that she did not want to live but, at the same time, did not think that she had the "nerve" to kill herself. The psychiatrist arranged hospitalization to increase the frequency of treatment, define her problems more precisely, and give her an opportunity to work through her current crisis.

She is described as an attractive woman who might be easily judged to be in her 20s. She has been very cooperative since her admission and seems eager to please those around her. She is the older of two siblings. Her 33-year-old brother is retarded and has lived in an institution since he was age 15. Her mother, age 67, is a housewife. Her stepfather, age 66, is a retired postal worker. Her biological father died of a heart attack when she was 9 years old. She says that she was close to both of her parents prior to her father's death and remained close to her mother until she remarried when the subject was age 14: "After that we didn't share as much, probably because I didn't like him very much." She graduated from high school at age 18 and then completed two years of secretarial school, after which she obtained a secretarial position in a government agency.

Her first marriage occurred when she was 22. Her husband, age 24, worked in industrial sales and she had recently been promoted to an advanced secretarial position. She states that she knew him for about one year prior to their marriage and felt that they had very compatible interests and objectives. She says that their sexual relationship was "very good," but trouble began during their second year of marriage when she became pregnant. She says that she had many physical problems during the pregnancy and, on her physician's advice, began a maternity leave early in her seventh month. Her husband was not very supportive because her leave involved a reduction in salary. She notes that he began working longer hours, "but he really seemed angry that I couldn't handle the pregnancy well. By my eighth month we hardly ever talked. I was in constant pain and really couldn't do anything around the house, and he hated getting meals ready." The child, a boy, was delivered by cesarean section early in the ninth month and her recovery was slow. The husband's mother cared for the child most of the time during the first six postdelivery months.

She returned to work three months after the birth, and her mother-in-law continued in a major child-rearing role. Her husband objected to this, and they quarreled frequently about her neglect of the child. She says that she found herself in a position where she really did not want to be a mother and was "sick and tired" of his complaining. At that point, they separated. He filed for divorce, to which she agreed and also afforded him full custody of their son, now age 13, with whom she has only infrequent contact: "He remarried and she seems to be a good mother. I've felt it's better not to get in the way."

She was 26 when the divorce became final, and she devoted herself almost exclusively to her work and dated only occasionally. During the following year, she began dating a supervisor regularly. He was 41 years old at that time. After a year, they began living together and married three months later. She states, "My entire life changed for the better at that time. We were really in love, and I felt wanted for the first time." For the next three years, both continued working and both received promotions. Shortly after beginning their fourth year of marriage, he was killed in a head-on automobile collision that was determined to be the fault of the other driver, who was intoxicated. She received a $500,000 insurance settlement, part of which ($100,000) she used to create an educational trust fund for her son.

She says that she was very depressed following her husband's death and did not work for about a month. Then she decided to immerse herself in her work and also began taking some adult education courses at a local university to develop management skills. She was promoted again and currently is an office supervisor, responsible for overseeing the activities of 17 employees. She began dating again after about a year, "Most were pretty casual." When she was 32, she met a 30-year-old building contractor who had recently been divorced after five years of marriage: "We really seemed to hit it off, although I know it was mainly sexual." After dating for six months, they moved in together and married one month later. She says, "It didn't take long for me to know it was a mistake. I guess I was just lonely and dissatisfied with life and saw a new marriage as an opportunity for change. The sex was great, but we hadn't been together even six months when everything else became stormy. We didn't like the same things and we argued about almost everything. It seemed like my first marriage all over again." She believes that he began seeing other women sometime during their second year, and she decided to leave the marriage saying, "I really didn't care by that time."

Her second divorce has been final for about two months. She says that since being separated 18 months ago, she has had difficulty concentrating on her work, has lost approximately 25 pounds, and feels a sense of futility. She notes that she has a few friends, but does not see them often. "I just sit around at night and sometimes I cry for no reason. During the past month, I've neglected almost everything. Right now my best friend is my cat." She has considered changing jobs, but does not want to lose her civil service rating.

The referral asks: (1) To what extent should she be considered as a suicidal risk? (2) Is the current depression reactive or is this a more endogenous condition? (3) Is there any evidence of an underlying psychotic or borderline condition that might warrant a different medication routine? (4) What recommendations for a treatment plan and treatment objectives seem appropriate?

CASE FORMULATION AND RELEVANT LITERATURE

Self-destructive risk is the most immediate consultation question this case presents. The psychiatrist arranged hospitalization because of the patient's suicidal rumination, a particular concern in a woman who is encountering increasing difficulties at work and is socially isolated. The secondary question of whether her depression is reactive or endogenous also has significant implications for treatment planning. A review of the Rorschach literature about these two questions will be helpful as the psychologist integrates the test findings and prepares a consultation.

Assessment of Suicide Risk

Because suicide potential is a compelling clinical issue, its assessment was one of the first topics that Rorschach researchers investigated (Fisher, 1951; Hertz, 1948). Initially, there was an attempt to identify single-sign Rorschach suicide indicators. Appelbaum and Colson (1968) presented data indicating that color-shading blends occur more frequently in hospitalized patients who had made suicide attempts. Blatt and Ritzler (1974) found significantly more transparency and cross-section percepts in suicidal individuals, a finding replicated by Rierdan, Lang, and Eddy (1978).

Exner and Wylie (1977) moved beyond this single-sign approach, empirically identifying a constellation of 11 Rorschach variables that discriminated individuals who had killed themselves within 60 days after taking a Rorschach from control groups of nonsuicidal inpatient depressives and schizophrenics, and from nonpatients. Using a cutoff of eight or more variables, the constellation identified 75% of the effected suicides. Interestingly, this empirically developed Suicide Constellation (S-CON) included vista percepts, which are similar to the transparency answers described by Blatt and Ritzler (1974), and a more inclusive version of the color-shading blend identified by Appelbaum and Colson (1968).

The current S-CON (Exner, 1986) has 12 variables, and a study by Fowler, Piers, Hilsenroth, Holdwick, and Padawer (2001) provides a comprehensive assessment of its predictive validity. The authors used detailed medical record documentation extending up to 60 days after Rorschach administration to classify their predominantly female inpatient sample into three groups: nonsuicidal, parasuicidal, and near-lethal suicidal. These three clinical groups did not differ in age, education level, full-scale IQ, or diagnoses, but there were highly significant differences among groups on their total Rorschach S-CON score.

Fowler, Piers, et al. (2001) found that a total S-CON score of seven or more discriminated those patients who later made near-lethal suicide attempts from those who either made low-level (parasuicidal) attempts or were nonsuicidal. When comparing the near-lethal group with the other two groups, an S-CON cutoff of seven or more accurately identified 81% of the patients who made near-lethal attempts and 78% of those who did not, for an overall correct classification rate of 79%.

Fowler, Piers, et al. (2001) also investigated the S-CON's relation to documented specific self-destructive behaviors, thus eliminating any subjective component that might have been involved in the researchers' chart review ratings of each patient's level of lethality. Total S-CON scores were significantly correlated with serious overdose attempts and emergency transfers to a medical facility. The S-CON was not significantly correlated with superficial wrist-cutting incidents, providing the sort of discriminant validity data that supports interpreting the S-CON as a predictor of potentially lethal self-destructive behavior. The authors conclude, ". . . the total S-CON score is associated with ecologically valid, real-world behaviors of serious suicide attempts, rather than assessing general impulsivity or self-destructive trends" (p. 347).

In an overlapping study, Fowler and his colleagues (Fowler, Hilsenroth, & Piers, 2001) took another approach to the Rorschach assessment of suicide risk, attempting to identify variables consistent with a psychoanalytic understanding of the conscious and unconscious components of self-destructive behavior. They hypothesized that morbid content is the Rorschach analog of self-hate and fantasies about death; that transparency and cross-section responses are the Rorschach analog of boundary confusion; and that color-shading blends in which the shading occurs in chromatic areas (Appelbaum & Colson, 1968) are the Rorschach analog of overwhelming immersion in psychological conflict and pain, with little ability to sustain effective defenses.

Fowler, Hilsenroth et al. (2001) found significant differences in the expected direction for each of the hypothesized Rorschach variables among groups of seriously disturbed psychiatric inpatients who were classified as nonsuicidal, parasuicidal, or near-lethal suicidal on the basis of extensive medical record documentation for the 60 days after they had taken a Rorschach. The authors then created a composite index (the Riggs Index), calculated as the sum of all color-shading blends, transparencies, morbid contents, and cross-section responses. They found that a total score of 5 or greater on this index yielded an overall correct classification of 80% when comparing the near-lethal group with the parasuicidal patients and a correct classification rate of 81% when contrasting the near-lethal group with nonsuicidal patients.

Fowler, Hilsenroth et al. (2001) then conducted an analysis to determine whether the Riggs Index added incremental validity to the empirically derived Suicide Constellation (S-CON), which was able to predict membership in the near-lethal and nonsuicidal groups with 75% accuracy. When the Riggs Index was entered into the equation, ability to predict which patients were in each of the two groups increased to 80%. Post hoc analyses indicated that Appelbaum's color-shading blend variable (coded only if the light-dark variation occurs in a chromatic area) was a more sensitive single-sign predictor of near-lethal attempts than the *Comprehensive System*'s more inclusive definition (light-dark variation can occur in either chromatic or achromatic areas). The authors suggest that the Riggs Index is a useful adjunct to the S-CON as one component of a comprehensive clinical assessment of suicide risk.

Assessment of Depression

A specific referral question in this case asked whether the patient's depression was reactive or involved more long-standing, endogenous components. There is only one Rorschach study in the literature that specifically addresses endogenous versus reactive depression. Modestin, Gruden, and Spielmann (1990) attempted to classify 37 depressed Swiss inpatients as endogenous versus nonendogenous with the Rorschach, the dexamethasone suppression test, and two structured interviews. The only agreement they found was between the two sets of interview criteria, leading the authors to conclude, "The clinical concept of the endogeneity in the depressive illness apparently resists confirmation by nonclinical methods" (p. 300).

There have, however, been suggestions throughout the Rorschach literature of variables associated with depression. Hartmann and her colleagues (Hartmann, Wang, Berg, & Saether, 2003) compared Norwegian samples of clinically depressed individuals, previously but not currently depressed individuals, and never depressed individuals on 13 theoretically selected Rorschach variables and on the Beck Depression Inventory (BDI; Beck, Rush, Shaw, & Emery, 1979). The

Rorschach variables covered a range of cognitive, affective, and coping processes that the authors hypothesized would be compromised in depressive disorders.

Hartmann et al. (2003) found that the currently depressed patients differed significantly from the combined previously depressed and never depressed individuals in the pathological direction on 8 of the 13 variables. These included the weighted sum of cognitive slippage special scores (*WSum6*), *X+%*, *X−%*, *C, SumY, AG*, MOR, and *EBPer*. They also found that the combined currently and previously depressed groups differed significantly from the never depressed group on *SumY,* MOR, and *EBPer.* BDI scores were also significantly different in both comparisons.

The authors then conducted a logistic regression to evaluate whether the Rorschach variables added incremental validity beyond the BDI, whose overall accuracy was 70%. Entering the Rorschach variables in a stepwise fashion after the BDI increased the overall correct classification to 85%, with *SumY* and *WSum6* accounting for the increased predictive accuracy. The authors concluded, ". . . the Rorschach provided substantial information about cognitive, affective, and coping disturbances in major depression not available by the BDI, whereas the BDI exhibited limited predictive power in classifying major depression" (p. 252).

Interestingly, the Depression Index (DEPI; Exner, 1991) did not significantly differentiate the groups in the Hartmann et al. (2003) study. This finding is consistent with other studies that have suggested that the DEPI has limited ability to diagnose depression (Carlson, Kula, & St. Laurent, 1997; Greenwald, 1997; Ritsher, Slivko-Kolchik, & Oleichik, 2001). A comprehensive review of the DEPI's efficiency in diagnosing depression (Jorgensen, Andersen, & Dam, 2000) suggested that the index may be relatively more accurate in identifying nonpsychotic and unipolar depression than psychotic and bipolar presentations but that ". . . DEPI scores should be interpreted with considerable caution when applied for diagnostic purposes" (p. 278). The conclusion is similar to that of Meyer and Archer (2001), who point out that the variables in the DEPI are less directly related to the sort of observable behavior necessary for a diagnosis. Although they speculate that it may be possible to conceptualize the DEPI as assessing implicit depressive predispositions, they conclude that ". . . the evidence clearly indicates that psychologists should not use the DEPI on its own to diagnose a major depressive disorder from the *Diagnostic and Statistical Manual of Mental Disorders*" (p. 499). Exner (2003) has agreed and recommended, ". . . positive DEPI values are probably best interpreted as representing an affective problem rather than specifically equating positive values with diagnostic categories" (p. 312).

It would appear that the Rorschach's value in the assessment of depression is at the level of individual variables as opposed to a constellation designed to yield a *DSM* diagnosis. For example, a study by Khouri and Greenway (1996) found a significant relationship between the Rorschach variable Blends < 4 and the Harris-Lingoes Mental Dullness and Subjective Depression subscales on the MMPI-2.

Card	Response	Inquiry
I	1. A bat	**E:** Rpts Ss resp **S:** It ll a bat, the wgs, the body, its all dark colord, lik a bat
	Tak ur time & look more, I thk u'll find smthg else	
	2. I supp it cb a bf	**E:** Rpts Ss resp **S:** All of it too, if u disreg the color it cb a bf, w the wgs spread out lik flyg
II	3. 2 kinds of A's, mayb littl bears holdg their noses togthr	**E:** Rpts Ss resp **S:** It's 2 little black bears, just their heads & necks, here's the ear (points), & it ll thyr holdg their noses togethr, I dk why, mayb bears do tht som times when thyr playg
	4. The cntr ll a lamp of ss	**E:** Rpts Ss resp **S:** Not the whole lamp, just a globe, a white globe lik mite b on a post by a door or on the ceiling in an office
III	5. 2 ppl bendg ovr smthg mayb a fishbowl	**E:** Rpts Ss resp **S:** Here r the ppl, the head, body, legs, shoes, & thyr bendg ovr ths fishbowl lookg for the fish I guess **E:** I c the ppl ok but I'm not sur about the fishbowl **S:** I'm not eithr, I just said tht, it cb a fishbowl, the way it's shaped, sorta round on each end but I don't c any fish
	6. Thes cb red lanterns hangg up	**E:** Rpts Ss resp **S:** Well, thyr red lik lanterns fr a boat or train, thyr round at the bttm, & have ths long part, mayb lik a long wick in there, thy ll thyr just hangg dwn on the wall **E:** On the wall? **S:** Yes, lik u hang on the wall, the white wb the wall but disregard the ppl
	7. Ths cb a bow, lik an old fashion hair ribbon	**E:** Rpts Ss resp **S:** A red one, if u look at old movies u c wm used to wear thm, u never c them anymore, a bow, I guess u'd use it nowdays on a pkage
IV	8. A prehistoric monster w big feet & short arms	**E:** Rpts Ss resp **S:** It just ll a monster standg there, w littl slanty eyes, short arms, big legs & feet & a big tail behind it in the middl **E:** Behind it in the middl? **S:** U can c it here (D1) betwn his legs, it's behind the rest of his body **E:** U said slanty eyes? **S:** Yes, thes littl marks up here (Dd25) cb his eyes
	<9. It cb a snake here, on the othr side too	**E:** Rpts Ss resp **S:** It ll he's coiled up & he's stickg his neck out lik he's ready to strike at smthg **E:** U said coiled up? **S:** Well u only c the neck & head & here it wb the rest of him but more lik a hump or coil, its the sam on the othr side
V	10. Back to your bat	**E:** Rpts Ss resp **S:** Its wgs r spread & its got those horns lik som bats & its all black too **E:** U said the wgs r spread? **S:** Lik in flight
	11. If u just study the cntr it cb a bug	**E:** Rpts Ss resp **S:** I dk wht kind, one w big antennae & little back legs, just a bug

Card	Response	Inquiry
VI	12. I dk what it is, the very top prt ll head of a snake	**E:** Rpts Ss resp **S:** Just the head of a snake, u can mak out the eyes **E:** I'm not sur I'm cg it rite **S:** Just ths top prt (Dd23) & thes tiny spots r the eyes
	13. If u just study the cntr it ll a river w a boat or raft in it	**E:** Rpts Ss resp **S:** Just the cntr part, all the way up (D5) has the effect of if u were hi up lookg dwn at a river, its dark, lik deep in a gorge **E:** U said a boat or raft in it **S:** Ths (Dd32) cb a raft, lik floatg dwn the river, it looks more lik a raft than a boat
VII	14. Som type of cloud formation	**E:** Rpts Ss resp **S:** Cuz somtims clds ll ths, billowy, it looks full, airy lik **E:** I'm not sur wht makes it ll tht **S:** Well, it goes up on the sides lik buildg up & the way it's colord gives it a full, thick look **E:** The way it's colord? **S:** Its drkr on the edges & liter in the middl, thers a space in the cntr now but it ll its going to fold ovr it as it builds up
	15. Two faces, lik littl girls who r makg faces at eo	**E:** Rpts Ss resp **S:** Here & here (D1), thy hav combs in their hair, the nose & jaw **E:** U said thyr makg faces at eo? **S:** The way the jaw sticks out maks me thk of 2 littl girls sayg naya naya to eo
	16. Thes ll evil faces, here lik a pencil sketch	**E:** Rpts Ss resp **S:** Sort of an artists pencil sketch of an evil face, somthg lik an A's face, I c teeth & a nose & an eye, one on each side **E:** U said a pencil sketch? **S:** It's done in grey, like a pencil sketch
VIII	17. 2 lizards on the outsid, lik climbg up smthg	**E:** Rpts Ss resp **S:** I lik those colors, pink lizards, here's their legs, head, ll thyr climbg up toward the top of ths plant **E:** Plant? **S:** Ths wb the base or pot (D2), its pink too & thes r leaves (D5) & mayb a flowr (D4) here
IX	18. Two space ppl w pointd hats & coats thyr all orange	**E:** Rpts Ss resp **S:** A big pointd hat on the head, lik the outline of sb w coat & hat on, it's all orange, lik silly, to repres space I supp, u can only c the head & hat & the upper prt of the body, the rest isn't there
	19. A candle inside of a glass candle holdr	**E:** Rpts Ss resp **S:** Ths is the candle (part of D5 in D8) & ths ll the glass (D8), there r holes at the base to give circulation, it's lik the candle is lit **E:** Lit? **S:** Yes, at top it looks sort of lik a yellow like candle light, u get the effect of the glow in the glass **E:** I'm not sur wht u mean **S:** It's a greenish blue, lik the lite effect fr the candle

(continued)

Card	Response	Inquiry
X	20. Two scfict creatures pushg on a tree	**E:** Rpts Ss resp **S:** Ther r 2 creatures, 1 on each side of the tree, the littl legs, tails, antennae, & it ll thyr tryg to push ths tree over
	21. Two grasshopprs r gettg caught by thes spiders	**E:** Rpt Ss resp **S:** There's 1 on each side (D12), lik the spider has grabbed thm & thyr tryg to get away **E:** Wht maks thm ll grasshopprs? **S:** Thy hav tht shape w the antennae & thyr green **E:** & the spiders? **S:** The blue but the color's wrong, thy hav a lot of legs & each one has caught a grasshoppr
	22. The pink is lik a bldstain on e side	**E:** Rpts Ss resp **S:** It just ll bldstains **E:** What maks it ll tht? **S:** Well thyr red but prts r drkr lik its dried, lik a stain

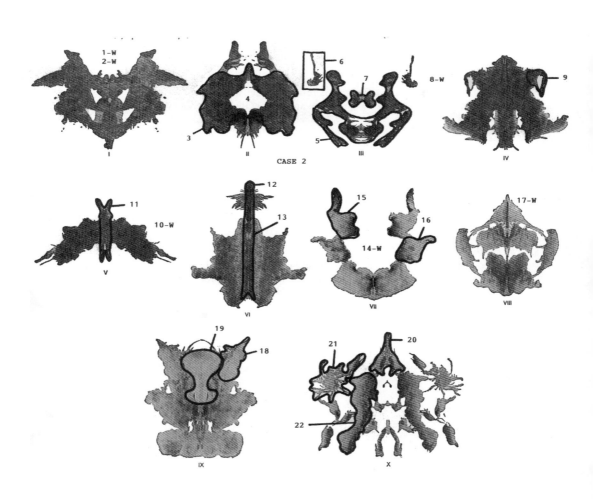

CASE 2

62

Case 2. Sequence of Scores.

Card	No.	Loc.	No.	Determinant(s)	(2)	Content(s)	Pop	Z	Special Scores
I	1	Wo 1		FC'o		A	P	1.0	
	2	Wo 1		FMao		A	P	1.0	
II	3	D+ 6		FMp.FC'o	2	Ad	P	3.0	COP,GHR
	4	DSo5		FC'o		Hh			
III	5	D+ 1		Mpo	2	H,Cg,Hh	P	3.0	GHR
	6	DdS+99		CF.mpu	2	Hh		4.5	
	7	Do 3		FCo		Cg			PER
IV	8	Wo 1		Mp.FDo		(H)	P	2.0	GHR
	9	Do 4		FMao	2	A			AG,PHR
V	10	Wo 1		FMa.FC'o		A	P	1.0	INC
	11	Do 7		Fu		A			
VI	12	Ddo 23		Fu		Ad			
	13	D+ 5		FV.mpo		Na,Sc		2.5	
VII	14	WS/ 1		mp.VFo		Cl		4.0	
	15	D+ 1		Mao	2	Hd,Cg	P	3.0	AG,GHR
	16	Do 3		FC'o	2	(Ad),Art			
VIII	17	W+ 1		FMa.FCu	2	A,Bt		4.5	INC
IX	18	D+ 3		CFo	2	(Hd),Cg	P	2.5	GHR
	19	DS+8		FV.mp.CFo		Fi,Hh		5.0	
X	20	D+ 11		Mau	2	(A),Bt		4.0	COP,AG,PHR
	21	D+ 12		FMa.FCu	2	A	P	4.0	AG,PHR
	22	Dv 9		C.Y	2	Bl			MOR

Case 2.   Structural Summary.

Location Features	Determinants Blends	Single	Contents	S-Constellation
				YES ..FV+VF+V+FD>2
			H = 1	YES ..Col-Shd Bl>0
Zf = 15	FM.FC′	M = 3	(H) = 1	YES ..Ego<.31,>.44
ZSum = 45.0	CF.m	FM = 2	Hd = 1	NO ...MOR > 3
ZEst = 49.0	M.FD	m = 0	(Hd) = 1	YES ..Zd > +– 3.5
	FM.FC′	FC = 1	Hx = 0	YES ..es > EA
W = 6	FV.m	CF = 1	A = 7	YES ..CF+C > FC
D = 14	m.VF	C = 0	(A) = 1	YES ..X+% < .70
W+D = 20	FM.FC	Cn = 0	Ad = 2	YES ..S > 3
Dd = 2	FV.m.CF	FC′ = 3	(Ad) = 1	YES ..P < 3 or > 8
S = 4	FM.FC	C′F = 0	An = 0	YES ..Pure H < 2
	C.Y	C′ = 0	Art = 1	NO ...R < 17
		FT = 0	Ay = 0	10 ...TOTAL
DQ		TF = 0	Bl = 1	**Special Scores**
		T = 0	Bt = 2	Lv1 Lv2
+ = 10		FV = 0	Cg = 4	DV = 0x1 0x2
o = 10		VF = 0	Cl = 1	INC = 2x2 0x4
v/+ = 1		V = 0	Ex = 0	DR = 0x3 0x6
v = 1		FY = 0	Fd = 0	FAB = 0x4 0x7
		YF = 0	Fi = 1	ALOG = 0x5
		Y = 0	Ge = 0	CON = 0x7
Form Quality		Fr = 0	Hh = 4	Raw Sum6 = 2
		rF = 0	Ls = 0	Wgtd Sum6 = 4
	FQx MQual W+D	FD = 0	Na = 1	
+ = 0 = 0 = 0		F = 2	Sc = 1	AB = 0 GHR = 5
o = 15 = 3 = 15			Sx = 0	AG = 4 PHR = 3
u = 6 = 1 = 4			Xy = 0	COP = 2 MOR = 1
− = 0 = 0 = 0		(2) = 11	Id = 0	CP = 0 PER = 1
none = 1 = 0 = 1				PSV = 0

Ratios, Percentages, and Derivations

R = 22	L = 0.10		FC:CF+C = 3:4	COP=2 AG=4
			Pure C = 1	GHR:PHR = 5:3
EB = 4: 6.0	EA = 10.0	EBPer = 1.5	SumC′:WSumC = 5:6.0	a:p = 7:7
eb = 10: 9	es = 19	D = −3	Afr = 0.38	Food = 0
	Adj es = 16	Adj D = −2	S = 4	SumT = 0
			Blends:R = 10:22	Hum Cont = 4
FM = 6	C′ = 5	T = 0	CP = 0	Pure H = 1
m = 4	V = 3	Y = 1		PER = 1
				Iso Indx = 0.27
a:p = 7:7	Sum6 = 2	XA% = 0.95	Zf = 15.0	3r+(2)/R = 0.50
Ma:Mp = 2:2	Lv2 = 0	WDA% = 0.95	W:D:Dd = 6:14:2	Fr+rF = 0
2AB+Art+Ay = 1	WSum6 = 4	X–% = 0.00	W:M = 6: 4	SumV = 3
MOR = 1	M– = 0	S– = 0	Zd = −4.0	FD = 1
	Mnone = 0	P = 9	PSV = 0	An+Xy = 0
		X+% = 0.68	DQ+ = 10	MOR = 1
		Xu% = 0.27	DQv = 1	H:(H)Hd(Hd) = 1:3

PTI = 0	DEPI = 6*	CDI = 4*	S-CON = 10*	HVI =YES	OBS = No

S-CON AND KEY VARIABLE

The Suicide Constellation value of 10 is positive and cause for concern. She has reported a preoccupation with dying, and this apparently prompted her hospitalization. The consultation should emphasize that she has many features that are commensurate with those found among persons who effect their own death. Some cautionary measures should be taken, and it is important that her inpatient care focus first on prevention. Typically, this will involve the creation of close supportive relationships between herself and various staff members, including her therapist.

The first positive Key variable is the DEPI value (6) greater than 5 and the CDI value (4) greater than 3. This suggests that the interpretation of the cluster data should begin with interpersonal relations, followed by self-perception, controls, affect, processing, mediation, and ideation.

INTERPERSONAL PERCEPTION

Case 2.   Interpersonal Perception Data for a 36-Year-Old Female.

R	= 22	CDI	= 4	HVI	= Yes	COP & AG Responses	
a:p	= 7:7	SumT	= 0	Fd	= 0	II	6. D+ FMp.FC'o 2 Ad P 3.0 COP,GHR
		[eb	= 10:9]			IV	9. Do FMao 2 A AG,PHR
Sum Human Contents = 4				H	= 1	VII	15. D+ Mao 2 Hd,Cg P 3.0 AG,PHR
[Style = Extratensive]						X	20. D+ Mau 2 (A),Bt 4.0 COP,AG,PHR
GHR:PHR = 5:3						X	21. D+ FMa.FCu 2 A P 4.0 AG,PHR
COP = 2		AG	= 4	PER	= 1		
Isolation Indx = 0.27							

The positive CDI value (4) indicates the likelihood that she is lacking in many social skills necessary to create and sustain mature relations with others. People lacking in these skills are more likely to have superficial relationships and frequently are regarded as distant or inept in their dealings with others. Vulnerability to rejection and a tendency to become dissatisfied with life are common by-products of this problem, and periodic emotional disruptions, especially depression, often result as social failures accumulate. This finding seems reasonably consistent with her interpersonal history. Her limited social skills may be a by-product of being hypervigilant. Hypervigilance is a traitlike feature that is usually well developed by early adulthood. People with this characteristic usually feel vulnerable and have a negative or mistrusting attitude toward their environment. As result, they are inclined to be overly cautious and conservative in relations with others. They do not display interest in affiliations in typical ways, and they usually do not permit close relationships unless they feel in control of the interactions. They do not expect closeness and sometimes become anxious about gestures of closeness by others.

Her 22-response protocol contains four human content responses. This is not an unusual finding for an individual with an extratensive style. However, only one of the four human contents is a Pure *H*. This suggests that, although she may be interested in others, she probably does not understand them very well. People like this often misinterpret social situations, and hypervigilance substantially increases that likelihood. This finding may seem somewhat contradictory to that for the GHR:PHR ratio (5:3), in which more good human representational answers exist. The Sequence of Scores reveals that two of the five *GHR* answers have parenthesized human contents, a third is an *Hd* answer, and a fourth is a response with an *Ad* content. Although none of the *GHR* responses include negative features, four have contents that convey a sense of interest but do not correlate well with interpersonal adaptiveness.

Similarly, her record includes the unusual mix of two COP answers and four *AG* responses. The COP answers suggest that she anticipates positive interactions among people, but the substantial frequency of *AG* indicates that she tends to be forceful or aggressive in her interactions and perceives such behaviors to be natural in interpersonal relations. People with this unexpected mixture of COP and *AG* answers usually do not understand people very well and are likely to be somewhat inconsistent in their interpersonal behaviors. Sometimes, they will maintain a superficial facade of being cooperative and outgoing that serves to conceal the more aggressive attitudes that they harbor.

There is likely a relationship between the findings regarding the features of the human content answers, the unusual COP and *AG* mix, the positive HVI, and the value for the Isolation Index (.27). It is marginally elevated and appears to reflect some reluctance about being routinely involved in social intercourse.

Her protocol contains seven *M* or *FM* answers that include pairs. They include little bears holding their noses together, playing (response 3), two people bending over a fishbowl (response 5), snakes coiled ready to strike (response 9), little girls making faces at each other (response 15), lizards climbing up something (response 17), science fiction creatures pushing on a tree (response 20), and grasshoppers getting caught by spiders (response 21). The first is positive, but none of the remaining six have positive features. In fact, four of those include aggressiveness and probably depict her more basic attitude toward or anticipation about relations with others.

Overall, it would appear that she is not very skilled with relationships, probably because she tends to be interpersonally guarded, mistrusting, and cautious. She is interested in people, but does not understand them very well. Her interest may represent defensiveness more than a desire for interaction, and it seems likely that many of her relationships will be marked by aggressiveness or superficiality.

SELF-PERCEPTION

Case 2.   Self-Perception Related Data for a 36-Year-Old Female.

			Human Content Responses
R = 22	OBS = No	HVI = Yes	III 5. D+ Mpo 2 H,Cg,Hh P 3.0 GHR
			IV 8. Wo Mp.FDo (H) P 2.0 GHR
Fr+rF = 0	3r+(2)/R = 0.50		VII 15. D+ Mao 2 Hd,Cg P 3.0 AG,GHR
			IX 18. D+ CFo 2 (Hd),Cg P 2.5 GHR
FD = 1	SumV = 3		
An+Xy = 0	MOR = 1		
H:(H)+Hd+(Hd) = 1:3			
[EB = 4:6.0]			

The positive HVI has been discussed earlier, but it warrants added consideration here. This is because hypervigilant people are concerned about protecting their integrity and are inclined to attribute difficulties or failures to external causes, regardless of the realities of the situation. They are overly preoccupied with the importance of avoiding situations in which they might be degraded or manipulated. This sort of self-concern is often reflected in a higher than average Egocentricity

Index, as is the case here (0.50). It does not necessarily signify positive self-esteem, but it definitely represents considerable self-involvement.

The findings regarding the HVI and the Egocentricity Index are important, because her protocol also includes three vista answers plus an *FD* response. She is involved in considerable self-examining behavior, much of which seems to include rumination about features that she regards negatively, and this is painful for her. This is an extremely unusual finding for a hypervigilant person and signifies that the style is not working well for her. This seems confirmed by her history. Despite being cautious and guarded about others, she has allowed herself to be manipulated into two failed marriages and appears to have no obvious supports in her life. It is a devastating situation that can easily breed emotional confusion and disarray.

Interestingly, there is only one MOR response in the record, suggesting that her self-image does not yet include markedly negative attributions. However, the *H:(H)+Hd+(Hd)* ratio (1:3) implies that her self-image is based more on imaginary impressions or distortions of experience. The codings for her human content answers are generally quite positive; three are Popular responses and all are coded *GHR*. At least superficially, they suggest a relatively positive self-image, but the projected material conveys a different picture.

The search for projected material focuses on the minus, MOR, and movement answers, plus any embellishments in other responses. There are no minus responses in the protocol, but the one MOR answer is dramatic. It is her final answer (Card X, 22), "a bloodstain on each side . . . like it's dried, like a stain." Stains are usually difficult to eliminate. In this instance, it may represent a well-fixed sense of damage or self-degradation. It might relate to traumatic past events, including her marriages or the lack of involvement with her child, or it may simply reflect a broader sense of futility about herself and her situation.

Her first *M* response (Card III, 5) is "Two people bending over something, maybe a fishbowl." In the Inquiry, she says they are "looking for the fish"; and when pressed, she becomes more cautious, indicating that it "could be a fishbowl . . . but I don't see any fish." It is a passive and possibly voyeuristic response. The second *M* (Card IV, 8) is "A prehistoric monster," which she elaborates as "standing there with little slanty eyes, short arms, big legs and feet, and a big tail in the middle." Although a common response, the addition of the slanty eyes is worth noting and may relate to her guardedness. The third *M* (Card VII, 15) is "little girls who are making faces at each other." It is an aggressive response. The last *M* answer (Card X, 20) is "Two science fiction creatures pushing on a tree . . . it looks like they are trying to push this tree over." It is also aggressive. As a collective, these four answers do not convey a very positive characterization of the self. Two are unreal, two are aggressive, and two are passive. The "big tail" and "tree" may hint at some sexual concern, but that is a very speculative suggestion.

Her record contains six *FM* answers. The first (Card I, 2) is "a butterfly . . . flying." It is a common answer. Her comment, "if you disregard the color," is true, but uncommon. It may reflect some concerns about being correct. The second *FM* (Card II, 3) is "maybe little bears holding their noses together," about which she later notes, "I don't know why, maybe bears do that sometimes when they are playing." It is a very cautious COP response. The third *FM* (Card IV, 9) is "a snake . . . coiled up . . . ready to strike at something." It is clearly an *AG* response, and the content is not very desirable. The fourth (Card V, 10) is "Back to your bat." Although a common response, she also notes, "it's got those horns like some bats and it's all black." By adding the horns, an INCOM, she adds a menacing or aggressive quality.

The fifth *FM* (Card VIII, 17) is "Two lizards . . . climbing up something." Lizards also are not very desirable, even though she suggests they may be: "I like those colors, pink lizards . . ." The last *FM* (Card X, 21) is also aggressive, "Two grasshoppers are getting caught by these spiders . . . like the spider has grabbed them and they are trying to get away." It represents malevolence and victimization. At least four of the six *FM* answers include defensive, negative, or aggressive features. They imply that her self-concept is more negative than positive and includes many defensive or aggressive features. This is consistent with her hypervigilance and highlights the insecurity that underlies it.

Three of her four *m* responses include white space, and three also have vista determinants. The first (Card III, 6) is one of the three *S* responses, "Lanterns hanging up . . . from a boat or a train . . . just hanging down on the wall." Lanterns on boats or trains are typically used as signals for defining space. In effect, they are warnings. The second (Card VI, 13) is a vista answer, "A river with a boat or raft in it . . . it's like dark, deep in a gorge . . . a raft, like floating down the river . . ." It conveys a lack of control and possibly a sense of helplessness. The third *m* answer includes both *S* and vista, "Some type of cloud formation." In the inquiry, she describes it as billowy, full, thick, and "it looks like it's going to fold over as it builds up." When clouds build and merge, or "fold over," to create a flat top, they become storm clouds that can be volatile. The fourth *m* answer also includes *S* and vista (Card IX, 19), "A candle inside of a glass candle holder . . . there are holes to give circulation . . . the candle is lit . . . you get the effect of the glow on the glass." Candles are a source of light, and this one is protected by a glass holder in which there are holes (*S*) to provide circulation. It is a defensive response that may also represent a sense of fragility, but that is a speculative interpretation. As a group, these answers seem to denote helplessness and irritation. They also convey defensiveness and lack or loss of control, but possibly more important, they impart a fairly marked sense of vulnerability. This may be an important finding in light of a possible potential for suicidal behavior.

Some of the seven answers that have not yet been reviewed contain elaborations or embellishments that may contribute to an understanding of her self-image. The first (Card I, 1), "A bat" does not include such material, but the second (Card II, 4) is more intriguing. It is "a lamp of some sort . . . a white globe like might be on a post by a door or on the ceiling of an office." It probably relates to the lantern and candle responses discussed earlier. All are light sources that attract attention, but in this case, all also include *S* locations. They may represent a subtle, unconscious way of drawing attention to her anger.

The third (III, 7) is "a bow, like an old fashion hair ribbon . . . you never see them anymore, I guess you would use it nowadays on a package." This is a positive response, but it does not yield any obvious information. The fourth (V, 11) and fifth (VI, 12) do not include embellishments but seem relevant because of the contents, a bug and the head of a snake, neither of which are very positive.

The sixth answer in this group (VII, 16) is a bit more revealing, "evil faces . . . an artist's pencil sketch of an evil face . . . I see teeth and a nose and an eye." It is interesting because of the descriptor, "evil," but also because it is not real. It is a pencil sketch, which is less durable than a painting. The last of these answers (IX, 18) is "Two space people with pointed hats and coats . . . it's all orange, like silly, to represent space . . ." It is also unreal.

None of these seven answers are markedly revealing, but they do add support for the notion that her self-image seems to be more negative than positive. In addition, three involve heads, faces, or upper bodies. One of those, the evil faces, includes teeth and eyes; and a second, the head of a snake, also emphasizes eyes. One of her *M* responses (15) also involves faces, which is common, but includes an uncommon emphasis on the jaw. A second *M* (8), also a common response, includes the uncommon report of slanty eyes. Additionally, two of her *FM* answers (3 & 9) elaborate just heads and necks.

When a protocol includes a substantial number of answers that are restricted to heads or faces, or when there is an unexpected frequency of answers that emphasize facial features such as eyes, jaws, and ears, paranoid-like ideation should be considered. It is difficult to ascertain whether that may be true in this case. The frequency by which these characteristics appear is notable, but not necessarily substantial. In addition, about half of these unusual elaborations occur in conventional responses. On the other hand, she is hypervigilant, and unusual stresses or substantial pathology often exacerbate guardedness in ways that promote more paranoid-like thinking.

Overall, her self-image seems to be far less sturdy or reality based than might be expected for an adult. She is inclined to view herself much more negatively than positively, and she appears to be involved with considerable rumination about features that she perceives as shortcomings. She may also have a sense of futility about herself. Certainly, she feels fragile and vulnerable. She is defensive about this and is not very confident about her controls. She is prone to use aggressiveness to fend off threats, but that approach is not very successful. It only serves to exacerbate her long-standing sense of mistrust and guardedness about her world.

CONTROLS

Case 2.   Control-Related Variables for a 36-Year-Old Female.

EB = 4:6.0	EA = 10.0		D = -3	CDI = 4
eb = 10:9	es = 19	Adj es = 16	AdjD = -2	L = 0.10
FM = 6 m = 4	SumC' = 5	SumT = 0	SumV = 3	SumY = 1

The Adj D Score of −2 indicates that she is highly vulnerable to a loss of control. People like this are often able to function adequately in structured and routine environments, but they become susceptible to disorganization when structure is lacking or when routines are interrupted. Her vulnerability is escalated because of limited social skills (CDI = 4). This deficit increases the likelihood of interpersonal problems, which can add stresses that she is unable to contend with easily.

The control problems are not caused by a lack of resources. The value for her *EA* (10) is in the average range, and the findings concerning the *EB* (4:6.0) and *Lambda* (0.10) offer no reason to challenge the validity of the *EA*. The basic cause of the problem is reflected in the high Adj *es* (16), which signifies the presence of some unusual psychological complexity that has created a stimulus overload within her. This complexity is well illustrated by the substantial values in the *eb* (10:9), and by three variables in particular. Her protocol includes six *FM*s, suggesting more ungratified needs than is typically expected, and which result in random or disconnected patterns of thinking that interfere with attention and concentration. More important, the right side *eb* value includes five achromatic color and three vista determinants. As a composite, they signal considerable distress, some of which is created by the suppression and internalization of feelings, and some of which results from the self-degrading rumination discussed earlier. These impairments will be reviewed again when data regarding affect and ideation are studied.

Her state of stimulus overload and the resulting limited controls are critical features to be considered when planning treatment and are especially important to any appraisal of a suicide potential. These problems seem to be magnified because she is burdened even more by the presence of situationally related stress.

SITUATIONALLY RELATED STRESS

Case 2.   Situational Stress Data for a 36-Year-Old Female.

EB	= 4:6.0	EA = 10.0		D	= −3	**Blends**	
eb	= 10:9	es = 19 Adj es = 16		AdjD	= −2	M.FD	= 1
						FM.FC	= 2
						FM.FC′	= 2
FM	= 6 m = 4	C′ = 5 T = 0 V = 3 Y = 1				m.VF	= 1
		(3r+(2)/R) = .50				C.Y	= 1
						CF.m	= 1
Pure C = 1 M− = 0		MQnone = 1			Blends = 10	FV.m.CF	= 1
						FV.m	= 1

The fact that the D Score (−3) is one point less than the Adj D Score suggests some mild or moderate situational stress elements. Although the stress may be moderate, or even mild, its impact is creating an even greater impairment to her already limited capacities for control. D Scores of this magnitude usually indicate that many of her decisions and behaviors will probably not be well thought through.

The protocol contains four *m* responses, as contrasted with only one diffuse shading (*Y*) answer, suggesting that the stress is having a substantial impact on her thinking. It has already been noted that the elevation in *FM,* apparently related to ungratified needs, could interfere with attention and concentration. The presence of the four *m* answers increases this likelihood considerably. Typically, they relate to patterns of random or disconnected thoughts that often occur when a person feels helpless or out of control. Although they usually exist at a subconscious level, they tend to break into consciousness from time to time. Under optimal conditions, these interruptions alert an individual to the need for action, but when they occur frequently, they may confuse, distract, and reduce attention or concentration spans substantially. When this occurs, it usually has a broad impact on the psychological operations of the individual.

Although the situational stress appears to be impacting mainly on her thinking, it probably is also affecting her emotions. The self-degrading rumination, indicated by the three vista answers in the record, has been discussed previously with the implication that this process has been ongoing for some time. While this is likely, it may have been exacerbated by a sense of guilt or remorse about her most recent marital failure. If this is true, the added negative emotions that result simply serve to increase her vulnerability to control problems.

In a related context, her control problems, plus the presence of a Pure *C* response in the record, imply that she is susceptible to impulsive episodes that can manifest in either her ideational or emotional activities. This notion is also supported by the striking complexity in her current psychological makeup. Her 22 responses include 10 blended answers, of which four are created by *m* or *Y* variables. Two of these include vista determinants and a third (*C.Y*) is the second of two Color Shading blends in the record. These findings strongly suggest that the stress has not only created much more complexity than is common for her, but has also increased a preexisting confusion that she has about her feelings.

Even without consideration of any situational elements, at best, she is vulnerable to control problems because of a substantial overload state. Current stresses are making this problem worse, and it seems reasonable to conclude that she is in a precarious situation regarding her ability to maintain control when forming or implementing behaviors. The situational stresses are not precisely identified, but it seems likely that the decree ending her most recent marriage, the difficulties she seems to be having at work, and the overall lack of any obvious external support system, may all be contributing.

AFFECT

Case 2.   Affect-Related Data for a 36-Year-Old Female.

						Blends	
EB	= 4:6.0			EBPer	= 1.5	**Blends**	
eb	= 10:9	L	= 0.10	FC:CF+C	= 3:4	M.FD	= 1
DEPI	= 6	CDI	= 4	Pure C	= 1	FM.FC	= 2
						FM.FC′	= 2
SumC′ = 5	SumT = 0			SumC′:WSumC	= 5:6.0	m.VF	= 1
SumV = 3	SumY = 1			Afr	= 0.38	C.Y	= 1
						CF.m	= 1
Intellect	= 1	CP	= 0	S = 4 (S to I,II,III	= 2)	FV.m	= 1
Blends:R	= 10:22			Col-Shad Bl	= 2	FV.m.CF	= 1
m + y Bl	= 4			Shading Bl	= 0		

The combination of a positive DEPI value (6) and a positive CDI value (4) clearly indicates that a substantial, and probably disabling, affective problem exists. Some aspects of this problem have already been discussed. For example, persons who have limited social skills are prone to experience bouts of distress or depression because their interpersonal lives are often inconsistent and less rewarding. That is likely to be true for this woman, but other findings concerning her self-image and her overload state intimate that her affective problem has several etiological tentacles. Thus, any conclusions about it, and recommendations regarding treatment, can be derived only after studying the full context of her psychology, including the broad aspects of her emotional structure and functioning.

The *EB* (4:6.0) indicates an extratensive style, signifying that she is inclined to merge her feelings into her thinking during problem solving or decision making. In effect, her feelings usually influence her quite a bit, and she is probably comfortable about relying on an intuitive approach when deciding things. People like this are disposed to test out postulates and assumptions through trial-and-error behaviors and rely a great deal on external feedback. The *EBPer* value of 1.5 indicates that she is not inflexible in her decision-making habits, and when circumstances make it obvious that more delay and thoughtfulness might be effective, she is likely to push her feelings aside and use that different approach.

The substantial right-side value of the *eb,* though discussed previously, warrants added consideration here. The five achromatic color responses are especially important because they signal a process that is somewhat contrary to her extratensive style. Extratensive people are inclined to display their feelings openly and, typically, are less concerned than others about carefully modulating those displays. The marked elevation in achromatic color answers indicates that she often suppresses feelings and, by holding them in, creates considerable discomfort for herself. This adds to the disquieting feelings that are generated by her frequent self-degrading rumination, as reflected by the three vista answers.

Although the *SumC′*:*WSumC* ratio (5:6.0) does not confirm excessive emotional constraint, the very low value for the *Afr* (.38) indicates a marked tendency to avoid emotional stimulation. This is quite unusual for an extratensive person. It suggests the likelihood of emotional constraint or, at the very least, a notably defensive avoidance of situations that might require emotional exchange.

The $FC:CF+C$ ratio (3:4) seems antithetical to the findings concerning the C' responses and the low *Afr,* but that may not be true. It suggests that, like many extratensive people, she is not very stringent about modulating emotional discharges. Her expressions of feelings tend to be obvious or intense and, at times, the magnitude of these expressions may even be inappropriate for the situation. This is not necessarily a liability for some people, especially if there are no control problems and the person is socially adept. However, if control problems exist, or if the individual is limited in social skills—both of which are the case here—a tendency to be overly intense when expressing feelings can often be viewed negatively by others. Assuming that she has some awareness of this, a tendency to be constrained or to avoid emotional exchanges is a natural defensive consequence, even though it runs contrary to her extratensive style. Constraint and avoidance are also consistent with her hypervigilance, and these tendencies require careful consideration when planning treatment.

The fact that her Pure C response is also her only MOR answer also deserves attention. It is bloodstains, a primitive and negative answer which, when considered in light of her control problems, suggests that some of her lapses in modulating emotions can easily yield inappropriate or maladaptive behavior. The potential for such behavior is made more important because of the four S responses in her protocol. They signify that she has a negativistic set about her environment and probably harbors a noticeable level of anger. This is not uncommon for a hypervigilant person, and tends to reflect the attitude that she holds about her world. Thus, when her emotional discharges become intense, they are likely to include manifestations of this negativism or hostility.

The unexpectedly large number of blend answers (10) has been noted earlier, and the number has been increased substantially by situationally related factors. The 10 include two Color Shading blends. They also include all three of her vista determinants and five of her seven chromatic color determinants. As a group, they serve well to illustrate the complexity and intricacies of the turmoil that she is experiencing.

There seems little doubt that she is in affective disarray. Her depression seems real and intense. It appears to be marked by many more endogenous than reactive features, including the accumulation of considerable dissatisfaction that has resulted from social failures. She seems confused about her feelings and works hard to suppress them, or to avoid situations that might exacerbate them. She tends to degrade herself much more than most people, and this creates a difficult emotional burden for her. She is angry, probably both at herself and the world which she mistrusts. This sort of turmoil can easily breed self-destructive thinking.

PROCESSING

Case 2.   Processing Variables for a 36-Year-Old Female.

EB = 4:6.0	Zf = 15	Zd = −4.0	DQ+ = 10
L = 0.10	W:D:Dd = 6:14:2	PSV = 0	DQv/+ = 1
HVI = YES	W:M = 6:4		DQv = 1
OBS = NO			

Location & DQ Sequencing

I: Wo.Wo	VI: Ddo.D+
II: D+.DSo	VII: WSv/+.D+.Do
III: D+.DdS+.Do	VIII: W+
IV: Wo.Do	IX: D+.DS+
V: Wo.Do	X: D+.D+.Dv

Hypervigilance usually fosters added effort and great care when processing new information. The *Zf* value (15) suggests she invests considerable effort to organize new information, but other data in the cluster seem antithetical to that conclusion. The *W:D:Dd* ratio (6:14:2) signifies a very economical processing approach, and this conclusion is supported by a review of her location sequence. Four of the six *W* answers are to Cards I, IV, and V, which are relatively solid figures and tend to promote whole responses. Her answers to the more broken or complex figures are mainly *D* or *Dd* responses. Likewise, the *W:M* ratio (6:4) reflects a more conservative striving than expected for an extratensive person, and suggests that she is cautious when setting processing objectives. Nonetheless, her processing approach is reasonably consistent, with all but one of her *W*'s being first answers.

Possibly the most surprising finding in this data set is the *Zd* value of −4.0, indicating that she is an underincorporator. Apparently, she scans new fields of information somewhat hastily and haphazardly, and she may often neglect critical cues in a field. This is inconsistent with hypervigilance, and raises the likelihood that the situational stress she is experiencing, or a more chronic pathology, is causing some impairment to her typical processing habits. On the other hand, 10 of her answers have *DQ+* codings, signaling that the yield of her processing is often complex. Most of her *DQ+* responses are given to the more broken figures (II, III, VII, VIII, & X), which tend to be more amenable to *DQ+* answers. Nevertheless, the quantity and regularity with which they occur suggests that the overall quality of her processing is probably quite good.

In effect, the processing data are a bit contradictory. She seems to exert considerable effort when processing, but also seems very economical or conservative in applying the effort, usually preferring to contend with obvious distal properties of a field. The yield of the effort is often complex and probably commendable. These findings are not surprising for a hypervigilant person, but the finding that she seems to scan hastily and may miss important details is surprising. It suggests that, although her current processing habits are adequate, she may have processed at a more sophisticated level earlier. In this context, it is reasonable to assume that some impairment to her processing habits has occurred, possibly because of situational factors, but more likely because of the turmoil that she has been experiencing for some time.

MEDIATION

Case 2. Mediation Variables for a 36-Year-Old Female.

R = 22		L = 0.10		OBS = No	**Minus & NoForm Features**
FQx+	= 0		XA%	= .95	X 22. Dv C.Y 2 Bl MOR
FQxo	= 15		WDA%	= .95	
FQxu	= 6		X–%	= .00	
FQx–	= 0		S–	= 0	
FQxnone	= 1				
(W+D	= 20)		P	= 9	
WD+	= 0		X+%	= .68	
WDo	= 15		Xu%	= .27	
WDu	= 4				
WD–	= 0				
WDnone	= 1				

The *XA%* (.95) and the *WDA%* (.95) are both higher than expected, indicating that she makes a special effort to ensure that she translates stimulus cues in a manner that is appropriate for the situation. She likes to be accurate, a notion also supported by the fact that there are no minus answers in her protocol.

However, she gave one NoForm answer (*C.Y*). Extratensives are more likely than others to give a Pure *C* answer but, usually when that occurs, it is in a record that does not include obvious evidence for concerns with accuracy. Thus, a Pure *C* response in her protocol suggests that, although her reality testing seems adequate most of the time, it can become impaired occasionally because of her intense feelings.

Her striving to be accurate or conventional is also suggested by the nine Popular answers, a finding considerably greater than average. When considered in light of the high *XA%* and *WDA%*, it raises a question about whether she has a perfectionistic tendency. However, the absence of *FQ+* answers, plus her somewhat haphazard scanning, argues against that conclusion. The fact that the *X+%* (.68) is not high and the *Xu%* (.27) is substantial also decries any such assumption. They suggest that her mediational decisions tend to disregard social demands or expectancies more than is the case for many people. Therefore, it seems reasonable to postulate that her endeavors to be accurate are related to defensiveness produced by her hypervigilance. If she translates events appropriately, she is able to reduce the possibility of being unexpectedly demeaned or threatened by them. Regardless of the antecedents, it is sensible to conclude that her mediational processes usually are intact and, as such, form the basis from which good reality testing can occur.

IDEATION

Case 2. Ideation Variables for a 36-Year-Old Female.

L	= 0.10	OBS	= No	HVI	= YES	**Critical Special Scores**			
						DV	= 0	DV2	= 0
EB	= 4:6.0	EBPer	= 1.5	a:p	= 7:7	INC	= 2	INC2	= 0
				Ma:Mp	= 2:2	DR	= 0	DR2	= 0
eb	= 10:9	[FM = 6 m = 4]				FAB	= 0	FAB2	= 0
				M−	= 0	ALOG	= 0	CON	= 0
Intell Indx = 1		MOR	= 1	Mnone	= 0	Sum6	= 2	WSum6	= 4
							(R = 22)		

M Response Features

III   5. D+ Mpo 2 H,Cg,Hh P 3.0 GHR
IV   8. Wo Mp.FDo (H) P 2.0 GHR
VII 15. D+ Mao 2 (Hd),Cg P 3.0 AG,GHR
X   20. D+ Mau (A),Bt 4.0 COP,AG,PHR

As noted earlier, the *EB* (4:6.0) indicates that this patient's thinking tends to be routinely influenced by her feelings. This does not mean that it is less consistent or more illogical, for that is not the case. It simply means that she is prone to rely on intuition when making decisions. However, the datum for the *EBPer* (1.5) suggests that there is no reason to believe she is inflexible about this approach, and she often may push her feelings aside when the circumstances of a situation seem to call for a more logical approach.

The regularity of her approach to decision making is an asset, but another element probably reduces its effectiveness. It is her hypervigilance. At its core is a negative or mistrusting attitude toward her environment that tends to be pervasively influential in much of her thinking. She feels insecure and vulnerable in her world, and these feelings prompt her to be cautious about making decisions or implementing behaviors. This hypervigilant set can easily lead to patterns of thinking that are less clear, less flexible, and even illogical at times. Thus, although her feelings are likely to influence her when making decisions or forming behaviors, the persistent undercurrent of guardedness and mistrust also will contribute to her feelings and decisions in ways that can lead to less effective behaviors, especially in social situations. This possibility of less effective decisions is also increased because her often influential emotions are in disarray, which can easily breed flawed intuitive judgments.

Usually, a single MOR answer adds no useful information about patterns of ideation but, in this instance, the dramatic substance of her MOR response, bloodstains, seems worth noting. It implies a sense of futility and suggests that, at times, her thinking will be marked by a pessimistic set that can easily influence her judgments. These may be fleeting events but, when they occur, they are likely to affect her thinking markedly. This seems particularly important now because of two other elements discussed earlier.

The first is the possibility of a suicidal preoccupation. Even brief episodes of extreme pessimism can be hazardous if an underlying concern with self-destruction exists. The second element is reflected in the left side *eb* value (10) that denotes considerable peripheral thinking, which has apparently been increased substantially by situational factors (four *m* responses). Although much of this subconscious or unconscious thinking seems related to need states, it apparently also includes a profusion of ideational activity that is being provoked by a sense of helplessness. This would not bode well for anyone. It can easily breed a substantial interference with attention and concentration, but the impact on conceptual thinking could be even greater for a person who is seriously depressed, mistrusting of the world around her, and prone to episodes of considerable pessimism.

On a more positive note, none of the other data concerning her thinking raise causes for concern. The value for the *Ma:Mp* ratio (2:2) does not signal any notable abuse of fantasy, and the Intellectualization Index (1) offers no hint that she strives to deny emotions by ideationally minimizing their importance. The relative absence of Critical Special Scores (two INCOMs), and the fact that none of her four *M* responses contain distortions, support the notion that her thinking is usually free of detachments from reality. In addition, her *M* responses, though not very sophisticated, are concise and on target.

The clarity of her thinking seems to be an asset for her, but some aspects of her ideation must be regarded as liabilities and should be considered carefully when planning treatment. One stems from her hypervigilance, which includes a guarded and mistrusting attitude about her world. This cannot help but influence the manner in which she conceptualizes things and can easily lead to flawed decisions or ineffective behaviors. Possibly of more immediate importance is a sense of situationally related helplessness. It is creating much more peripheral ideation than is customary and probably interferes significantly with her attention and concentration. It can also breed a sense of futility, and enhance any pessimistic ideation that may occur, either of which can have a hazardous influence on her decisions and behaviors.

SUMMARY

This woman is in serious psychological difficulty and there is no reason to challenge the validity of her stated preoccupation with suicide. She is in great turmoil and has many characteristics that are common among people who effect their own death. Several elements have caused the turmoil to build. Some have evolved over a lengthy time, and some appear to have more recent origins.

The condition overlies a long-standing feature of her personality that tends to influence much of her thinking and behavior. It is a state of hypervigilance that reflects an apprehensive or defensive attitude about the environment. It has a broad impact on much of her psychology, including a chronic tendency to view others with a guarded and mistrusting attitude. This creates problems in establishing or maintaining rewarding social or emotional relationships and predisposes that most of her interpersonal relations are likely to be superficial and not very satisfying. As her interpersonal relationships have generally failed to fulfill her needs, her mistrust of the world has intensified, and she has become somewhat negative and angered by the situation. As a result, she is prone to manifest more aggressiveness in her relationships than is expected for an adult, and this simply adds to the prospect for more unrewarding relationships.

Another result of her guardedness is that she does not understand people very well, and this contributes to a lack of understanding about herself. Her self-image is not very sturdy. She tends to perceive herself more negatively than positively and seems to ruminate a great deal about her shortcomings. She feels fragile and vulnerable and this tends to increase her defensiveness about others. Although she is an intuitive person who usually relies on feelings when making judgments or decisions, she has gradually become confused and wary about emotions. As a consequence, she overemphasizes concealing feelings by suppressing them and striving to avoid situations that might be emotionally provocative. This creates a discomforting burden that is increased by her self-degrading rumination and by the accumulated anger and distress that her social failures have produced.

The result is that her unfulfilled needs and disruptive emotions create a great deal more internal stimulation than is common for most adults. This stimulus overload sharply limits her capacity to control behaviors and contend effectively with stresses. It increases the likelihood that impulsiveness will mark her thinking and/or behavior, and it adds significantly to her sense of fragility and vulnerability. Moreover, the overload state is now being escalated by situationally related stresses, which add to the possibility that impulsiveness will mark her thinking or behaviors.

The end product is considerable depression. Although the depression has probably intensified recently, it seems to have been present, at least episodically, for some time. The level of intensity that currently marks this affective disarray is disabling, and it is somewhat surprising that she does not manifest more obvious disorganization in her everyday behaviors. This is probably because most of her cognitive processes remain essentially intact.

She continues to exert considerable effort when processing new information, but is also conservative about applying that effort. The overall yield is usually commendable, which is to be expected of a person who is guarded and mistrusting of her environment. On the other hand, some of her processing is more haphazard than would be expected. This suggests that some impairment to her usual processing habits may be occurring. If so, it may be caused by considerable peripheral ideation that she is experiencing, much of which seems related to situational elements. This sort of subconscious or unconscious thinking often intrudes on directed thinking and can interfere significantly with attention and concentration.

Another factor that helps her avoid greater disorganization is a habitual striving to be accurate or appropriate when translating events. This is also a probable consequence of her hypervigilance. If she interprets events appropriately, it reduces the possibility of being unexpectedly demeaned by them. This sort of orientation forms the basis for adequate reality testing, even though the hypervigilance tends to impair her ability to form enduring relations with others. Generally, her thinking is clear, and this is definitely an asset for her. It can be impaired from time to time by a sense of pessimism that she seems to harbor, or by her intense feelings, but this probably does not occur very often.

The composite of adequate processing, appropriate translations of new stimuli, and reasonably clear thinking permit her to maintain a relatively stable facade for interacting with others. However, the facade only serves to provide some concealment of the intense turmoil and sense of helplessness that she is experiencing and the feeling of futility that she reports.

RECOMMENDATIONS

The most important issue is the suicide potential and the necessity to treat her as a person in crisis by building a broad support system that she will not misinterpret as threatening. It is not easy to define current situational stresses. The legal finalization of her last marriage, even though separation occurred 18 months ago, may have triggered an acute awareness about her accumulation of social failures. However, other, less obvious factors, may also be contributing. There may be more problems at work than she has revealed, and there is very little information about her relationship with her son. Both of these issues should be explored more thoroughly, especially the latter, as an underlying sense of guilt about that relationship could have been exacerbated recently.

Once a system of support has been created, the matter of her emotional turmoil, especially her depression, can be addressed more directly. This will not be easy to accomplish. The basic ingredients are long standing, and she has worked hard to conceal them. When deciding on intervention strategies, it is important to consider her hypervigilance and the strong sense of guardedness and mistrust that it evokes. Even though she is a self-referral, she is likely to view any gestures of support by others with apprehension, and it is especially probable that she will resist sharing feelings. In this context, the intervention approach should be as structured and clear as possible, at least during the first several weeks of treatment.

Pharmacological intervention may have some usefulness, but it was not very effective when she was being treated as an outpatient. Her opinions about this issue should be afforded considerable weight. A reasonably well-structured cognitive approach to her social and emotional problems seems most viable, but both issues should be approached cautiously to avoid provoking any feelings that she will perceive as threatening. Continued hospitalization seems warranted until her current turmoil is noticeably eased and until plans for continued outpatient care are firmly in place.

Optimally, the transition from inpatient to outpatient care will not jeopardize her perception of the therapeutic process or the support that it offers. She is the type of person who seems to strive to identify things accurately. Thus, the continuation of a structured intervention format will be important. Assuming that both social and emotional issues will have been broached during her hospitalization, the therapist should strive for some balance in dealing with them during the early weeks of outpatient treatment. Her self-image and perceived frailties can be addressed in the context of these issues as the intervention proceeds.

EPILOGUE

This woman remained an inpatient for 17 days, during which time she was seen 14 times by a female staff psychiatrist and visited four times by her therapist. The staff psychiatrist broached the issue of self-destruction early on, and the patient readily conceded that she had considered the possibility of suicide often during the preceding three months. She also revealed that she had similar thoughts at an earlier time, following the death of her second husband, which coincided with her son's eighth birthday. She expressed considerable remorse about her "failures" as a mother and noted that, for a while, she harbored the belief that the death of her second husband was somehow related to this.

During her therapist's fourth visit, she raised a question about whether she might be able to discontinue treatment with him and work with the staff psychiatrist as an outpatient after her discharge. Both psychiatrists agreed to this arrangement. Following her discharge, she returned to the hospital twice weekly during the next six months for individual sessions. Antidepressant medication was continued during that time, and the therapy sessions focused mainly on the development of more effective social skills. According to the therapist, she began to share some of her feelings more openly during the third month of treatment, focusing mainly on her emotions as related to her marital failures and her limited contact with her son.

The therapist notes that her efforts to develop more rewarding interpersonal relationships have been mildly successful, although issues of mistrust of others have become more and more apparent during the treatment. She also has initiated more frequent contacts with her son and this appears to have been rewarding for her, although it was somewhat difficult for her ex-husband and his wife. They gradually were able to work out a satisfactory visitation schedule. At the end of the sixth month of treatment, the frequency of visits to the psychiatrist were reduced by mutual agreement to six per month because the patient has insisted that she would gradually like to become more independent and less directed in making decisions for herself.

The therapist acknowledges that many intrapsychic problems still have not been addressed adequately, or at all, but believes that the progress to this point has been quite favorable, and she expresses a sense of optimism concerning the patient's future.

REFERENCES

Appelbaum, S. A., & Colson, D. B. (1968). A reexamination of the color-shading Rorschach test response and suicide attempts. *Journal of Projective Techniques and Personality Assessment, 32*(2), 160–164.

Beck, A. T., Rush, A. J., Shaw, B. F., & Emery, G. (1979). *Cognitive therapy of depression.* New York: Guilford Press.

Blatt, S. J., & Ritzler, B. A. (1974). Suicide and the representation of transparency and cross-sections on the Rorschach. *Journal of Consulting and Clinical Psychology, 42*(2), 280–287.

Carlson, C. F., Kula, M. L., & St. Laurent, C. M. (1997). Rorschach revised DEPI and CDI with inpatient major depressives and borderline personality disorder with major depression: Validity issues. *Journal of Clinical Psychology, 53*(1), 51–58.

Exner, J. E. (1986). *The Rorschach: A comprehensive system: Vol. 1. Basic foundations* (2nd ed.). New York: Wiley.

Exner, J. E. (1991). *The Rorschach: A comprehensive system: Vol. 2. Interpretation* (2nd ed.). New York: Wiley.

Exner, J. E. (2003). *The Rorschach: A comprehensive system: Vol. 1. Basic foundations* (4th ed.). Hoboken, NJ: Wiley.

Exner, J. E., & Wylie, J. (1977). Some Rorschach data concerning suicide. *Journal of Personality Assessment, 41*(4), 339–348.

Fisher, S. (1951). The value of the Rorschach for detecting suicidal trends. *Journal of Projective Techniques, 15,* 250–254.

Fowler, J. C., Hilsenroth, M. J., & Piers, C. (2001). An empirical study of seriously disturbed suicidal patients. *Journal of the American Psychoanalytic Association, 49*(1), 161–186.

Fowler, J. C., Piers, C., Hilsenroth, M. J., Holdwick, D. J., Jr., & Padawer, J. R. (2001). The Rorschach suicide constellation: Assessing various degrees of lethality. *Journal of Personality Assessment, 76*(2), 333–351.

Greenwald, D. F. (1997). Comparison between the Rorschach depression index and depression-related measures in a nonpatient sample. *Psychological Reports, 80*(Pt. 2, 3), 1151–1154.

Hartmann, E., Wang, C. E., Berg, M., & Saether, L. (2003). Depression and vulnerability as assessed by the Rorschach method. *Journal of Personality Assessment, 81*(3), 242–255.

Hertz, M. R. (1948). Further study of suicidal configurations in Rorschach records. *American Psychologist, 3,* 283–284.

Jorgensen, K., Andersen, T. J., & Dam, H. (2000). The diagnostic efficiency of the Rorschach depression index and the schizophrenia index: A review. *Assessment, 7*(3), 259–280.

Khouri, S., & Greenway, A. P. (1996). Exner's depression index and the Harris-Lingoes MMPI-2 subscales for depression. *Perceptual and Motor Skills, 82*(1), 27–30.

Meyer, G. J., & Archer, R. P. (2001). The hard science of Rorschach research: What do we know and where do we go? *Psychological Assessment, 13*(4), 486–502.

Modestin, J., Gruden, D., & Spielmann, D. (1990). Identification of endogenous depression: A comparison of three diagnostic approaches. *Journal of Clinical Psychology, 46*(3), 300–305.

Rierdan, J., Lang, E., & Eddy, S. (1978). Suicide and transparency responses on the Rorschach: A replication. *Journal of Consulting and Clinical Psychology, 46*(5), 1162–1163.

Ritsher, J. B., Slivko-Kolchik, E. B., & Oleichik, I. V. (2001). Assessing depression in Russian psychiatric patients: Validity of MMPI and Rorschach. *Assessment, 8*(4), 373–389.

CHAPTER 5

An Issue of Panic Attacks

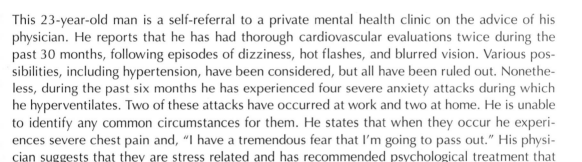

CASE 3

This 23-year-old man is a self-referral to a private mental health clinic on the advice of his physician. He reports that he has had thorough cardiovascular evaluations twice during the past 30 months, following episodes of dizziness, hot flashes, and blurred vision. Various possibilities, including hypertension, have been considered, but all have been ruled out. Nonetheless, during the past six months he has experienced four severe anxiety attacks during which he hyperventilates. Two of these attacks have occurred at work and two at home. He is unable to identify any common circumstances for them. He states that when they occur he experiences severe chest pain and, "I have a tremendous fear that I'm going to pass out." His physician suggests that they are stress related and has recommended psychological treatment that would focus on stress management.

He has been married for approximately 18 months. His wife is also age 23. He works as a bank teller, a position that he has had for about two years. His wife works as a receptionist in a dental office. They both completed $2^1/_2$ years at a state university and decided to drop out at the end of their fifth semester in accord with their plans for marriage. They met during their first year at the university and began dating regularly shortly thereafter. He says that they both plan to continue their education in night school and ultimately obtain degrees. He is interested in business and she is interested in environmental science. His wife is currently taking two evening courses, but he decided to defer enrollment until he is able to eliminate, or at least control, his anxiety attacks.

Since their marriage, they have been living in his mother's home. He says it is a good arrangement because it provides them with the opportunity to save money for their future. His mother, age 47, works as an office manager. His father, an industrial salesman, died at age 40 following a heart attack. He describes a normal developmental history with no unusual medical problems. He is an only child who graduated from high school at age 18 in the top 20% of his class. He says that he dated frequently while in high school and had his first sexual experience at age 17 with a girl of his own age. He describes that experience as confusing for him, "I probably did everything wrong, I was never much of a jock, and when it finally happened I was pretty uncomfortable about it."

He says that his marital relationship is "fine" and that he and his wife rarely disagree about anything: "We're really good partners." He states that when the episodes of dizziness first occurred and the possibility of hypertension was considered, he was concerned that there might be some genetic linkage to his father's coronary problems, but he has been reassured that is not the case. He was 15 when his father died. He notes, "We were pretty close and I was pretty depressed for a few months, but I got through it. I still miss him though."

He describes his work as "pretty routine, but it can be frustrating at times." He notes that he had expected to be promoted to a different level of responsibility at the bank "after a year or so," but suggests that has not happened because "they really expect people at the higher levels to be college graduates. It's made me have some second thoughts about dropping out of school to get married, but it was a good trade-off. I'll get there someday." He states that his wife and his mother are both very supportive about his difficulties and that his wife has been very encouraging about his decision to enter therapy.

Assessment issues include: (1) Is there any evidence of a serious psychiatric problem? (2) Is there any evidence of depression? (3) Is his tolerance for stress significantly limited? (4) Do any findings suggest logical antecedents for the panic attacks? (5) Does he seem to be a reasonable candidate for a cognitive approach to stress management?

CASE FORMULATION AND RELEVANT LITERATURE

The problem that brings this man into the mental health clinic involves severe panic attacks with hyperventilation. The *DSM-IV-TR* (American Psychiatric Association, 2000) stresses the importance of considering the context in which such attacks occur. His are recurrent, unexpected, and not situationally bound (they have occurred both at home and at work). On the other hand, he is not reporting agoraphobia or other behavioral changes along with these episodes, a positive finding in terms of severity. De Ruiter and her colleagues (de Ruiter, Rijken, Garssen, & Kraaimaat, 1989) have suggested that hyperventilation is ". . . perhaps best considered an epiphenomenon of panic, comparable to other signs of hyperarousal, such as heart rate accelerations and skin conductance fluctuations" (p. 654).

A review of the Rorschach literature on panic disorder will be helpful in directing the assessing psychologist's attention to potentially important variables and configurations. Other referral questions include stress tolerance and depression, topics about which current literature was reviewed in Case 1 (Chapter 3) and Case 2 (Chapter 4). The final referral question asks whether a cognitive stress-management approach would be appropriate. Relevant treatment literature can help in providing consultation about this decision.

Assessment of Panic Disorder

A 1990 Danish study (Rosenberg & Andersen, 1990) compared panic-disordered outpatients with two other outpatient groups (major depression and generalized anxiety disorder) and with nonpatients. Using the Rapaport/Gill/Schafer coding system for the Rorschach (Rapaport, Gill, & Schafer, 1984) as well as slight modifications of Z-scores and blends from the *Comprehensive System*, the authors suggested that the panic-disordered outpatients were characterized by difficulties in synthesizing and in concept formation.

De Ruiter and Cohen (1992) used the *Comprehensive System* to study 22 Dutch patients with panic disorder, 18 of whom also had agoraphobia. They hypothesized that their sample would manifest affective constriction, lowered receptivity to affective stimuli, and avoidance of complexity. Compared with several other clinical groups and a nonpatient group, the panic-disordered patients showed the lowest mean *WsumC* (1.55). Their mean *Afr* was .51, and 19 of the 22 patients (86%) had Rorschachs with *Lambda* greater than .99.

A significant study (Mavissakalian & Hamann, 1987) emphasizes the importance of considering coexisting personality difficulties when planning treatment for individuals experiencing panic attacks. The authors administered the Personality Diagnostic Questionnaire (Hyler, Rider, & Spitzer, 1978) to 33 panic-disordered patients with agoraphobia before a 16-week combined medication and structured behavioral treatment regimen. They found that 75% of initially low-scoring patients on the personality disorder measure responded successfully to treatment, whereas only 25% of the high-scoring patients were treatment responders.

Case 3. A 23-Year-Old Male.

Card	Response	Inquiry

I   1. Ll a bat to me, w its wgs spread out

E: Rpts Ss Resp
S: Well, th whole thg ll tht, th wgs r spread out lik its flyg, it has feelrs too. Ths cntr prt (D4) is th body

     2. It could also b a person tied to a stake w othr ppl dancg arnd

E: (Rpts S's Resp)
S: Th wm is in th cntr w her hands up. These side thngs r peopl dressd up in costumes dancg arnd her, I can't c thm too well cuz there's smoke all around her
E: U said thyr in costumes?
S: Yes, its lik animals but thy hav wgs too, its lik som theatrical thg w the wm tied to the stake & these peopl dancg arnd her & the smoke, it's all dark lik, it represents smthg, but I dkno wht, th smoke is all dark & hazy but I don't c any fire

II   3. Th cntr ll a delta wgd plane of ss

E: Rpts Ss Resp
S: It cb a rocket instead of a plane bec there's fire dwn here below it lik it was takg off
E: I'm not sure I c it
S: Well th shape of it is a littl fat for a rocket but if u use your imagination it cb one especially bec of th fire here, the red ll it cb fire, exhaust

III   4. It ll 2 wm pullg st apart

E: Rpts Ss Resp
S: Well these side thngs r wm & it ll thy'r fightg ovr st here in th cntr, I'm sur thyr wm cuz thy hav breasts & hi heels, it ll thy'll j pullg ths apart
E: Pullg it apart?
S: I dk wht it is, mayb a basket of food, thyr fiting about it

     5. Ths cntr prt ll lungs

E: Rpts Ss Resp
S: Its got th shape of lungs & I suppose th way its colord helps too
E: Th way its colord?
S: Well thy'r red lik internal prts wld b, I thk lungs r red

IV   6. Ll som big monstr out of scfic sittg on a stump & I'm lookg up at him

E: Rpts Ss Resp
S: Th W thg ll tht, ths (D1) is th stump & th rest is th monstr
E: Help me c it lik u r
S: Well its a grotesque shape & it looks furry all ovr, j som scfic ko indefinite thg w a pair of boots on
E: U said it looks furry?
S: Yes, its lik I was sittg or lying on th grd & lookg up at him & thy way the colors r maks me think its a furry monster

     7. Ths thg ll th head of a goose or sthg

E: Rpts Ss Resp
S: Well it ll th head of a goose lik it was hangg out of a basket lik u were takg it home frm th butcher
E: Show me so I can c it too
S: Its the head & beak (points) & neck & ths cb a basket, lik its been killed & smbody is takg it home
E: Somebody is takg it?
S: U can't c thm, just the goose & basket

V   8. It ll 2 wm sittg back to back

E: Rpts Ss Resp
S: Well there's one on e side, w their legs stretchd out j leang against eo. Thy hav funny tassled hats on, I'd say thy'r wm bec u can c th vague outline of breasts

     9. Th whole thg cb a bf

E: Rpts Ss Resp
S: Th wgs r spread out lik it was glidg & th body is in th cntr, just a bf

Case 3. Continued.

Card	Response	Inquiry
VI 10.	Ths top prt is lik som club	**E:** Rpts Ss Resp **S:** Well it j remnds me of a club (D6), u'd hav to exclude ths side stuff (Dd22) & it would hav th shape of a club lik th cavemen used to use
v11.	Ths ll a nest w 2 littl birds in it	**E:** Rpts Ss Resp **S:** Well its shapd lik a nest & u can c 2 littl birds heads stickg out lik thy had their mouths open waitg for th mother to feed them
VII 12.	Two littl girls talkg to eo, thy ll identical twins	**E:** Rpts Ss Resp **S:** Thy hav ponytails & thy ll thy'r talkg, u can j c th heads & shouldrs, thy'r mouths r here & these r th shouldrs, u can't c the rest of thm
VIII 13.	Ths thg ll sombody's insides	**E:** Rpts Ss Resp **S:** Well it j lik I think I'v seen in som medical books showg all th diff organs **E:** I'm not sure I c it lik u r, show me **S:** Th side thgs r lungs & here is prt of th ribs (D3) & here is a pipe dwn th middle lik th esophogas. Th color & th shape of it makes it ll a pict i mite c in a medical book tht illustrates sombdy's insides
IX <14.	Th head of a baby is in there if u turn it on its side	**E:** Rpts Ss Resp **S:** Well its ths pink prt here it ll a baby's head **E:** A baby's head? **S:** Th color makes it ll a newborn baby & thyr all pink lik ths & it has th form of a baby's head
>15.	Ths way th orange & green cb clds in the sunset when a storm is coming on	**E:** Rpts Ss Resp **S:** It j ll clouds w th sun shing thru thm, th green cb storm clds cause thy r shaded ko billowy & loomg & th orange one's cb liter clouds which r further away in th distance, yes thy look furthr away than th green ones **E:** U said the green ones r billowg & loomg? **S:** The color & form of them makes it ll that, mostly th color bec it really distinguishes betwn th lite clds & th storm clds, th storm clds hav color tht varies in its intensity, thy definitely ll storm clds to me
X 16.	Insides again	**E:** Rpts Ss Resp **S:** Well it j ll prts of th internal organs lik wb illustrated in a book, the colors & th shapes suggest tht, j organs I can't really name any tho
17.	Tht pink stuff cb paint	**E:** Rpts Ss Resp **S:** Its j paint lik it was droppd & took this form **E:** I'm not sur why it ll paint? **S:** I dk it j ll tht, mayb its on a palette lik a painter would use, its just red, it ll paint to me

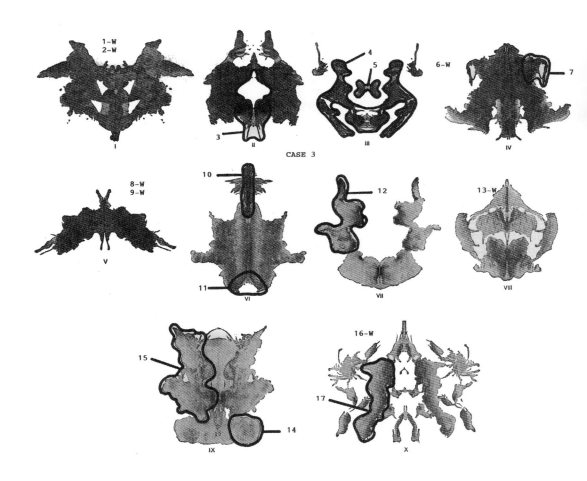

Case 3. Sequence of Scores.

Card	No.	Loc.	No.	Determinant(s)	(2)	Content(s)	Pop	Z	Special Scores
I	1	Wo	1	FMao		A	P	1.0	
	2	W+	1	Ma-p.YFo	2	H,Cg,Fi		4.0	COP,AG,PHR
II	3	DS+	5	ma.CFo		Sc,Fi		4.5	
III	4	D+	1	Mao	2	H,Cg,Fd P		3.0	AG,MOR,PHR
	5	Do	3	FCo		An			
IV	6	W+	1	Mp.FD.FTo		(H),Bt,Cg	P	4.0	GHR
	7	Dd+	99	mpo		Ad,Hh		4.0	MOR
V	8	W+	1	Mpo	2	H,Cg		2.5	COP,GHR
	9	Wo	1	FMpo		A	P	1.0	
VI	10	Do	6	Fu		Ay			
	11	Dd+	33	FMpo	2	A,Bt		2.5	
VII	12	D+	2	Mpo	2	Hd	P	3.0	GHR
VIII	13	W+	1	FC−		An,Art		4.5	PER
IX	14	Do	4	FCo		Hd			PHR
	15	Dv/+	12	mp.CF.VFu		Cl,Na		2.5	
X	16	Wv	1	CFu		An,Art			
	17	Dv	9	C		Art			

Case 3. Structural Summary.

Location Features	Determinants Blends	Single	Contents	S-Constellation
				NO . . .FV+VF+V+FD>2
		H = 3		YES . .Col-Shd Bl>0
Zf = 12	M.YF	M = 3	(H) = 1	YES′. .Ego<.31,>.44
ZSum = 36.5	m.CF	FM = 3	Hd = 2	NO . . .MOR > 3
ZEst = 38.0	M.FD.FT	m = 1	(Hd) = 0	NO . . .Zd > +− 3.5
	m.CF.VF	FC = 3	Hx = 0	NO . . .es > EA
W = 7		CF = 1	A = 3	YES . .CF+C > FC
D = 8		C = 1	(A) = 0	NO . . .X+% < .70
W+D = 15		Cn = 0	Ad = 1	NO . . .S > 3
Dd = 2		FC′ = 0	(Ad) = 0	NO . . .P < 3 or > 8
S = 1		C′F = 0	An = 3	NO . . .Pure H < 2
		C′ = 0	Art = 3	NO . . .R < 17
		FT = 0	Ay = 1	3 . . . .TOTAL

	Single	Contents	Special Scores		
DQ	TF = 0	Bl = 0		Lv1	Lv2
+ = 9	T = 0	Bt = 2	DV = 0x1		0x2
o = 5	FV = 0	Cg = 4	INC = 0x2		0x4
v/+ = 1	VF = 0	Cl = 1	DR = 0x3		0x6
v = 2	V = 0	Ex = 0	FAB = 0x4		0x7
	FY = 0	Fd = 1	ALOG = 0x5		
	YF = 0	Fi = 2	CON = 0x7		
	Y = 0	Ge = 0	Raw Sum6 = 0		
Form Quality	Fr = 0	Hh = 1	Wgtd Sum6 = 0		

	FQx	MQual	W+D	Single	Contents		
				Fr = 0	Ls = 0		
+	= 0	= 0	= 0	rF = 0	Na = 1		
o	= 12	= 5	= 10	FD = 0	Sc = 1	AB = 0	GHR = 3
u	= 3	= 0	= 3	F = 1		AG = 2	PHR = 3
−	= 1	= 0	= 1	Sx = 0		COP = 2	MOR = 2
none	= 1	= 0	= 1	Xy = 0		CP = 0	PER = 1
				Id = 1			PSV = 0
				(2) = 5			

Ratios, Percentages, and Derivations

R = 17	L = 0.06		FC:CF+C = 3:4	COP = 2 AG = 2	
			Pure C = 1	GHR:PHR = 3:3	
EB = 5:6.0	EA = 11.0	EBPer = N/A	SumC′:WSumC = 0:6.0	a:p = 4:8	
eb = 6:3	es = 9	D = 0	Afr = 0.42	Food = 1	
	Adj es = 7	Adj D = +1	S = 1	SumT = 1	
			Blends:R = 4:17	Hum Cont = 6	
FM = 3	C′ = 0	T = 1	CP = 0	Pure H = 3	
m = 3	V = 1	Y = 1		PER = 1	
				Iso Indx = 0.35	

a:p	= 4:8	Sum6 = 0	XA% = 0.88	Zf = 12.0	3r+(2)/R	= 0.29	
Ma:Mp	= 2:4	Lv2 = 0	WDA% = 0.87	W:D:Dd = 7:8:2	Fr+rF	= 0	
2AB+Art+Ay	= 4	WSum6 = 0	X−% = 0.06	W:M = 7:5	SumV	= 1	
MOR	= 2	M− = 0	S− = 0	Zd = −1.5	FD	= 1	
		Mnone = 0	P = 5	PSV = 0	An+Xy	= 3	
			X+% = 0.71	DQ+ = 9	MOR	= 2	
			Xu% = 0.18	DQv = 2	H:(H)Hd(Hd)	= 3:3	

PTI = 0	DEPI = 5*	CDI = 3	S-CON = 3	HVI = No	OBS = No

S-CON AND KEY VARIABLES

The S-CON value of three is not positive. The first positive Key variable is $D <$ Adj D, indicating that the interpretation should begin with a review of the data regarding controls and situational stress. This variable does not identify the entire interpretive routine, and the order for interpreting the other clusters is decided on the basis of a second Key variable or from the table of Tertiary variables. In this instance, a second Key variable, $p > a+1$, is positive, suggesting that the remainder of the interpretive routine should begin with the cluster regarding ideation, followed by processing, mediation, self-perception, interpersonal perception, and ending with the data concerning affect.

CONTROLS

Case 3.   Control-Related Variables for a 23-Year-Old Male.

EB = 5:6.0	EA = 11.0		D = 0	CDI = 3
eb = 6:3	es = 9	Adj es = 7	AdjD = +1	L = 0.06
FM = 3 m = 3	SumC' = 0	SumT = 1	SumV = 1	SumY = 1

The Adj D value of +1 signifies that he usually has a sturdy tolerance for stress and is less likely to experience problems with control than do many people. The *EA* (11.0) reveals substantial resources, and the data for the *EB* (5:6.0) and *Lambda* (0.06) suggest that there is no reason to question the reliability of the *EA*. Likewise, the Adj *es* (7) is in the expected range for adults, offering no data that would challenge the reliability of the *EA*. The *eb* (6:3) does contain some data of importance that will be addressed with the findings concerning situational stress.

SITUATIONALLY RELATED STRESS

Case 3.   Situational Stress Data for a 23-Year-Old Male.

EB	= 5:6.0	EA = 11.0		D	= 0	**Blends**	
eb	= 6:3	es = 9 Adj es = 7		AdjD = +1		M.FD.FT	= 1
						M.YF	= 1
FM	= 3 *m* = 3	C' = 0 T = 1 V = 1 Y = 1				M.CF.VF	= 1
		(3r+(2)/R) = .24				m.CF	= 1
Pure C = 1 M– = 0		MQnone = 0		Blends = 4			

The fact that the D Score (0) is less than the Adj D (+1) signals some mild-to-moderate situationally related stress that is impinging on his typically sturdy capacity for control. It is not disorganizing or disabling, but it is creating an unwanted psychological burden for him. The values for *m* and *SumY* (3:1) suggest that the impact of the stress tends to be diffuse, but it may be having a greater influence on his thought processes and could affect his attention and concentration.

There is no obvious information concerning the nature of the stress. It may simply relate to the suggestion by his physician that his difficulties are psychologically related. The vista response could be situationally related, but that seems unlikely as the Egocentricity Index (.24) is low. It is probable that the stress has increased his psychological complexity substantially. Two of his four blend answers (*M.YF* and *m.CF*) are created by stress-related variables. Nonetheless, there are no indications of an overload state and no reason to believe that his decisions or behaviors will be significantly influenced by the presence of stress.

IDEATION

Case 3. Ideation Variables for a 23-Year-Old Male.

L	= 0.06	OBS	= No	HVI	= No	Critical Special Scores			
						DV	= 0	DV2	= 0
EB	= 5:6.0	EBPer	= N/A	a:p	= 4:8	INC	= 0	INC2	= 0
				Ma:Mp	= 2:4	DR	= 0	DR2	= 0
eb	= 6:3	[FM = 3 m = 3]				FAB	= 0	FAB2	= 0
				M−	= 0	ALOG	= 0	CON	= 0
Intell Indx	= 4	MOR	= 2	Mnone	= 0	Sum6	= 0	WSum6	= 0
							(R = 17)		

M Response Features

I	2.	W+ Ma-p.YFo 2 H,Cg,Fi P 4.0 COP,AG,PHR
III	4.	D+ Mao 2 H,Cg,Fd P 3.0 AG,MOR,PHR
IV	6.	W+ Mp.FD.FTo 2 (H),Bt,Cg P 4.0 GHR
V	8.	W+ Mpo 2 H,Cg 2.5 COP,PHR
VII	12.	D+2 Mpo 2 Hd P 3.0 GHR

The *EB* (5:6.0) suggests that he is not very consistent in the way he uses conceptual thinking in making decisions. At times, his judgments and decisions will result from thinking that is reasonably free of emotional influence but, in other instances, they will be formed much more intuitively and will be influenced considerably by emotion. This inconsistency reduces efficiency and can be a liability because more time and effort are often required to contend with the demands of everyday life.

Although unusual from an interpersonal perspective, the values in the *a:p* ratio (4:8) are not sufficiently disparate to suggest that his thinking and values are less flexible or more well fixed than for most people. Similarly, none of the data for the HVI, OBS, or sum MOR indicate unusually strong sets that might affect conceptual thinking. The value for the left side of the *eb* (6) is in the expected range, but the presence of three *m*s is unexpected and indicates that situational stress is increasing peripheral mental activity. As noted, this could have a negative impact on his attention and concentration, but he offers no report of this.

The data for the *Ma:Mp* ratio (2:4) are more important. They indicate a stylistic orientation to use flights into fantasy as a routine tactic for dealing with unpleasantness. This action is likely to deny or disregard reality, and people who defensively abuse fantasy usually prefer to avoid responsibility for decision making. As a coping method, it creates a self-imposed helplessness that requires dependency on others. Although it usually brings relief in short-term situations, it can often be counterproductive to the long-term fulfillment of one's needs.

Another defensive tactic that he appears to use with regularity is indicated by the value for the Intellectualization Index (4). It signifies that he is more prone than most to intellectualize feelings as a way of denying their importance. This process requires a pseudo-intellectual form of conceptual ideation that distorts or denies the true emotional impact of a situation.

On a more positive note, the absence of critical special scores ($WSum6 = 0$) indicates that there is no reason to question the clarity of his conceptual thinking. His five M responses have ordinary form quality and three are Popular answers. Four are relatively commonplace for conceptual quality (responses 4, 6, 8, & 12) and one, (response 2) tends to be somewhat more complex and sophisticated.

Although he may be less efficient in his decision-making routines, there is no reason to question the clarity of his thinking. He probably uses fantasy excessively to escape burdens that he judges to be not easily resolvable. He is also prone to deny the impact of some emotions by dealing with them on a pseudo-intellectual level. This suggests that feelings may be more of a problem for him than he is willing to admit.

PROCESSING

Case 3.   Processing Variables for a 23-Year-Old Male.

EB	= 5:6.0	Zf	= 12	Zd	= -1.5	DQ+	= 9
L	= 0.06	W:D:Dd	= 7:8:2	PSV	= 0	DQv/+	= 1
HVI	= NO	W:M	= 7:5			DQv	= 2
OBS	= NO						

Location & DQ Sequencing

I: Wo.W+		VI: Do.Dd+	
II: DS+		VII: D	
III: D+.Do		VIII: W+	
IV: W+.Dd+		IX: Do.Dv/+	
V: W+.Wo		X: Wv.Dv	

The Zf (12) and $W:D:Dd$ (7:8:2) are both within the expected range, indicating that he usually makes an adequate effort to process new information. There is nothing unusual in the location sequence to suggest otherwise. Five of his seven W responses are first answers and both Dd responses are last answers. The $W:M$ (7:5) is a bit more conservative than might be expected for an ambitent, but his protocol is not very long, only 17 responses. It seems clear that he does not invest great effort in processing, but neither does he seem prone to avoid processing tasks.

The Zd score (−1.5) is within the average range and affords no reason to question his scanning efficiency, but the DQ distribution yields an unexpected finding. Nine of his answers are coded as $DQ+$, slightly more than expected, suggesting that the quality of his processing is usually good and probably somewhat complex. However, two of his answers are coded DQv, and a third is coded $DQv/+$. Even in a longer protocol, the composite of three vague and vague/plus answers would be cause for concern, suggesting that his processing activity sometimes becomes very flawed, and a much less mature form of processing occurs. The significance of this postulate is magnified because the record contains only 17 answers.

His less mature forms of processing occurred on Cards IX and X, which are completely chromatic. Interestingly, he did give one answer, a $W+$ response, to Card VIII, but the form quality for the answer is minus. It has the same contents (An, Art) that appear in the Wv answer given to Card X as response 16. The unusual sequence of answers to the last three figures suggests that, when a field consists mainly of emotionally toned stimuli, some sort of disarray associated with emotion causes his typically good processing activities to become somewhat impaired. It has been noted that he intellectualizes feelings more than most people. It will be important to determine if the impairment that emotion seems to cause in his processing activities has a significant impact on how he mediates inputs.

MEDIATION

Case 3.   Mediation Variables for a 23-Year-Old Male.

R = 17	L = 0.06		OBS = No	**Minus & NoForm Features**
FQx+	= 0	XA%	= .88	VIII 13. W+ FC– An,Art 4.5 PER
FQxo	= 12	WDA%	= .87	X 17. Dv C Art
FQxu	= 3	X–%	= .06	
FQx–	= 1	S–	= 0	
FQxnone	= 1			
(W+D	= 20)	P	= 5	
WD+	= 0	X+%	= .71	
WDo	= 10	Xu%	= .18	
WDu	= 3			
WD–	= 1			
WDnone	= 1			

The *XA%* (.88) and *WDA%* (.87) are both in the expected range, signifying that his translations of inputs are usually appropriate for the situation. This is a basic ingredient for good reality testing. However, his record also contains a NoForm answer (Pure *C*) that appears as the last response to the test.

Usually, a single NoForm answer adds little information concerning mediation, but in this instance it takes on added importance in light of the sequencing of responses and the findings from the processing data. The form quality of the 12 answers that he gave through Card VII includes 11 *o* responses and one unusual answer. The five answers that he gave to the last three cards includes one *o* response (Card IX), his only minus response (Card VIII), two unusual responses (Cards IX and X), and the NoForm answer (Card X). This composite supports the postulate that his reality testing may become more limited when he is confronted with emotional stimulation. Three of the five answers to Cards VIII, IX, and X are marked by contents that imply efforts to intellectualize (*Art*).

On the other hand, the *X–%* of .06 indicates that events of serious mediational dysfunction occur no more frequently than for most people. The single minus answer, "somebody's insides" (response 13), does not represent a severe distortion of the distal field. The five Popular answers in the record are in the expected range and suggest that he will make customary or conventional responses when the cues to expected or acceptable responses are easily identified. This notion is also supported by the *X+%* (.71) and the *Xu%* (.18) which intimate that he has a notable proclivity to form behaviors that are in accord with social demands or expectations.

Although the basic data concerning mediation seem to rule out any significant problems that might impair reality testing, there are clear hints in both the processing and mediation findings that emotion tends to negatively affect his cognitive operations. When this occurs, his mediational activities seem to deviate from his normal striving to render conventional or acceptable behaviors. In this context, it seems reasonable to alter the planned order for reviewing the data clusters and study the findings concerning affect before moving to the self-perception and interpersonal perception clusters.

AFFECT

Case 3.   Affect-Related Data for a 23-Year-Old Male.

EB	= 5:6.0			EBPer	= N/A	**Blends**	
eb	= 6:3	L	= 0.06	FC:CF+C	= 3: 4	M.FD.FT	= 1
DEPI	= 5	CDI = 3		Pure C	= 1	M.YF	= 1
						m.CF.VF	= 1
SumC' = 0	SumT = 1			SumC':WSumC	= 0:6.0	m.CF	= 1
SumV = 1	SumY = 1			Afr	= 0.42		
Intellect	= 4	CP	= 0	S = 1 (S to I,II,III	= 1)		
Blends:R	= 4:17			Col-Shad Bl	= 1		
m + y Bl	= 2			Shading Bl	= 0		

The DEPI value (5) indicates that his psychological features are organized in a way that creates a potential for frequent experiences of affective disruption. When such episodes occur, they may manifest in the forms of obvious emotional distress, such as sadness or moodiness. But it is equally likely that the manifestations will be less obviously related to emotions, such as in experiences of tension, anxiety, easy distractibility, or even somatic problems. In this instance, his past complaints of dizziness, hot flashes, and blurred vision, and his present complaints of anxiety and hyperventilation are probably related to these characteristics.

In studying the data concerning ideation, it was noted the *EB* (5:6.0) signified that he is not consistent in solving problems or making decisions. In some instances, he tries to push his feelings aside and deal with issues in a conceptually logical manner, whereas in similar situations, he may become involved with his feelings, leading him to make intuitive judgments. This inconsistency in using his feelings increases the likelihood that he will be confused by them, which can lead to inconsistency in the way he manifests his emotions.

The right side value of the *eb* (3) is unremarkable, but it does include a vista answer. As noted, there is no apparent reason to assume that it involves situationally related feelings of guilt or remorse. More likely, it is associated with rumination about personal features that he judges negatively. Regardless of the antecedent, the vista answer indicates that self-examining behavior is producing considerable discomfort. The absence of achromatic color answers affords no evidence of unusual emotional constraint. However, the *Afr* value (.42) is quite low for an ambient and signals a marked tendency to avoid emotional stimulation. People with this tendency are typically uncomfortable when dealing with emotion, and they often become more socially isolated or constrained.

The Intellectualization Index (4) has been noted previously, suggesting that he is more inclined than most people to deal with feelings on an intellectual level. This process reduces or neutralizes the impact of emotions, but it distorts the full meaning of an emotional situation. Interestingly, the *FC:CF+C* ratio (3:4) suggests that he may be somewhat less stringent in modulating his emotional displays than might be expected. In other words, when he displays his feelings, they often are likely to be obvious or intense.

Usually, an *FC:CF+C* in which the right side value is only one point greater than the left is not a negative finding, but in this instance, it may be. Consider the substance of his single Pure *C* (response 17), "The pink stuff could be paint." (Inquiry) "It's just paint that was dropped and took this form." (E: I'm not sure why it looks like paint) "I don't know, it just looks like that, maybe it's on a palette like a painter would use, it's just red, it looks like paint to me." It is a defensive and immature answer that is not very effective as a last response to the test.

There is no unusual use of white space and the number of blends (4) falls within the expected range for this modest length protocol. However, two of those blends (*M.FY, m.CF*) apparently are situationally related and might not have occurred if his current experience of stress was less. If that is true, it signifies that his usual level of psychological complexity is modest compared with that expected for an adult. He does have a Color Shading blend (*m.CF.VF*), suggesting that he is sometimes uncertain or confused by emotion or emotional situations.

Emotions seem to be a problem for him. He does not use them in a consistent manner and seems disposed to episodes of emotional disruption. He has a marked tendency to avoid emotional situations, probably because they make him uncomfortable, and he also is prone to neutralize feelings by dealing with them on an intellectual level more than most people do. It is likely that he may have some difficulty modulating the displays of his feelings. In some instances, their intensity seems to limit his judgment markedly. This probably relates to his tendency to avoid emotional situations and his proneness to intellectualize feelings. He experiences considerable discomfort as a result of self-inspecting behavior, and although he is usually less psychologically complex than most adults, feelings tend to increase that complexity and also create confusion for him.

SELF-PERCEPTION

Case 3.   Self-Perception Related Data for a 23-Year-Old Male.

R	= 17	OBS	= No	HVI	= No	Human Content, An & Xy Responses
						I 2. W+ Mp-a.YFo 2 H,Cg,Fi 4.0 COP,AG,PHR
Fr+rF	= 0	3r+(2)/R	= 0.29			III 4. D+ Mao 2 H,Cg,Fd P 3.0 AG,MOR,PHR
						III 5. Do FCo An
FD	= 1	SumV	= 1			IV 6. W+ Mp.FD.FTo (H),Bt,Cg 4.0 GHR
						V 8. W+ Mpo 2 H,Cg 2.5 COP,GHR
An+Xy	= 3	MOR	= 2			VII 12. D+ Mpo 2 Hd P 3.0 GHR
						VIII 13. W+1 FC– An,Art 4.5 PER
H:(H)+Hd+(Hd) = 3:3						IX 14. Do FCo Hd PHR
[EB = 5:6.0]						X 16. Wv1 CFu An,Art

The value for the Egocentricity Index (.29) suggests that his estimates of personal worth are likely to be more negative than positive and that he tends to perceive himself less favorably when compared with others. This finding seems consistent with the vista response in his record. It signals the likelihood of rumination about features that he perceives negatively, and as noted, it is yielding painful feelings for him.

The three *An* responses highlight the body concerns with which he has been struggling for the past three years. All three involve color, and one includes his only minus answer. This seems to emphasize the emotional undercurrent that is associated with his somatic preoccupation. The fact that his symptoms changed seems important. Originally, he presented symptoms of dizziness, hot flashes, and blurred vision, but after cardiovascular problems were ruled out, he began to experience anxiety attacks that include hyperventilation and chest pain. The implication is that it is important for him to have somatic symptoms, and there appears to be a linkage between those symptoms and the emotional problems cited earlier. Obviously, it will be important to seek out the purpose that his symptoms serve.

There are two MOR responses, indicating that some negative features exist in his self-concept that tend to promote a more pessimistic view of himself than may be readily apparent. The ratio $H:(H)+Hd+(Hd)$ (3:3) is in the expected range for an ambitent, suggesting that social interactions have contributed substantially to his impressions of himself. An inspection of the codings for his six human content answers reveals no obviously negative features. Four of the six contain passive movement that may have negative implications for self-concept, but that remains to be seen as the substance of the answers are reviewed more carefully.

The search for projected materials yields some interesting findings. His single minus answer (response 13) is "somebody's insides," which, in the inquiry, he describes as "like I've seen in some medical books showing all the different organs." The basic response, "insides," implies a sense of vulnerability, but he tends to neutralize the intensity by dealing with it on a more intellectual level (*Art*). His first MOR answer (response 4) has good form quality, but the substance is negative, "two women pulling something apart." In the inquiry, he describes them as "fighting" and identifies the "something" as a basket of food. Food is usually associated with dependency needs. It is tempting to speculate that the two women may represent his wife and/or his mother but, more conservatively, they may simply reflect an internal conflict concerning dependence versus independence.

His second MOR answer (response 7), "the head of a goose or something," also seems food related, although not coded *Fd*. In the inquiry, he describes it as "hanging out of a basket like you were taking it home from the butcher . . . it's been killed and somebody is taking it home." In both MOR responses, the dependency-related object is being or has been destroyed, leading to the possible implication that he is finding it difficult to maintain sources on which he can be dependent.

As noted, four of his five *M* responses include passive features. The first (response 2) is "a person tied to a stake with other people dancing around." The possibility for the answer to be morbid exists, but he neatly sidesteps that possibility in the inquiry, even though he says, "There is smoke all around her." He notes, "[the] side things are people dressed up in costumes . . . it's like some theatrical thing . . . the smoke is dark and hazy but I don't see any fire." His second *M* (response 4), "women pulling something apart," has already been discussed. The third (response 6) is "some big monster out of science fiction sitting on a stump and I'm looking up at him." In the inquiry, he describes it as having a "grotesque shape and it looks furry all over . . . ." This is a Popular answer, and caution is required about any interpretation. Probably the words, "grotesque" and "furry" are most important because they are somewhat contradictory and may reflect impressions that he has about himself.

The fourth *M* (response 8), "two women sitting back to back," is a relatively straightforward passive and dependent answer, elaborated in the inquiry as "with their legs stretched out just leaning against each other." The final *M* in this group (response 12), "little girls talking to each other, they look like identical twins," is a Popular answer and also requires a cautious interpretation. Probably the most important aspect is the passivity involved.

It may seem intriguing that all the figures identified, except the Card IV monster, are women, but this factor should not be translated to suggest that his own identity is more feminine. It is common for female figures to be identified in three of the four responses in which he reported female figures (Cards I, III, & VII). If any interpretive postulate is to be derived from this finding, it should simply be that women are somehow important in his life.

The first of his three *FM* answers (response 1), "a bat with its wings spread out . . . like it's flying" is a Popular answer and has no unusual characteristics. Likewise, the second *FM* (response 9), "a butterfly . . . like it was gliding," is Popular and not especially revealing except for the word "gliding," which is consistent with his tendency to describe passive movement. The third *FM* (response 11) is more unusual and revealing, "a nest with two little birds in it," elaborated in the inquiry as "two little bird heads sticking out like they had their mouths open waiting for their mother to feed them." Its obvious passive-dependent features are easily identified, and the fact that it is given to a *Dd* area lends credence to the notion that it a fairly direct self-representation.

His first *m* answer (response 3), "a delta winged plane of some sort . . . a rocket instead of a plane because there's fire down here . . ." is a common answer with no unusual features. The second *m* (response 7), "the head of a goose," has been discussed earlier. The third *m* (response 15) is intriguing: "The orange and green could be clouds in the sunset when a storm is coming on." It is his vista response, described in the inquiry as, "clouds with the sun shining through, the green could be storm clouds cause they are shaded kind of billowy and looming and the orange ones could be lighter clouds which are further away . . . the storm clouds have color that varies in its intensity, they definitely look like storm clouds to me." The fact that the storm clouds are closer and "looming" probably has importance, as does his mention that they vary in intensity. It seems likely that the answer represents some sort of pessimistic anticipation.

Five other answers have not been reviewed. Two (responses 5 & 16) are anatomy responses (lungs & insides again) and do not contain unusual embellishments. Response 17 is his Pure *C* answer, and also does not contain unusual embellishments. The remaining two (responses 10 & 14) have interesting content. Response 10 is "some club . . . like the cavemen used to use." On a speculative level, it may have some sexual connotations. Response 14 is "the head of a baby . . . the color makes it look like a newborn baby."

It seems reasonable to conclude that his self-image is not very sturdy. He does not regard himself very positively and appears to ruminate about his perceived negative features. He is not very self-confident, and there are strong hints that he is reluctant to assume responsibilities. As a result, he has cast himself in a more passive or dependent role in the world. In fact, it seems realistic to postulate that his symptoms reflect a way of maintaining a dependency role. There are indications that he may be aware of this and is struggling with some sort of dependence versus independence conflict.

INTERPERSONAL PERCEPTION

Case 3.   Interpersonal Perception Data for a 23-Year-Old Male.

R = 17	CDI = 3	HVI = No	**COP & AG Responses**
a:p = 4:8	SumT = 1	Fd = 1	I 2. W+ Ma-p.YFo 2 H,Cg,Fi 4.0 COP,AG,PHR
	[eb = 6:3]		III 4. D+ Mao 2 H,Cg,Fd P 3.0 AG,MOR,PHR
Sum Human Contents = 6		H = 3	V 8. W+ Mpo 2 H,Cg 2.5 COP,GHR
[Style = Ambitent]			
GHR:PHR = 3:3			
COP = 2	AG = 2	PER = 1	
Isolation Indx = 0.35			

The CDI and HVI are not positive, but the $a:p$ ratio (4:8) stands out like a beacon, confirming that he usually prefers to adopt a passive, though not necessarily submissive, role in his interpersonal relations. He prefers to avoid responsibility for decision making and is not very prone to seek solutions or initiate new behaviors on his own. The food response implies that, instead, he is inclined to depend on others to make decisions and take responsibility. This postulate is strengthened considerably by two other food-related answers (response 7—goose hanging from a basket and response 11—birds waiting for their mother to feed them) discussed in the self-perception section.

The single texture answer conveys the notion that he probably acknowledges and expresses his needs for closeness as openly as do most people, and the six human content answers, including three Pure H, signify that he is interested in people and probably conceptualizes them realistically. The GHR:PHR ratio (3:3) has equal values suggesting that he may tend to engage in interpersonal behaviors that are less likely to be as adaptive for the situation than might be desired.

The two COP and two AG suggest that he is open and interested in positive interactions, but many of them may be marked by forcefulness or aggressiveness. This is apparently because he perceives aggressiveness as a natural mode of exchange among people. This may seem inconsistent for a person who is passive and dependent, but it is not. Aggressiveness can manifest in many subtle ways that are not always obvious. The Isolation Index value (.35) is higher than anticipated and implies that he may be more socially isolated than might be expected. This could be because he finds it difficult to sustain smooth relations with others. Being passive and somewhat dependent often creates obstacles to close relations with others and can limit the frequency of rewarding relations.

Five M and FM answers contain pairs. The first (response 2) involves two people in costume dancing around a third person tied to a stake. The second (response 4) describes two women fighting over a basket of food and pulling it apart. The third (response 8) entails two women sitting back to back. The fourth (response 11) is a nest with two little birds in it, waiting for the mother to feed them, and the fifth (response 12) is two little girls talking to each other. It seems to represent the most positive interaction of the five, as the others are noticeably passive or aggressive.

Overall, his interpersonal world is probably more narrow and superficial than he might prefer. There seems to be little doubt that he is a very passive and dependent individual. It is probable that he is not disliked, but it is also probable that he is not sought out by others.

SUMMARY

Any description of this man and consideration of his symptoms must begin with an emphasis on his passive and dependent features. They are core elements of his personality and give rise to most of his other negative characteristics. Apparently, his reluctance to be less dependent on others and become more self-assertive in making decisions has existed for some time.

There is nothing in the history that supports this contention, but the history is rather sparse about his relations with others, and about his relations with his parents. Thus, it can only be speculated that during his developmental years he found it rewarding to rely on others for direction and reassurance. As a result, he became prone to avoid or limit the extent to which he would express ideas or engage in behaviors that were not sanctioned first by significant others. The end product is a person who has many assets but is probably unable to take full advantage of them because of psychological timidity.

He is not very confident about himself and tends to judge his worth more negatively than positively. Apparently, he ruminates about his perceived shortcomings, and this causes considerable discomfort for him. His prolonged reluctance to be more independent and assume responsibility for himself has simply strengthened the more passive and dependent role that he has assumed in the world. There are indications that he may be aware of this and is struggling internally with the problem. Nonetheless, a direct result of his passivity is an interpersonal world that is probably more narrow and superficial than he might prefer.

A by-product of his passive-dependent orientation is problems with emotions. They apparently confuse him, and he uses them in an inconsistent manner. In fact, the way in which his personality structure is currently organized creates a potential for episodes of emotional disruption. He has a noticeable tendency to avoid emotional situations, probably because they make him uncomfortable. He tries to neutralize feelings by dealing with them on a pseudo-intellectual level more often than do most people. This tactic serves to neutralize and, in effect, deny the true impact of emotions or emotional situations. He also may have difficulty modulating the displays of his feelings and, at times, the intensity of his feelings can limit his judgment markedly.

Actually, he has considerable resources available and is less likely to experience difficulties in managing stress than most people. He is under some situational stress now, probably related to the suggestion that his physical difficulties may be psychologically related, but it is not causing any significant impairment or disorganization. It is creating a bit more complexity in his psychological activities and could have affected his attention and concentration, but he does not report any such problems.

He is not very consistent in his decision-making routines. Sometimes he pushes feelings aside and thinks things through, and at other times, feelings merge into his thinking and become influential as he is forming judgments. This inconsistency is not uncommon, but it sometimes can be a liability because reaching decisions often requires more time and effort. Nevertheless, his thinking is usually clear, and he often conceptualizes in reasonably sophisticated ways. On the other hand, there is a negative aspect in the way he uses his thinking. It involves an excessive use of fantasy to escape the perceived harshness of reality. This defensiveness includes a denial or disregard for reality and typically entails an avoidance of responsibility and a dependence on others for the resolution of problems.

He usually makes an adequate effort to process and organize new information, but when emotion is involved, his processing becomes less mature and more disorganized. He strives to translate inputs in a conventional manner, and there are no reasons to question his reality testing. However, there are clear hints that his processing and translations of inputs tend to become impaired when they involve emotions.

RECOMMENDATIONS

This man's passivity and tendency to be dependent on others probably were not significant liabilities during childhood and adolescence. In fact, they may have been rewarded often. However, when he left his student role and was confronted more directly by the challenges of adulthood, his passive and dependent tendencies became less acceptable, and this has probably been confusing for him.

His symptoms first appeared after he left college and a few months before being married. It seems realistic to postulate that they reflected a psychological reaction to the necessity to take on a less passive and more independent role.

This is not to suggest that he would prefer to remain in a passive-dependent role *ad infinitum*. That is probably not true. There is no reason to question the sincerity of his motivation to be successful in his marriage and in his occupational choice. However, it is likely that the demands of adulthood, especially those requiring more independence, have exceeded his expectations by a considerable margin.

The onset of episodes of dizziness, hot flashes, and blurred vision probably represent reactions to those demands, and when those symptoms were discounted as having a cardiovascular basis, new symptoms of anxiety, hyperventilation, and chest pains evolved. In effect, they serve to maintain a passive and dependent role.

This is not simply a stress management case, although some of the strategies in a cognitive approach to stress management can be useful in an overall treatment plan. The primary treatment objective involves the development of a more mature and confident self-image and, concurrently, the evolution of interpersonal behavior patterns that entail greater independence and assertiveness, especially in decision making. In that context, the early therapeutic sessions should focus as much as practical on the origins and consequences of day-to-day decisions, both at work and in the home. This process should provide avenues for addressing some of his passivity and proneness to avoid dealing directly with feelings.

It also seems important to evaluate his marital relationship more closely at the earliest possible time, and ultimately explore the relationships that he and his wife have with his mother. Optimally, this might involve some conjoint sessions in which his wife is present, but if possible, that decision should be instigated by him. Those sessions should provide a clearer picture about the current living relationships. It seems very possible that, although living in his mother's home may have financial benefits, it is also likely to inhibit some of the growth that is desirable for this man, his marriage, and his future.

EPILOGUE

Follow-up information about this case was provided by his primary therapist after seven months of treatment. Initially, he was provided feedback concerning the assessment findings by his prospective therapist at the clinic. He readily confirmed that he tended to feel insecure about some of his decisions and often sought reassurance from others. However, he expressed a sense of doubt and dismay that this insecurity might be contributing to some of his physical difficulties. Nonetheless, he agreed to weekly individual sessions with the understanding that, during the first month or two, they would focus mainly on his work, including his relationships with coworkers and supervisors, and issues of job-related stresses.

During the next eight weeks, he reported feeling more comfortable at work, but also emphasized his irritation about the limited possibilities for advancement. Concurrently, he expressed concerns that his wife might be regarding him more negatively. Apparently, she had become involved with her evening courses and was already planning to take two or three more courses the following semester in her quest for a degree in environmental science. He noted that she had suggested that he investigate the bank's continuing education support program with the notion of enrolling in night school the following semester. This complaint opened an avenue for the therapist to explore the marital relationship and his relation with his mother more extensively.

During the third treatment month, the patient raised a question about marital therapy, and it was arranged for him and his wife to work with a different therapist weekly while he continued in individual treatment. During the third and fourth marital therapy sessions the wife focused extensively on the fact that she and her mother-in-law were often at odds. She described the mother-in-law as a controlling and dominating person. She stated that it had been her understanding that they would live with his mother for only about six months until they could become financially able to be self-supporting. He reluctantly acknowledged this had been their plan, but noted that his physical problems had prevented them from leaving the parental home. Shortly after this confrontation in marital therapy, he had a mild panic attack at home. It involved extreme tension, dizziness, and chest pain, but without hyperventilation.

The marital therapy confrontation also caused him to attend much more in the individual treatment sessions to his relationship with his mother and his feelings of a "torn allegiance" between his mother and his wife. At the end of the fifth month of treatment, he and his wife made arrangements for their own apartment, apparently with the reluctant agreement of the mother. Marital therapy was discontinued at that time. He also registered to take an evening course at the same university that his wife was attending. According to the therapist, considerable progress was obvious by the seventh month of treatment. No additional episodes of physical symptoms had occurred, and the marital relationship seems reasonably sound. However, the therapist noted that some issues concerning his self-esteem remained unresolved, and the patient apparently continued to harbor some remorse about moving from the parental home.

REFERENCES

American Psychiatric Association. (2000). *Diagnostic and statistical manual of mental disorders* (4th ed., text rev.). Washington, DC: Author.

de Ruiter, C., & Cohen, L. (1992). Personality in panic disorder with agoraphobia: A Rorschach study. *Journal of Personality Assessment, 59*(2), 304–316.

de Ruiter, C., Rijken, H., Garssen, B., & Kraaimaat, F. (1989). Breathing retraining, exposure and a combination of both, in the treatment of panic disorder with agoraphobia. *Behaviour Research and Therapy, 27*(6), 647–655.

Hyler, S. E., Rider, S. O., & Spitzer, R. L. (1978). *Personality diagnostic questionnaire.* New York: New York State Psychiatric Institute.

Mavissakalian, M., & Hamann, M. S. (1987). *DSM-III* personality disorder in agoraphobia. II. Changes with treatment. *Comprehensive Psychiatry, 28*(4), 356–361.

Rapaport, D., Gill, M. M., & Schafer, R. (1984). *Diagnostic Psychological Testing.* New York: International Universities Press.

Rosenberg, N. K., & Andersen, R. (1990). Rorschach-profile in panic disorder. *Scandinavian Journal of Psychology, 31*(2), 99–109.

CHAPTER 6

An Issue of Delusional Thinking

This 31-year-old male has agreed to a psychiatric evaluation after his twin brother encouraged him to do so. Apparently the brothers are very close and recently he has confided to his brother about events that seem peculiar and have caused him to raise questions about his sanity. The brother, who is an attorney, reports that they are fraternal twins and are the oldest of seven children.

The brother describes the family as being close but also notes that the patient "has been somewhat of a loner since we were in high school. He was the quiet one, into math and studying and almost always got As in everything. I was into basketball and girls and had to rely on him to get me through some of the tougher courses that we took together. I'd try to get him to go out with me, or fix him up with a date, but it was like pulling teeth. He just didn't want to do it."

They went to different universities but usually talked by phone two or three times a month. The brother reports, "I can remember a few times that I thought he was kind of obsessed about classmates who he said were cheating, but I never thought there was anything really wrong with him though. When I got married four years ago, he was my best man, and he comes over to dinner a couple of times a month. He's just quiet."

The referral has been provoked by recent discussions between the brothers in which the patient insists that his colleagues at work are trying to get him to resign and that, somehow, his oldest sister's husband may be involved. He is aware that his preoccupations seem delusional and has expressed a fear to his brother that he may be losing contact with reality.

The psychiatrist has arranged for him to be hospitalized for five days in a general medical facility to complete physical, neurological, and psychological evaluations. The patient has reluctantly agreed to the hospitalization to "make sure that I'm not crazy." He has done this under guarantees of privacy so that no other members of his family, supervisors, or colleagues at work, or his girlfriend will know.

Both parents are living. The father, age 60, has retired from a middle management position in state government. His mother, age 59, has worked as a legal secretary for the past 11 years, having completed training for such a position after her youngest child entered school. The younger children in the family include a brother, age 28, who works in automotive sales. He is married and has one child. Another brother, age 27, is single and works as a landscape architect. The youngest brother, age 20, completed one year of college and joined the navy. He had treatment as an adolescent for behavior problems. A sister, age 22, completed one year of college and married about a year ago. Her husband manages a seafood distribution warehouse which, purportedly, is owned by an "organized crime family." The parents were opposed to the marriage and, together with the older siblings, including the subject, tried hard to discourage it. This created an animosity between the sister's husband and the family and, currently, they have little contact. The youngest sister, age 16, is in high school.

The patient graduated from high school at age 18 and was admitted on full scholarship to a prestigious university from which he received a BS degree in computer science at age 21. He remained at the university for an additional two years to complete an MS degree in computer theory and communications. Shortly thereafter, he accepted a position with a firm specializing in microchip design. He states that for the first five or six years he usually enjoyed his work, mainly because he was given a great deal of creative freedom.

About 10 months ago, he was transferred into a more structured department of the firm, and his work is routinely shared with and evaluated by a seven-person team of which he is a member. He does not like this arrangement and says that he has felt depressed since having been assigned to the team. He feels that other team members are overly critical and often uncooperative, "sometimes they are really stupid." He notes that while he was working alone, he received substantial bonuses annually, but he has been cautioned recently not to expect such rewards because his work has not shown the creative effort that was manifest in the past. He states, "I'm sure that my so-called colleagues are deliberately making my life more difficult. They're trying to get me to resign, or fired. I know that sounds paranoid, but I don't really think it is. They really want to use my ideas as their own."

When the interviewer explored the problems he was having with his colleagues further, he stated, "Every now and then I get the feeling that [the sister's husband] and those Mafia people are involved, too. He doesn't like me and I think he's somehow been able to influence some of the people at work. They can do that you know. I know that may sound crazy, but I really get that feeling."

He lives alone and speaks freely about the lack of close friendships, "I've never really felt the need to be with people, except probably my brother and my girlfriend. I don't really understand the things that interest most people, and they don't understand the things that interest me. I'm more into the universe and they're more into a little narrow world." He says that his relationship with his twin brother is the "closest I've ever felt to anyone until just recently. He's my best friend." He did not date during high school, "I just didn't want to. I tried it in college a few times because he said I really should, but I didn't know what to say. The girls all probably thought I was a nerd, and they weren't anything special. I only did it three or four times to get him off my back." His first sexual experience was at age 22, "I was goaded by a roommate into going to a prostitute. It was okay I guess, but I never went back."

Approximately five months ago, he became interested in a technical assistant who works with him. He says, "It began during coffee breaks. She seemed easy to talk with, and we started having lunch together." They began social dating about a month later and have seen each other regularly since then. He describes their current relationship as being "very close, and sometimes a little scary. She really understands what I'm thinking, about my work and all. I can talk to her." She is 33 years old and he says that she was a virgin until they began a sexual relationship about three months ago. He is insistent that she not be interviewed regarding his evaluation.

He states that he usually sleeps well and has a good appetite, but admits to having reasonably "serious episodes" of depression from time to time. He is quick to note that he has never contemplated suicide and injects, "I always know that when I get depressed it will ultimately end. It's usually because I get frustrated because of some problem that I am working on." The psychiatrist overseeing the evaluation has asked for a personality description and has raised specific questions about: (1) the possibility of a schizophreniform problem, (2) the magnitude of any depression, (3) the possibility of suicide, and (4) an opinion about whether the apparent delusions concerning his work situation and the activities of his brother-in-law are indications of paranoia or may have a reality base, and (5) recommendations concerning treatment if necessary.

CASE FORMULATION AND RELEVANT LITERATURE

The questions raised by this young man and his referring psychiatrist revolve around his preoccupation with the motives of his fellow workers. He has some awareness that these concerns may have a paranoid delusional quality, and he worries about whether he is "losing contact with reality." The Rorschach can be of some utility in assessing delusional thinking, and a review of the literature will provide focus for the psychologist analyzing this patient's protocol. Other questions raised by the psychiatrist include depression and suicide risk. Literature concerning those topics was reviewed in relation to Case 2 (Chapter 4).

Assessment of Paranoid Delusional Thinking

Kleiger (1999) has pointed out that delusional and obsessional thinking share some important structural features. Both involve careful attention to detail, both can occur in individuals who are functioning adequately in at least some areas of their lives, and both typically occur without grossly disorganized thought processes. Consequently, even in psychosis we would expect fewer indications of poor reality testing and serious cognitive slippage in the Rorschachs of individuals whose thinking is organized around a delusional system, and a number of studies support that assumption.

Auslander, Perry, and Jeste (2002) compared 27 medically stable outpatients with paranoid schizophrenia to 17 outpatients with nonparanoid schizophrenia and to 45 normal comparison participants. The paranoid patients showed significantly less impairment on a Rorschach measure of perceptual inaccuracy and cognitive slippage [the Ego Impairment Index (EII); Perry & Viglione, 1991] and were similar in their performance to the normal comparison group. An earlier study with younger schizophrenic patients (Perry, Viglione, & Braff, 1992) resulted in a similar finding when comparing paranoid patients with a nonparanoid (disorganized and undifferentiated) group.

Belyi (1991) found that the Rorschachs of patients with systematized delusions were similar to those of normal controls and were distinguished only by greater attention to detail. Kleiger (1999) reports a case of a frankly delusional woman whose Rorschach had no indications of perceptual inaccuracy or cognitive distortion, noting, "Somehow, the stimulus demands of the Rorschach bypassed her encapsulated delusionality . . ." (p. 310).

What we might expect in well-organized paranoid delusional systems is a cautious and detail-oriented Rorschach information processing style. Rapaport, Gill, and Schafer (1968) suggested that this caution might show up in a low number of responses, card rejections, and fewer color determinants. Exner's Hypervigilance Index (2003) contains several variables suggestive of a detail-oriented approach. They include high Zf, an overincorporative Zd, and a disproportionate amount of human and animal detail ($H+A:Hd+Ad < 4:1$).

Case 4. A 31-Year-Old Male.

Card	Response	Inquiry
I	1. A bat. Basically, tht's it. I don't feel into this today	**E:** (Rpts Ss Resp) **S:** The whole thng (outlines), j this whole shape, c the wgs (points) & the body **E:** If u look longr I thnk u'll find st else too
	2. It ll a man parachuting	**E:** (Rpts Ss Resp) **S:** Ths middle prt **E:** Help me to c it lik u r **S:** The form, lik when u jump out and free fall, it ll a man doing tht w his arms up, the chute hasn't opend yet, he's just in free fall
	3. A devil's face, tht's it	**E:** (Rpts Ss Resp) **S:** J rite here (circles the cntr), j the shape of the eyes rite here **E:** The shape of the eyes? **S:** Theyr slantd, lik the eyes of the devil **S:** Are there many inkblots to do? **E:** Not too many
II	4. A wound, a bloody wound	**E:** (Rpts Ss Resp) **S:** The blood, the gash, its all red and bloody lik a wound, it must b a wound bec its bleedg **E:** U said there's a gash? **S:** Ths liter prt in the middl (Dd24) ll skin & the gash is rite in the middl, ths littl white line ll a cut dwn in the flesh & its bleedg all around it
	5. A clash betwn 2 adversaries, thts it	**E:** (Rpts Ss Resp) **S:** Two individuals engaged in combat, the hands up against one anothr, and the red is the blood, it's on their heads & their feet
III	6. A man and wm about to embrace	**E:** (Rpts Ss Resp) **S:** Ths is the man (left D9) and this is the wm (rite D9), the shape of them, the heads & legs **E:** U said about to embrace? **S:** Thy r bendg towd eo lik thy r going to embrace, lik thyr r going to reach out to embrace
	7. Two hearts comg togthr, tht's it	**E:** (Rpts Ss Resp) **S:** Rite here (D3), thyr shaped like hearts & thyr red lik hearts **E:** U said thyr togthr? **S:** Thyr abt to get togthr, they'r lookg at ech othr, thy want to get togthr, lik 2 hearts will become one
IV	8. A large ogre, its going to beat evrythg in its path, thts it	**E:** (Rpts Ss Resp) **S:** The whole blot, the overbearg size and black lik a monstr, j walkg ominously, it ll he's puttg one foot in frnt of the othr (demo's w hands), towrd u, lik comg towd u
V	9. A bf, a free and easy bf, thts it	**E:** (Rpts Ss Resp) **S:** The entire blot, the shape of the wngs, antenna **E:** U said free and easy? **S:** It j looks graceful lik a bf
VI	10. A bear mat, u know when u carve up a bearskin? Tht's it	**E:** (Rpts Ss Resp) **S:** It ll a bearskin, the arms, legs, tail, and the off gray color **E:** Off gray color? **S:** Well, u kno, thts pretty much the color of bears

Case 4. Continued.

Card	Response	Inquiry
VII	11. A referee signalg a touchdown	**E:** (Rpts Ss Resp) **S:** From here up (D2's), these ll 2 hands going up, sombdy lik scored & thes r the referee's arms going up to confirm tht
	12. It cb a letter U also, tht's it	**E:** (Rpts Ss Resp) **S:** The whole blot, the shape of it ll a letter U to me
VIII	13. Fire	**E:** (Rpts Ss Resp) **S:** Here (D2), it's the color of fire, lik a fire burng, it sort of is moving up lik fire does **E:** Moving up? **S:** Fire rises, it ll it is rising
	14. Two dead rats	**E:** (Rpts Ss Resp) **S:** On the side here, j the shape of a dead rat, the legs & the head **E:** U say thyr dead? **S:** Thyv been skinned, thy'r pink, lik dead skinned rats
	15. Mayb a depressed hand too, tht's all I c	**E:** (Rpts Ss Resp) **S:** Here (Dd22), outstretched, lik reachg aimlessly, not graspg on anythng. Lik a depressed person has nothng to touch, j reachg out hopelessly **E:** U say lik a depressed person? **S:** Yes, its lik tht but there's no person, just the arm, outstretched, just reachg out
IX	16. Jesus Christ, wht the hell is ths? Confusion, mass confusion, thts it	**E:** (Rpts Ss Resp) **S:** The entire blot looks strange, diffrnt colors, disorganized, no shapes, j a mishmash, lik the insides of a person tht r boiling w anger & hate. He's disorganized & filled w fury **E:** I'm not sur I'm seeg it lik u r, help me **S:** Think of it as wht goes on in your insides when u boil w anger, it's j a mess of stuff tht happens, I thk of it as evrythg boiling, nothing is calm, it's all disorganized
X	17. Marriage, 2 bodies married, thts it	**E:** (Rpts Ss Resp) **S:** Two bodies here (D9) holdg hands, movg forward to happiness **E:** Happiness? **S:** The colors, the red, yellow, blue, green, thy all signal happiness. The bodies hav found tht & now thy r bonded togthr. The minister has fused them togthr **E:** Fused them? **S:** This (D6) is lik cartilage tht will hold them togthr

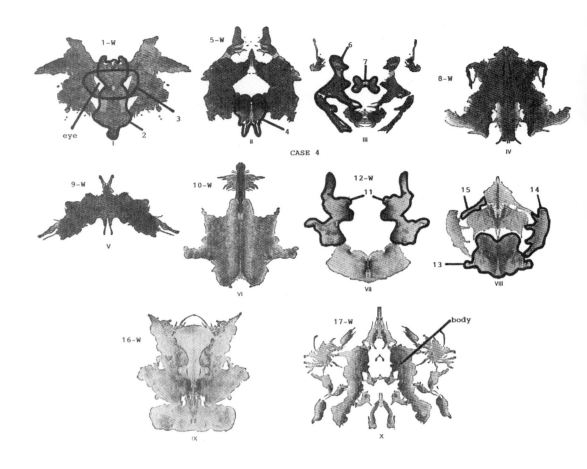

CASE 4

Case 4. Sequence of Scores.

Card	No.	Loc.	No.	Determinant(s)	(2)	Content(s)	Pop	Z	Special Scores
I	1	Wo	1	Fo		A	P	1.0	
	2	Do	4	Mpu		H			GHR
	3	DdSo	99	F–		(Hd)		3.5	PHR
II	4	Dv	3	CF.mp.VFu		Bl,An			MOR
	5	W+	1	Ma.CFo	2	H,Bl		4.5	AG,MOR,PHR
III	6	D+	9	Mpo		H	P	4.0	COP,GHR
	7	D+	3	Mp.FC–	2	An		3.0	FAB2,COP,PHR
IV	8	Wo	1	FC'.Ma.FDo		(H)	P	2.0	AG,GHR
V	9	Wo	1	Fo		A	P	1.0	
VI	10	Wo	1	FC'o		Ad	P	2.5	MOR,INC
VII	11	Do	2	Ma–		Hd			PHR
	12	Wo	1	Fu		Art		2.5	
VIII	13	Dv	2	CF.mau		Fi			
	14	Do	1	FCo	2	Ad	P		MOR
	15	Ddo	22	Mau		Hd,Hx			DR2,MOR,PHR
IX	16	Wv	1	Ma.C		Hx			AB,DR2,PHR
X	17	W+	1	Ma.C–	2	H		5.5	AB,COP,FAB2,PHR

Case 4. Structural Summary.

Location Features	
Zf	= 10
ZSum	= 29.5
ZEst	= 31.0
W	= 8
D	= 7
W+D	= 15
Dd	= 2
S	= 1

DQ

+	= 4
o	= 10
v/+	= 0
v	= 3
YF	= 0

Form Quality

	FQx	MQual	W+D
+	= 0	= 0	= 0
o	= 7	= 3	= 7
u	= 5	= 2	= 4
–	= 4	= 3	= 3
none	= 1	= 1	= 1

Determinants

Blends
CF.m.VF
M.CF
M.FC
FC′.M.FD
CF.m
M.C
M.C

Single	
M	= 4
FM	= 0
m	= 0
FC	= 1
CF	= 0
C	= 0
Cn	= 0
FC′	= 1
C′F	= 0
C′	= 0
FT	= 0
TF	= 0
T	= 0
FV	= 0
VF	= 0
V	= 0
FY	= 0
Fi	= 1
Y	= 0
Fr	= 0
rF	= 0
FD	= 0
F	= 4
(2)	= 4

Contents	
H	= 4
(H)	= 1
Hd	= 2
(Hd)	= 1
Hx	= 2
A	= 2
(A)	= 0
Ad	= 2
(Ad)	= 0
An	= 2
Art	= 1
Ay	= 0
Bl	= 2
Bt	= 0
Cg	= 0
Cl	= 0
Ex	= 0
Fd	= 0
Ge	= 0
Hh	= 0
Ls	= 0
Na	= 0
Sc	= 0
Sx	= 0
Xy	= 0
Id	= 0

S-Constellation
NO . . .FV+VF+V+FD>2
YES . .Col-Shd Bl>0
YES . .Ego<.31,>.44
YES . .MOR > 3
NO . . .Zd > +- 3.5
NO . . .es > EA
YES . .CF+C > FC
YES . .X+% < .70
NO . . .S > 3
NO . . .P < 3 or > 8
NO . . .Pure H < 2
NO . . .R < 17
5 . . . .TOTAL

Special Scores

	Lv1	Lv2
DV	= 0x1	0x2
INC	=1x2	0x4
DR	= 0x3	2x6
FAB	= 0x4	2x7
ALOG	= 0x5	
CON	= 0x7	
Raw Sum6	= 5	
Wgtd Sum6	= 28	

AB	= 2	GHR = 3
AG	= 2	PHR = 7
COP	= 3	MOR = 5
CP	= 0	PER = 0
		PSV = 0

Ratios, Percentages, and Derivations

R	=17	L	=0.31		
EB	=9:7.0	EA	=16.0	EBPer	=N/A
eb	=2:3	es	=5	D	=+4
		Adj es	=4	Adj D	=+4
FM	=0	C′	=2	T	=0
m	=2	V	=1	Y	=0

FC:CF+C	=2:5
Pure C	=2
SumC′:WSumC	=2:7.0
Afr	=0.42
S	=1
Blends:R	=7:17
CP	=0

COP = 3	AG=2
GHR:PHR	=3:7
a:p	=7:4
Food	=0
SumT	=0
Human Cont	=8
Pure H	=4
PER	=0
Iso Indx	=0.00

a:p	=7:4	Sum6	= 5	XA%	=0.71	Zf	=10.0	3r+(2)/R	=0.24
Ma:Mp	=6: 3	Lv2	= 4	WDA%	=0.73	W:D:Dd	=8:7:2	Fr+rF	=0
2AB+Art+Ay	= 5	WSum6	=28	X–%	=0.24	W:M	=8:9	SumV	=1
MOR	=5	M–	= 3	S–	=1	Zd	=–1.5	FD	=1
		Mnone	= 1	P	=6	PSV	=0	An+Xy	=2
				X+%	=0.41	DQ+	=4	MOR	=5
				Xu%	=0.29	DQv	=3	H:(H)Hd(Hd)	=4:4

PTI = 3	DEPI = 6*	CDI = 1	S-CON = 5	HVI = No	OBS = No

S-CON AND KEY VARIABLES

The S-CON value of five is not positive. The first positive Key variable is the DEPI value of six. It indicates that the interpretation should begin with a review of the data concerning affect. That review should be followed by an evaluation of the data for controls, then self-perception, interpersonal perception, and the three clusters that comprise the cognitive triad, processing, mediation, and ideation.

AFFECT

Case 4.   Affect-Related Data for a 31-Year-Old Male.

EB	= 9:7.0			EBPer	= N/A	**Blends**	
eb	= 2:3	L	= 0.31	FC:CF+C	= 2:5	M.CF	= 1
DEPI	= 6	CDI = 1		Pure C	= 2	M.C	= 2
						M.FC	= 1
SumC' = 2	SumT = 0			SumC':WSumC	= 2:7.0	CF.m.VF	= 1
SumV = 1	SumY = 0			Afr	= 0.42	CF.m	= 1
						FC'.M.FD	= 1
Intellect	= 5	CP = 0		S = 1 (S to I,II,III = 1)			
Blends:R	= 7:17			Col-Shad Bl	= 1		
m + y Bl	= 2			Shading Bl	= 0		

The DEPI value of six signals the likelihood of a potentially disabling affective problem. It is not surprising that he reports having had "serious" episodes of depression "from time to time." The *EB* (9:7.0) value indicates that he is an ambitent. As such, he is likely to be inconsistent in his approach to making decisions. At times, he may push feelings aside and approach decision making very thoughtfully, but in similar instances, he may become influenced by feelings and rely much more on them to arrive at a decision. This lack of consistency in the use of feelings frequently causes the ambitent to become confused by them. It can lead to erratic forms of emotional display and often breeds an ideational inefficiency that increases the possibility of judgmental errors.

Although the *EB* data indicate that he is an ambitent, it seems appropriate to question or qualify that conclusion. In this case, the *EB* data may be somewhat misleading. It is unusual for a person to give nine *M* responses in a modest length record (*R* = 17) and not be identified as introversive. A review of the *Structural Summary* and Sequence of Scores reveals that the large right side *EB* value (7.0) is created by a noticeable failure to modulate his chromatic color use. Seven answers of his 17 responses include chromatic color. Two of the seven are blended Pure *C* responses, and three others are blended *CF* responses. Four of the seven, including both Pure *C*s, also contain *M*. If more modulation in the use of chromatic color had occurred in any one of his five Pure *C* and *CF* answers, the right side *EB* value would be reduced by at least one-half point. Thus, it seems reasonable to speculate that he probably has been more consistently ideational (introversive) in his decision-making habits, but some sort of psychological disarray is interfering with that consistency and creating the previously described tendency to vacillation and inefficiency.

The right side value of the *eb* (3) is not unusual, but it does include one variable that is relevant to the study of his affects. It is the vista variable, suggesting that he often experiences some negative feelings because of a persistent tendency to berate or degrade himself. The *Afr* (.42) is unexpectedly low, regardless of whether he is considered to be an ambient or an introversive. It signals a marked tendency to avoid emotional stimuli and suggests that he is probably uncomfortable dealing with emotion. That postulate is also supported by the Intellectualization Index value (5), which implies that he is more prone than most people to reduce or neutralize the impact of feelings by dealing with them on an intellectual level. It is a form of denial that tends to distort the true experience of emotions or emotional situations.

The data in the *FC:CF+C* ratio (2:5) seem contrary to the postulate developed from the *Afr* and the Intellectualization Index. The ratio signifies that he is lax about modulating his emotions or their display, and this should be considered a significant liability because two Pure *C* responses are involved. Often, persons with this characteristic are regarded by others as being impulsive, or at least, emotionally immature. Modulation failures such as implied by the data usually have a negative effect on social adjustment. If he is introversive, as has been speculated, this finding implies a serious problem concerning the effectiveness of his ideational style.

Neither of his Pure *C* responses include primitive features. On the contrary, both contain *M,* and both have a pseudo-intellectual quality. In response 16, the color is used to represent "confusion . . . like the insides of a person that are boiling with anger and hate." In response 17, the color is used to "signal happiness." The way in which the color is used in these answers implies that failures to modulate emotions may be less obvious in his behaviors and more obvious in some of his ideational activity.

The seven blends in the record comprise slightly more than 40% of his responses, which is substantial for an ambient, and much more so for an introversive person. This suggests that his psychological organization is unusually complex, a notion also supported by the fact that two of the seven blends contain three determinants. One is a color-shading blend (*CF.m.VF*), which probably denotes a sense of confusion about feelings.

Overall, it appears as if emotions are troublesome and somewhat disorganizing for him. It is probable that he has felt threatened by or fearful of feelings for some time. It is also likely that he has been able to avoid emotions or maintain control over their impact by relying primarily on a logical, ideational approach to the world. However, for reasons that are unclear at the moment, that approach has faltered. As a result, his feelings seem to have become intense and appear to be creating a considerable disorganizing influence, which includes a marked proclivity for depression or depression-like experiences.

CONTROLS

Case 4. Control-Related Variables for a 31-Year-Old Male.

EB = 9:7.0	EA = 16.0		D = +4	CDI = 1
eb = 2:3	es = 5	Adj es = 4	AdjD = +4	L = 0.31
FM = 0 m = 2	SumC' = 2	SumT = 0	SumV = 1	SumY = 0

The Adj D value of +4 suggests that he has a more sturdy tolerance for stress than do most people. As such, he is far less likely to experience problems in control. The *EA* (16.0) is well above average, signifying considerable resources and offering no reason to question the validity of the Adj D Score. Likewise, the data for the *EB* (9:7.0) and *Lambda* (0.31) provide no basis to challenge the validity of the Adj D.

On the other hand, the value for the Adj *es* (4) is lower than expected, mainly because the protocol contains no *FM* answers. The absence of *FM* in the record is discussed in detail when the data concerning ideation are reviewed. It is relevant here because it raises a question of whether the Adj D is spuriously elevated due to the absence of *FM*. Assuming that the record contained three, four, or five *FM*s, the Adj *es* would increase accordingly to seven, eight, or nine, yielding Adj D scores of +3, or +2. The absolute value of the Adj D would be lowered by a point or two, but the resulting value would still be in the *plus* range, and the hypothesis about his capacity of control and tolerance for stress would remain unchanged.

At the same time, it seems important to inject a caution. Good stress tolerance, a sturdy capacity for control, and the presence of substantial resources do not necessarily yield good adjustment or freedom from pathology. They simply indicate a greater capacity for the volitional control of behavior.

SELF-PERCEPTION

Case 4.   Self-Perception Related Data for a 31-Year-Old Male.

R	= 17	OBS	= No	HVI = No	**Human Content, Hx, An & Xy Responses**
					I 2. Do Mpu H GHR
Fr+rF	= 0	3r+(2)/R	= 0.24		I 3. DdSo F– (Hd) 3.5 PHR
					II 4. Dv CF.m.VFu Bl,An MOR
FD	= 1	SumV	= 1		II 5. W+ Ma.CFo 2 H,Bl 4.5 AG,MOR,PHR
					III 6. D+ Mpo 2 H P 4.0 COP,GHR
An+Xy	= 2	MOR	= 5		III 7. D+ Mp.FC– 2 An 3.0 FAB2,COP,PHR
					IV 8. Wo FC'.Ma.FDo (H) P 2.0 AG,GHR
H:(H)+Hd+(Hd) = 4:4					VII 11. Do Ma– Hd PHR
[EB = 9:7.0]					VIII 15. Ddo Mau Hd,Hx AB,DR2,PHR
					IX 16. Wv Ma.C Hx AB,DR2,PHR
					X 17. W+ Ma.C– 2 H 5.5 AB,COP,FAB2,PHR

The Egocentricity Index (.24) is well below average, indicating that he tends to view his personal worth more negatively than positively and is likely to regard himself less favorably when making comparisons with others. The vista response was noted earlier. It connotes a preoccupation with features that he perceives to be negative, and this yields painful feelings.

His record also includes two *An* contents, one of which has a special score of MOR and the second a form quality of minus. They signify the presence of some unusual body concern that is probably important to him. The protocol also includes five MOR answers, a substantial number for any protocol, but especially so for one of modest length. Their presence indicates that his self-image is marked by some very serious negative attributions that tend to affect his thinking and create a noticeably pessimistic view of himself.

There are eight responses in which human or humanlike figures are reported. Four of the eight are Pure *H* answers. If he is an introversive person, this suggests that much of his self-image has developed from imaginary impressions or distortions of real experience. The codings for the eight answers that include human or humanlike figures tend to be more negative than positive. The four answers that contain Pure *H* include two that are coded *FQo* (responses 5 & 6), one coded *FQu* (response 2), and one (response 17) coded *FQ–*. One of those coded *FQo* (response 5) also has the special scores MOR and *AG*. Two of the four that contain *(H), Hd,* or *(Hd)* contents are minus answers (responses 3 and 11). Two of the eight also include serious critical special scores, *DR2* and *FAB2* (responses 15 and 17). In addition, two answers (responses 15 and 16) have *Hx* contents, suggesting that he probably attempts to deal with self-concept issues in an overly intellectualized manner that may ignore reality. As a collective, these findings suggest that his self-image is not very positive.

The hypothesis that his self-image is rather negative gains considerable support from the search for projected material in the protocol. Each of the four minus answers contains interesting material. The first (Card I, response 3) is "A devil's face," justified as such because of the "the shape of the eyes . . . they are slanted like the eyes of the devil." Minus responses sometimes convey something about internal sets, and this one may imply an ominous or even evil sense about himself.

The second minus (Card III, response 7) is more dramatic and bizarre, "Two hearts together . . . they are about to get together . . . looking at each other, they want to get together, like two hearts will become one." It implies an intense longing or struggle to achieve emotional closeness. The third minus (Card VII, response 11) "A referee signaling a touchdown . . . somebody like scored and these are the referee's arms going up to confirm that." It is a strange response that involves considerable distortion of the distal field. It seems to connote a need for affirmation. On a speculative level, this answer may have some relation to his unusual sexual history.

The fourth minus (Card X, response 17) is, in some ways, similar to the Card II (hearts) response, "Marriage, two bodies married . . . moving forward toward happiness . . . bonded together . . . the minister has fused them together . . . like cartilage that will hold them together." It is bizarre yet, like response 7, it contains a COP. It involves a sense of closure regarding his striving for closeness. It is difficult to avoid some speculation that at least two and possibly all of these minus answers reflect emotional turmoil that he has been experiencing as a result of his relatively newfound relationship with his 33-year-old girlfriend.

As would be expected, his five MOR responses present a much more negative picture. The first (Card II, response 4) is "a bloody wound, like flesh has been cut into and it's bleeding." It is a fairly direct answer, possibly related to some perceived traumatic experience. The second (Card II, response 5) is "A clash between two adversaries . . . individuals engaged in combat . . . the blood, it's on their heads and their feet." Like the preceding response, it involves injury. In this instance, the injury occurs because of a combat between individuals, raising a question about whether the combat is intrapsychic or between himself and the environment.

The third MOR (Card VI, response 10) is less dramatic, "A bear mat, you know when you carve up a bearskin," and has no obvious meaning. However, the fourth and fifth MOR responses seem to be much more revealing about his self-concept. The fourth is "dead rats . . . like skinned dead rats." It conveys a sense of damage and futility. The fifth MOR (Card VIII, response 15) is probably the most directly revealing: "a depressed hand . . . reaching aimlessly, not grasping on anything . . . like a depressed person has nothing to touch, just reaching out hopelessly."

The collective of the MOR responses imparts the notion of a self-image that is clearly marked by a sense of damage, futility, and a pessimistic view of himself. It may be of interest to review the form quality of the MOR responses, all of which relate to negative features. Four of the five are coded *FQo,* and one is *FQu.* In contrast, three of the four minus answers (hearts together, touchdown, marriage) relate to positive features or experiences. This hints at the notion that positive views of himself and his relation to the world require some noticeable bending or distorting of reality, but this hypothesis should be tested further as the *M* responses are studied.

The first *M* (Card I, response 2), "a man parachuting . . . the chute hasn't opened yet, he's just in free fall," seems to imply a sense of optimistic helplessness (the chute will open). The second *M* (Card II, response 5) "a clash between two adversaries," was discussed earlier and has an ominous quality. The third (Card III, response 6) is much more positive, "A man and woman about to embrace," but it is also quite unusual because the figures are differentiated. It is unfortunate that the examiner did not pursue this a bit more in the inquiry. The response seems to imply the same sort of optimism noted in response 2, that is, something positive is about to happen. This same theme seems evident in the fourth *M* (Card III, response 7), "Two hearts . . . about to get together," which has also been discussed earlier.

The fifth *M* (Card IV, response 8), "A large ogre, it's going to beat everything in its path," has a markedly ominous quality and conveys intense aggressiveness, similar to that noted in response 5. Three of the remaining four *M* answers have been discussed earlier, but all four are worth study again because of the sequencing effect. The first of the four (Card VII, response 11) contains positive material, involving a referee signaling that someone has scored. The next two *M*s are very negative. One (Card VIII, response 15) is the depressed hand reaching out hopelessly. The second (Card IX, response 16) is "mass confusion . . . like the insides of a person that are boiling with anger and hate . . . filled with fury . . . nothing is calm, it's all disorganized." It is an extremely labile response marked by a complete absence of control. Interestingly, it is followed by an *M* with positive features (Card X, response 17), "two bodies married . . . moving forward to happiness . . . bonded together."

In all, four of the nine *M*s focus on positive emotional interactions or events; people are about to embrace, hearts are about to get together, a referee confirms a touchdown, and bodies are being married and moving forward to happiness. They convey a positive sense of self, but unfortunately, all involve detachment from or distortion of reality. Four of the remaining five *M*s connote a much more angry, negative, or confused sense of the self; adversaries are in combat, an ogre is going to beat everything in its path, a depressed hand is reaching out hopelessly, and the insides of a person are boiling with anger and hate.

There are two responses that include *m*'s. The first (Card II, response 4), "a bloody wound . . . it's bleeding," has been noted earlier, and may signify some traumatic event. The second (Card VIII, response 13) is "Fire . . . moving up like fire does." It is an intense, labile answer that has an ominous quality; the fire is rising. There are three responses that have not been reviewed, but none contain any obvious embellishments. Response 1 is a bat, response 9 is a butterfly, and response 12 is the letter U.

The 14 responses that appear to contain projective features provide glimpses of self-representation that are contradictory and suggest that he is in great conflict about himself. On a basic level, he seems to perceive himself as an angry, confused, damaged, and disorganized person. Apparently, he is sometimes tormented by the impulses that rise from this picture of the self.

On another level, he has devised a way of defending against these negative impressions and the manifestations of chaotic thoughts and feelings that they provoke by focusing on the anticipation of a strong and enduring emotional relationship. Unfortunately, the latter requires a pseudo-intellectual bending or distorting of reality.

His history indicates that he has been somewhat of a social isolate for much of his life. His experiences with women are limited and he has never had an enduring relationship, except with his brother, until about five months ago. He says that his relationship with his newfound girlfriend is very close—"I can talk to her"—but he is also insistent that she not be told of his current evaluation. This suggests that the relationship might not be as close as he claims, and actually may be more fragile than he is willing to concede. Ultimately, more information about the relationship may be pivotal in understanding his problems and making recommendations. Possibly the data concerning interpersonal perception will shed added light on this issue.

INTERPERSONAL PERCEPTION

Case 4.   Interpersonal Perception Data for a 31-Year-Old Male.

R	= 17	CDI	= 1	HVI	= No	**COP & AG Responses**	
a:p	= 7:4	SumT	= 0	Fd	= 0	II	5. W+ Ma.CFo 2 H,Bl 4.5 AG,MOR,PHR
		[eb	= 2:3]			III	6. D+ Mpo H P 4.0 COP,GHR
Sum Human Contents = 8				H	= 4	III	7. D+ Mp.FC– 2 An 3.0 FAB2,COP,PHR
[Style = Ambitent, possibly introversive]						IV	8. Wo FC'.Ma.FDo (H) P 2.0 AG,GHR
GHR:PHR = 3:7						X	17. W+ Ma.C– 2 H 5.5 AB,COP,FAB2,PHR
COP = 3		AG	= 2	PER	= 0		
Isolation Indx = 0.00							

The CDI and HVI are not positive, and the $a:p$ ratio (7:4) is in the expected direction. The first datum of importance is the absence of texture answers. The value of zero for *SumT* suggests that he is likely to acknowledge or express his needs for closeness in more cautious ways than are expected for most people. He is probably conservative in close interpersonal situations, especially those implying or involving tactile exchange, and he may be overly concerned with issues of personal space. This is not surprising in light of his reported history about interpersonal relations.

There is little doubt that he is interested in people. This is signified by the eight human contents in the protocol, which is at the upper end of the expected range for an introversive person, and more than expected for an ambitent. If he is introversive, the fact that only four of the eight are Pure *H* answers implies that, despite his considerable interest, he probably does not understand people very well. This notion is afforded support by the data for the GHR:PHR ratio (3:7). Typically, persons giving a substantial number of *PHR* responses will have histories of failed or conflicted relations and are often shunned or rejected by others.

The protocol contains three COP and two *AG* answers. Usually this suggests that the person is open to and interested in positive interactions, but many of those may be marked by more aggressive or forceful forms of exchange. In this instance, however, that hypothesis requires elaboration and qualification because two of the three COP responses have a minus form quality (responses 7 & 17) and both include the special score FABCOM2. This does not negate the hypothesis, but strongly implies that his conceptualizations about positive interactions may not be very realistic, and this can easily breed social behaviors that others deem inappropriate.

In addition, the two *AG* answers (responses 5 & 8) are fairly intense. They involve a clash between adversaries and an ogre that is going to beat everything in its path. Both suggest that, if aggressiveness manifests in his interpersonal behaviors, it is likely to be more obvious, direct, and possibly asocial instead of simply reflecting a playful or competitive forcefulness.

Only three of his nine *M* responses are coded for a pair. All were studied during the review of data concerning self-perception, but they warrant added consideration here to determine if there is any consistency in the way that interactions are described. One of the three is negative. It is the clash between adversaries engaged in combat (Card II, response 5). The remaining two are very positive but also convey a bizarre naivete. They are the hearts together (Card III, response 7), and the two bodies married and moving forward to happiness (Card X, response 17).

In general, the findings from this cluster suggest that he is interested in relations with people but apparently is very naive and inexperienced about social interaction. This seems consistent with the social history that he reports. He has had very limited dating experience and regards his interests as being different from those around him. He is annoyed that he cannot work alone and criticizes his coworkers as being uncooperative and "stupid" at times.

PROCESSING

Case 4. Processing Variables for a 31-Year-Old Male.

EB = 9:7.0	Zf = 10	Zd = −1.5	DQ+ = 4
L = 0.31	W:D:Dd = 8:7:2	PSV = 0	DQv/+ = 0
HVI = NO	W:M = 8:9		DQv = 3
OBS = NO			

Location & DQ Sequencing

I: Wo.Do.DdSo	VI: Wo
II: Dv.W+	VII: Do.Wo
III: D+.D+	VIII: Dv.Do.Ddo
IV: Wo	IX: Wv
V: Wo	X: W+

The *Zf* value of 10 is within the expected range, suggesting a processing effort similar to that of most people. The *W:D:Dd* ratio (8:7:2) shows a slightly greater proportion of *W* answers, which could signal more processing effort than expected, but that hypothesis does not seem supported by a review of the location sequencing. This is a not a long record, only 17 responses. His eight *W* answers include five that are only responses (Cards IV, V, VI, IX, and X), and a sixth is the first answer to Card I. His *Dd* answers are both last responses. These findings suggest that the processing effort is not overly conservative, but it would be misleading to suggest that he works harder than most people when processing new information. Instead, it seems more reasonable to note that he is relatively consistent in his approach.

Actually, the *W:M* ratio (8:9) implies a more cautious or conservative approach to processing if he is considered to be an ambient, but not so if he is introversive. The *Zd* value (−1.5) falls in the expected range, suggesting that his scanning efficiency is similar to that of most people.

Probably the most important data in the processing cluster concern the *DQ* distribution. There are only four *DQ+* responses, which is less than expected for an adult. There are also three *DQv* responses, substantially more than expected from an adult. It is an unusual mix for a person who has a graduate degree and for a protocol that contains nine *M* responses. These findings suggest some impairment to the quality of his processing. A review of the *DQ* sequencing seems to support this notion but also raises a question about whether mediation or conceptualization problems may be causing his apparent processing difficulties.

His three *DQv* answers are all first or only responses to broken or semibroken figures (Cards II, VIII, X) that contain chromatic color features. All three also include some form of movement. Likewise, his four *DQ+* answers occur to broken or semibroken figures that contain chromatic color features (Cards II, III, and X), and all contain *M*. Thus, it can only be concluded that he has some processing difficulty, the cause of which is unclear at this time.

MEDIATION

Case 4.   Mediation Variables for a 31-Year-Old Male.

R = 17		L = 0.31		OBS = No	**Minus & NoForm Features**
FQx+	= 4		XA%	= .89	II 3. WS+ CF.FT.Mp– Hd,Bl 4.5 MOR,PER,PHR
FQx+	= 0		XA%	= .71	I 3. DdSo F– (Hd) 3.5 PHR
FQxo	= 7		WDA%	= .73	III 7. D+ CF.Mp– 2 An 3.0 FAB2,COP,PHR
FQxu	= 5		X–%	= .24	VII 11. Do Ma– Hd PHR
FQx–	= 4		S–	= 1	IX 16. Wv Ma.C Hx AB,DR2,PHR
FQxnone	= 1				X 17. W+ Ma.C– 2 H 5.5 AB,COP,FAB2,PHR
(W+D	= 20)		P	= 6	
WD+	= 0		X+%	= .41	
WDo	= 7		Xu%	= .29	
WDu	= 4				
WD–	= 3				
WDnone	= 1				

The values for the *XA%* (.71) and *WDA%* (.73) indicate a moderate level of mediational dysfunction that can have a noticeable effect on his reality testing. That likelihood seems supported by the significant *X–%* (.24). His four minus answers are spread across four cards. Three of the four (responses 7, 11, and 17) include human movement, and two of the four (responses 7 and 17) also include *CF* or *C* determinants. In addition, there is one NoForm answer (response 16) that contains *M* and *C* determinants. Collectively, these findings suggest that his mediation may be impeded either by strange conceptualizations or by poorly contained emotions.

The levels of distortion included in the four minus responses are varied. The first (Card I, response 3—a devil's face) uses two of the white space areas of the figure appropriately, but the actual contours used for the face do not exist. He creates them. The second minus answer (Card III, response 7—two hearts together) generally avoids major distortions of the distal field. The third (Card VII, response 11—a referee signaling) involves more distortion of the distal features. It requires considerable stretching of the imagination to think of the *D2* areas of the figure as upraised arms. The last minus (Card X, response 17—two bodies married) includes less distortion than response 11, but some does exist. The use of the *D9* areas as bodies is appropriate, but the identification of the center *D6* area as connecting cartilage bends reality noticeably. None of the minus answers include a severe disregard for the stimulus fields that are involved, and at least one, the bodies on Card X would have been coded as *unusual* if he had not spoiled the answer by adding features that require distortion of the distal properties. Nonetheless, the characteristics of the four minus answers raise serious questions about the integrity of his reality testing.

On a positive note, the record includes six Popular answers, signifying that expected or acceptable translations or behaviors are likely to occur when the cues for those behaviors are obvious. However, the *X+%* (.41) is noticeably low, and the *Xu%* (.29) is higher than expected. Both imply the probability of more unconventional translations or behaviors because of a tendency to disregard social demands or expectations. The tendency to do so is likely to be increased because of his difficulties with reality testing. A review of data concerning his thinking should shed more light on this issue.

IDEATION

Case 4.   Ideation Variables for a 31-Year-Old Male.

							Critical Special Scores			
L	= 0.31	OBS	= No	HVI	= No					
							DV	= 0	DV2	= 0
EB	= 9:7.0	EBPer	= N/A	a:p	= 7:4		INC	= 1	INC2	= 0
				Ma:Mp	= 6:3		DR	= 0	DR2	= 2
eb	= 2:3	[FM = 0 m = 2]					FAB	= 0	FAB2	= 2
				M−	= 3		ALOG	= 0	CON	= 0
Intell Indx	= 5	MOR	= 5	Mnone	= 1		Sum6	= 5	Sum6	= 28
								(R = 17)		

M Response Features

I	2.	Do Mpo H GHR
II	5.	W+ Ma.CFo 2 H,Bl 4.5 AG,MOR,PHR
III	6.	D+ Mpo 2 H P 4.0 COP,GHR
III	7.	D+ CF.Mp− 2 An 3.0 COP,FAB2,PHR
IV	8.	Wo FC'.Ma.FDo (H) P 2.0 AG,GHR
VII	11.	Do Ma− Hd PHR
VIII	15.	Ddo Mau Hd,Hx DR2,MOR,PHR
IX	16.	Wv Ma.C Hx AB,FAB2,PHR
X	17.	W+ Ma.C− 2 H 5.5 AB,COP,FAB2,PHR

The *a:p* ratio (7:4) offers no information to suggest that he is notably inflexible in his thinking or values. However, the five MOR responses in the record signify the presence of a markedly pessimistic set that causes him to conceptualize his relationships with the world with a sense of doubt and discouragement. This sort of pessimism often leads to narrow and concrete thinking and foments an expectation of gloomy outcomes, regardless of one's effort. It is a basic element that frequently promotes sadness and/or depression.

The left side *eb* value (2) comprises two *m*'s. The absence of *FM* responses is a very unusual finding, suggesting that he somehow minimizes or avoids the naturally alerting mental intrusions that are caused by need states. Some people do this by acting quickly to reduce needs when they are experienced. Others develop conceptual tactics by which the peripheral mental intrusions are merged into the stream of controlled and directed thinking. In that he is likely an introversive person, he probably does the latter, thereby reducing the impact of need states temporarily. It is a form of overcontrol that can serve as an asset at times, but it also creates a distinct possibility of ignoring needs that may intensify and ultimately become disruptive.

The value for the Intellectualization Index (5) supports the notion that he may strive to overcontrol some of his natural impulses, especially those involving emotions. It suggests that he uses his directed conceptual thinking more often than most people to intellectualize feelings. This defensive process often requires a distorted form of thinking to deny and attempt to offset the true impact of emotions. It may occur even more often than implied by the Index value of five as there are at least two other answers in the protocol (responses 7—hearts together; and 15—a depressed hand) that have marked intellectualization qualities, but are not coded in ways that would contribute to the Index.

Assuming that intellectualization is a major component in the network of defensive tactics that he uses to maintain control over impulses, the clarity and quality of his thinking become quite important. Intellectualization does not work well for people whose thinking is clouded or peculiar. Unfortunately, that seems to be true in this case. The *Sum6* is only five, which might be unremarkable but, in this instance, four of the five are Level 2 special scores, two *DR2* and two FAB-COM2. The yield is a *WSum6* value of 28, which is very high and, typically, signifies that thinking is seriously impaired. Impairments of this magnitude usually impact on reality testing because thinking tends to be disorganized, inconsistent, and marked by flawed judgments. Bizarre conceptualizations are not uncommon, and people with this level of impairment usually find it difficult to contend with the demands of everyday living.

The verbiage related to the coding of the five critical special scores provides some insights about the characteristics of his thinking problem. One of the five, the INCOM, is coded because arms are included in his description of a bearskin. It is not bizarre and probably represents the kind of casual neglect of reality that is most common among persons who are not very mature. The material prompting the coding of the remaining four critical special scores is quite different. All are marked by inappropriate forms of intellectualization in which the task at hand becomes neglected and a spewing forth of intense feeling occurs. The first (response 7) is the hearts "about to get together . . . looking at each other . . . want to get together, like two hearts will become one." Even though positive in tone, it is flawed in substance and, at best, seems to reflect a very loose and naive kind of judgment. The second (response 15) is the depressed hand, "reaching aimlessly, not grasping anything . . . just reaching out hopelessly." It is clearly negative and seems to emphasize a preoccupation with a very lonely and painful state of pessimism.

The third (response 16) is even more intense in substance and more detached from the reality of the task, "mass confusion, insides, boiling with anger and hate . . . filled with fury . . . nothing is calm." The fourth (response 17) is the next and last answer. It seems to revert to the sort of loose and naive thinking that marked the first of the four responses, "two bodies married, moving forward to happiness . . . the minister has fused them." He describes them as "bodies" rather than people, and it seems important to him to emphasize that they are bonded or fused together.

While these four answers fall short of exhibiting a detached psychotic rambling, they intimate a sort of delusional thinking that can occur when cognitive operations are overwhelmed by preoccupations or intense feelings. In this case, the degree of cognitive slippage appears to be particularly serious because the preoccupations reflect extreme opposites and both involve intense feelings. At one extreme, the feelings manifest in forms of anger, confusion, and hopelessness. At the other extreme, the feelings are identified in relation to a joyful, happy, interpersonal merging.

SUMMARY

Apparently, this man has been predisposed to psychological trouble for some time because of a self-image that is much more negative than positive. His self-esteem is low and he tends to regard himself less favorably when he compares himself to others. The negative attributions that he has developed about himself have an adverse impact on his thinking. They create a notably pessimistic view of himself and his relation to the world. A by-product of this view is a chronic tendency to avoid close interpersonal relationships or, at least, to keep contacts with others on a superficial level. He has difficulty expressing his needs and this has contributed significantly to his cautious attitude about relations with others. Thus, although he is interested in people, he is naive about ways to create and sustain close relations with others. His inexperience about social relations and his negative self-concept have caused him to adopt an isolated lifestyle that has tended to limit his opportunities for personal and social growth.

This semi-isolated existence has apparently been at least marginally satisfying for him, although it has also disposed him to experience bouts of emotional turmoil that usually manifest as depression. Some of those experiences have probably been relatively serious, and he seems to have contended with them by relying mainly on his own logic to suppress or minimize their impact. It is unlikely that this tactic has been as effective as he reports, and it does seem clear that this strategy is no longer successful.

He is now being more and more victimized by his feelings, mainly because he is not accustomed to dealing with them, or the feelings of others, very directly. Instead, he has used his considerable resources and good capacity for control to avoid emotions or, when that is not possible, to deal with them in intellectual ways that reduce their impact. In fact, it seems likely that he has relied extensively on a markedly ideational approach to decision making and problem solving much of his life. This overly ideational approach has become less and less effective, and he currently seems to vacillate, somewhat inefficiently, when decision making or problem solving is required. In this state, his feelings play a much more important role and often cause his thinking to become flawed or disorganized.

His inability to deal with his feelings effectively has caused them to intensify and become more disruptive for him. He seems to have some awareness that he is becoming a confused and disorganized individual, and this has bred a sense of anger and also a sense of futility and hopelessness.

Gradually, this composite of liabilities has caused some impairment to his cognitive functioning. He does not process new information as well as should be the case, and his reality testing often is compromised, either because of strange thoughts or unusually intense feelings. Although he is still likely to respond in acceptable or conventional ways when the cues for such responses are obvious, he also has a notable tendency to interpret more ambiguous cues in ways that disregard social expectancies. The most obvious negative impact of his current situation is on his thinking. The pessimistic view that he holds about himself appears to have intensified, and he now seems to have a gloomy outlook about himself and the world around him.

Evidently, he has been attempting to deal with these disruptive thoughts and feelings, at least in part, by focusing extensively on a current relationship with a woman. Emotional relations can often ease misery, but in this instance, his preoccupation about the relationship may well be more delusional than real. It seems to include a naive optimism that the relation will be a source for resolving all of his difficulties. This problem also ties closely to the intensity of his feelings. They are very strong and he does not appear to know how to modulate them or express them in effective ways. In his confused thinking, he may become prone to vent them without adequate regard for the consequences.

RECOMMENDATIONS

It seems likely that the bouts of depression that he reports have been more severe and disabling than he concedes. In fact, they may have affected his work productivity and contributed to the change in his work status that occurred about 10 months ago, forcing him to work with a team rather than independently. Regardless of whether that is true, the change has forced him into an interpersonal network that runs contrary to his customary mode of work, and for which he is not well prepared. The referral questions whether his apparent delusions about his work status are indications of paranoia or may have a reality base. Both are possible. It may be that his colleagues have not found him easy to work with or very likable. If that is true, there is probably a kernel of truth in his complaints about them, but that does not account for his belief that his brother-in-law is somehow involved.

A more important key to understanding his current situation is the relationship with his girlfriend, which he describes as "very close." It is a new kind of experience for which he also is not very well prepared. If this relationship is as open and as close as he implies, it can be of considerable value in helping him sort through the emotional turmoil that he is experiencing. However, he may be distorting the true nature of the relation. His insistence that she not be interviewed regarding his evaluation suggests that their affiliation may be superficial or fragile. If that is the case, it gives greater credence to the likelihood that he is delusional.

The referral asks about the possibility of a schizophreniform problem and for information about the magnitude of any depression and the possibility of suicide. Although his thinking is sometimes disturbed, and his reality testing moderately impaired, it would be unrealistic to think of him as having a schizophreniform problem. His speech and behavior are not markedly disorganized and there is no evidence from which to suspect hallucinatory experiences. On the other hand, many of his characteristics are similar to those commonly noted among persons who are described as being schizoid or schizotypal. These include his solitary life, the lack of close friendships, social discomfort, some unusual speech patterns, a tendency to avoid or constrain emotions, a tendency to be overly ideational at times, and the current presence of some delusionlike thinking.

However, his major problem lies in the affective domain. He is psychologically organized in ways that make him vulnerable to frequent and intense experiences of affective disruption, which are most likely to manifest as depression. In fact, he is probably depressed now, although not as much as may have been the case in the past. Nonetheless, it seems serious and should be considered as a primary target for early intervention efforts. A potential problem concerning this recommendation is that he does not concede to any affective disruption at this time. He questions his sanity, but bases that question on the suspicion that his colleagues, and possibly his brother-in-law, are trying to get him to resign from work. This may be an intellectualizing way of reaching out for help, and if so, affective issues can be broached easily. However, his need to control or contain his feelings is strong, and it will be important to avoid any challenges to his integrity at the onset of treatment.

There is no clear evidence to suggest that he may be suicidal, but the potential volatility of his emotions should not be ignored. They can be dangerous to him, especially when considered in light of his thinking and reality-testing problems, his negative self-image, and his feelings of futility and hopelessness. Such a mixture can easily breed self-destructive thoughts. The sturdiness of his relationship with his girlfriend, and the extent of support from his family, especially his brother, should be regarded as key elements in this context.

As a bright and complex person who seems to be aware that he has problems, the prospects for treatment seem favorable, but it is important to recognize that he is emotionally fragile. He is not used to sharing much with others, and if pressured prematurely, he could easily bolt from treatment.

EPILOGUE

Findings from the physical and neurological examinations were unremarkable as were the results of a neuropsychological screening. Feedback concerning the various evaluations was provided to him by the attending psychiatrist, who recommended a trial period of antidepressive medication and weekly sessions of individual psychotherapy. He was skeptical about some of the feedback and especially defensive about the need for medication, but he did agree to follow the recommendations for an undetermined period.

According to his therapist, the first two months of outpatient care had modest results. Most of the sessions focused mainly on his problems at work and the exploration of tactics that might be used to interact more effectively with his coworkers and supervisor. However, he remained dissatisfied with his work situation and began to consider seeking a position with a different company. This seemed to reduce some of the stress he was experiencing at work, but he persisted in avoiding emotional issues altogether. During the third and fourth months, he began discussing his interest in marrying his girlfriend and his fears that she might reject such an overture. Concurrently, he began considering the possibility of discussing his work dissatisfaction with his supervisor. He also reported having two episodes of feeling depressed, which lasted two or three days. This provided an entry into more discussions about his feelings.

During the fifth month, he confronted his supervisor about his work dissatisfaction. The response of the supervisor was sympathetic and favorable, and a decision was made to move him into a new position that involved working with two technicians and provided him with more creative freedom. In the sixth month, he raised the prospect of marriage with his girlfriend. Although she discounted that possibility for the immediate future, she agreed that they might consider it in the future. Subsequently, she began accompanying him when he visited his brother or his parents for dinner.

The patient is currently in the eighth month of treatment and, according to the therapist, continues to make slow but positive progress. He apparently feels more confident and has become somewhat more socially active. His medication was discontinued during the sixth month of care. He has expressed some suspicions about others at work from time to time, but usually discounts them as being unimportant. His relationship with his girlfriend continues to be reasonably stable although there have been no further discussions about marriage possibilities.

REFERENCES

Auslander, L. A., Perry, W., & Jeste, D. V. (2002). Assessing disturbed thinking and cognition using the Ego Impairment Index in older schizophrenia patients: Paranoid vs. nonparanoid distinction. *Schizophrenia Research, 53*(3), 199–207.

Belyi, B. I. (1991). Interpretation of Rorschach ink blots by patients with delusional forms of schizophrenia. *Zhurnal Nevropatologii i Psikhiatrii, 91*(7), 97–104.

Exner, J. E. (2003). *The Rorschach: A comprehensive system: Vol. 1. Basic foundations* (4th ed.). New York: Wiley.

Kleiger, J. H. (1999). *Disordered thinking and the Rorschach: Theory, research, and differential diagnosis.* Hillsdale, NJ: Analytic Press.

Perry, W., & Viglione, D. J. (1991). The Ego Impairment Index as a predictor of outcome in melancholic depressed patients treated with tricyclic antidepressants. *Journal of Personality Assessment, 56*(3), 487–501.

Perry, W., Viglione, D. J., & Braff, D. (1992). The Ego Impairment Index and schizophrenia: A validation study. *Journal of Personality Assessment, 59*(1), 165–175.

Rapaport, D., Gill, M. M., & Schafer, R. (1968). *Diagnostic psychological testing.* New York: International Universities Press.

CHAPTER 7

An Issue of Dissociation

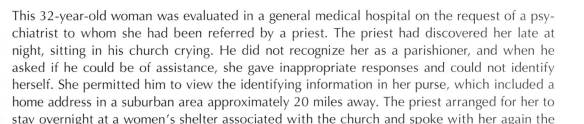

CASE 5

This 32-year-old woman was evaluated in a general medical hospital on the request of a psychiatrist to whom she had been referred by a priest. The priest had discovered her late at night, sitting in his church crying. He did not recognize her as a parishioner, and when he asked if he could be of assistance, she gave inappropriate responses and could not identify herself. She permitted him to view the identifying information in her purse, which included a home address in a suburban area approximately 20 miles away. The priest arranged for her to stay overnight at a women's shelter associated with the church and spoke with her again the next morning.

At that time, her mind seemed clear, and she readily gave her name and address. She denied drug use but admitted that she had no memory for any events of the preceding two days. She was reluctant to have anyone contact her husband but agreed to speak with a psychiatrist who consults for the shelter. During her interview with the psychiatrist, she reported that she has had several episodes for which she has no memory. She shared with the psychiatrist the thought that she may have some sort of multiple personality in which "someone else takes over my body." She agreed to a brief hospitalization, for two or three days, for the purpose of neurological and psychological evaluation. She also agreed to have her husband contacted.

As it turned out, her husband had reported her missing during the second day of her absence. He said that she had been upset because he had decided that they should visit his parents a few weeks hence, and he believed that she left "to emphasize that she didn't want to go, but when she hadn't come back by the next day I called the police."

She has been married for 10 years. The marriage occurred when she was 22 years old, eight months after she graduated from college with a degree in political science. Her husband is three years older than herself and is a certified public accountant. He is the co-owner of an accounting firm and reports a substantial income. He concedes that he and his wife have disagreed for the past six years about whether to have children. He notes that she became pregnant during their second year of marriage, but she miscarried during her third month after tripping on some stairs. He says that, after the miscarriage, his wife has persistently stated that she does not want children, and when she became pregnant again during their fourth year of marriage, she decided to have an abortion. He says that he has been encouraging her to try to become pregnant again but that she rejects this appeal. He readily acknowledged, "We've had a troubled marriage for the past three or four years."

In the second interview with the psychiatrist, the patient gave a very different story. She says that the miscarriage occurred after her husband struck her several times during an argument about money. She states that she considered leaving him at that time but did not, and she concedes that their relationship improved during the next year. She says that she was happy when she became pregnant again, but her husband forced her to have the abortion because "we weren't financially ready to have a family." She says that he now wants her to become pregnant, but she feels confused about the prospect. She says that most of their past five marital years have been tumultuous: "We don't fight about money anymore, it's other things, the house, his parents, vacations, children, almost anything. We just don't have much to be happy about."

She is the younger of two children. Her older brother, age 35, lives in a distant city, is married, and has two children. He is an electrical contractor. She has little contact with him. Her father, age 66, is a retired postmaster. Her mother, age 64, is a housewife. They live in a distant city and she has infrequent contact with them except during holiday periods. Following her graduation from college, she accepted a position as a legal aide and met her future husband at work. He was working at the law firm while finishing course work necessary for certification as a CPA. She says that she had intended to work for about two years and then apply to law school, "but we got involved. It was a whirlwind romance, and we married about five months after we met."

She continued to work for another two years. She says that she liked the work, but after her husband became certified, they bought a home and she found that she didn't have as much time as she would like to organize and maintain her new residence, "We didn't need my income anymore so I decided to quit."

She reports that she has always been fearful about becoming pregnant and attributes this to having been raped at the age of 13 by two 16-year-old friends of her brother. She did not report the rape to her parents or anyone else, but she has always been tormented by memories of the event. She says that she believes her brother was aware of the event, which occurred after a high school baseball game, but they have never spoken about it. She says that she accompanied the two boys to an area near the baseball field, "I thought we'd fool around, but they got rough and held me down, it was terrible and I was so ashamed."

She says that she avoided any sexual contact during her high school years but had intercourse in college "several times, but I never really liked it much." She says these events usually occurred after using drugs or alcohol, "I did that too much during college; everybody was trying something and I did, too. It affected my grades for awhile and that's when I quit." She states that she told her husband about her drug/alcohol involvement during college and he frequently berates her because of this. She denies any current use of drugs and says that she drinks an occasional glass of wine or a beer, but never more than one or two.

She estimates that she has had six or seven episodes of memory loss. Most have been for intervals of 6 to 12 hours, after which she finds herself in an unfamiliar location. They have included a bar, a theater, a motel, and a rest area near a lake about 50 miles from her home. In each case, her car was nearby. On one occasion, the episode apparently lasted for nearly a full day, ending when she found herself on a street corner. She took a taxi home and found that her car was there.

The most recent episode apparently lasted for two or three days. She says that it is the first time that she has ever found herself "awakening" during the night. She reluctantly admits that she has some reason to believe that she may have been drinking more than usual and may have engaged in sexual activity during some or all of these episodes, but she has no recollection for these events. When her suspicion was pursued, she notes that she has "felt like I had a hangover," at least twice, and once she was not wearing underwear.

She is unable to identify any common elements that precede her episodes of amnesia, "they just occur." She says that, usually, her life is fairly ordinary, "shopping, cooking, going out with friends from time to time, probably like most other people." She says that her relationship with her husband has been more strained during the past two or three years, "We seem to argue a lot." She says that she gets depressed "sometimes," but those episodes do not last very long. She has been thinking about seeking employment, but has not taken any action about that interest.

In her referral, the psychiatrist notes that she was impressed by the sincerity of the patient, but wonders about the possibility of malingering amnesia to conceal some planned behaviors. She asks (1) if a diagnosis of dissociative fugue reaction is appropriate, (2) if there is any evidence to account for the memory lapses, (3) if there is any evidence for a dissociative identity disorder, and (4) she requests advice concerning immediate and long-term treatment objectives plus, if possible, a review of obstacles to treatment.

CASE FORMULATION AND RELEVANT LITERATURE

The patient experienced a traumatic sexual assault at age 13, and it would appear that sexuality, pregnancy, and any suggestion of drug or alcohol involvement have been sources of ongoing conflict for her. She and her husband both report a troubled marriage, although with very different accounts about the part each has played in their difficulties. The patient estimates that she has had six or seven memory loss incidents similar to the one for which she is currently being evaluated. She wonders if "someone else takes over my body" during these episodes. The referring psychiatrist asks about the possibility of a dissociative disorder and, although the patient's presentation seems candid and straightforward, also questions whether the amnesia serves to defend against having to acknowledge planned acting out.

The current edition of the *Diagnostic and Statistical Manual of Mental Disorders* (*DSM-IV-TR*; American Psychiatric Association, 2000) presents the dissociative disorders as a spectrum of syndromes defined by ". . . a disruption in the usually integrated functions of consciousness, memory, identity, or perception" (p. 519). Within the dissociative disorder spectrum, the circumstances of this case are probably best encompassed under the Dissociative Fugue category, in which there is sudden and unplanned travel away from one's home with inability to recall some aspects of one's past and confusion about identity. Although the patient wonders about the possibility of "someone else" taking over her body, her presentation does not seem consistent with Dissociative Identity Disorder (formerly Multiple Personality Disorder). This more pathological dissociative syndrome involves the presence of two or more distinct and well-defined personalities who recurrently control the person's behavior. The *DSM-IV-TR* (p. 525) cautions that it is important to evaluate for malingering and secondary gain with individuals who report dissociative experiences.

There is a substantial literature concerning the dynamics of dissociation and how they manifest on the Rorschach. A survey of these studies can provide perspective for the psychologist in reviewing this patient's protocol and providing diagnostic and treatment planning consultation.

Assessment of Dissociation

Several Rorschach researchers have theorized about the psychodynamics of dissociation. Wagner (1978) hypothesized that, in contrast to the less complex psychology of patients with conversion syndromes, those who dissociate would have Rorschachs characterized by greater elaboration, introspection, and conflict. Armstrong and Loewenstein (1990) evaluated 14 inpatients diagnosed with dissociative disorder, and their results support Wagner's "greater complexity" hypothesis. Nine of their 14 participants were introversive, four were ambitents, and only one was extratensive. The authors suggest that these patients displayed a unique Rorschach configuration ". . . markedly different from those of schizophrenics and borderlines," and note, ". . . they show psychological complexity, human relatedness, and highly developed self-observing capacity" (p. 452). They further suggest, ". . . the surface instability seen in dissociative disorder patients frequently belies a much more developed and stable personality organization . . ." (p. 453). Armstrong (1991) noted that these patients' predominantly ideational and obsessional coping style can be distinguished from the more emotional response patterns seen in post-traumatic stress disorder.

Consistent with the hypothesis of complexity and conflict as the defining characteristics of dissociative dynamics, Wagner and his colleagues (Wagner, Allison, & Wagner, 1983; Wagner & Heise, 1974; Wagner, Wagner, & Torem, 1986) proposed five Rorschach features indicative of Dissociative Identity Disorder: (1) at least six movement ($M+FM+m$) determinants; (2) at least two qualitatively opposite M percepts ("two people planning a party" versus "two people arguing"); (3) at least one movement response involving oppression ("that shark is about to attack those smaller fish"); (4) at least three chromatic color determinants with $CF+C > FC;$ and (5) at least one positive ("red butterfly") and one negative ("blood") chromatic color percept.

Other researchers have also proposed constellations of Rorschach variables suggestive of dissociative disorder. Labott and her colleagues (Labott, Leavitt, Braun, & Sachs, 1992; Leavitt & Labott, 1997) hypothesized that dissociation would manifest in two distinct types of percepts. The first (Dissociation percepts) involve the following criteria: (1) seeing the world through some sort of obscuring element that renders objects unclear or blurry ("like looking through something cloudy toward a mountain"); (2) reporting very exaggerated distance ("the people look like they're a long way off"); or (3) reporting a sense of disorientation in which the percepts are unstable or changing rapidly ("a tornado blowing everything apart"). The second type of percept the authors propose (Splitting percepts) would manifest in split or pulled-apart images ("looks like a person just fragmenting into pieces"). These two types of percepts have become known as the Labott signs.

Barach (1986) theorized that the presence of conflicting personality components would result in Hiding responses (one blot element is hidden behind another; one element is unaware of another element; masks) or in Denial responses (an element reported during the response phase is denied during the inquiry; the person has difficulty finding an element mentioned during the response phase; the person confabulates to explain an element reported during the response phase).

Labott and her colleagues evaluated these proposed constellations in a series of studies. Labott et al. (1992) tested 16 female inpatients diagnosed with Multiple Personality Disorder and 16 female psychiatric controls. They found that the dissociative patients were significantly higher on Wagner's Total Movement and Oppression variables and on Labott's Dissociation and Splitting responses. The Wagner signs correctly classified 45% of the patients, the Barach Hiding plus Denial responses classified 66% of the patients correctly, and the Labott Dissociation plus Splitting signs correctly classified 94% of the patients.

Leavitt and Labott (1997) next evaluated the Rorschach Dissociation percept against a self-report measure, the Dissociative Experience Scale (DES; Bernstein & Putnam, 1986). The DES is a factorially complex 28-item questionnaire whose dimensions include amnesia, derealization/depersonalization, and the capacity for fantasy-based absorption (Carlson et al., 1993). The authors compared 89 patients referred for evaluation of dissociation with 36 patients who had been referred for nondissociative reasons such as depression or anxiety. The results indicated a highly significant relationship between DES scores and Rorschach Dissociation percepts. The mean DES for individuals with no Dissociation percepts was 10.11. For individuals with one Dissociation percept, it increased to 25.48; and for individuals with two Dissociation percepts, the mean DES score was 35.86. A similar pattern was observed for DES subscales measuring the factors of Amnesia, Derealization/Depersonalization, and Absorption. Carlson et al. (1993), on the basis of a large multisite sample, have suggested that a cutscore of 30 discriminates patients with dissociative disorder from both nondissociative psychiatric patients and nonpatients.

Leavitt and Labott (1997) concluded that Rorschach Dissociation percepts can be understood as test analogues of dissociation, ". . . visual representations of mental processes exposed to view by Rorschach stimuli that provide important information about dissociative symptomatology" (pp. 247–248). The authors go on to suggest that these Rorschach percepts ". . . distinguish well between low and high dissociative patients and as such provide a basis for evaluating dissociative processes void of the usual biases of self-report" (p. 248). They suggest that these percepts can distinguish three categories of dissociative status: minimal (no Dissociation percepts), intermediate (one Dissociation percept), and high (two or more Dissociation percepts).

In 1998, Leavitt and Labott cross-validated their findings, comparing 27 women admitted to an inpatient dissociative disorders unit with 72 inpatient psychiatric controls. The Labott signs (Dissociation plus Splitting percepts) demonstrated sensitivity of 78%, specificity of 97%, and overall correct classification of 92%. The Barach Hiding plus Denial signs obtained a sensitivity rate of 63%, specificity of 89%, and overall correct classification of 82%. The Wagner signs were able to assign participants to the dissociative or control groups with sensitivity of 67%, specificity of 90%, and overall correct classification of 84%.

Scroppo, Drob, Weinberger, and Eagle (1998) compared 21 adult female psychiatric patients with Dissociative Identity Disorder with 21 female nondissociative psychiatric patients. The dissociative group had significantly more movement ($M+FM+m$) responses, incongruous and fabulized combinations, and blood, anatomy, morbid, and nonwhole human ($Hd+(Hd)$) content. They also exhibited significantly more Labott Dissociation percepts and a significantly lower $X+\%$. The authors summarized their findings by suggesting that the two groups could be differentiated by Rorschach complexity, noting that the dissociative patients exhibited ". . . a comparatively greater use of imaginative and projective operations, inasmuch as they tended to mentally endow the inkblot with features (movement, dimensionality, morbidity) that notably exceeded its manifest characteristics . . ." (pp. 280–281).

Scroppo et al. (1998) also found that the Dissociative Identity Disorder group reported significantly higher levels of childhood sexual and physical abuse than did the controls. This finding is consistent with results reported by Sandberg and Lynn (1992). These researchers compared 33 female college students who scored in the upper 15% on the DES with 33 female students who were below the DES mean. The high-DES students reported more psychological, physical, and sexual maltreatment than did the controls.

As noted, it is important to evaluate for issues of secondary gain and malingering when patients describe dissociative experiences. Many of the self-report and structured interview techniques include items with high face validity, and as Scroppo et al. (1998) noted, their lack of "opacity" makes them vulnerable to impression management.

Labott and Wallach (2002) investigated whether dissociative identity disorder could be successfully malingered on the Dissociative Experiences Scale (DES) and the Rorschach. They assigned 50 undergraduate women either to a malingering or to a control group. Those in the malingering group were given a definition of Dissociative Identity Disorder and a description of common dissociative features and were asked to take both the DES and the Rorschach as if they were attempting to convince the examiner that they suffered from the disorder. The students in the control group were instructed to answer as honestly as possible. The malingering group had a significantly higher mean DES score than did the controls (51.3 versus 14.4), placing them well within the pathological range. There were no differences between the two groups on Rorschach variables for either the Wagner, Barach, or Labott constellations, leading the researchers to conclude that their malingering group participants were ". . . unable to produce responses to the Rorschach Test that were indicative of Dissociative Identity Disorder" (pp. 536–537).

Labott and Wallach (2002) note that asking college students to simulate dissociation is probably different from situations in which individuals in clinical or forensic settings attempt to malinger. Also, there are no studies in the current literature evaluating whether coached malingerers can produce Rorschachs containing some of the variables that have been associated with dissociative psychopathology.

In summary, the Rorschachs of individuals with dissociative disorders appear to be characterized by cognitive complexity and extensive content elaboration. The constellation of variables Wagner and his colleagues have proposed are Rorschach analogues of complexity and conflict, whereas those proposed by Barach and by Labott and her colleagues are hypothesized to reflect dissociative phenomena. The literature suggests that these variables add incremental validity beyond interview and self-report approaches in the assessment of dissociation.

Card	Response	Inquiry
I	1. Cld b a bf	**E:** Rpts Ss resp **S:** Th W thg, it has wgs, body, & the littl antennae at the top
	2. A carving of 2 gargoyle creatures holdg onto ea side of a huge beetle	**E:** Rpts Ss resp **S:** It's the W thg too, the gargoyles r on e side, c the wgs r pronounced & the legs & the cntr ll a beetle, it ll thy r holdg onto it **E:** U said it's a carving? **S:** It wld hav to be, none of them r real so I thot of some art work lik a statue on a church or bldg
	>3. An elephant w his ears up stndg on the edge of a pond, lookg in & seeg his reflection	**E:** Rpts Ss resp **S:** This is the waterline (midln), these r shrubs, & ths is the elephant (D2), c the big ear (Dd34) & its all reflected dwn here
	v 4. Sthg dead, lik a bat, a black bat, bats r black lik ths but thy don't hav holes	**E:** Rpts Ss resp **S:** The tail, wgs, but it has holes in it, thts why I thot it was dead, I supp it cb asleep, thy sleep hangg dwn, but not the holes, so I thk it wb dead
II	5. 2 bears finger paintg on the wall	**E:** Rpts Ss resp **S:** Bears r on each side, c the heads & their bodies, there's a paw or hand print up above thm & thy spilled paint on the floor, the red dwn here is the paint
	6. It cb lik s.k. of black magic ritual too, w 2 peopl in frt of ths white altar making a bld offering	**E:** Rpts Ss resp **S:** Two peopl wearg black cloaks, & red hats, their hands r togthr, thyr kneelg in frnt of ths white altar & the bld's dwn here **E:** U said it is a ritual? **S:** Tht white altar in the cntr, & the bld, it has to b one, lik black magic
III	7. 2 natives beatg a drum w dead monkeys hangg upside dwn in the bkgrnd	**E:** Rpts Ss resp **S:** Thy'r naturalists, wm naturalists, u can c their breasts, here r their heads, necks, arms & legs & thes ll dead monkeys here, hangg upside dwn, c the long tail & here is the littl head **E:** U said thyr naturalists? **S:** Sur, thyr naked, lik nudists, thy call thmselvs naturalists
	8. A set of lungs in the middl	**E:** Rpts Ss resp **S:** Thy hav 2 spheres connected in the middl & thy r red lik lungs
IV	9. A very large anteater lying on its back	**E:** Rpts Ss resp **S:** U can c the nose & arm, big feet, tail **E:** U said lying on its back? **S:** Its on his back bc u can c his belly not c his face, it's like ur standg hi above lookg dwn
	10. Cb a tree if u r lookg up through the leaves	**E:** Rpts Ss resp **S:** If the ground was glass & u were undr tht glass lookg up, it wld b lik ths lookg up, the trunk (points) & out here is the branches & leaves
	v11. Ths way it ll an IUD, I thk	**E:** Rpts Ss resp **S:** I nevr used one but I've seen them, thy hav ths littl head & jagged edges, it has tht general shape
	12. Cb a pelt of an A tht has been skinned	**E:** Rpts Ss resp **S:** Lik the texture, the colors, lik fur, & it ll a pelt lik u c in the movies, in thos films about trappers

(continued)

Card	Response	Inquiry
V 13.	A bf	**E:** Rpts Ss resp **S:** Ths is the body & here r the wgs
14.	2 A's crashg their heads tog	**E:** Rpts Ss resp **S:** Thy ll rams or deer, the back feet, frnt feet, & thyr comg tog here, its a side view of thm
VI 15.	Lik the female organ, not the top tho	**E:** Rpts Ss resp **S:** The lips spread out here, open lik pulled apart, u can c the gradation of colors going out from the seam or the slit, a vagina
v16.	An A hide lik hung on a wall	**E:** Rpts Ss resp **S:** The legs, the tail dwn here, it looks all furry the way the diff colorg in there
VII 17.	Smthg broken	**E:** Rpts Ss resp **S:** Pieces r missg, it was smthg but its broken, mayb a vase or smthg but u can't tell, just pieces of smthg, just layg ther
v18.	Lik a crab w nothg in the middl	**E:** Rpts Ss resp **S:** Lik the back of a crab but nothg in the middl, lik part of the shell of a crab w the middl part gone, decayed
v19.	Oh, or mayb 2 native blk wm dancg back to back w their hair touchg	**E:** Rpts Ss resp **S:** U can c their legs, dress, their heads r touchg, lik thyr doing som exotic dance
VIII 20.	A scarab	**E:** Rpts Ss resp **S:** A very colorful beetle lik pin, it's lik a piece of jewelry
>21.	A pink cat w 1 foot on a rock & 1 foot on a stump seeg his reflect in the water	**E:** Rpts Ss resp **S:** A pink cat, c the eye & nose, the legs, & ths wb a foot & the wtr is the blue, ths is the rock & he's reflectd dwn here
22.	Insides, lik in the stomach a pict lik fr a med book	**E:** Rpts Ss resp **S:** Guts, it ll a chart, the colored picts lik in thos Time-Life books to show insides, the pink is the stomach & the rest is lik guts & fluid, its like the bile & stuff
IX >23.	A fat elf sittg by a pink rock smokg a pipe by the side of the water	**E:** Rpts Ss resp **S:** A hunched up elf w a pipe, smoke comg out of it, he's by the water & its all reflectd, c the pipe here (points) & all the orange prt cb the smoke
v24.	Sk of bomb blast	**E:** Rpts Ss resp **S:** Its lik force comg from the blast, from below a mushroom cloud, the orange fire & the green smoke r pushg up the mushroom cld
X 25.	A mardi gras mask, very colorful	**E:** Rpts Ss resp **S:** All of it is a wild mask, a wild colorful mask w ths pointd top & ths grn droopy mustache effect & a lot of colorful thgs hangg off each sid, lik u'd c at mardi gras
26.	A lot of colorful undersea creaturs all moving around	**E:** Rpts Ss resp **S:** The blu & the grey & the brown all ll crabs, the green ll ss of eel, th pink is lik coral, som coral is pink lik ths, I'v seen it, thyr all moving arnd the coral

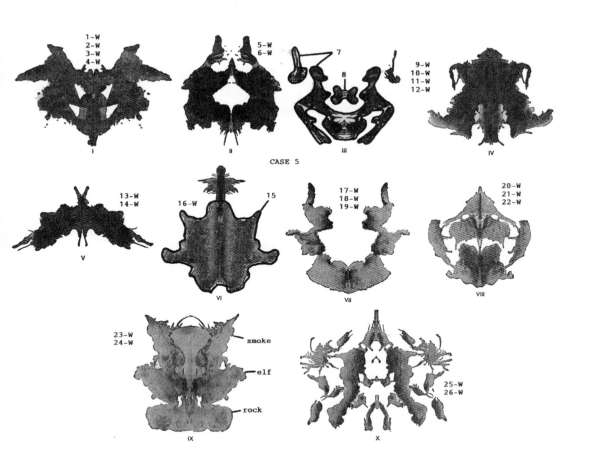

CASE 5

Case 5. Sequence of Scores.

Card	No.	Loc.	No.	Determinant(s)	(2)	Content(s)	Pop	Z	Special Scores
I	1	Wo		Fo		A	P	1.0	
	2	W+	1	FMpo	2	Art,(A)		4.0	
	3	W+	1	FMp.Fro		A,Na		4.0	
	4	WSo	1	FC'o		A	P	3.5	MOR
II	5	W+	1	Ma.CFo	2	A,Art	P	4.5	FAB,PHR
	6	WS+	1	Mp.FD.FC'.CFo	2	H,Bl,Cg,Id		4.5	AB,ALOG,COP,PHR
III	7	D+	1	Ma.mp.FD+	2	H,Id,A,Sx	P	4.0	COP,DV,MOR,GHR
	8	Do	3	FCo		An			
IV	9	Wo	1	FMp.FDu		A		2.0	INC
	10	Wo	1	FDo		Bt		2.0	
	11	Wo	1	F−		Sc,Sx		2.0	PER
	12	Wv	1	TFo		Ad			PER
V	13	Wo	1	Fo		A	P	1.0	
	14	W+	1	FMao	2	A		2.5	AG,PHR
VI	15	Do	1	FVu		Hd,Sx			PHR
	16	Wo	1	mp.FTo		Ad	P	2.5	
VII	17	Wv	1	F−		Hh			MOR
	18	WSo	1	Fu		Ad		4.0	MOR
	19	W+	1	FC'.Mao	2	H,Cg		2.5	COP,GHR
VIII	20	Wo	1	CFu		Art,(A)		4.5	
	21	W+	1	FMp.Fr.CF+		A,Na	P	4.5	INC
	22	Wo	1	CF−		Art,An		4.5	
IX	23	W+	1	Mp.FC.Fr.mpu		(H),Fi,Na		5.5	INC,PHR
	24	Wo	1	ma.CFo		Ex,Fi		5.5	
X	25	WSo	1	CF.mp−		(Hd),Art		5.5	PHR
	26	W+	1	CF.FMao	2	A,Bt	P	5.5	PER

Case 5. Structural Summary.

Location Features	Determinants Blends	Single	Contents	S-Constellation
				YES . .FV+VF+V+FD>2
		H = 3		YES . .Col-Shd Bl>0
Zf = 22	FM.Fr	M = 0	(H) = 1	YES . .Ego<.31,>.44
ZSum = 79.5	M.CF	FM = 2	Hd = 1	YES . .MOR > 3
ZEst = 73.5	M.FD.FC′.CF	m = 0	(Hd) = 1	YES . .Zd > +- 3.5
	M.m.FD	FC = 1	Hx = 0	YES . .es > EA
W = 23	FM.FD	CF = 2	A = 10	YES . .CF+C > FC
D = 3	m.FT	C = 0	(A) = 2	YES . .X+% < .70
W+D = 26	FC′.M	Cn = 0	Ad = 3	YES . .S > 3
Dd = 0	FM.Fr.CF	FC′ = 1	(Ad) = 0	NO . . .P < 3 or > 8
S = 4	M.FC.Fr.m	C′F = 0	An = 2	NO . . .Pure H < 2
	m.CF	C′ = 0	Art = 5	NO . . .R < 17
	CF.m	FT = 0	Ay = 0	9 . . . .TOTAL
DQ	CF.FM	TF = 1	Bl = 1	**Special Scores**
		T = 0	Bt = 2		Lv1	Lv2
+ = 10		FV = 1	Cg = 2	DV = 1x1 0x2
o = 14		VF = 0	Cl = 0	INC = 3x2 0x4
v/+ = 0		V = 0	Ex = 1	DR = 0x3 0x6
v = 2		FY = 0	Fd = 0	FAB = 1x4 0x7
		YF = 0	Fi = 2	ALOG = 1x5
		Y = 0	Ge = 0	CON = 0x7
Form Quality		Fr = 0	Hh = 1	Raw Sum6 = 6
		rF = 0	Ls = 0	Wgtd Sum6 = 16
	FQx	MQual	W+D	FD = 1	Na = 3
+ = 2	= 1	= 2	F = 5	Sc = 1	AB = 1 GHR = 2
o = 15	= 3	= 15		Sx = 3	AG = 1 PHR = 6
u = 5	= 1	= 5		Xy = 0	COP = 3 MOR = 4
− = 4	= 0	= 4	(2) = 7	Id = 2	CP = 0 PER = 3
none = 0	= 0	= 0			PSV = 0

Ratios, Percentages, and Derivations

R = 26	L = 0.24		FC:CF+C = 2: 8	COP = 3 AG = 1
			Pure C = 0	GHR:PHR = 2:6
EB = 5:9.0	EA = 14.0	EBPer = 1.8	SumC′:WSumC = 3:9.0	a:p = 6:10
eb = 11:6	es = 17	D = −1	Afr = 0.37	Food = 0
	Adj es = 13	Adj D = 0	S = 4	SumT = 2
			Blends:R = 12:26	Hum Cont = 6
FM = 6	C′ = 3	T = 2	CP = 0	Pure H = 3
m = 5	V = 1	Y = 0		PER = 3
				Iso Indx = 0.31

a:p	= 6:10	Sum6 = 6	XA% = 0.85	Zf = 22.0	3r+(2)/R	= 0.62
Ma:Mp	= 3: 2	Lv2 = 0	WDA% = 0.85	W:D:Dd = 23:3: 0	Fr+rF	= 3
2AB+Art+Ay	= 7	WSum6 = 16	X−% = 0.15	W:M = 23:5	SumV	= 1
MOR	= 4	M− = 0	S− = 1	Zd = +6.0	FD	= 4
		Mnone = 0	P = 8	PSV = 0	An+Xy	= 2
			X+% = 0.65	DQ+ = 10	MOR	= 4
			Xu% = 0.19	DQv = 2	H:(H)Hd(Hd)	= 3:3

PTI = 0	DEPI = 6*	CDI = 3	S-CON = 9*	HVI = No	OBS = No

S-CON AND KEY VARIABLE

The S-CON value of nine is positive and cause for concern. It signals the presence of many features that are found among persons who effect their own death, and the report on this case should emphasize this finding. She offers no hint of a preoccupation with self-destruction, and the high S-CON value could represent a false positive finding created by the presence of considerable turmoil. However, it would be foolish to make such an assumption without exploring the issue carefully. Thus, the report should urge that the possibility of a preoccupation with death be thoroughly explored. In addition, the referring therapist should be encouraged to take all practical measures to create a strongly supportive relationship with her and consider increasing the frequency of visits until it is clear that the possibility of a self-destructive preoccupation does not exist or has been contended with effectively.

The first positive Key variable is the DEPI, which has a value of six. This indicates that the interpretive routine should begin with a study of the data concerning affect and then move on to the data regarding controls. Subsequently, the clusters concerning self and interpersonal perception should be reviewed, followed by an interpretation of the clusters comprising the cognitive triad, processing, mediation, and ideation.

AFFECT

Case 5.   Affect-Related Data for a 32-Year-Old Female.

							Blends	
EB	= 5:9.0			EBPer	= 1.8			
eb	= 11:6	L	= 0.24	FC:CF+C	= 2:8		M.FD.FC'.CF	= 1
DEPI	= 6	CDI	= 3	Pure C	= 0		M.FC.Fr.m	= 1
							M.m.FD	= 1
SumC' = 3	SumT = 2			SumC':WSumC	= 3:9.0		M.CF	= 1
SumV = 1	SumY = 0			Afr	= 0.37		FC'.M	= 1
							FM.Fr.CF	= 1
Intellect	= 7	CP	= 0	S = 4 (S to I,II,III	= 2)		FM.Fr	= 1
Blends:R	= 12:26			Col-Shad Bl	= 1		FM.FD	= 1
m + y Bl	= 3			Shading Bl	= 0		CF.FM	= 1
							CF.m	= 1
							m.CF	= 1
							m.FT	= 1

The DEPI value of six suggests a significant and potentially disabling affective problem. It is important to note that she does not provide any information that might confirm such a problem. There is no evidence of indirect symptoms such as sleep problems, weight loss, poor appetite, lethargy, or difficulties with concentration. She does not complain about anxiety, unusual tension, or moodiness and, while conceding that she is depressed occasionally, she says that the episodes do not last very long. She does admit to confusion about the pregnancy issue and notes that she and her husband argue frequently, but both fall short of confirming a significant affective problem. Thus, the possibility that the DEPI value is misleading should be considered carefully as the interpretation unfolds.

The *EB* (5:9.0) signifies that, usually, she tends to merge her feelings with her thinking during problem-solving or decision-making activities. She uses and is strongly influenced by her feelings, and she is disposed to test out postulates and assumptions in a trial-and-error manner to gain feedback concerning her decisions. People like this tend to display feelings openly and sometimes are less concerned about modulating those displays. On the other hand, the value for *EBPer* (1.8) offers no evidence to suggest that she is inflexible in her coping or decision-making habits.

The right side *eb* value of six is considerably less than the left side value, but it contains some unusual findings. The first is the presence of vista, suggesting that she experiences some irritating feelings because of a tendency to ruminate about perceived negative characteristics or, in this instance, possibly because of a sense of guilt or remorse concerning her recent behavior. The second is the presence of two texture answers, which probably signify feelings of loneliness or emotional neediness. The third is the value for *SumC'* (3), which implies negative emotions are being created by a tendency to inhibit the release of some feelings by internalizing or suppressing them. These findings are not inconsistent with her history, but they suggest that she may experience more painful feelings than she readily concedes. On the other hand, the data for the *SumC' : WSumC* ratio (3:9.0) offer no evidence to suggest that she is overly constraining or suppressing her emotions.

The value for the *Afr* (.37) is of considerable interest because it implies a marked tendency to avoid emotional stimuli. It signifies that she usually is very uncomfortable about dealing with emotion and may be prone to social constraint or isolation. This is an incongruous finding because she is an intuitive person who tends to rely considerably on her feelings when making decisions. It suggests that, for some reason, her typical way of coping or decision making may not be working very well for her. There can be several possible reasons for this, but it would be premature to speculate about them before considering additional findings.

In a related context, the Intellectualization Index value (7) is substantial and seems consistent with the low *Afr*. It suggests that she has a marked tendency to deal with emotions or emotional situations on an ideational rather than an affective level. This tactic tends to reduce the impact or importance of emotions by denying or distorting their meaning. Her excessive use of intellectualization also signifies that she is not very comfortable when dealing with feelings.

The data for the *FC : CF+C* (2:8) ratio may shed some light about findings from the *Afr* and the Intellectualization Index. It indicates that she modulates her emotional displays much less than do most people. Adults who do this usually call attention to themselves because of the intensity with which they express their emotions. This is not necessarily a liability if others accept her less restrained displays of affect, but if that is not the case, the intensity of her emotions could easily alienate people. Her tendency to avoid emotions or emotional situations or neutralize their impact may be the result of some recognition of this potential.

Interestingly, she also has four space responses, suggesting the likelihood of considerable anger or, at least, a marked sense of alienation that has produced a negative set toward her environment. This could relate to her marital conflict but might also have broader implications concerning her interpersonal world.

Twelve of her 26 responses include blends, indicating much more psychological complexity than is expected. Three of her 12 blend answers seem situationally related, having been created by the presence of *m*. However, even if these situationally related blends are disregarded, the remaining nine would still represent more complexity than expected for an extratensive person. In addition, four of the nine have more than two determinants, and two of those include four determinants. Usually, an array such as this indicates an inordinate level of complexity that is almost always related to some sort of emotional turmoil. The blends include one color shading blend, which is not uncommon for extratensive people, but it suggests that she experiences episodes of uncertainty about her feelings from time to time.

The composite of data concerning her affect strongly suggests that she probably experiences much more emotional turmoil than she seems ready to admit. She is a lonely person who likely suffers from feelings of guilt or remorse. In addition, she tends to rely on her feelings when making decisions, but she does not seem to modulate her emotions very well much of the time. Interestingly, she also appears to avoid or neutralize emotions whenever possible. This tendency is incongruous with her natural coping style and suggests that the style may not be very effective. This probably contributes to the considerable complexity that marks her psychology and is likely to create more chaos than adaptiveness.

CONTROLS

Case 5.   Control-Related Variables for a 32-Year-Old Female.

EB = 5:9.0	EA = 14.0		D = −1	CDI = 3
eb = 11:6	es = 17	Adj es = 13	AdjD = 0	L = 0.24
FM = 6 m = 5	SumC′ = 3	SumT = 2	SumV = 1	SumY = 0

The Adj D Score (0) implies that, ordinarily, her capacity for control and tolerance for stress is similar to that of most others. The *EA* value (14.0), plus the fact that the *EB* (5:9.0) has substantial values on each side of the ratio, suggests that there is no reason to question the reliability or validity of the Adj D Score. However, the Adj *es* (13) is higher than usually expected. This intimates that the Adj D of zero may actually underestimate her typical control capabilities. This issue must be explored further, and because there is a difference between the D Score and the Adj D Score indicating the presence of situationally related stress, it should be done in that context.

SITUATIONAL STRESS

Case 5.   Situational Stress Data for a 32-Year-Old Female.

EB	= 5:9.0	EA = 14.0		D = −1	**Blends**	
eb	= 11:6	es = 17	Adj es = 13	AdjD = 0	M.FD.FC′.CF= 1	
					M.FC.Fr.m = 1	
FM	= 6 *m* = 5	C′ = 3 T = 2	V = 1 Y = 0		M.m.FD = 1	
			(3r+(2)/R) = .62		M.CF = 1	
					FC′.M = 1	
Pure C = 0 M− = 0		MQnone = 0		Blends = 12	FM.Fr.CF = 1	
					FM.Fr = 1	
					FM.FD = 1	
					CF.FM = 1	
					CF.m = 1	
					m.CF = 1	
					m.FT = 1	

As noted, the D Score (−1) is less than the Adj D Score (0), signifying the presence of some situationally related stress. This is not surprising in light of her recent experience, plus the fact that she is now entering treatment. The difference between the two scores is one point, implying that the impact of the stress is mild to moderate. However, that may be an underestimate when the variables related to the *es* and Adj *es* are considered.

The *es* (17) is elevated primarily because of the five *m* determinants in the record. There are no responses containing diffuse shading determinants. Therefore, it is reasonable to assume that the stress is impacting mainly on her ideational activities. In such a state, peripheral or subconscious thoughts, probably related to a sense of helplessness created by the stress, tend to intrude into her conscious stream of ideation. These intrusions can easily interfere with attention or concentration.

Her record also contains two texture responses and one vista answer that require some review to determine if an additional adjustment to the Adj *es* might be appropriate. There is no indication in the history of recent emotional loss. Therefore, it is not appropriate to readjust the Adj *es* on the basis of the texture data. On the other hand, her vista answer may be related to a sense of guilt or remorse about her behaviors. As such, it is probably contributing to the present stress experience. If it is also subtracted out of the *es,* the resulting Adj *es* becomes 12, only one point higher than the criterion for the Adj D Score to be +1.

This review tends to strengthen the postulate that her capacity for control is like that of most others, and may be even sturdier. It also provides some clarity from which to understand the potential consequences implied by her D Score (−1), which signifies an overload state. She is experiencing more internal demands than she can contend with easily or effectively. The current stresses have added considerably to her complexity, as noted by the fact that 3 of her 12 blends (*CF.m, m.CF,* and *m.FT*) are situationally related. In effect, the current stress impact is probably more moderate than mild and creates a clear vulnerability. She can probably function effectively in familiar settings, but the potential exists for her to become disorganized easily in unfamiliar or unusually complex situations. If that occurs, the likelihood of impulsive thinking or behavior is substantial. Earlier, it was recommended that strong supports be provided early in treatment to contend with a possible suicide preoccupation. The findings here obviously support that recommendation and suggest that, to the extent possible, the initial focus of treatment should be on her current experience of stresses.

SELF-PERCEPTION

Case 5. Self-Perception Related Data for a 32-Year-Old Female.

R	= 26	OBS	= No	HVI = No	**Human Content, An & Xy Responses**
				II	6. WS+ Mp.FD.FC.CF'o 2 H,Bl,Cg,Id 4.5 AB,ALOG,COP,PHR
Fr+rF	= 3	3r+(2)/R	= 0.62	III	7. D+ Mp.mp.FD+ 2 H,Id,A,Sx P 4.0 COP,DV,MOR,GHR
				III	8. Do FCo An
FD	= 4	SumV	= 1	VI	15. Do FVu Hd,Sx PHR
				VII	19. W+ FC'.Mao 2 H,Cg 2.5 COP,GHR
An+Xy	= 2	MOR	= 4	VIII	22. Wo CF− Art,An 4.5
				IX	23. W+ Mp.FC.Fr.mpu (H),Fi,Na 5.5 INC,PHR
H:(H)+Hd+(Hd) = 3:3				X	25. WSo CF.mp− (Hd),Art 5.5 PHR
[EB = 5:9.0]					

The presence of three reflection answers indicates that she has an exaggerated sense of self-worth and self-involvement that strongly affects the way she perceives and interacts with the world. This feature influences her decisions and behaviors because it creates a need for frequent reaffirmation of her worth. When this is not forthcoming, she is likely to become negative, frustrated, and prone to rely on defenses to protect her integrity. Typically, rationalization, externalization, and denial make up the core of these defensive operations.

The high Egocentricity Index (0.62) tends to reaffirm the notion that she is very involved with herself. In fact, when it is considered in light of the three reflection answers, it seems reasonable to postulate that narcissistic features are strongly embedded in her basic psychology. If her reports about episodes of amnesia are valid, it seems likely that these narcissistic features will have played a major role in provoking them.

Interestingly, her record also contains four *FD* responses plus a vista answer. It has been postulated earlier that the vista answer may relate to a sense of guilt or remorse about her recent behaviors. That may or may not be true, but the four *FD* answers cannot be attributed to situational factors. They indicate an uncommon concern for her self-image and imply that a ruminative kind of self-inspection is occurring. Whether the vista answer is situationally provoked or represents a more persistent feature, it suggests a self-denigrating preoccupation that produces considerable discomfort. This finding is unusual for a narcissistic person and seems to indicate that she is involved in a serious conflict about herself and her self-image.

The presence of two *An* responses raises the possibility that some body concern may be present, but there is no direct evidence to support that notion. It could relate to her preoccupation about pregnancy, but that is speculative. She also has four MOR answers in her record, implying that her self-image includes some significant negative attributions. This finding also signals that her thinking often includes a pessimistic view of herself and her world. This is unusual for a person who has marked narcissistic features and may depict a conflict concerning self-image and self-value. Alternatively, it could represent an effort to exaggerate impressions of distress or helplessness.

Her six human contents include three that are Pure *H,* suggesting that her self-image has evolved mainly from social experiences. However, the codings for the six human content answers are generally more negative than positive. Three of the six, including two of the Pure *H* answers have critical special scores (ALOG, *DV,* and INCOM). A fourth has a vista determinant, and a fifth has a minus form quality. Two of the six include sex content, and three of the six have at least three determinants. Overall, this composite of findings conveys the notion that her conceptions about herself tend to be complex and are likely to be somewhat confused. A search through the projected material in her answers should provide some clarification about this.

There are four minus answers in her protocol. The first (Card VI, response 11) is "an IUD. . . . I've never used one but I've seen them," seems to convey her stated preoccupation about sexuality and pregnancy. The second (Card VII, response 17) is "Something broken . . . pieces are missing, it was something but it's broken . . . just laying there." It strongly implies an experience of serious damage and intimates a sense of futility. The third minus (Card VIII, response 22) is "Insides, like in the stomach, a picture . . . like guts and fluid, it's like the bile and stuff." Anatomy responses to Card VIII are not unique, but this one stands out because of the unusual elaborations about guts, fluid, and bile, which seem to connote a marked intensity that is toned down by making it a picture from a medical book. The last minus (Card X, response 25) is a "Mardi Gras mask . . . a wild colorful mask . . . a lot of colorful things hanging off." Masks conceal and present a facade that often misrepresents whatever is beneath them. On a speculative level, these last two responses appear to relate to earlier findings about the way in which she displays her feelings, that is, intense but often intellectualized.

Her four MOR responses are much more homogeneous. The first (Card I, response 4) is a dead bat. The second (Card III, response 7) includes dead monkeys. The third (Card VII, response 17) is something broken with pieces missing, and the fourth (Card VII, response 18) is a crab with nothing in the middle, decayed. Collectively, they convey the ominous implication of a seriously damaged self-image, and suggest a marked sense of futility. Although the antecedents of this negative self-perception are not crystal clear, the rape, abortion experience, and the seemingly failed marriage offer grist for speculation.

The five *M* responses are less homogeneous, but they have some common elements. The first (Card II, response 5) is "bears finger painting . . . they spilled paint on the floor." It is a nonhuman, anthropomorphic response in which an accident (spilling paint) has happened. The second (Card II, response 6) is a "black magic ritual, with two people in front of this white altar making a blood offering." It reflects a sinister act, and it is difficult to avoid speculating about whether this may relate to her abortion experience. The third (Card III, response 7) is one of her MOR responses, "Two natives beating a drum with dead monkeys hanging upside down in the background." She defines them as "naturalists" [naturists] because they are nude. It is somewhat similar to the preceding response as it also has a ritualistic quality. Although humans are involved, she takes some distance from them by identifying them as natives. She does the same in her fourth *M* answer (Card VII, response 19), "maybe two native black women dancing back to back . . . doing some exotic dance." Her final *M* (Card IX, response 23) is a mythical human, "A fat elf, sitting by a pink rock smoking a pipe." It is a fantasy response and one of her reflection answers.

As a collective, none of these five answers convey a very positive sense of self. Two are nonhuman, two are natives, and the fifth involves people in a malevolent act. Likewise, neither of the two remaining human content answers conveys very positive features. The first (Card VI, response 15) is her vista answer, "the female organ . . . open like pulled apart." The second (Card X, response 25) is the previously discussed Mardi Gras mask.

Eleven of her 26 responses contain *FM* or *m* determinants. The first *FM* (Card I, response 2) is, "A carving of two gargoyle creatures holding onto each side of a huge beetle." It has no obvious implication; however, gargoyles usually are thought of as ugly or grotesque figures. It is followed (Card I, response 3) by, "An elephant with his ears up, standing on the edge of a pond, looking in and seeing his reflection." It is a more positive answer. The third *FM* (Card IV, response 9) is, "A very large anteater lying on its back . . . you can see his belly not his face, it's like you are standing high above looking down." It conveys a sense of vulnerability. The fourth (Card V, response 14) is, "Two animals crashing their heads together," represents conflict and aggressiveness. The fifth (Card VIII, response 21) is another reflection, "A pink cat with one foot on a rock and one foot on a stump seeing his reflection in the water." Although seemingly positive, it has no obvious meaning. The last *FM* (Card X, response 26), "A lot of colorful undersea creatures all moving around," also seems to be positive, but again with no obvious meaning.

The contents and verbiage in the five responses containing *m* determinants are also heterogeneous. The first (Card III, response 7) refers to dead monkeys hanging upside down. The second (Card VI, response 16) involves an animal hide hung on a wall. The third (Card IX, response 23) refers to smoke coming out of the pipe of the elf. The fourth (Card IX, response 24) is the only active *m*, a "bomb blast . . . force coming from the blast . . . pushing up the mushroom cloud." The last *m* (Card X, response 25) refers to the "colorful things hanging off each side . . ." of the Mardi Gras mask. The only common element among these answers is that four of the five are passive. There are five other responses (8, 10, 12, 13, & 20) that have not been reviewed. They include lungs, a tree, a pelt, a butterfly, and a scarab. None appear to include any unusual embellishments. However, response 10, "a tree if you are looking up through the leaves," comes close to meeting the criterion for one category of dissociative responses described by Labott et al (1992).

The composite of answers that apparently contain projected elements portray a much more negative than positive self-image. There are clear connotations of damage and a sense of helplessness or futility in some, and a lack of a firm sense of self in others. This is unusual for a person who also seems to hold herself in very high regard. It suggests the presence of considerable conflict and possible disorganization concerning self-concept. If this is a valid assumption, the existence of such disarray could easily serve as a precursor to dissociative reactions.

INTERPERSONAL PERCEPTION

Case 5.   Interpersonal Perception Data for a 32-Year-Old Female.

R = 26	CDI = 3	HVI = No	**COP & AG Responses**
a:p = 6:10	SumT = 2	Fd = 0	II 6. WS+ Mp.FD.FC'.CFo 2 H,Bl,Cl,Id 4.5 AB,ALOG,COP,PHR
	[eb = 11:6]		III 7. D+ Ma.mp.FD+ 2 H,Id,A,Sx P 4.0 COP,DV,MOR,GHR
Sum Human Contents = 6	H = 3		V 14. W+ FMao 2 A 2.5 AG,PHR
[Style = Extratensive]			VII 19. W+ FC'.Mao 2 H,Cg 2.5 COP,GHR
GHR:PHR = 2:6			
COP = 3	AG = 1	PER = 3	
Isolation Indx = 0.31			

The data for the *a:p* ratio (6:10) strongly suggest that she is likely to assume a passive role in her interpersonal relations. This does not necessarily mean that she will be submissive to others, but it implies that she prefers to avoid responsibilities and tends to avoid seeking out new solutions to problems or engaging in new or unfamiliar behaviors.

The presence of two texture answers signals strong unfulfilled needs for closeness. There is no indication of any recent emotional loss. Therefore, it seems reasonable to assume that this represents a persistent state that has developed because of an accumulation of losses or disappointments that have never been contended with adequately. Possibly, this state could relate to her previously noted narcissistic features. If those around her have failed to provide reassurance about her worth, this could create a sense of rejection or abandonment.

The six human content responses imply that she is interested in people, and the fact that three of the six are Pure *H* suggests that she tends to conceptualize them in the context of reality. However, the GRH:PHR ratio (2:6) indicates that many of her interpersonal behaviors are unlikely to be very adaptive for the situation and, in fact, may often be regarded unfavorably by others. On the other hand, she has one *AG* and three COP responses, which suggests that she perceives interaction with others to be an important component in her daily routine and is likely to be regarded as outgoing by others. These are seemingly contradictory findings, but that is not necessarily the case. Two of the three COP responses involve ritualistic-like behaviors, and two of the three identify the human figures as natives. Only one of the three can be regarded as clearly positive (native black women dancing back to back). Thus, while she may be very interested in interpersonal exchange, her social behaviors may not be as outgoing and positive as the COP finding implies.

There are three PER answers in the protocol, suggesting that she is somewhat more defensive in interpersonal situations than most people. It is likely that she often relies on displays of information as a way of maintaining security in those situations. This does not necessarily impair social relationships but can be regarded unfavorably by others if overdone. In a similar context, the Isolation Index value (.31) suggests that she is somewhat reluctant to be involved in social intercourse routinely. It is another finding that seems contradictory to the COP datum.

The seven movement answers involving pairs do not provide much additional information from which to speculate about her interpersonal world. The first (response 2) is a carving of two gargoyles holding onto each side of a huge beetle. The second (response 5) is two bears finger painting. The third and fourth (responses 6 and 7) are the ritualistic COP answers, people making a blood offering and natives beating a drum with dead monkeys hanging in the background. The fifth (response 14) is two animals crashing their heads together. The sixth (response 19) is two native black women dancing back to back, and the last (response 26) is undersea creatures all moving around. None are markedly negative, but none are markedly positive.

The findings from the interpersonal data seem to indicate that her interpersonal world is not very satisfying for her. She seems interested in people and appears to have strong needs for closeness or reassurance. However, she tends to be passive and defensive when interacting, and it seems probable that others may regard some of her behaviors unfavorably. The result appears to be a social world that generally is superficial and unrewarding.

PROCESSING

Case 5.   Processing Variables for a 32-Year-Old Female.

EB	= 5:9.0	Zf	= 22	Zd	= +6.0	DQ+	= 10
L	= 0.24	W:D:Dd	= 23:3:0	PSV	= 0	DQv/+	= 0
HVI	= NO	W:M	= 23:5			DQv	= 2
OBS	= NO					

Location & DQ Sequencing

I: Wo.W+.W+.WSo	VI: Do.Wo
II: W+.WS+	VII: Wv.WSo.W+
III: D+.Do	VIII: Wo.W+.Wo
IV: Wo.Wo.Wo.Wv	IX: W+.Wo
V: Wo.W+	X: WSo.W+

The processing data are intriguing and somewhat unexpected. The *Zf* value of 22 is substantial, suggesting that she makes a considerable effort to organize new information. This is also indicated by the *W:D:Dd* ratio of 23:3:0, signifying that she strives to assimilate all aspects of a new stimulus field with little concern about economizing energy. The location sequence reveals that she gave *W* answers to every figure except Card III. The *W:M* ratio (23:5) implies that she endeavors to accomplish more than may be reasonable in light of her functional capabilities. Similarly, the *Zd* value (+6.0) indicates a traitlike characteristic that prompts her to invest considerable effort and energy into scanning activities. Usually, persons with this feature are concerned about avoiding careless mistakes.

A composite of findings such as these is not unusual when marked perfectionism or even obsessiveness is present or when a person is very guarded and concerned about safeguarding his or her integrity. There is no evidence in the history, or in previously reviewed Rorschach findings, to suggest that she may be perfectionistic or obsessive. Thus, it may be that this unusual processing effort is related more to her inflated sense of personal worth and the need to protect it.

Despite her somewhat remarkable processing effort, the quality of her processing is not especially striking. The *DQ+* value (10) is slightly above average for an extratensive adult, but well within the expected range for a college graduate and less than expected for a record with a *Zf* value of 22. The two *DQv* responses are not unusual for an extratensive person, but they suggest that the quality of her processing is not always as mature as might be expected. Neither of these findings would be consistent for a perfectionistic individual.

It is also of interest that five of her 10 *DQ+* answers occurred in her first seven responses, while the remaining five are scattered, with one each appearing in answers to Cards V, VII, VIII, IX, and X, with three being last responses. This hints that some sort of mental shifting may have occurred as she became more involved with the task. Possibly the data regarding mediation and ideation will shed more light on this premise.

MEDIATION

Case 5. Mediation Variables for a 32-Year-Old Female.

R = 26	L = 0.24	OBS = No	**Minus & NoForm Features**
FQx+	= 2	XA% = .85	IV 11. Wo F– Sc,Sx 2.0 PER
FQxo	= 15	WDA% = .85	VII 17. Wv F– Hh MOR
FQxu	= 5	X–% = .15	VIII 22. Wo CF– Art,An 4.5
FQx–	= 4	S– = 1	X 16. WSo CF.mp– (Hd),Art 5.5 PHR
FQxnone	= 0		
(W+D	= 26)	P = 8	
WD+	= 2	X+% = .65	
WDo	= 15	Xu% = .19	
WDu	= 5		
WD–	= 4		
WDnone	= 0		

The *XA%* (.85) and *WDA%* (.85) are well within the expected range and indicate that her translations of inputs are usually appropriate for the situation. The *X–%* of .15 is marginally elevated. It is created by four minus answers in her 26-response protocol. There is no distinct homogeneity among the coding for the minus answers, or among the contents (IUD, something broken, picture of insides, and a Mardi Gras mask). This finding suggests that, occasionally, some mediational dysfunction occurs, but there is no obvious reason why this happens. None of the four minus answers, except possibly the IUD response to Card IV, involve severe distortions of distal features. Thus, in most instances, the basic ingredient for adequate reality testing is likely to be intact.

Her eight Popular responses, slightly more than expected, indicate that she strives to detect clues related to socially expected or acceptable behaviors. This is not surprising in light of the findings from the processing data. Similarly, the two *FQ+* responses in her record are not unexpected and suggest that she is oriented toward being precise or correct. On the other hand, the *X+%* (.65) and the *Xu%* (.19) imply that, by no means, is she a slave to conventionality. As with most people, her individuality will often be apparent in the way she contends with reality. Overall, there is no reason to question the integrity or effectiveness of her mediational operations.

IDEATION

Case 5.   Ideation Variables for a 32-Year-Old Female.

L	= 0.24	OBS	= No	HVI	= No	**Critical Special Scores**			
						DV	= 1	DV2	= 0
EB	= 5:9.0	EBPer	= 1.8	a:p	= 6:10	INC	= 3	INC2	= 0
				Ma:Mp	= 3:2	DR	= 0	DR2	= 2
eb	= 11:6	[FM = 6 m = 5]				FAB	= 1	FAB2	= 2
				M–	= 0	ALOG	= 1	CON	= 0
Intell Indx	= 7	MOR	= 4	Mnone	= 0	Sum6	= 6	WSum6	= 16
							(R = 19)		

M Response Features

II 5. W+ Ma.CFo 2 A,Art P 4.5 FAB,PHR
II 6. WS+ Mp.FD.FC'.CFo 2 H,Bl,Cg,Id 4.5 AB,ALOG,COP,PHR
III 7. D+ Ma.mp.FD+ 2 H,Id,A,Sx P 4.0 COP,DV,MOR,GHR
VII 19. W+ FC'.Mao 2 H,Cg 2.5 COP,GHR
IX 23. W+ Mp.FC.Fr.mpu (H),Fi,Na INC,PHR

As noted when reviewing the findings about affect, the data for the *EB* (5:9.0) indicate that she is prone to merge her emotions into her thinking during problem solving or decision making. She relies considerably on her feelings when forming concepts or making judgments, and she often uses external feedback as a source of evaluations and reassurance for her decisions. On the other hand, she is not a rigidly intuitive person. The *EBPer* (1.8) suggests that there are instances in which she pushes feelings aside in favor of an ideational approach that involves a systematic consideration of options before reaching a decision or implementing behaviors. In a similar context, the data for the *a:p* ratio (6:10) offer no reason to suspect that her ideational sets or values are usually fixed or inflexible.

The four MOR answers are important because they signify that a very pessimistic set marks much of her conceptual thinking. It influences her view of the world by promoting doubt and discouragement that often create an anticipation of unwanted outcomes, regardless of the quality of her efforts. It can also have a significant impact on some of her judgments.

The substantial left side *eb* value (11) consists of six *FM*s and five *m* responses. This finding signals an unusual level of potentially intrusive ideation, which seems related to both internal need states and a sense of helplessness created by situational stress. This form of mental activity is likely to intrude into her conscious, directed thinking frequently, and the resulting distractions impact negatively on attention and concentration. Another finding is also important to understanding her thinking. It is the value for the Intellectualization Index (7), which signifies the use of intellectualization as a major defensive tactic in situations that she perceives as stressful or emotionally challenging. It is a way of denying, distorting, or neutralizing feelings and reduces the likelihood that they will be dealt with directly. It tends to promote false or misleading concepts that often lead to flawed judgments.

Six of her responses contain critical special scores yielding a *WSum6* of 16. This could represent a serious thinking problem, but in this instance, they seem to reflect a casual negligence in her conceptualizations. The *FABCOM* is coded for bears finger painting. The *DV* (response 7) is assigned for her misuse of the term *naturalists* instead of naturists. One of the INCOMs (response 9) is coded for noting arms on an anteater, while the remaining two INCOMs are assigned because she identifies a pink cat (response 21) and a pink rock (response 23). None of these signify serious cognitive slippage, but all convey naive judgments. The most serious of the six critical special scores is the ALOG (response 6), because she insists that the people "must be" engaged in a black magic ritual. It is a concrete judgment that is unexpected for an intelligent adult and tends to illustrate the pseudo-intellectual defensiveness that marks much of her thinking.

The form quality of her *M* responses is quite respectable. One is an *FQ+,* three are *FQo,* and one is *FQu.* Likewise, her *M* answers, with the exception of the bears finger painting (response 5), have a reasonably sophisticated quality. They include people in a black magic ritual (response 6), natives beating a drum with dead monkeys in the background (response 7), native black women dancing back to back (response 19), and a fat elf sitting by a pink rock smoking a pipe by the water (response 23).

Overall, she is usually somewhat intuitive when making decisions or judgments, relying extensively on her feelings, but not inordinately so. Typically, her thinking is reasonably clear, although often naive and concrete, mainly because her tendency to intellectualize clouds and distorts her judgments. Currently, she is likely to be easily distracted by considerable peripheral ideation prompted by an unusual level of unfulfilled needs and ongoing stresses. Possibly more important, much of her thinking is influenced by a notably pessimistic set that can easily influence many of her decisions and judgments.

SUMMARY

This is a complex woman who presents a picture that includes several seemingly contradictory features and, overall, conveys the impression of considerable dysfunction. She relies extensively on her feelings to guide her thinking, yet she also seems uncomfortable about emotions and usually tries to avoid or neutralize them. At the same time, her displays of emotion are usually intense and not always well modulated. It seems likely that she experiences much more emotional disruption than she readily admits.

Similarly, findings indicate that she is a very self-centered, narcissistic person, yet her overall self-image seems to be much more negative than positive. There are clear indications that she feels damaged and has a sense of helplessness and futility about herself. She appears to be involved in considerable rumination about herself and probably harbors feelings of guilt or remorse.

She is interested in people and probably conveys the impression, at least superficially, of being an outgoing person. However, she is also a lonely person who apparently is prone to be passive in her interpersonal relations. In fact, she appears somewhat reluctant to be routinely involved in social interaction, and it is probable that others may find some of her social behaviors unappealing and unfavorable. This may be because she is passive and defensive, tends to intellectualize a great deal, and may exude a pessimistic outlook. Regardless of the causes, it is likely that her social world is superficial and unrewarding, contributing to a noticeable sense of alienation or anger that she harbors.

Another seeming enigma concerns her remarkable processing effort when confronted with new information. She works very hard to organize inputs, yet the overall quality of her effort is not particularly striking and, in fact, is sometimes marked by less maturity than expected. She strives to identify cues related to socially expected or acceptable behaviors, yet this process of mediating new information sometimes seems to falter for no obvious reason. Likewise, her thinking is generally clear and often reasonably sophisticated, but sometimes it seems unexpectedly naive and concrete.

Presently, she is likely to be easily distracted because of intrusive subconscious thoughts that are created mainly by ungratified needs and ongoing stresses. In fact, the latter have accumulated to the extent of creating a considerable stimulus overload for her. Thus, while her capacity for control usually is adequate, situational stresses have caused it to become more limited, and forms of impulsiveness in her thinking or behaviors are possible.

The current limitations to her capacity for control are important because she also has many of the characteristics that are common among suicidal persons. She offers no hints of such a preoccupation, but the findings are compelling and should be afforded substantial weight when making decisions about a plan of treatment for her.

RECOMMENDATIONS

The referral asks if either dissociative fugue reaction or dissociative identity disorder is an appropriate diagnosis. As reported earlier, Rorschach research concerning dissociation has identified several variables that appear frequently in the Rorschachs of those with confirmed histories of such problems. Although none should be used as a basis from which to form a definitive diagnostic conclusion, they create a useful composite of indicators in addressing questions concerning diagnosis.

Her protocol includes a large number of movement determinants (16), has a low *Lambda* value (.24), and is complex as signified by her numerous blends (12 of 26 responses). These findings are commensurate with those noted among patients with dissociation by Wagner et al. (1983) and Scroppo et al. (1998). Her record also contains four MOR responses, and five answers that are coded *FD* or vista, findings that are also commensurate with those reported by Scroppo et al. (1998). In addition, there are two *An* answers and one *Bl* response (Scroppo et al., 1998; Wagner et al., 1983), both positive and negative color responses (Wagner et al., 1983), and one answer that may meet the criterion for a dissociative content response (Labott et al., 1992; Leavitt & Labott, 1997). Her history also includes a report of sexual abuse, which is a frequent finding reported by researchers of dissociative disorders. These empirically related indicators confirm that she has several features that are common among those with dissociative disorders.

Additionally, some of the data from her protocol, especially those yielding apparently contradictory findings concerning her emotions, her self-image, her interpersonal world, and her cognitive functioning can easily be conceptualized as the sort of nuclear elements that might predispose dissociation. However, the referral also raises a question about the possibility of malingering, and many of the apparent contradictions cited previously can also be perceived as the products of efforts to simulate more serious problems than really exist.

Efforts at malingering serious affective problems such as illustrated in this record are often difficult to detect from Rorschach data taken alone. It is an issue that is addressed most realistically when a much more detailed history and, at the very least, other test findings, especially the MMPI-2, are merged with the Rorschach findings. Such a collective of information increases the level of certainty when attempting to confirm or reject the likelihood that an attempt to simulate a serious affective problem has occurred.

Assuming that the Rorschach findings present a valid picture of her psychology, the most important of these concern a possible self-destructive preoccupation. This is particularly troublesome because she is an outpatient, and it should be the focus of immediate intervention efforts. Frequent close and supportive contact is necessary with the main objectives of reducing the impact of currently experienced stresses and creating reassurance about the intervention process. Other treatment objectives are more varied and complex. They include her affective disarray, her confused self-image, and her superficial and unrewarding interpersonal world. The latter includes specific focus on her tendency to assume a passive role with others, and her seemingly unstable marriage.

It is important to note that she has some features that are common among patients who terminate treatment prematurely. The most prominent of these is her exquisite self-centeredness and her confusion about her self-image. In this context, it is essential that early intervention tactics do not threaten her personal integrity. Probably, her unhappiness and the broad issues pertaining to her interpersonal world and her marriage are the most appropriate topics to address early in the treatment process. They are issues least likely to threaten her personal integrity and can provide useful avenues for some ventilation of her disruptive feelings. They also provide opportunities for strengthening intervention supports. It seems probable that the strength, or lack thereof, of her marital relationship will have much to do with her potential for progress in treatment. That relationship should be evaluated as thoroughly as practical early in the intervention process.

Intervention topics, such as the trauma related to her rape, miscarriage, and abortion should be deferred until she raises them. Likewise, any attempts to focus on long-term treatment objectives, such as her defensiveness and issues regarding her confused self-image and self-esteem should be avoided until there is clear evidence that she is comfortable in, and allied with, the intervention routine. Considerable time may elapse before this occurs.

EPILOGUE

The results of the assessment were reviewed with her by the attending psychiatrist. She reaffirmed having frequent episodes of depression, noting that she usually contended with them by shopping or housecleaning. She stated that they usually lasted no longer than two or three days. She denied having any serious suicidal thoughts but noted, "It has crossed my mind a few times when things are especially bad." She also spoke at length about her dissatisfaction with her marriage. She described her husband as dominant and indifferent and admitted that she had considered leaving him on several occasions.

She was agreeable to outpatient treatment and the psychiatrist arranged for her to be seen weekly by a female colleague. After six months of treatment, her therapist noted that progress had been very slow during the first 10 weeks, mainly because the patient was passive and frequently sought direction concerning the substance of the sessions. During this time, focus was mainly on her marital problems and her interests in seeking employment or further education.

Near the end of the third treatment month, the patient became noticeably depressed and reported insomnia and midnight awakening. Antidepressant medication was considered, but the decision to prescribe it was deferred as the patient began recalling some events that had occurred during amnestic episodes. During the next four weeks, she described numerous events for which she had no memory previously. Typically, the events she was able to recall happened after she had been intensely depressed. During these episodes, she would usually seek out social contacts in bars or restaurants and at least three times engaged in sexual relations with men that she met. As these memories unfolded, her depression became more intense and the therapist began seeing her more frequently to contend with the guilt that also was emerging.

This crisis period lasted for nearly one month and, at one point, hospitalization was considered. After having recovered and reported many memories concerning her amnestic episodes, she began to broaden the substance of her therapeutic sessions considerably. She was able to revisit her rape and abortion experiences at length and began talking much more optimistically about her future. During this time, she also decided to separate from her husband, and the therapist anticipates that they will divorce. Currently, the focus in most of the intervention sessions is on concrete issues regarding employment and self-sufficiency.

REFERENCES

American Psychiatric Association. (2000). *Diagnostic and statistical manual of mental disorders* (4th ed., text rev.). Washington, DC: Author.

Armstrong, J. G. (1991). The psychological organization of multiple personality disordered patients as revealed in psychological testing. *Psychiatric Clinics of North America, 14*(3), 533–546.

Armstrong, J. G., & Loewenstein, R. J. (1990). Characteristics of patients with multiple personality and dissociative disorders on psychological testing. *Journal of Nervous and Mental Diseases, 178*(7), 448–454.

Barach, P. (1986). *Rorschach signs of MPD in multiple personality disorder and nonmultiple personality disorder in victims of sexual abuse.* Paper presented at the Third International Conference on Multiple Personality/Dissociative States, Chicago.

Bernstein, E. M., & Putnam, F. W. (1986). Development, reliability, and validity of a dissociation scale. *Journal of Nervous and Mental Diseases, 174*(7), 727–735.

Carlson, E. B., Putnam, F. W., Ross, C. A., Torem, M., Coons, P., Dill, P., et al. (1993). Validity of the Dissociative Experiences Scale in screening for multiple personality disorder: A multicenter study. *American Journal of Psychiatry, 150,* 1030–1036.

Labott, S. M., Leavitt, F., Braun, B. G., & Sachs, R. G. (1992). Rorschach indicators of multiple personality disorder. *Perceptual and Motor Skills, 75*(1), 147–158.

Labott, S. M., & Wallach, H. R. (2002). Malingering dissociative identity disorder: Objective and projective assessment. *Psychological Reports, 90*(2), 525–538.

Leavitt, F., & Labott, S. M. (1997). Criterion-related validity of Rorschach analogues of dissociation. *Psychological Assessment, 9*(3), 244–249.

Leavitt, F., & Labott, S. M. (1998). Rorschach indicators of dissociative identity disorders: Clinical utility and theoretical implications. *Journal of Clinical Psychology, 54*(6), 803–810.

Sandberg, D. A., & Lynn, S. J. (1992). Dissociative experiences, psychopathology and adjustment, and child and adolescent maltreatment in female college students. *Journal of Abnormal Psychology, 101*(4), 717–723.

Scroppo, J. C., Drob, S. L., Weinberger, J. L., & Eagle, P. (1998). Identifying dissociative identity disorder: A self-report and projective study. *Journal of Abnormal Psychology, 107*(2), 272–284.

Wagner, E. E. (1978). A theoretical explanation of the dissociative reaction and a confirmatory case presentation. *Journal of Personality Assessment, 42*(3), 312–316.

Wagner, E. E., Allison, R. B., & Wagner, C. F. (1983). Diagnosing multiple personalities with the Rorschach: A confirmation. *Journal of Personality Assessment, 47*(2), 143–149.

Wagner, E. E., & Heise, M. R. (1974). A comparison of Rorschach records of three multiple personalities. *Journal of Personality Assessment, 38*(4), 308–331.

Wagner, E. E., Wagner, C. F., & Torem, M. (1986). *Contraindications of MPD based on psychological test data and behavioral inconsistencies.* Paper presented at the Third International Conference on Multiple Personality/Dissociative States, Chicago.

CHAPTER 8

An Issue of Anxiety and Sleep Problems

This 30-year-old man was referred for evaluation by a prospective therapist with whom he has met following the recommendation of a supervisor at work. He has been employed for the past six years as an investments analyst for a large brokerage firm. He accepted that position after completing an MBA at a prestigious university and has expected rapid advancement. He was given a substantial salary increase after one year and, for the past 18 months, has expected reassignment to a more senior level position, but this has not occurred even though two vacancies have existed.

In discussing the reasons for his failure to be promoted with the supervisor, he was informed that his presentations to various committees have not been well organized and that the justifications for many of his recommendations concerning investments have not been well developed. In addition, the supervisor suggested that his coworkers tend to regard him as being inflexible and slow to recognize obvious market trends. He says he was surprised by the supervisor's feedback.

He claims that he gets along well with most of the people with whom he works and is confused and anxious about the evaluation of his performance. He notes that he works "long days" to make sure that he has organized all the necessary information for making a report or a presentation and believes that he considers all options very carefully before forming a recommendation. He states, "I think my reports are among the best, and I certainly have trouble believing that some people think they are not well organized. I know that, sometimes, people may disagree with my recommendations, but that's their problem. It's not because I didn't do my job well."

He says that he is now having trouble sleeping and that he experiences considerably more anxiety at work than was formerly the case. He also notes that he is having some difficulties in his marriage of four years. His wife, who is age 28, works as a legal secretary. He says that she seems less supportive of him concerning his failures than he expects, and that during the past four to six months they have argued frequently about financial matters. Apparently, she wants to spend more of their money while he argues in favor of investing it. They have also had some heated discussions lately about his difficulties at work, and she has expressed the opinion that it might be better for him to consider a different kind of employment.

He is described as an attractive and well-groomed man who often seems intense as he describes his difficulties. He is precise in identifying his work routines, but far less so with regard to other aspects of his life. He states that he usually awakens about 5 A.M. so that he can check on progress in the European markets, and because of this, usually he is in bed before 10 P.M. His wife often stays up later to watch television or to read, and she has openly challenged the necessity for him to keep such an unusual schedule. He justifies this routine by saying that if he has sound knowledge about European markets it makes his work much easier.

He is the only child in a professional family. His father, age 59, is an attorney specializing in corporate law. His mother, age 57, is a physician specializing in obstetrics. He reports a normal developmental history and says that he has always been close to his parents. He graduated from high school at age 18 with above-average grades and then attended a small liberal arts college, receiving a bachelor's degree in economics and graduating with honors. He devoted the next two years to graduate school and states that he received excellent recommendations from his professors when seeking employment after receiving his MBA.

He says that he began "casual dating" when he was about 16 but was never seriously interested in a long-term relationship until he began dating his wife during his senior year in college. She had dropped out of college after two years to accept a secretarial position with a law firm. They met through a mutual friend and dated regularly for the next three years. After he completed his MBA, they became engaged and lived together for about a year before marrying. He says that they have always gotten along well until the past year. She chides him about being too preoccupied with work. He strongly maintains that his wife's suggestions that he may be in the wrong occupation are completely "off base," but he admits that he might have progressed more rapidly had he accepted employment with a smaller firm where, "I could have had more responsibility for decisions from the beginning."

He states forcefully that he feels certain that he has no deep-seated problems, but admits to concerns about controlling his tension and anxiety at work and also wants to investigate whether he really is more disorganized than he believes to be the case. He maintains that once he is able to "control this tension problem and make better progress at work," his current marital difficulties, "which are no big deal," will subside rapidly.

The prospective therapist asks: (1) Is there any evidence of a serious psychiatric disturbance? (2) How acute is the current anxiety and how disabling is it to his functioning? (3) What are the short-term versus long-term treatment potentials? and (4) How strongly motivated is he for change?

Case Formulation and Relevant Literature

This man feels that most of his problems, including his sleep disturbances and marital difficulties, result from the tension and anxiety he is experiencing at work. His prospective therapist wonders whether this current level of anxiety is increasingly immobilizing and indicative of more long-standing problems. There is a suggestion that this man's coworkers find him poorly organized and inflexible, and he seems defensive about these criticisms. Although he did very well in his undergraduate and graduate training in economics and business administration, his wife now questions whether some other professional area might be more appropriate for him.

The Rorschach literature associated with the assessment of anxiety, stress, and interpersonal competence was reviewed in Case 1 (Chapter 3). There are a few studies relevant to assessing sleep difficulties, and the Rorschach has also been used in research about vocational adaptation. A review of these studies may be of value in providing consultation for the prospective therapist.

Assessment of Sleep Difficulties

Mattlar et al. (1991) compared the Rorschachs of 18 Finnish adult nonpatients who described themselves as poor sleepers with those of 20 adult nonpatients who identified themselves as good sleepers. There were no statistically significant differences on basic *Comprehensive System* variables between the two groups, but the authors did find that 17% of the poor sleepers, compared with none of the good sleepers, were positive on the Suicide Constellation.

de Carvalho et al. (2003) evaluated the Rorschachs of 32 Brazilian patients with insomnia and suggested that their range of problem-solving options was more limited than those of nonpatients. Vincent and Walker (2000) studied the relationship between chronic insomnia and perfectionism as measured by two self-report measures (Frost, Marten, Lahart, & Rosenblate, 1990; Hewitt & Flett, 1989) in a sample of 32 adult insomniacs and 26 healthy controls. The insomnia group was higher on an index of "maladaptive" perfectionism, leading the authors to speculate, ". . . some individuals who doubt their own actions, who feel frequently criticized by important others, and who frequently worry about making mistakes may be in a heightened state of arousal during the evening, which may lead to difficulty with falling asleep at night" (p. 353). The authors also noted these patients ". . . will need extra education, reassurance, and support when receiving either psychological and/or medication treatment for insomnia" (p. 353).

There are no current studies relating insomnia to Rorschach variables associated with perfectionism, such as the Obsessive Style Index, but Vincent and Walker's (2000) findings suggest the potential utility of research in this area.

Assessment of Vocational Adaptation

Although there was early interest in the Rorschach's use in vocational settings (Piotrowski & Rock, 1963; Steiner, 1953), there is little in the recent literature that relates psychological variables to vocational function. One exception is the longitudinal work of Heath (1976, 1977), who evaluated 80 male college students with a comprehensive battery that included the Rorschach. He then reevaluated 68 of these men for occupational satisfaction when they were in their early 30s. Heath's Rorschach measures were drawn from the work of Holt (Holt & Havel, 1960) and assess the extent to which primary process material intrudes on thinking. Heath found that greater vocational adaptation was positively correlated with Holt's measures of ability to control primary process content and with judges' Rorschach ratings of healthy self-organization. He suggested that the overarching construct predictive of vocational adjustment is psychological maturity, which he conceptualized as the ability to symbolize personal experience and to integrate the perspectives and viewpoints of self and others into an increasingly robust and autonomous problem-solving style. A potentially useful extension of Heath's work would involve studying the relationship between vocational adjustment and Rorschach variables that measure some of these elements of maturity.

Case 6.   A 30-Year-Old Male.

Card	Response	Inquiry
I	1. Well it ll a mask l an A mask, lik a cat or st	**E:** Rpts Ss Resp **S:** It has th ears out hre (Dd34) & th whit prts r lik eyes & th mouth but its not real, mor lik a mask lik for Halloween
		S: How many shld I find **E:** Its up to u most peopl c mor thn 1 thg
	2. It cld b a bat too	**E:** Rpts Ss Resp **S:** Well th ear prts fr th mask cld b wgs & th body in th midl ll a bat to me
		S: Can u turn it around **E:** If u lik
	< 3. Ths way it ll a dog tht is runng along & his ear is floppg up	**E:** Rpts Ss Resp **S:** Ths prt is his body & legs & his ear is up in air ths why I thot he wld b runng, our dog has big ears & thy always flop around whn he runs sort of lik ths
II	4. Tht ll 2 dogs w their noses togethr, smellg at eo	**E:** Rpts Ss Resp **S:** Not any of th red j th dark prt it ll 2 dogs c th noses r touchg lik smellg at eo, th head & th uppr prt of th body u cant c thr bodys j fr th neck up lik
	5. Ths bottm red cb sk of bf	**E:** Rpts Ss Resp **S:** Well it doesnt realy ll 1 vry much except u cld say ths r wgs & th liter cntr is lik th narrow body & its diff shades of all red u kno I've seen thm in the Natl Geographic
	6. Ths litl prt sorta ll a rocket sittg on a launch pad	**E:** Rpts Ss Resp **S:** Well ths prt (D4+S) ll a rocket & ths whit prt is th pad c thes litl lines (top of DS5) sho wher it meets th ground tht extends out in frnt of it & th rocket is pointd upward lik ready for firing
III	7. Ths ll a cpl of peopl wrkg on a machine	**E:** Rpts Ss Resp **S:** C 1 hre & hre th head leg & thr arms r hre & ths cb a machin tht thy r wrkg on I dk wht kind mayb thyr putg a tire on a rim, u kno, thyr st tht it lets u strip th tire off or remount it easy u kno wht I mean **E:** Yes
	8. Ths upr red prts ll 2 guys who r doing sk of gymnastics	**E:** Rpts Ss Resp **S:** Lik in a gym on th mats lik acrobats, it ll thy r doing ss of act lik a team togethr whr thy r flipg towrd eo c th legs r stretchd up & th arms & heads u gotta forget ths othr prt is hre & j thk of thm separately
IV	9. Ths ll som big giant sittg on a tree stump or st	**E:** Rpts Ss Resp **S:** Hes got big feet stickg out in frnt of him & ths hre is th stump lik hes sitg on it leang back & his arms r hangg down lik
	< 10. Ths way ths prt ll th head of a goose or snake I gues a goose	**E:** Rpts Ss Resp **S:** It has th long neck & th beak j shapd lik a goose's head & neck
V	11. Tht ll a cpl of rams buttg thr heads togethr lik th wild ones in th mts do whn thy fite ovr territory	**E:** Rpts Ss Resp **S:** Th cntr is whr th horns r hitg & u can c th rear lgs strtchd out lik thy r straing to knock eo ovr, u c thm on th TV stimes on natur programs, thy ll ths thy realy bang eo

Card	Response	Inquiry
	12. Ths top prt also ll a hand lik smbody givg a victory sign	**E:** Rpts Ss Resp **S:** Well its lik ths (demos) lik u curl all ur fingrs in except th 2 tht u point up lik victory lik a V, c ths is th hand & ths r th fingers I rem Nixon used to do tht hold both hands up lik tht & whn peopl imitate him thy always do tht
VI	13. Tht ll a carcass lik a skin or hide of an A it kinda ll 1 tht got run ovr	**E:** Rpts Ss Resp **S:** Its j all flatnd out 1 som poor A tht got run ovr c th head & th legs, j th skin is left u can thk of it as mayb a cat markgs **E:** Markgs? **S:** Yeah u kno th way cats fur is lik a tabby cat th fur is lik ths, diff colors lik tht
	<14. Ths prt re m of a seal or a walrus	**E:** Rpts Ss Resp **S:** It j re m of it th way its shapd ll one
	v15. Ths ll th heads of a cpl of birds	**E:** Rpts Ss Resp **S:** Th beaky ths ll birds j ll tht to m ths litl prt rt hre, ll a bird head c **E:** Yes
	v16. Ths drk prt in hr re m of a candle	**E:** Rpts Ss Resp **S:** Well realy lik a candle holdr w a candl u cant thk of a candl lik ths so it wld hav to b a holdr, but u can c th flame up at th top hre lik comg out of the candl prt th holdr is lowr dwn
VII	17. Ths ll 2 litl girls who r squattg on a rock & playg som game	**E:** Rpts Ss Resp **S:** C their faces, the hair, nose, chin & the body & its lik a game thy r playg & eo is pointg bhind thm lik in a game of ss, c here r their arms & ths is th rock
	18. I thk of an island too w a harbor there	**E:** Rpts Ss Resp **S:** Its lik lkg dwn a it ths wld all b th island & th whit prt th harbor lik an aerial view of 1 I've seen ones sorta l ths whn we fly dwn to th Caribbean on vacation
VIII	19. It ll 2 A's climbg up st	**E:** Rpts Ss Resp **S:** Th A's r on th side c th legs & heads & ths cntr is lik a tree but its strang lkg (pause) I supp it cb a tropical tree bec its got several diff colrs
	20. Ths cntr prt ll a rib cage	**E:** Rpts Ss Resp **S:** Well it j ll tht u can c th spaces betwn th ribs
	21. U kno ths litl whte prt ll a tooth I lost last yr	**E:** Rpts Ss Resp **S:** Yeah I had to hav it pulld bec it was infectd & thy wre gonna j tak th roots out but it was crackd & thy pulld it it was th first one I evr lost it lkd alot lik ths
IX	22. Tht ll a mask a vry fancy one sort of lik a Chinese one, u kno a dragon mask	**E:** Rpts Ss Resp **S:** Well if uv evr seen th Chinese New Year celebration thy wear a lot of masks lik ths we go evry yr almost thy hv pointd ears & big cheeks & litl slits lik ths (S) for th person to c thru & thy paint em all diff colrs lik ths is it realy has tht shape I bought one sthg lik it for my daughter 1 yr
	< 23. Ths way it ll a guy sort of squattg dwn by som watr & being reflectd in th watr	**E:** Rpts Ss Resp **S:** Well hres his head thts mostly wht u c & th rest is a scrunchd dwn body lik hesin a squattg position, heres the waterlin (midln) & dwn hre its all reflectd

(continued)

Card	Response	Inquiry
X	24. Well lets c, I gues up at th top it ll 2 ants fightg ovr ths stalk or smthg	**E:** Rpts Ss Resp **S:** Yeah ths (D8) ll ants c th litl antena on em & thr legs & in th midl of em is ths stalk tht thy r fightg ovr, a stem of a flowr or wheat stalk or sthg
	25. Ths brown thgs ll 2 crabs	**E:** Rpts Ss Resp **S:** Well thy hav th spindley legs lik a crab altho I dont thk crabs r brown
	26. Th blue thgs cld b crabs 2	**E:** Rpts Ss Resp **S:** Well thy hav more legs lik some crabs but I kno tht thy arent blue altho I guess thy call em blue crabs down in Washington but I dont thk tht thy really blue at least I nvr saw one & I dkno anybody tht has & even if thy r thy wldnt b ths color of blue
	27. Ths litl thg in th cntr ll a maple seed	**E:** Rpts Ss Resp **S:** It has tht shap to it lik whn thy fall off th tree thy whirl around we get alot of thm in our yard in th fall
	v28. Whn u lk ths way ths prt ll a guy holdg up a cpl of big flags or smthg lik big	**E:** Rpts Ss Resp **S:** Well u can c his head, legs, arms & body & th green thgs r lik banners lik green banners hes waving thm up in th air lik holdg one w each hand big green ones lik mayb at a fair or sthg

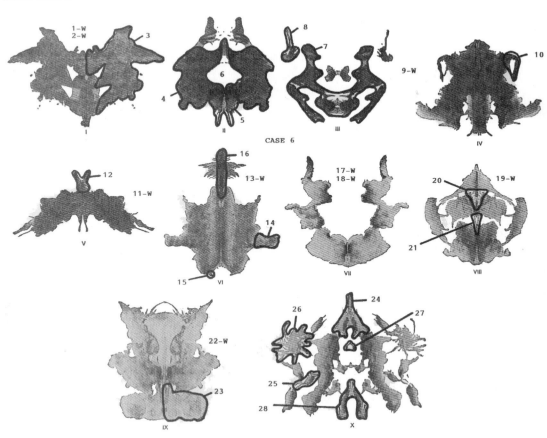

CASE 6

Case 6.   Sequence of Scores.

Card	No.	Loc.	No.	Determinant(s)	(2)	Content(s)	Pop	Z	Special Scores
I	1	WSo	1	Fo		(Ad)		3.5	
	2	Wo	1	Fo		A	P	1.0	
	3	Do	2	FMao		A			PER
II	4	D+	6	FMpo	2	Ad	P	3.0	
	5	Do	3	FC.FYo		A			PER
	6	DdS+	99	mp.FDu		Sc		4.5	
III	7	D+	1	Mao	2	H,Sc	P	3.0	PER,COP,GHR
	8	D+	2	Mao	2	H		4.0	COP,GHR
IV	9	W+	1	Mp.FDo		(H),Bt	P	4.0	GHR
	10	Do	4	Fo		Ad			
V	11	W+	1	FMao	2	A		2.5	PER,AG,PHR
	12	Do	6	Mao		Hd			PER,AB,PHR
VI	13	Wo	1	FTo		Ad	P	2.5	MOR
	14	Ddo	24	Fo		A			
	15	Ddo	21	Fo	2	Ad			
	16	D+	2	mpo		Hh,Fi		2.5	
VII	17	W+	1	Ma+	2	H,Ls	P	2.5	COP,GHR
	18	WS/	1	FDo		Ls		4.0	PER
VIII	19	W+	1	FMa.FCo	2	A,Bt	P	4.5	
	20	DSo	3	Fo		An			
	21	DdSo	29	F−		Hd			PER,PHR
IX	22	WSo	1	FCo		(Ad)		5.5	PER
	23	D+	6	Mp.Fro		H,Na		2.5	GHR
X	24	D+	11	FMao	2	A,Bt		4.0	AG,PHR
	25	Do	7	Fo	2	A			
	26	Do	1	Fo	2	A	P		DR,PER
	27	Do	3	Fo		Bt			PER
	28	D+	10	Ma.FC+	2	H,Id		4.0	GHR

Case 6.   Structural Summary.

Location Features	Determinants Blends	Single	Contents	S-Constellation
				YES . .FV+VF+V+FD>2
		H = 5		YES . .Col-Shd Bl>0
Zf = 17	FC.FY	M = 4	(H) = 1	YES . .Ego<.31,>.44
ZSum = 57.5	M.FD	FM = 4	Hd = 2	NO . . .MOR > 3
ZEst = 56.0	FM.FC	m = 1	(Hd) = 0	NO . . .Zd > +- 3.5
	M.Fr	FC = 1	Hx = 0	NO . . .es > EA
W = 9	M.FC	CF = 0	A = 9	NO . . .CF+C > FC
D = 15	m.FD	C = 0	(A) = 0	NO . . .X+% < .70
W+D = 24		Cn = 0	Ad = 4	YES . .S > 3
Dd = 4		FC' = 0	(Ad) = 2	NO . . .P < 3 or > 8
S = 6		C'F = 0	An = 1	NO . . .Pure H < 2
		C' = 0	Art = 0	NO . . .R < 17
		FT = 1	Ay = 0	4 . . . .TOTAL
DQ		TF = 0	Bl = 0	**Special Scores**

		T = 0	Bt = 4		Lv1	Lv2
+ = 12		FV = 0	Cg = 0	DV	= 0x1	0x2
o = 15		VF = 0	Cl = 0	INC	= 0x2	0x4
v/+ = 1		V = 0	Ex = 0	DR	= 1x3	0x6
v = 0		FY = 0	Fd = 0	FAB	= 0x4	0x7
		YF = 0	Fi = 1	ALOG	= 0x5	
		Y = 0	Ge = 0	CON	= 0x7	
		Fr = 0	Hh = 1	Raw Sum6 = 1	

Form Quality					
	FQx	MQual	W+D	rF = 0	Ls = 2	Wgtd Sum6 = 3
+	= 2	= 2	= 2	FD = 1	Na = 1	
o	= 24	= 5	= 22	F = 10	Sc = 2	AB = 1	GHR = 6
u	= 1	= 0	= 0		Sx = 0	AG = 2	PHR = 4
−	= 1	= 0	= 0		Xy = 0	COP = 3	MOR = 2
none	= 0	= 0	= 0		Id = 1	CP = 0	PER = 10
				(2) = 11		PSV = 0	

Ratios, Percentages, and Derivations

R = 28	L = 0.56		FC:CF+C = 4:0	COP = 3 AG = 2	
			Pure C = 0	GHR:PHR = 6:4	
EB = 7:2.0	EA = 9.0	EBPer = 3.5	SumC':WSumC = 0:2.0	a:p = 9:5	
eb = 7:2	es = 9	D = 0	Afr = 0.56	Food = 0	
	Adj es = 8	Adj D = 0	S = 6	SumT = 1	
			Blends:R = 6:28	Hum Con = 8	
FM = 5	C' = 0	T = 1	CP = 0	Pure H = 5	
m = 2	V = 0	Y = 1		PER = 10	
				Iso Indx = 0.29	

a:p	= 9:5	Sum6 = 1	XA% = 0.96	Zf = 17.0	3r+(2)/R	= 0.50
Ma:Mp	= 5:2	Lv2 = 0	WDA% = 1.00	W:D:Dd = 9:15:4	Fr+rF	= 1
2AB+Art+Ay	= 2	WSum6 = 3	X−% = 0.04	W:M = 9:7	SumV	= 0
MOR	= 1	M− = 0	S− = 1	Zd = +1.5	FD	= 3
		Mnone = 0	P = 8	PSV = 0	An+Xy	= 1
			X+% = 0.93	DQ+ = 12	MOR	= 1
			Xu% = 0.04	DQv = 0	H:(H)Hd(Hd)	= 5:3

PTI = 0	DEPI = 3	CDI = 2	S-CON = 4	HVI = No	OBS = YES

S-CON AND KEY VARIABLES

The S-CON value (3) is not positive. The first positive Key variable is identified by one reflection response. It signifies that the interpretation should begin with a review of the clusters concerning self-perception, interpersonal perception, and controls. The remainder of the search routine should be decided by the next positive Key or Tertiary variable. In this instance, it is that he is introversive ($EB = 7:2.0$). Thus, the review of the remaining clusters will begin with ideation and proceed through processing, mediation, and end with the data regarding affect.

SELF-PERCEPTION

Case 6. Self-Perception Related Data for a 30-Year-Old Male.

R	= 28	OBS	= Yes	HVI = No	**Human Content, An & Xy Responses**
					III 7. D+ Mao 2 H,Sc P 3.0 PER,COP,GHR
Fr+rF	= 1	3r+(2)/R	= 0.50		III 8. D+ Mao 2 H 4.0 COP,GHR
					IV 9. W+ Mp.FDo (H),Bt P 4.0 GHR
FD	= 3	SumV	= 0		V 12. Do Mao Hd PER,AB,PHR
					VII 17. W+ Ma+ 2 H,Ls P 2.5 COP,GHR
An+Xy	= 1	MOR	= 1		VIII 20. DSo Fo An
					VIII 21. DdSo F– Hd PER,PHR
H:(H)+Hd+(Hd) = 5:3					IX 23. D+ Mp.Fro H,Na 2.5 GHR
[EB = 7:2.0]					X 28. D+ Ma.FC+ 2 H,Id 4.0 GHR

The Obsessive Style Index is positive, indicating a preoccupation with perfectionism. Seeking to be correct or precise is a way of protecting one's integrity and, if not carried to an extreme, it is not necessarily a liability. However, it represents a predisposition to problems if significant failures are experienced or if others are unaccepting of this characteristic. Usually, obsessional people do not overestimate their personal worth, but in this case the presence of a reflection response suggests that his self-image includes a narcissistic tendency to value himself highly. The Egocentricity Index (.50) is also above average, implying that this high self-value is well embedded and usually causes him to judge himself more favorably than he judges others. This also is not necessarily a liability but, when considered in light of his obsessive style, it connotes a noticeable status or achievement orientation.

When important mistakes or failures occur in his life, he will usually externalize the blame rather than criticize himself. Mistakes or failures also tend to exacerbate his strivings to be precise. This is a customary way for him to protect his high self-value, but it can also create a proclivity to become overly involved in details and/or vacillate about decisions. If such behaviors occur frequently, there is a potential for more failures and a risk of alienating those around him. This probably accounts for some of the difficulties that he is having at work.

Interestingly, there are three *FD* responses in his record, suggesting that he is quite involved with self-examination. This is a positive finding, especially if treatment is recommended. Another positive finding is the presence of eight human content responses, of which five are Pure *H*. This suggests that his self-image has evolved mainly from experiences rather than from fantasy. The codings for the human content answers also are generally positive. Seven of the eight have a form quality of plus or ordinary, with three involving uncomplicated blends and three involving cooperative movement. This also suggests that his self-image is based largely on social experiences.

The projected material in the record provides some interesting glimpses about his self-concept. The single minus answer (Card VIII, response 21) is "this little white part looks like a tooth I lost last year . . . it was infected and . . . it was cracked and they pulled it, it was the first one I ever lost." It is intriguing because he uses a *DdS* area, and this is the third and last response to the card. It is almost a MOR response, and conveys a sense of damage and loss that runs contrary to his high self-esteem. His single MOR answer (Card VI, response 13), "a carcass like a skin or hide of an animal, it kinda looks like one that got run over . . . some poor animal that got run over . . . just the skin is left." It is a common answer, but it is also similar in substance to the "tooth" response. It connotes damage caused by others.

The *M* responses are generally positive, but also somewhat conservative. They include all the human content answers except the tooth response discussed earlier. The first (Card III, response 7) is "a couple of people working on a machine . . . maybe putting a tire on a rim . . ." Although a positive response, most of the verbiage focuses on the machine rather than the people. The second (Card III, response 8) is "two guys doing some kind of gymnastics . . . it looks like they are doing some sort of act like a team together where they are flipping toward each other . . ." This answer seems more positive than the first. The third involves a single figure (Card IV, response 9), "some big giant sitting on a tree stump or something . . . big feet sticking out in front of him . . . his arms are hanging down like." It is a passive response.

The fourth *M* (Card V, response 12) is an *Hd* response, "a hand like somebody giving a victory sign . . . you curl all your fingers in except two that you point up like victory, like a V . . . Nixon used to do that. . . ." It probably implies a status orientation. The fifth (Card VII, response 17), a Popular response, is "two little girls who are squatting on a rock and playing some game . . . they are playing and each one is pointing behind them like in a game of some sort . . ." It is another positive response. The sixth (Card IX, response 23) involves his reflection answer, "a guy sort of squatting down by some water and being reflected in the water . . . his head is mostly what you see and the rest is a scrunched down body like he's in a squatting position . . ." It is another passive answer. The last *M* (Card X, response 28) is also his last response. It is, "a guy holding up a couple of big flags or something like big green banners . . . he's waving them up in the air . . . one in each hand . . . maybe at a fair or something." He is calling attention to himself.

Overall, the *M*s convey the notion of a relatively positive self-image, but there is also a sense of conservatism about them. Two of the seven are dynamic (guys doing gymnastics and a guy waving banners), but the remaining five are much less so (people working on a machine, a giant sitting with his arms hanging down, holding two fingers in the air, squatting and playing, and squatting and being reflected). Only two of the five are passive but all five are less dynamic than might be expected of a bright, achievement-oriented person. They are adequate, but they are also cautious and suggest that his self-image may not be as sturdy as superficially implied. This is speculative, but worth considering further as the interpretation unfolds.

The material from the five *FM* responses adds a bit to the picture. The first two (Card I, response 3 and Card II, response 4) are somewhat nondescript, "a dog running along and his ear is flopping up . . . that's why I thought he'd be running," and "two dogs with their noses together smelling at each other . . . you can't see their bodies. . . ." Very little, if any, projection is involved. The third (Card V, response 11) is more revealing, "a couple of rams butting their heads together like the wild ones in the mountains do when they fight over territory . . . their horns are hitting and you can see the rear legs stretched out like they are straining to knock each other over . . . they really bang each other." It is his first aggressive response and seems to connote his achievement striving.

The fourth *FM* (Card VIII, response 19), "two animals climbing up something," is interesting because of the inquiry in which he struggles a bit with the tree, "but it's strange looking (pause). I suppose it could be a tropical tree because it's got several colors." It illustrates his tendency to be as precise as possible.

The last *FM* (Card X, response 24) is his second aggressive response, "two ants fighting over this stalk or something . . . in the middle of them is this stalk that they are fighting over, a stem of a flower or a wheat stalk or something." Again, achievement seems to be emphasized.

The two *m* answers are both passive. The first (Card II, response 6) is intriguing because of the way that the space is used. The response is, "rocket sitting on a launch pad." Typically, people report the entire *DS5* area as a rocket and, often, it is reported as taking off. In this instance, the *D4* area plus a small part of the center white area (*DS5*) is used as the rocket and the remaining part of *DS5* is the pad, "that extends out in front of it." It is an unusual answer that illustrates his orientation to be precise. The second *m* (Card VI, response 16) conveys the same tendency, "a candle . . . really like a candle holder, you can't think of a candle like this so it would have to be a holder, but you can see the flame up at the top . . ." It is cautious and precise. That both answers are like this suggests that his obsessional features become more dominant as he experiences stress.

There are 12 other responses that have not been studied. None have especially unusual embellishments that convey self-image features, but five (responses 5, 18, 22, 26, & 27) are coded as PER. The verbiage in those answers tends to highlight a kind of authoritarian defensiveness: I've seen them in the *National Geographic*; I've seen ones sort of like this when we fly down to the Caribbean on vacation; I bought one something like it for my daughter; I guess they call them blue crabs in Washington but I don't think they are blue, at least I never saw one and I don't know anyone who has, and even if they are they wouldn't be this color of blue; we get a lot of them in our yard.

In general, he appears to view himself with high regard, but he is also cautious and defensive about doing this. Whether this is because his personality is marked by an obsessiveness with perfectionism that causes him to be wary about his own judgments or because he feels vulnerable to criticism by others is not clear. Both postulates are viable. In reality, his self-image seems to be reasonably well established and not marked by serious flaws. However, he does not regard himself as adequate. His failure to view himself realistically promotes a lack of confidence and gives rise to substantial defensiveness which creates the potential for more difficulties in life than should be the case. On a more positive note, he is involved in introspective behavior and his willingness to undergo evaluation is to his credit.

INTERPERSONAL PERCEPTION

Case 6.   Interpersonal Perception Data for a 30-Year-Old Male.

					COP & AG Responses
R = 28	CDI = 1		HVI = No		III 7. D+ Mao 2 H,Sc P 3.0 PER,COP,GHR
a:p = 9:5	SumT = 1		Fd = 0		III 8. D+ Mao 2 H 4.0 COP,GHR
	[eb = 7:2]				V 11. W+ FMao 2 A 2.5 PER,AG,PHR
Sum Human Contents = 8			H = 5		VII 17. W+ Ma+ 2 H,Ls P 2.5 COP,GHR
[Style = Introversive]					X 24. D+ FMao 2 A,Bt 4.0 AG,PHR
GHR:PHR = 6:4					
COP = 3	AG = 2		PER = 10		
Isolation Indx = 0.29					

A review of the first few variables in this cluster yields seemingly positive findings. The CDI and HVI are not positive. The $a:p$ ratio is greater on the active side, and there are no food responses. There is one texture response, the Popular *FT* commonly given to Card VI. It suggests that he probably acknowledges and expresses needs for closeness in ways similar to most people. There are eight human content responses, which is in the expected range for an introversive person, implying a typical interest in people. In addition, five of the eight human contents are Pure *H* answers, suggesting that he tends to conceptualize others in reality-based ways.

The GHR:PHR ratio (6:4) is in the favorable direction, intimating that he usually engages in interpersonal behaviors that are likely to be adaptive for the situation. The first potentially negative finding is the presence of three COP and two *AG* responses. This is an unusual combination implying that, while open and interested in positive relations with others, many of his interactions will be marked by forceful or aggressive forms of exchange. Typically, these are not antisocial or asocial behaviors. Ordinarily, persons with this characteristic seem to perceive forcefulness or aggressiveness as a natural component in interpersonal relations. Often, these individuals are regarded favorably, but sometimes they are likely to alienate others because of their tendency to strive for dominance or control in relationships.

A tendency to be dominating or controlling in relationships is also suggested by the inordinate number of PER responses (10) in his protocol. Previously, this has been interpreted as a sort of defensive authoritarianism, and that hypothesis continues to be viable. However, when considered in the context of relations with others, it also suggests that he is often emphatic and inflexible. These characteristics may not be well received by others, creating substantial potential for limiting the extent to which he can maintain deep and mature relations.

Some added support for the postulate that his interpersonal relations are more superficial than deep and enduring is also implied by the value for the Isolation Index (0.29). It suggests that he may be less active or open in social relations than might be expected. There are four *M*s (responses 7, 8, 17, and 28) and four *FM*s (responses 4, 11, 19, & 24) that contain pairs. Three of the *M* responses involve cooperative movement (people working on a machine; guys doing gymnastics; girls playing), while two of the *FM* answers contain aggressive movement (rams butting their heads; ants fighting over a stalk). As a group, these responses do not appear to contain any consistent or unusual verbiage regarding interactions that could clarify or add to previously developed postulates.

Overall, it seems that this man is interested in positive relations with others and, at least superficially, probably interacts adaptively with people. However, his defensiveness about himself and his tendency to be dogmatic are likely to limit the extent to which his relations will be more than superficial. He may be somewhat reluctant about engaging routinely in social intercourse, and it seems unlikely that others will seek him out routinely for friendships. In fact, his tendency to be inflexible can easily alienate those around him. This problem may be contributing significantly to his current occupational difficulties.

CONTROLS

Case 6.   **Control-Related Variables for a 30-Year-Old Male.**

EB = 7:2.0	EA = 9.0		D = 0	CDI = 1
eb = 7:2	es = 9	Adj es = 8	AdjD = 0	L = 0.56
FM = 5 m = 2	SumC' = 0	SumT = 1	SumV = 0	SumY = 1

The Adj D Score (0) indicates that his capacity for control and tolerance for stress is similar to that of most people. There is no reason to challenge the validity of this assumption, derived from the Adj D value of zero, as the *EA* (9.0) is in the average range, the *EB* (7:2.0) does not contain any zero values, and the *Lambda* value (0.56) is less than 1.0. In addition, the Adj *es* (8) is in the expected range, and there are no unusual values for any of the six variables that contribute to it.

These findings indicate that there is no reason to believe that he has any problems with his controls. Typically, he is able to formulate decisions and direct behaviors without unusual interference. Likewise, the findings suggest that his tolerance for stress usually will be adequate.

IDEATION

Case 6.   Ideation Variables for a 30-Year-Old Male.

						Critical Special Scores			
L	= 0.56	OBS	= Yes	HVI	= No				
						DV	= 0	DV2	= 0
EB	= 7:2.0	EBPer	= 3.5	a:p	= 9:5	INC	= 0	INC2	= 0
				Ma:Mp	= 5:2	DR	= 1	DR2	= 0
eb	= 7:2	[FM = 5 m = 2]				FAB	= 0	FAB2	= 0
				M−	= 0	ALOG	= 0	CON	= 0
Intell Indx	= 2	MOR	= 2	Mnone	= 0	Sum6	= 1	WSum6	= 3
							(R = 28)		

M Response Features

```
III    7. D+ Mao 2 H,Sc P 3.0 PER,COP,GHR
III    8. D+ Mao 2 H 4.0 COP,GHR
 IV    9. W+ Mp.FDo (H),Bt P 4.0 GHR
  V   12. Do Mao Hd PER,AB,PHR
VII   17. W+ Ma+ 2 H,Ls P 2.5 COP,GHR
 IX   23. D+ Mp.Fro H,Na 2.5 GHR
  X   28. D+ Ma.FC+ 2 H,Id 4.0 GHR
```

The *EB* values (7:2.0) signal that he is an ideational person who delays decisions or behaviors until he can think things through and consider various options. He tends to push his emotions aside and rely on his internal evaluations instead of on external feedback when making decisions. This form of coping and decision making can be effective, provided his thinking is clear and he is somewhat flexible about the use of the style.

Unfortunately, the latter does not appear to be true in this case. The value for *EBPer* (3.5) indicates that he will usually persist in his ideational style, even in circumstances where a more intuitive or trial-and-error approach is clearly preferable. Although this is not necessarily a liability, it signifies that he is not very flexible in his coping and decision-making activities. This is consistent with his obsessional style. People with this feature usually take great care when forming concepts and applying them, and they are reluctant to make decisions without careful thought about consequences. This can require much effort and sometimes can be inefficient. Some of his occupational difficulties, particularly his inability to reach what should be obvious conclusions quickly, are likely related to this obsessional lack of flexibility.

On a positive note, the other variables in this cluster have values or findings that are within expected limits for an adult. The values for the $a:p$ ratio (9:5) are not unusually disparate. The HVI is not positive. There are two MOR answers, but this is no reason to suspect that a pessimistic set marks his thinking consistently. The value for the left side eb (7) is slightly above average because of two m responses. It signifies some increase in peripheral mental activity caused by situational stress, but this is not a serious problem. It probably relates to the fact that he is being evaluated because of difficulties at work. The value for the Intellectualization Index (2) is not significant and the $Ma:Mp$ ratio (5:2) is in the desired direction.

There is only one critical special score (DR) in the protocol, yielding a $WSum6$ of three. It was coded because of his rambling during the inquiry for response 26 (Card X), "I guess they call them blue crabs down in Washington, but I don't think they are really blue, at least I never saw one and I don't know anybody that has, and even if they are, they would not be this color of blue." It does not represent slippage as much as his already noted tendency to authoritatively defend his decisions. The form quality of all of his human movement responses is o or $+$, and the quality of his M answers is reasonably concise and, often, somewhat sophisticated. This is to be expected from a relatively intelligent college graduate.

Overall, there is no reason to question the clarity of his thinking, and there is no evidence from which to suspect flawed judgment or unusual instances of cognitive slippage. The only negative finding concerning his ideation is his cautious inflexibility in his decision-making habits, which can make for a sort of ideational inefficiency.

PROCESSING

Case 6.   Processing Variables for a 30-Year-Old Male.

EB	= 7:2.0	Zf	= 17	Zd	= +1.5	DQ+	= 12
L	= 0.56	W:D:Dd	= 9:15:4	PSV	= 0	DQv/+	= 1
HVI	= NO	W:M	= 9:7			DQv	= 0
OBS	= YES						

Location & DQ Sequencing

I: WSo.Wo.Do	VI: Wo.Ddo.Ddo.D+
II: D+.Do.DdS+	VII: W+.WSv/+
III: D+.D+	VIII: W+.DSo.DdSo
IV: W+.Do	IX: WSo.D+
V: W+.Do	X: D+.Do.Do.Do.D+

The Zf value (17) indicates that he invests considerable effort in processing new information. Although the $W:D:Dd$ ratio (9:15:4) includes proportions for W and D (1:1.7) that suggest reasonably economical processing strategies, the four Dd selections cast doubt on that assumption. They imply that he tends to become unnecessarily preoccupied with the minor details of a stimulus field. This is consistent with his obsessive tendencies. However, two of the four Dd answers include white space, raising the issue of whether a significant negativistic set may be exacerbating his obsessive style.

The location sequence suggests that this is probably not the case. It does include six S responses, but as noted, only two are Dd. Actually, the sequence is consistent. He makes W selections for his first responses to 7 of the 10 figures. On the two most broken figures (Cards III and X), he gives *D* answers exclusively, and his *Dd* responses are always second or third answers. Thus, while the *S* selections are important and will be considered when the data regarding affect are studied, there is no reason to suspect that a negative set is influencing his processing behaviors markedly.

The *W*:*M* ratio (9:7) is well within the expected range, and the *Zd* value (+1.5) connotes that his scanning efficiency is similar to that of most people. The value for *DQ*+ (12) is greater than expected and there is one *DQv/*+ answer. He gave synthesis answers to all cards except one, and typically they occur as first or last responses. These findings suggest that the quality of his processing is good, and probably complex.

The composite of processing-related data appears to indicate that his processing habits are adequate. Although he may become overly involved with details at times, this does not seem to be a serious liability in light of the considerable effort that he invests when dealing with new information.

MEDIATION

Case 6. Mediation Variables for a 30-Year-Old Male.

R = 28		L = 0.56		OBS = Yes	**Minus & NoForm Features**
FQx+	= 2		XA%	= .96	VIII 21. DdSo F– Hd PER,PHR
FQxo	= 24		WDA%	= 1.00	
FQxu	= 1		X–%	= .04	
FQx–	= 1		S–	= 1	
FQxnone	= 0				
(W+D	= 24)		P	= 8	
WD+	= 2		X+%	= .93	
WDo	= 22		Xu%	= .04	
WDu	= 0				
WD–	= 0				
WDnone	= 0				

The *XA%* (.96) and the *WDA%* (1.00) are very high, and indicate that it is customary for him to make a special effort to ensure that his translations of inputs are appropriate. This is not surprising in light of his obsessive style. The *X–%* (.04) is very low, implying that events of mediational dysfunction are unusual for him. Interestingly, the single minus answer (Card VIII, response 21) involves the use of white space and, as with some of the processing data, raises a question about whether a sense of anger or alienation may predispose his infrequent episodes of mediational dysfunction. Actually, the minus answer (a tooth) is not a serious distortion of the distal field.

There are eight Popular answers, which is slightly more than given by most adults, but not at all unusual for a person who is concerned with being correct. No doubt, his obsessive style prompts him to search out cues related to socially acceptable or expected responses. Likewise, the two *FQ*+ responses signify that he is oriented to being precise when translating inputs. The very high *X+%* (.93) and noticeably low *Xu%* (.04) connotes an unusual commitment to conventionality and a probable sacrifice of much of his individuality. While this is not unusual for obsessive people, the cost to them can be considerable because of their preoccupation with correctness and conformity.

AFFECT

Case 6.   Affect-Related Data for a 30-Year-Old Male.

EB	= 7:2.0			EBPer	= 3.5	**Blends**	
eb	= 7:2	L	= 0.56	FC:CF+C	= 4:0	M.FD	= 1
DEPI	= 3	CDI = 2		Pure C	= 0	M.Fr	= 1
						M.FC	= 1
SumC′ = 0	SumT = 1			SumC′:WSumC	= 0:2.0	FM.FC	= 1
SumV = 0	SumY = 1			Afr	= 0.56	m.FD	= 1
						FC.FY	= 1
Intellect	= 2	CP	= 0	S = 6 (S to I,II,III	= 2)		
Blends:R	= 6:28			Col-Shad Bl	= 1		
m + y Bl	= 2			Shading Bl	= 0		

As noted, the *EB* (7:2.0) indicates that he is the type of person who prefers to delay, push emotions aside, and think things through carefully before reaching a decision or initiating a behavior. Unfortunately, as also noted, he is not very flexible about this approach (*EBPer* = 3.5) and is likely to make a considerable effort to avoid being overly influenced by feelings. In the same context, he is probably loathe to try out possibilities and rely much on external feedback, even though such an approach could be beneficial in some situations. This inflexibility can be a substantial liability at times. It may reflect a core issue concerning some of his current problems because it requires close control over his feelings and the way in which he interacts with his environment.

The right side *eb* value (2), consisting of one texture answer and one diffuse shading response, is relatively low for a 28-response protocol. It offers no evidence of affective discomfort which, for a person in his circumstance, seems unusual. It is also inconsistent with his report that he is tense and anxious about his work situation. The *SumC′:SumC* ratio (0:2.0) suggests no indication of unusual affective constriction, and the *Afr* value (.56) is in the average range for an introversive person. It implies that he is as willing as most others with a similar coping style to process and become involved with emotional stimulation.

The previously discussed postulate that he may closely control manifestations of his emotions is clearly supported by the *FC:CF+C* ratio (4:0). The absence of at least one *CF* answer in a relatively long record is unusual and typically signals a mistrust about displaying intense feelings openly. Usually, it connotes a noticeable form of emotional constraint. On the other hand, his protocol includes six space responses, four of which appear after Card III. Ordinarily, this signifies considerable anger or at least a strong sense of alienation. Usually, this is a traitlike feature that affects the coping and decision-making activities of the person. However, in this case, some of these negative feelings may have a situational relationship.

Typically, when a person harbors considerable anger or a marked sense of alienation, it manifests in ways that are obvious to others, but the history suggests that is not true for this man. In addition, there are no other indications in the protocol of unusual negativism. Thus, it may be reasonable to speculate that these substantial negative feelings have some relationship to his current difficulties. He has been strongly cautioned about his work effectiveness, and it has been recommended that he see a therapist. In addition, he is receiving very little support from his wife, and they have been arguing frequently about financial matters. Either or both of these circumstances represent forms of serious insult, especially for a person who holds himself in high regard.

Thus, it seems possible that the anger or alienation that he is experiencing is being constrained and is manifesting in ways that he interprets as tension and anxiety. Regardless of whether this is true, these feelings are likely to cause him to be less willing to make some of the routine compromises that mark sustained and meaningful relations with others.

There are six blends in his 28-response protocol (21%). This is an expected proportion for an introversive person and implies that his psychology is not marked by unusual complexity. Two of those blends (*FC.FY* and *m.FD*) suggest some modest increase in complexity as the result of situational factors, but this is not excessive and no cause for concern. However, one of those is a color shading blend, implying that current stresses may be causing some confusion for him about his feelings.

There are some notable problems about the way he handles his feelings, most of which are probably related to his obsessive style. He works hard to avoid being influenced by emotions in his routine coping and decision-making activities, and he is not very flexible about this. In a similar context, he maintains fairly close control over any displays of his feelings, apparently because of the mistrust that he has about emotions in general. Beneath the surface, however, he seems to experience considerable anger or, at least, a marked sense of alienation concerning his environment. There is no clear evidence to indicate how this manifests in his thinking or behavior, but it must be having some effects, especially in his interpersonal life.

SUMMARY

This is a man who appears to be very self-centered. He has some narcissistic features that breed a high regard for himself, but he also seems very defensive about this. Some of his defensiveness may have existed for some time, having been prompted by his obsessiveness and concerns with correctness. This could easily cause him to be cautious about his judgments. However, it also seems likely that recent events have exacerbated this defensiveness considerably, as his occupational and marital difficulties represent serious challenges to his sense of high self-value.

In effect, although continuing to regard himself highly, he does not feel as confident or secure in his environment as he would prefer, and he is concerned about avoiding criticism by others. This concern tends to promote considerable introspection on his part which, apparently, is partly responsible for his willingness to be evaluated. Actually, his self-image seems to be reasonably well established and not marked by serious flaws, but his substantial defensiveness takes a psychological toll and creates the potential for more difficulties in life than should be the case.

He appears to be interested in positive relations with others and probably strives to interact adaptively with most people. However, his defensiveness about himself, and a noticeable tendency to be dogmatic, are likely to limit the extent to which his relations will be more than superficial. He seems to have some reluctance about engaging extensively in social intercourse, and this makes it somewhat unlikely that others will seek him out for close friendships. In fact, his tendency to be dogmatic and inflexible may alienate those around him, and this is probably contributing significantly to his current occupational difficulties.

There is no reason to believe that he has any problems with his controls. Typically, he is able to form decisions and direct behaviors without unusual interference, and the findings suggest that his tolerance for stress usually will be adequate. Likewise, there is no reason to question the clarity of his thinking, and there is no evidence from which to suspect flawed judgment or unusual instances of cognitive slippage. The only negative finding concerning his ideation is his relative inflexibility in his decision-making habits, which can make for considerable inefficiency.

The tactics that he uses to process new information are adequate. He makes a commendable effort to be thorough and, although at times he tends to become overly involved with details, this does not seem to be a serious liability. He also strives to ensure that his translations of inputs are appropriate. In fact, he probably works too hard to be conventional. This unusual commitment to conventionality causes him to sacrifice much of his individuality. Although this is not surprising in light of his obsessiveness, the cost can be considerable because of the expectations and constraints that he places on himself.

A notable illustration of this is the way in which he deals with feelings. He works hard to avoid being influenced by emotions in his routine coping and decision-making activities, and he is not flexible about this. He also maintains fairly close control over any displays of his feelings, apparently because of his mistrust about emotions in general. This emotional constraint appears to be a direct by-product of his obsessiveness, but beneath the surface, he seems to be experiencing considerable anger or, at least, a marked sense of alienation concerning his environment.

Some of these negative feelings probably have developed over time because the environment may not have afforded him the recognition that he believes he deserves. More recently, these feelings have probably intensified as the result of experiencing serious criticism at work and discord in his marriage. Both challenge his integrity, and this is likely to have exacerbated any preexisting negative sets or given rise to more indignation and irritation. They create discomfort that he probably experiences as tension and anxiety. These irritating feelings affect his thinking and behavior, and they must be having some counterproductive effects in his interpersonal life.

Although he has many assets, his obsessiveness, inflexibility, sense of defensiveness, and affective constraint limit the extent to which those assets can be fully exploited. He is overly preoccupied with doing things correctly, and he seems to be naively convinced that his thoughts and feelings must be closely controlled regardless of the situation, including the very negative feelings that he works hard to conceal from others. In effect, he is his own worst enemy. His inflexibility and need for control have fomented a potential for both personal and interpersonal calamity. He has become more defensive about himself and less willing to strive for relations with others that will be meaningful and rewarding.

RECOMMENDATIONS

His proneness to self-examination and his willingness to be evaluated are positive elements. They imply that he may be open to seek some changes that can be beneficial for him. However, it is also important to avoid excessive optimism about his openness to change. The referral is work related, and he attributes his tension and anxiety problems to that source. He seeks to control those features, but also fails to acknowledge some of the negative feelings, anger, and alienation that he has about his situation and, possibly, about the environment in general. Likewise, he is somewhat casual about his marital difficulties (they are "no big deal") and assumes they will subside with success at work.

At least superficially, he seems to be naive about his obsessiveness, his defensiveness, his anger or irritation, and his marked tendencies toward emotional constraint. This sort of naiveté or denial is an obstacle to the treatment of any obsessive person, but even more so when the individual is narcissistic. The latter is a basic ingredient that will cause him to bolt from treatment if seriously threatened. Thus, any intervention model will require the careful development of a reasonably positive working relationship before specific issues can be broached in depth.

Despite his apparent naiveté, it is almost certain that he has some awareness of his concerns with correctness. This issue and its relation to tension may be the least threatening topic to use as an entrée to treatment. It is unlikely that his concerns with perfection or correctness will diminish. However, it may be possible to assist him in finding ways to use those concerns to his advantage and minimize their potential for creating excessive cautiousness and disorganization at work. In particular, it may be beneficial to help him identify instances in which his inflexibility becomes a liability and encourage routines for the consideration of alternatives. Optimally, focus on this issue might also create an avenue for him to identify and possibly ventilate some of the anger or irritating feelings that he is experiencing about his interpersonal relationships.

If he responds positively to a review of his perfectionistic features and conveys some sense of trust about the therapeutic relationship, broader issues such as his emotional constraint and his interpersonal relationships, including his marriage, may be amenable to consideration. However, this will not occur early in treatment, and the therapist will often be hard pressed to contend effectively with his tendencies to be dogmatic about issues. This feature is likely to be one of the greatest obstacles to the development of a positive working relationship. In that context, it seems important to emphasize that he is the type of person who needs to feel reassured about his efforts, and the intervention strategy should be designed to afford some reassurance regularly.

EPILOGUE

Feedback concerning the assessment results was provided by the therapist, who used the information as a basis from which to discuss treatment options and suggestions. The therapist noted that the patient seemed impressed by the findings and readily agreed that he might be overly concerned with correctness. However, he expressed skepticism about the findings regarding emotional constraint and defensiveness, suggesting that these findings were probably related to his concerns about making a "good impression." Nonetheless, he stated an interest in trying out weekly therapeutic sessions "for awhile" with the objective of improving his work performance.

The therapist noted that the substance of the first five sessions focused mainly on work-related issues. During the sixth session, he shifted the main topic from work to his marriage and the persistent complaints of his wife about his work schedule. Marital issues remained a basic focal point during the next month and, during the 11th session, he inquired about the possibility of marriage therapy. The therapist offered information about the marriage therapy process and provided names of therapists for consideration. Subsequently, the patient terminated individual treatment, and he and his wife entered marriage therapy.

Approximately six months later, he contacted his primary therapist again. He reported that he and his wife had separated and that he wanted to begin individual treatment again because he was experiencing frequent episodes of anxiety and depression. During the first month of renewed treatment, he noted that his situation at work had not improved and he worried about keeping his job. He also ventilated considerably about his wife and tended to blame her for many of his difficulties. The therapist noted that he was much more open and direct about emotions, and about relations with others.

During the second month, the patient requested that the frequency of visits be increased to twice per week, while also reporting that the incidents of depression had subsided considerably and that he was feeling a renewed sense of confidence about his work situation. He stated that he would like to be seen more often to learn more about himself and to explore various ways to improve his life situation. He was seen twice weekly for the next three months, during which time he and his wife agreed to divorce. Beginning with the fourth month, he no longer complained about episodes of anxiety and he shifted to a once-per-week routine again.

He has continued in treatment for about 16 additional months. In the course of treatment, his work situation improved considerably and he received his long-awaited promotion. He also became more socially active and has begun talking cautiously about the possibility of marrying again. The therapist noted that he remains somewhat obsessional but has learned to use his strivings for correctness more to his advantage. The therapist also noted that he continues to be overly defensive with people but has devised several effective tactics to reduce the negative impact of this. The therapist has expressed the belief that termination will occur within three or four additional months.

REFERENCES

de Carvalho, L. B., Lopes, E. A., Silva, L., de Almeida, M. M., Silva, T. A., Neves, A. C., et al. (2003). Personality features in a sample of psychophysiological insomnia patients. *Arquivos de Neuropsiquiatria, 61*(3), 588–590.

Frost, R. O., Marten, P., Lahart, C., & Rosenblate, R. (1990). The dimensions of perfectionism. *Cognitive Therapy Research, 14*(5), 449–468.

Heath, D. H. (1976). Adolescent and adult predictors of vocational adaptation. *Journal of Vocational Behavior, 9,* 1–19.

Heath, D. H. (1977). Some possible effects of occupation on the maturing of professional men. *Journal of Vocational Behavior, 11,* 263–281.

Hewitt, P. L., & Flett, G. L. (1989). The Multidimensional Pefectionism Scale: Development and validation. *Canadian Psychologist, 30,* 339.

Holt, R. R., & Havel, J. A. (1960). A method for assessing primary and secondary process in the Rorschach. In M. A. Rickers-Ovsiankina (Ed.), *Rorschach psychology* (pp. 263–315). New York: Wiley.

Mattlar, C.-E., Carlsson, A., Kronholm, E., Rytöhonka, R., Santasalo, H., Hyyppä, M. T., et al. (1991). Sleep disturbances in a community sample investigated by means of the Rorschach. *British Journal of Projective Psychology, 36*(2), 15–34.

Piotrowski, Z. A., & Rock, M. R. (1963). *The perceptanalytic executive scale: A tool for the selection of top managers.* Oxford, England: Grune & Stratton.

Steiner, M. E. (1953). The search for occupational personalities: The Rorschach test in industry. *Personnel, 29,* 335–343.

Vincent, N. K., & Walker, J. R. (2000). Perfectionism and chronic insomnia. *Journal of Psychosomatic Research, 49,* 349–354.

CHAPTER 9

Issues Regarding an Acute Psychotic Episode

CASE 7

This 23-year-old woman was evaluated 12 days after an involuntary admission to a public psychiatric facility. Initially, she had been admitted to a general medical facility by her parents' physician following a two-day episode of chaotic behavior during which she attempted to isolate herself in her room and refused to eat. She seemed disoriented, frequently tearful, and possibly hallucinatory. She was transferred to the psychiatric unit the next day. On admission, she identified herself correctly, but she was disoriented for time and place. Shortly thereafter, she became withdrawn and nontalkative.

On the fifth day following her admission (the sixth day of hospitalization), she began to carry on limited conversations with staff, ate willingly, and the sedative that had been prescribed for her was discontinued. Shortly thereafter, she became cooperative with hospital staff and participated willingly in interviews. On the seventh day after admission, she signed herself to a voluntary status, but only after assurance that she could leave the hospital of her own accord at any time thereafter.

She has been living with her father and mother, both age 48, for the past three months following her release from a general medical hospital. That admission resulted from an automobile accident in which her husband of two years was seriously injured and remains comatose. He shows no signs of meaningful brain activity and is being sustained on life support. The accident occurred following the wedding reception of a close friend for whom the husband served as best man. According to witnesses and the patient, both she and her husband consumed large quantities of wine and also used cocaine. When they prepared to leave the reception, an argument ensued about who would drive. A friend offered to drive them home or call a taxi, but the husband refused and they set out together in their own car.

She says that her husband did not seem to be driving badly, but approximately three miles from the wedding reception he crossed the center line of the road and had a head-on collision with a delivery van. The driver of the van was killed. She was wearing a seatbelt, but her husband was not. He was thrown partially through the windshield, while she suffered fractures of the left arm and ankle and minor abrasions. Her parents have cared for her since the accident. Both fractures have healed satisfactorily and casts have been removed. She began working again, part time, in her secretarial position about six weeks ago and assumed her full-time work responsibilities three weeks ago.

She has visited her husband's bedside daily since she has been mobile, a period of about 10 weeks. According to her parents, her grief has been intense and obvious, and it has increased recently as his attending physicians have raised the issue of how long to sustain her husband on life support. About two weeks ago, she decided to leave the final decision about this to the attending neurologist, a decision supported by her husband's parents.

Her father, a highway maintenance supervisor, expresses disbelief at her breakdown. He states that she has "held up" very well through this trying situation and finds her current state difficult to understand. Her mother, a housewife, attributes her daughter's condition to some sort of head injury suffered during the accident. Neurological and neuropsychological evaluations conducted two days prior to the personality assessment yield no positive findings. Medical records concerning her hospitalization following the accident are consistent with these findings.

She is the older of two children, having a sister, age 19, who is a freshman at a state university. According to her and her parents, the family was always close, and both parents describe her as a lively, independent person. Her mother describes a normal developmental history. The patient began menstruation late in her twelfth year, but reports no problems related to it. Her grades in both elementary and high school were above average. She was a cheerleader in high school, a member of the school choir, and active in a social services club involved in soliciting funds for meals for the elderly. After high school, she decided against entering a university and completed a one-year secretarial course in a local business college. Her grades there were A's and B's. On completing that course, she obtained a position as a receptionist-secretary in a law firm and, after one year, was selected to be a personal secretary for two attorneys. She continues to hold that position.

She and her husband were classmates in high school, although they dated only occasionally. She reports that she dated "many" fellows during her high school years and had her first sexual experience at age 16. She reports that it was disappointing because "he was awfully gross, and I guess I wasn't ready." During the next two years, she had sexual relationships with at least four other men and reports experiencing her first orgasm during her senior year in a relationship with her husband-to-be. They began dating regularly following high school and considered the possibility of living together, but she declined, assuming that her parents would strenuously object. They became engaged a few months before she completed her business school course and married shortly after she took her job with the law firm. Her husband also had decided against college and accepted a position in a firm manufacturing canned food products. He had done well in that position and was promoted twice, ultimately becoming an assistant foreman, overseeing an assembly line.

She says that she is puzzled and embarrassed by her psychotic behavior. She denies any abuse of alcohol or drugs, although she admits that she and her husband used cocaine on several occasions, including the wedding reception. She hints at being in agreement with her mother's postulate that she may have experienced some undiagnosed head injury. She expects to be discharged soon and seeks assurance that this will not happen again.

The assessment is part of a routine procedure. Several staff have been impressed by the lack of clarity in her thinking and a tendency to become detached during interviews or conversations. Thus, the issue of an affective psychosis or schizophreniform disturbance has been raised in the referral. The referral also requests specific treatment recommendations, both in the hospital and following her discharge.

Case Formulation and Relevant Literature

This young woman suffered a serious breakdown after more than three months of unremitting but mostly unacknowledged stress. Now nearly two weeks later, she is puzzled and embarrassed by a psychotic episode that required hospitalization and that she and her parents view with disbelief. She wonders if there was a neurological cause, perhaps a subtle head injury she sustained during the car accident. She expects to be discharged soon and wants to put the episode behind her as a temporary aberration that will not occur again. It would appear that her response to this disquieting episode is to minimize its significance and to look for other than emotional reasons for its occurrence. A first step in providing useful treatment recommendations is to review the literature about the different ways people reconsolidate after a psychotic break and what the therapeutic implications are for these various styles. A second step is to review the Rorschach literature about the assessment of psychological disorganization and psychotic-level function.

Assessment of Recovery Style

McGlashan and his colleagues (Levy, McGlashan, & Carpenter, 1975; McGlashan, Levy, & Carpenter, 1975; McGlashan, Docherty, & Siris, 1976) have written extensively about recovery styles after an acute psychotic break. They suggest that there is a continuum ranging from integration to sealing over. Integration involves an active interest in the psychotic episode during recovery and a willingness to discuss the experience as a road toward self-understanding. Sealing over involves a "less said the better" approach in which the patient prefers not to engage the psychotic experience during recovery, focusing instead only on the present and future.

McGlashan et al. (1975) note that integrators see the psychotic episode as a valuable source of information that makes sense in the overall context of their lives. Patients who seal over minimize the episode's importance and view it as a circumscribed, ego-alien event caused by an outside force.

These differences in recovery style are illustrated in a study by Levander and Werbart (2003). The authors followed two men who had experienced first-time psychotic breaks, using data from interviews of the patients and their therapists and from each patient's Rorschach. The first patient, whose style approximated that of an integrator, viewed the psychotic break as part of a long-standing problem. The introversive problem-solving style on his Rorschach was consistent with content suggesting a damaged self-concept that only he would be able to repair. His therapist, in contrast, viewed the patient's difficulties as the result of insensitive and unsupportive parents. Follow-up at 18 months indicated little therapeutic progress.

The second patient described by Levander and Werbart (2003) moved quickly to seal over the experience, noting that he would talk with his therapist "in the evenings, but otherwise I want to work with my hands and with the books I am working with . . . I want to be in the present and to forget what's behind" (p. 169). He saw his psychotic break as the result of a complex conspiracy in which he had been poisoned with a drink laced with cocaine. He was unwilling to look at previous life experiences, and his therapist felt that he lacked curiosity about himself as a person. His Rorschach was characterized by an extratensive style and a tentative uncertainty in his responses. Although the therapist felt that an uncovering approach was indicated, he allowed the patient to develop a theory that encapsulated the psychotic episode as an ego-alien experience that could now be controlled. The patient and therapist agreed that he had made a good recovery and terminated therapy after 6 months, with continuing good function at 18-month and 7-year follow-up.

Levander and Werbart (2003) point out that patients' opinions about what constitutes helpful intervention are related to their theories about the cause of the psychotic break. Integrators see continuity between the break and other parts of their lives, whereas patients who seal over will assign the cause to external sources. These different stances imply different therapeutic approaches, ranging from the careful working through of a potentially insight-providing experience to pragmatic support for a present- and future-oriented stance.

Assessment of Psychotic Disorganization

The *DSM-IV-TR* (American Psychiatric Association, 2000, pp. 329–332) defines Brief Psychotic Disorder as a disturbance involving the sudden onset of positive psychotic symptoms such as grossly disorganized or catatonic behavior. The episode lasts less than a month and can occur in response to a markedly stressful event or events. During the episode, the person typically experiences overwhelming confusion with rapid shifts between intense emotions. The Rorschach can be helpful in evaluating level of disorganization during such an episode, particularly for individuals whose recovery style involves sealing over.

The most comprehensive approach to the Rorschach assessment of disorganization can be found in the work of Perry and his colleagues (Perry & Viglione, 1991; Perry, Viglione, & Braff, 1992; Perry, McDougall, & Viglione, 1995; Perry, Minassian, Cadenhead, Sprock, & Braff, 2003; Viglione, Perry, & Meyer, 2003). Beginning with their 1991 development of the Ego Impairment Index (EII), Perry and Viglione attempted to create an index that uses *Comprehensive System* variables to provide information about an individual's level of ego organization. They define organization as ". . . one's ability to meet internal and external demands and stressors," noting that ". . . personality traits and defensive styles can be called on to interact with the external world with varying degrees of success, depending on the ego's capacity to utilize internal processes and the environment" (1991, p. 488).

Drawing on Beres's (1956) delineation of six interrelated ego functions, Perry and Viglione (1991) identified a composite of Rorschach variables that provide information about poor relation to external reality (*FQ*−), cognitive slippage and primary process thinking (*WSum6*), inability to inhibit instinctual needs and urges (Critical Contents: anatomy, blood, explosions, fire, food, sex, and X-ray content, and aggressive and morbid special scores), interpersonal distortion (*M*−), and quality of interpersonal relationships (*GHR* and *PHR*). Factor analysis of these Rorschach variables yielded a single significant factor and provided the weights for each of the Rorschach variables that allow the computation of the EII.

Viglione et al. (2003) refined the EII by recalculating the factor coefficients with a sample of Rorschachs from 363 individuals ranging from nonpatients through character disorder patients and offenders to psychiatric outpatients and inpatients. The algorithm for calculating this refined index (EII-2) is $.141(Sum\ FQ-) + .049(WSum6) + .072(\text{Critical Contents}) + .198(M-) + .117(PHR) - .104(GHR) - .066(R) - .038$. Higher scores are associated with greater levels of ego impairment, and the authors suggest that EII-2 scores greater than +1.3 indicate significant disorganization. They also suggest that comparison of each variable's contribution (excluding the control variable R) to the final EII-2 score allows a more fine-grained understanding of the causes of an individual's disorganization.

Extensive factor analytic, reliability, and validity studies with the EII suggest that it is a robust index. Repeated factor analyses of the EII components (Perry & Viglione, 1991; Perry et al., 1992;

Viglione et al., 2003) have yielded a single replicable factor that accounts for approximately 60% of the variance among these Rorschach variables. Several studies (e.g., Adrian & Kaser-Boyd, 1995; Perry & Viglione, 1991) have demonstrated excellent intercoder agreement for the EII's components. A five-year follow-up with 17 depressed patients (Perry et al., 1995) yielded a rank order test-retest correlation of .68, leading the authors to conclude that the EII ". . . may be addressing a stable core component of personality that endures in the face of symptomatic change" (p. 116).

Several validity studies have associated the EII with level of psychological disorganization as measured either by outpatient versus inpatient status or by severity of psychiatric diagnosis. Adrian and Kaser-Boyd (1995) found higher EII scores among a heterogeneous group of male and female inpatients compared with outpatients. Although the EII did not distinguish between psychotic and nonpsychotic patients, the *GHR* variable was able to discriminate between these two groups. Perry et al., (1992) found that EII scores were significantly higher for undifferentiated and disorganized schizophrenic patients when they were compared with paranoid schizophrenic patients matched for age and education. Perry et al. (2003) tested six groups, ranging from nonpatients through first-degree relatives of schizophrenics and patients with schizotypal personality disorder to outpatient and hospitalized schizophrenics. The authors found a significant linear increase in EII scores as the level of pathology increased, ranging from a mean of −0.35 for the nonpatients to 1.21 for the inpatient schizophrenia patients.

In summary, it would appear that the EII provides a useful assessment of a person's level of adaptive psychological organization. As Viglione et al. (2003) concluded, "[Elevations]. . . suggest problem-solving failures or ineffective and idiosyncratic thinking in complex and demanding life situations" in an index that is ". . . sensitive to impairment and limitations in thinking in relatively well-functioning individuals as well as in severely disordered individuals" (p. 154).

Case 7. A 23-Year-Old Female.

Card	Response	Inquiry
I	1. I dk, mayb two birds r flyg off w a carcass of ss, I dk, prob a cow or horse	**E:** (Rpts Ss resp) **S:** It ll lik a bird on each side & thyr pickg up ths dead thg in the cntr, it ll a carcus of som A, lik a cow or horse, I guess a cow **E:** I'm not sur I'm seeg it rite, help me **S:** There's a bird on each side, c the wgs r out lik birds get when thy pick on smthg or thyr ready to fly w it lik these, ths is their body **E:** And the carcus? **S:** It's smthg dead, I thot of a cow bec of the horns on top & it's pretty fat too lik a cow
	2. It cb a face too, it must b a wolf	**E:** (Rpts Ss resp) **S:** Well, it has the big ears & the eyes (S) and mouth is curled up lik it's wolves growling, wolves r always growling **E:** U said it must be a wolf? **S:** Yeah, lik I said wolves r always growling, thts why I said a wolf
II	3. Some A's r fiting & thyr both hurt, pretty bad	**E:** (Rpts Ss resp) **S:** Thy cb bears I guess, thyr big enuff to b, but thyv got blood all over, on their feet & on their heads, I don't thk either one will live, it's gory **E:** I'm not sur wht makes them ll bears? **S:** I guess thy just ll bears, u cld c them better but all ths red, ths bld covers their faces
III	4. Ths one's gory too, it ll a cpl skeletons lik thyr dancg around som pot, lik thy killed smthg	**E:** (Rpts Ss resp) **S:** There's one on each side, lik thyr dancing around this pot tht thyr cookg som poor A tht thy killed, c all the blood around them **E:** Wht maks them ll skeletons? **S:** Thyr all thin, bony lookg, lik skeletons **E:** And the blood? **S:** All ths red, it's blood & ths is the pot
IV	5. Thts ugly, sk of monster, mayb a gorilla, yes thts it	**E:** (Rpts Ss resp) **S:** It's big, huge, lik I'm layg under it lookg up, it has big feet & its, I dk, all fur w a littl head, mayb its sittg on smthg **E:** U said all fur? **S:** It's all dark & fuzzy lookg lik fur, lik gorilla's hav **E:** U said it's sittg on smthg? **S:** Lik a stool I guess, no a stump of a tree, yeah, a tree stump
	6. I suppose it cb one of thos Darth Vader masks too	**E:** (Rpts Ss resp) **S:** It has those thgs tht come dwn around the ears, lik flaps & ths straight piece over the mouth and it's black...my husband really liked those movies (cries)...cld we stop **E:** Take u'r time we're in no hurry (the subject stood for about a minute and then) **S:** Ok, I'm ok
V	7. A moth, tryg to keep away fr the flame	**E:** (Rps Ss resp) **S:** U can't really c the flame, jst the moth flyg upward **E:** I'm not sur what makes it ll a moth **S:** It's dreary lookg, grey, its got it's wgs stretched out lik it was flyg upward lik thy do whn thyr too near a lite or flame
	8. It cb 2 people too, thyv fallen asleep, leaning on each othr	**E:** (Rpts Ss esp) **S:** Thy just hav their legs sprawled out in frnt of them & their head r kind of bent ovr lik thyr sleeping, propped up against eo, c the leg here & the heads

Card	Response	Inquiry
VI	9. Tht's strange, it's lik a crucifix, a medal like u wear	**E:** (Rpts Ss resp) **S:** Just the top, it ll a crucifix, its elaborate showing Christ's body & it has a sunburst design, u can c the darker outline of the body, lik a human, lik the Turin cross, all dark lik tht, imprinted on the cross
	v10. Ths way it ll a cat tht got run ovr by a car or truck	**E:** (Rpts Ss resp) **S:** It's all flattened out, like it was run over by a car or smthg, u can still c the head & the whiskers & I guess these wld b the legs all flattened & the rest is just a furry mess **E:** Furry mess? **S:** It just looks lik fur, all the lines & dots lik the fur of a cat
VII	v11. Ugh, it sorta ll bones	**E:** (Rpts Ss resp) **S:** Just smthg lik bones, thy seem connected but I can't tell very much about them, maybe it's lik one piece of the rib cage of a big A, lik if u go to a museum and look at a dinosar's bone ths is lik tht, sorta lik one huge piece
	12. It's better ths way, it ll 2 littl girls going up & dwn on a teeter-totter	**E:** (Rpts Ss resp) **S:** It's happy times, thyr playg togethr on the teeter, a see-saw, I used to lov to do tht w my friends when I was littl, u just didn't hav any cares, just had fun **E:** I'm not sur I'm seeg it rite, can u help? **S:** There's one here (D2) & here, c the nose & their hair is flyg up & dwn here is the teeter
VIII	13. Smthgs been all tore apart, its just insides, lik a carcus	**E:** (Rpts Ss resp) **S:** It looks horrible, just remains of some poor A, there's ribs & lungs & I guess wht's left of the stomach, part is decayed **E:** Decayed? **S:** All the blue, thgs get blue when thy decay, the rest is still bloody but the cnter is all decayed **E:** The rest is all bloody? **S:** Oh God, I dk, it just is, it's colored lik blood, alright!
	v14. It's better ths way, but I dk wht it is, a top, yes, a kid's top	**E:** (Rpts Ss resp) **S:** Well ths pointed part is wht it spins on, it's round & it's diff colors, it's lik I got my nephew, he's only 3
IX	15. I don't lik ths one, it re me of a woman's insides	**E:** (Rpts Ss resp) **S:** It's lik the lower parts, the center is the uterus & there's a tube in there, inside of it, & the pink is down around the vagina and the rear, I dk wht the green is, part of the stomach I guess & the orange is nothing, maybe heartburn **E:** I'm not sur I followed all of tht, the uterus is the center & there's a tube in there and the pink? **S:** It's pink, lik the vagina is pink & the rear is pink, it's all pink there **E:** And U said the orange is hearburn? **S:** I dk, I just said heartburn bec its orange, lik fire, tht's wht hearburn is, all fire in your stomach
X	16. I c 2 littl yellow birds	**E:** (Rpts Ss resp) **S:** One on each side, thyr just sitting there lik on ths limb here, ths brown part **E:** Wht maks them ll birds? **S:** Thy hav tht form, thyr yellow, lik yellow birds

(continued)

Card Response	Inquiry
17. These mite be spiders, blue spiders	**E:** (Rpts Ss resp) **S:** Thy do, thy hav a lotta legs lik spiders, one on each side, I've always hated spiders but I guess u shouldn't hate anythg cuz it will come home to haunt u. I'm not gonna hate spiders anymore, at least I'll try to lik blue ones
18. Ths ll a sad rabbit, he's crying green tears	**E:** (Rpts Ss resp) **S:** His head, it's rite here (D5), but he's cryg, all this green (D4) is his tears, he's really sad
v 19. Ths way is better, it's a lot of flowers, all diff colors, just scattered	**E:** (Rpts Ss resp) **S:** Just a lot of flowers, all diff colors but some r wilting, thyr fading, c the pink one's hav diff shades of pink, & dwn here thes r grey already. It's lik smbody just thru them away

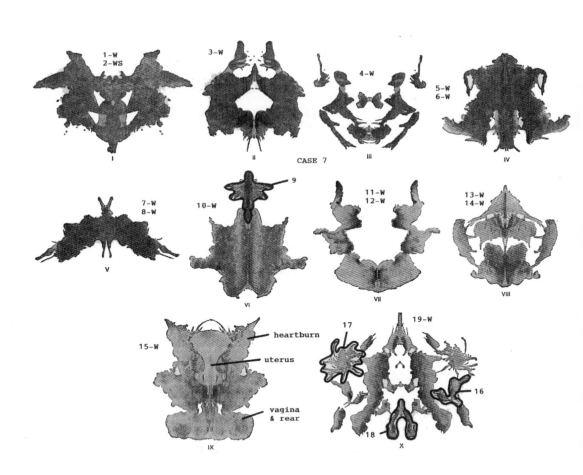

176

Case 7. Sequence of Scores.

Card	No.	Loc.	No.	Determinant(s)	(2)	Content(s)	Pop	Z	Special Scores
I	1	W+	1	FMa–	2	A,Ad		4.0	FAB2,MOR,COP,PHR
	2	WSo	1	FMao		Ad		3.5	AG,ALOG,PHR
II	3	W+	1	FMa.CFo	2	A,Bl		4.5	AG,MOR,PHR
III	4	W+	1	Ma.Cu	2	(H),Bl,Hh	P	5.5	COP,MOR,FAB2,PHR
IV	5	W+	1	FD.FT.FMpo		A,Bt		4.0	
	6	Wo	1	FC'u		(Hd)		2.0	PER,GHR
V	7	Wo	1	FMa.FC'o		A		1.0	
	8	W+	1	Mpo	2	H		2.5	COP,GHR
VI	9	Do	3	FYo		Art,H			DV,GHR
	10	W+	1	FTo		Ad	P	2.5	MOR
VII	11	Wo	1	Fu		An,Ay		2.5	PER
	12	W+	1	Ma.mpo	2	H,Sc	P	2.5	COP,PER,GHR
VIII	13	Wo	1	CF–		An,Bl		4.5	MOR
	14	Wo	1	FCu		Sc		4.5	PER
IX	15	Wo	1	FD.CF.Ma–		An,Hx,Sx		5.5	DR,MOR,PHR
X	16	D+	15	FC.FMpo	2	A,Bt		4.0	
	17	Do	1	FCo	2	A	P		INC,DR
	18	D+	10	Mp.FC–		Ad,Hx,Id		4.0	FAB2,MOR,PHR
	19	Wv/+	1	CF.mp.YF.C'Fo		Bt		5.5	MOR

Case 7. Structural Summary.

Location Features	Determinants Blends	Single	Contents	S-Constellation
				NO . . .FV+VF+V+FD>2
			H = 3	YES . .Col-Shd Bl>0
Zf = 17	FM.CF	M = 1	(H) = 1	NO . . .Ego<.31,>.44
ZSum = 62.5	M.C	FM = 2	Hd = 0	YES . .MOR > 3
ZEst = 56.0	FD.FT.FM	m = 0	(Hd) = 1	YES . .Zd > +−3.5
	FM.FC′	FC = 2	Hx = 2	YES . .es > EA
W = 15	M.m	CF = 1	A = 6	YES . .CF+C > FC
D = 3	FD.CF.M	C = 0	(A) = 0	YES . .X+% < .70
W+D = 18	FM.FC	Cn = 0	Ad = 4	NO . . .S > 3
Dd = 1	M.FC	FC′ = 1	(Ad) = 0	NO . . .P < 3 or > 8
S = 1	CF.m.YF.C′F	C′F = 0	An = 3	NO . . .Pure H < 2
		C′ = 0	Art = 1	NO . . .R < 17
		FT = 1	Ay = 1	6 . . . .TOTAL

DQ			Single	Contents	Special Scores
			TF = 0	Bl = 1		Lv1	Lv2
+ = 8			T = 0	Bt = 3	DV = 1x1	0x2
o = 10			FV = 0	Cg = 0	INC = 1x2	0x4
v/+ = 1			VF = 0	Cl = 0	DR = 2x3	0x6
v = 0			V = 0	Ex = 0	FAB = 0x4	3x7
			FY = 1	Fd = 0	ALOG = 1x5	
			YF = 0	Fi = 0	CON = 0x7	
			Y = 0	Ge = 0	Raw Sum6 = 8	

Form Quality				Single	Contents	Special Scores	
	FQx	MQual	W+D	Fr = 0	Hh = 1	Wgtd Sum6 = 35	
+	= 0	= 0	= 0	rF = 0	Ls = 0		
o	= 11	= 2	= 10	FD = 0	Na = 0	AB = 0	GHR = 4
u	= 4	= 1	= 4	F = 1	Sc = 2	AG = 2	PHR = 6
−	= 4	= 2	= 4		Sx = 1	COP = 4	MOR = 8
none	= 0	= 0	= 0		Xy = 0	CP = 0	PER = 4
				(2) = 7	Id = 1	PSV = 0	

Ratios, Percentages, and Derivations

R = 19	L = 0.06		FC:CF+C = 4:5	COP = 4 AG = 2
			Pure C = 1	GHR:PHR = 4:6
EB = 5:7.5	EA = 12.5	EBPer = 1.5	SumC′:WSumC = 3:7.5	a:p = 7:6
eb = 8:7	es = 15	D = 0	Afr = 0.58	Food = 0
	Adj es = 13	Adj D = 0	S = 1	SumT = 2
			Blends:R = 9:19	Hum Con = 5
FM = 6	C′ = 3	T = 2	CP = 0	Pure H = 3
m = 2	V = 0	Y = 2		PER = 4
				Iso Indx = 0.16

a:p	= 7:6	Sum6 = 8	XA% = 0.79	Zf = 17.0	3r+(2)/R	= 0.37
Ma:Mp	= 3:2	Lv2 = 3	WDA% = 0.78	W:D:Dd = 15:3:1	Fr+rF	= 0
2AB+Art+Ay	= 2	WSum6 = 35	X−% = 0.21	W:M = 15:5	SumV	= 0
MOR	= 8	M− = 2	S− = 0	Zd = +6.5	FD	= 2
		Mnone = 0	P = 4	PSV = 0	An+Xy	= 3
			X+% = 0.58	DQ+ = 8	MOR	= 8
			Xu% = 0.21	DQv = 0	H:(H)Hd(Hd)	= 3:2

PTI = 3	DEPI = 3	CDI = 1	S-CON = 6	HVI = No	OBS = No

S-CON AND KEY VARIABLES

The S-CON value (6) is not significant. The first positive Key variable is the *EB* (5:7.5) indicating that she is extratensive. Thus, the interpretation should begin with a review of the data concerning affect and then proceed to the data regarding self and interpersonal perception. This should be followed by studying the data concerning controls and moving on to a review of the clusters that compose the cognitive triad.

AFFECT

Case 7.   Affect-Related Data for a 23-Year-Old Female.

							Blends	
EB	= 5:7.5			EBPer	= 1.5			
eb	= 8:7	L	= 0.06	FC:CF+C	= 4:5		M.C	= 1
DEPI	= 3	CDI = 1		Pure C	= 1		M.FC	= 1
							M.m	= 1
SumC′ = 3	SumT = 2			SumC′:WSumC	= 3:7.5		FD.CF.M	= 1
SumV = 0	SumY = 2			Afr	= 0.58		FM.CF	= 1
							FM.FC	= 1
Intellect	= 2	CP	= 0	S = 1 (S to I,II,III	= 1)		FM.FC′	= 1
Blends:R	= 9:19			Col-Shad Bl	= 1		FD.FT.FM	= 1
m + y Bl	= 1			Shading Bl	= 1		CF.m.YF.C′F	= 1

In that a question has been raised about a possible affective psychosis, it is somewhat surprising that the DEPI value (3) is not significant. The *EB* (5:7.5) signifies that, usually, she merges her feelings with her thinking during decision making. She is likely to display her feelings openly, and she prefers to test out decisions and rely on feedback as the basic source from which to evaluate their efficacy. The value for *EBPer* suggests that she is not inflexible about the use of this intuitive coping style and, in some circumstances, she may take a more ideational approach in which emotions are pushed aside and possible decisions or behaviors are carefully considered before any action occurs.

The right side *eb* value (7) is not, as might be predicted, greater than the left side value (8), but it is more substantial than usually expected. It suggests that she is experiencing considerable internal emotional aggravation from two main sources. One, signified by the *SumC′* value (3), is related to an excessive internalization of feelings that she would prefer to discharge. On a speculative level, this finding raises a question about whether she has been able to ventilate her grief satisfactorily and whether she feels able to deal with emotions effectively. The second, illustrated by the two texture responses, seems likely to have a direct relation to her marked sense of loss and loneliness, and a corresponding increase in her needs for closeness.

The *Afr* (.58) is slightly lower than expected for an extratensive person, and implies that she may be somewhat uncomfortable about processing emotional stimulation. It is impossible to state with certainty whether this is a long-standing characteristic or has evolved recently as a result of her trauma. In any event, it does not appear to be a liability unless she is having difficulty with her controls or if she is having problems modulating her emotional displays. In this context, the *FC:CF+C* ratio (4:5), which includes one Pure *C* response, suggests that she is prone to be obvious and intense when displaying her feelings. This is not unusual for extratensive people, and is not necessarily a negative finding if she has no significant problems in control. It is of interest, however, because of her previously noted tendency to withhold and internalize feelings, and her possible tendency to avoid emotional stimulation. This composite of findings conveys the notion that she may be having more difficulties handling her feelings than ordinarily might have been the case.

Her single Pure *C* answer (Card III, response 4) of blood has a primitive quality, but it is tempered to some extent because of the greater emphasis on two formed objects (skeleton and pot) in the response. However, it is also a response that includes notable cognitive slippage and may signify that she is having some difficulties managing her emotions. This is not surprising in light of her traumatic experience and her recent psychotic behaviors, but it raises a question about the integrity of her controls.

Nine of her nineteen answers (47%) are blend responses, a higher proportion than expected from most extratensives. It denotes that her psychology is marked by substantial complexity. Only one of her nine blends (*M.m*) can be attributed to situational factors with certainty, but it seems important to note that two of the nine contain three determinants (*FD.FT.FM* and *FD.CF.M*), and a third contains four determinants (*CF.mp.YF.C'F*). The first of these three contains one of her two texture answers and the third contains two variables that are situationally related. Thus, it seems reasonable to suggest that her present circumstance has contributed significantly to her concurrent level of unusual complexity, which might have a negative impact on her ability to control her feelings. Also, her four-variable blend includes both color and shading and is also a shading blend. It connotes a sense of confusion about her feelings and the presence of intense pain that probably is situationally related.

Overall, there are indications of affective disarray and irritation. This is probably disruptive for her as she relies extensively on her feelings during decision making. She is experiencing considerable emotional discomfort that results from the internalization of feelings plus a strong need for closeness or experience of loneliness that is probably the result of her recent tragedy. She may be more prone than has been the case in the past to avoid processing emotions or being in emotionally loaded situations, and she seems burdened by considerable complexity that includes some confusion about her feelings and substantial pain, much or all of which is probably situationally related.

Some of the interpretive postulates derived from the affect-related data (*SumC'*, *Afr*, *FC:CF+C* ratio, her pure *C* response, and the findings concerning blends) have raised issues about the integrity of her controls. In that context, it seems reasonable to deviate from the planned interpretation strategy and review the data concerning controls before moving on to the clusters concerning self and interpersonal perception.

CONTROLS

Case 7.   Control-Related Variables for a 23-Year-Old Female.

EB = 5:7.5	EA = 12.5		D = 0	CDI = 1
eb = 8:7	es = 15	Adj es = 13	AdjD = 0	L = 0.06
FM = 6 m = 2	SumC' = 3	SumT = 2	SumV = 0	SumY = 2

The D Score and Adj D Score are both zero, indicating that her capacity for control and tolerance for stress are similar to that of most people. This finding, despite the high value for *es* (15), indicates she is experiencing considerably more internally irritating demands than are typical. Apparently, as indicated by the *EA* value (12.5), she has access to substantial resources and is able to tolerate these demands without being thrown into overload. However, some caution seems warranted about casually accepting that conclusion in the context of the D Score.

The D Score of zero, derived from the difference between the *EA* and *es,* is −2.5. If the *EA* had been 0.5 lower or the *es* 1.0 higher, the D Score would be −1. Although all the codings related to *EA* and *es* are technically correct, one answer, coded as *M,* may be equivocal. It is response 15, to Card IX, scored as *M* for her inquiry comment, ". . . and the orange is nothing, maybe heartburn." Two questions later, the examiner asked, "And you said the orange *is* heartburn," to which she replied, "I don't know, I just said heartburn because it's orange, like fire, that's what heartburn is, all fire in your stomach."

The question is whether the examiner's use of the word *is,* rather than the subject's word *maybe,* forced the agreement, or whether she would have reaffirmed the area as heartburn if the correct wording had been used? For instance, had she replied, "I really don't know, I wasn't thinking that when I first looked, I suppose it could be," the *M* might not have been coded. In such an event, the *EA* value would be 11.5, yielding an *EA–Adj es* difference of 2.0 and an Adj D Score of zero, but the *EA–es* difference would be −3.5, which equates with a D Score of −1.

In light of this speculative review of the *EA* and *es* data, conclusions regarding her capacity for control should be framed cautiously. It seems reasonable to propose that, ordinarily, her capacity for control and tolerance for stress are similar to most people. Currently, however, her capacity for control seems fragile, and the potential exists for a loss of control if even a modest increase occurs in the level of stress that she is experiencing.

This proposition is not only supported by the *EA–es* difference of −2.5 (or possibly −3.5), but also by several features that contribute to the unusually high *es* value (15). The left side *eb* value (8) consists mainly of six *FM*s and two *m*s. The former suggests that she has a higher level of ungratified need experiences than expected, and they are promoting more peripheral or subconscious patterns of ideation than is customary. The latter relates to current feelings of stress and helplessness, which also promotes ideational activity outside the focus of attention. Collectively, these ideational experiences often create seemingly random thoughts that tend to interfere with directed patterns of thinking and impact negatively on attention and concentration. The right side *eb* value (7) was discussed earlier. It was noted that she seems to be holding in unpleasant emotions and also is experiencing some painful feelings that apparently relate to her sense of loss and corresponding experience of loneliness.

If any of these negative aspects of her psychology intensify, an overload state and the sort of disorganization associated with it can easily occur. It seems very possible that her fragile capacity for control is related to her recent episode of psychotic behavior, but that postulate cannot be addressed adequately until all the data from the protocol have been reviewed.

SELF-PERCEPTION

Case 7.   Self-Perception Related Data for a 23-Year-Old Female.

R = 19	OBS = No	HVI = No	**Human Content, Hx, An & Xy Responses**
			III 4. W+ Ma.Cu 2 (H),Bl,Hh P 5.5 COP,MOR,FAB2,PHR
Fr+rF = 0	3r+(2)/R = 0.37		IV 6. Wo FCxu (Hd) 2.0 PER,GHR
			V 8. W+ Mpo 2 H 2.5 COP,GHR
FD = 2	SumV = 0		VI 9. Do FYo Art,H DV,GHR
			VII 11. Wo Fu An,Ay 2.5 PER
An+Xy = 3	MOR = 8		VII 12. W+ Ma.mpo 2 H,Sc P 2.5 COP,PER,GHR
			VIII 13. Wo CF− An,Bl 4.5 MOR
H:(H)+Hd+(Hd) = 2:3			IX 15. Wo FD.CF.Ma− An,Hx,Sx 5.5 DR,MOR,PHR
[EB = 5:7.5]			X 18. D+ Mp.FC− Ad,Hx,Id 4.0 FAB2,MOR,PHR

The Egocentricity Index (0.37) suggests that she is no more or less concerned with herself than are most people. The two *FD* answers imply that she engages in self-examination somewhat routinely, but not excessively. The value for *An+Xy* (3) is higher than expected and indicates some unusual body or self-image concerns. Two of the three *An* answers are coded *FQ*–, and both are MOR responses, implying considerable rumination about these issues and intimating a marked sense of vulnerability. This may be a chronic feature, but it seems equally plausible that it may have evolved more recently as a result of her trauma experience. Some clarification about this may occur when the verbiage of the responses is reviewed.

Another negative finding concerns the extraordinarily large number of MOR responses (8). MOR is a relatively stable variable over time, mainly because most people give protocols in which the MOR value is zero, one, or two. Values greater than two are more frequent among people who perceive themselves negatively but, even among that group, values greater than five are uncommon and values greater than six are rare. In this case, the high value appears to represent some very negative conceptualizations about herself, as well as a strong sense of pessimism, helplessness, or possibly even hopelessness. The magnitude of the MOR value, considered in light of her pretrauma history, makes it unlikely that this is a chronic feature. Instead, it has probably evolved from the trauma that she has experienced and her inability to contend with it. This feature should be critically important in any planning for intervention.

A more positive finding is that the number of responses containing human contents (5) is in the expected range for an extratensive person, and the number of Pure *H* contents (3) represents more than half of the human content answers. This finding implies that her self-image probably has developed primarily as the result of social interactions. The *FQ* codings for the three Pure *H* responses are all ordinary, suggesting that the core elements of her self-image are likely to have a favorable reality basis.

Her four minus responses include two of her three *An* answers and all four are coded as MOR. They consist of (Card I, response 1) "two birds flying off with a carcass"; (Card VIII, response 13) "Something's been tore apart, it's just insides like a carcass . . . remains of some poor animal . . . part is decayed"; (Card IX, response 15) "a woman's insides . . . the pink is down around the vagina and the rear . . . the orange is nothing, maybe heartburn"; and (Card X, response 18) "a sad rabbit, he's crying green tears . . . he's really sad." Collectively, they seem to highlight the devastating effects that she has experienced and her preoccupation with them.

The characteristics of her remaining four MOR responses seem commensurate with that postulate. They include (Card II, response 3) "animals fighting and they're both hurt pretty bad . . . they've got blood all over. . . . I don't think either one will live,"; (Card III, response 4) "a couple of skeletons dancing around some pot, like they killed something . . . they're cooking some poor animal that they killed, see all the blood around them"; (Card VI, response 10) "a cat that got run over by a car or truck . . . just a furry mess,"; and (Card X, response 19) "a lot of flowers . . . just scattered . . . but some are wilting, they're fading . . . like somebody just threw them away." Six of the eight MOR responses are marked by death or decay, and the remaining two are both human experience (*Hx*) answers, heartburn and sadness. The projections in these responses portray a damaged, tormented, and helpless sense of self that seems directly related to her husband's condition. He is brain-dead and decaying, and she is torn apart by the experience. Although there is no clear evidence regarding feelings of guilt, some of her torment and negative view of herself may have evolved from her recent decision to abrogate decision making about her husband's life support or from a series of "if" questions that people invariably ask when a tragedy occurs (if we had taken a taxi, if we had let a friend drive us, if I had been driving, etc.).

While three of her *M* responses are included in the eight MOR answers (skeletons cooking some poor animal, heartburn, and sad rabbit), the remaining two offer more favorable connotations regarding her self-image. They include (Card V, response 8) "two people too, they've fallen asleep, leaning on each other," and (Card VII, response 12) "two little girls going up and down on a teeter-totter . . . it's happy times, they're playing together . . . I used to love to do that with my friends . . . you just didn't have any cares, just fun." There are two other human content answers that have not been included in the review of the minus, MOR, and *M* responses. Neither is very positive. The first (Card IV, response 6) is "one of those Darth Vader masks." In *Star Wars,* Darth Vader represents the adversarial dark side. The second (Card VI, response 9) is, "a crucifix, a medal like you wear . . . showing Christ's body . . . all dark like that, imprinted on the cross." It has both positive and negative implications.

Two of the six *FM* responses (birds flying off with a carcass; animals fighting, hurt badly) have already been reviewed as they are MOR answers. A third *FM* answer (Card I, response 2) is intriguing because of its aggressive or angry feature, "a wolf . . . it has big ears and the eyes and the mouth is curled up like it's wolves growling, wolves are always growling." This could relate to being examined, or it may reflect a more broadly based sense of anger or aggressiveness. One of the remaining three *FM* responses (Card IV, response 5) is common, but interesting because of her articulations, "That's ugly, some kind of monster, maybe a gorilla. . . . It's big, huge, like I'm laying under it looking up . . . all fur with a little head . . . sitting on something." It may connote a sense of fragility (laying under it) and her strong feelings of loneliness (all fur with a little head). Fragility also seems implied in another *FM* answer (Card V, response 7) "a moth trying to keep away from the flame . . . like they do when they're too close to a light or a flame." The final *FM* response (Card X, response 16), "two little yellow birds . . . just sitting there like on this limb," is passive. Both answers that include inanimate movement codings have been discussed previously. The first (Card VII, response 12) denotes "hair flying up" in relation to the positive teeter-totter response. The second (Card X, response 19) is more ominous, referring to the wilting flowers.

There are two other answers that have not been reviewed. The first (Card VIII, response 14) is "a top, yes, a kid's top." It is given with the card inverted, following a minus-MOR answer (carcass decayed) and is positive in the sense of recovery from a mediational dysfunction, but not necessarily positive in the context of self-concept. The second (Card X, response 17) is intriguing because of the embellishment, "blue spiders. . . . I've always hated spiders but I guess you shouldn't hate anything cuz it will come home to haunt you, I'm not going to hate spiders anymore . . ." It implies a sense of guilt.

A firm and reliable characterization of the basic self-image of this woman is difficult to generate because so much of the current picture appears to have been sharply impacted by the ongoing tragedy that she is experiencing. It seems likely that, historically, she has been no more or less concerned with herself than most people and that her self-value has been similar to that found among most adults. She is prone to engage in self-examination somewhat routinely, but not excessively, and it appears probable that the core of her self-concept has evolved realistically from her social experiences. However, she has some substantial somatic concerns that appear to convey a marked sense of vulnerability. It is unlikely that this is a chronic preoccupation. Instead, it is probably related to her recent physical injury or a preoccupation with her husband's current status.

In that same context, she has negative feelings about herself, as well as a strong sense of damage. Both appear to be situationally provoked. In effect, she now conveys a tormented, fragile, possibly guilt ridden, and miserable sense of self, apparently produced by a preoccupation with her recent tragedy and its devastating effects on her.

INTERPERSONAL PERCEPTION

Case 7.   Interpersonal Perception Data for a 23-Year-Old Female.

R = 19	CDI = 1	HVI = No	**COP & AG Responses**
a:p = 7:6	SumT = 2	Fd = 0	I 1. W+ FMa– 2 A,Ad 4.0 FAB2,MOR,COP,PHR
	[eb = 8:7]		I 2. WSo FMao Ad 3.5 AG,ALOG,PHR
Sum Human Contents = 5		H = 3	II 3. W+ FMa.CFo 2 A,Bl 4.5 AG,MOR,PHR
[Style = Extratensive]			V 8. W+ Mpo 2 H 2.5 COP,GHR
GHR:PHR = 4:6			VII 12. W+ Ma.mpo 2 H,Sc P 2.5 COP,PER,GHR
COP = 4	AG = 2	PER = 4	
Isolation Indx = 0.16			

The elevation in *SumT* (2) is the first significant feature in this cluster. As mentioned, it implies that she is a needy, lonely person who is struggling with the consequences of her loss. While this is almost certain to be a situation-related phenomenon, it is likely to have an impact on her current and future interpersonal behaviors. The presence of five human contents suggests that she is interested in people, and the fact that three of the five are coded *H* implies that she probably conceptualizes others in a reality-based manner. The GHR:PHR ratio (4:6) indicates that she is likely to engage in interpersonal behaviors that are less adaptive for the situation than might be desired. However, an inspection of the *GHR* and *PHR* responses suggests that proposition requires an amendment. The *GHR* value is created from the codings for four of her five human content answers (responses 6, 8, 9, & 12), while the higher *PHR* value is created by composite of one of her five human content answers (response 4) and five anatomy or animal content answers (responses 1, 2, 3, 15, & 18) that include *AG* or MOR special scores. It has been noted that most, or all, of the *PHR* answers have some situational relationship.

Thus, her current interpersonal behaviors may be less adaptive than desirable, but it seems equally likely that her pretragedy behaviors were much more adaptive. This proposition seems supported by the four COP responses in her record. They denote that others probably regard her as likable and gregarious. She seems to anticipate that most of her exchanges will be positive, and she usually strives to create and maintain harmonious relationships.

The elevation in PER responses (4) indicates that she tends to be defensive with others. It seems unlikely that this is a chronic feature. Instead, it is probably a situationally developed tactic that helps her contend with the bad feelings she has about herself and helps defend against her sense of vulnerability.

There are three *M* and three *FM* responses that are coded for a pair. They represent a mixture of both favorable and unfavorable connotations about interpersonal perceptions and behaviors. The three *M*s are all coded COP, but one of the three is very unrealistic (skeletons dancing around some pot, like they killed something). Two of the three *FM* answers with a pair are coded MOR (birds flying off with a carcass; animals are fighting and they're both hurt pretty bad), while the third is a passive answer (yellow birds sitting on a limb). The composite of the six answers implies that her current interpersonal perceptions and behaviors are often less adaptive and possibly marked by some pathological features.

It seems reasonable to speculate that, in the past, her interpersonal behaviors have usually been adaptive and effective. Others have probably regarded her as likable and gregarious, but the recent trauma she has experienced is undoubtedly affecting her interpersonal perceptions and behaviors. She tends to be more defensive and pessimistic about relationships and may harbor a sense of hopelessness about her contacts with others.

PROCESSING

Case 7.   Processing Variables for a 23-Year-Old Female.

EB = 5:7.5	Zf = 17	Zd = +6.5	DQ+ = 8
L = 0.06	W:D:Dd = 15:3:1	PSV = 0	DQv/+ = 1
HVI = NO	W:M = 15:5		DQv = 0
OBS = NO			

Location & DQ Sequencing

I: W+.WSo	VI: Ddo.Wo
II: W+	VII: Wo.W+
III: W	VIII: Wo.Wo
IV: W+.Wo	IX: Wo
V: Wo.W+	X: D+.Do.D+.Wv/+

The very low *Lambda* value (0.06) indicates that she becomes overly immersed in stimulus complexity. It represents a failure to economize while processing new information. This can result from an overincorporative processing style but, more often, it is produced because of some disorganization in thinking or the unusual influence of broadly pervasive emotions. When the latter is true, it becomes a liability because overinvolvement creates more demands on cognitive activity that, in turn, can provoke more complexity in emotion.

Her failure to economize is also reflected in her processing effort. The high *Zf* (17) and the disproportionate relationship in the *W:D:Dd* ratio (15:3:1) signify a commendable but demanding effort. A review of the location sequencing illustrates this. Fourteen of her first fifteen answers, to Cards I through IX, are *W*. The single exception is a *Dd* response given as the first answer to Card VI. It is a response that mainly involves the *D3* area, but she extends a small bit into the *D1* area to be more precise. Her *D* responses are the first three answers to Card X, followed by another *W* answer. Patterns such as this seem to be obsessive, especially when they include several *FQ+* responses. However, when not marked by *FQ+* answers, they are more likely to represent individuals driven by a great deal of complexity in their psychology.

Some of this striving may be more long-standing than situationally provoked. The value for the *Zd* score (+6.5) confirms an overincorporative style that usually is a traitlike feature involving the investment of considerable energy into scanning activities. Likewise, the quality of her processing seems respectable, as indicated by the eight *DQ+* answers. Thus, it is not unreasonable to suspect that her preexisting orientation to process thoroughly may have been exacerbated by her current confusion, but it has not been impaired.

Overall, she seems to become overly involved in her efforts to process stimuli, investing more energy than most people to ensure that all aspects of a field are processed. This style can be effective if there are no significant problems in mediation or ideation, but if such problems exist, the overinvolvement in processing can tend to increase the levels of dysfunction.

MEDIATION

Case 7.   Mediation Variables for a 23-Year-Old Female.

R = 19		L = 0.06		OBS = No	**Minus & NoForm Features**
FQx+	= 0		XA%	= .79	I 1. W+ FMa– 2 A, Ad 4.0 FAB2,MOR,COP,PHR
FQxo	= 11		WDA%	= .78	VIII 13. Wo CF– An,Bl 4.5 MOR
FQxu	= 4		X–%	= .21	IX 15. Wo FD.CF.Ma– An,Hx,Sx 5.5 DR,MOR,PHR
FQx–	= 4		S–	= 0	X 18. D+ Mp.FC– Ad,Hx,Id 4.0 FAB2,MOR,PHR
FQxnone	= 0				
(W+D	= 18)		P	= 4	
WD+	= 0		X+%	= .58	
WDo	= 10		Xu%	= .21	
WDu	= 4				
WD–	= 4				
WDnone	= 0				

The *XA%* (.79) and *WDA%* (.78) indicate that, usually, her translations of information are appropriate for the situation. This is a favorable finding because it implies that the basic elements necessary for adequate reality testing have not been significantly impaired. On the other hand, the value for the *X–%* (.21) is higher than desirable and indicates that there may be a pervasive tendency toward some sort of mediational dysfunction.

In the referral, issues of an affective psychosis or a latent schizophreniform disturbance were raised. Two elements concerning form quality seem to make the likelihood of a schizophreniform disturbance very low. First, the sequence of the minus answers shows that first is response 1, followed by a series of 11 answers across seven cards in which no distortions occur. In fact, 8 of the 11 have *ordinary* form quality. Such a sequence is highly unusual in a schizophreniform record. Second, as noted, all four of her minus responses include MOR content, and two of the four include *An* content, representing her pessimistic sense of vulnerability and damage to her self-image. In addition, two of the four minus answers are coded *Hx* (heartburn and sad rabbit, crying green tears). *Hx* responses usually reflect attempts to deal with self-image issues in an unrealistic, intellectualized manner that tends to ignore reality.

Also, although the levels of distortion represented in two of her minus answers are considerable (Card I—the carcass of a cow; Card IX—a woman's insides), in at least three of the four minus answers, the response becomes minus because of something that is added to an otherwise *ordinary* answer. In response 1, the major features are two birds, the carcass creates the minus. In response 13, the minus occurs only because specific organs or parts were identified, and in response 18, the major element is the head of a rabbit. It is the addition of tears that causes the minus to be assigned. This seems to highlight her preoccupation and the devastating effects that it is having.

The lower than average number of Popular responses (4) indicates that she is less likely than others to make conventional responses, even when cues concerning the obvious are readily apparent. Likewise, the low $X+\%$ (.58) indicates that the tendency to make less conventional translations of stimuli is pervasive, regardless of whether obvious cues are present. However, the value for the $Xu\%$ (.21) is not higher than expected. It seems probable that the main reason for the low $X+\%$ is the higher than expected frequency of minus answers.

Thus, while many of her pretrauma behaviors may have been more idiosyncratic than is typical for most adults, that proposition cannot be supported firmly by the data. Obviously, she is having difficulties in mediation that, at times, are serious and set the stage for maladaptive behaviors. However, it seems improbable that these difficulties are chronic. It seems much more likely that they can be attributed to the extensive affective, and probably ideational, disarray that she is experiencing.

IDEATION

Case 7.   Ideation Variables for a 23-Year-Old Female.

L	= 0.06	OBS	= No	HVI	= No	**Critical Special Scores**		
						DV	= 1	DV2 = 0
EB	= 5:7.5	EBPer	= 1.5	a:p	= 7:6	INC	= 1	INC2 = 0
				Ma:Mp	= 3:2	DR	= 2	DR2 = 0
eb	= 8:7	[FM = 6 m = 2]				FAB	= 0	FAB2 = 3
				M–	= 2	ALOG	= 1	CON = 0
Intell Indx	= 2	MOR	= 8	Mnone	= 0	Sum6	= 8	WSum6 = 29
							(R = 19)	

M Response Features

    III   4. W+ Ma.Cu 2 (H),Bl,Hh P 5.5 COP,MOR,FAB2,PHR
     V   8. W+ Mpo 2 H 2.5 COP,GHR
    VII 12. W+ Ma.mpo 2 H,Sc P 2.5 COP,PER,GHR
     IX 15. Wo FD.CF.Ma– An,Hx,Sx 5.5 DR,MOR,PHR
     X   18. D+ Mp.FC– Ad,Hx,Id 4.0 FAB2,MOR,PHR

As noted in the study of findings concerning affect, the *EB* (5:7.5) reveals that she is an intuitive person who usually permits her feelings to influence her decisions and who also relies extensively on feedback from her actions. She is not inflexible about this approach, however; and as indicated by the *EBPer* value (1.5), she can push emotion to a peripheral level and rely more on an internal evaluation of various alternatives before forming behaviors when that is appropriate. When thinking is reasonably clear, this form of coping and decision making can be quite effective, but several elements indicate that is currently not the case.

The eight MOR responses signal that a pessimistic set pervades much of her thinking. It causes her to conceptualize herself and her world with a sense of doubt and discouragement. It promotes a tendency to anticipate negative outcomes, regardless of her actions, and it can easily induce her to misread stimuli. This set can often create concrete thinking that tends to disregard flawed logic.

It represents a significant potential for impairment to the quality of the conceptualizing and can easily breed disorganized thinking.

Additionally, the left side *eb* value (8) suggests that her ideational world is marked by more peripheral, potentially distracting thought than is common for most people. This is being created by a composite of unmet needs, some of which are probably situation related, and by a noticeable sense of helplessness. A third, and possibly most serious problem in her thinking, is indicated by the values for *Sum6* (8) and *WSum6* (35). They imply that her thinking tends to be disorganized, inconsistent, and marked by faulty judgment. When the conceptualization process is impaired at this level, reality testing usually is marginal.

Three of the eight critical special scores are coded as FABCOM2, signifying that, at times, she makes some irrational and bizarre associations (birds flying off with the carcass of a cow or horse; skeletons dancing around a pot; a sad rabbit crying green tears). In a similar vein, her single ALOG response (it must be a wolf . . . wolves are always growling that's why I said a wolf) intimates that her judgment often becomes more concrete than should be the case. Two of her answers are coded *M*−, and the contents of those responses (heartburn; a sad rabbit crying green tears) hint that at least some of her peculiar thinking may be related to the considerable emotional pain that she is experiencing. Despite the apparent bizarreness that marks her thinking, the quality of human movement answers suggests that her ideation is reasonably sophisticated at times (skeletons dancing around a pot; people fallen asleep leaning on each other; little girls going up and down on a teeter-totter).

Four of the seven responses coded for critical special scores, including the three FABCOM2 codings, also contain MOR coding. This denotes that her strange and sometimes concrete thinking is likely to be trauma related. This notion seems supported by the fact that there are no reports in the history to suggest that her pretrauma thinking was strange or bizarre.

SUMMARY

Unquestionably, this young woman is in a great deal of disarray. She is burdened by painful feelings that she cannot handle easily, and they are a constant source of irritation. This creates much confusion for her, as she usually relies on her feelings as an important input when making judgments or decisions.

Her emotional disruption has had a broad impact on her psychology, affecting her sense of self and others, her thinking, and her reality testing. The magnitude of her disarray is emphasized when the Ego Impairment Index is calculated. It is 2.893, which falls well into the range suggested by Viglione et al. (2003) as indicating significant disorganization.

It seems likely that, historically, she has been a resourceful and likable person who has been reasonably confident about herself, conscientious in her efforts, and adaptive in her relations with others. However, the trauma that she is experiencing has extracted a high toll on her assets. Not only is she emotionally confused, but her controls have become marginal, and her self-image is marked by notable feelings of vulnerability, a strong sense of pessimism and helplessness, and possibly even feelings of hopelessness. Her logic is often strained and her thinking sometimes becomes disorganized and bizarre.

Many of the favorable core features of her personality continue to exist. Although she sometimes becomes overly involved when dealing with new information, she continues to process new inputs reasonably well and, typically, is able to translate information appropriately using reasonably sophisticated forms of conceptualizing. However, the burdens of loss, loneliness, and probable guilt that she is experiencing cause much more complexity in her psychology than she can handle easily, and this often clouds her reality testing and leads to considerable dysfunction.

There is no evidence to suggest that this is a long-standing condition. On the contrary, many findings suggest a direct relation to her ongoing trauma. She is preoccupied and easily distracted, and this often promotes a view of herself and her world through a distorted psychological lens. The end product is a woman in misery and torment.

RECOMMENDATIONS

There are no findings to support the notion of a schizophreniform disturbance. When considered in light of the history, the findings strongly suggest a reactive psychosis that has not fully subsided. It would be unreasonable to describe her as a posttraumatic stress psychosis because the trauma continues. Her husband remains on life support and no closure has occurred for her. In fact, her considerable distress, her marked sense of pessimism and vulnerability, and her periodic episodes of strange thinking all have some relation to this fact, plus whatever guilt she may have accumulated since the onset of the tragedy.

She has tried to return to work and, according to father, has "held up well" since the accident, but it seems likely that this has been a facade designed to conceal the torment inside. Her parents also report that she has grieved "intensively," but it seem obvious that it has not been sufficient to relieve the considerable distress that she has experienced.

She needs considerable assistance to deal more directly with her guilt and grief. Some decision should soon be forthcoming about the life support for her husband. This is crucial to help her experience closure and set the stage from which supportive psychotherapy can begin to provide direction for the decisions she must make in reconstructing her life. Continued hospitalization seems warranted until some sense of closure can be experienced. However, hospitalization should not be prolonged as it risks exacerbating her pessimistic state and adding to her already excessive confusion. Optimally, it will be for a brief period during which a posthospitalization support structure can be defined and organized. This should include planning for an indefinite period of outpatient care designed primarily to provide support as she strives to reconstitute from her current state of disarray.

EPILOGUE

The patient remained hospitalized for an additional 10 days following the psychological evaluation. During that time, which included daily individual therapy, her improvement was marked. Two days prior to being discharged she met with the neurologist who had been monitoring her husband's condition, and plans were formulated to remove him from life support during the first two weeks after she returned home. She was present at that event and at his funeral three days later.

Following her discharge from the hospital, she continued in individual treatment twice weekly for three months and once weekly for an additional three months. Her therapist reported that she was able to contend with her feelings about the accident and her husband's death reasonably well during this time. She returned to work two weeks after her husband's funeral. A second round of psychological tests was administered at the end of six months at the request of her therapist. The second Rorschach showed remarkable improvement and was essentially free of any indices of pathology. An elevated *SumT* persisted, and some of the findings suggested a sense of cautiousness about social relationships, but otherwise the findings were similar to those of a well-adjusted non-patient. Following the retest, she and the therapist agreed to continue with weekly visits for at least three months.

REFERENCES

Adrian, C., & Kaser-Boyd, N. (1995). The Rorschach Ego Impairment Index in heterogeneous psychiatric patients. *Journal of Personality Assessment, 65*(3), 408–414.

American Psychiatric Association. (2000). *Diagnostic and statistical manual of mental disorders* (4th ed., text rev.). Washington, DC: Author.

Beres, D. (1956). Ego deviation and the concept of schizophrenia. *Psychoanalytic Study of the Child, 11*, 164–235.

Levander, S., & Werbart, A. (2003). Different views of a psychotic breakdown: Complementary perspectives of a bewildering experience. *Psychoanalytic Psychotherapy, 17*(2), 163–174.

Levy, S., McGlashan, T., & Carpenter, W. (1975). Integration and sealing-over as recovery styles from acute psychosis. *Journal of Nervous and Mental Diseases, 161*, 307–312.

McGlashan, T., Docherty, J., & Siris, S. (1976). Integrative and sealing-over recoveries from schizophrenia: Distinguishing case studies. *Psychiatry, 39*, 325–338.

McGlashan, T., Levy, S., & Carpenter, W. (1975). Integration and sealing-over: Clinically distinct recovery styles from schizophrenia. *Archives of General Psychiatry, 32*, 1269–1272.

Perry, W., McDougall, A., & Viglione, D. J. (1995). A five-year follow-up on the temporal stability of the Ego Impairment Index. *Journal of Personality Assessment, 64*(1), 112–118.

Perry, W., Minassian, A., Cadenhead, K., Sprock, J., & Braff, D. (2003). The use of the Ego Impairment Index across the schizophrenia spectrum. *Journal of Personality Assessment, 80*(1), 50–57.

Perry, W., & Viglione, D. J. (1991). The Ego Impairment Index as a predictor of outcome in melancholic depressed patients treated with tricyclic antidepressants. *Journal of Personality Assessment, 56*(3), 487–501.

Perry, W., Viglione, D. J., & Braff, D. (1992). The Ego Impairment Index and schizophrenia: A validation study. *Journal of Personality Assessment, 59*(1), 165–175.

Viglione, D. J., Perry, W., & Meyer, G. (2003). Refinements in the Rorschach Ego Impairment Index incorporating the Human Representational variable. *Journal of Personality Assessment, 81*(2), 149–156.

CHAPTER 10

An Evaluation Related to Substance Abuse

———————————————— C A S E 8 ————————————————

This 24-year-old man was evaluated in conjunction with his entry into a substance abuse program. He had been using cocaine almost daily for 18 to 24 months. Recently, on a weekend, he had an episode of serious disorientation that lasted several hours. According to his girlfriend, he was alternately violent and suicidal, striking her several times and threatening her with a knife. Subsequently, he became very tearful and apologetic and sat on a window ledge for about 45 minutes threatening to jump. She called his brother who was able to subdue him and took him to an emergency room. He was admitted overnight, sedated, and the next morning signed himself out and returned home. He found his girlfriend packing to move out and she says that he pleaded with her to stay. She agreed, with the proviso that he seek help. She has agreed to enter treatment with him.

He is the younger of two sons, having a brother, age 26, who is a certified public accountant. His father, age 48, is also a certified public accountant and owns his own small firm. His mother, age 48, is a college graduate and has taught elementary school for the past five years. She did not finish her degree until the patient had graduated from high school, although she had completed two years of college before her older son was born. There is no reported psychiatric history in the immediate family.

The patient graduated from college at age 21, having majored in business administration. He reports that his grades were, "a bit above average. I could have done better if I worked at it, but I wasn't very interested." Since graduation, he has been employed as an industrial salesman for a chemical firm that manufactures solvents. His work history is reported to be good and he has received three salary increases during his three years of employment, plus a bonus during the past year. He says that he enjoys his work and expects to become an assistant sales manager in the near future. He has asked for and received a one-month unpaid leave of absence to enter treatment.

He reports an unremarkable developmental history and has been free of serious injuries or illnesses. He states that he was close to both parents and especially close to his brother, with whom he shared a bedroom until age nine. They enjoyed playing baseball together in Little League and in high school. They also were both active in the Boy Scouts during their teen years. He states that he had many high school and college friends and was in a fraternity in college.

His brother reports that they see each other three or four times a month but denies any awareness of the patient's drug involvement, "I know he got into it in college, but I thought that was all over." He describes the patient as, "A pretty easygoing guy. He really doesn't work up to his potential. He could do a lot more if he tried." The brother also tends to blame the girlfriend for the drug involvement, "I don't know her well, but I don't really like her. She seems like a loser to me, and I'll bet she's been using a lot longer than he has. He could do a lot better if he got rid of her."

The patient reports that his first sexual experience occurred when he was age 15. He denies any homosexual experiences. He says that he became serious about one girl during his sophomore year in college, but she broke up with him before the end of that year. He met his current girlfriend about 18 months ago at a party given by a mutual friend. They dated regularly for about eight months and, when the lease on her apartment expired, they decided to live together in his apartment. He states that she has raised the possibility of marriage but says, "I'm not ready for something like that yet." He notes that their sexual relationship is, "not always good," but attributes this to his cocaine addiction. She has reported that he has frequently been impotent and sometimes has ejaculated prematurely. She also notes that he often asks her to dress and dance in "see through" underwear to stimulate him.

He says that he became casually involved with cocaine during his senior year in college, although he has been using marijuana since high school and experimented with other drugs during his college years. He reports that he found cocaine helpful in dealing with the pressures of his job and ultimately began using it almost every day. He says that he usually did not use it during the day, except during the past month, but did use it in the evenings at home. He says that he also drinks one or two glasses of wine daily. He states that he had never before experienced disorientation while using drugs and that the recent episode has frightened him, "I never want that to happen again. I've really got to get away from this stuff."

He is described as an athletic looking, attractive, and neatly dressed young man. During the initial interview, he often asked that questions be repeated, but when responding he seemed open and cooperative. He was especially cautious in describing his feelings for his girlfriend and hesitant about the possibility that she might also enter treatment: "She's just great, I don't know how she's put up with me. She really deserves better. She probably should get dried out, too, but I don't think we should be joined at the hip right now. I hope everything works out for her, I owe her a lot." If his girlfriend enters treatment, she would not go through the inpatient routine but, instead, would begin an eight-week outpatient sequence of individual and group sessions.

The treatment program that he is entering requires a minimum 14-day inpatient stay followed by a minimum six-week outpatient treatment consisting of one individual session and one group session per week. Drug screening prior to the evaluation was positive, but levels were not toxic. Neuropsychology screening was essentially negative.

The assessment issues are as follows: (1) Is there any serious psychiatric disturbance? (2) How well will he respond to a highly structured inpatient program? (3) What is the prognosis for completing the outpatient treatment? (4) Are there any specific recommendations for focus in individual treatment?

CASE FORMULATION AND RELEVANT LITERATURE

Although this young man's drug history extends back several years, the recent episode of violent and suicidal disorientation now substantiates the seriousness of his addiction problem. He has arranged to take a month off work and has agreed to enter an intensive inpatient program followed by individual and group outpatient sessions. The Rorschach literature specific to cocaine abuse is relatively limited, but a review can alert the psychologist to concerns associated with serious abuse.

Because the overall dropout rate for substance abuse programs is at least 50% (Baekeland & Lundwall, 1975), staff members are understandably concerned about this man's ability to handle the structured inpatient routine and to continue through outpatient treatment. A substantial Rorschach literature about continuation versus premature termination in mental health services has evolved, and its review will be helpful in providing consultation about how best to ensure effective treatment.

Assessment of Cocaine Addiction

Dougherty and Lesswing (1989) evaluated 100 inpatient cocaine abusers and found Rorschach indicators associated with narcissism, anger, and oppositionalism as well as difficulties with reality testing and cognitive slippage. Although there were suggestions of reactive distress, the authors note that the Rorschach findings were not suggestive of more chronic dysphoric or depressive difficulties. They conclude that the patients in their sample were not using cocaine to self-medicate a primary affective disorder.

In a related study, Lesswing and Dougherty (1993) compared 99 cocaine-dependent inpatients with 94 alcoholic inpatients in a chemical dependency program. Interestingly, 85% of the cocaine-dependent patients also abused other substances, contrasted with only 18% for the alcohol-dependent individuals. Rorschach comparisons indicated that the alcohol-dependent group had ". . . longer Rorschachs, clearer reality testing operations, and better controlled emotionality" (p. 56). The authors suggest that the cocaine-dependent patients' combination of polysubstance abuse and poorer cognitive and emotional control increases the likelihood of relapse.

A few other Rorschach studies also describe the potential damage associated with hard-core substance abuse. Cipolli and Galliani (1990) compared 25 short-term (1–3 years) with 25 long-term (5+ years) heroin users and found significantly lower Zd values for the long-term group. Kobayashi et al. (1995) studied adolescents with long-term organic solvent abuse and found increased reality testing problems.

In summary, these limited Rorschach findings suggest that serious substance abuse may have the potential for impairing higher-level cognitive operations and may also be related to difficulties with reality testing and impulse control. When hard-core or long-term substance abuse is part of a patient's history, both neuropsychological screening and personality assessment represent necessary components of comprehensive multimethod evaluation.

Assessment of Capacity to Engage in Treatment

Assessing an individual's capacity to remain in treatment and use it productively has been a significant Rorschach focus since early in the test's history (e.g., Kotkov & Meadow, 1953; Rogers, Knauss, & Hammond, 1951). A study by Alpher, Perfetto, Henry, and Strupp (1990) investigated the relationship between Rorschach predictors and judges' ratings on a measure of ability and willingness to address affective and interpersonal issues (Capacity for Dynamic Process Scale; Thackrey, Butler, & Strupp, 1985). The authors used a semistructured interview that covers a broad range of interpersonal issues to evaluate 42 adult patients who responded to advertisements offering treatment at a university-based clinic. Both the interviewing clinician and an independent judge, who watched a videotape of the interview, then rated the patient on the Capacity for

Dynamic Process Scale for attributes such as ability to integrate affect insightfully and to collaborate therapeutically.

Alpher et al. (1990) found that Rorschach variables accounted for 43% of the variance in the interviewing clinician's ratings and 51% of the variance in the ratings of the independent judge. Three common predictors (*Zf, DR, & ep*) emerged for both groups of raters. *Zf* was the single best predictor for both groups, and the authors suggest that it provides an index of ". . . how willing patients are to attempt to synthesize their worlds in a meaningful way, to look beyond the surface features of the field to attempt to organize the underlying relationships among elements therein" (p. 227). They speculate that *Zf* involves ". . . intellectual activity, psychological mindedness, and the capacity for insight" (p. 227).

An earlier study (Thornton, Gellens, Alterman, & Gottheil, 1979) also found that a cognitive measure of the level of differentiation, articulation, and integration of Rorschach percepts predicted alcohol-related outcomes (reduction in drinking and days not intoxicated) following inpatient alcohol treatment. However, a study by Alterman, Slap-Shelton, and DeCato (1992) with Veterans Administration alcohol-dependent male patients did not replicate this finding.

Ackerman, Hilsenroth, Clemence, Weatherill, and Fowler (2000) conceptualized the number of psychotherapy sessions attended as a measure of involvement in treatment for 76 personality-disordered outpatients at a university-based community clinic. They used Urist's (1977) Mutuality of Autonomy Scale (MOA), a seven-point scale that rates Rorschach percepts on their level of separation-individuation, ranging from well-differentiated descriptions of self and other (e.g., "two people dancing with each other at a party," scale score 1) to primitively engulfing representations (e.g., "two people with two creatures coming down to envelop them, like monsters that will suck them up into themselves," scale score 7). The authors found that the MOA PATH score, the sum of all percepts at the pathological end of the scale (scale points 5, 6, & 7), was positively and significantly predictive of number of psychotherapy sessions attended.

Ackerman et al. (2000) also found that therapy attendance was related to a Thematic Apperception Test (TAT; Murray, 1943) measure of expectation and experience of relationships as unpleasant, but simultaneously with a TAT measure of capacity and desire for emotional connection with others. The authors conclude that patients who continue in therapy longer ". . . may have more disturbed object representations . . . and more negative expectations and/or painful affect in relationships, but also the capacity and/or desire to invest emotionally in a relationship" (p. 398).

The finding that disturbed but ambivalent interpersonal relationships predict continuation in psychotherapy runs through numerous Rorschach studies. Hilsenroth, Handler, Toman, and Padawer (1995) compared the pretreatment Rorschachs of 97 outpatients at a university-based psychological clinic who dropped out of treatment within eight sessions, against the advice of clinic staff, to those of 81 outpatients who remained in individual insight-oriented psychotherapy for at least six months and 24 sessions. The continuation group had significantly fewer COP responses and trends toward more aggressive responses (*AG*) and cognitive slippage (*Sum6*), but also a trend toward more texture (*SumT*).

The converse of a focus on Rorschach correlates of continuation in psychotherapy involves identifying variables associated with premature termination. Horner and Diamond (1996) compared borderline personality-disordered women who dropped out of a treatment program with those who completed the program. They found that the Rorschach Separation-Individuation Scale (S-I Scale; Coonerty, 1986) differentiated dropouts from continuers. The dropouts were characterized by more percepts with narcissism/practicing themes ("a girl looking at herself in the mirror, like she's transfixed"). The ratio of narcissism/practicing themes to rapprochement themes ("two people facing each other, not sure about each other") was three to four times higher for the dropout group than for those who continued in therapy. The authors conclude, "Those who dropped out of treatment appeared to be more narrowly and rigidly organized around narcissistic issues of self-absorption, self-reliance, and envious attacks on others. . . . In contrast, those who completed treatment demonstrated the flexibility to struggle with a wide range of separation-individuation issues, including both autonomy and relatedness" (p. 219).

A study by Hilsenroth, Holdwick, and Castlebury (1998) supports the association of narcissistic features with a heightened potential for psychotherapy dropout. They evaluated 90 outpatients who met the *DSM-IV* criteria for an Axis II personality disorder and found that five specific *DSM-IV* descriptors accounted for 31% of the variance in predicting number of psychotherapy sessions attended. Among the five descriptors, "requires excessive admiration" ranked highest in its relationship (negative) to number of psychotherapy sessions attended. The descriptors positively related to treatment attendance ("frantic efforts to avoid real or imagined abandonment," "inappropriate, intense anger or difficulty controlling anger," and "considers relationships to be more intimate than they really are") again reflect the disturbed but ambivalent interpersonal stance that appears related to remaining in treatment.

In summary, the literature suggests that the Rorschach can be helpful in identifying three major characteristics associated with continuation versus premature termination for mental health services. Active cognitive involvement (indicated by *Zf*) and disturbed but ambivalent interpersonal representations (suggested by the paradoxical combination of low COP, more *AG,* and MOA PATH scores, but simultaneously by elevated *SumT*) are positive predictors of engagement in psychotherapy. Narcissistic features, on the other hand, appear to predict a heightened likelihood of dropout.

Case 8.   A 24-Year-Old Male.

Card	Response	Inquiry
I	1. A bf, sbody told me tht thy all ll bf's	**E:** (Rpts Ss resp) **S:** Well its got the wgs, thyr out lik it is in flight & the body in the cntr & the littl antennae, jus a bf **E:** Tak ur tim & look som more, I thk u'll find sthg else too
	v2. Ths way it ll a pagoda	**E:** (Rpts Ss resp) **S:** U kno lik thy hav thos thgs going up & weird designs & the crown is at the top, it comes to a point & it has thes opengs in it (S) not windows but opengs tht r part of the design, I'v seen em in magazines
II	3. Two people at a party or sthg, it ll thyr shaking hands	**E:** (Rpts Ss resp) **S:** Mayb a costume party cuz u can't mak out a lot of features. It ll thyv got their hands togethr lik thyr shaking hands, it ll thyr wearing cloaks or big coats & thyr bending forward, lik greeting e.o. **E:** U said thyr at a party or sthg **S:** Well thyr wearing red hats & those big cloaks so I figure a party
	4. The red down here ll a crab, lik a horseshoe crab but I don't thk thy have 2 tails	**E:** (Rpts Ss resp) **S:** Well it has tht shape except for the 2 tails & the variations in the coloring gives it the impression of a hard shell **E:** A hard shell? **S:** The lite & dark variations give it a kind of a shiny appearance lik it is a hard surface
III	5. Ths ll a wm lookg in the mirror kinda checking herself out	**E:** (Rpts Ss resp) **S:** Ths stuff down here (D7) doesn't count, just this part (D9), she's bendg forward a littl lik she's just checkg herself out, c her head & neck, she's got a big nose & her arm, leg & her breast & she's wearg hi heels
IV	6. I'd say a tree at night	**E:** (Rpts Ss resp) **S:** Ths is the trunk & the big arching top, big maple or oak, we hav alot on our street tht hav ths shape **E:** U said at nite? **S:** Well its all black, lik a silhouette
V	7. A bird, no wait I'll say a bf	**E:** (Rpts Ss resp) **S:** It really looks more lik a bf w the wgs extended lik thy do when the air lifts them & the antennae r here
	v 8. When I look ths way it looks mor lik a bird	**E:** (Rpts Ss resp) **S:** Well the othr way the wgs were rite for a bf but ths way thy come forward, lik a bird thts flapping its wgs & ths (D9) is the beak is open, it re me of a swallow, I'v seen pict's lik ths of them
VI	< 9. Ths re me of an iceberg thts floatg in the water & its reflectd dwn here	**E:** (Rpts Ss resp) **S:** Well it has an irreg shape & ths line is lik the water & down here its the same, it has a cold look to it, thts why I thot of an iceberg **E:** I'm not sur what there is tht gives it a cold look **S:** Its all diff shades of grey & blk lik a big huge chunk of ice, lik it wld really b cold if u sat on it
VII	10. Ths ll a weird statue of 2 peopl w their heads turned bkward lookg at eo	**E:** (Rpts Ss resp) **S:** Ths cb their arms & noses & faces & ths is ss of hair style if thyr wm or mayb a feather if thyr supp t b kids, thy cb either, just statues

Card	Response	Inquiry
v 11.	Ths way it re me of one of thos arch thgs lik u grow flowrs on, usually roses or smthg, we had one in our backyrd tht my mother was always trimming	**E:** (Rpts Ss resp) **S:** Well it has the gen shape of an arch & thes thgs cb the flowrs stickg out out on the sides & ths white cntr is where u can walk thru, its lik a trellis tht u can walk thru, we used to run thru it playg tag & my mothr wld hav a fit cuz we'd grab it & she was always worried we'd pull it down
VIII 12.	Well, the first thg I thot of was a big birthday cake	**E:** (Rpts Ss resp) **S:** It has all different colors of icing on it & it has 2 little candles on top **E:** I'm not sur I'm seeg it lik u r **S:** Well it has three layers, c here (D4), here (D5) & here (D2) & each is a diff color & then there's pink designs out here & white frosting too, sort of lik in between the layers, its very pretty & up here it ll 2 littl candles (Dd24)
13.	It cb a crown too, lik one u c in Nat'l Geographic tht som oriental prince mite wear at special occasions	**E:** (Rpts Ss resp) **S:** Well it has all the diff colors & the designs on the sides ll 2 A's, mayb dogs or wolves & it has ths peak, it all looks glittery lik it had a look of glass or jewels in it **E:** Glass or jewels? **S:** Well each section, it has 3 sections, has various shades of the coloring, it gives it a glittery look, Iv seen some lik ths in Nat'l Geographic
IX 14.	Up here it ll a cpl of wizards or witches making sthg in ths cauldron lik makg magic	**E:** (Rpts Ss resp) **S:** Well thyv got pointed hats & orange robes & it ll thy hav got their arms out ovr ths caludron, c ths round cntr thg, its all white lik it contains magic fog or smoke, lik u can c in it, & its all hazy lik u c in the movies **E:** U can c thru it? **S:** Not thru it, in it, lik its transparent, c the white looks hazy, lik smthg is bubblg in it & thyv got their arms ovr it lik thyr makg smthg
v 15.	Ths way ths part ll a corkscrew	**E:** (Rpts Ss resp) **S:** C ths part (D5) is what goes into the bottl & here (D6) is the handle, just lik a corkscrew lik to open wine
X 16.	The 1st thg I thk of here is a firewrks display, lik on the 4th of July	**E:** (Rpts Ss resp) **S:** It just ll its bursting outward, all of the colors are going outward in a symmetrical fashion, lik to represent a celebration, just a lot of colors exploding outward at the same time lik u c if u watch fireworks
17.	Ths part up here re me of the Eiffel Tower	**E:** (Rpts Ss resp) **S:** It just has that shape to it, I've been to Paris & it looks very much lik ths
18.	These thgs cb fancy blue earrings	**E:** (Rpts Ss resp) **S:** Yes, lik made out of some pretty blue sapphires, its a blue jewel, thyr irregular in shape & thy hav a shimmery effect to them **E:** Shimmery effect? **S:** The diff variations of blue mak them ll thyr moving slightly, sort of the way jewels sparkle as lite hits thm differntly

(continued)

Card	Response	Inquiry
19.	Ths othr blue cb a wm's bra	**E:** (Rpts Ss resp) **S:** Sort of a fancy one, blu, it just ll tht, I'd guess about a 36C
20.	U kno w the symmetrical effect & all the colors it ll a mobile, lik abstract art w all the pieces hangg in a symmetrical pattern	**E:** (Rpts Ss resp) **S:** If u'v evr been to a museum where thy specialize in abstracts thy hav mobiles, ths one is very colorful, mor lik a child mite do, most of the ones I'v seen by artists r made of metal but ths one is just loaded w colors & up here is where it wld hang from & evthg goes out fr these lrge pink thgs alth u can't c all of the connections, lik ths green dwn here ll its suspended by itself, evythg is interconnected

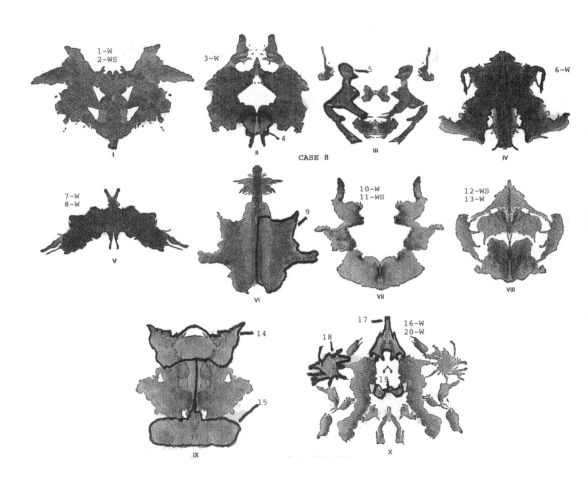

CASE 8

Case 8. Sequence of Scores.

Card	No.	Loc.	No.	Determinant(s)	(2)	Content(s)	Pop	Z	Special Scores
I	1	Wo	1	FMao		A	P	1.0	
	2	WSo	1	Fu		Ay		3.5	PER
II	3	W+	1	Ma.FCo	2	H,Cg		4.5	COP,GHR
	4	Do	3	FTo		A			
III	5	D+	9	Mp.Fr+		H,Cg	P	4.0	GHR
IV	6	Wo	1	FC'o		Bt		2.0	PER
V	7	Wo	1	FMpo		A	P	1.0	
	8	Wo	1	FMao		A		1.0	PER
VI	9	Dv/+	4	mp.rF.TFo		Na		2.5	
VII	10	W+	1	Mpo	2	Art,(H)	P	2.5	GHR
	11	WS+	1	Fu		Sc,Bt		4.0	PER
VIII	12	WS+	1	CF.C'F–		Fd,Sc		4.5	
	13	Wo	1	CF.YFu	2	Art,(A)	P	4.5	PER
IX	14	DS+	3	Ma.FC.FVo	2	(H),Na,Cg		5.0	AB,COP,GHR
	15	Do	9	Fu		Hh			
X	16	Wo	1	ma.CFo		Ex		5.5	
	17	Do	11	Fo		Art			PER
	18	Do	1	CF.YF.mpu	2	Art			
	19	Do	6	FCu		Cg,Sx			
	20	Wo	1	CF.mpu		Art		5.5	

Case 8. Structural Summary.

Location Features	Determinants Blends	Single	Contents	S-Constellation
				NO . . .FV+VF+V+FD>2
			H = 2	YES . .Col-Shd Bl>0
Zf = 15	M.FC	M = 1	(H) = 2	YES . .Ego<.31,>.44
ZSum = 48.5	M.Fr	FM = 3	Hd = 0	NO . . .MOR > 3
ZEst = 49.0	m.rF.TF	m = 0	(Hd) = 0	NO . . .Zd > +- 3.5
	CF.C'F	FC = 1	Hx = 0	YES . .es > EA
W = 12	CF.YF	CF = 0	A = 4	YES . .CF+C > FC
D = 8	M.FC.FV	C = 0	(A) = 1	YES . .X+% < .70
W+D = 20	m.CF	Cn = 0	Ad = 0	YES . .S > 3
Dd = 0	CF.YF.m	FC' = 1	(Ad) = 0	NO . . .P < 3 or > 8
S = 4	CF.m	C'F = 0	An = 0	NO . . .Pure H < 2
		C' = 0	Art = 5	NO . . .R < 17
		FT = 1	Ay = 1	6 . . . .TOTAL

DQ		Single	Contents	**Special Scores**
		TF = 0	Bl = 0	Lv1 Lv2
+ = 6		T = 0	Bt = 2	DV = 0x1 0x2
o = 13		FV = 0	Cg = 4	INC = 0x2 0x4
v/+ = 1		VF = 0	Cl = 0	DR = 0x3 0x6
v = 0		V = 0	Ex = 1	FAB = 0x4 0x7
		FY = 0	Fd = 1	ALOG = 0x5
		YF = 0	Fi = 0	CON = 0x7
		Y = 0	Ge = 0	Raw Sum6 = 0
Form Quality		Fr = 0	Hh = 1	Wgtd Sum6 = 0

	FQx	MQual	W+D			
				rF = 0	Ls = 0	
				FD = 0	Na = 2	
+	= 1	= 1	= 1	F = 4	Sc = 2	AB = 1 GHR = 4
o	= 11	= 3	= 11		Sx = 1	AG = 0 PHR = 0
u	= 7	= 0	= 7		Xy = 0	COP = 2 MOR = 0
–	= 1	= 0	= 1		Id = 0	CP = 0 PER = 6
none	= 0	= 0	= 0	(2) = 5		PSV = 0

Ratios, Percentages, and Derivations

R = 20	L = 0.25		FC:CF+C = 3:5	COP = 2 AG = 0
			Pure C = 0	GHR:PHR = 4:0
EB = 4:6.5	EA = 10.5	EBPer = 1.6	SumC':WSumC = 2:6.5	a:p = 5:6
eb = 7:7	es = 14	D = −1	Afr = 0.82	Food = 1
	Adj es = 10	Adj D = 0	S = 4	SumT = 2
			Blends:R = 9:20	Hum Con = 4
FM = 3	C' = 2	T = 2	CP = 0	Pure H = 2
m = 4	V = 1	Y = 2		PER = 6
				Iso Indx = 0.30

a:p = 5:6	Sum6 = 0	XA% = 0.95	Zf = 15.0	3r+(2)/R = 0.55
Ma:Mp = 2:2	Lv2 = 0	WDA% = 0.95	W:D:Dd = 12:8:0	Fr+rF = 2
2AB+Art+Ay = 8	WSum6 = 0	X–% = 0.05	W:M = 12:4	SumV = 1
MOR = 0	M– = 0	S– = 1	Zd = +2.0	FD = 0
	Mnone = 0	P = 5	PSV = 0	An+Xy = 0
		X+% = 0.60	DQ+ = 6	MOR = 0
		Xu% = 0.35	DQv = 0	H:(H)Hd(Hd) = 2:2

| PTI = 0 | DEPI = 4 | CDI = 1 | S-CON = 6 | HVI = No | OBS = No |

S-CON AND KEY VARIABLES

The S-CON value (6) is not significant. The first positive Key variable is that the D Score (−1) is less than the Adj D Score (0). This only identifies the search strategy for the first two groups of data, the cluster regarding controls and the array of data concerning situational stress. The second positive Key variable is that *Fr+rF* is greater than zero. This indicates that the next two clusters to be studied should be self-perception and interpersonal perception. A third positive Key variable, the *EB* (4:6.5) is extratensive; it signifies that the interpretive procedure should continue with a review of data concerning affect and end with a study of the three clusters that comprise the cognitive triad.

CONTROLS

Case 8.   Control-Related Variables for a 24-Year-Old Male.

EB = 4:6.5	EA = 10.5		D = −1	CDI = 1
eb = 7:7	es = 14	Adj es = 10	AdjD = 0	L = 0.25
FM = 3 m = 4	SumC′ = 2	SumT = 2	SumV = 1	SumY = 2

The Adj D Score is zero and the CDI value (1) is not positive. This indicates that, typically, this young man has enough resources accessible to participate meaningfully in the formulation and direction of decisions and behaviors. His usual tolerance for stress is like that of most people; that is, controls typically will not falter unless the stress is unexpected and intense or prolonged. The *EA* value (10.5) is well into the average range and the *EB* (4:6.5) contains no zero values. The Adj *es* (10) is slightly higher than expected, mainly because of a substantial right side value in the *eb* (7). This elevation seems to be the result of higher than expected values for *SumT* (2) and *SumV* (1). Even so, there is no reason to challenge the reliability of the Adj D Score.

Thus, a basic premise that, ordinarily, his capacities for control and tolerance for stress are like that of most people seems reasonable. He has enough resource accessible to formulate and implement responses, and his stress tolerance is likely to be exceeded only under unusual conditions. However, there is evidence indicating that, currently, his capacity for control is not as sturdy as is usually the case, and this requires further study.

SITUATION-RELATED STRESS

Case 8.   Situational Stress Data for a 24-Year-Old Male.

				Blends	
EB = 4:6.5	EA = 10.5		D = −1	M.FC.FV	= 1
eb = 7:7	es = 14 Adj es = 10		AdjD = 0	M.FC	= 1
				M.Fr	= 1
FM = 3 m = 4	C′ = 2 T = 2 V = 1 Y = 2			CF.YF.m	= 1
	(3r+(2)/R) = .55			CF.m	= 1
				CF.C′F	= 1
Pure C = 0 M− = 0	MQnone = 0		Blends = 9	CF.YF	= 1
				m.rF.TF	= 1
				m.CF	= 1

The difference between the D Score (−1) and the Adj D Score (0), plus the fact that the D Score is in the minus range, indicates that he is experiencing a notable increase in stimulus demands as a result of situationally related stress and is in a state of stimulus overload. The D Score is −1 suggesting that he is not necessarily disorganized, but some of his decisions or behaviors may not be well thought through, and he is vulnerable to impulsiveness in thinking, emotions, and behaviors.

The main elements causing the overload are represented by the values for *m* (4) and *SumY* (2), both of which are generally related to thoughts or feelings caused by a sense of helplessness. The values for these two variables intimate that the effects of the stress are diffuse, although there may be a notable increase in peripheral thinking that probably will affect his attention and concentration. In addition, the elevated value for *SumT* (2) implies that some of this vulnerability is generated by a sense of emotional neediness or loneliness. This may relate to his girlfriend's threat to move out, but that is speculative. It seems likely that this feature may be more chronic than situational. On the other hand, the one vista answer, when considered in light of the high Egocentricity Index (.55), seems more situational than persistent. It suggests that he may be experiencing a current sense of guilt or remorse that is contributing to the overload.

The fact that four of his nine blends are created by *m* or *Y* determinants emphasizes that the current stress is creating substantially more psychological complexity than is common. Additionally, two of these four blends involve color and shading (*CF.YF.m, CF.YF*) suggesting that one result of his current condition is an increase in confusion about feelings.

It seems logical to suspect that his recent experience of drug-induced disarray, the hospitalization that followed, and the need to enter treatment have prompted much or all of the stress that he is experiencing. When considered in the context of intervention, his sense of helplessness and possible guilt may well serve as positive sources of motivation to participate actively in treatment.

SELF-PERCEPTION

Case 8.   Self-Perception Related Data for a 24-Year-Old Male.

R	= 20	OBS	= No	HVI = No	**Human Content, Hx, An & Xy Responses**
					II 3. W+ Ma.FCo 2 H,Cg 4.5 COP,GHR
Fr+rF	= 2	3r+(2)/R	= 0.55		III 5. D+ Mp.Fr+ H,Cg P 4.0 GHR
					VII 10. W+ Mpo 2 Art,(H) P 2.5 GHR
FD	= 0	SumV	= 1		IX 14. DS+ Ma.FC.FVo 2 (H),Cl 2.5 AB,COP,GHR
An+Xy	= 0	MOR	= 0		
H:(H)+Hd+(Hd) = 2:2					
[EB = 4:6.5]					

The two reflection answers indicate that a core element of his personality is a narcissistic tendency to overvalue his personal worth. This seems supported by the Egocentricity Index (0.55), and the composite suggests that a tendency to sustain favorable judgments of himself, as contrasted with others, is strongly embedded in his psychology. It tends to be a dominant influence that affects his thinking and perceptions of the world and, in turn, influences his decisions and behaviors.

This narcissistic feature creates a stylistic orientation to reaffirm his exaggerated sense of self-value, and this often serves in a positive way to promote motivations for achievement and status. In a less positive context, it also creates a need to protect the exaggerated sense of personal worth and usually leads to the formation of an elaborate defense system. Typically, this involves an unreasonable reliance on denial, rationalization, and externalization to avoid responsibility for flawed judgments or behavioral blunders. The abuse of these defenses tends to create barriers that reduce the likelihood of forming and maintaining close, meaningful interpersonal relationships. Possibly the greatest liability of this narcissistic feature is an increase in the potential to develop asocial or antisocial sets when the environment is unrewarding.

There are no *FD* responses in the protocol, implying that he may be somewhat naive about himself. However, there is one vista response, signifying that he is probably involved in some preoccupation with perceived negative features. This is an unusual finding for a narcissistic person and, because it is yielding some painful feelings, could serve as an asset to treatment. On the other hand, there are no MOR responses in the record, which is not an unusual finding for a devoutly self-centered person. Thus, it seems probable that the painful feelings that are resulting from his self-examination are associated with some guilt or remorse about his recent episode and, as such, are likely to be short-lived.

The presence of four human content responses, including two pure *H* answers, is in the expected range for an extratensive person and implies that his self-concept is based more on experience and less on imagination than might be suspected. The codings for the four human content answers are generally positive, even though one includes a reflection and a second contains a vista determinant. They also suggest a reasonably well developed self-concept. Some clarification of these issues may be gleaned from the projected material in his protocol.

His single minus response (Card VIII, response 12), is "a big birthday cake . . . all different colors of icing on it and it has two little candles on top." Although a reasonably sophisticated answer, it also has a juvenile quality and represents a form of self-glorification. The first of his four human movement answers (Card II, response 3), "Two people at a party or something, it looks like they are shaking hands . . . maybe a costume party cuz you can't make out a lot of features . . . like greeting each other" is positive and sophisticated. The notion that it is a "costume party" may imply some need to conceal, but that is speculative. The second of his *M* answers (Card III, response 5) is clearly self-focusing, "a woman looking in the mirror kind of checking herself out." The third (Card VII, response 10), "a weird statue of two people with their heads turned backward looking at each other," is interesting because the statue is described as "weird," and the people are described as having their "heads turned backward" to look at each other. It has a stilted, concrete quality to it that raises a question about whether his own self-concept is stilted or concrete. The fourth *M* (Card IX, response 14) connotes special power: "a couple of wizards or witches making something in this cauldron, like making magic . . . like it contains magic fog or smoke . . . like something is bubbling in it . . . like they are making something."

The three animal movement answers do not contain any readily detectable projected material: Card I, response 1, "A butterfly . . . it's got the wings, they are out like it is in flight"; Card V, response 7, "a butterfly . . . with the wings extended like they do when the air lifts them"; Card V, response 8, "like a bird . . . that's flapping its wings . . . like the beak is open."

The four inanimate movement answers are more idiosyncratic. The first (Card VI, response 9) is, "an iceberg that is floating in the water and it's reflected down here . . . it has a cold look to it . . . like it would be really cold if you sat on it." It conveys concealment, impenetrability, and possibly threat. The remaining three were all given to Card X, and all have ornate, exhibitionistic qualities that seem commensurate with his narcissistic features: response 16, ". . . a fireworks display, like on the 4th of July . . . like to represent celebration"; response 18, "fancy blue earrings . . . it's a blue jewel . . . they have a shimmery effect to them . . . moving slightly . . . the way jewels sparkle as light hits them"; and response 20. "a mobile, like abstract art with all the pieces hanging in a symmetrical pattern . . . like a child might do . . . loaded with colors . . . this green thing down here looks like it's suspended by itself . . . everything is interconnected."

Five of the eight remaining answers are also impressive for their ornate contents: Card I, response 2, "a pagoda . . . it has openings, not windows but openings that are part of the design"; Card VII, response 11, "one of those arch things like you grow flowers on, usually roses"; Card VIII, response 13, "a crown . . . that some oriental prince might wear at special occasions . . . glittery like it had the look of glass or jewels in it"; Card X, response 17, "the Eiffel Tower. . . . I've been to Paris"; and Card X, response 19, "a woman's bra . . . sort of a fancy one . . . I'd guess about a 36C." The remaining three have much the same impenetrable feature as the iceberg: Card II, response 4, "a horseshoe crab . . . it gives the impression of a hard shell"; Card IV, response 6, "a tree at night . . . the trunk and the big arching top, big maple or oak"; and Card IX, response 15, "a corkscrew . . . like to open wine."

His texture answers are unusual and raise a question about his sense of loneliness or neediness. The first (horseshoe crab) is described as, "a shiny appearance like it was hard." The second (iceberg) is described as, "like it would really be cold if you sat on it." On a speculative level, it may be that he is prone to regard or experience tactile exchange very differently from those who give the more common soft or furry descriptions that characterize most texture answers.

It seems clear that his personality is marked by much self-centeredness and a tendency to overvalue his own worth. This feature exerts a dominating influence on his perceptions of the world, as well as on decisions and behaviors. He appears to have developed a substantial motive for status but is also defensive about this and tries to remain somewhat aloof to conceal the detection of any flaws. There are hints that he may be experiencing some guilt or remorse about his recent episode of disarray, but this may be short-lived. His main goal for intervention is likely to be oriented toward a reaffirmation of his exquisite self-centeredness. The magnitude of his self-involvement suggests that it may be difficult for him to create or maintain mature relationships with others. It also seems likely that he may tend to use his interpersonal skills to manipulate others for his own gains.

INTERPERSONAL PERCEPTION

Case 8.   Interpersonal Perception Data for a 24-Year-Old Female.

R = 20	CDI = 1	HVI = No	**COP & AG Responses**
a:p = 5:6	SumT = 2	Fd = 1	II 3. W+ Ma.FCo 2 H,Cg 4.5 COP,GHR
	[eb = 7:7]		IX 14. DS+ Ma.FC.FVo 2 (H),Cl 2.5
Sum Human Contents = 4		H = 3	
[Style = Extratensive]			
GHR:PHR = 4:0			
COP = 2	AG = 0	PER = 6	
Isolation Indx = 0.30			

The $a:p$ ratio (5:6) is not definitive, but the preponderance of passive movement answers hints that he may be reluctant to assume responsibility and tends to rely on others to resolve problems. This speculation seems supported by the presence of a Food response, implying that he may engage in more dependency behaviors than might be expected, relying on others for support. People who do this often tend to be naive in their expectations about interpersonal relationships.

As noted, the two texture responses indicate a sense of loneliness or emotional neediness. This can be influential in his interpersonal relations. As also mentioned, however, the unusual characteristics of these two answers raise a question about how this feature manifests in his behavior. The first, a horseshoe crab, was described as having, "a shiny appearance like it was hard." The second, an iceberg, was described as, "like it would really be cold if you sat on it." If these answers are considered in the context of Barrier-Penetration concepts, such as those put forth by Fisher and Cleveland (1958), it seems reasonable to conjecture that he expresses his needs for closeness in ways that are self-protective and controlling. The report of his girlfriend that he often asks her to dress in unusual ways to arouse him may have a relation to this finding.

The four human contents in the record, including two Pure H responses, suggest that he has as much interest in others as do most people, and that his conceptions of people are likely to be reality based. The GHR:PHR ratio (4:0) indicates that he generally engages in interpersonal behaviors that are likely to be adaptive for the situation. Likewise, the presence of two COP answers and no AG responses connotes that he usually anticipates positive interactions among people and has an interest in participating in them. However, a review of the specific descriptions in the four human content answers, three of which contain pairs, yields impressions that are less positive and convey less maturity than might be expected.

The first of the four (response 3) represents a positive view of interpersonal contact, "two people at a party . . . shaking hands," but the answer is also marked by guardedness. It is a costume party and both are wearing cloaks or big coats. The remaining three tend to convey less mature impressions of others: (response 5) "a woman looking in the mirror," (response 10) "a statue of two people with their heads turned backward," (response 14) "two wizards or witches . . . making magic."

In a somewhat related context, the six PER responses indicate that he is somewhat insecure about his personal integrity and tends to be defensively authoritarian to thwart or control situations that he perceives as challenging to his self-value. Others often see people who do this to excess as being rigid or narrow, and they frequently have difficulties in maintaining close relations, especially with those who are not submissive to them. In light of these findings, it is not surprising to note a positive Isolation Index (.30). It implies that he is prone to be less involved in social interactions than most people. This does not necessarily mean that he avoids social relationships, but it suggests that they will be less broad or diversified than might have been expected from earlier findings.

Overall, it seems probable that he is much more naive in his expectations about relationships than might be anticipated for an intelligent adult. Although he appears to feel lonely or emotionally needy, this feature is likely to manifest in ways that are less typical than expected. Although he seems interested in people and appears to anticipate that most interpersonal relations will be positive, he probably is not involved more than superficially in a broad social network. This is because he is unsure, or possibly insecure, about his personal integrity and tends to be overly authoritarian when interpersonal situations pose challenges to him. In fact, those who know him reasonably well probably regard him as narrow or rigid. This creates difficulties in maintaining close relations with those who are not submissive to him, and also reduces the likelihood that his relationships will be marked by depth and maturity.

AFFECT

Case 8.   Affect-Related Data for a 24-Year-Old Male.

								Blends	
EB	= 4:6.5				EBPer	= 1.6		Blends	
eb	= 7: 7	L	= 0.25		FC:CF+C	= 3:5		M.FC.FV	= 1
DEPI	= 4	CDI	= 1		Pure C	= 0		M.FC	= 1
								M.Fr	= 1
SumC' = 2	SumT = 2				SumC':WSumC	= 2:6.5		CF.YF.m	= 1
SumV = 1	SumY = 2				Afr	= 0.82		CF.C'F	= 1
								CF.YF	= 1
Intellect	= 8	CP	= 0		S = 4 (S to I,II,III	= 1)		CF.m	= 1
Blends:R	= 9:20				Col-Shad Bl	= 4		m.rF.TF	= 1
m + y Bl	= 4				Shading Bl	= 0		m.CF	= 1

The *EB* (4:6.5) indicates that feelings usually play an important role in his problem solving or decision making. He is prone to test out postulates through trial-and-error behaviors and is likely to display feelings openly. The *EBPer* value (1.6) suggests that he is somewhat flexible about the use of this style and at times will push feelings aside in favor of an ideational approach.

As noted previously, the right side value of the *eb* (7) is substantial, indicating considerable irritating emotions. However, much of the elevation in this variable appears to be created by a sense of helplessness regarding his current situation (*SumY* = 2), and probably feelings of guilt or remorse about it (*SumV* = 1). Some elevation is also being generated by feelings of unexplained loneliness or neediness (*SumT* = 2). However, there is no indication of unusual emotional constriction (*SumC'* : *WSumC* = 2:6.5). In fact, the *Afr* (.82) is in the expected range for an extratensive person, denoting that he seems willing to process and become involved with emotions or emotional situations.

On the other hand, the value for the Intellectualization Index (8) is high. It signifies that he is prone to use intellectualization as a tactic to deal with emotions that he identifies as unwanted or threatening. This form of denial reduces or neutralizes the intensity of negative or confusing emotions. It can be a useful defense, but it requires distortions of reality and, when done to excess, creates a vulnerability to become emotionally overwhelmed if the defense is not effective.

The *FC*:*CF+C* ratio (3:5), and the Pure *C* value of zero indicate that he is not very stringent about modulating his emotional displays, but this is not unusual for an extratensive person. When considered in light of his considerable use of intellectualization, it is doubtful that they will seem overly intense to most observers. A much more important finding is the elevated value for *S* (4). It signifies a sense of alienation about the environment, and possibly an angry attitude toward it. This appears to be a traitlike feature that can easily promote an oppositional influence in his decision making and coping activities, impeding the development of close relations with others. It is also likely to limit his tolerance for the routine compromises that are often required in social intercourse.

The substantial number of blends (9) in this 20-response record, three of which contain three determinants, signals that his psychological functioning is markedly more complex than ordinarily expected. As noted, four of these blends appear to be situationally related. Nonetheless, this level of complexity increases the potential for emotions to have a detrimental influence on his behavioral consistency. Moreover, the four color shading blends indicate that he often finds emotions confusing and may frequently experience both positive and negative reactions to the same feelings. Two of the four color shading blends include YF determinants, suggesting that this confusion or ambivalence has been increased by situational stress, but it is also likely to have existed at a lower level prior to his current state.

The findings regarding affect yield both positive and negative features when considered in the context of treatment prospects. His relatively consistent intuitive coping style, in which feelings usually play an important role in his thinking, is an asset, especially in that he seems to be flexible about using this style. Additionally, he is experiencing more negative feelings and encountering more discomfort than usual, which can also be assets to intervention. His current functioning is much more complex than usual, and this has exacerbated a long-standing confusion that he has about feelings. It may also serve to motivate active participation in treatment.

On the negative side, a marked tendency to deal with upsetting or unwanted feelings on an intellectual level, requiring denial and a bending of reality will, no doubt, limit the extent to which he will be open with others. Finally, and possibly most important, he harbors a negative, oppositional attitude toward the world, and this too will limit the extent to which he is willing to share thoughts and feelings with others, especially persons he perceives as threatening or controlling.

PROCESSING

Case 8.   Processing Variables for a 24-Year-Old Male.

EB	= 4:6.5	Zf	= 15	Zd	= +2.0	DQ+	= 6
L	= 0.25	W:D:Dd	= 12:8:0	PSV	= 0	DQv/+	= 1
HVI	= NO	W:M	= 12:4			DQv	= 0
OBS	= NO						

Location & DQ Sequencing

I:	Wo.WSo	VI:	Dv/+
II:	W+.Do	VII:	W+.WS+
III:	D+	VIII:	WS+.Wo
IV:	Wo	IX:	DS+.Do
V:	Wo.Wo	X:	Wo.Do.Do.Wo

The values for Zf (15) and the $W:D:Dd$ ratio (12:8:0) indicate that he makes a considerable effort to process new information, especially when it relates to problem solving or decision making. This motivation is also implied by the $W:M$ ratio (3:1) and reflected in the consistent location sequencing. His 12 W answers were given to 7 of the 10 figures, with seven being first responses and five being last responses.

The *Zd* value (+2.0) is in the expected range and denotes a scanning efficiency similar to that of most adults. The distribution of *DQ* codes includes six *DQ+* responses, which is in the average range for an adult extratensive. Six *DQ+* answers, however, are fewer than might be expected for a person who works diligently to process inputs, as implied by the 15 *Zf*. It is not necessarily inconsistent, but it conveys the notion that, while the quality of his processing effort is adequate, it may also be somewhat more conservative than expected.

For example, he gave synthesis answers to only 5 of the 10 cards, and although he gave five responses to Card X, none are coded *DQ+*. This is not a liability, but this finding tempers the notion that he is strongly motivated to process new information. He probably does work hard to identify components of new information, but he does not really strain his resources to make sure that the new information is organized.

MEDIATION

Case 8.   Mediation Variables for a 24-Year-Old Male.

R = 20		L = 0.25		OBS = No	**Minus & NoForm Features**
FQx+	= 1		XA%	= .95	VIII 12. WS+ CF.C'F– Fd,Sc 4.5
FQxo	= 11		WDA%	= .95	
FQxu	= 7		X–%	= .05	
FQx–	= 1		S–	= 1	
FQxnone	= 0				
(W+D	= 20)		P	= 5	
WD+	= 1		X+%	= .60	
WDo	= 11		Xu%	= .35	
WDu	= 7				
WD–	= 1				
WDnone	= 0				

The substantial values for the *XA%* (.95) and *WDA%* (.95) signify that he makes a concerted effort to ensure that his translations of inputs are appropriate for the situation. This indicates that the basic element critical to adequate reality testing, that is, competent mediation, is firmly intact. When the values for these variables are higher than expected, it often connotes a person who is concerned with avoiding errors and their potential consequences.

His relatively low *X–%* (.05) is created by a single minus answer that involves *S* (Card VIII, response 12, a birthday cake). It also includes a color shading blend (*CF.C'F*) and has a Food content. The distortion may have evolved as a result of his negativism, or his confusion about feelings, both of which were noted during the study of his affective features. Alternatively, the distortion might have been prompted by his excessive self-involvement or his tendency to seek the support of others. Regardless of the antecedents, the degree of distortion in the answer is modest.

The value for Popular responses (5) is in the expected range and suggests that he is likely to translate stimuli in common ways when the cues for such responses are reasonably obvious. Likewise, the presence of one *FQ+* answer implies that he is oriented to be precise in his mediational efforts. On the other hand, the *X+%* (.60) is a bit lower and the *Xu%* (.35) is somewhat higher than might be anticipated in light of the substantial values for the *XA%* (.95) and *WDA%* (.95). This composite of findings signifies that, while he does not appear to seriously bend or distort reality very often, he has a tendency to disregard conventionality a bit more frequently than most people. He is prone to overpersonalize or individualize translations of new information. This is not really a liability, but his tendency to interpret the world through his own set of psychological lenses increases the likelihood for behaviors that ignore social expectations.

IDEATION

Case 8.   Ideation Variables for a 24-Year-Old Male.

L	= 0.25	OBS	= No	HVI	= No	**Critical Special Scores**			
						DV	= 0	DV2	= 0
EB	= 4:6.5	EBPer	= 1.6	a:p	= 5:6	INC	= 0	INC2	= 0
				Ma:Mp	= 2:2	DR	= 0	DR2	= 0
eb	= 7:7	[FM = 3 m = 4]				FAB	= 0	FAB2	= 0
				M−	= 0	ALOG	= 0	CON	= 0
Intell Indx	= 8	MOR	= 0	Mnone	= 0	Sum6	= 0	WSum6	= 0
							(R = 20)		

M Response Features

II   3. W+ Ma.FCo 2 H,Cg 4.5 COP,GHR
III   8. D+ Mp.Fr+ H,Cg P 4.0 GHR
VII   10. W+ Mpo 2 Art,(H) P 2.5 GHR
IX   14. DS+ Ma.FC.FVo 2 (H),Cl 5.0 AB,COP,GHR

As noted, the *EB* (4:6.5) and *EBPer* (1.6) reveal that his ideational activity associated with decision making usually is intuitive, influenced by the merging of feelings into his thinking. He is likely to be accepting of logic systems that are not precise, but he is not inflexible in applying this coping style. The value for the left side of the *eb* (7) indicates that, currently, his thought processes are marked by a higher than expected level of subconscious or peripheral ideation, much of which seems to be situationally provoked. Although this often serves as a positive stimulus to action, it can also become distracting when it is excessive, and when that is the case, a pattern of more limited concentration and interruptions in the flow of deliberate thinking will be present.

The value for the Intellectualization Index (8) is important because it reveals intellectualization as a major defensive tactic. This pseudo-intellectual process conceals and/or denies unwanted or stressful emotion and, as a result, reduces the likelihood that feelings will be dealt with directly or realistically, even if his thinking is clear. The excessive use of this defense tends to cloud thinking when emotional experiences are intense because this tactic becomes less effective as the magnitude of affective stimulation increases.

On a positive note, there are no critical special scores in the protocol, indicating that there is no reason to question the clarity of his conceptual thinking. Additionally, the codings for all four of his *M* answers are appropriate and conventional. An evaluation of his human movement responses, which have previously been studied, also suggests that there is no reason to be concerned about the quality of his conceptual thinking.

Three of the four *M* responses have a relatively sophisticated quality (response 3, "Two people at a party or something, it looks like they are shaking hands . . . maybe a costume party . . . they are bending forward, like greeting each other"; response 5, "a woman looking in the mirror kinda checking herself out"; response 14, "a couple of wizards or witches making something in this cauldron, like making magic . . . they've got pointed hats and orange robes and it looks like they have got their arms out over this cauldron, like it contains magic fog or smoke.") The fourth is somewhat more stilted and unique, but of reasonably good quality (response 10, "a weird statue of two people with their heads turned backward looking at each other"). It could be argued that one or two have some juvenile features, but all are elaborate and conceptually well developed.

The findings concerning his thinking are generally positive. He is consistent, but not rigid, in the use of an intuitive approach to decision making. His thinking seems clear and his conceptualizations tend to be of good quality. He currently may experience difficulties in attention and concentration because of an increase in peripheral ideation, but this appears to be situationally related and not a significant liability. A more chronic problem with his ideation concerns his proclivity to intellectualize unwanted emotions. This may not affect his day-to-day functioning very much, but it can impede therapeutic efforts, especially in the short term, because it provides a convenient way for him to avoid confrontations with some of his own problems.

SUMMARY

This young man is in a stimulus overload state that seems situational and probably related to his recent episode of disorganization and the pending entry into treatment. He is not disorganized, but his controls are fragile; he is somewhat vulnerable to impulsiveness in his thinking and/or in the way that he handles emotions. He seems to be experiencing more distracting thoughts than is usually the case, and the stresses that he is encountering have made him more confused about his feelings. As a result, some of his actions may not be well thought through.

Ordinarily, his resources are sufficient to ensure adequate controls, and his stress tolerance is likely to be exceeded only under unusual conditions. Nonetheless, the way that his personality is organized includes a potential for stresses, such as he is experiencing, to increase his vulnerability for disorganization. The core of this potential is a very noticeable narcissistic tendency to overglorify his own worth. This feature has a dominant influence on his thinking—the way that he perceives the world—and it has created a strong motivation for status. A product of this characteristic is a self-image that includes some less mature and exhibitionistic-like features that are part of a support system for his exquisite self-centeredness.

He has also developed an elaborate system of defense to protect his overvalued self-image, and it tends to conceal flaws and ensure his own aloofness and impenetrability. It involves rationalization and denial to avoid responsibility, a marked abuse of intellectualization to minimize or neutralize the impact of negative affects, and a form of authoritarianism that he employs to ward off challenges to his integrity. This system of interrelated defenses probably serves him well much of the time, but if any of these tactics falter in their effectiveness, the result is a sharp increase in negative emotions. In such a circumstance, he tends to feel helpless and more confused than usual about his emotions. In turn, his ability to maintain control over his thinking and behavior is lessened.

Such events are particularly detrimental for him, as emotions play a significant role in his thinking and decision making. This intuitive coping style can be effective if there are no problems in control and if emotions do not become overly confusing or intense. However, if either occur, the potential for loss of control and the onset of inappropriate behaviors increases considerably.

His elaborate system of defenses also tends to create obstacles that affect his relations with others. He is prone to rely on others as sources of support and reassurance for his inflated sense of self, but his perceptions of people and expectations of them are not very realistic. As a result, most of his relations with others will be more superficial than close. In fact, it seems likely that he is often regarded as being rigid or narrow, especially by those who are not submissive or easily manipulated by him.

He feels emotionally lonely or needy, and this may be a long-standing characteristic. In any case, regardless of whether that is true, he is experiencing more negative emotion than is typical for him, and this seems to include a sense of guilt or remorse about his situation. He also appears to harbor a negative and possibly angry attitude toward the environment. This is probably a long-standing characteristic that invariably has some impact on his functioning. This sense of alienation or anger may not manifest overtly, but it contributes to his defensiveness and his tendency to be intolerant of those around him. The current stress has also exacerbated his tendency to be confused by his feelings.

On a positive note, his cognitive activities are intact and function well. He makes a considerable effort to process new information accurately and translates inputs appropriately. Some of his translations tend to be more individualistic than might be expected, probably because of his excessive self-involvement, but this is not a problem. His ideation usually is clear, and although some of his conceptualizations include juvenile features that appear related to his extreme self-centeredness, his thinking is often elaborate, well developed, and reasonably sophisticated. In effect, his reality testing is adequate, despite his emotional burdens and the elaborate defenses on which he relies.

RECOMMENDATIONS

The referral questions whether there is any serious psychiatric disturbance and, technically, the answer is no. There is a personality problem, but the focus of planned treatment concerns substance abuse, with little regard for potential long-term treatment issues. Thus, his narcissistic personality is relevant only in the context of the planned intervention. A second issue raised in the referral asks about his probable response to the highly structured two-week inpatient program. It seems feasible to assume that he will respond favorably to the structured program. He feels helpless and vulnerable and seeks support from others and relief from his emotional distress. Thus, it is likely that he will be cooperative in the program, at least until he experiences relief. In light of his elaborate system of defenses, he will probably exhibit considerable intellectualization during this phase of treatment and couple this with his authoritarian dogmatism as he becomes more accustomed to the routines. At that point, he is likely to begin competing directly with his therapists.

Another issue raised in the referral concerns a prognosis about the likelihood that he will complete the six-week outpatient program. He has received a one-month leave of absence to involve himself in treatment, probably with the naive and somewhat grandiose expectation that such a treatment effort will bring satisfactory resolution to his problems. Brief treatment can work wonders at times, but not when seeking changes in the basic personality structure. Thus, the probability that he will complete the six-week outpatient program seems equivocal, and much depends on the focus of the individual and group sessions. If the focus is on abstinence and support, his persistence will depend mainly on the extent to which he experiences relief and feels confident about his ability to control the situation. Conversely, if the focus is on change, once he experiences relief, the prognosis for persisting in treatment becomes relatively poor as the prospects of change will be very threatening to him.

A fourth issue raised in the referral concerns recommendations for focus in the individual treatment sessions. In that only six weeks are involved, any targets should be reasonably simple and not threatening. His sense of negativism about the environment might be a springboard to review his interpersonal behaviors but, at best, it will be difficult to create a close working relationship with him. On the other hand, should such a relationship be created, he has numerous assets in the event that he might be interested in remaining in treatment for a longer time. He processes well. His thinking is clear and can be sophisticated, and his reality testing is appropriate. He is interested in people and has substantial needs for status. In addition, his sense of guilt or remorse might prompt him to search out ways to avoid repeating his recent disorganization. However, keeping him motivated for treatment will require a skillful therapist who can handle two important but delicate issues, control and self-integrity. In other words, if he perceives himself as losing control over his behavior, or relinquishing his overglorified sense of self, he is likely to bolt the therapeutic situation.

EPILOGUE

He was accepted into the relatively brief substance abuse program. He was judged to be very co-operative during the 14 inpatient days, and described by at least two staff members as being outgoing, likable, and helpful with other patients. It was noted that he organized at least three interward basketball games during his second week of hospitalization. Following his discharge, he returned to work and participated in all six individual therapy sessions, but only the first four of the six group therapy sessions that were a formal part of the program. His therapist noted that much of the time during the individual sessions was devoted to complaints by the patient about the hospital routine and about the extreme pressures that are experienced when working as a salesman. The therapist felt that it was difficult to create a working relationship with him and apparently was not surprised when the patient opted not to continue treatment after the sixth session. According to his girlfriend, the patient began using cocaine occasionally about one month after the termination.

REFERENCES

Ackerman, S. J., Hilsenroth, M. J., Clemence, A. J., Weatherill, R., & Fowler, J. C. (2000). The effects of social cognition and object representation on psychotherapy continuation. *Bulletin of the Menninger Clinic, 64*(3), 386–408.

Alpher, V. S., Perfetto, G. A., Henry, W. P., & Strupp, H. H. (1990). The relationship between the Rorschach and assessment of the capacity to engage in short-term dynamic psychotherapy. *Psychotherapy, 27*(2), 224–229.

Alterman, A. I., Slap-Shelton, L., & DeCato, C. M. (1992). Developmental level as a predictor of alcoholism treatment response: An attempted replication. *Addictive Behaviors, 17*(5), 501–506.

Baekeland, F., & Lundwall, L. (1975). Dropping out of treatment: A critical review. *Psychological Bulletin, 82,* 738–783.

Cipolli, C., & Galliani, I. (1990). Addiction time and value of Z indicators in Rorschachs of heroin users. *Perceptual & Motor Skills, 70*(3, Pt. 2), 1105–1106.

Dougherty, R. J., & Lesswing, N. J. (1989). Inpatient cocaine abusers: An analysis of psychological and demographic variables. *Journal of Substance Abuse Treatment, 6*(1), 45–47.

Coonerty, S. (1986). An exploration of separation-individuation themes in the borderline personality disorder. *Journal of Personality Assessment, 50*(3), 501–511.

Fisher, S., & Cleveland, S. E. (1958). *Body image and personality.* New York: Van Nostrand.

Hilsenroth, M. J., Handler, L., Toman, K. M., & Padawer, J. R. (1995). Rorschach and MMPI-2 indices of early psychotherapy termination. *Journal of Consulting and Clinical Psychology, 63*(6), 956–965.

Hilsenroth, M. J., Holdwick, D. J., & Castlebury, F. D. (1998). The effects of *DSM-IV* Cluster B personality disorder symptoms on the termination and continuation of psychotherapy. *Psychotherapy, 35*(2), 163–176.

Horner, M. S., & Diamond, D. (1996). Object relations development and psychotherapy dropout in borderline outpatients. *Psychoanalytic Psychology, 13*(2), 205–223.

Kotkov, B., & Meadow, A. (1953). Rorschach criteria for predicting continuation in individual psychotherapy. *Journal of Consulting Psychology, 17,* 16.

Kobayashi, T., Fukui, K., Hayakawa, S., Koga, E., Ono, I., Fukui, Y., et al. (1995). Psychological problems due to long-term organic solvent abuse. *Arukoru Kenkyuto Yakubutsu Ison, 30*(5), 356–358.

Lesswing, N. J., & Dougherty, R. J. (1993). Psychopathology in alcohol- and cocaine-dependent patients: a comparison of findings from psychological testing. *Journal of Substance Abuse Treatment, 10*(1), 53–57.

Murray, H. A. (1943). *Manual for the Thematic Apperception Test.* Cambridge, MA: Harvard University Press.

Rogers, L. S., Knauss, J., & Hammond, K. R. (1951). Predicting continuation in therapy by means of the Rorschach Test. *Journal of Consulting Psychology, 15,* 368.

Thackrey, M., Butler, S., & Strupp, H. (1985, June). *Measure of patients' capacity for dynamic process.* Paper presented at the meeting of the Society for Psychotherapy Research, Evanston.

Thornton, C. C., Gellens, H. K., Alterman, A. I., & Gottheil, E. (1979). Developmental level and prognosis in alcoholics. *Alcoholism: Clinical and Experimental Research, 3*(1), 70–77.

Urist, J. (1977). The Rorschach Test and the assessment of object relations. *Journal of Personality Assessment, 41*(1), 3–9.

CHAPTER 11

An Issue of Motivation for Substance Abuse Treatment

 CASE 9

This 25-year-old woman is the companion of the 24-year-old patient described in Case 8 (Chapter 10). As noted in that history, she expressed a willingness to enter treatment with him, and she was evaluated in conjunction with her application for outpatient treatment in the substance abuse program. She admits to the frequent use of cocaine with her boyfriend. She says that she wants to enter treatment to help with his rehabilitation and because she feels unable to say no when drugs are offered to her by others, especially when her boyfriend encourages their use. She does not want to go through the inpatient treatment program because she is unable to take time away from her work. She fears that if she were to do so she might lose her job. She emphasizes that she does not feel "hooked like [her boyfriend] seems to be, but I want to learn how to avoid using [drugs]." If she is accepted into the outpatient program, she would be seen twice per week, once individually and once in a group for a minimum of eight weeks.

She is the only child of a couple who divorced when she was nine. She lived with her mother, who is now age 47, and an aunt, now age 51, until she was 22 years old. Her mother works as an assistant manager in a bookstore, and her aunt is a secretary. She has had no contact with father, age 50, for the past six years except for occasional letters or notes that he encloses with birthday and Christmas gifts. He remarried and moved to a distant state shortly after her high school graduation. Prior to that time, she would stay with him on five to eight weekends per year, and he usually would take her out to dinner on special occasions such as her birthday. He apparently was treated for alcoholism when she was in junior high school, and to the best of her knowledge, he has not used alcohol since that time. He works for an oil company in a blue-collar position. She is vague about the reasons for her parents' divorce, but she suspects that the main causes were his alcoholism and that he was unfaithful.

She reports that a series of upper respiratory infections caused her to be bedridden often when she was between the ages of 3 and 6, and she entered school a year late. She had problems with skin rashes between the ages of 13 and 15. These were identified as being caused by allergies, and for that reason she was exempt from physical education classes. That problem cleared by the time she entered high school, although she continued with allergy shots until age 16.

She graduated from high school at age 19. Her grades were mostly Cs and Bs. She worked one year in the bookstore where her mother is employed and then began training to become a dental technician. She completed that two-year course, was certified at age 21, and obtained a position as dental assistant in a group practice. She continues in that position, which she says she likes, and she anticipates staying on indefinitely.

She says that, because she was frail, she often did not join in the games of other children during elementary school. Because of her allergy problems, she did not have many friends while in junior high school or in her first two years of high school. She began menstruation at age 13 and had serious cramping problems for the next two years. She went to her first school dance at age 16. Not long after, at another dance, a boy kissed and fondled her, and she had her first experience of intercourse with him about four months later. She says it was not a very pleasant experience for her. She abstained from further sex until she was in dental training.

She notes that, during her dental technician training, she began dating regularly, "but with no one special person." She also indicates that it was during those two years that she began using marijuana, "usually at parties." After completing her training, she began sharing an apartment with two other women. One was a 27-year-old secretary and the other a 25-year-old who worked as an airline agent, "We often went to parties together, and I tried several other drugs, but not regularly, and didn't do any of them very much."

She states that, during that time, she had sexual relations with 8 or 10 men, but did not experience orgasm until she met her current boyfriend at a party about 18 months ago. They began living together when the lease on her shared apartment expired about nine months ago. She says, "He's the first guy I ever really loved, and he loves me. It's been bad sometimes, but if we didn't do all the coke we'd get along a lot better. When we get high, things just don't go right, and he loses his temper a lot when that happens." She says that sex with him is "really good except when he has trouble and then he makes me do a lot of weird things." She reports that he buys exotic underwear for her and asks her to dance in it, and he has also bought her a vibrator. She states that if she seems reluctant about his sexual suggestions, "He loses his temper sort of quickly, but he has never hit me until he went crazy last week." She adds, "He needs to get better, to really get clean. I don't know what we'll do if he doesn't. I can't think about losing him, but things have to change for our future."

She is described as a neatly dressed, reasonably attractive person who is slightly overweight. She was cooperative during the evaluation and appeared to smile a great deal when talking about herself. Drug screening was essentially negative, although some trace findings were noted. Neuropsychological screening was negative.

The assessment issues are: (1) Is there any evidence of a serious psychiatric disturbance? (2) How sincere is her motivation for intervention and what is the likelihood that she will complete the minimum of eight weeks in outpatient treatment? (3) Are there any specific short-term treatment objectives? (4) Should couples therapy be considered?

CASE FORMULATION AND RELEVANT LITERATURE

As noted in the case formulation for this young woman's boyfriend, the potential for dropout is significant in substance abuse programs. The Rorschach literature relevant to continuation versus premature termination of mental health services was reviewed for that case. Additionally, staff members are asking whether a couples component should be added to the individual and group therapy that is standard in the outpatient substance abuse program for which she is being considered. A review of the relatively limited Rorschach literature specific to couples therapy may help in treatment planning for this woman and her boyfriend.

Assessment of Couples

There are two ways in which the Rorschach can be used in therapeutic work with couples. One focuses on the individual and the implications of his or her personality style for interpersonal function. The other involves a focus on the couple's relationship, using a "consensus" technique in which the two partners work together to produce a conjoint protocol.

Blake, Humphrey, and Feldman (1994) studied married couples, examining the relationship between each partner's Rorschach and his or her style during a problem-solving discussion. They used four subscales from the Psychoanalytic Rorschach Profile (PRP; Burke, Friedman, & Gorlitz, 1988) thought to be related to robustness of self-concept: adequacy of Boundary for objects, Differentiation of separate objects, Stability and integrity of objects, and Mutuality and quality of emotional relatedness between separate objects. Each subscale rates responses along a four-point continuum ranging from well delineated self-concept to severe impairment. The authors used the four PRP subscales to derive two measures of healthy self-delineation (percentage of *very good* Differentiation and Stability responses) and two measures of impaired self-delineation (percentage of *very poor* Boundary and Mutuality responses).

The couples were then asked to discuss two problems in their marriage, and judges rated segments from verbatim transcripts of their audiotaped conversation using the Structural Analysis of Social Behavior (SASB; Benjamin, 1974, 1993). The SASB places interactions on a matrix formed by two orthogonal but intersecting dimensions: affiliation-disaffiliation and independence-interdependence. The affiliation dimension ranges from loving to hostile, and the independence dimension ranges from extreme independence to enmeshment.

Blake et al. (1994) reported significant relationships between the Rorschach self-concept measures and observed marital interactions. Specifically, they found that as healthy Differentiation and Stability percepts increased, the likelihood of SASB ratings for deferring and submitting interpersonal behavior decreased. Conversely, they found that Rorschach impaired Boundary percepts were significantly and positively correlated with SASB ratings of resentful compliance and defensive self-justification. The authors conclude that their results demonstrate ". . . clear and meaningful relationships between intrapsychic self-delineation and observed marital interaction" (p. 161).

A second way to use the Rorschach with couples involves asking the two partners to work together to produce a consensus protocol. Several variations of this approach have been developed (e.g., Bauman & Roman, 1968; Blanchard, 1968; Loveland, Wynne, & Singer, 1963; Magni, Ferruzza, & Barison, 1982; Nakamura & Nakamura, 1987; Willi, 1979), each focusing either on some aspect of the couple's interaction or on the structure or content of their individual and agreed-on Rorschachs.

Handler (1997) illustrates a consensus approach that may be of particular value in working with couples. Each partner takes the Rorschach individually, and then the two are asked to take the test together, arriving at agreed-on responses for each card. This approach produces three Rorschachs whose structural and content comparison allows a description of ". . . the ways in which the interaction either enhances or detracts from the personalities, as they are portrayed in the individual records" (p. 502).

Handler (1997) presents data for a couple being evaluated for marital therapy, and his findings demonstrate the potential utility of this approach. For example, a comparison of structural data for the individual and consensus Rorschachs found that the husband's protocol had five vague Developmental Quality answers, the wife's had three, and the consensus protocol had none. Handler suggests that the wife may exert ". . . a controlling, defining, and sharpening effect on her husband's perceptual world; she helps him to clarify what he sees and to organize his world" (p. 504). Noting that the consensus protocol contains no vague Developmental Quality percepts, he suggests that " . . . the couple collaborate to be more focused and less diffuse than either is capable of being individually" (p. 504). In another example of a structural comparison, the *Lambda* of 1.14 that the couple produced in their consensus Rorschach was markedly higher than either of their individual findings (.60 and .42). Handler suggests that they ". . . agreed to narrow their approach to the world, oversimplifying complex stimulus demand situations" (p. 505) and wonders if their agreed-on avoidance of complexity will present difficulties in the marital therapy.

Handler (1997) also illustrates how the consensus approach can be used in analyzing content. As an example, the husband's response on card VIII was creative and highly elaborated, the wife's more aggressive, and their agreed-on percept a more prosaic one. Handler suggests that the couple's interaction serves to modulate the wife's aggressiveness but, in the process, ". . . the responses appear less creative and original, indicating that the cost to the marriage is a loss of spontaneity and creativity" (p. 517).

In summary, the Rorschach—used both in its standard way to describe individual personality and with the consensus approach to describe interaction dynamics—can be useful in working with couples. At present, consensus Rorschach techniques do not have the validity support provided by studies like those of Blake et al. (1994), which relate individual Rorschach findings to observed interpersonal behavior. This is an area in which future research will be helpful.

Case 9.   A 25-Year-Old Female.

Card	Response	Inquiry
I	1. 1. It ll a person in a costume, lik a ballerina, mayb lik fr Swan Lake or sthg	**E:** (Rpts Ss resp) **S:** Well u can c her outline here (D4) & ths wb wgs, lik a costume, it's lik she's standg w the wgs out, u can c her outlin thru the costume **E:** Thru the costume? **S:** Well c here (D3) is the outline of her legs lik her costume was transparent, lik u can c thru it **E:** Look som more, I thk u'll find smthg else too
	2. Ths mite be a bell, just ths part	**E:** (Rpts Ss resp) **S:** Well, it has the outline of a bell & ths wld be the clapper, lik a church bell or the Liberty bell
II	3 Ths part up here ll 2 chickens sorta looking at eo	**E:** (Rpts Ss resp) **S:** Well thy hav the outline of chickens (D2) & thyr facing eo, thts why I thot thyd b lookg at eo
	4. Ths part ll a partly decayed tooth	**E:** (Rpts Ss resp) **S:** Well u c some pretty strange lookg teeth if u work for a dentist & ths re me of one tht we had to reconstruct last wk, it had decayed more on the outside & it was all black lik ths one **E:** I'm not quite sur I'm seeg it lik u r **S:** Rite here (D4) & c the littl cone shaped edges, lik decay
III	5. Ths ll 2 wm talking to eo	**E:** (Rpts Ss resp) **S:** Well thy ll wm to me, c their heads & breasts & legs & thyr standg ovr some pot or sthg & tallkg to eo
IV	6. Ths part up here ll a fan, lik an oriental fan	**E:** (Rpts Ss resp) **S:** Well u can c the folds in it, c the lines, lik it is opened up, at least partially but mayb not all the way, thy usually mak them out of paper, at least the ones tht don't cost much are made out of paper **E:** I'm not sur about the folds **S:** C these dark lines mak it ll folds lik when u begin to open one up
	7. Ths dark cntr part in here ll an x-ray of the spine	**E:** (Rpts Ss resp) **S:** Well, it just has tht shape to it, when I looked it just re me of tht, its dark lik an xray of a spine
V	8. Tht re me of a bat	**E:** (Rpts Ss resp) **S:** Its lik when thy hav their wgs way out lik when thy fly real fast, I guess when thyr swooping & ths is his hands out here in front & the little feet
	9. Ths part out here ll a leg but u can't c a foot, lik its been cut off	**E:** (Rpts Ss resp) **S:** Well it really has the shape of a leg to it but u can't c a foot, its lik it was severed & it stops at the ankle **E:** What kind of leg? **S:** A person's leg, I dk of any A legs lik tht
VI	10. I dkno about all ths (D1) but up here it ll a fly	**E:** (Rpts Ss resp) **S:** Well it just does, it has wgs & the body, just lik a fly
VII	11. Ths ll 2 littl rabbits sittg on a ledge	**E:** (Rpts Ss resp) **S:** Well thy hav their ears & the littl tails & the round face lik a rabbit face & thyr sittg on ths thg, it ll a piece of rock lik a rocky ledge or smthg lik tht

(continued)

Card Response	Inquiry
12. Down here it ll 2 people standg nxt to eo, lik thy hav formal clothg on	**E:** (Rpts Ss resp) **S:** U can just barely make them out, its lik thyr both dressed in dark clothg & thyr standg there, lik at a ceremony, mayb its a couple gettg married or smthg but she ought to b in white if thy r **E:** I'm not sur I'm seeg it lik u, help me **S:** Look, rite here, standg next to eo, its lik a man on the left & a wm & ths cb a big train from her gown but it shld b white, mayb it looks dark cuz thyr in the shadows
VIII 13. Tht looks lik sbody's insides	**E:** (Rpts Ss resp) **S:** Well ths cb the rib cage (D3) & the stomach (D2) & the lungs & smthg else up here (D4) mayb a neckbone **E:** I'm not sur why it ll tht **S:** I don't either, its ugly, it just ll smbody was opened up & u c all the parts
14. If u just tak the pink it cb a cpl of A's	**E:** (Rpts Ss resp) **S:** Sort lik dogs or cats, c the legs & the head & the body, I thk mor lik a dog
IX 15. A clown's face lik u'd c on a circus poster	**E:** (Rpts Ss resp) **S:** Well its painted all diff colors, c his ears r orange & his cheeks r green & his his neck is pink, & he's got orange hair arranged to stick up lik clown's do, its lik a poster more than real, lik thy show to advertise the circus
X 16. Well up here it ll 2 littl bugs tryg to lift up this stick	**E:** (Rpts Ss resp) **S:** Well thy ll littl ants or sthg c the antennae & the legs & thyr tryg to lift ths pole or stick or smthg up or at least thry pushg on it. Thyr prob ants cuz thyr grey colored lik ants
17. Ths ll the face of a rabbit	**E:** (Rpts Ss resp) **S:** Well it just does, c the ear & the eyes, just lik a rabbits face
18. Ths part ll one of those spaceships lik u c in science fiction movies, its lik coming toward u	**E:** (Rpts Ss resp) **S:** It has the big pods on each side (D3) & the littl cabin in the middl, it ll it's traveling in space **E:** Traveling in space? **S:** Yes if u thk of the white prt as being space, ths ll its coming toward u, way off in the distance, its so littl it wb far off
19. Ths part ll 2 cherubs or smthg lik thyr drinking smthg out of a straw, thy havpointy caps on	**E:** (Rpts Ss resp) **S:** Well thy hav littl pudgy noses & the forehead & ths blue is lik a straw & thy littl each r sharing whtevr is in the container, ths othr blue prt **E:** U said thyr cherubs or sthg? **S:** Well thyr pink, I guess cherubs cb pink & thy hav littl pointy caps on, lik nitecaps, mayb its fr a cartoon or smthg, u can't c the rest of their bodies

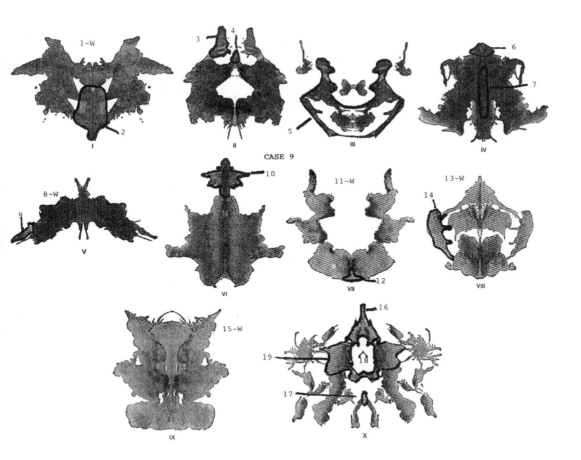

CASE 9

Case 9. Sequence of Scores.

Card	No.	Loc.	No.	Determinant(s)	(2)	Content(s)	Pop	Z	Special Scores
I	1	W+	1	Mp.FVo		H,Cg		4.0	GHR
	2	Ddo	24	Fo		Sc			
II	3	D+	2	FMpu	2	A		5.5	
	4	Do	4	FC'–		Hd			PER,MOR,PHR
III	5	D+	1	Mpo	2	H,Hh	P	3.0	GHR
IV	6	Do	3	FV.mpu		Id			DR
	7	Ddo	33	FYo		Xy			
V	8	Wo	1	FMao		A	P	1.0	INC
	9	Do	1	Fo		Hd			MOR,PHR
VI	10	Do	3	Fu		A			
VII	11	W+	1	FMpo	2	A,Ls		2.5	
	12	Dd+	28	Mp.FC'u		H,Cg		1.0	AB,COP,GHR
VIII	13	Wo	1	F–		An		4.5	MOR
	14	Do	1	Fo	2	A	P		
IX	15	Wo	1	CFu		Art,(Hd)		5.5	GHR
X	16	D+	11	FMa.FC'o	2	A,Bt		4.0	COP,GHR
	17	Do	5	Fo		Ad			
	18	DdS+	29	ma.FDu		Sc,Na		6.0	PER
	19	Dd+	99	Mp.FCo	2	(Hd),Fd		4.0	COP,GHR

221

Case 9. Structural Summary.

Location Features	Determinants Blends	Single	Contents	S-Constellation
				YES . .FV+VF+V+FD>2
		H = 3		NO . . .Col-Shd Bl>0
Zf = 11	M.FV	M = 1	(H) = 0	NO . . .Ego<.31,>.44
ZSum = 41.0	FV.m	FM = 3	Hd = 2	NO . . .MOR > 3
ZEst = 34.5	M.FC′	m = 0	(Hd) = 2	YES . .Zd > +− 3.5
	FM.FC′	FC = 0	Hx = 0	YES . .es > EA
W = 5	m.FD	CF = 1	A = 6	NO . . .CF+C > FC
D = 9	M.FC	C = 0	(A) = 0	YES . .X+% < .70
W+D = 14		Cn = 0	Ad = 1	NO . . .S > 3
Dd = 5		FC′ = 1	(Ad) = 0	NO . . .P < 3 or > 8
S = 1		C′F = 0	An = 1	NO . . .Pure H < 2
		C′ = 0	Art = 2	NO . . .R < 17
		FT = 0	Ay = 0	4 . . . .TOTAL

DQ

		Single	Contents	Special Scores
+ = 8		TF = 0	Bl = 0		Lv1	Lv2
o = 11		T = 0	Bt = 1	DV	= 0x1	0x2
v/+ = 0		FV = 0	Cg = 2	INC	= 1x2	0x4
v = 0		VF = 0	Cl = 0	DR	= 1x3	0x6
		V = 0	Ex = 0	FAB	= 0x4	0x7
		FY = 1	Fd = 1	ALOG	= 0x5	
		YF = 0	Fi = 0	CON	= 0x7	
		Y = 0	Ge = 0	Raw Sum6 = 2	
		Fr = 0	Hh = 1	Wgtd Sum6 = 5	

Form Quality

	FQx	MQual	W+D	Single	Contents	Special Scores
+	= 0	= 0	= 0	rF = 0	Ls = 1	
o	= 11	= 3	= 8	FD = 0	Na = 1	AB = 1	GH = 6
u	= 6	= 1	= 4	F = 6	Sc = 2	AG = 0	PHR = 2
−	= 2	= 0	= 2		Sx = 0	COP = 3	MOR = 3
none	= 0	= 0	= 0		Xy = 1	CP = 0	PER = 2
				(2) = 6	Id = 0	PSV = 0	

Ratios, Percentages, and Derivations

R = 19	L = 0.46			FC:CF+C = 1:1	COP = 3 AG = 0
				Pure C = 0	GHR:PHR = 6:2
EB = 4:1.5	EA = 5.5	EBPer = 2.7		SumC′:WSumC = 3:1.5	a:p = 3:7
eb = 6:6	es = 12	D = −2		Afr = 0.58	Food = 1
	Adj es = 11	Adj D = −2		S = 1	SumT = 0
				Blends:R = 6:19	Hum Con = 7
FM = 4	C′ = 3	T = 0		CP = 0	Pure H = 3
m = 2	V = 2	Y = 1			PER = 2
					Iso Indx = 0.21

a:p	= 3:7	Sum6 = 2	XA% = 0.89	Zf = 11.0	3r+(2)/R = 0.32
Ma:Mp	= 0:4	Lv2 = 0	WDA% = 0.86	W:D:Dd = 5:9:5	Fr+rF = 0
2AB+Art+Ay	= 4	WSum6 = 5	X−% = 0.11	W:M = 5:4	SumV = 2
MOR	= 3	M− = 0	S− = 0	Zd = +6.5	FD = 1
		Mnone = 0	P = 3	PSV = 0	An+Xy = 2
			X+% = 0.58	DQ+ = 8	MOR = 3
			Xu% = 0.32	DQv = 0	H:(H)Hd(Hd) = 3:4

PTI = 0	DEPI = 4	CDI = 4*	S-CON = 4	HVI = No	OBS = No

S-CON AND KEY VARIABLE

The S-CON value (4) is not significant. The first positive Key variable is the CDI value (4), indicating that the interpretive routine should begin with a study of the data regarding controls. Subsequently, the clusters concerning interpersonal perception, self-perception, and affect should be reviewed; and the routine should end by examining the data in the three clusters that compose the cognitive triad.

CONTROLS

Case 9.   Control-Related Variables for a 25-Year-Old Female.

EB = 4:1.5	EA = 5.5		D = −2	CDI = 4
eb = 6:6	es = 12	Adj es = 11	AdjD = −2	L = 0.46
FM = 4 m = 2	SumC′ = 3	SumT = 0	SumV = 2	SumY = 1

The positive CDI value (4) and Adj D Score (−2) indicate that she is vulnerable to disorganization under stress. The CDI finding connotes that she is somewhat less mature than might be expected for an adult, which makes her susceptible to problems in coping with the demands of everyday living, especially in the interpersonal sphere. The Adj D Score indicates that her capacity for control and tolerance for stress are fragile because her psychological organization is more complicated and demanding than she can contend with easily. It creates a substantial potential for impulsiveness in her thinking, decisions, and behaviors.

The modest *EA* value (5.5), plus the fact that neither side of the *EB* (4:1.5) contains a zero value, signals that the Adj D Score is probably reliable, supporting the postulate that she is likely to be less mature than expected for her age. She simply has fewer resources organized in ways that make them easily available to her. This creates a proclivity for a psychological overload that increases her susceptibility to disorganization. In her case, this susceptibility appears to be chronic. It is caused mainly by the combination of her limited resources and discomforting emotions that she does not deal with effectively.

This is revealed by the value for the Adj *es* (11), which is slightly higher than average for an adult, and the *eb* (6:6), in which the right side value is also higher than expected. It is elevated primarily because of two elements. The first is the value for *SumC′* (3), indicating that she suppresses the release of emotions more often than most people. This is a persistent source of irritation. The second is the value for *SumV* (2), signifying that she apparently ruminates a great deal about personal features that she judges to be negative. This also breeds upsetting feelings. Thus, she is burdened by unwanted emotions and has limited resources with which to deal with these irritating feelings. This can cause anyone to be susceptible to problems in control, but in her case, the susceptibility is more profound because of her immaturity.

It seems likely that her tenuous state prompts her to seek out structured and routine environments, in which she can rely on others for support. However, even in those supportive situations, some of her decisions and behaviors will not be well thought through or implemented very effectively because of her persistent overload state and the confusion that it breeds for her.

INTERPERSONAL PERCEPTION

Case 9.   Interpersonal Perception Data for a 25-Year-Old Female.

R = 19	CDI = 4	HVI = No	**COP & AG Responses**
a:p = 3:7	SumT = 0	Fd = 1	VII 12. Dd+ Mp.FC'u H,Cg 1.0 AB,COP,GHR
	[eb = 6:6]		X 16. D+ FMa.FC'o 2 A,Bt 4.0 COP,GHR
Sum Human Contents = 7		H = 3	X 19. Dd+ Mp.FCo (Hd),Fd 4.0 COP,GHR
[Style = Introversive]			
GHR:PHR = 6:2			
COP = 3	AG = 0	PER = 2	
Isolation Indx = 0.21			

As noted, the positive CDI (4) signals that she is prone to experience frequent difficulties when interacting with the environment, especially in the interpersonal sphere. Most of her interpersonal relationships are likely to be more superficial and less mature than desirable. Moreover, the substantial value for passive movement answers, as indicated by the $a:p$ ratio (3:7), signifies that she usually assumes a somewhat passive role in her relations with others. Apparently, she has become accustomed to avoiding responsibility for making decisions and is not very likely to seek new solutions to problems.

The Food response in her record suggests that much of her interpersonal passivity is probably related to notable dependency needs. She needs the support of others, and her behaviors are likely to be marked by more dependency gestures than are typical for adults. This has become a natural coping style that serves as a compensation for her immaturity and reduces the probability that she will be overwhelmed by complex decision-making situations.

The finding concerning her passive-dependent coping style is especially interesting when considered in light of the absence of any texture responses ($SumT = 0$). This suggests that she does not experience needs for emotional closeness in the same ways as most people. This does not mean the needs are not present but, rather, that she probably is somewhat uncomfortable in close relations, especially those involving tactile exchange. When considered in light of her dependency needs, this could create a conflict for her as, optimally, it is likely that she would prefer being dependent while maintaining some distance or safety in her relations. However, her immaturity and probable naïveté make it unlikely that this is a major concern for her.

The presence of seven human content responses, about the value expected from an introversive adult, signifies that she is interested in people. However, only three of those seven responses are pure H answers, implying that she may not understand people very well. If this is true, she may be prone to have greater expectations for her relationships than is reasonable, and she also may have a tendency to misinterpret social gestures.

On the other hand, the data for the GHR:PHR ratio (6:2) indicate that she is likely to engage in behaviors that are adaptive in a broad range of interpersonal relations. This finding, plus the fact that her protocol includes three COP and no AG answers, strongly suggests that others probably regard her as likable and outgoing. The two PER answers hint that she may be a bit more defensive in some of her relations with others, probably because of a sense of insecurity, but this is not likely to occur often. The overall implication of the findings is that she tends to view interpersonal activity as an important part of her daily routine and that others identify her as being gregarious.

At first glance, the likelihood that she is adaptive and gregarious in her interpersonal relations may seem contradictory to other findings concerning her immaturity, her vulnerability to impulsiveness or disorganization, and her passive-dependent style, but this is not necessarily so. Much depends on how she manifests her passivity and quest for dependence, and if done in an adaptive and seemingly gregarious manner, her behaviors can be perceived as acceptable and even rewarding to others. She has selected an occupation that is structured, involves controlled interpersonal exchange, and permits her to be dependent on the direction provided by others. Under those circumstances, features that might otherwise be liabilities can become assets. Thus, if her immaturity and dependency orientation pose hazards for her, they are most likely to occur in relationships that involve close and varied emotional exchanges.

The sorts of activity that probably mark her interpersonal behaviors seem to be illustrated by the five movement answers that include pairs: Card II, response 3, "two chickens sort of looking at each other"; Card III, response 5, "two women talking to each other"; Card VII, response 11, "two little rabbits sitting on a ledge"; Card X, response 16, "two little bugs trying to lift up a stick"; and Card X, response 19, "two cherubs . . . drinking something out of a straw . . . sharing whatever is in the container." All but one (bugs) are passive, but none are negative. In fact, two (women talking, cherubs sharing) are positive, and this composite of answers implies that her perceptions of people tend to be more positive than negative.

Thus, although her immaturity and limited resources make her susceptible to difficulties when interacting with the environment, it appears unlikely that those difficulties are readily apparent to others. This is probably because she is interested in people and usually views them positively, even though she often may not understand them very well. This interest, plus her need to be dependent, appear to have promoted patterns of interpersonal behavior that lead others to regard her as likable and outgoing. These behaviors usually include a noticeably passive, dependent role in her relations, permitting her to avoid responsibility for decision making and reducing the likelihood of conflict with others. She probably makes few demands for closeness with others and seems likely to fulfill her own emotional needs through dependency rather than through elaborate emotional exchanges. This permits her to take from others while also usually remaining at a seemingly safe distance from them.

SELF-PERCEPTION

Case 9. Self-Perception Related Data for a 25-Year-Old Female.

R	= 19	OBS	= No	HVI = No	Human Content, Hx, An & Xy Responses
					I 1. W+ Mp.FVo 2 H,Cg 4.0 GHR
Fr+rF	= 0	3r+(2)/R	= 0.32		II 4. Do FC'– Hd PER,MOR,PHR
					III 5. D+ Mpo 2 H,Hh P 3.0 GHR
FD	= 1	SumV	= 2		IV 7. Ddo FYo Xy
					V 9. Do Fo Hd MOR,PHR
An+Xy	= 2	MOR	= 3		VII 12. Dd+ Mp.FC'u H,Cg 1.0 AB,COP,GHR
					VIII 13. Wo F– An 4.5 MOR
H:(H)+Hd+(Hd) = 3:4					IX 15. Wo CFu Art,(Hd) 5.5 GHR
[EB = 4:1.5]					X 19. Dd+ Mp.FCo 2 (Hd),Fd 4.0 COP,GHR

The marginally low Egocentricity Index (0.32) suggests that she tends to regard herself less favorably in comparison with others. The composite of one *FD* and two vista answers indicates that she engages in much more self-examining behavior than is customary. This probably relates to her low self-esteem; much of the focus is on features of herself that she regards negatively.

There is a slight elevation in *An+Xy* answers (2), which hints at some unusual body concern. Although the source is not obvious, it seems probable that this relates to a sense of vulnerability that may be provoked by her considerable self-examining. On a speculative level, recent events may have exacerbated her introspective preoccupations, and she may be aware that her current relationship is somewhat precarious. The three MOR contents indicate that her self-image includes some negative attributions and she probably harbors a fairly pessimistic view of herself.

Only three of her seven human content responses are Pure *H* implying that her self-image contains many features based on imagination or distortions of real experience. Although the codings for those three answers (responses 1, 5, & 12) are not markedly negative, one contains a vista determinant, a second is AB, and all three include passive movement. The other four answers that contain human content (responses 4, 9, 15, & 19) include one of her two minus responses and two of her three MOR codings. In effect, the composite of codings for the seven responses strongly hints that she has a negative and possibly distorted notion of herself.

Her two minus responses include dramatic forms of projection regarding her impressions of self. The first (Card II, response 4) is, "a partly decayed tooth . . . you see some pretty strange looking teeth if you work for a dentist . . . we had to reconstruct last week, it has decayed more on the outside and it was all black like this one." The second (Card VIII, response 13) is, "somebody's insides . . . it's ugly . . . somebody was opened up and you can see all the parts." Both are MOR and emphasize a sense of vulnerability. This is also conveyed by her third MOR answer (Card V, response 9), "a leg but you can't see a foot, like it's been cut off . . . it's like it was severed and it stops at the ankle." All three connote serious damage and imply strong feelings of fragility.

All four of her *M* responses are passive, but the features are more positive than the minus and MOR answers. The first, (Card I, response 1) is, "a person in costume, like a ballerina, maybe from *Swan Lake* or something . . . standing with the wings out, you can see her outline through the costume." It represents a fantasy facade, but also suggests vulnerability (through the costume). The second (Card III, response 5) is, "two women talking to each other . . . standing over some pot or something." It is a common answer, but described in a passive and conservative manner.

The third *M* response (Card VII, response 12) is the most intriguing of the four. It is, "two people standing next to each other . . . both dressed in dark clothing . . . like at a ceremony, maybe it's a couple getting married . . . but she ought to be in white if they are." It has a positive, fantasylike element (maybe getting married), but it also includes a somber feature that implies some uncertainty (she ought to be in white . . . maybe they are in the shadows). The final *M* answer (Card X, response 19) is ". . . two cherubs . . . drinking something out of a straw . . . sharing whatever is in the container . . . maybe it's from a cartoon." It is also a fantasylike response that is possibly most notable for the "sharing" concept. This probably relates to her previously noted dependency orientation.

None of the four *FM* responses include negative attributions. Two are passive (Card II, response 3), "two chickens sort of looking at each other," and (Card VII, response 11), "two little rabbits sitting on a ledge." One of the remaining two (Card V, response 8), "a bat . . . like when they have their wings way out when they fly real fast," does not contain any obvious interpretive substance. The fourth *FM* (Card X, response 16) is probably the most positive, "two little bugs trying to lift up this stick." The two *m* answers are interesting because both include dimensional features. The first (Card IV, response 6) is one of her two vista answers, "an oriental fan . . . it is opened up, at least partially . . . the ones that don't cost much are made out of paper."

On a speculative level, two implications are possible. One is that more development (opening) may occur but, more negatively, there is a suggestion of fragility (made of paper) and low self-worth (don't cost much). The second (Card X, response 18) seems more positive, "one of those spaceships like you see in science fiction movies . . . it's coming toward you, way off in the distance." It also appears to convey a sense of things yet to come and, as with the fan response, might reflect optimism that she harbors about herself.

The remaining six answers, (response 2), "a bell," (response 7), "an X-ray of the spine," (response 10), "a fly," (response 14), "a couple of animals," (response 15), "a clown's face . . . on a circus poster," and (response 17), "the face of a rabbit," do not contain any unusual wording or embellishments. The X-ray response is congruent with earlier hypotheses about fragility and/or vulnerability, and the clown's face answer seems to be of interest because of the implication about a facade, ". . . it's painted all different colors . . . it's like a poster more than real, like they show to advertise the circus."

Overall, her view of herself seems to reflect cautiously naive positive features based mainly on fantasy that, like a facade, overlay a distinctive sense of vulnerability or apprehension and view of being damaged. It is likely that she regards herself unfavorably in comparison with others and that she engages in much self-examining, that focuses on the perceived negative features of her self-image. Despite these negative features, she appears to have molded a self-concept that includes many fantasy-based expectations that ignore reality. This is not unexpected in light of her immaturity, and it provides her with a positive but naive optimism about herself. At the same time, there is a clear impression that she harbors an awareness that the optimism is not well founded in reality.

AFFECT

Case 9.   Affect-Related Data for a 25-Year-Old Female.

						Blends	
EB	= 4:1.5			EBPer	= 2.7		
eb	= 6:6	L	= 0.46	FC:CF+C	= 1:1	M.FV	= 1
DEPI	= 4	CDI = 4		Pure C	= 0	M.FC'	= 1
						M.FC	= 1
SumC' = 3	SumT = 0			SumC':WSumC	= 3:1.5	FM.FC'	= 1
SumV = 2	SumY = 1			Afr	= 0.58	FV.m	= 1
						m.FD	= 1
Intellect	= 4	CP	= 0	S = 1 (S to I,II,III	= 0)		
Blends:R	= 6:19			Col-Shad Bl	= 0		
m + y Bl	= 2			Shading Bl	= 0		

The *EB* (4:1.5) indicates that, typically, she approaches decision-making tasks in an ideational manner during which she tends to push emotions aside to avoid being influenced by them. The datum for the *EBPer* (2.7) suggests that this is a persistent style, regardless of its effectiveness. This is a bit unusual for an immature person and implies that her emotional history may have been marked by dubious and confusing experiences. In light of the positive CDI value (4), it seems reasonable to speculate that many or most of these experiences have occurred in the interpersonal sphere and have gradually created a tendency to mistrust her feelings. This postulate seems supported by the data for three other variables.

The first is the right side value for the *eb* (6:6), which indicates that she is experiencing more discomforting emotions than might be expected. These feelings appear to be generated mainly from two sources, the two vista answers signaling a tendency to self-examine and focus on her perceived shortcomings, and the *SumC'* value (3) indicating a proneness to hold in and suppress emotions that she would prefer to express. The former usually breeds sadness or unhappiness, while the latter usually creates sensations of tension, uneasiness, or anxiety.

A second variable suggesting some mistrust of feelings is the *SumC':WSumC* ratio (3:1.5). Higher left side values in this ratio are unusual and signify an emotional constraint that leads to irritating feelings. When considered with regard to findings about her interpersonal characteristics, it seems reasonable to speculate that she has found that her passive-dependent orientation is accepted most often when she conceals or constrains displays of her feelings.

In that context, it is not surprising that the value for the *Afr* (.58) is in the expected range. It implies that she is as willing as most others to become involved with emotional situations. This is consistent with findings concerning the adaptability of her interactions with others. She is probably quite willing to share in the feelings of others, but less willing to share her own feelings with them.

A third variable that provides some support for the notion that she mistrusts her feelings is the Intellectualization Index value (4). It is slightly higher than expected and suggests that she is inclined to deal with emotions on an intellectual level more often than most people. This process permits her to deny or neutralize the impact of feelings. In a similar context, the low values in the *FC:CF+C* ratio (1:1) suggest that she does not display her feelings freely, but when she does, they are probably modulated as well as those of most adults.

The six blends in this 19-response protocol (32%) connotes more psychological complexity than is usual for an introversive person. This can create difficulties for her because of her somewhat limited resources. However, two of her six blends (*FV.m, m.FD*) appear to be situationally related, creating more complexity than she is accustomed to dealing with.

Her tendency to constrain expressions of her feelings is likely related to uncertainty about how others will receive them and whether they might jeopardize her dependency opportunities. As a result, she seems to burden herself with much irritating emotion that increases her vulnerability to becoming overwhelmed and limits the probabilities of her being able to establish and maintain the sorts of relationships that she would prefer.

PROCESSING

Case 9.   Processing Variables for a 25-Year-Old Female.

EB = 4:1.5	Zf = 11	Zd = +6.5	DQ+ = 8
L = 0.46	W:D:Dd = 5:9:5	PSV = 0	DQv/+ = 0
HVI = NO	W:M = 5:4		DQv = 0
OBS = NO			

Location & DQ Sequencing

I: Wo.Ddo	VI: Do
II: D+.Do	VII: W+.Dd+
III: D+	VIII: Wo.Do
IV: Do.Ddo	IX: Wo
V: Wo.Do	X: D+.Do.DdS+.Dd+

Although the value for Zf (11) is in the expected range, indicating a processing effort that is similar to most people, the data for the $W:D:Dd$ ratio (5:9:5) conveys a somewhat different impression. At first glance, the higher value for D selections connotes an economizing form of processing. However, when this is considered with regard to the substantial number of Dd locations, a more atypical processing is implied that involves considerable scanning activity and a focus on minute or unusual details. This suggests the presence of a guarded or mistrusting set that prompts her to minimize or avoid involvement with perceived ambiguity and orients her to deal with less complex, more easily managed stimulus fields. This finding is not unusual in light of her passive style and probably represents an inclination to feel uncomfortable about her decision-making capabilities.

This tactic could reduce her processing effectiveness, but other data indicate that this is not the case. The Location sequencing is consistent. All of her first responses are given to W or D locations, while four of her five Dd responses are last answers, and the fifth is a third response to Card X. This suggests a concerted effort and seems to imply that she feels more confident when she perceives the stimulus field to be more easily defined.

Her considerable effort is also noted by the Zd value (+6.5), indicating an overincorporative style that requires the investment of considerable energy and effort into scanning activities. Usually, this signifies a need to avoid being careless and to ensure that she is not making processing errors. The adequacy of her processing tactics is also reflected by the distribution of DQ codes. Eight of her nineteen responses are synthesized. They include five of her first responses, involving W or D areas, and three of her five Dd answers. None of her responses are coded as DQv or $DQv/+$.

In effect, although guarded when dealing with new information, she makes a considerable effort to do so. Her processing habits are reasonably consistent, yielding inputs that are adequate and possibly even sophisticated at times.

MEDIATION

Case 9.   Mediation Variables for a 25-Year-Old Female.

R = 19	L = 0.46	OBS = No	**Minus & NoForm Features**
FQx+	= 0	XA% = .89	II 4. Do FC'– Hd PER,MOR,PHR
FQxo	= 11	WDA% = .86	VIII 13. Wo F– An 4.5 MOR
FQxu	= 6	X–% = .11	
FQx–	= 2	S– = 0	
FQxnone	= 0		
(W+D	= 14)		
WD+	= 0	P = 3	
WDo	= 8	X+% = .58	
WDu	= 4	Xu% = .32	
WD–	= 2		
WDnone	= 0		

The substantial values for the $XA\%$ (.89) and the $WDA\%$ (.86) indicate that her translation of inputs is usually appropriate for the situation. Likewise, the modest $X-\%$ value (0.11) suggests that instances of mediational dysfunction occur no more frequently than for most people. Although the content codes of her two minus answers (*Hd* & *An*) are dissimilar, the actual contents (decayed tooth & somebody's insides) seem to correspond. This homogeneity implies that instances of dysfunction are most likely provoked by her previously noted concerns with fragility or vulnerability. Although neither of her minus answers represents a severe departure from reality, their similarity should be noted when treatment options and objectives are considered.

The low number of Popular responses (3) seems somewhat contrary to the substantial *XA%* and *WDA%* findings. This composite of data suggests that, even though she translates inputs appropriately, she often disregards obvious or commonplace translations in situations where cues regarding them are easily identified. Similarly, the modest values for the *X+%* (.58) and the substantial values for the *Xu%* (.32) support the notion that she tends to make more mediational decisions that disregard social demands or expectations than do most people. These findings connote that she has a marked tendency to overpersonalize when translating inputs and is probably very influenced in doing so by her own needs, sets, and attitudes. If she does this to excess, as seems the case, it creates a potential for others to regard her as being eccentric, out of step, or overly individualistic. This has important implications for treatment planning, especially in light of earlier findings that she seems lacking is social skills and has settled on a passive mode of interacting with others.

IDEATION

Case 9.   Ideation Variables for a 25-Year-Old Female.

								Critical Special Scores			
L	= 0.46	OBS	= No	HVI	= No			DV	= 0	DV2	= 0
EB	= 4:1.5	EBPer	= 2.7	a:p	= 3:7			INC	= 1	INC2	= 0
				Ma:Mp	= 0:4			DR	= 1	DR2	= 0
eb	= 6:6	[FM = 4 m = 2]						FAB	= 0	FAB2	= 0
				M−	= 0			ALOG	= 0	CON	= 0
Intell Indx	= 4	MOR	= 3	Mnone	= 0			Sum6	= 2	WSum6	= 5
									(R = 19)		

M Response Features

I   1. W+ Mp.FVo 2 H,Cg 4.0 GHR
III   5. D+ Mpo 2 H,Hh P 3.0 GHR
VII 12. Dd+ Mp.FC'u H,Cg 1.0 AB,COP,GHR
X 19. Dd+ Mp.FCo 2 (Hd),Fd 4.0 COP,GHR

As noted during the review of data concerning her emotions, the *EB* (4:1.5) indicates that she prefers to delay formulating decisions or initiating behaviors until she has considered all apparent alternative possibilities. She relies heavily on internal evaluation in forming judgments, and usually, her feelings play only a limited role in decision-making activity. Moreover, the datum for *EBPer* (2.7) suggests that she is not flexible about this decision-making approach and is likely to use it in most situations regardless of indications that a different approach might be more effective.

The notion that she lacks flexibility in decision making tends to be supported by the data for another variable, the *a:p* ratio (3:7). This finding suggests that her ideational sets and values are reasonably well fixed and would be difficult to alter. Her tendency to be inflexible in her thinking probably contributes to her apparent immaturity and social difficulties and should be considered as an important issue when planning for treatment objectives.

This problem also appears to be compounded by a moderate elevation in the frequency of MOR responses (3). It signals another source that can limit the effectiveness of her ideational style. The presence of a pessimistic set prompts her to conceptualize her relationship with the environment with some apprehension and discouragement. A potential result is that some of her decision making will be marked by doubt and the anticipation that her actions will have little effect on the outcome of a situation.

The left side *eb* value (6), comprising four *FM* and two *m,* is not inordinately high, but it signifies a modest increase in peripheral ideation due to situational stress. This could have a negative impact on her current attention and concentration operations.

A more negative finding concerns the *Ma:Mp* ratio (0:4). It connotes a stylistic proneness to take flight into fantasy as a routine tactic for dealing with unpleasant situations. This *Snow White syndrome* is characterized mainly by the avoidance of responsibility and decision making through an abusive use of fantasy. This feature is not surprising because it coincides with a self-imposed helplessness that requires dependency on others. It also makes her vulnerable to the manipulations of others, and the pervasiveness of this tactic is likely to cause her basic conceptualizations to be strongly influenced by this fantasy orientation.

In a related context, the Intellectualization Index (4), discussed earlier in relation to her affects, implies a distinctive tendency to intellectualize feelings. This also involves reliance on a form of conceptual thought that serves to deny or distort the true impact of a situation. When considered with regard to her persistent tendency to abuse fantasy defensively, it seems reasonable to postulate that much of her directed thinking is used in ways that help her deny or avoid any harsh or threatening realities of her world.

Interestingly, her thinking seems to be reasonably clear. Only two answers are coded for critical special scores (responses 6 & 8), yielding a *WSum6* (5), which is unremarkable. The two special scores (*DR* and INCOM) reflect mild cognitive slips, and an evaluation of them seems to indicate more immature judgment than problems in thinking ("they usually make them out of paper, at least the ones that don't cost much are made out of paper"; "this is [the bat's] hands").

In addition, all four of her *M* answers have appropriate form quality (three ordinary and one unusual). The general quality of her conceptualizations, as reflected in those *M* responses, also tends to be adequate and even a bit sophisticated, although some appear to reflect the juvenile fantasy that characterizes much of her thinking: (response 1) "a ballerina, . . . standing with the wings out, maybe in a pose"; (response 5) "two women talking to each other . . . standing over some pot"; (response 12) "two people standing next to each other . . . like at a ceremony, maybe . . . getting married . . . but she ought to be in white"; (response 19) "two cherubs . . . drinking something out of a straw . . . sharing whatever is in the container."

Thus, while her thinking is clear, she does not always use it to her advantage. Her ideational sets, attitudes, and values are reasonably well fixed; and an underlying current of pessimism marks many of her internal evaluations. Collectively, these sets breed a sense of insecurity that leads her to employ much of her deliberate thinking in defensive ways. This involves the use of an elaborate fantasy world into which she takes flight as a routine tactic for dealing with unpleasant situations, and a proneness to neutralize or deny unwanted feelings with intellectualizing tactics. These tactics permit her to avoid responsibility for decision making and to depend on others for security and direction. This thwarts growth possibilities and perpetuates a sort of immature psychological existence.

SUMMARY

This 25-year-old woman seems considerably less mature than expected. Her resources are somewhat limited, but she experiences as many demands on those resources as do most adults. The disparity between resources and demands creates a persistent state of overload for her which, in turn, causes problems in everyday living. Her capacity for control is fragile, and the persistent overload often causes some of her decisions to be poorly formulated or implemented.

Her immaturity and limited resources make her especially susceptible to difficulties in the interpersonal sphere. She seems to have an awareness of her limitations and vulnerability and has tried to compensate by adopting a passive-dependent role in her interpersonal relations. This role appears to serve her reasonably well. In it, she probably makes few demands for closeness and tends to fulfill her needs through dependency. She is interested in people, and although her perceptions of them are somewhat naive, they are generally positive. Thus, she presents an interpersonal facade that is usually adaptive, and others are likely to regard her as gregarious and likable. Her passive-dependent role affords her a sense of structure and security and permits her to rely on others for decisions and direction. It creates a kind of safe haven that allows her to take from others while also usually remaining at a safe distance from them.

There is a significant cost for this form of structure and security. While it reduces the likelihood of becoming overwhelmed or disorganized by the complexities of life, it perpetuates her immaturity and forces her to seek out environments with predictable demands and expectations. It also requires that she sacrifice some of her own wants and interests in favor of those defined by others, and this has a negative impact on her self-image.

Her view of herself seems to reflect a mixture of naively positive features that are linked together with a sense of vulnerability, apprehension, and pessimism. She tends to regard herself unfavorably in comparison to others and seems involved in considerable self-examining, much of which focuses on features that she perceives to be negative. This gives rise to conflictual, painful feelings because she does not handle emotions very well. In fact, she seems to mistrust her ability to do so and often suppresses or conceals her feelings, which easily leads to tension, anxiety, or sadness.

Often, when unwanted feelings occur, she tries to deny or neutralize them through intellectualization, but she also relies extensively on an abusive use of fantasy as a defensive tactic to help her contend with irritations in her life. It allows her to easily take flight to avoid situations that are seemingly harsh or potentially overwhelming. This tactic permits her to maintain a positive but naive sense of optimism about herself and her world even though, at a different level, she has some awareness that this optimism is not well founded in reality.

Actually, she has many more assets than she seems to be aware of. Although she is not especially comfortable with complexity or ambiguity, she processes new information reasonably well. She invests considerable effort and energy into scanning activity, and this tends to ensure that the yield from her processing efforts is consistent, and even sophisticated at times. Likewise, she translates new inputs appropriately. Many of those translations tend to disregard social conventions or expectations, but this does not involve significant distortions of reality. Instead, she tends to yield to her own individuality more than most people, and she translates information in the context of her own needs, sets, and attitudes.

She is an ideational person who, when forced to make decisions, delays forming them or implementing behaviors until she has considered all apparent alternatives. Unfortunately, she is not very flexible about using the strategy, in part because her ideational sets, attitudes, and values are reasonably well fixed, but mainly because she has learned to rely more on others for decisions and seems less experienced in decision making than should be the case. Nonetheless, her thinking is reasonably clear and, although often involved in juvenile fantasies, holds the potential for good reality testing. Her thinking is marked by more pessimism than should be the case, and this often gives rise to the notion that her actions will have little effect on the outcome of a situation. Much of this is because she has become accustomed to a passive role in life that makes her quite vulnerable to the manipulations of others.

RECOMMENDATIONS

The referral asks if a serious psychiatric disturbance is present. This question probably should be addressed somewhat equivocally. There is no evidence of a major disturbance, but there are some significant personality problems that relate mainly to her passive dependent features. They should be weighed carefully when considering her request to enter a treatment program that is mainly focused on substance abuse.

The referral asks for estimates regarding her motivation for treatment and a prognosis for staying in treatment. In reality, she is probably fairly naive about various treatment options. Her current motivation about treatment seems based on her belief that she has a substance abuse problem, which may or may not be true. However, it is doubtful that she would recognize it as being important if it were not that her boyfriend appears to need treatment. Apparently, he is her main source of emotional support and her prognosis for staying in treatment will depend largely on his reactions. He probably not only permits her to be dependent on him, but also encourages that behavior. In effect, she seems to be a victim of a relationship that she needs and, for the moment, she sees substance abuse treatment to be a part of that relationship.

The referral also asks for recommendations concerning treatment objectives. There are many, but none seem easily achievable in a brief treatment regimen. Obviously, her immaturity and persistent overload state are prime treatment targets, as are her notable passivity and her extensive fantasy abuse. She really does not know who she is or what she is, and she will remain vulnerable to the manipulations of others until she resolves those issues. In addition, she appears to be naive about social behaviors that might not involve submissiveness.

A realistic treatment plan should have a developmental focus and would require considerable time and effort, much more than is usually possible in an eight-week program. Optimally, it should begin with a focus on her interpersonal perceptions and behaviors and gradually work into a review of her concerns about emotion. However, neither of these is likely to be accomplished in a brief period. In fact, a brief program focusing on substance abuse could be counterproductive for her. A women's group could be beneficial, but not at the onset of intervention. It might supplement progress from individual treatment at whatever time she feels comfortable about the possibility. It should not be undertaken, however, until she has identified more resources with which to ward off some of the everyday stresses of living that threaten to overwhelm her.

The referral also asks whether couples therapy might be appropriate. This raises an ethical question. Surely, she wants to continue in her somewhat pathological relationship with her boyfriend (Case 8, Chapter 10), who appears to be manipulating her at will. To interfere with the relationship violates her own wishes, yet to encourage the continuance of, or strengthening of the relationship, will doom her to continue her fragile passive-dependent role. If her best interests are to be given proper weight, any consideration of couples therapy would be deferred at the onset.

As noted, she has numerous assets, especially involving her cognitive functioning; also, she tends to regard others positively and probably is perceived by them as a likable person. The key to therapeutic success with her will lie in the development of a working relationship with someone with whom she feels comfortable and can identify. This suggests a female therapist who can employ the skills necessary to instill and maintain motivation for change and can assist her, when necessary, in evaluating any pathologically dependent relationships that she may create.

EPILOGUE

She was accepted into the substance abuse program with the proviso that she participate in at least eight weekly individual and group psychotherapy sessions. She did so and, at the end of the eighth week, asked to continue in individual treatment. Her therapist, a woman, notes that much of the time in the early sessions focused on her relationship with her boyfriend, but that as time progressed the main topic gradually shifted to concerns about her social fears and feelings of insecurity. Apparently, the group interactions also played a significant role in provoking her to look more closely at herself, so that when she requested continuation in treatment, she was able to identify objectives that seemed realistic in the opinion of the therapist.

During the twelfth week of treatment, she decided to move out of her boyfriend's apartment after he became angry when she refused to use cocaine. She moved to her parents' home, where she remained for three weeks, after which she moved into an apartment shared by a female medical technician. She was seen twice each week during that interval. The therapist reports that, after seven months of treatment, the patient is progressing slowly but favorably. She has two dating relationships, has remained drug free, has developed a close relationship with her roommate, and is actively expanding her social network and experience. She is currently considering taking some evening courses at a local university.

REFERENCES

Bauman, G., & Roman, M. (1968). Interaction product analysis in group and family diagnosis. *Journal of Projective Techniques and Personality Assessment, 32*(4), 331–337.

Benjamin, L. S. (1974). Structural analysis of social behavior. *Psychological Review, 18,* 392–425.

Benjamin, L. S. (1993). *Interpersonal diagnosis and treatment of personality disorders.* New York: Guilford Press.

Blake, S. E., Humphrey, L. L., & Feldman, L. (1994). Self-delineation and marital interaction: The Rorschach predicts structural analysis of social behavior. *Journal of Personality Assessment, 63*(1), 148–166.

Blanchard, W. H. (1968). The Consensus Rorschach: Background and development. *Journal of Projective Techniques and Personality Assessment, 32*(4), 327–330.

Burke, W. F., Friedman, G., & Gorlitz, P. (1988). The Psychoanalytic Rorschach Profile: An integration of drive, ego, and object relations perspectives. *Psychoanalytic Psychology, 5*(2), 193–212.

Handler, L. (1997). He says, she says, they say: The Consensus Rorschach. In J. R. Meloy, M. W. Acklin, C. B. Gacono, & J. F. Murray (Eds.), *Contemporary Rorschach interpretation* (pp. 499–533). Mahwah, NJ: Erlbaum.

Loveland, N., Wynne, L., & Singer, M. (1963). The Family Rorschach: A new method for studying family interaction. *Family Process, 2,* 187–215.

Magni, G., Ferruzza, E., & Barison, F. (1982). A preliminary report on the use of a new method of presenting the Rorschach Test to evaluate the relationship of couples. *Journal of Family Therapy, 4*(1), 73–91.

Nakamura, S., & Nakamura, N. (1987). The Family Rorschach Technique. *Rorschachiana, 16,* 136–141.

Willi, J. (1979). The Rorschach as a test of direct interaction in groups. *Bulletin de Psychologie, 32,* 279–282.

CHAPTER 12

An Issue of Impulse Control

This 29-year-old single woman was referred for evaluation by a consulting psychiatrist. She has completed approximately 15 months of a three-year residency program in internal medicine. This is her second psychiatric evaluation while in this program, both resulting from conflicts that occurred at work. She is challenging her probable dismissal from the program based on various reports concerning her work behaviors, which have been summarized as follows: "Her performance is often marked by intense anger and rage, anxiety, and possible depression, any of which could represent a potential threat to the well-being of patients because of apparently impaired judgments during these episodes of emotional lability."

Previously, she was dismissed during her first year of a residency program in pediatrics after it was noted that she had obvious difficulties relating effectively to young patients and often seemed insensitive during her interactions with parents. Apparently, after being evaluated negatively in that program, she agreed that pediatrics was not an appropriate choice for her and was given a cautious but generally favorable recommendation that emphasized her extensive medical knowledge and skills.

Her current conflicts began approximately nine months prior to this evaluation when she was allegedly slapped on the hands by an attending physician during her training program. About a month later, she was accused by the same physician of altering a medical record, a charge that she disputes. She believes she is now scrutinized much more closely than anyone else in the program and that there is a concerted effort "to get rid of me."

Her program is at a large midwestern university that has outreach clinics in surrounding farming communities. She has been very vocal regarding what she considers unreasonable travel requirements, little sleep, poor program administration, and chauvinistic attitudes. She has had various difficulties with other staff. On one occasion, she borrowed a nurse's stethoscope without asking, which resulted in a heated exchange between them. On another occasion, she was reported as being verbally abusive to a cafeteria worker who she felt did not treat her appropriately. She was also accused of negligence when she missed a page one day after going home early and got into a heated discussion with a supervisor. She states, "When I think I've been wronged, I lose it, I feel they want to get rid of me because I'm making waves."

She was raised in a small town in the northwest. Her father, age 55, is a line supervisor in a manufacturing plant and mother, age 52, is a licensed practical nurse. She has a younger sister, age 26, who is a teacher in an elementary school. She describes her father as, "a lot like me, stubborn, hotheaded. If he believes in something, he is not going to give it up. He works hard." She states she never found it easy to talk with her father because he would scream at her when there was a problem rather than discussing it. She says her mother is "stubborn, set in her ways, and she won't change her mind. I'm not as close to her as I am to my dad."

She says her family is poor financially and describes herself as an "outsider kid" in school. She graduated from high school as salutatorian and was active in tennis and basketball. She states that she did well in college, but admits that she had some difficulties in her medical school studies, especially those involving hands-on requirements, "I know all of the concepts, but I don't like to have to make quick judgments."

Her relationships with men have been less than satisfactory. In high school, she was "dumped" by her boyfriend for one of her friends. She says that, as an undergraduate, she dated irregularly but not more than once or twice with any one person. In medical school, she met a man at an athletic event; they began dating, then moved in together. He proved to be abusive, pushing her down the stairs, running over her foot with a car, and squandering their money. She stayed until he left her ". . . because he was better than nothing." Most recently, she had been dating an MRI technician who terminated the relationship because "he felt I was too good for him."

She presented for the evaluation casually dressed in jeans and a shirt and with no makeup. She is described as generally attractive and in good physical condition. During the interviews, her mood varied considerably. At times she seemed friendly and cooperative, but in other instances she seemed sad and became tearful. When discussing her performance evaluations, she became enraged and yelled several times. Although she tried to be cooperative during the evaluation, there were instances during which she became hostile, sullen, and evasive.

She describes her health as "generally good" but admits to frequent headaches and sleep difficulties. She currently takes birth control pills and Vistaril for sleep. She does not smoke and drinks only about one glass of wine per week. She denies any drug use. As a result of the first evaluation, a brief period of inpatient psychiatric hospitalization was recommended with participation in a Dialectical Behavior Therapy (DBT) program to help her identify conflicts in her life and deal with them more effectively. She refused the inpatient stay, but did agree to a modified outpatient DBT program that involved individual sessions twice weekly for six weeks. She states that the treatment was "helpful and gave me some direction that I needed."

The results of intelligence testing (WAIS-R) yielded a Verbal IQ of 114, with subtest scaled scores ranging from 11 to 13, and a Performance IQ of 118, with subtest scaled scores ranging from 11 to 14. The validity scales derived from her performance on the MMPI-2 have T-Scores between 48 and 57. Most of the clinical scales have T-Scores between 47 (Si) and 63 (Ma); however, elevations are noted on scales 6 (Pa), which has a T-Score of 74, and 4 (Pd), which has a T-score of 66. All the Content and Supplementary Scales have T-Scores less than 65.

The following specific questions have been put forth in the referral: (1) Is she a danger to herself or others? (2) Is there a psychiatric diagnosis that should be considered as likely to interfere significantly with her capability to maintain a medical practice, treat patients appropriately, and interact adequately with colleagues and coworkers? (3) Should she be permitted to continue in the residency program? and (4) What recommendations seem practical concerning such matters as inpatient or outpatient treatment, medication, type of treatment, duration, and treatment goals?

Case Formulation and Relevant Literature

This woman's internal medicine residency performance evaluations include descriptions of "intense anger and rage." She has been involved in heated confrontations with colleagues and supervisors, and she notes that she can be emotional when she feels she has been treated unfairly. Although she was trying to remain calm during this assessment, she became actively enraged when the interview turned to the topic of her performance evaluations.

She feels that her program has made unreasonable demands in terms of work schedules and travel requirements. At present, she thinks she is being monitored closely to accumulate information that would justify her dismissal from the residency. Her MMPI-2 profile falls into the 6-4 code type, which Graham (2000) notes often includes individuals who resent any demands made on them, particularly by authority figures. He describes this code type as one in which the person has poor social skills, is suspicious of others, feels that life is often unfair, and consequently avoids significant emotional involvement. Typical defensive operations include denial of difficulties and externalization of blame.

Faced with their current observations and a history of similar concerns about this woman's judgment and impulse control in interpersonal situations, staff members in the residency program are understandably worried about whether her "episodes of emotional lability" could place patients at risk. Because medical practice involves extensive interaction with patients and colleagues, they have also raised concerns about the implications of her abrasive interpersonal style. Although there are apparently no questions about her general medical competence, these concerns are serious enough that staff members are considering terminating her from the residency.

A review of the Rorschach literature about impulse control can alert the psychologist to variables that may be associated with ability to inhibit and delay. Additionally, Case 1 (Chapter 3) reviewed the literature relevant to the assessment of interpersonal competence, another area that seems important in responding to the referral questions staff members have raised.

Assessment of Impulse Control

As this case demonstrates, problems with impulse control can have serious implications for an individual's personal and professional life. Many clinical and forensic referrals revolve around this aspect of psychological function; and the assessment of motoric, cognitive, and affective inhibition has been a significant focus of Rorschach research since early in the test's history.

Rorschach (1942/1981, p. 78) suggested that percepts involving human movement were associated with "measured, stable motility," and he noted, "Kinaesthetic engrams, therefore, act as inhibitors of physical activity; motor activity inhibits kinaesthetic engrams" (p. 80). Several studies have tested this hypothesis, investigating the relation between human movement (M) determinants and motoric inhibition. In a counterbalanced design, Singer, Meltzoff, and Goldman (1952) asked male undergraduates to respond to pairs of Rorschach cards in an initial baseline condition and then after a motor inhibition condition (standing without moving for a five-minute period) and after a hyperactivity condition (five minutes of vigorous calisthenics). Although the number of responses did not vary significantly among the various conditions, M determinants increased significantly from baseline after the motor inhibition condition. There was no difference in M frequency between the baseline and hyperactivity conditions.

Singer and Spohn (1954) divided 50 male VA schizophrenic patients into two groups based on whether their Rorschachs contained more than one M determinant and observed them during a

15-minute waiting room period. The patients were rated on degree of motor activity on a six-point scale ranging from no gross motor activity to considerable restless activity and manipulation of objects on a nearby table. The high-*M* group had significantly lower motor activity levels. Within the high-*M* group, those patients with two or more active *M* responses had significantly lower motor activity ratings than patients with fewer than two active *M* percepts.

In a second condition, Singer and Spohn (1954) tested motor inhibition by asking the high-*M* and low-*M* patients to write the phrase "New Jersey Chamber of Commerce" as slowly as possible without stopping or lifting the pencil from the paper. The high-*M* group had a significantly longer mean inhibition time (277 versus 138 seconds). Within the high-*M* group, the active *M* patients had significantly longer inhibition times.

Levine and Meltzoff (1956) extended the study of the human movement determinant by investigating its relation to cognitive inhibition. They began by giving a 10-item paired associate task to VA psychiatric patients. After achieving a perfect recitation of the 10 pairs, the patients were asked to give any word *other* than the one they had learned when presented with the stimulus word. In a median split, patients with *M* greater than one were significantly faster in their ability to inhibit the learned response and produce a new one.

The relation of the human movement determinant to ability to inhibit an overlearned task was also partially supported in a study by Levine, Spivack, and Wight (1959). They tested groups of adolescents at a residential facility and VA schizophrenic and nonschizophrenic inpatients. One of the symbols in the Wechsler Digit Symbol subtest was the mirror image of the letter "N," and the authors divided participants into those who wrote the letter "N" instead of its mirror image at least once. For the adult hospitalized group, but not for the adolescents, patients who wrote the overlearned "N" instead of the correct symbol had significantly fewer *M* percepts in their Rorschach protocols.

Consistent with these earlier findings, a study by Darby, Hofman, and Melnick (1967) found that college students who engaged in a response inhibition task gave significantly more human movement responses than participants who performed tasks that did not involve having to delay responses. Their finding was consistent with a conceptualization of *M* as representing a volitional decision to use ideation to delay responding to the immediate demands of the stimulus field.

Pantle, Ebner, and Hynan (1994) studied the relationship of a rationally selected group of Rorschach variables (*D*, Adj D, *Afr*, *X+%*, *M*, *FC*:*CF+C*, and *Lambda*) to a behavioral task involving response delay and inhibition in a group of 55 adolescent psychiatric inpatients. The adolescents completed the Gordon Diagnostic System (GDS; Gordon, 1983), a microprocessor-based task in which participants press a button in response to visual input on a small screen. The GDS includes three separate tests. Two of them involve attentiveness during nine-minute continuous performance tasks with increasing levels of distractibility, and one involves an eight-minute test of ability to delay output while formulating a response strategy that uses feedback effectively.

Pantle et al. (1994) categorized the participants' findings on the three GDS tests as either "abnormal" (25th percentile or below) or "normal" and performed discriminant analyses to determine the Rorschach's ability to distinguish between the groups on each test. The discriminant function for the GDS delay task was statistically significant and correctly classified 76% of the participants. The three Rorschach variables with the highest correlations in the discriminant function were *D*, *FC*:*CF+C*, and *M*. No Rorschach variables discriminated normal from abnormal performances on the two GDS continuous performance tests of attentiveness. The authors suggest that those tasks involved other abilities, such as freedom from distractibility, in addition to impulse control. In contrast, they view the GDS delay task as a more homogeneous measure of impulse control, requiring specifically the ability to inhibit responding while generating a response strategy that integrates ongoing feedback.

Meltzoff and Litwin (1956) studied the relation of human movement percepts to ability to inhibit affect. They played a humorous recording [a record by Spike Jones and his orchestra, described as ". . . a recording of contagious laughter with an accompaniment of humorous background music and assorted noises" (p. 463)] to college students and asked them *not* to smile or laugh while listening to it. Participants were then administered Cards III and VII of the Rorschach and divided at the median into High (two or more *M* percepts) and Low groups. Of the 34 participants in the High *M* group, 20 were able to listen to the record without smiling or laughing, whereas only 11 of the 34 participants in the Low *M* group were able to inhibit this expression of affect ($p = .03$).

Gardner (1951) asked long-term acquaintances to rate 10 university students on an impulsivity-inhibition continuum. He found significant correlations (.705 to .879) between these rankings and Rorschach variables associated with the form dominance of chromatic color determinants (*FC:CF+C*), the percentage of chromatic color determinants in the record (*FC+CF+C:R*), and the ratio of chromatic color and human movement determinants (*M:WSumC*). These results are similar to those of Gill (1966), who found that individuals who delayed their responses to a geometric figure problem-solving task produced significantly more *FC* than *CF+C* percepts, whereas participants who responded more spontaneously produced significantly more *CF+C* answers.

In summary, the Rorschach variables most directly relevant for assessing impulse control are those associated with motoric, cognitive, or affective inhibition (*M*), and with ability to modulate output when affect is involved (*FC:CF+C*). As noted in Chapter 1, however, it is important to take a configural approach as opposed to a single variable by single variable focus. Although higher frequencies of *M* are generally related to ability to inhibit and delay, when interpreting an individual record, it is crucial to consider the person's human movement responses in light of their form quality, their active versus passive content, and their relationship to other Rorschach variables such as chromatic color.

Case 10.   A 29-Year-Old Female.

Card	Response	Inquiry
I	v1. Well it doesn't ll a bat to me, it ll the one on the computer game	**E:** (Rpts Ss Resp) **S:** The w thg, the shape of it ll th thg tht goes across th computer game, lik on the Space Invader game
	2. I really dk, a bug	**E:** (Rpts Ss Resp) **S:** It really doesn't ll a bug, its the best thg I cld come up w **E:** Rem, I need to c wht maks it ll tht & where it is **S:** I was lookg at that (D1), its antennae, thats about it **E:** Where r u seeg the bug? **S:** Sort of the w thg I guess (points), th tail, body, I dk
II	3. We'll do th pelvis thg, why not	**E:** (Rpts Ss Resp) **S:** The black is sort of th shape of th pelvis, of a pelvic bone
	[**S:** Do we have to use the w thg? **E:** Its up to u]	
	v4. Thes teeny littl points cb antennae	**E:** (Rpts Ss Resp) **S:** Thes 2 littl thgs **E:** Wht maks it ll antennae? **S:** Thyr stickg out from evrythng else
III	5. Two people	**E:** (Rpts Ss Resp) **S:** I guess tht's right there (D9) **E:** And wht maks it ll two peopl? **S:** Not a lot, I guess head, arms & legs, lik peopl
	v6. Thes littl thgs cb kidneys w a ureter	**E:** (Rpts Ss Resp) **S:** There is kidney & that's ureter **E:** I'm not sur why thy ll kidneys? **S:** Both of 'em do, thy hav tht shape
IV	v7. Ths ll a blob, it doesn't ll athg to me, looks even less lik st than the othr 2 did. A crinkled up oak leaf, how's tht?	**E:** (Rpts Ss Resp) **S:** Oak leaves hav 3 thngs, thers sort of 3 thgs here, lik the stem & the leaves going out, sort of crinkled up **E:** Crinkled up? **S:** The diff shadows, this (D6) is bent over, it looms lik crinkled
	[**S:** Do I need to come up wth anothr? **E:** If u lik **S:** Man u'r killing me]	
	8. Another bug	**E:** (Rpts Ss Resp) **S:** Yes **E:** Rem, I need to c it lik u do **S:** It really doesn't ll athg **E:** Where on th blot did u c a bug & wht maks it ll that? **S:** Never really did, mayb little antennae here (Dd28) & mayb arm or st (D4) I dk **E:** I'm not sure I c it **S:** The W thg cb I guess
V	9. A bf	**E:** (Rpts Ss Resp) **S:** It has the little antennae & big wgs
	>10. One of those thgs tht flick dwn fr trees, u kno wht I mean. I dk wht thyr calld, thos seed thgs	**E:**(Rpts Ss Resp) **S:**Lik th w thg, ko wing-shaped, sk of seed tht falls off the trees
VI	<11. Yes, right (laughing), a stingray	**E:**(Rpts Ss Resp) **S:**It's got a long tail (outlining it), th whole thing ll a stingray

Case 10. Continued.

Card	Response	Inquiry
	<12. A neural tube, I bet tht would b a very common answer	**E:** (Rpts Ss Resp) **S:** J this littl thg j ll dark electron pictures thy show us in school, j tht centr part **E:** Dark? **S:** Thy show us those black & white electron pictures in school
VII	13. Bunny rabbits [**S:** There is supposedly some validity to this test? **E:** Yes]	**E:** (Rpts Ss Resp) **S:** There is little ears **E:** Help me c it lik u do **S:** Here's head, rest of it really doesn't ll much, j the heads
	14. Two women wth their arms out	**E:** (Rpts Ss Resp) **S:** This ll an arm & that cb mayb a nose, I dk, j 2 wm w their arms out
VIII	<15. A little A here	**E:** (Rpts Ss Resp) **S:** That (points to D1) **E:** Rem, I need to c it lik u do **S:** The 4 legs, ll it has an eye, I dk wht kind
	>16. Som rocks wth an A crawlg on it, is tht good enough? [**E:** Is ths a separate resp? **S:** Yes]	**E:** (Rpts Ss Resp) **S:** Yes, these **E:** Help me c it lik u do **S:** Thes thgs here ll rocks (half of D5&D2), th shape of 'em & this is the A, mayb a lion or fox, a bigger A than the first one I saw
IX	>17. Some mtns reflectg on a lake, I guess tht can b th shoreline there [**S:** Need more? **E:** Its up to u]	**E:** (Rpts Ss Resp) **S:** I dk, ko blue here, lik water **E:** I'm not sur I c it lik u do **S:** Ok, heres th mtns, & green is lik trees, & its all reflectd in th lake—th blue prt
	18. Part of a map, the colors r ko map-lik	**E:** (Rpts Ss Resp) **S:** Yes, its colors u'd c on a map **E:** Where r u seeg it? **S:** The W thg. I had an Old World Map when I was little. Tht orange really ll one of the colors & the pink too
X	19. The pink ll Italy	**E:** (Rpts Ss Resp) **S:** J tht half, needs a little more shore built in it, but even without it it ll Italy to me
	20. And this will b a common answr, a tip here ll a Bouie tip [**E:** Spell it, please] **S:** B-o-u-i-e, it's a surgical instrument	**E:** (Rpts Ss Resp) **S:** J that little thing, this here (D14) **E:** Why does it ll a Bouie tip? **S:** It j ll the instrument, it's tht shape

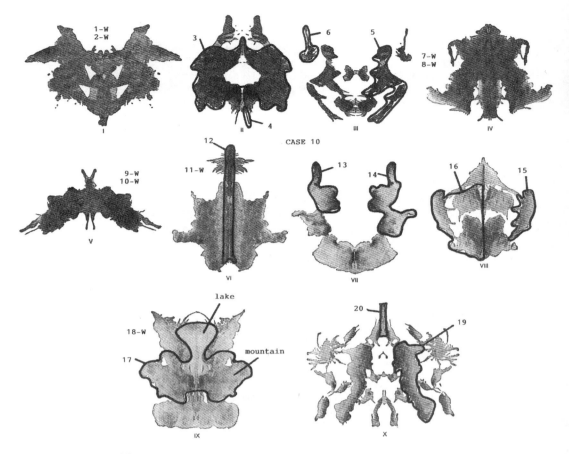

Case 10. Sequence of Scores.

Card	No.	Loc.	No.	Determinant(s)	(2)	Content(s)	Pop	Z	Special Scores
I	1	Wo	1	Fu		(H),Sc		1.0	GHR
	2	Wo	1	F–		A		1.0	
II	3	Do	6	Fo		An			
	4	Ddo	25	Fo		Ad			
III	5	Do	9	Fo	2	H	P		GHR
	6	Do	2	Fu	2	An			
IV	7	Wo	1	FVo		Bt		2.0	
	8	Wo	1	F–		A		2.0	INC
V	9	Wo	1	Fo		A	P	1.0	
	10	Wo	1	Fu		Bt		1.0	
VI	11	Wo	1	Fu		A		2.5	
	12	Do	5	FC'u		An,Art			PER
VII	13	Do	1	Fo	2	Ad			
	14	Do	2	Mpo	2	H	P		GHR
VIII	15	Do	1	Fo		A	P		
	16	Dd+	99	FMau		A,Ls	P	3.0	
IX	17	Dv/+	1	rF.CFu		Na		2.5	
	18	Wv	1	C		Ge			PER
X	19	Do	9	F–		Ge			
	20	Do	14	Fu		Sc			

Case 10.   Structural Summary.

Location Features	Determinants Blends	Single	Contents	S-Constellation
				YES . .FV+VF+V+FD>2
		H = 2		NO . . .Col-Shd Bl>0
Zf = 9	rF.CF	M = 1	(H) = 1	NO . . .Ego<.31,>.44
ZSum = 16.0		FM = 1	Hd = 0	NO . . .MOR > 3
ZEst = 27.5		m = 0	(Hd) = 0	YES . .Zd > +− 3.5
		FC = 0	Hx = 0	NO . . .es > EA
W = 8		CF = 0	A = 6	YES . .CF+C > FC
D = 10		C = 1	(A) = 0	YES . .X+% < .70
W+D = 18		Cn = 0	Ad = 2	NO . . .S > 3
Dd = 2		FC′ = 1	(Ad) = 0	NO . . .P < 3 or > 8
S = 0		C′F = 0	An = 3	NO . . .Pure H < 2
		C′ = 0	Art = 1	NO . . .R < 17
		FT = 0	Ay = 0	3 . . . .TOTAL

DQ

		Single	Contents	Special Scores
		TF = 0	Bl = 0		
+ = 1		T = 0	Bt = 2		Lv1	Lv2
o = 17		FV = 1	Cg = 0	DV = 0x1	0x2
v/+ = 1		VF = 0	Cl = 0	INC = 1x2	0x4
v = 1		V = 0	Ex = 0	DR = 0x3	0x6
		FY = 0	Fd = 0	FAB = 0x4	0x7
		YF = 0	Fi = 0	ALOG = 0x5	
		Y = 0	Ge = 2	CON = 0x7	
		Fr = 0	Hh = 0	Raw Sum6 = 1	

Form Quality

	FQx	MQual	W+D		Contents	Special Scores
				rF = 0	Ls = 1	Wgtd Sum6 = 0
+	= 0	= 0	= 0	FD = 0	Na = 1	
o	= 8	= 1	= 7	F = 14	Sc = 2	AB = 0 GHR = 3
u	= 8	= 0	= 7		Sx = 0	AG = 0 PHR = 0
−	= 3	= 0	= 3		Xy = 0	COP = 0 MOR = 0
none	= 1	= 0	= 1		Id = 0	CP = 0 PER = 2
				(2) = 4		PSV = 0

Ratios, Percentages, and Derivations

R = 20	L = 2.33		FC:CF+C = 0:2	COP = 0 AG = 0
			Pure C = 1	GHR:PHR = 3:0
EB = 1:2.5	EA = 3.5	EBPer = N/A	SumC′:WSumC = 1:2.5	a:p = 1:1
eb = 1:2	es = 3	D = 0	Afr = 0.43	Food = 0
	Adj es = 3	Adj D = 0	S = 0	SumT = 0
			Blends:R = 1:20	Hum Con = 3
FM = 1	C′ = 1	T = 0	CP = 0	Pure H = 2
m = 0	V = 1	Y = 0		PER = 2
				Iso Indx = 0.35

a:p	= 1:1	Sum6	= 1	XA% = 0.80	Zf = 9.0	3r+(2)/R	= 0.35
Ma:Mp	= 0: 1	Lv2	= 0	WDA% = 0.78	W:D:Dd = 8:10:2	Fr+rF	= 1
2AB+Art+Ay	= 1	WSum6	= 2	X−% = 0.15	W:M = 8:1	SumV	= 1
MOR	= 0	M−	= 0	S− = 0	Zd = −11.5	FD	= 0
		Mnone	= 0	P = 5	PSV = 0	An+Xy	= 3
				X+% = 0.40	DQ+ = 1	MOR	= 0
				Xu% = 0.40	DQv = 1	H:(H)Hd(Hd)	= 2:1

PTI = 0	DEPI = 4	CDI = 4*	S-CON = 3	HVI = No	OBS = No

S-CON AND KEY VARIABLE

The S-CON value (3) is not actuarially meaningful. The first positive Key variable is the CDI (4). This signals that the interpretation should begin with a study of data concerning controls and then proceed to an evaluation of the findings regarding interpersonal perception, self-perception, and affect, ending with a review of the data for the three clusters that comprise the cognitive triad.

CONTROLS

Case 10.   Control-Related Variables for a 29-Year-Old Female.

EB = 1:2.5	EA = 3.5		D = 0	CDI = 4
eb = 1:2	es = 3	Adj es = 3	AdjD = 0	L = 2.33
FM = 1 m = 0	SumC' = 1	SumT = 0	SumV = 1	SumY = 0

Although the Adj D Score (0) implies an adequate capacity for control, findings for three other variables suggest that the interpretive usefulness of the Adj D is, at best, limited and probably not valid. The first of the three is the positive CDI (4). It signifies a substantial likelihood that she is less mature than might be expected. If so, this creates a vulnerability to problems in coping with everyday living, especially in the interpersonal sphere. Such problems often promote difficulties in control. The second of the three is the *EA* of 3.5. It is much lower than expected for a reasonably intelligent adult, indicating a notably limited access to resources. If this is a valid finding, it connotes a chronic proclivity to becoming disorganized by many of the stresses that exist in a complex society.

The third variable is probably the most important in the context of attempting to study control issues. It is the substantial *Lambda* value (2.33). It reveals an avoidant response style. There is a possibility that this style is the product of situational defensiveness, as she is being evaluated in an adversarial circumstance. However, this is not a brief protocol. She gave 20 responses, and a high *Lambda* score in a record of average or greater length usually signals a chronic traitlike tendency to ignore or minimize complexity and ambiguity. Regardless of whether her presentation represents a situationally defensive or traitlike tendency to avoid and simplify complexity, the combination of the high *Lambda* and the low *EA* strongly suggest that the Adj D Score cannot be considered as a reliable or valid source from which to identify her true capacity for control.

Nonetheless, if she has a traitlike avoidant style, it has notable consequences regarding controls. The avoidance of complexity represents an indirect form of control because it reduces the possibility of being overwhelmed by complexity. This form of control usually works well in structured or predictable situations. However, unfamiliar situations are often intrinsically complex and demanding, and avoidance or oversimplification is ineffective in contending with them. In those circumstances, the likelihood of loss of control increases substantially, especially if resources are limited or social skills are lacking. Although there is no clear evidence that she has frequent control problems, there are strong suggestions that this is likely to be the case, and some of her reported behaviors support that contention.

INTERPERSONAL PERCEPTION

Case 10.   Interpersonal Perception Data for a 29-Year-Old Female.

R = 20	CDI = 4	HVI = No	**No COP or AG Responses**
a:p = 1:1	SumT = 0	Fd = 0	
	[eb = 1:2]		
Sum Human Contents = 3		H = 2	
[Style = Avoidant]			
GHR:PHR = 3:0			
COP = 0	AG = 0	PER = 2	
Isolation Indx = 0.35			

The previously noted positive CDI (4) connotes the presence of features that typically indicate social immaturity or ineptness. It suggests that she has difficulty creating or maintaining close relations with others. It is not surprising that her history includes reports of unsatisfying relations, and it seems likely that much of her adult life has been marked by dissatisfaction about her relations with others. It is also probable that she harbors a naive sense of confusion about this.

The absence of texture answers, although she gave two responses involving grey-black or shading features, implies that she perceives or expresses her needs for interpersonal contacts in ways that are unlike those of most people. It does not mean that she fails to have such needs but, instead, that she is probably much more conservative in interpersonal situations and is somewhat cautious about creating close emotional ties with others. In fact, the low frequency of human content answers (3) hints at the distinct possibility that she is not very interested in people. If true, this lack of interest is likely to have developed as a result of numerous failed or unrewarding relations with others. Interestingly, two of her three human content responses are pure *H*, suggesting that her impressions of people are likely to be reality based.

The GHR:PHR ratio (3:0) seems to indicate that most of her interpersonal behaviors are adaptive for the situation. However, the absence of interactive exchanges in her responses, that is, COP or *AG* answers, tends to support the notion that most of her relations with others are likely to be superficial. There is a slight elevation in PER responses (2), implying that she may be more defensive or insecure in social situations that involve challenge. This does not necessarily impede interpersonal relations, but may cause her to be overly cautious with others.

On the other hand, the Isolation Index (.35) is high connoting that she probably finds it difficult to create smooth or meaningful relations with others and may tend toward more social isolation than would be expected. Moreover, there is only one movement answer containing a pair (response 14), "two women with their arms out." It lacks any dynamic features and appears to support the notion that her interpersonal world is, at best, superficial.

SELF-PERCEPTION

Case 10. Self-Perception Related Data for a 29-Year Old Female.

					Human Content, Hx, An & Xy Responses
R	= 20	OBS	= No	HVI = No	I 1. Wo Fu (H),Sc 1.0 GHR
					II 3. Do Fo An
Fr+rF	= 1	3r+(2)/R	= 0.35		III 5. Do Fo 2 H P GHR
					III 6. Do Fu 2 An
FD	= 0	SumV	= 1		VI 12. Do FC'u An,Art PER
					VII 14. Do Mpo 2 H P GHR
An+Xy = 3		MOR	= 0		

H:(H)+Hd+(Hd) = 2:1
  [EB = 1:2.5]

There is one reflection response, and it is her only blended answer. It signifies the likelihood of a marked tendency to value herself highly. This exaggerated self-involvement is influential in her decisions and behaviors, and can easily add to any difficulties that she may have in her interpersonal relationships. Interestingly, her Egocentricity Index (.35) is in the average range. This is an unusual finding in light of the reflection response and indicates that she may have some awareness that her assumed high personal worth is not well founded.

There is also a vista answer (response 7). It may denote a sense of guilt or remorse about her recent inappropriate actions, or it may signal a preoccupation with negative features that she perceives in herself. In either instance, it conflicts with her exaggerated sense of worth and hints that she may be struggling with this. There are also three *An* responses. Usually this indicates unusual body concern, which could be related to her complaints of frequent headaches. However, it seems equally likely that she has drawn on her medical knowledge to formulate reasonably safe and familiar answers.

The finding for the ratio *H:(H)+Hd+(Hd)* (2:1) suggests that her self-image is largely based on experience, but that conclusion probably should be regarded as tenuous in light of earlier findings, plus the nature of the three answers. Two of the three (responses 1 & 5) are pure *F* answers, and although the third (response 14) is coded *M,* it has little substance.

Her three minus responses include two answers that she tends to deny in the inquiry, and justifies in a limited way. In the first (Card I, response 2), she states, "I really don't know, a bug." In the inquiry, she reports, "It really doesn't look like a bug. . . . I was looking at that, it's antennae." When pressed for location, she states, "Sort of the whole thing I guess, the tail, body, I don't know." The second (Card IV, response 8) is, "another bug . . . it really doesn't look like anything." When the examiner asks, "Where on the blot did you see a bug and what makes it look like that?," she replies, "Never really did, maybe little antennae here and maybe an arm or something." Her elusiveness illustrates her defensive avoidant style. She simply does not want to commit and focuses on small areas that she defines as antennae, as basic justifications to generalize to the whole figure. Antennae are sensory organs used for processing inputs and often are critical for defensive purposes.

Assuming that minus answers do include projected elements of the self, it is of interest that she focuses on antennae, raising a question about whether she is more defensively hyperalert than the structural data indicate. She also gives antennae as a separate answer (Card II, response 4). A second question is whether the "bug" selections somehow represent a component of her self-image.

Her third minus answer (Card X, response 19), a geography response, is less defensive, "The pink looks like Italy . . . it needs a little more shore built in, but even without it, it looks like Italy to me." It is a concrete response.

Her single *M* (Card VII, response 14), "Two women with their arms out, and her other two human content answers" (Card I, response 1), "one on the computer game . . . the thing that goes across the computer game . . . like the Space Invader game," and (Card III, response 5), "Two people . . . head, arms, and legs, like people," are essentially barren for meaningful projected information. Her single *FM* response (Card VIII, response 16), "Some rocks with an animal crawling on it . . . maybe a lion or fox," also seems void of projected material.

As might be expected, there is little embellishment in her other responses. There are three answers in which her comments may be of interest. The first (Card IV, response 7) is not very revealing except that she precedes it with another defensive comment, "This looks like a blob, it doesn't look like anything to me, looks even less like something than the other two did, a crinkled up oak leaf, how's that?" Crinkled could imply a MOR answer, but in this instance her articulation is not convincing. Nonetheless, especially as it is a vista answer, it hints at the possibility of more negative self-perceptions than are readily apparent in other data sources. The remaining two answers are (Card VI, response 12), "A neural tube, I bet that would be a very common answer," and (Card X, response 20), "And this will be a common answer, a tip here looks like a Bouie tip." The notion that either of these answers is commonplace seems inappropriate and raises a question about her judgment.

Overall, it is difficult to develop a useful picture of her self-image from the material in this cluster. It seems likely that she is self-centered and struggling with that issue. The magnitude of her defensiveness suggests considerable insecurity, and the manner by which she reports her answers, especially her human content responses tends to imply an apparent naiveté about herself as well as others.

AFFECT

Case 10.   Affect-Related Data for a 29-Year-Old Female.

EB	= 1:2.5			EBPer	= NA	**Blends**	
eb	= 1:2	L	= 2.33	FC:CF+C	= 0:2	rF.CF	= 1
DEPI	= 4	CDI	= 4	Pure C	= 1		
SumC' = 1	SumT = 0			SumC':WSumC	= 1:2.5		
SumV = 1	SumY = 0			Afr	= 0.43		
Intellect	= 1	CP	= 0	S = 0 (S to I,II,III	= 0)		
Blends:R	= 1:20			Col-Shad Bl	= 0		
m + y Bl	= 0			Shading Bl	= 0		

The high *Lambda* value (2.33), plus the data for the *EB* (1.2.5) signals that she has an avoidant-ambitent coping style. This suggests that the influence of her feelings on her decision making varies considerably, and that the frequency of incidents in which her emotions are not well controlled, or overly constricted, is probably substantially greater than expected for most adults. The *eb* ratio is 1:2. Usually, a higher right side *eb* indicates distress or discomfort, but in this instance, the left side value (1) is very low and raises a question about whether this hypothesis is viable. The only support for it is the previously noted vista answer, which may relate to situational elements or could be associated with a more persistent preoccupation that causes negative feelings. In either event, the evidence supporting the notion of frequent distress or discomfort is sparse. The *Afr* (.43) is slightly lower than expected for an avoidant-style person, and may connote a tendency to avoid affectively toned situations. However, this also may reflect her proneness to avoid complexity.

The *FC:CF+C* ratio (0:2) is of interest because, although the frequency of chromatic color answers is low for a 20-response protocol, neither of the two that were given is *FC*, and one of the two is a pure *C* response. This suggests that she may be lax about modulating her emotional displays and may be more obvious or intense in expressing her feelings than are most people. Her pure *C* answer (Card IX, response 18) is, "Part of a map, the colors are map-like . . . I had an old world map when I was little. That orange really looks like one of the colors and the pink, too." Although it is only a single answer, it is somewhat concrete and immature, hinting that when she fails to modulate her feelings they are likely to manifest in inappropriate and potentially maladaptive ways. The fact that there is only one blend (*rF.CF*) in her record is not unusual because of her avoidant style and her resulting proneness to avoid complexity.

Overall, the findings concerning her emotions are not very revealing. It seems probable that she does not control her feelings very effectively and is likely to be expressive or intense in her emotional displays. She may have a sense of discomfort that could have a situational basis or may be related to a struggle that she is having about her self-image. However, this is speculative.

PROCESSING

Case 10.   Processing Variables for a 29-Year-Old Female.

EB	= 1:2.5	Zf	= 9	Zd	= –11.5	DQ+	= 1
L	= 2.33	W:D:Dd	= 8:10:2	PSV	= 0	DQv/+	= 1
HVI	= NO	W:M	= 8:1			DQv	= 1
OBS	= NO						

Location & DQ Sequencing

I:	Wo.Wo	VI:	Wo.Do
II:	Do.Ddo	VII:	Do.Do
III:	Do.Do	VIII:	WSo.Dd+
IV:	Wo.Wo	IX:	Dv/+.Wv
V:	Wo.Wo	X:	Do.Do

The findings regarding *Zf* (9) and the *W:D:Dd* ratio (8:10:2) imply that her processing effort is similar to that for most adults. However, a review of the Location Sequence reveals that seven of her eight *W* responses were given to Cards I, IV, V, and VI, which are more solid figures that facilitate the formation of *W* answers. The eighth *W* was given to Card IX, which usually requires considerable effort, but in this instance a response was given that has no form demand (*Wv*). Although some of the data suggest a reasonable effort, the sequence connotes a conservative approach that only involves a modest effort. Interestingly, the *W:M* ratio (8:1) implies that she may strive to achieve more than is reasonable in light of her current functional capabilities.

The value for the *Zd* score (−11.5) is striking and signifies that she tends to scan hastily and haphazardly. This often causes her to neglect critical cues in a stimulus field. This finding, which is consistent with the notion that she may be less mature than expected for an adult, is unusual for an intelligent adult in a professional role. In a related context, the value for *DQ+* (1) is much lower than expected. In addition, there is one *DQv* response and one *DQv/+* answer. This composite indicates that the quality of her processing is considerably less than adequate, and probably even more compromised in complex situations. Interestingly, her single *DQ+* answer occurred when she used a *Dd* area (Card VIII, response 16) and the *DQv/+* response involved her reflection answer.

The findings regarding her processing activities are likely to be cause for concern, especially her underincorporative approach and her persistent failure to integrate processed information. These negatives relate to her avoidant style, but they should not be simply attributed as being products of it. They represent a special kind of problem that requires more study through additional cognitive evaluation. It appears to represent a feature that handicaps her markedly and should be regarded as an important issue if intervention is considered.

MEDIATION

Case 10.   Mediation Variables for a 29-Year-Old Female.

R = 20		L = 2.33		OBS = No	**Minus & NoForm Features**
FQx+	= 0		XA%	= .80	I 2. Wo F– A 1.0
FQxo	= 8		WDA%	= .78	IV 8. Wo F– A 2.0 INC
FQxu	= 8		X–%	= .15	IX 18. Wv C Ge PER
FQx–	= 3		S–	= 0	X 19. Do F– Ge
FQxnone	= 1				
(W+D	= 18)		P	= 5	
WD+	= 0		X+%	= .40	
WDo	= 7		Xu%	= .40	
WDu	= 7				
WD–	= 3				
WDnone	= 1				

The *XA%* (.80) and *WDA%* (.78) are nearly equal and signify that her translations of inputs are usually appropriate for the situation. However, the presence of one *FQnone* answer and three minus responses (*X–%* = .15) warrants concern because it indicates slightly more mediational dysfunction than is expected, especially for a person with an avoidant style. There is no clear homogeneity among her minus responses except that two of the three are the "bug" responses, discussed previously, in which she emphasized that the figures did not look like bugs and reportedly generalized from antennae. This may intimate that mediational dysfunction is most likely to occur when she is rigidly defensive in the use of her avoidant style. However, none of her minus answers involve serious or bizarre distortions of the figures.

She gave five Popular answers, although two involve a redundant use of the *D1* animal on Card VIII, and the remaining three are among the most commonly given by adults (Cards III, V, and VII). In other words, she seems likely to make conventional or expected responses when the distal features promoting such responses are clear. On the other hand, the value for the *X+%* (.40) is low and the value for the *Xu%* (.40) is substantial. This strongly suggests that many of her mediational decisions will be unconventional. This does not imply a reality-testing problem, but indicates that she is not greatly influenced by social demands or expectations.

Generally, her excessive self-involvement, plus her noticeably defensive avoidant style, tends to limit the extent to which she is concerned with social expectations. As a result, she is likely to formulate many of her decisions and behaviors in accord with her own needs and wants, and she probably does not weigh issues of social convention very strongly.

IDEATION

Case 10.   Ideation Variables for a 29-Year-Old Female.

L	= 2.33	OBS	= No	HVI	= No	Critical Special Scores			
						DV	= 0	DV2	= 0
EB	= 1:2.5	EBPer	= NA	a:p	= 1:1	INC	= 1	INC2	= 0
				Ma:Mp	= 0:1	DR	= 0	DR2	= 0
eb	= 1:2	[FM = 1 m = 0]				FAB	= 0	FAB2	= 0
				M–	= 0	ALOG	= 0	CON	= 0
Intell Indx	= 1	MOR	= 0	Mnone	= 0	Sum6	= 1	WSum6	= 2
								(R = 20)	

M Response Features

VII 14. Do Mpo 2 H P GHR

As noted, the composite of the *EB* (1.2.5) and substantial *Lambda* (2.33) represents an avoidant-ambitent style. This psychological feature usually includes less sophisticated forms of conceptual thinking, and less consistency in the employment of conceptual thinking. In effect, it represents an ideational inefficiency that often breeds difficulty adapting to a complex environment. Because the applications of conceptual thinking tend to be inconsistent, there is an increased vulnerability for incidents in which emotions are poorly modulated.

The low *FM* value (1) is probably related to her avoidant style, and suggests that she often acts quickly to reduce need experiences when they occur. When she employs this tactic, there is an increased likelihood that some of the behaviors she selects to reduce her needs may not be well thought through. On a positive note, there is only one critical special score (INCOM) among her 20 answers. It is an unremarkable finding and signifies that her conceptual thinking is usually clear. In a related context, her single *M* response has appropriate form quality (*o*), but the quality of the answer (response 16) is stilted and concrete, "Two women with their arms out."

Although there is no reason to question the clarity of her thinking, many of her conceptualizations are much more concrete and simplistic than is expected of a reasonably intelligent person. Moreover, she apparently fails to use her directed thinking in a consistent way. The composite of her simplistic thinking, plus her inconsistent use of it, creates a handicap for her, especially as she strives to function effectively in complex situations.

SUMMARY

It is difficult to formulate a detailed picture of her personality structure because much of the Rorschach data are sparse. Her current functioning is marked by considerable defensiveness and a stylistic tendency to avoid complexity and ambiguity. This may be a reaction to the adversarial situation in which she finds herself for a second time during this residency. However, that proposition seems unlikely in light of the test findings and the history that is provided.

Several of the incidents that have led to her current evaluation appear to involve a naive negligence, which is not uncommon among those with an avoidant style when functioning in complex or demanding situations. They can be characterized as the result of poor judgments, but more precisely, they are likely to be the products of haphazard processing, oversimplification of complex cues, and hasty decision making. These flaws in her everyday approach to the world are exacerbated by two interrelated features that seem to have a persistent influence on her behaviors. The first is her tendency to exaggerate her personal worth in a seemingly naive manner. Her self-image does not seem to be well developed or realistic, and her proneness to focus excessively on herself often creates an insensitivity to others that can contribute to less than effective interpersonal behaviors. She is defensive about herself, suggesting that she may be questioning her sense of worth, and if true, this serves to increase an underlying sense of insecurity that she has about herself.

The second is a more general social immaturity that is likely to prompt others to regard her somewhat negatively. She does not understand people very well and, because she probably feels insecure around them, has difficulty creating or sustaining close relations. In effect, she tends to feel alienated in her world. As a result, her social interactions are prone to be superficial, somewhat guarded, and unrewarding. This appears to be confirmed by the history in which she notes being an "outsider kid" in high school, "dumped" by a boyfriend, and dating irregularly as an undergraduate. In medical school, she became involved in an abusive relationship that she did not end, and more recently, she was involved with a technician who terminated their relationship because, according to her, he believed that she was "too good" for him.

These problems are compounded because she does not control her feelings very well. Much of the time her emotional displays are likely to be noticeably intense and impulsive. This can easily breed less effective or even inappropriate behaviors. Moreover, many of her decisions and behaviors appear to be formulated to meet her own needs and wants and show less concern for social convention than should be the case for someone with her occupational aspirations. She does not have any significant problems with reality testing, but she tends to disregard reality often in her quest to avoid the demands of complex situations. Her thinking is reasonably clear, but less sophisticated than expected for one of her intellectual level. Also, she is inconsistent in the way that she thinks through issues, and this inefficiency makes it more difficult for her to deal effectively with complex situations.

This is a reasonably intelligent person who seems well motivated toward success. However, her developmental experiences have not prepared her to deal with the intricacies and demands of the adult world. She is less mature and more socially inept than should be the case. She becomes easily threatened by complexities and ambiguities and strives to defend herself against them by avoiding or disregarding them, while struggling to retain a substantial sense of personal integrity. It is an impossible task because of her naive view of herself and of others. Although her reality testing is generally adequate, she does not process new information effectively and she often translates new cues in a more personalized manner than should be the case. As both personal and interpersonal failures have accumulated, she feels a sense of alienation and has become exquisitely defensive. This only serves to reduce her potential for success. Her controls seem fragile. Her emotions often are not well controlled, and her interpersonal world is, at best, a shambles. Although her thinking is clear, she does not use it to her advantage much of the time because of her marked defensiveness and a corresponding sense of insecurity.

RECOMMENDATIONS

The referral questions whether she is a danger to herself or others. There is no evidence to suggest this may be true. The referral also asks whether a psychiatric diagnosis should be considered as likely to interfere significantly with her capability to maintain a medical practice and interact adequately with colleagues and coworkers. She has some significant personality problems, but they do not fall neatly into a *DSM* classification. In effect, there is no severe psychiatric disability but she is immature. Her problems do not necessarily limit her capacity to practice medicine, especially if the routines required are structured and reasonably predictable. However, her effectiveness as a person, and as a practitioner, probably can be enhanced substantially if some of her current liabilities can be altered or eliminated.

The referral also questions whether she should be allowed to continue in her residency program. This is not a question that can be addressed adequately from the test data. She seems to have sufficient potential and motivation, and there are no indications in the history that she is lacking in medical skills. The complaints about her are largely interpersonal. She has been described as insensitive, inappropriately emotional, and negligent, and as exhibiting poor judgment. These features are not surprising in the context of her psychology. She probably is not easy to like or respect because of her self-centered defensiveness and lack of mature social skills, but whether these elements should prompt dismissal must be evaluated in a broader evaluation of her overall performance.

Another issue in the referral seems related to the question of dismissal. It is the request for recommendations concerning treatment. The questions regarding inpatient versus outpatient treatment and the need for medication seem to imply the anticipation of more serious findings than are the case. Her basic problem appears to one of immaturity and a marked lack of social development. Inpatient care is not indicated and there are no medications that purport to produce greater maturity. In fact, unless there are behavioral circumstances that have not been reported, it is difficult to understand the previous recommendation for inpatient care and participation in Dialectical Behavior Therapy for a brief period of six weeks. Neither could be expected to contend effectively with her problems, and those recommendations probably intensified any sense of threat and alienation that she had at the time.

Optimally, she should be in outpatient care for an extended period, as the fundamental goal is developmental. There are issues that should be addressed early on during the intervention, and fortunately, they are problems for which good progress can be expected, assuming the patient is reasonably cooperative. The first concerns her ineffective processing habits, especially her hasty and haphazard scanning of new information, which can easily lead to flawed decisions and behaviors. Some additional cognitive evaluation should be accomplished to study this issue in more detail. However, even without additional information, it is likely that training in delay tactics and reprocessing habits will promote much better processing activity in a relatively short period.

The second early intervention target is social skill development. This cannot be accomplished as quickly as changes in her processing habits, but it can be a reasonably nonthreatening form of intervention in which the focus is on the tactics of effective interpersonal behaviors, including re-dundant reviews of interpersonal experiences. Emphasis on social skills and behaviors also creates an entry for contending with other important issues, especially the use, control, and expression of feelings and, most important, a gradual study of self-image. These issues ultimately become more time consuming and, typically, lengthen the duration of treatment.

EPILOGUE

She was placed on a probationary status for the remaining nine months of her second residency year with the stipulations that she enter outpatient therapy and be reevaluated after eight months with regard to continuation in the residency program. She was seen twice per week by a female therapist for the eight months. According to the therapist, she was very defensive during the first several treatment sessions but gradually adapted favorably to sessions focusing on her processing habits and issues of emotional constraint. She responded less favorably when issues of interper-sonal effectiveness were broached and became noticeably depressed during the fourth treatment month. At that time, she considered resigning from the residency program in favor of seeking a pharmacy degree. The therapist noted that the depression subsided after about one month and that subsequent progress increased considerably. At the eight-month reevaluation, her performance in the residency program was judged to be satisfactory and she was permitted to continue into the third year. No additional information is available.

REFERENCES

Darby, J., Hofman, K., & Melnick, B. (1967). Response inhibition and the Rorschach "M" response. *Journal of Projective Techniques and Personality Assessment, 31*(5), 29–30.

Gardner, R. (1951). Impulsivity as indicated by Rorschach test factors. *Journal of Consulting Psychology, 15,* 464–468.

Gill, H. (1966). Delay of response and reaction to color on the Rorschach. *Journal of Projective Techniques and Personality Assessment, 30,* 545–552.

Gordon, M. (1983). *The Gordon Diagnostic System.* DeWitt, NY: Gordon Systems.

Graham, J. (2000). *MMPI-2: Assessing personality and psychopathology.* New York: Oxford University Press.

Levine, M., & Meltzoff, J. (1956). Cognitive inhibition and Rorschach human movement responses. *Journal of Consulting Psychology, 20,* 119–122.

Levine, M., Spivack, G., & Wight, B. (1959). The inhibition process, Rorschach human movement re-sponses, and intelligence: Some further data. *Journal of Consulting Psychology, 23,* 306–311.

Meltzoff, J., & Litwin, D. (1956). Affective control and Rorschach human movement responses. *Journal of Consulting Psychology, 20,* 463–465.

Pantle, M. L., Ebner, D. L., & Hynan, L. S. (1994). The Rorschach and the assessment of impulsivity. *Journal of Clinical Psychology, 50*(4), 633–638.

Rorschach, H. (1981). *Psychodiagnostics* (9th ed.). Berne: Hans Huber. (Original work published 1942)

Singer, J. L., Meltzoff, J., & Goldman, G. D. (1952). Rorschach movement responses following motor inhi-bition and hyperactivity. *Journal of Consulting Psychology, 16,* 359–364.

Singer, J. L., & Spohn, H. E. (1954). Some behavioral correlates of Rorschach's experience-type. *Journal of Consulting Psychology, 18,* 1–9.

CHAPTER 13

Problems with Interpersonal Relations

---------------------------------- C A S E 1 1 ----------------------------------

This 27-year-old man is a self-referral, having arranged an appointment with a psychologist who was recommended by a friend. He states that he has been bothered for some time because it is difficult for him to sustain relationships with women. He reports that he finds this confusing as he usually has no difficulty in establishing initial contacts, but he has had four relationships each of which lasted less than one year and, in each, it has been the woman who terminated the relationship.

He describes himself as usually easygoing. He notes that sometimes he may be outspoken about things that he likes or dislikes, but he says that this usually does not lead to arguments. He says that he has numerous friends and acquaintances but admits that he does not feel really close to any of them. He denies aggressiveness and emphasizes that when he is with a woman he is concerned about her well-being and happiness.

He notes that his concerns about his social relations have increased following the recent termination of a relationship with a 26-year-old woman who is a set designer. During their time together, he found that, for the first time, he had difficulties in sexual function. In several instances, he has experienced premature ejaculation and, at other times, he found that he was unable to maintain an erection during intercourse. He states that she was probably more sexually demanding than any of his prior girlfriends because "she seemed to expect sex more frequently and tried to make sure it lasted." On two occasions, she gave him Viagra to increase his endurance, "but I really didn't like that. I was embarrassed and she knew it. We didn't really argue about it, but I guess that ended things."

He is the second of three children, and the only son of parents who have been married for more than 35 years. His father, age 61, owns a restaurant. His mother, age 55, is primarily a housewife, but sometimes works as a cashier in the restaurant. His older sister, age 30, is married to an attorney and has three children. His younger sister, age 24, is recently divorced after two years of marriage to a naval officer. She has recently returned to college to complete a degree in fine arts. There is no psychiatric history in the immediate family.

He completed high school at age 18 with above-average grades and went to a technical institute for three years, specializing in communications and photography. He received an Associate of Arts degree at the age of 21. He reports that, at that time he gave serious thought to the possibility of entering the priesthood. He says, "I've always been quite religious and I really admired the priest in our church." His first job after graduating was as a commercial photographer for an advertising firm. Concurrently, he began to explore religious training and accumulated considerable information about the priesthood during the next several months. He reports that he decided against entering the priesthood because, "I began to question the strength of my faith." He is still active in a church auxiliary group, but he argues that he feels certain that he made the proper decision in staying with photography.

During the past four years, most of his work has involved the creation of television commercials under the direction of others. He emphasizes that he is a very good photographer and notes that he has received substantial salary increases and has been given royalties on two television ads that he helped create. He notes, "I have a good eye for light and depth and someday I expect to have my own crew for shooting advertisements."

He says that most of his relationships have developed through his work and that, for the past few years, he has been "looking for the right girl." He describes the right girl as "attractive, intelligent, supportive, and interested in the same things I am." He lists his own interests as motion picture arts, jogging, travel, and attending political discussion groups. He describes himself as being "pretty flexible, sensitive, and I think I read people well."

He defines his objectives for treatment as finding ways to understand himself better and to improve his ability to sustain relationships. He notes that he is open to the possibility that, for some reason, "I may be picking the wrong kind of women," and states that if that is true he would like to be able to become more discriminating.

The prospective therapist asks these questions: (1) Is there any evidence of serious psychopathology? (2) To what extent might direct treatment concerning his sexual dysfunction be appropriate, or should that be delayed? (3) What are short-term and long-term treatment objectives? (4) How well motivated is he for intervention?

CASE FORMULATION AND RELEVANT LITERATURE

This man has referred himself because of increasing interpersonal concerns, intensified most recently by sexual difficulties and the termination of the fourth in a series of failed relationships. He finds this history confusing, because he sees himself as an easygoing and flexible person who reads people well and is sensitive to their needs.

Although his presenting problems are interpersonal and he wonders if he is "picking the wrong kind of women," there is some suggestion that he is also interested in understanding himself better and examining the part he has played in the relationship failures. His thoughtful consideration about entering the priesthood also indicates some potential for self-exploration. The therapist is questioning whether a comprehensive, insight-oriented approach would be more appropriate than a symptom-oriented one that begins with a direct focus on his sexual dysfunction.

The Rorschach literature on interpersonal competence was surveyed in Case 1 (Chapter 3), and a review of those variables can provide useful information about a person's interpersonal skills and accuracy. Because this case raises questions about the appropriateness of long-term insight-oriented psychotherapy, it will be helpful to review the Rorschach literature about ability to benefit from psychodynamic treatment.

Assessment of Psychodynamic Capacity

Nygren (2004) reviewed the psychotherapy literature and found that measures of psychological mindedness, quality of interpersonal relations, and motivation have been useful in predicting the effectiveness of psychodynamic therapy. However, she notes that there are few *Comprehensive Sys-*

tem studies whose focus has been whether psychodynamic approaches would be the most appropriate therapeutic intervention.

One such study (Alpher, Perfetto, Henry, & Strupp, 1990) investigated the relationship between 15 rationally chosen *Comprehensive System* predictors and interviewer and independent judge ratings on a measure of willingness and ability to address affective and interpersonal topics therapeutically during a semistructured intake interview. The authors found that the Rorschach variables accounted for 43% of the variance in interviewer ratings and 51% of the variance in the independent judge ratings of the videotaped interviews. *Zf* was the single best positive predictor for both groups of raters, and the authors view it as a measure of both motivation and psychological mindedness. High *Lambda* values, seen by the authors as suggesting emotional constriction, were negatively related to interviewer ratings of potential for engaging in dynamic psychotherapy.

Nygren (2004) used a format similar to the study by Alpher et al. (1990), but studied 17 *Comprehensive System* variables rationally chosen to reflect aspects of two overarching constructs: Dynamic Capacity and Ego Strength. She tested 52 self-referred nonpsychotic individuals who had applied for psychodynamic therapy and had been interviewed extensively as part of the intake process. Each interviewer rated the applicants he or she had seen on three 7-point Dynamic Capacity scales (psychological mindedness, motivation, and cooperation) and on seven 7-point Ego Strength scales (reality testing, interpersonal capacity, self and object constancy, impulse control, defense structure, realistic self-evaluation, and global ego strength). The Rorschach findings were not used in the intake team's decision to accept ($n = 29$) or suggest other treatment ($n = 23$) for the 52 applicants.

The age range of participants in Nygren's (2004) study was 20 to 57 and, interestingly, age correlated negatively with the sum of subscale scores for both the Dynamic Capacity and the Ego Strength ratings. She found that *EA, FC, Blends, Zf,* and *MQo* correlated positively with interviewer overall ratings of Dynamic Capacity. *EA, FC,* and *Blends* correlated positively and *YFY* (nonform dominant diffuse shading determinants) and *F%* (a research version of *Lambda*) correlated negatively with interviewer overall ratings of Ego Strength. The mean *EA* was markedly higher for the group selected for psychodynamic therapy than for the nonselected group (12.29 vs. 9.59) as was the mean *Zf* (16.24 vs. 13.04).

In summary, the combination of higher *Zf* and lower *Lambda,* particularly in the context of higher *EA* and good form *M,* may constitute the basic elements necessary for psychological mindedness, motivation, and adequate interpersonal skills. As part of a comprehensive multimethod evaluation, assessment of those attributes provides a foundation for predicting whether psychodynamic treatment approaches will be helpful.

Card	Response	Inquiry
I	1. It ll a statue, birds & an angel, lik at a church	E: Rpts Ss resp S: It re me of st on the frnt of a church E: Help me c it too
	E: If u tak ur tim I thk u'll find st else too	S: These figurs (D2) cb statues of birds, & thyr on e side of ths religious fig in the middl, lik a statue of a saint, or a monk, he has his hands raised lik callg to the faithful E: Can u tell me about the birds? S: Thy just do, the shape, c the wgs r outstretched lik thy hav flown dwn in response to being called & thyr hangg on him
	2. I suppose it cb a blk bird too	E: Rpts Ss resp S: The shape of it ll a bird, lik a crow or smthg, its black so it cb a crow
II	3. I get a sense of two dogs, I supp u cld thk of thm as playg	E: Rpts Ss resp S: Yeah, thyr hav thyr noses together here (D4) lik dogs do when thyr playful, sort of sniffing, so if u don't count the red I wld thk thyr playg
	4. but if u includ the red thy cb fiting	E:Rpts Ss resp S: Well, the dark prts r the dogs, mayb dogs or bears & the red dwn here (D3) cb blood lik thyr hurt as the result of fiting, it seems to be out in frnt of them, mayb thy killed smthg & now thyr fiting ovr it E: Out in frnt of thm? S: Yes, it looks in frnt of thm to me, mayb its what's left of sm A thy killed, its red so it cld just a bloody carcass tht thyr fiting about
III	5. ll 2 wm carryg sthg, a basket	E: Rpts Ss resp S: These 2 shapes r the wm & ths (D7) cb a basket tht thyr liftg or carryg, c the head & legs & the arms
IV	6. ll sk of monster sort of standg ther lik u'r lookg up at it	E: Rpts Ss resp S: Just ll u'r lookg up at sk of strange A creature, a weird monster it has a small head & a very large tail (D1) & little arms, thes r the ft, thyr way out of proportion, thts why I thot of it in som sort of perspective as if u were lookg up at the ft
V	7. A dead bf or smthg	E: Rpts Ss resp S: It has the wgs & the body but it's decayed lookg, the color givs tht impression, as if its dead, & the ends of the wgs look torn
	8. It cb a repres of the devil also, lik a paintg of him	E: (Rpts Ss resp) S: Lik a pict of him standg w his wg lik arms out, the dark color thr make it look sinister lik evil thts why I thot of a repres of the devil E: I'm not sur I c it lik u do S: Its all dark & gloomy lookg lik to giv an evil impression, here's the slender body in the center, thr horns, & the wg-lik arms
VI	9. It ll a bearskin, just the bottm prt	E: Rpts Ss resp S: Ths prt (outlines D1), ths looks to me as a rug a bearskin rug w the legs out here, no head to it, just a furry like pelt tht u mite c in a movie in frnt of a fireplace or on a wall E: U said furry like? S: The colorg rem me of tht, it has all diff shades of grey in it, lik fur looks sometimes & the gen shape conforms to tht, lik u'd c sittg next to a a fireplace in a den sm where

Case 11. Continued.

Card	Response	Inquiry
	10. The top actually ll an abstract of the crucifix	**E:** Rpts Ss resp **S:** It's sort of a modernistic one, some of the young kids wear them, its not really a good portrayal but it still has the meaning of Christ on the cross, c thy use rays for the arms & the body isn't as distinct as it shld b but it still repres the crucifix
VII	11. It ll a young boy lookg in the mirror	**E:** Rpts Ss resp **S:** Ll a young boy w a feather in his hair, just ths upper prt is the boy, the bottm ll he's kneeling on whatevr ths base prt is, mayb a cushion **E:** U said he's lookg in the mirror **S:** Yes, its all the same ovr here, as in a reflection
VIII	12. It cb 2 wm stretchg some cloth across a pole	**E:** Rpts Ss resp **S:** These figs (D1) cb wm & thy ll thyr stretchg or pullg ths cloth (D5) across, don't count the bottm, c the wm r on each side & thyr pullg ths blue & ths grey up here, lik stretchg it across ths pole in the middl **E:** I'm not sur I'm seeg it rite **S:** Ths wb pcs of cloth, som is blu, som is grey, & thyr separating it, mayb thy dyed it & thyr stretchg it out on the pole in the middl to dry out
	13. Or it cb 2 rats dragg som animal away	**E:** Rpts Ss resp **S:** Cb these r rats (D1) if u want to call thm rats, thy thy r pullg on ths object in the cntr. It ll thyr lik dragg it **E:** U said its an animal? **S:** I dkno, a carcus, lik bones here (D3) and guts & stuff, just alot of diff colored insides of whatevr is left of an A, alot of guts & stuff
IX	14. I get the impress of a delicate flowr somehow the colors look very soft	**E:** Rpts Ss resp **S:** Thes (D3) r the orange flowers & here (D1) r the green leaves, lik it is in ths pinkish pot dwn here **E:** U said it's delicate & the colors look soft **S:** I'm not sur why but it looks very fragile, the shades in the orange & green make it look very soft, I guess thts why I said delicate, lik smthg u shouldn't touch
	15. Ths cntr white re me of a skull, dried out	**E:** Rpts Ss resp **S:** It ll an A skull, lik a cow or horse, it looks weatherd, lik all dried out **E:** Weathered? **S:** It has diff shades of whiteness in it
X	16. I c insects dancg around, lik havg a party	**E:** Rpts Ss resp **S:** All thes thgs cb sk of littl insects, bugs, thy look lik thyr all havg a good time, lik thyr in a festive mood. Thyr all brightly colored lik bugs mite look I guess **E:** U said thy r havg a party? **S:** I suppose, just havg fun for a change, all gettg togethr for a good time

(continued)

Card Response	Inquiry
v17. If u look ths way its lik a face or mayb a mask, yes a devil mask	**E:** Rpts Ss resp **S:** Its lik a devil mask or smthg tht is supposed to represent somethg associated w the devil or evil, lik satanical thgs **E:** I don't think I c it lik u r **S:** It has all diff colored parts, ths is a beard part (D11) & a littl mouth area & pink sides here & thn all of these exterior thgs r lik colored symbols tht hang off the side, so tht when u move they move & thes r painted green eyebrows
v18. The pink alone ll sthg too, mayb worms, red worms	**E:** Rpts Ss resp **S:** Thy just rem me of red worm, long & fat, lik good sand worms, good for fishing, u c them along the sand by the ocean **E:** U say thyr fat? **S:** Yeah, thy look big there, lik fat ones
19. Ths top prt ll 2 littl gnomes holdg up a stick	**E:** Rpts Ss resp **S:** Thy hav littl legs & heads & the white spot is their eye, thyr seem to be struggling to hold up ths big stick or post or whtever

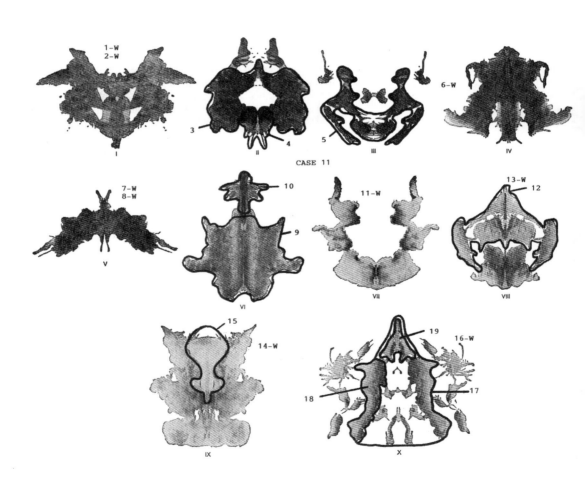

CASE 11

Case 11. Sequence of Scores.

Card	No.	Loc.	No.	Determinant(s)	(2)	Content(s)	Pop	Z	Special Scores
I	1	W+	1	Mpo	2	Art,(H),(A)		4.0	GHR
	2	Wo	1	FC'o		A		1.0	
II	3	D+	6	FMao	2	A	P	3.0	COP,GHR
	4	D+	6	FMa.CF.FDo	2	A,Ad,Bl	P	3.0	AG,MOR,PHR
III	5	D+	1	Mao	2	H,Hh	P	3.0	COP,GHR
IV	6	Wo	1	FMp.FD+		(A)		2.0	
V	7	Wo	1	FYo		A	P	1.0	MOR
	8	Wo	1	Mp.FC'u		Art,(H)		1.0	GHR
VI	9	Do	1	FTo		Ad,Hh	P		PER
	10	Do	3	Fo		Art			AB,PER
VII	11	W+	1	Mp.Fro		H,Cg,Hh	P	2.5	GHR
VIII	12	D+	1	Ma.mp.CF.FC'–	2	H,Hh		3.0	COP,PHR
	13	W+	1	FMa.CFo	2	A,An	P	4.5	MOR,COP,GHR
XI	14	W+	1	CF.TFo		Bt,Hh		5.5	
	15	DSo	8	FC'.FY–		An			MOR
X	16	Wv/+	1	Ma.CFo		A,Hx		5.5	FAB,COP,GHR
	17	DdSo	22	CF.mp–		(Hd)			AB,PHR
	18	Do	9	FCo	2	A			PER
	19	DS+	11	Mau	2	(H),Bt		6.0	COP,GHR

Case 11.   Structural Summary.

Location Features	Determinants Blends	Single	Contents	S-Constellation
			H = 3	YES . .Col-Shd Bl>0
Zf = 14	FM.CF.FD	M = 3	(H) = 3	YES . .Ego<.31,>.44
ZSum = 45.0	FM.FD	FM = 1	Hd = 0	YES . .MOR > 3
ZEst = 45.5	M.FC'	m = 0	(Hd) = 1	NO . . .Zd > +− 3.5
	M.Fr	FC = 1	Hx = 1	YES . .es > EA
W = 9	M.m.CF.FC'	CF = 1	A = 7	YES . .CF+C > FC
D = 9	FM.CF	C = 0	(A) = 2	NO . . .X+% < .70
W+D = 18	CF.TF	Cn = 0	Ad = 2	NO . . .S > 3
Dd = 1	FC'.FY	FC' = 1	(Ad) = 0	NO . . .P < 3 or > 8
S = 3	M.CF	C'F = 0	An = 2	NO . . .Pure H < 2
	CF.m	C' = 0	Art = 3	NO . . .R < 17
		FT = 1	Ay = 0	5 . . . .TOTAL

DQ					
+ = 9		TF = 0	Bl = 1	**Special Scores**	
o = 9		T = 0	Bt = 2	Lv1	Lv2
v/+ = 1		FV = 0	Cg = 1	DV = 0x1	0x2
v = 0		VF = 0	Cl = 0	INC = 0x2	0x4
		V = 0	Ex = 0	DR = 0x3	0x6
		FY = 1	Fd = 0	FAB = 1x4	0x7
		YF = 0	Fi = 0	ALOG = 0x5	
		Y = 0	Ge = 0	CON = 0x7	
Form Quality			Hh = 5	Raw Sum6 = 1	
		Fr = 0	Ls = 0	Wgtd Sum6 = 4	

	FQx	MQual	W+D				
+	= 1	= 0	= 1	rF = 0	Na = 0		
o	= 13	= 4	= 13	FD = 0	Sc = 0	AB = 2	GHR = 8
u	= 2	= 2	= 2	F = 1	Sx = 0	AG = 1	PHR = 3
−	= 3	= 1	= 2		Xy = 0	COP = 6	MOR = 4
none	= 0	= 0	= 0		Id = 0	CP = 0	PER = 3
				(2) = 8		PSV = 0	

Ratios, Percentages, and Derivations

R = 19	L	= 0.06	FC:CF+C = 1:6	COP = 6 AG = 1
			Pure C = 0	GHR:PHR = 8:3
EB = 7:6.5	EA = 13.5	EBPer = N/A	SumC':WSumC = 4:6.5	a:p = 7:6
eb = 6:8	es = 14	D = 0	Afr = 0.73	Food = 0
	Adj es = 12	Adj D = 0	S = 3	SumT = 2.
			Blends:R = 10:19	Hum Con = 6
FM = 4	C' = 4	T = 2	CP = 0	Pure H = 3
m = 2	V = 0	Y = 2		PER = 3
				Iso Indx = 0.11

a:p = 7:6	Sum6 = 1	XA% = 0.84	Zf = 14.0	3r+(2)/R = 0.58
Ma:Mp = 4:3	Lv2 = 0	WDA% = 0.89	W:D:Dd = 9:9:1	Fr+rF = 1
2AB+Art+Ay = 7	WSum6 = 4	X−% = 0.16	W:M = 9:7	SumV = 0
MOR = 4	M− = 1	S− = 2	Zd = −0.5	FD = 2
	Mnone = 0	P = 7	PSV = 0	An+Xy = 2
		X+% = 0.74	DQ+ = 9	MOR = 4
		Xu% = 0.11	DQv = 0	H:(H)Hd(Hd) = 3:4

PTI = 0	DEPI = 3	CDI = 1	S-CON = 5	HVI = No	OBS = No

S-CON AND KEY VARIABLES

The S-CON value (5) is not significant. The first positive Key variable is $Fr+rF > 0$, indicating that the first three data clusters to be reviewed should be self-perception, interpersonal perception, and controls. Ordinarily, the remainder of the interpretive approach is decided by a second Key variable but, in this instance, there is none. Using Tertiary variable guidelines, either of two alternatives seems reasonable.

The first, based on the findings that the *EA* is 13.5 and the value for MOR (4) is greater than two, suggests that the interpretation should continue with a study of data concerning ideation, then move to the findings regarding processing and mediation, and end with a review of findings concerning affect. However, three other Tertiary variables are also positive. The *eb* has a higher right side value (6:8), *CF* is greater than *FC+1,* and the value for *SumT* is greater than one. In addition, a cursory review of the *Structural Summary* reveals that his 19 responses include 10 blended answers, of which eight contain affect-related variables. These findings imply the possibility of some emotional difficulties and tend to favor a decision to review the data concerning affect after studying controls, and before contending with the findings about cognition.

Either routine is logical, that is, following the study of controls with a review of data about ideation, or a review of findings concerning affect. In this case, however, the positive Tertiary variables regarding affect seem more compelling. Thus, after the findings for self-perception, interpersonal perception, and controls have been reviewed, the interpretation will move on to the data cluster concerning affect; and then the data related to ideation, processing, and mediation will be studied.

SELF-PERCEPTION

Case 11.   Self-Perception Related Data for a 27-Year-Old Male.

R	= 19	OBS	= No	HVI = No	**Human Content, Hx, An & Xy Responses**
				I	1. W+ Mpo 2 Art,(H),(A) 4.0 GHR
Fr+rF	= 1	3r+(2)/R = 0.58		III	5. D+ Mao 2 H,Hh P 3.0 COP,GHR
				V	8. Wo Mp.FC'u Art,(H) 1.0 GHR
FD	= 2	SumV	= 0	VII	11. W+ Mp.Fro H,Cg,Hh P 2.5 GHR
				VIII	12. D+ Ma.mp.CF.FC'– 2 H,Hh 3.0 COP,PHR
An+Xy	= 2	MOR	= 4	VIII	13. W+ FMa.CFo 2 A,An P 4.5 MOR,COP,GHR
				IX	15. DSo FC'.FY– An MOR
H:(H)+Hd+(Hd) = 3:4				X	16. Wv/+ Ma.CFo A,Hx 5.5 FAB,COP,GHR
[EB = 7:6.5]				X	17. DdSo CF.mp– (Hd) AB,PHR
				X	19. DS+ Mau 2 (H),Bt 6.0 COP,GHR

The presence of one reflection response plus the substantial value for the Egocentricity Index (0.58) indicates that he is much more involved with himself than are most others. These findings imply that a narcissistic feature is embedded in his psychology. It prompts him to value himself highly and probably promotes a need for status. It has probably contributed to his decision to seek therapy because his persistent difficulties with women, and his more recent problems in sexual functioning, are significant challenges to his high self-regard. Usually, inflated self-involvement breeds a proneness to rationalize mistakes or failure, and it is interesting to note that he suggests "I may be picking the wrong kind of women," implying that it is the women who are at fault.

The two *FD* answers in his protocol indicate that he is involved routinely in self-inspecting behaviors. This can be a positive feature in treatment motivation, provided his reality testing is intact. Interestingly, he also has two *An* responses, which comprise half of his four MOR answers. These findings are atypical for someone who has an inflated sense of self-worth. They suggest the possibility of some unusual body preoccupation and the notion that his self-image includes impressions of markedly negative features. It seems likely that these are the results of the social failures about which he complains and his more recent sexual concerns. Regardless of whether they are recent or long standing, they tend to promote an irritating sense of pessimism about himself.

The *H:(H)+Hd+(Hd)* ratio (3:4) suggests that his self-concept probably includes some features that are based more on imagination or distortions of real experience than should be the case. This tends to breed unrealistic notions about self-image, either favorable or unfavorable, that can impact negatively on his relations with others. Moreover, two of his seven human content responses have a minus form quality, one of which is a pure *H* response (D+ *Ma.mp.CF.FC'*− 2 *H, Hh* 3.0 COP, PHR). It is a very complex response that appears to support the postulate that there is some confusion about self-image. In addition, there is an *Hx* response in the record (response 16) that also includes his only critical special score (*FABCOM*). It suggests that he may be prone to deal with issues of self-image in an overly intellectualized manner that tends to bend or ignore reality.

His three minus answers were given to chromatically colored figures (VIII, IX, & X) and, interestingly, two of the three include the use of white space. This suggests that his emotions, probably caused by a sense of alienation, are likely to have a substantial influence in defining some aspects of his self-image. There is seemingly little homogeneity in the substance of these answers, but all three appear to contain useful projected material. The first (Card VIII, response 12) is one of his seven *M* responses, "two women stretching some cloth across a pole . . . stretching or pulling this cloth . . . they're separating it, maybe they dyed it and they're stretching it out on the pole in the middle to dry out." It is an unusual response because the *D1* areas of Card VIII are rarely reported to be human figures. It is difficult to avoid speculating that it may be a direct representation of his presenting complaints, implying a sense of threat from, and control by others that is greater than he prefers, "stretching it out on the pole . . . to dry out."

The second minus (Card IX, response 15) is, "a skull, dried out . . . it looks weathered like all dried out." It is one of his four MOR responses, and is the second reference among the minus responses to being "dried out." That description is intriguing, but unclear. It may imply a loss of integrity or a diminished sense of self or, alternatively, may connote a feeling of hopelessness. The third minus (Card X, response 17) is, "a devil mask . . . something that is supposed to represent something associated with the devil or evil, like satanical things." It is a concealment object that presents a facade, and may raise a question about whether, at some level, he perceives himself to be in conflict with his religious concerns and commitments.

The remaining three MOR answers are homogeneous, as each involves dead objects. The first (Card II, response 4) was given as an alternative to response 3 (dogs playing) in which he says, "but if you include the red they could be fighting . . . the red could be blood like they're hurt . . . it seems to be out in front of them, maybe they killed something and now they're fighting over it . . . maybe it's what's left of some animal they killed . . . just a bloody carcass that they're fighting over." The second (Card V, response 7) is, "A dead butterfly or something . . . it's decayed looking . . . as if it's dead, and the ends of the wings look torn." The third is much like the first

(Card VIII, response 13), "Or it could be two rats dragging some animal away . . . pulling on this object . . . like dragging it . . . a carcass, like bones and stuff . . . different colored insides of whatever is left of an animal."

These three MOR answers represent products of violence. An issue to be considered is whether he identifies with the aggressor or the victim. The latter seems more likely in light of his presenting problem and, if so, conveys the notion that he has a sense of having been damaged by the actions of others. In either event, they denote a preoccupation with aggressiveness and its harmful consequences and, as with two of the three minus answers, suggest that his self-image includes negative features that probably result from actions over which he has no control. This postulate seems important in light of his marked self-centeredness and the tendency that it creates to attribute external rather than self-created causes for problems.

His seven *M* responses are more heterogeneous for substance. One (women stretching cloth across a pole) has been discussed previously. Two of the remaining six have somewhat antithetical religious connotations. One (Card I, response 1) is, "statue, birds and an angel, like at a church . . . like the statue of a saint or monk . . . calling to the faithful." It is a positive response, but neutralized (a statue). The second (Card V, response 8) is much more negative, but also neutralized, "It could be a representation of the devil, like a painting . . . sinister like evil . . . dark and gloomy looking to give an evil impression." It has been noted that he may have some conflicts about his religious concerns, and these answers seem to add support to that notion.

One of the remaining four *M*'s (Card III, response 5) is positive, "two women carrying something, a basket." However, it is not very dynamic, as he provides little elaboration in the inquiry. The second of the four (Card VII, response 11) is his reflection answer, "a young boy looking in the mirror . . . he's kneeling on whatever this base part is, maybe a cushion." The kneeling aspect of the response seems intriguing and might relate to some of his religious concerns. The third of these four answers (Card X, response 16) is the most positive and is his single *Hx* response, but it also involves a distortion of reality, "insects dancing around, like having a party . . . having a good time . . . in a festive mood . . . having fun for a change." Insects, not people, are "having fun for a change." It is an intellectualized response that raises a question about acceptable roles that he perceives for himself. The final *M* (Card X, response 19) also does not involve people, "two gnomes holding up a stick . . . they seem to be struggling to hold up this big stick or post or whatever." The symbolic connotation is impossible to avoid in light of his reported sexual difficulties, even though it is a positive answer.

Two of his four *FM* responses (dogs fighting & rats dragging an animal) have been noted earlier. The remaining two include (Card II, response 3), "I get a sense of two dogs, I suppose you could think of them as playing . . . like dogs do when they're playful," and (Card IV, response 6), "some kind of monster standing there, you're looking up at it . . . it has a small head and a large tail and little arms." The first is somewhat tentative (I suppose you could think of them), while the second is more ominous (a monster, you're looking up at it), but it is difficult to identify projective components as both are relatively common answers. The two *m* responses are much less common. Both (cloth being stretched; a devil mask with colored symbols that hang off the side) have been noted earlier.

Thus far, 14 of his 19 responses have been examined for substance. Two of the remaining five (Card I, response 2), "a black bird, too . . . like a crow," and (Card VI, response 9), "a bearskin . . . a bearskin rug . . . that you might see in a movie in front of a fireplace or on a wall" are somewhat meager for projected material. The third (Card VI, response 10), is, "an abstract of the crucifix . . . a modernistic one . . . not really a good portrayal but it still has the meaning." Although projected material is less direct than might be preferred, it is intriguing for the comment, "it still has the meaning," which seems in line with his other religious content answers and the question about whether religious concerns contribute in some ways to his difficulties.

The fourth (Card IX, response 14) is the most obvious of the five when self-concept is considered, "a delicate flower, somehow the colors look very soft . . . it looks very fragile, the shades in the orange and green make it look soft . . . that's why I said delicate, like something you shouldn't touch." It conveys the notion of an attractive but vulnerable sense of self. The last of these five answers (Card X, response 18) also implies a sense of vulnerability, "maybe worms, red worms . . . like good sand worms, good for fishing."

The overall picture of his self-image is marked by contradictory features. On the one hand, he appears to be self-involved and holds himself in high regard. On the other hand, he seems to judge himself as a fragile, vulnerable, and damaged person who has been, or can be, easily victimized by others. He seems introspective, but his conceptualizations of himself are strongly influenced by his imagination or misinterpretations of experience. It also seems likely that he has a conflict in values that is created mainly by strong religious concerns. It may be contributing to some of his self-perceptions regarding vulnerability and damage. It also probably plays an important role in fomenting the interpersonal difficulties that he identifies as being his main source of concern.

INTERPERSONAL PERCEPTION

Case 11.   Interpersonal Perception Data for a 27-Year-Old Male.

R =19	CDI = 1	HVI = No	**COP & AG Responses**
a:p = 7:6	SumT = 2	Fd = 0	II 3. D+ FMao 2 A P 3.0 COP,GHR
	[eb = 6:8]		II 4. D+ FMa.CF.FDo 2 A,Ad,Bl P 3.0 AG,MOR,PHR
Sum Human Contents = 7		H = 3	III 5. D+ Mao 2 H,Hh P 3.0 COP,GHR
[Style = Ambitent]			VIII 12. D+ Ma.mp.CF.FC'– 2 H,Hh 3.0 COP,PHR
GHR:PHR = 8:3			VIII 13. W+ FMa.CFo 2 A,An P 4.5 MOR,COP,GHR
			X 16. Wv/+ Ma.CFo A,Hx 5.5 FAB,COP,GHR
COP = 6	AG = 1	PER = 3	X 19. DS+ Mau 2 (H),Bt 6.0 COP,GHR
Isolation Indx = 0.11			

There are no distinctive features that automatically suggest probable interpersonal problems. The CDI and HVI are both negative and the $a:p$ ratio (7:6) offers no meaningful information. The first hint of possible difficulties is the value for *SumT* (2), which signifies fairly strong, but unfulfilled, needs for closeness. It seems possible that this represents an irritating sense of loneliness caused by his most recently terminated relationship, but an alternative hypothesis is also worth consideration. He reports four unsuccessful adult relationships, each lasting less than one year. Thus, it may be equally plausible to suspect that his yearnings may be more persistent, resulting from an accumulation of losses and disappointments.

The seven human contents in his protocol denote a reasonable interest in people, but the fact that only three are pure *H* implies that he does not understand people very well. When this is considered in the context of his substantial self-centeredness, it seems possible that he may expect more than is reasonable of his social relations. Such expectations, plus his naive impressions of others, can easily lead to misinterpretations of social gestures and increase the potential for blunders that can alienate others.

On the other hand, the GHR:PHR ratio (8:3) signifies that most of his interpersonal behaviors are likely to be adaptive across a broad spectrum of social situations. This may appear to contradict findings about his naive impressions of people and his high expectations about relationships. However, these apparent contradictions may simply connote that he is effective in superficial relationships, but is less so in more personal and emotionally demanding associations. Certainly, the presence of six COP responses implies that he usually anticipates harmonious interactions, and others probably regard him as outgoing and likable. However, one of the six COP answers has a minus form quality (response 12) and a second contains a *FABCOM* (response 16), suggesting that his anticipations may not always be well grounded in reality.

In a related context, the three PER responses imply that he may feel less secure and more defensive than he prefers in social situations, especially those that he perceives as challenging. Although there are no data to suggest that he is prone to avoid social intercourse, there are some suggestions that his social relations are not as mature as might be expected. His seven *M* responses include four that are coded for a pair, and three of the four contain COP. However, one of those three is a minus response (women stretching something), and neither of the remaining two (women carrying something; gnomes holding up a stick) is very dynamic. The most positive of his *M*'s involves insects having a party. Likewise, three of his four *FM* answers are coded for a pair, and two of the three include COP, but two are MOR, and the one positive *FM* is tentative ("I suppose you could think of them [dogs] as playing"). Overall, the composite of his paired movement responses intimates that his social relations are likely to be somewhat lacking in depth or richness.

Generally, the findings connote that he is interested in people and in developing meaningful relationships. However, he does not seem to understand people very well, and it is likely that many of his social interactions are more superficial than might be expected. Although most of his relations are positive and adaptive, they are probably immature and potentially fragile. In part, this can be attributed to his self-centeredness, but he also may be attempting to present a social facade that runs contrary to some of his religious concerns. This postulate is based mainly on some of the findings about his self-concept. Either, or both, of these features can easily increase the likelihood that close relationships will not endure and, as they fail, he experiences an increasingly significant sense of confusion, frustration, and loneliness.

CONTROLS

Case 11.   Control-Related Variables for a 27-Year-Old Male.

EB = 7:6.5	EA = 13.5		D = 0	CDI = 1
eb = 6:8	es = 14	Adj es = 12	AdjD = 0	L = 0.06
FM = 4 m = 2	SumC′ = 4	SumT = 2	SumV = 0	SumY = 2

The Adj D Score of zero indicates that his capacities for control and tolerance for stress are similar to that of most adults. The values for the *EB* (7:6.5) and *Lambda* (0.06) suggest that there is no reason to question the validity of the *EA* or the integrity of the Adj D. However, his *EA* value (13.5) is well above average, while the Adj D Score is only zero, signaling that the *es* (14) is unexpectedly elevated. This implies that the Adj D Score may reflect a conservative estimate of his typical control capacities.

Lending support for that notion is that the Adj *es* (12) is more substantial than expected. The main cause for this elevation is in the right side *eb* data, which includes atypical values for both *SumC'* (4) and *SumT* (2). The former may represent a persistent tendency to internalize feelings and, as noted, the *SumT* finding may reflect a more chronic sense of need and loneliness. Nonetheless, if either of these features has a situationally related basis, it is reasonable to speculate that his capacities for control have been somewhat sturdier than currently indicated by the Adj D of zero. In any event, there are no reasons to assume that problems with control or tolerance for stress exist.

AFFECT

Case 11.   Affect-Related Data for a 27-Year-Old Male.

EB	= 7:6.5			EBPer	= NA	**Blends**	
eb	= 6:8	L	= 0.06	FC:CF+C	= 1:6	M.m.CF.FC'	= 1
DEPI	= 3	CDI	= 1	Pure C	= 0	M.Fr	= 1
						M.FC'	= 1
SumC' = 4	SumT = 2			SumC':WSumC	= 3:6.5	M.CF	= 1
SumV = 0	SumY = 2			Afr	= 0.73	FM.CF.FD	= 1
						FM.CF	= 1
Intellect	= 7	CP	= 0	S = 3 (S to I,II,III	= 0)	FM.FD	= 1
Blends:R	= 10:19			Col-Shad Bl	= 2	CF.TF	= 1
m + y Bl	= 2			Shading Bl	= 1	CF.m	= 1
						FC'.FY	= 1

The findings for the *EB* (7:6.5) and *Lambda* (0.06) indicate that he has not developed a consistent approach to problem solving or decision making. One result is that his emotions vary considerably in their influence on his thinking, especially when making decisions. In some instances, they may have a substantial impact and promote an intuitive strategy in which external feedback and trial-and-error tactics are prominent. In another instance, even though it may be similar to the first, he may push his feelings aside and adopt a more thoughtful strategy in which he tries to delay decision making until he has considered all seemingly possible alternatives.

Although this inconsistency is not very efficient, it does not necessarily breed problems in adjustment. However, the failure to use his feelings consistently creates a potential for emotions to become somewhat confusing for him. He may weigh similar feelings differently at different times. He is also likely to be somewhat erratic about how he modulates his emotional displays; that is, sometimes he is too controlled and at other times he is overly intense.

The higher right side *eb* value (6:8) connotes the presence of distress or some other emotional discomfort. Part of the elevation in that value is created by the two texture answers that, as noted, imply neediness or loneliness. This could be a reaction to his recently terminated relationship, but it seems equally likely that it is a persistent feature. In either event, it is contributing to his distress. However, much of his discomfort appears generated by a tendency to inhibit or suppress feelings, as suggested by the *SumC'* value (4). The *SumC':WSumC* ratio (4:6.5) indicates that this is not an extreme form of constraint, but it implies that he is conservative about displaying or sharing his feelings openly. The question of why this may be true is not answered easily.

The value for the *Afr* (.73) connotes that he is as willing as most others to process and become involved with emotions and emotionally toned situations. On the other hand, the value for the Intellectualization Index (7) indicates a very notable tendency to deal with emotions by contending with them defensively on an ideational level rather than more directly as they are experienced. This is most likely to occur when feelings are perceived as potentially threatening or stressful; when done to excess, it can create a potential for emotional disorganization. Findings regarding a third variable, the *FC:CF+C* ratio (1:6) cloud the issue further. They signify that he is somewhat lax in modulating the displays of his feelings and probably calls attention to himself because of the intensity with which he expresses his emotions. This seems contrary to his proneness to suppress or intellectualize feelings.

The apparent contradictions about how he handles his feelings may simply represent an extension of his inconsistency in the use of emotions when making decisions. However, it also may represent a more distinctive kind of naiveté that he has about emotions, which parallels his apparent confusion about himself and about others, and how best to interact with them. Some indirect support for this postulate is noted by his three *S* responses. They suggest irritation with, or alienation about, his environment that may breed a negativistic set about his world. The fact that all three *S* responses were given to the last two figures may imply that this irritation is most likely to occur when he is confronted with emotionally loaded stimulation.

There are 10 blended answers (53%) in his 19-response protocol. Although two are probably related to current stresses (*FC'.FY* and *CF.m*), the remaining eight still comprise 42% of the record. One of the eight contains four variables and a second includes three variables. Collectively, these findings signify that he is an inordinately complex individual. As might be expected, six of those eight blends include affect-related variables and tend to highlight the significant role that emotions are playing in his psychology. Moreover, two of the eight (*M.m.CF.FC'* and *CF.TF*) are color shading blends suggesting that he is often confused by feelings. In addition, one of the situationally related blends has both grey-black and shading variables (*FC'.FY*), which is unusual and typically signals stressful emotional experiences.

Some of the findings regarding his emotions are not surprising or inconsistent with findings about his self-concept or his view of people and relations with them. These include the irregular influence of feelings in his thinking, his interest in being involved in emotional situations, and his excessive use of intellectualization. Although the inconsistent influence of emotion in his decisions and his excessive intellectualization are negative features, they are not necessarily major or disabling liabilities. On the other hand, some of the findings regarding his emotions are unexpected. These include his marked tendency to constrain or suppress feelings, his inclination to display emotions more intensely than expected, his substantial emotional complexity, and the evidence (right side *eb* and blend findings) suggesting that he is in considerable emotional distress.

These unexpected findings all have negative implications and, collectively, represent a group of features that can easily lead to disorganization. They are especially interesting because he has offered no information from which to suspect that he might be in emotional turmoil. On the contrary, he has presented himself as a person who is simply interested in discovering why his relationships do not endure. It seems reasonable to speculate that this may be a classic illustration of how intellectualization serves to conceal or deny true feelings. However, such a postulate should be deferred until more information is reviewed concerning his cognitive operations, especially his reality testing.

IDEATION

Case 11.   Ideation Variables for a 27-Year-Old Male.

L	= 0.06	OBS	= No	HVI	= No	**Critical Special Scores**		
						DV	= 0	DV2 = 0
EB	= 7:6.5	EBPer	= NA	a:p	= 7:6	INC	= 0	INC2 = 0
				Ma:Mp	= 4:3	DR	= 0	DR2 = 0
eb	= 6:8	[FM = 4 m = 2]				FAB	= 1	FAB2 = 0
				M–	= 1	ALOG	= 0	CON = 0
Intell Indx	= 7	MOR	= 4	Mnone	= 0	Sum6	= 1	WSum6 = 4
						(R = 19)		

M Response Features

I   1. W+ Mpo 2 Art,(H),(A) 4.0 GHR
III   5. D+ Mao 2 H,Hh P 3.0 COP,GHR
V   8. Wo Mp.FC'u Art,(H) 1.0 GHR
VII   11. W+ Mp.Fro H,Cg,Hh P 2.5 GHR
VIII   12. D+ Ma.mp.CF.FC'– 2 H,Hh 3.0 COP,PHR
X   16. Wv/+ Ma.CFo A,Hx 5.5 FAB,COP,GHR
X   19. DS+ Mau 2 (H),Bt 6.0 COP,GHR

As noted during the study of his affect, the *EB* (7:6.5) reveals that the characteristics of his ideation are probably not very consistent when he is involved in problem solving or decision making. At times, his directed thinking will be reasonably free of emotional influences as he thinks things through. In other instances, his thinking is more swayed by his feelings and his decisions become more intuitively formulated. Although this lack of consistency is not necessarily a liability, it is somewhat inefficient and can be a disadvantage in situations that are unexpectedly complex or stressful. This may be especially important for him. As noted, he is a very complex person, and as indicated by the very low *Lambda* value (0.06), he has a notable tendency to become involved in complex situations.

An even more distinctive liability is noted by the four MOR answers in his record. It signifies that much of his thinking is marked by pessimism. It influences him to conceptualize his relation with the world in a more negative than positive way. It breeds doubts and the anticipation of gloomy outcomes, regardless of his own efforts. It can also lead to narrow and concrete patterns of thought. Despite his pessimistic set, there is no evidence of unusual levels of peripheral or subconscious ideation that might interrupt his directed thinking more often than is common. The left side *eb* value (6) consists of four *FM*'s, which is average, and two *m* responses, which is slightly elevated because of situational factors.

The importance of his excessive use of intellectualization has already been emphasized (Intellectualization Index = 7), but seems worth noting again. At least in part, the impact of his pessimistic set is probably contained by his use of intellectualization to deny or neutralize the intensity of the unwanted emotions. In effect, it is a way of ignoring internal reality.

The *WSum6* (4) is modest, representing a single *FABCOM* that occurred in response 16, "insects dancing around, like having a party . . . they're in a festive mood . . . just having fun for a change." It does not reflect serious ideational slippage, but tends to connote less sophisticated judgment than expected for an intelligent adult. This is probably because, as noted, it is an *Hx* response (in a festive mood, just having fun for a change), which is usually a form of intellectualizing related to self-image.

Six of his seven *M* answers have appropriate form quality (*o* = 4; *u* = 2) and most are marked by reasonably sophisticated forms of conceptualizing (a saint or monk calling to the faithful; women carrying a basket; a devil with his winglike arms out; a young boy looking in the mirror, kneeling; insects dancing around having a party; gnomes holding up a stick). Even his single *M*– response, "two women stretching some cloth across a pole . . . separating it, maybe they dyed it and they're stretching it out on the pole in the middle to dry out," is conceptually sophisticated.

Although the basic ingredients that influence the formulations of his directed thought are not very consistent, there is no reason to question the integrity or clarity of his ideation. Some of his thinking is overly pessimistic, and he is far too defensively intellectualized in dealing with his feelings. Both of these features are significant liabilities that should be considered as important treatment objectives. However, the basic elements of his ideation seem intact and should contribute to adequate reality testing.

PROCESSING

Case 11. Processing Variables for a 27-Year-Old Male.

EB	= 7:6.5	Zf	= 14	Zd	= –0.5	DQ+	= 9
L	= 0.06	W:D:Dd	= 9:9:1	PSV	= 0	DQv/+	= 1
HVI	= NO	W:M	= 9:7			DQv	= 0
OBS	= NO						

Location & DQ Sequencing

I: W+.Wo	VI: Do.Do
II: D+.D+	VII: W+
III: D+	VIII: D+.W+
IV: Wo	IX: W+.DSo
V: Wo.Wo	X: Wv/+.DdSo.Do.DS+

The *Zf* (14) and *W:D:Dd* (9:9:1) signify that he tends to invest more effort than is customary in processing new information. This postulate is generally supported by the location sequencing. Although five of his *W* answers were given to the more solid figures (I, IV, & V), four were also given to more complex figures (VII, VIII, IX, & X). At the same time, the *W:M* ratio (9:7) is somewhat more conservative than is typical for an ambient, suggesting that he is also cautious about processing.

The *Zd* value (−0.5) offers no reason to question the efficiency of his scanning activities. There are nine synthesis answers in the records, which is slightly more than expected and indicates that the quality of his processing is very good and probably rather complex. The answers appear across seven of the ten figures and, as has been noted from the study of findings concerning ideation, many of these are reasonably sophisticated responses.

MEDIATION

Case 11.   Mediation Variables for a 27-Year-Old Male.

R = 19		L = 0.06		OBS = No	**Minus & NoForm Features**
FQx+	= 1		XA%	= .84	VIII 12. D+ Ma.mp.CF.FC′− 2 H,Hh 3.0 COP,PHR
FQxo	= 13		WDA%	= .89	IX 15. DSo FC′.FY− An MOR
FQxu	= 2		X−%	= .16	X 17. DdSo CF.mp− (Hd) AB,PHR
FQx−	= 3		S−	= 2	
FQxnone	= 0				
(W+D	= 18)		P	= 7	
WD+	= 1		X+%	= .74	
WDo	= 13		Xu%	= .11	
WDu	= 2				
WD−	= 2				
WDnone	= 0				

The *XA%* (.84) and *WDA%* (.89) are both within the expected range and indicate that his translations of stimuli are usually appropriate for the situation. The *X−%* (.16), created by three minus answers, is slightly elevated. The dysfunction appears to be clearly affect related. All appeared in Cards VIII, IX, and X; all three include situational stress-related variables (*m* or *Y*); and all three include chromatic color variables (*FC* or *CF*). Two of the three include *S,* and in addition, one contains a color shading blend (*M.m.CF.FC′*) and a second is a shading blend (*FC.FY*).

Two of the three minus answers (Card IX, a skull, and Card X, a devil mask) are not severe distortions. However, the third, (Card VIII, women stretching cloth) represents a marked distortion of the distal features present in the *D1* area. The composite of findings concerning his minus answers is particularly important with regard to an issue raised earlier during the review of his affective features, that is, whether his apparent emotional turmoil has a significant impact on his reality testing. Although it does not occur often, it does happen in some instances and can be somewhat disorganizing. This should be weighed carefully when possible treatment regimens are considered.

In a more favorable context, he gave seven Popular answers, denoting that he is likely to translate situations in a conventional manner when the cues to do so are obvious. Likewise, the *X+%* (.74) is substantial, indicating a proclivity to formulate decisions and behaviors that are in accord with social demands or expectations.

In effect, no findings regarding his cognitive operations suggest marked problems with his reality testing. His thinking is generally clear, he works hard to process new information, and he translates situations or events in a fairly customary manner. His emotions sometimes interfere with his reality testing, and he intellectualizes too much in ways that tend to deny or bend reality; but to this point in time, they do not appear to have a substantial disorganizing impact on the efficacy of his cognitive operations.

SUMMARY

This is a very complex man who is apparently experiencing much more emotional turmoil than he readily admits. In fact, he appears to make a considerable effort to deny, neutralize, or control unwanted feelings by suppressing them, or by contending with them intellectually instead of more experientially. However, this only serves to increase his complexity and the potential for discomfort. The origins of his emotional strife are varied but appear to have evolved mainly because his psychology includes several seemingly conflicting or contradictory features.

For instance, he is a noticeably self-centered person, prone to hold himself in high regard, but his self-concept also includes a sense of being somewhat fragile and vulnerable, and possibly even damaged. He appears to be reasonably introspective and yet is naive about himself. Likewise, he goes to great lengths to constrain and minimize negative or threatening feelings, but when he displays his emotions, he seems to do so more intensely than would be expected.

In a similar context, he is quite interested in people and apparently has developed many social skills that usually serve him well. As a result, his interactions with others are generally adaptive, and it seems likely that people regard him favorably. Nonetheless, it seems probable that he does not understand people very well, and it is likely that most of his relationships are superficial rather than deep or mature. There is some evidence hinting that religious values or concerns may be contributing to his difficulties. In essence, he may have adopted an overt role in dealing with others that tends to run contrary to some of his values or to a model of conduct that he might prefer.

As noted by the history, and some of the test data, he does not handle close relationships effectively. It seems clear that he would like to have a deep and meaningful relationship and becomes lonely and distraught when the possibility of such a relation dissipates, yet the basic cause for such failures seem to be more internal than external. Emotional commitment is probably confusing for him; as emotional demands become more frequent or intense, they threaten his self-image and he becomes cautious and defensive. In part, this is because he does not understand or handle emotions very well, but his self-centeredness and the likelihood that some of his basic values are not very flexible also contribute to the problem.

For many, the extent of his emotional turmoil might lead to considerable disorganization. However, he has good capacities for control and tolerance for stress, and his cognitive functions are respectable. His thinking is sophisticated, even though it is sometimes overly pessimistic. He processes new information well, and his overall reality testing is generally more than adequate. His emotions tend to cause occasional dysfunction in his thinking, but this does not occur to a disabling level, mainly because his defenses are sturdy and easily employed.

On a speculative level, he appears to have naive expectations about relationships that tend to run contrary to social reality. He holds himself in high regard and probably expects others to do so as well. When that does not occur, he becomes threatened and is likely to adopt behavioral routines that are defensively intense and convey a subtly negative or resistive picture to anyone close to him. The end product is a substantial probability for a failed relationship.

RECOMMENDATIONS

This man presents some intriguing challenges for treatment planning. On the surface, his problem is interpersonal. He is frustrated and lonely because of a series of unsuccessful relationships and implies that his objective for treatment is to learn how to pick the "right" woman—one who is attractive, intelligent, supportive, and shares common interests. He offers no hint about being emotionally distraught and, in fact, describes himself in ways that seem commensurate with his inflated sense of self, as flexible, sensitive, and able to read people well.

He gives no implication of intrapersonal problems, and raising that issue very directly with him risks the possibility of premature termination, as it would be an affront to the high value he places on himself. Nevertheless, the basic problems seem to be intrapersonal and, at the moment, involve a great deal of emotional chaos that is having a much greater impact on him than he openly admits. Thus, the therapist will have to maintain his interest and motivation for treatment without becoming overly threatening.

This probably requires some attention to, and consideration of his interpersonal complaints while casually but persistently raising emotional issues as opportunities are presented. Ultimately, his religious concerns and whether some of his behaviors conflict with those values should become a focus in treatment, but this should not be done early and must be approached cautiously.

An alternative is a therapeutic assessment feedback approach as an entry to treatment. This would involve a reasonably direct review of assessment findings, especially those concerning his emotions. It might serve to lessen some of his emotional defensiveness and create an opportunity to deal more directly with emotional issues early. However, the risk that this model could be threatening should not be ignored. If it is employed, it will probably be important to sidestep or minimize the issues of his self-involvement and his religious concerns because perceived criticisms of either could easily cause him to become more defensive and use such criticisms as a rationalizing basis to discontinue.

EPILOGUE

Feedback concerning the assessment findings was provided by his therapist, who emphasized the relationship between his difficulties in dealing with emotions and the superficiality of his relationships with women. The therapist noted that the patient entered a dynamically oriented form of treatment, involving two sessions per week, somewhat optimistically with high expectations, even though cautioned to the contrary. During the first four months he focused extensively on his interpersonal relations but persisted in dealing with emotional issues in naive and indirect ways.

During the fifth month of treatment, he began to explore his religious interests and beliefs at length and contrasted them with his own lifestyle and the lifestyles of those with whom he associated most frequently through his work. This process continued for several weeks and frequently led to a more direct consideration of his feelings than had been the case previously. During his seventh month of treatment he participated in a religious retreat in which he met a woman whom he found to be very appealing. They began a dating relationship that included many situations in which he could explore issues concerning interpersonal and emotional habits that he had discussed in treatment. The therapist noted that, at the end of one year in treatment, considerable progress had been made specifically in the emotional sphere. His dating relationship continued to flourish, and he was actively considering the prospect of marriage.

REFERENCES

Alpher, V. S., Perfetto, G. A., Henry, W. P., & Strupp, H. H. (1990). The relationship between the Rorschach and assessment of the capacity to engage in short-term dynamic psychotherapy. *Psychotherapy, 27*(2), 224.

Nygren, M. (2004). Rorschach *Comprehensive System* variables in relation to assessing dynamic capacity and ego strength for Psychodynamic Psychotherapy. *Journal of Personality Assessment, 83*(3), 277–292.

PART THREE

Using the Rorschach in Forensic Consultation

CHAPTER 14

An Issue of Danger to the Self or Others

―――――――――――――――――――― C A S E 1 2 ――――――――――――――――――――

This 22-year-old single man was referred for evaluation by the court prior to a bail hearing. He was apprehended by campus police, responding to a silent alarm, while he was entering a second-floor window near a fire escape in a women's residence hall at a small liberal arts college near his home. When he was searched, a large switchblade knife was found in his possession. Subsequently, each of four female students identified him as the man who had followed them frequently while they were walking alone on campus.

He is described as being of medium height and build, dressed in jeans and a T-shirt and generally unkempt. During the evaluation, his speech and performance were slow, his affect was flat, and he appeared depressed. He claims that he does not remember why he decided to break open the window and enter the dormitory, but he admits that he often frequents the campus "when there is nothing else to do."

He has been charged with illegal entry, a misdemeanor, but because of the stalking allegations and possession of the knife, the court has raised an issue of whether the subject is dangerous to himself or others. He has a previous psychiatric history. After graduating from high school with above-average grades at the age of 18, he entered a state university with the intention of majoring in political science. During his first year, he became depressed and sought assistance at the university mental health center. He was treated there on a weekly basis, and according to his report, the depression subsided. During his second year at the university, the depression recurred in a more intense form, and he solicited the assistance of a priest who contacted his parents. Subsequently he was hospitalized for 33 days, most of which were during the Christmas vacation. At that time, he was treated with an antidepressant and psychotherapy and released to outpatient care, which continued once per week through the completion of his second academic year.

He reports that his grades in college were generally good, "some Cs, but mostly Bs. I never got an A though." He states that, despite his adequate performance, "I wasn't very interested, I couldn't find peace or happiness in what I was doing." He says that when he was hospitalized he thought about suicide a lot but decided that he could never initiate the act. He admits that he also has considered hurting people, "but nobody in particular." He dropped out of college at the end of the second year. Since then he has worked irregularly as a waiter in each of three restaurants and most recently part time at a car wash.

He says that he feels depressed again, and for the past four or five months, he has experienced fears, "but I don't exactly know about what, that's why I carry the knife." He notes that there have been times in the past where he felt it was important to go through some ritualistic behavior such as counting the number of trees on the street where his home is located before leaving the street. He also admits that when he first went to college he felt that he had to touch the doorknob of his room three times before turning it. He denies any drug or alcohol history.

His father, age 56, is a retired Army Colonel and now works in an editorial position for a magazine. His mother, age 53, is a housewife who completed two years of college. He is the fifth of six children. His oldest brother, age 29, is married and teaches math and physics in a high school. Another brother, age 28, completed two years of college. He is single and currently works as a professional musician. His oldest sister, age 25, married recently. She is a college graduate and now works in a government position. His third brother, age 23, graduated from college about a year ago and works as a commercial artist. His younger sister, age 18, is a freshman in college. He is the only child living at home.

He claims that he had a happy childhood until he was 14 or 15 years old, when he became more fearful of things. He has never dated but has had two sexual experiences with prostitutes. In discussing his social history, he states "I have a history of masturbating frequently and having lusting thoughts." He says that he likes to sleep, watch television, and listen to music, but he has no real hobbies. He claims that he likes to walk on the local campus because "It gives me the feeling of being intelligent, and if I walk around enough, I can work everything out." When confronted with the fact that four women have identified him as having followed them several times, he says, "Maybe, I don't remember, but I do like to be around beauty, it makes me feel good, but I would never hurt anyone or anything that's beautiful. I'm not like that."

The court has raised three assessment issues: (1) Is he a danger to himself or others? (2) Is there any evidence to suggest that he is a sexual predator? (3) Is there any evidence of a significant psychiatric disturbance that should be considered in relation to the breaking and entering charges?

CASE FORMULATION AND RELEVANT LITERATURE

This man's behavior has escalated from "lusting thoughts" and frequent masturbation to following female students and now to entering a women's residence hall while in possession of a switchblade. The judge in charge of the case has appropriately asked for a dangerousness assessment and has also raised a more specific concern about sexual predation. A review of the Rorschach literature on aggression and on sexual acting out can be of value as the psychologist formulates a consultation for the court.

Assessment of Aggression

Aggressive potential is a significant concern in many clinical and forensic settings, and its assessment has been a part of the Rorschach literature since early in the test's history. Finney (1955) found that a group of Rorschach variables, which he called the Palo Alto Destructive Content Scale, could differentiate male Veterans Administration psychiatric inpatients who had made homicidal attempts in the hospital from a matched group of nonassaultive inpatients. The variables included objects described in a derogatory, contemptuous, or hostile manner; objects destroyed, crippled, damaged, or injured by an aggressive act; objects in the process of escaping, avoiding, or anticipating injury; objects with a high likelihood of attacking, injuring, harming, or destroying; objects that are typically used for aggression or are generally considered to be frightening or dangerous; and movement responses in which an explicitly destructive act is occurring.

Rose and Bitter (1980) used the Palo Alto Destructive Content Scale in a state hospital setting to compare male assaultive non-reoffenders, assaultive reoffenders, rapists, murderers, and non-assaultive child molesters. The rapists, murderers, and assaultive reoffenders were significantly higher than the non-reoffenders and child molesters on the scale.

The *Comprehensive System* (Exner, 2003) limits the coding of the special score *AG* to responses in which an aggressive act is occurring in the present. Drawing on the work of Finney (1955) and others, Meloy and Gacono (1992) proposed four additional codes that they suggested were also indicative of aggressive dynamics. These included Aggressive Content (*AgC*), objects that most people would view as predatory, dangerous, malevolent, injurious, or harmful; Aggressive Potential (*AgPot*), responses in which an aggressive act is about to happen; Aggressive Past (*AgPast*), responses in which an aggressive act has occurred or the object has been the victim of aggression; and Sado-masochisitic (*SM*), responses in which the person expresses pleasure or positive affect when giving devalued, aggressive, or morbid content.

Numerous studies have investigated the reliability and validity of Rorschach aggression variables. In their initial article, Meloy and Gacono (1992) reported interjudge agreement between 92% and 100% for *AG, AgC, AgPast,* and *AgPot* in a sample of incarcerated men. Because the coding of *SM* involves observing the person at the time of administration, it was not possible to determine interjudge agreement for this variable.

Baity and Hilsenroth (1999), working with Rorschach data from a university-based outpatient psychological clinic, investigated interjudge agreement for the *Comprehensive System* variables MOR and *AG* and the Meloy and Gacono variables *AgC* and *AgPast*. They also included two variables proposed by Holt (1956): primary process aggression (*A1*), defined as intense, overwhelming, murderous, or sadomasochistic, and secondary process aggression (*A2*), defined as nonlethal and more socially appropriate. Interjudge agreement ranged from 86% for *A2* to 100% for *AgPot*.

In a study that provides additional support for Meloy and Gacono's aggressive content (*AgC*) variable, Baity, McDaniel, and Hilsenroth (2000) asked college students to score 126 words on a Likert-type scale in terms of how closely each word fit the definition (predatory, dangerous, malevolent, injurious, or harmful) of *AgC*. They then asked the students to classify words that had been rated at least moderately consistent with the definition into five qualitative categories: weapons, animal/part of animal, environmental danger, fictional creature, and other. The level of agreement initially and also at a one-month retest was extremely high, leading the authors to conclude that aggressive content could be reliably rated with very high consistency across time.

Mihura, Nathan-Montano, and Alperin (2003) tested 70 college students and coded their Rorschachs for *AG, AgPot, AgC,* and *AgPast*. They also coded the Rorschachs for Urist's (1977) Mutuality of Autonomy (MOA) scale. The MOA assesses interpersonal function and ranges from relationships that are described as mutual and autonomous to those that are actively enveloping and destructive. Interscorer agreement was high, with kappa coefficients ranging from .74 for *AG* to .94 for *AgPast*.

These studies suggest that there are several reliably scorable Rorschach variables associated with the destructive content Finney (1955) initially identified. Researchers have gone on to investigate the validity of these variables by relating them to each other, to other test measures, and to diagnostic and behavioral criteria.

Baity and Hilsenroth (1999) studied Holt's primary and secondary process aggression variables (*A1* and *A2*) and *AG,* MOR, *AgC,* and *AgPast* in outpatients who met the *DSM-IV* (American Psychiatric Association, 1994) criteria for an Axis II personality disorder. A factor analysis of the six aggression variables yielded two factors that accounted for 77% of the total variance. The first factor (MOR, *AgPast,* and *A1*) appears to involve more intense and primitive aggression, while the second factor (*AG, AgC,* and *A2*) reflects higher level, more socially appropriate aggressive representations.

Baity and Hilsenroth (1999) next conducted stepwise regression analyses to study the relationship of the six Rorschach aggression variables with *DSM-IV* histrionic, narcissistic, borderline, and antisocial personality disorder descriptors. The variables had no relationship to the total criteria for histrionic or narcissistic personality disorder, but increased *AgC* and decreased MOR were nonredundant significant predictors of the total number of antisocial personality disorder criteria. Increased MOR was the only significant predictor for the total number of borderline personality disorder descriptors. The authors suggest that the inverse relation of MOR to the antisocial criteria and its positive relation to borderline descriptors reflect the identification with victimization and damage that characterizes borderline but not antisocial dynamics.

The authors also studied the relation of the Rorschach variables to three Minnesota Multiphasic Personality Inventory-2 (MMPI-2; Butcher, Dahlstrom, Graham, Tellegen, & Kaemmer, 1989) scales: psychopathic deviance (*Pd*), anger (*ANG*), and antisocial practices (*ASP*). *AgPast* significantly predicted scores on the *ANG* scale, and *AgC* significantly predicted *ASP* scores. The relation of *AgC* with both the total number of antisocial personality disorder descriptors and with a self-report measure of antisocial behavior provides important validation for this variable's association with acting-out psychopathology.

Mihura and Nathan-Montano (2001) tested college students to investigate the relation of *AG, AgPast, AgC,* and *AgPot* with a self-report measure, the Structural Analysis of Social Behavior (SASB; Benjamin, 2000) which includes scales related to aggression and interpersonal control. In summarizing their findings, the authors note, "*AG* was supported as a measure of ego-dystonic aggressive tension, *AgPast* as a victimized view of self (submitting to the other), and a combined *AgPot/AgC* variable as a feared loss of interpersonal (external) control" (p. 622).

In a further study, Mihura et al. (2003) studied the relation of college students' Rorschach aggression variables with another self-report measure, the Personality Assessment Inventory (PAI; Morey, 1991). They also investigated whether the addition of a Rorschach measure of emotional impulsivity based on the level of form dominance of chromatic color answers (*FC* versus *CF* versus *C* and *Cn*) would incrementally improve prediction of self-reported physical aggression potential, impulsive suicidal ideation, and borderline features on the PAI. The authors found that self-reported physical aggression on the PAI was significantly correlated with *AgPot, AgC,* and a combined *AgPot/AgC* variable, and that self-reported impulsive self-destructive behaviors on the PAI were related to *AgPast.* The level of form dominance for chromatic color responses accounted for additional variance above and beyond the Rorschach aggression variables for PAI measures of self-reported physical aggression potential and suicidal ideation with impulsivity.

A study by Baity and Hilsenroth (2002) provides data on the relation between real-world aggressive behavior and *AG, AgC,* and MOR. They rated the level of aggressive behavior reported during interviews with 94 inpatients and outpatients referred for psychological assessment. The ratings were done using a 7-point scale that ranged from consistently able to express anger appropriately to physically assaultive or impulsively aggressive. Regression analysis indicated that *AgC* was the only nonredundant significant predictor of real-world aggressiveness. *AG* and MOR did not account for significant predictive ability beyond that provided by *AgC.* Although the study indicated a relationship between *AgC* and aggressive behavior, mixed findings on the variable's ability to discriminate patients who reported more active forms of aggression from those who did not led the authors to caution: ". . . at this time it is premature to consider *AgC* as indicating anything other than a preoccupation with aggressive objects. A greater number of *AgC* responses on a given protocol does not indicate that an individual's hostile ideation will necessarily translate to aggressive behavior" (p. 285).

In summary, it would appear that several Rorschach variables can be reliably coded and are relevant in the assessment of a patient's aggressive dynamics. Within this group of variables, MOR and *AgPast* may be more specifically related to an angry sense of victimization, whereas *AgC* may reflect identification with more overt aggressive behavior. There is also some suggestion that *AG* may be associated with tension about aggressive impulses that the person views as ego-dystonic.

Assessment of Sexual Acting Out

Because forensic evaluation for sexual offending frequently creates a strong set to minimize psychopathology, the Rorschach's susceptibility to impression management becomes an important issue. Grossman, Wasyliw, Benn, and Gyoerkoe (2002) compared Rorschach data for alleged male sex offenders who minimized psychiatric symptoms on the MMPI or MMPI-2 with a group who presented themselves accurately. The minimizers were able to produce significantly less pathological MMPI or MMPI-2 profiles (74% of the minimizers produced normal-limits profiles compared with 38% for the nonminimizers). However, there was no difference between minimizers and nonminimizers on Rorschach indicators of distress (*D* and AdjD), reality testing and cognitive precision (*X+%, X−%, WSum6,* Intellectualization Index), or interpersonal function (H and M−). The two groups also did not differ on the Schizophrenia Index, Suicide Constellation, Coping Deficit Index, or the Depression Index. The authors concluded, "In contrast to our findings on the MMPI, we found that on the Rorschach minimizers were not able to appear more psychologically healthy than nonminimizers. Moreover, minimizers were not able to appear normal on the Rorschach, that is, similar to the general population" (p. 496).

Two studies have investigated whether sexual offenders differ from nonsexually offending individuals on Rorschach variables. Gacono, Meloy, and Bridges (2000) compared nonsexually offending psychopaths with sexual homicide perpetrators and nonviolent pedophiles. The two sexually deviant groups produced more responses, and the sexual homicide offenders were more likely to have *Lambda* less than 1.0 and to be introversive. Both sexually offending groups were markedly more likely to have at least one texture response in their Rorschachs. The nonsexually offending psychopaths appeared less interested in human interaction (*SumT* = 0 and *H* = 0), and they tended to be more affectively avoidant (*Afr* < .40). The authors speculate that the individuals in the two sexually offending groups experienced much more interpersonal interest, conflict, and ambivalence than the nonsexually offending psychopaths, whose Rorschachs suggest an almost total lack of attachment capacity.

In a follow-up study, Huprich, Gacono, Schneider, and Bridges (2004) used the Rorschach Oral Dependency Scale (ROD; Masling, Rabie, & Blondheim, 1967) to compare the three groups identified in the Gacono et al. (2000) article. The pedophiles demonstrated significantly higher levels of pure oral dependency, while the sexual homicide perpetrators' dependency answers were more frequently paired with aggressive content. The authors note that this highly conflictual mix of dependency and aggression is well encapsulated in the response of one of their sexual homicide perpetrators: "a lonely bird of prey out looking for a relationship" (p. 353).

In summary, the Rorschach can provide useful data for assessing sexual acting out, even in the context of strong needs to minimize psychopathology. Sexual offenders are frequently characterized by interpersonal interest and marked dependency. In the case of sexual homicide perpetrators, this heightened interpersonal engagement has the potential for fusing with aggressive impulses.

Case 12. A 22-Year-Old Male.

Card	Response	Inquiry
I	1. A bf	**E:** (Rpts Ss Resp) **S:** Wgs out here & 2 littl antennae up here, the W thg **E:** If u look longr I think u'll find smthg else too
	2. Lik a crab	**E:** (Rpts Ss Resp) **S:** Yeah, pinchers rite here (D1), sort of arms & hands stickg out all ovr like ths (extends arms) w the body in the middl
	3. It ll an angry cat's face	**E:** (Rpts Ss Resp) **S:** Eyes & mouth & there r ears, & littl horns **E:** U mentiond it looks angry? **S:** The way the eyes r slantd & the mouth, lik its hissing
	4. And it ll a beetle	**E:** (Rpts Ss Resp) **S:** Um hum, arms r here (D2) & body lik tht (outlines D4) & head wb rite up here (top of D4)
	5. Lik a wolf's face	**E:** (Rpts Ss Resp) **S:** J lik the cat's face but the nose is pointg down, lik it's lookg dwn, the ears, the slanted eyes look mean
II	6. A black fly smashd against a wall	**E:** (Rpts Ss Resp) **S:** Thrs bld splatterd all ovr there, all the red, & the blk wgs, lik a fly was . . . smeared **E:** I'm not sure why it looks smeared? **S:** The way the lines r there in the red, the way the colors r thr, just all smeared togethr
	7. A jet going thru space	**E:** (Rpts Ss Resp) **S:** Tht prt (DS5) ll a jet & the outside is all black so tht it must b space arnd it, all drk lik tht, lik space
III	8. Two ppl facg ech othr, grabg 4 a bowlg ball	**E:** (Rpts Ss Resp) **S:** Um hum, both r bent forwrd, there's the legs, arms, necks, heads, & thy'r facg ech othr. This dwn her (D7) cb bowlg balls & the rack thy'r on
IV	9. A monster w big feet	**E:** (Rpts Ss Resp) **S:** The big feet, clompg along, head up there, littl eyes, its big on the bottom & slims at the top, head pointd downwrd, the arms r stickg out
	10. Som ko flyg bug	**E:** (Rpts Ss Resp) **S:** It's upside down, the head (D1) w antennas, the wgs r out & it ll its in the air, flyg, it's symmetrical in shape
V	11. It ll a bf	**E:** (Rpts Ss Resp) **S:** 2 wgs, 2 antennae, it j ll a bf to me
	12. Or it ll a wolf on its tippy-toes, w big	**E:** (Rpts Ss Resp) **S:** 2 ears, 2 feet lik on tippy-toes, arms stickg out, the w thg ll tht
VI	13. It ll a jet who's cockpit is blowg up	**E:** (Rpts Ss Resp) **S:** The wgs of the jet, here's the front of it (D3), it's flyg in the air & & here (D3) all of it is blowg up lik the cockpit prt
VII	14. Two ladies facg ech othr, ech w one hand out behnd her, lik ready to throw a pie in the othrs face	**E:** (Rpts Ss Resp) **S:** These ll faces, thy'r facg ech othr, hair is stickg up, their arms r back lik thy'r throwg a pie at the othr person, c the littl flat prt (Dd21) cb the pie, thyr lik squattg on smthg (D4)

Card	Response	Inquiry
VIII 15.	A tree or plant & 2 bears r climbg up ech side of it	**E:** (Rpts Ss Resp) **S:** These r the bears, their heads & legs & this is the plant rite here, stickg out lik tht, lik u c in somones house, its ko green at the top
IX 16.	Two wise men w machine guns & flares pointd at eo, & standg on green rocks	**E:** (Rpts Ss Resp) **S:** These r the wise men, thy hav pointd hats so thy'r wise, the machine guns & flares, shootg at ech othr. I j called tht a rock cause he was standg on it **E:** I"m not sur about the flares **S:** Ths orange arc (Dd25) is lik fire in the air, lik a flare whn u thro it
17.	A horse's face, frm the front	**E:** (Rpts Ss Resp) **S:** It ll 2 nostrils, thes white slots, & tht ll its head, the shape
X 18.	A big fight betwn 2 bugs, on a mt, each has a blue crab on his side, each hav a reindeer runng away fr him	**E:** (Rpts Ss Resp) **S:** It ll 2 bugs (D8) opposing ech othr, on top of this mt (D9) thes r the blue crabs (D1), tht's the reindeer (D7) runng away, the feet & legs r sprawled out in a runng position & the color of it is lik a deer **E:** U say the bugs r having a big fight? **S:** Yes, it's lik a war of the bugs on a mt

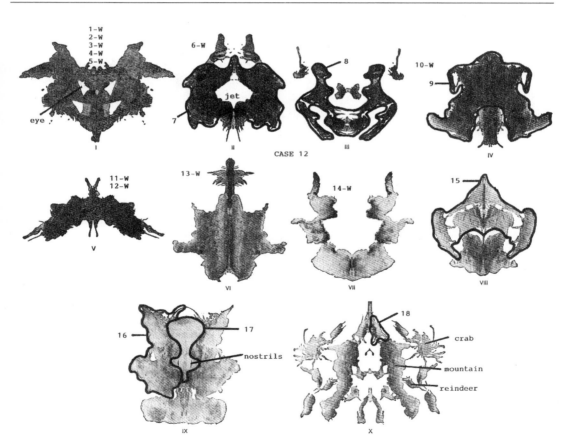

CASE 12

Case 12.   Sequence of Scores.

Card	No.	Loc.	No.	Determinant(s)	(2)	Content(s)	Pop	Z	Special Scores
I	1	Wo	1	Fo		A	P	1.0	
	2	Wo	1	FMpu		A		1.0	INC
	3	WSo	1	FMao		Ad		3.5	INC2,AG,PHR
	4	Wo	1	Fu		A		1.0	INC
	5	WSo	1	FMpo		Ad		3.5	
II	6	W+	1	C'F.CF.YF–		A,Bl		4.5	MOR
	7	DS+	5	ma.C'Fo		Sc,Na		4.5	ALOG
III	8	D+	1	Ma+	2	H,Sc	P	3.0	GHR
IV	9	Do	7	Mao		(H)	P		GHR
	10	Wo	1	FMau		A		2.0	
V	11	Wo	1	Fo		A	P	1.0	
	12	Wo	1	FMa–		A		1.0	INC
VI	13	Wo	1	mau		Sc,Ex		2.5	MOR
VII	14	W+	1	Mao	2	H,Fd,Id	P	2.5	AG,GHR
VIII	15	D+	1	FMa.FCo	2	A,Bt	P	3.0	FAB
IX	16	D+	3	Ma.CF.mpo	2	H,Cg,Ls,Fi	P	4.5	ALOG,AG,PHR
	17	DSo	8	F–		Ad		5.0	
X	18	D+	8	Ma.FMa.FCu	2	A,Ls	P	4.5	FAB2,AG,PHR

Case 12. Structural Summary.

Location Features	Determinants Blends	Single	Contents	S-Constellation
				NO . . .FV+VF+V+FD>2
		H = 3		YES . .Col-Shd Bl>0
Zf = 17	C'F.CF.YF	M = 3	(H) = 1	YES . .Ego<.31,>.44
ZSum = 48.0	m.C'F	FM = 5	Hd = 0	NO . . .MOR > 3
ZEst = 56.0	FM.FC	m = 1	(Hd) = 0	YES . .Zd > +− 3.5
	M.CF.m	FC = 0	Hx = 0	YES . .es > EA
W = 11	M.FM.FC	CF = 0	A = 9	NO . . .CF+C > FC
D = 7		C = 0	(A) = 0	YES . .X+% < .70
W+D = 18		Cn = 0	Ad = 3	YES . .S > 3
Dd = 0		FC' = 0	(Ad) = 0	NO . . .P < 3 or > 8
S = 4		C'F = 0	An = 0	NO . . .Pure H < 2
		C' = 0	Art = 0	NO . . .R < 17
		FT = 0	Ay = 0	6 . . . .TOTAL

DQ

		Single	Contents	**Special Scores**	
+ = 7		TF = 0	Bl = 1	Lv1	Lv2
o = 11		T = 0	Bt = 1		
v/+ = 0		FV = 0	Cg = 1	DV = 0x1	0x2
v = 0		VF = 0	Cl = 0	INC = 3x2	1x4
		V = 0	Ex = 1	DR = 0x3	0x6
		FY = 0	Fd = 1	FAB = 1x4	1x7
		YF = 0	Fi = 1	ALOG = 2x5	
		Y = 0	Ge = 0	CON = 0x7	
Form Quality		Fr = 0	Hh = 0	Raw Sum6 = 8	
		rF = 0	Ls = 2	Wgtd Sum6 = 31	

	FQx	MQual	W+D				
				FD = 0	Na = 1		
+	= 1	= 1	= 1	F = 4	Sc = 3	AB = 0	GHR = 3
o	= 9	= 3	= 9		Sx = 0	AG = 4	PHR = 3
u	= 5	= 1	= 5		Xy = 0	COP = 0	MOR = 2
−	= 3	= 0	= 3		Id = 1	CP = 0	PER = 0
none	= 0	= 0	= 0	(2) = 5		PSV = 0	

Ratios, Percentages, and Derivations

R = 18	L = 0.29		FC:CF+C = 2:2	COP = 0 AG = 4
			Pure C = 0	GHR:PHR = 3:3
EB = 5:3.0	EA = 8.0	EBPer = 1.7	SumC':WSumC = 2:3.0	a:p = 12:3
eb = 10:3	es = 13	D = −1	Afr = 0.29	Food = 1
	Adj es = 11	Adj D = −1	S = 4	SumT = 0
			Blends:R = 5:18	Hum Con = 4
FM = 7	C' = 2	T = 0	CP = 0	Pure H = 3
m = 3	V = 0	Y = 1		PER = 0
				Iso Indx = 0.28

a:p	= 12:3	Sum6 = 8	XA% = 0.83	Zf = 17.0	3r+(2)/R = 0.28
Ma:Mp	= 5:0	Lv2 = 2	WDA% = 0.83	W:D:Dd = 11:7:0	Fr+rF = 0
2AB+Art+Ay	= 0	WSum6 = 31	X−% = 0.17	W:M = 11:5	SumV = 0
MOR	= 2	M− = 0	S− = 1	Zd = −8.0	FD = 0
		Mnone = 0	P = 8	PSV = 0	An+Xy = 0
			X+% = 0.56	DQ+ = 7	MOR = 2
			Xu% = 0.28	DQv = 0	H:(H)Hd(Hd) = 3:1

PTI = 1	DEPI = 4	CDI = 3	S-CON = 6	HVI = No	OBS = No

S-CON AND KEY VARIABLES

The S-CON (6) is not positive. The first positive Key variable is the Adj D Score of −1, indicating that the interpretation should begin with a review of the cluster regarding controls. However, that variable does not provide a guideline for the order in which the remaining clusters should be studied. That decision should be based on the next positive Key variable or, if necessary, the first positive Tertiary variable. In this case, there is another positive Key variable. It is the introversive *EB* of 5:3.0, suggesting that the interpretation of the other clusters should begin with ideation, then proceed through processing, mediation, and affect, and end with a review of the data concerning self-perception and interpersonal perception.

CONTROLS

Case 12.   Control-Related Variables for a 22-Year-Old Male.

EB = 5:3.0	*EA* = 8.0		D = −1	CDI = 3
eb = 10:3	*es* = 13	Adj *es* = 11	AdjD = −1	*L* = 0.29
FM = 7 *m* = 3	*SumC′* = 2	*SumT* = 0	*SumV* = 0	*SumY* = 1

The Adj D value of −1 indicates that he is in a chronic state of stimulus overload that limits his capacity to deal with stress effectively. Usually, he will be able to function adequately in routine or structured circumstances. However, as demands on him, either internal or external, become more substantial or complex, his controls are likely to falter. In those circumstances, he becomes susceptible to disorganization and impulsiveness, and this can have marked effects on both his thinking and behavior.

There is no reason to doubt the integrity of the Adj D Score as the *EA* value (8.0) is in the average range for an adult and the *EB* (5:3.0) contains no zero values. Those findings imply that his resources should be sufficient to routinely form decisions and direct behaviors. However, that capacity is sometimes limited because of the unexpectedly high level of persistent demands that he experiences. These are indirectly represented by the elevated Adj *es* (11), the bulk of which consists of seven *FM* and a *SumC′* value of two. The former indicates that he often experiences seemingly disconnected patterns of thinking that are prompted by ungratified needs. The latter implies a tendency to internalize and suppress feelings that he would prefer to release openly. These features impinge on him in a way that limits his attention and concentration and interferes with his capacity to control his thinking and behavior, especially in complex situations.

IDEATION

Case 12. Ideation Variables for a 22-Year-Old Male.

							Critical Special Scores			
L	= 0.29	OBS	= No	HVI	= No					
							DV	= 0	DV2	= 0
EB	= 5:3.0	EBPer	= 1.7	a:p	= 12:3		INC	= 3	INC2	= 1
				Ma:Mp	= 5:0		DR	= 0	DR2	= 0
eb	= 10:3	[FM = 7 m = 3]					FAB	= 1	FAB2	= 1
				M–	= 0		ALOG	= 2	CON	= 0
Intell Indx	= 0	MOR	= 2	Mnone	= 0		Sum6	= 8	WSum6	= 31
								(R = 18)		

M Response Features

```
III    8. D+ Ma+ 2 H,Sc P 3.0 GHR
IV     9. D+ Mao (H) P GHR
VII   14. W+ Mao 2 H,Fd,Id P 2.5 AG,GHR
IX    16. D+ Ma.CF.mpo 2 H,Cg,Ls,Fi P 4.5 ALOG,AG,PHR
X     18. D+ Ma.FMa.FCu 2 A,Ls P 4.5 FAB2,AG,PHR
```

The *EB* (5:3.0) implies that he is inclined to delay decisions and behaviors until he can think things through and consider various options. He is likely to rely much more on his internal evaluations than external feedback, and he tries to minimize emotional influences on his thinking. This general form of coping can be effective if he is somewhat flexible about its use and if his thinking generally is logical, clear, and reasonably consistent.

The value for the *EBPer* (1.7) gives no indication that he is inflexible about the use of his ideational style and, in some instances, he may adopt a more intuitive approach when the circumstances of a situation seem to favor a trial-and-error tactic. On the other hand, the data for the *a:p* ratio (12:3) are markedly disparate, with the left side value being four times that of the value on the right. This strongly intimates that his ideational sets and values are well fixed and unlikely to be altered easily. This is not necessarily a liability if his thinking is clear and logical, but it can be a serious problem if his thinking is muddled or illogical.

The left side *eb* value (10), consisting of seven *FM* and three *m,* is of particular interest. As noted, features related to it are contributing substantially to his limited control capacity, and those features also are having a significant impact on his thinking. They represent a great deal of intrusive mental activity. In this case, much seems to be provoked by unmet need states, and that is being increased by situationally related stress elements. The magnitude of this nonvolitional mental activity is more than can be handled easily by most adults who do not have an abundance of resources. As a result, he is likely to experience frequent distractions from his consciously directed thinking, and some of his conceptualizations may not be well formulated. This sort of ideational overload can easily breed less mature or less effective forms of thinking.

Some of the products of his difficulty in thinking are reflected by the values for *Sum6* (8) and *WSum6* (31). Both are well above average, especially for an 18-response protocol. They suggest that his thinking tends to be disorganized and inconsistent, and is often marked by flawed judgments. People with limitations such as this often are unable to contend with the demands of everyday living in ways that will be persistently effective. An evaluation of the responses containing the eight critical special scores should provide some clarification about the extent of his faulty judgments.

Three of the eight answers are coded as INCOM (Card I, responses 2 and 4, and Card V, response 12). In each, he reports an incongruous feature to a perceived animal. He reports arms and hands, instead of legs and pinchers, on a crab (response 2), arms, instead of legs, on a beetle (response 4), and arms, instead of legs on a wolf (response 12). They are not bizarre, but tend to represent the naive, casual, and simplistic forms of conceptualization that are often found in the unsophisticated answers of children. They occur occasionally, but not very frequently, in some answers of adults.

The other five answers containing critical special scores are much more indicative of faulty judgments and a more substantial detachment from reality. In Card I, response 3 is coded as an INCOM2 because it includes "little horns" on an angry cat's face. He does this almost casually in the inquiry and the examiner failed to prompt for further elaboration about this cognitive slip. Thus, it is difficult to speculate about the extent to which bizarreness may have been included in his thinking for this answer. An ALOG is coded for his second answer to Card II (response 7) in which he notes in the inquiry, "The outside is all black so it must be space around it. . . ." It is not an unrealistic answer, but he is concrete in the definitive way that he translates the distal features of the figure, "it must be space."

There is a greater detachment from reality in his first answer to Card VIII (response 15), which is coded as *FABCOM*. In the basic response, he describes "a tree or plant and two bears are climbing up each side." In the inquiry, he describes the bears and then settles on a plant, "sticking out like that, like you see in someone's house. . . ." Bears do climb trees, but not house plants, and it seems intriguing that he selected the unrealistic option when given the opportunity to elaborate on his answer during the inquiry. Actually, to this point in the record, all the verbal material that is the basis for the coding of critical special scores occurred in the inquiry.

His second ALOG, coded for response 16 to Card IX, is more implicit in the basic response, "Two wise men with machine guns and flares. . . ." He elaborates in the inquiry, stating "they have pointed hats so they are wise. . . ." It is fairly clear in illustrating very concrete and flawed judgment. His final answer (Card X, response 18), coded as FABCOM2, is the most unrealistic, "A big fight between two bugs on a mountain, each has a blue crab on his side, each has a reindeer running away from him." In the inquiry, he describes each of the objects involved; and when asked about the big fight, he states, ". . . it's like a war of the bugs on a mountain." It is an unrealistic and somewhat disconnected response that, unfortunately, was not pursued adequately in the inquiry. Thus, as with his Card I INCOM2 answer, the issue of bizarreness remains somewhat speculative.

The evaluation of these eight answers suggests that his thinking is, at best, naive and simplistic. His conceptualizations often are immature and concrete, and there are hints of bizarreness (horns on a cat's face; a war of the bugs). The data are insufficient to conclude that his thinking is seriously disturbed, but if his ideation is routinely marked by this sort of cognitive slippage, it is likely that many of his decisions and behaviors will be inappropriate for some situations. This is especially probable in complex situations. An important issue is the extent to which this naive and strained sort of thinking affects his overall reality testing. Data from the other clusters in the cognitive triad should shed light on this issue.

PROCESSING

Case 12.   Processing Variables for a 22-Year-Old Male.

EB	= 5:3.0	Zf	= 17	Zd	= -8.0	DQ+	= 7
L	= 0.29	W:D:Dd	= 11:7:0	PSV	= 0	DQv/+	= 0
HVI	= NO	W:M	= 11:5			DQv	= 0
OBS	= NO						

Location & DQ Sequencing

I:	Wo.Wo.WSo.Wo.WSo	VI:	Wo
II:	W+.DS+	VII:	W+
III:	D+	VIII:	D+
IV:	Do.Wo	IX:	D+.DSo
V:	Wo.Wo	X:	D+

The data for Zf (17) and the $W:D:Dd$ ratio (11:7:0) indicate that he invests considerable effort when processing new information. However, those data may tend to exaggerate his effort level as nine of his 11 W answers are given to fairly solid figures (I, IV, V, & VI) for which W answers are easy to create. The remaining two W responses were given to figures II and VII, which have only a moderate difficulty level for W answers. This suggests that, while he may be willing to invest considerable effort, he often modulates it when the field is complex.

A question is whether the modulation of effort is sufficient, as the $W:M$ ratio (11:5) implies that he may often aspire to accomplish more than is reasonable in light of his functional capabilities. One source from which an answer to this question may be gleaned is the Zd score. It is -8.0, which signals an underincorporative form of scanning. It indicates that he scans new information hastily and haphazardly and often neglects critical cues that exist in the field. This creates the potential for faulty mediation, which can easily lead to flawed judgments and ineffective behaviors. This might account for some of the concreteness in his thinking that was noted earlier.

To his credit, his record includes seven synthesized ($DQ+$) answers, which is in the expected range for an introversive person, and there are no DQv or $DQv/+$ responses. Usually this indicates that the quality of processing is adequate, but when the sequence of scores is reviewed, that notion seems less viable. Four of the seven $DQ+$ answers (7, 15, 16, & 18) contain critical special scores. Interestingly, all four were given to figures containing chromatic color (Cards II, VIII, IX, & X). In the review of data concerning ideation, it was noted that much of his thinking is naive and simplistic, and it is not unreasonable to assume that his haphazard processing habits may be contributing to this. An important issue that remains to be addressed concerns the extent to which his thinking and processing problems affect the way that he translates new inputs.

MEDIATION

Case 12.   Mediation Variables for a 22-Year-Old Male.

R = 18		L = 0.29		OBS = No	**Minus & NoForm Features**	
FQx+	= 1		XA%	= .83	II 6. W+ C'F.CF.YF– A,Bl 4.5 MOR	
FQxo	= 9		WDA%	= .83	V 12. Wo FMa– A 1.0 INC	
FQxu	= 5		X–%	= .17	IX 17. DSo F– Ad 5.0	
FQx–	= 3		S–	= 1		
FQxnone	= 0					
(W+D	= 18)		P	= 8		
WD+	= 1		X+%	= .56		
WDo	= 9		Xu%	= .28		
WDu	= 5					
WD–	= 3					
WDnone	= 0					

The *XA%* (.83) and *WDA%* (.83) indicate that his translations of new inputs are usually appropriate for the situation. This is somewhat unexpected in light of the previously identified problems with his thinking and processing. In effect, these data strongly suggest that his mediational operations should ordinarily promote adequate reality testing.

The value for the *X–%* (.17) is slightly elevated, but this is only an 18-response record, with each response contributing more than five percentage points. In this instance, there are three minus responses, which may be worrisome, depending on how much distortion is involved. The first minus is a *W* response (Card II, response 6), "A black fly smashed against a wall." It is not a serious distortion of the distal field, especially because he identifies the *D6* area as the "black wings." The second (Card V, response 12) is also a *W* response, "A wolf on its tippy-toes, with big arms." It involves a moderate distortion of the field, and is one of the answers that illustrate his concrete or simplistic thinking. The third (Card IX, response 17) is to the *DS8* area, "A horse's face, from the front." It is also only a moderate distortion of the field. Had he identified the area as a horse's nose instead of a face, it would have been coded unusual. It could easily be a product of his underincorporative processing or his simplistic thinking.

Another element in the mediational data supporting the notion that generally his reality testing is intact is the value for Popular responses (8). This is slightly above average and implies that, when the cues for customary or conventional responses are reasonably obvious, he will translate them appropriately. On the other hand, the *X+ %* (.56) and *Xu%* (.28) connote that he is more prone than most adults to make mediational decisions that disregard social demands or expectations. Usually, this reflects a greater emphasis on individualism than is typical, but in this instance, it may represent the casual and simplistic way that he conceptualizes.

A Summary Concerning Cognition

In most cases, findings gleaned from the clusters in the cognitive triad merge in a homogeneous way, but when that does not occur, an overview of the findings can be helpful. Such an overview seems warranted here because the findings about his cognitive operations seem, at least at first glance, contradictory. The processing data indicate that he makes a considerable effort to input new information, but the quality of that effort is, at best, modest and often limited, mainly because of hasty and haphazard scanning. Typically, faulty processing has a negative effect on mediation but, in this case, the findings regarding mediation imply that, while he is somewhat individualistic, he usually translates new information appropriately. In fact, he seems especially alert for cues that identify acceptable or conventional translations.

The findings regarding his thinking also tend to be somewhat inconsistent with the mediation findings. It seems clear that he is an ideational person with well-fixed attitudes and values. However, his thinking is marked by frequent episodes of cognitive slippage. Some of this muddled ideation appears to be the product of naive and concrete thinking, but some may be caused by bizarre conceptualizing. The examiner did not pursue some of the seemingly bizarre answers adequately, making it difficult to be precise about the latter. The question of why his strange thinking and faulty processing did not interfere more with his mediational activities during the test can be addressed only on a speculative level, but it seems likely that defensiveness played a role.

He gave 18 responses, technically an average length record. However, five of those answers were given to Card I, all involving W and animal contents, and three have critical special scores. He gave 13 answers to the remaining nine cards, one response to each of five (III, VI, VII, VIII, and X) and two answers to each of four (II, IV, V, and IX). Interestingly, his minus answers occurred to three of the four cards in which he gave two answers. Apparently, as he permitted himself to become more involved with the task, some mediational dysfunction occurred. It seems reasonable to postulate that, after Card I, or possibly after giving his first answer to Card II, a minus, he made an effort to restrain his involvement with the test. Nonetheless, his strange thinking persisted and may represent considerably more pathology than is immediately obvious from the structural data.

Two of his three minus answers and four of his five more serious special scores (2 ALOG, *FABCOM*, and FABCOM2) appear in responses to four of the five chromatically colored cards (II, VIII, IX, X). This raises a question about whether affective stimulation may be contributing to his episodes of cognitive inefficiency.

AFFECT

Case 12.   Affect-Related Data for a 22-Year-Old Male.

EB	= 5:3.0			EBPer	= 1.7	**Blends**	
eb	= 10:3	L	= 0.29	FC:CF+C	= 2:2	M.FM.FC	= 1
DEPI	= 4	CDI	= 3	Pure C	= 0	M.CF.m	= 1
						FM.FC	= 1
SumC′ = 2	SumT = 0			SumC′:WSumC	= 2:3.0	C′F.CF.YF	= 1
SumV = 0	SumY = 1			Afr	= 0.29	m.C′F	= 1
Intellect	= 0	CP	= 0	S = 4 (S to I,II,III = 3)			
Blends:R	= 5:18			Col-Shad Bl	= 1		
m + y Bl	= 1			Shading Bl	= 1		

As noted, he has an ideational coping style ($EB = 5:3.0$) that usually involves keeping emotions aside so that they do not become influential in his decision making. However, the datum for *EBPer* (1.7) provides no basis to suspect that he is inflexible in this approach. Thus, on some occasions, he may form decisions or behaviors more intuitively and rely on trial-and-error feedback more than is usual for him.

The right side value for the *eb* (3) is much lower than the left side value (10) and offers no hint of unusual emotional distress. Similarly, the data for the *SumC':WSumC* ratio (2:3.0) give no reason to suspect unusual emotional suppression or constraint. Conversely, the *Afr* datum is quite low (.29), even for an introversive person, indicating that he has a marked tendency to avoid emotions or emotionally toned situations. It implies that he is probably uncomfortable and defensive about dealing with feelings and possibly suggests that he may have some awareness that emotions tend to have a negative impact on his cognitive functioning, especially his thinking. Usually, people with such a strong tendency to avoid emotion also avoid social contacts. Moreover, the *FC:CF+C* ratio (2:2) suggests that he does not modulate his emotional displays as much as most introversive people do. This is not necessarily a liability but, when considered in light of his defensiveness about emotion, it tends to highlight the potential for the control problems identified earlier.

An equally and possibly a more important finding concerning affect are the four *S* responses in this modest-length protocol. They connote a fairly strong sense of alienation or negativism concerning the environment. Usually, this manifests psychologically as animosity or anger and can have a significant influence on decision making and coping activities. There are five blends in the record (28%), slightly more than expected, but not necessarily significant in light of the fact that one blend is situationally related (*m.C'F*). On the other hand, three of the five blends each contain three determinants. It is an unusual proportion and suggests that his psychological functioning is often quite complex. This can be a problem for him because of his difficulties with controls, his strange thinking, and the considerable anger or resentment that he seems to harbor. Moreover, one of these blends (*C'F.CF.YF*) is both a color shading blend and a shading blend. The former signifies that emotions or emotional situations often confuse him, while the latter is much more unexpected and connotes the presence of very painful emotions.

The composite of data regarding affect indicates that he is uncomfortable with and probably confused about feelings. He does not seem to deal with them easily or effectively and usually tries to avoid them. Nonetheless, he is currently burdened by some painful and confusing feelings with which he cannot contend easily. These feelings apparently include considerable resentment or anger generated by a sense of alienation. They influence much of his decision making. When this problem is considered in light of his difficulties with controls, his potential for impulsiveness, and his strange thinking, it makes for an unwanted psychological mix that can easily lead to inappropriate behaviors.

SELF-PERCEPTION

Case 12. Self-Perception Related Data for a 22-Year-Old Male.

				Human Content, An & Xy Responses
R	= 18	OBS	= No	HVI = No	
				III 8. D+ Ma+ 2 H,Sc P 3.0 GHR
Fr+rF	= 0	3r+(2)/R	= 0.28		IV 9. Do Mao (H) P GHR
				VII 15. W+ Mao 2 H,Fd,Id P 2.5 AG,GHR
FD	= 0	SumV	= 0		IX 16. D+ Ma.CF.mpo 2 H,Cg,Ls,Fi ALOG,AB,PHR
An+Xy	= 0	MOR	= 2		
H:(H)+Hd+(Hd) = 3:1				
[EB = 5:3.0]				

The Egocentricity Index (0.28) is below average. It indicates that he tends to judge himself more negatively in comparisons with others. It usually connotes low self-esteem. The absence of *FD* or vista answers suggests that he is also probably rather naive about himself. There are two MOR responses in his record, signifying that there are some negative features in his self-concept that may be promoting a pessimistic view of himself. There are four human contents in the protocol, which is less than expected for an introversive person. Three of the four are pure *H,* implying that his self-image is likely to have evolved more from social interaction than from imagination, but this does not necessarily mean that his impressions of himself are realistic. In fact, although all three of his pure *H* answers are Popular, all contain some unusual verbiage and one contains an ALOG special score. The projected material in the record should provide some additional clarification about the substance of his self-image.

The first of his three minus answers (Card II, response 6) is the most complex, "A black fly smashed against a wall . . . like a fly was smeared. . . ." It is also the first of his two MOR answers, and conveys a marked sense of damage. The second minus (Card V, response 12), "A wolf on its tippy-toes, with big arms," is interesting because of the way in which he anthropomorphizes a predatory animal (tippy-toes, big arms). Assuming this is a self-representation, it is intriguing to speculate about other features he might have attributed to the wolf, had he been prompted for more elaboration (You said he is on tippy-toes?). Would he have associated the response with fantasy (Red Riding Hood, Three Little Pigs, a cartoon character); would he have corrected the slippage or added more humanlike features; or would he have simply reaffirmed that the features look like toes? The third minus (Card IX, response 17) is the least revealing of the three, "A horse's face, from the front." It is probably the result of faulty processing or mediation and seems to have little or nothing to do with projection.

The first of his two MOR responses (smashed fly) has already been studied, but the second (Card VI, response 13) is, at least, equally important from a self-image perspective. It is "a jet whose cockpit is blowing up . . . all of it is blowing up like the cockpit part." Controls are located in the cockpit of an airplane, and this answer appears to convey some awareness of his own control problems. The severity of the morbidity in both of his MOR answers is also of interest. The damage is not reversible. It is always risky to form a postulate based on two MOR answers but, in this instance, it seems reasonable to suspect that he is very pessimistic about himself.

His five human movement answers also contain some striking characteristics, even though all five are coded as Popular. The first (Card III, response 8), is "Two people facing each other, grabbing for a bowling ball." It seems to denote a competitive, possibly aggressive activity, but in the inquiry he seems to modify the answer by identifying *D7* as, "could be bowling balls and the rack they are on." This is another instance in which a question (you said they are grabbing?) might have prompted some clarification of the basic answer. The second *M* (Card IV, response 9) is "A monster with big feet." It is a fairly common answer, except for his description of "clomping along," which could be speculated as denoting his overall approach to life. He describes it as being big on the bottom and "slim at the top, head pointed down." This may represent dimensionality, but was not inquired.

His third *M* (Card VII, response 14) is "Two ladies facing each other, each with one hand behind her, like ready to throw a pie in the other's face . . . like they're throwing a pie at the other person." It seems to be an incongruous conceptualization of aggressiveness. Ladies usually do not throw pies at each other. It is not clear whether this represents the anticipation of aggressiveness from others or an anticipation of being aggressive toward others. The fourth *M* (Card IX, response 16) includes an obvious flawed judgment, "Two wise men with machine guns and flares pointed at each other, and standing on green rocks." In the inquiry, he confirms the faulty logic, "they have pointed hats on so they're wise. . . ." It seems to be a fantasy response, yet he never identifies it as such. As with the third *M* (ladies and pies), it includes something of an incongruity: Wise men are not known for shooting at each other. It is another instance in which the examiner might have pursued the issue a bit more (You say they are wise men because of their pointed hats?). Nonetheless, it conveys a fairly clear preoccupation with aggressiveness. The same is true of the last *M* answer (Card X, response 18), "A big fight between two bugs on a mountain, each has a blue crab on his side, each have a reindeer running away from him . . . it's like a war of the bugs on a mountain." Again, the concept involves aggressiveness and seems to be a serious distortion of reality. Unfortunately, the examiner settled on only one inquiry question, instead of attempting to investigate the probable pathology in the concept further.

The strange conceptualizing that is included in at least four of the five *M* answers implies that unusual thinking probably influences the way in which he views himself, and a preoccupation with aggressiveness is likely to play a prominent role in his self-image.

The seven *FM* and three *m* answers are somewhat less revealing, but some include projected material. Three of the *FM* responses were given to Card I. The first, a crab with arms and hands sticking out (response 2) does not have much interpretive substance. However, the next two—an angry cat's face . . . hissing (response 3), and a wolf's face . . . looking down, the slanted eyes look mean (response 5)—are both consistent with the aggressive preoccupation previously noted. The fourth *FM* (Card IV, response 10) is a flying bug, which he describes as "upside down" rather than turning the card. It may represent a sense of confusion. The fifth *FM* (wolf on tippy-toes) has already been studied. The sixth (Card VIII, response 15) also reflects his strange thinking, "A tree or plant and two bears climbing up each side." In the inquiry, he identifies it as a house plant, apparently ignoring the implausibility of his selection. The final *FM* (response 18) is the reindeer running away from the war of the bugs which, again, seems to illustrate the unrealistic way in which he conceives himself and his world.

Two of the three answers containing *m* determinants (jet with the cockpit blowing up; flares being thrown by wise men) have been reviewed. The third (Card II, response 7) is, "A jet going through space . . . the outside is all black so it must be space." It is not an uncommon answer, but the absolute way in which he accounts for the space illustrates the concreteness of his judgment. On a speculative level, he may feel this way about himself in his world and, if considered in light of response 13 (cockpit), he may judge himself to be in considerable jeopardy. There are three other answers that have not been reviewed (responses 1, 4, and 11), but none include unusual embellishments.

It seems clear that he is not very secure about himself. His self-esteem appears to be much more negative than positive and he seems to be confused about who he is. Not only does he tend to perceive himself negatively, but he also appears to be pessimistic about himself. He may harbor much more of a sense of helplessness or hopelessness than he readily admits. He has a strong preoccupation with aggressiveness that is likely to have evolved from his perceived need to defend himself against a sense of alienation from the world. This has been exacerbated by his feelings of fragility or vulnerability. Some of the findings regarding interpersonal perception may offer clarification about the aggression issue.

INTERPERSONAL PERCEPTION

Case 12. Interpersonal Perception Data for a 22-Year-Old Male.

R = 18	CDI = 3	HVI = No	**COP & AG Responses**
a:p = 12:3	SumT= 0	Fd = 1	I 3. WSo FMao Ad 3.5 INC,AG,PHR
	[eb = 10:3]		VII 14. W+ Mao 2 H,Fd,Id P 2.5 AG,GHR
Sum Human Contents = 4		H = 3	IX 16. D+ Ma.CF.mpo 2 H,Cg,Ls,Fi 4.5 ALOG,AG,PHR
[Style = Introversive]			X 18. D+ Ma.FMa.FCu 2 A,Ls P 4.5 FAB2,AG,PHR
GHR:PHR = 3:3			
COP = 0	AG = 4	PER = 0	
Isolation Indx = 0.28			

Neither the CDI nor HVI is positive and the data for the $a:p$ ratio offer no reason to suspect passivity. Interestingly, there is one *Fd* content, implying that he is inclined to rely on others for direction and support. This is an unusual finding for a person who feels alienated from his world and may represent naiveté in his expectations about social relations. On the other hand, the absence of any texture answers suggests that he acknowledges or expresses his own needs for closeness in ways that are unlike that of most people. He is likely to be conservative in interpersonal situations and overly concerned with issues of personal space.

As noted, he has fewer human contents (4) than expected for an introversive person, indicating that he is not as interested in others as most people are. This seems especially important because three of the four human contents are pure *H,* indicating that his conceptions about others tend to be reality based. In other words, even though he seems to perceive people in a realistic way, he is not very interested in or at least is very cautious about interacting with them. The GHR:PHR ratio (3:3) is of interest because the value for *PHR* is equal to that for *GHR*. This strongly suggests that many of his interpersonal behaviors are likely to be less adaptive for the situation than is desirable.

There are no COP answers in his protocol, an unusual finding for an introversive person, but there are four *AG* responses. This composite signifies that he is probably distant and aloof from others and perceives aggressiveness as a natural component in social relations. Typically, people like this are noticeably forceful or aggressive when dealing with others. When this feature is considered in light of the several problems in his psychological makeup that have been identified earlier, it does not bode well for social adaptation. It is not surprising that the datum for the Isolation Index (0.28) implies that he is somewhat reluctant to engage in social exchanges routinely.

The substance of the five *M* and *FM* answers that contain a pair seem to illustrate the sort of social confusion that marks his life. Three of the five (responses 14, 16, & 18) are coded *AG* (ladies throwing pies, wise men shooting; war of the bugs), two of the five (responses 15 & 18) include fabulized combinations (bears climbing a plant; war of the bugs), and one (response 16) contains an ALOG (wise men shooting). Only one (response 8) of the five (people grabbing a bowling ball) is free of unwanted special scores and, in that instance, there is a hint of aggressiveness.

SUMMARY

This young man has a multitude of troubles. He appears to be in a state of chronic stimulus overload, created mainly by internal irritations that are prompted by unmet needs and confusion about his feelings. These irritations interfere with his attention and concentration and breed a significant potential for loss of control, especially in complex situations. When this occurs, episodes of impulsiveness are likely to mark his thinking and behavior.

Other liabilities magnify the potential problems caused by his difficulties with control. Probably the most important of these concerns his cognitive functioning. He does not process new information very well. He tends to scan things in a hasty and haphazard manner that can easily lead to the misidentification or misinterpretation of cues. More importantly, his thinking is naive and concrete, and it often includes faulty judgment and strange conceptualizations. The latter border on being bizarre.

This situation is further compounded because he is uncomfortable and defensive about dealing with emotions and works hard to avoid them. This may have a relationship to some of his thinking problems. He seems naive about himself and feels insecure and confused about his role in life. This tends to breed feelings that are confusing and sometimes quite painful for him. He is also naive about others and appears to have developed a strong sense of alienation from his world. This has resulted in reasonably strong feelings of resentment or anger that he probably does not handle very well. He is not very socially adept and probably avoids people much of the time or, at least, keeps relations with other on a superficial level.

He apparently lives a schizoid kind of life that includes some potentially serious pathology. Parts of his Rorschach strongly hint at more problems in thinking than are readily apparent in the record and suggest that he is in a fragile state that can easily produce disorganized and inappropriate behaviors.

RECOMMENDATIONS

Three questions have been asked in the referral. The first is whether he is a danger to himself or others. There is no evidence in the protocol to suggest that he may be a danger to himself, but this cannot be ruled out with certainty. He has a potential for impulsiveness, his thinking is peculiar, he is confused about feelings, and probably he is experiencing considerable pain. These are ingredients that could contribute to self-destructive thoughts or actions. In addition, he was hospitalized, apparently for depression, during his second college year and reports thinking about suicide at that time. Information about that episode and his subsequent treatment could be important in attempting to address this question.

There is also the issue of his strong preoccupation with aggression and his noticeable sense of resentment or anger. While these are elements that could contribute to self-destructive thoughts or acts, they are much more likely to promote behaviors that could be harmful to others, especially when considered in light of his potential for impulsiveness and his peculiar thinking. There is no information in the available history to suggest that he has been overtly aggressive toward others. Nonetheless, the basic ingredients exist and concern is warranted. This is especially important because some of his recent behaviors appear to have involved stalking.

The second question posed in the referral asks whether he is a sexual predator. This is a very difficult issue to address from Rorschach data alone. As emphasized earlier, he is preoccupied with aggression, but that can take many forms. There is no evidence of a sexual preoccupation in the Rorschach data and only implications from the history that one may exist. Nonetheless, the possibility cannot be ruled out.

The third question in the referral asks whether there is a significant psychiatric disturbance that should be considered. As noted, he has numerous psychological handicaps that, at the very least, merge into a condition that can easily be described as approaching a personality disorder. There are hints that more serious pathology may be present than is readily apparent from the protocol. He seemed to be defensive throughout much of the test, and the examiner did not pursue some incidents of cognitive slippage adequately during the administration. Thus, the issue of whether a significant psychiatric disturbance exists requires additional evaluation. Such an evaluation might consist of more testing and interviewing, plus the retrieval of information about his previous hospitalization and treatment. However, optimally, it would also include a reasonable period of observation such as might occur during 10 to 14 days as an inpatient in an evaluation center.

EPILOGUE

He was released on bail but instructed to make himself available for two additional interviews with a court-appointed psychiatrist. The report from the psychiatrist emphasized a proclivity for depression but was equivocal regarding dangerousness. A recommendation for further treatment was included. He pleaded guilty to the misdemeanor charge of illegal entry for which he was placed on probation for 18 months with the provision that he reenter treatment. His parents arranged for him to be seen weekly by a psychiatrist at a private mental health clinic.

During his second month of treatment he obtained full-time employment in the shipping department for a department store. During his fourth month of treatment, he reported that he was considering quitting his job because his coworkers disliked him and he had a growing fearfulness that some of his female coworkers were planning to hurt him because his work was not satisfactory. He was encouraged to keep his job, and he was prescribed an antipsychotic medication. Two weeks later, he was apprehended by the neighbors of one of his female coworkers, who were alerted by her screams after he forced her into her apartment when she was returning home from shopping. His probation was revoked, and he was sentenced to an indefinite confinement in a state mental institution.

REFERENCES

American Psychiatric Association. (1994). *Diagnostic and statistical manual of mental disorders* (4th ed.). Washington, DC: Author.

Baity, M. R., & Hilsenroth, M. J. (1999). Rorschach aggression variables: A study of reliability and validity. *Journal of Personality Assessment, 72*(1), 93–110.

Baity, M. R., & Hilsenroth, M. J. (2002). Rorschach Aggressive Content (AgC) variable: A study of criterion validity. *Journal of Personality Assessment, 78*(2), 275–287.

Baity, M. R., McDaniel, P. S., & Hilsenroth, M. J. (2000). Further exploration of the Rorschach Aggressive content (AgC) variable. *Journal of Personality Assessment, 74*(2), 231–241.

Benjamin, L. S. (2000). *SASB interpreter's manual for short, medium, and long form questionnaires.* Salt Lake City, UT: University of Utah.

Butcher, J., Dahlstrom, W., Graham, J., Tellegen, A., & Kaemmer, B. (1989). *MMPI-2: Manual for administration and scoring.* Minneapolis: University of Minnesota Press.

Exner, J. E. (2003). *The Rorschach: A comprehensive system: Vol. 1. Basic foundations and principles of interpretation* (4th ed.). New York: Wiley.

Finney, B. C. (1955). Rorschach test correlates of assaultive behavior. *Journal of Projective Techniques, 19,* 6–16.

Gacono, C. B., Meloy, J. R., & Bridges, M. R. (2000). A Rorschach comparison of psychopaths, sexual homicide perpetrators, and nonviolent pedophiles: Where angels fear to tread. *Journal of Clinical Psychology, 56*(6), 757–777.

Grossman, L. S., Wasyliw, O. E., Benn, A. F., & Gyoerkoe, K. L. (2002). Can sex offenders who minimize on the MMPI conceal psychopathology on the Rorschach? *Journal of Personality Assessment, 78*(3), 484–501.

Holt, R. R. (1956). Gauging primary and secondary processes in Rorschach responses. *Journal of Projective Techniques, 20,* 14–25.

Huprich, S. K., Gacono, C. B., Schneider, R. B., & Bridges, M. R. (2004). Rorschach oral dependency in psychopaths, sexual homicide perpetrators, and nonviolent pedophiles. *Behavioral Sciences and the Law, 22,* 345–356.

Masling, J., Rabie, L., & Blondheim, S. H. (1967). Obesity, level of aspiration, and Rorschach and TAT measures of oral dependence. *Journal of Consulting Psychology, 31*(3), 233–239.

Meloy, J. R., & Gacono, C. B. (1992). The aggression response and the Rorschach. *Journal of Clinical Psychology, 48*(1), 104–114.

Mihura, J. L., & Nathan-Montano, E. (2001). An interpersonal analysis of Rorschach aggression variables in a normal sample. *Psychological Reports, 89,* 617–623.

Mihura, J. L., Nathan-Montano, E., & Alperin, R. J. (2003). Rorschach measures of aggressive drive derivatives: A college student sample. *Journal of Personality Assessment, 80,* 41–49.

Morey, L. C. (1991). *Personality Assessment Inventory: Professional manual.* Odessa, FL: Psychological Assessment Resources.

Rose, D., & Bitter, E. J. (1980). The Palo Alto Destructive Content Scale as a predictor of physical assaultiveness in men. *Journal of Personality Assessment, 44*(3), 228–233.

Urist, J. (1977). The Rorschach Test and the assessment of object relations. *Journal of Personality Assessment, 41*(1), 3–9.

CHAPTER 15

Issues of Sanity and Competency

The subject is a 25-year-old single man who was administered the Rorschach as part of a forensic assessment. He is charged with three homicides, each of which involved the mutilation and death of a young woman whose photographs he had taken while working as a freelance photographer.

He has no prior psychiatric or criminal history. He is an only child. His father and mother are ages 49 and 50 respectively. His parents were divorced when he was 10, after which he continued to live with his mother and saw his father only infrequently. After graduating from high school at age 18, he worked one year in a photography shop and then went on to complete two years at a technical institute and received an AA degree in commercial photography at age 21. After obtaining his degree, he moved out of his mother's home into his own small apartment.

During the next two years he was employed full time in the camera and photography section of a large department store, specializing in family and children's portraits and making passport photos. He resigned from that position at age 23, and for the next nine months toured a large section of the United States taking photographs of landscape and wildlife that he hoped to sell to nature magazines. Although he was able to sell a few photos, the majority of his pictures were not accepted. About 15 months ago, he took a part-time position with a firm specializing in wedding pictures and has used the remainder of his time doing freelance photography.

Information collected from high school and technical institute records is unremarkable. His grades were slightly above average. He worked as a photographer on the high school newspaper during his junior and senior years. He was described by teachers as quiet and conscientious. He apparently had several friends in high school, but no obvious close buddy or girlfriend relationships. He is known to have dated during high school, but there is little information concerning his social activities while at the technical institute. He is described by those with whom he has been working recently as a quiet person but a capable photographer. As part of his freelance activities, he has solicited modeling agencies and has been employed to create portfolios for more than two dozen male and female models. Models who have been interviewed uniformly describe him as helpful, mild mannered, concerned, and competent. Several commented about the detailed notes that he took concerning their modeling experience and the impressions that they hoped to convey in the portfolio photos.

He was apprehended during a break-in to the apartment of a female model by two of her male neighbors. She had left to go grocery shopping a short time before. At first, he claimed he was there to inspect the air conditioning system but became silent after a small bag that he was carrying was opened and revealed some of her undergarments and two necklaces. He continued to remain silent after being arrested by police and after being identified by the victim as having created a photo portfolio for her. A subsequent search of his apartment uncovered several undergarments and pieces of jewelry that were identified as articles belonging to three women who had been murdered in their homes during the preceding 18 months. In each instance, the victim was apparently strangled and then stabbed numerous times. Forensic experts believe that all three were attacked while sleeping. There was no evidence of sexual assault in any of the cases.

When confronted with these findings, he confessed to the murders. He maintained that they were not really models but had been working as prostitutes. He further maintains that he was able to detect their involvement in prostitution by viewing several of their photographs, which, when placed in a particular relationship to each other, provided the revelation. He states that he felt selected by some *special force* to take action, and found that he could not sleep until he had completed the act. His court-appointed attorney states that the subject looks forward to the possibility of a trial because it will provide him with an opportunity to explain the special force.

The assessment was conducted in conjunction with routine procedures with special focus on the issue of whether he is competent to stand trial and whether the court might accept a plea of not guilty by reason of insanity.

CASE FORMULATION AND RELEVANT LITERATURE

This man has no prior criminal or psychiatric history, is described by former teachers and current coworkers as quiet and conscientious, and has a stable and generally positive employment history. He has now confessed to three brutal homicides over the past 18 months, justifying them with a bizarre explanation that includes a revelation about his victims' involvement in prostitution and a special force that directed his actions. His attorney, faced with this paradoxical history, has requested consultation about his competency to stand trial and also asks whether it would be appropriate to consider an insanity defense. The Rorschach is not the primary instrument for responding to these psycholegal questions, but it may be of adjunctive help for the attorney. A review of the relevant literature about the specific psycholegal issues can orient the psychologist in providing this consultation.

Assessment of Competency to Stand Trial

The landmark *Dusky v. United States* (1960) decision of the United States Supreme Court articulated the legal standard for competency to stand trial in the following terms:

> The test must be whether he has sufficient present ability to consult with his lawyer with a reasonable degree of rational understanding—and whether he has a rational as well as factual understanding of the proceedings against him. (p. 789)

Rogers, Tillbrook, and Sewell (1998, 2004) developed a psychometrically robust standardized semistructured interview, the Evaluation of Competency to Stand Trial-Revised (ECST-R), to evaluate the three major elements of *Dusky:* (1) rational ability to consult with an attorney, (2) factual understanding of the charges and the responsibilities of the individuals involved in the proceedings, and (3) rational understanding of appropriate defense strategies and possible outcomes. A further study (Rogers, Jackson, Sewell, & Harrison, 2004) indicated that the ECST-R also serves as a screening measure for feigned incompetence to stand trial, an important concern in settings that may push for negative impression management.

When specific psycholegal questions are at issue, a psychometrically sound forensic instrument like the ECST-R that explicitly addresses those questions and screens for malingering is the most appropriate primary assessment technique. As Cruise and Rogers (1998) point out, standard cognitive and personality measures do not directly assess the very specific impairments necessary for a determination of incompetence to stand trial under the *Dusky* guidelines. However, standard clinical instruments could elaborate some of the explicit findings in ways that might be helpful for attorneys and judges. Rorschach $X+\%$, $X-\%$, *WSum6*, and GHR:PHR and HVI data could be helpful in providing general information about the overall accuracy and conventionality of an individual's reality testing, thought processes, fund of interpersonal information, and interpersonal hypervigilance.

Assessment of Criminal Responsibility

A defendant is responsible for his or her criminal acts unless it can be proved that an excusing condition, such as legal insanity, was present at the time of the crime (Morse, 1999). There is some variation in the United States on the guidelines for evaluating criminal responsibility, but the formulation presented by the American Law Institute (ALI) in section 4.01 of the Model Penal Code contains many of the elements commonly used in making this determination:

> A person is not responsible for criminal conduct if at the time of such conduct as a result of mental disease or defect he lacks substantial capacity either to appreciate the criminality (wrongfulness) of his conduct or to conform his conduct to requirements of law.

Severe mental illness at the time of the offense does not necessarily negate criminal responsibility. Instead, the evaluation of criminal responsibility and the potentially excusing condition of legal insanity must be organized around whatever psycholegal guidelines, such as the ALI insanity standard, are in effect in the jurisdiction in which the case is being tried.

Because they do not address these guidelines explicitly, traditional clinical personality assessment measures cannot be the primary techniques employed in criminal responsibility evaluations. Rogers and Sewell (1999) reviewed various approaches to conducting sanity evaluations and concluded:

> . . . both the MMPI-2 and the Rorschach are unable to differentiate between sane and insane defendants. This statement is not a condemnation of these measures, which may provide useful ancillary data in forensic assessments. Rather, it is an unassailable conclusion that current research on these measures does not provide any reliable classifications on the matter of criminal responsibility. (p. 192)

Rogers developed the Rogers Criminal Responsibility Assessment Scales (R-CRAS; 1984) to quantify symptomatology relevant to the elements of this legal construct and to screen for malingering. A review of reliability and validity studies (Rogers & Sewell, 1999) suggested that the R-CRAS is ". . . a reliable measure for the retrospective assessment of symptoms and characteristics associated with evaluations of criminal responsibility" (p. 184).

As noted, traditional personality measures like the Rorschach can provide adjunctive material that may be helpful in consultation with attorneys and judges during insanity evaluations. As examples, Rorschach findings about significant psychopathology (PTI, DEPI, HVI), available resources contrasted with experienced demands (D Score and Adjusted D Score), emotional control (*Afr* and *FC:CF+C*), and conventionality (Populars and $X+\%$) could allow the psychological consultant to develop a more fine-grained description of features that may be relevant to an insanity defense.

Case 13.   A 25-Year-Old Male.

Card	Response	Inquiry
I	1. A bird taking off, mayb its a queen crow E: Tak ur time, I'm sur u find st else too	E: (Rpts Ss resp) S: It's a big one, with great big wings, lik a special crow, these r the big wgs E: A special crow? S: Well crows don't hav big wgs so this must b a special one, lik a queen crow, the size of it lets the other crows know that she is majestic
	2. A face of a frog too	E: (Rpts Ss resp) S: Here (outlines), u can c the eyes & the forehead, he's got his mouth open but I can't c his chin E: I c the eyes but I'm not sur about the mouth or why it ll a frog S: It's round lookg lik a frog & it's lik he's got big eyes there, frogs always have very big eyes if theyr open E: The mouth open? S: Right here, ths darkr part (points)
II	3. A torn up body, prob an A	E: (Rpts Ss resp) S: It's got a hole & it's torn apart & there's a lot of blood E: A lot of blood? S: This red is all blood, up here & dwn here E: I'm not sur why it ll it's torn apart S: There's half on each side, lik sb tore som A apart
III	4. Some bones, lik the pelvis & the kidney too	E: (Rpts Ss resp) S: These (D1) r all bones of the pelvis & the upper part of the legs & the kidney is in the middl there, in the middl of the pelvis E: Wht maks it ll the kidney? S: Thts where thy r & thyr red & thyr shaped lik ths
	5. Some shoes, lik witches shoes	E: (Rpts Ss resp) S: Thy hav the shape lik shoes tht u c on witches, lik in the movies, thy hav a hi heel & a pointd toe, one on each side. I'v done halloween layouts & I always put boots in lik thes
IV	6. A gorilla wearing lumberjack boots, sittg on a stump	E: (Rpts Ss resp) S: He's a big hulk lik gorilla's, w a littl head & kinda scrawny arms & he's got these boots on, thy ll the lumberjacks wear, I'v seen lots of thm E: U said he's sittg on a stump? S: Here (D1) in the middl, he's just resting
	7. There's a face too, lik an evil lookg guy	E: (Rpts Ss resp) S: Up here (D3), u can c him squinting & his mouth looks angry, he's a mean person, lik evil just glaring lik he's really mad at smthg
V	v8. It ll some bone, a chicken bone	E: (Rpts Ss resp) S: It ll a wishbone tht has been pulled, it's still connected but it's partly broken, lik u make a wish and 2 peopl pull, well ths one was pulled but didn't break cuz it wasn't dry enuff so nobody will get a wish
VI	9. A high speed photo of a fist smashg thru smthg, mayb a wall or a board	E: (Rpts Ss resp) S: Ths is the negative, the fist & the arm is up here & it just smashed thru ths thg dwn here (D1), u can get the force of the action by ths stuff spatting out by the arm it's a real good shot taken w hi speed film, u hav to really plan them rite to catch all the action, I'v done it a few times

Case 13. Continued.

Card	Response	Inquiry
VI	9. *Continued.*	**E:** U said it's a negative? **S:** It's all black & grey lik a negative, I'd lik to c the print, I'll bet it's really a good one
	v10. It ll sbody was crucified & thy cut off his head & legs	**E:** (Rpts Ss resp) **S:** The pole in the cntr, the arms r out here, lik thyr nailed to the crosspole & the rest is the body but the head & legs aren't there, lik smbody wanted to make a point, to show that if u do wrong thy'll really get u & cut u up & cut off u'r head & leav u hangg there lik this
VII	11. Two littl girls who hav a secret	**E:** (Rpts Ss resp) **S:** Thyr just sittg there lookg at e.o., lik thy hav a secret, c ths is the nose & the hair & thyr sittg on ths thg, mayb a big cushion **E:** A big cushion? **S:** Mayb, or mayb a rock or a board, I dkno **E:** U said thy hav a secret? **S:** Thy just ll thy cb sharing smthg secret, u kno lik thy hav a secret between them, littl girls do tht
	v12. Ths ll a negative of a woman wearg a big hat or scarf	**E:** (Rpts Ss resp) **S:** The white is her face, u can't c the features bec it's not exposed enuff & the othr prt is som weird hat or scarf tht she's got wrapped around her head & it comes dwn around her neck **E:** U said a negative? **S:** Yeah, it's reversed, lik a negative, the scarf is dark colored & the face is lite colored
VIII	13. A Star Wars mask	**E:** (Rpts Ss resp) **S:** It's lik a mask, the white slit is for the eyes & it's pointed at the top & fat at the bottom & it's all diff colors lik some masks, lik in the sc. fict. movies lik Star Wars or smthg, I saw all those movies
	v14. Tht ll smbody mooning	**E:** (Rpts Ss resp) **S:** Smbody w pink drawers, I guess a woman, leaning forward, thes r her arms or elbows (Dd26) & the pink is her drawers & the rest is her ass & her privates, she's doing it on purpose, lik to shock people, mak fun of them
IX	15. Tht's a mask too, prob fr New Orleans or Venice whn thy hav thos celebrations	**E:** (Rpts Ss resp) **S:** It's lik an A mask, w the big ears & the big and little holes out here (DdS29) for the eyes, it's all diff colors lik the other one. It's lik thy buy for celebrations, it's not a scary one, just smthg to hide behind
X	16. Smbody is taking revenge, lik judgement day, it has a message	**E:** (Rpts Ss resp) **S:** Everything is being disintegrated, it's all being ripped apart and scattered, lik a quick glimpse of what will happen on judgment day, thts wht it represents, it's people & the world all disintegrating in the picture **E:** I'm not sur I'm seeing it lik u r **S:** Everything is coming apart, lik its all disintegrating, people, trees, houses, things, everythg, it's just all coming apart there as if some force is causing everything to be scattered, it's not very nice to look at

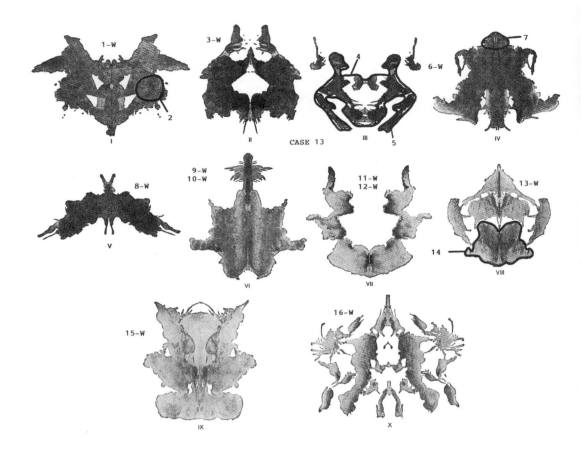

Case 13. Sequence of Scores.

Card	No.	Loc.	No.	Determinant(s)	(2)	Content(s)	Pop	Z	Special Scores
I	1	Wo	1	FMau		A		1.0	ALOG
	2	Ddo	99	FMp–		Ad			
II	3	WSv/+	1	CF–	2	Ad,Bl		4.5	MOR
III	4	DS+	1	FCu		An		4.5	FAB
	5	Ddo	33	Fo	2	Cg			PER
IV	6	W+	1	FMpo		A,Cg,Bt		4.0	FAB,PER
	7	Do	3	Ma–		Hd,Hx			AG,PHR
V	8	Wo	1	F–		An		1.0	MOR,DR
VI	9	W+	1	Mp.C'F.mpu		Art,Hd,Sc		2.5	AG,MOR,PER,PHR
	10	W+	1	mp–		Hd,Id		2.5	MOR,DR,PHR
VII	11	W+	1	Mpo	2	H,Hh	P	2.5	COP,GHR
	12	WS+	1	FC'u		Art,Hd,Cg		4.0	PHR
VIII	13	WSo	1	FCu		(Hd)		4.5	PER,GHR
	14	D+	2	Mp.FC.FD–		Hd,Cg,Sx		3.0	AG,PHR
IX	15	WSo	1	FCo		(Ad)		5.5	
X	16	W/+	1	Ma.mp–		(H),Hx,Bt,Sc		5.5	AB,AG,MOR,DR,PHR

Case 13. Structural Summary.

Location Features	Determinants Blends	Determinants Single	Contents	S-Constellation
				NO . . .FV+VF+V+FD>2
		H = 2		NO . . .Col-Shd Bl>0
Zf = 13	M.C'F.m	M = 2	(H) = 0	YES . .Ego<.31,>.44
ZSum = 45.0	M.FC.FD	FM = 3	Hd = 5	YES . .MOR > 3
ZEst = 41.5	M.m	m = 1	(Hd) = 1	NO . . .Zd > +– 3.5
		FC = 3	Hx = 2	NO . . .es > EA
W = 11		CF = 1	A = 2	NO . . .CF+C > FC
D = 3		C = 0	(A) = 0	YES . .X+% < .70
W+D = 14		Cn = 0	Ad = 2	YES . .S > 3
Dd = 2		FC' = 1	(Ad) = 1	YES . .P < 3 or > 8
S = 5		C'F = 0	An = 2	YES . .Pure H < 2
		C' = 0	Art = 3	YES . .R < 17
		FT = 0	Ay = 0	7 . . . .TOTAL

DQ

		Determinants Single	Contents	Special Scores
+ = 7		TF = 0	Bl = 1	Lv1 Lv2
o = 7		T = 0	Bt = 2	DV = 0x1 0x2
v/+ = 2		FV = 0	Cg = 4	INC = 0x2 0x4
v = 0		VF = 0	Cl = 0	DR = 3x3 0x6
		V = 0	Ex = 0	FAB = 2x4 0x7
		FY = 0	Fd = 0	ALOG = 1x5
		YF = 0	Fi = 0	CON = 0x7
		Y = 0	Ge = 0	Raw Sum6 = 6
		Fr = 0	Hh = 1	Wgtd Sum6 = 22

Form Quality

	FQx	MQual	W+D	Determinants Single	Contents	Special Scores
				rF = 0	Ls = 0	
+	= 0	= 0	= 0	FD = 0	Na = 0	
o	= 4	= 1	= 3	F = 2	Sc = 0	AB = 1 GHR = 2
u	= 5	= 1	= 5		Sx = 1	AG = 4 PHR = 6
–	= 7	= 3	= 6		Xy = 0	COP = 1 MOR = 5
none	= 0	= 0	= 0		Id = 2	CP = 0 PER = 4
				(2) = 3		PSV = 0

Ratios, Percentages, and Derivations

R = 16   L = 0.14

				FC:CF+C = 4:1		COP = 1 AG = 4
				Pure C = 0		GHR:PHR = 2:6
EB = 5:3.0	EA = 8.0	EBPer = 1.7		SumC':WSumC = 2:3.0		a:p = 3:8
eb = 6:2	es = 8	D = 0		Afr = 0.33		Food = 0
	Adj es = 6	Adj D = 0		S = 5		SumT = 0
				Blends:R = 3:16		Hum Con = 8
FM = 3	C' = 2	T = 0		CP = 0		Pure H = 2
m = 3	V = 0	Y = 0				PER = 4
						Iso Indx = 0.13

a:p	= 3:8	Sum6 = 6	XA% = 0.56	Zf = 13.0	3r+(2)/R = 0.19
Ma:Mp	= 2:3	Lv2 = 0	WDA% = 0.57	W:D:Dd = 11:3:2	Fr+rF = 0
2AB+Art+Ay	= 4	WSum6 = 22	X–% = 0.44	W:M = 11:5	SumV = 0
MOR	= 5	M– = 3	S– = 1	Zd = +3.5	FD = 1
		Mnone = 0	P = 1	PSV = 0	An+Xy = 2
			X+% = 0.25	DQ+ = 7	MOR = 5
			Xu% = 0.31	DQv = 0	H:(H)Hd(Hd) = 2:6

PTI = 4*	DEPI = 5*	CDI = 2	S-CON = 7	HVI = YES	OBS = No

S-CON AND KEY VARIABLES

The S-CON of seven, while not actuarially significant, should not be casually disregarded. This is a brief protocol, containing only 16 answers. Thus, when reviewing the record, the interpreter should be alert for hints of a self-destructive potential. This seems especially important because the first positive Key variable (PTI > 3) suggests problems in mediation and thinking that can breed considerable disarray. Using that Key variable as a guideline, the interpretation should begin with a review of the three clusters that comprise the cognitive triad: processing, mediation, and ideation. The interpretation will proceed with a study of the data regarding controls, move on to a review of the cluster concerning affect, and end with an interpretation of the data involving self-perception and interpersonal perception.

PROCESSING

Case 13.   Processing Variables for a 25-Year-Old Male.

EB = 5:3.0	Zf = 13	Zd = +3.5	DQ+ = 7
L = 0.14	W:D:Dd = 11:3:2	PSV = 0	DQv/+ = 2
HVI = YES	W:M = 11:5		DQv = 0
OBS = NO			

Location & DQ Sequencing

I: Wo.Ddo	VI: W+.W+
II: WSv/+	VII: W+.WS+
III: DS+.Ddo	VIII: WSo.D+
IV: W+.Do	IX: WSo
V: Wo	X: Wv/+

Information about processing is always important, but more so when the possibility of a serious disturbance exists. This is because some serious conditions can cause havoc in processing activity that can promote faulty mediational activities. In this case, the *Lambda* value (0.14) is very low, suggesting more involvement with stimuli than is usual for most adults. This is probably related to the positive HVI, signifying hyperalertness. Hypervigilant people tend to mistrust the environment and seek to ensure that they survey all features of a field carefully to avoid being victimized by surprise elements. To do so, requires considerable effort.

The *Zf* value (13) is at the upper end of the expected range, but more substantial when considered in light of the fact that this is a brief protocol. Considerable effort is also reflected by the *W:D:Dd* ratio (11:3:2), which has a disproportionately high value for *W.* In addition, this substantial effort is illustrated by the Location Sequence, which reveals a generally consistent approach in which he gave *W* responses as first answers to nine of the ten figures. Likewise, the *W:M* ratio (11:5) is unusual for an introversive person, suggesting that his strivings may be greater than reasonable in light of his capacities. A substantial processing motivation is also reflected by the *Zd* score (+3.5), suggesting a traitlike tendency to invest considerable effort and energy into scanning activities. This is consistent with his hypervigilance and his set to avoid being careless.

In light of this substantial effort, it is surprising that the overall quality of his processing yield is modest, and possibly flawed. His 16 answers do include seven *DQ+* responses, which is in the expected range for an introversive person. However, two answers are coded *DQv/+*, which is unusual for an introversive person, especially with a relatively brief record. These findings imply that, while the quality of his processing is usually adequate, it also may falter at times to an unsophisticated, less mature level. Thus, although seemingly well motivated to contend with new information and willing to invest considerable effort in organizing activity, he is not very efficient. The quality of this effort is generally good, but his strivings or his conceptual sets sometimes may lead to inefficient and faulty processing that may have an undesirable influence on some of his mediational activities.

MEDIATION

Case 13.   Mediation Variables for a 25-Year-Old Male.

R = 16		L = 0.14		OBS = No	**Minus & NoForm Features**
FQx+	= 0	XA%	= .56		I 2. Ddo FMp– Ad
FQxo	= 4	WDA%	= .57		II 3. WSv/+ CF– 2 Ad,Bl 4.5 MOR
FQxu	= 5	X–%	= .44		IV 7. Do Ma– Hd,Hx AG,PHR
FQx–	= 7	S–	= 0		V 8. Wo F– An 1.0 MOR,DR
FQxnone	= 0				VI 10. W+ mp– Hd,Id 2.5 MOR,DR,PHR
(W+D	= 14)	P	= 1		VIII 14. D+ Mp.FC.FD– Hd,Cg,Sx 3.0 AG,PHR
WD+	= 0	X+%	= .25		X 16. Wv/+ Ma.mp– (H),Hx,Bt,Sc 5.5 AB,AG,MOR,DR,PHR
WDo	= 3	Xu%	= .31		
WDu	= 5				
WD–	= 6				
WDnone	= 0				

The *XA%* (.56) and *WDA%* (.57) are both low and signify a serious mediational dysfunction and the likelihood that his reality testing is noticeably impaired. This is also indicated by the substantial *X–%* (.44), which implies that his mediational translations are abundant with distortion and, as a result, many of his behaviors will probably be inappropriately formulated. Most of these distortions do not appear to be rooted in anger. Seven of his 16 answers are coded minus, but only one includes the use of white space. He simply distorts many inputs and, in light of the findings about the general adequacy of his processing activities, it seems likely that these distortions result mainly from faulty conceptualizations. Regardless of the cause, the end result is potentially disastrous.

There is no obvious homogeneity in the sequencing of his seven minus responses. Three are only answers, while four are second responses. They were given to seven of the 10 figures. On the other hand, there is some rather distinct homogeneity in the characteristics of the seven minus answers. Four of the seven include human content, and five of the seven contain movement determinants. Moreover, four of the seven contain MOR special scores, and three of the seven are coded *AG*. This collective of findings strongly suggests that strange conceptualizations or sets involving aggressiveness and/or damage are in some way contributing to marked distortions of reality.

The levels of distortion vary considerably. Three of the seven, responses—3 (torn-up body), 8 (chicken bone), and 10 (somebody was crucified)—are Level 1 distortions in that some features are readily identifiable. In two of the remaining four, response 2 (face of a frog) and 7 (an evil-looking guy), a substantial use of imaginary lines is involved. Another, response 14 (somebody mooning), is also difficult to perceive. None of these three are complete detachments from the distal properties of the field, but they are more serious distortions than most Level 1 answers and, as such, tend to emphasize his mediational problem.

The last minus, "somebody taking revenge" (response 16, Card X) is bizarre, but also equivocal when the distortion is considered. In the inquiry, he implies that it is a representation with "people and the world all disintegrating." If taken as an abstract, there is little distortion, but if taken as "revenge" with "a message," involving people, trees, and houses, the detachment from the distal field is considerable. In any event, the composite of minus answers seems to confirm that he experiences frequent and serious departures from reality.

The presence of only one Popular answer is also cause for concern. It suggests the likelihood of unconventional translations of inputs, even in situations where cues regarding acceptable or expected responses are obvious. Likewise, the $X+\%$ (.25) is very low, indicating that regardless of cues in a situation, he simply does not translate inputs in a very conventional manner. The value for the $Xu\%$ (.31) is elevated and conveys the notion that he makes more mediational decisions that disregard social expectations. However, in this instance, it is not his tendency to be more individualistic that is at issue.

The collective of findings highlights a serious reality testing problem. He is prone to disregard or fail to perceive the conventional, and he may translate some inputs in an overly personalized manner. In many instances, however, his mediational efforts are marked by a serious perceptual inaccuracy that promotes a notable distortion of reality. Whenever overpersonalization and distortion occur with a high frequency, as is the case here, it usually leads to patterns of behavior that run contrary to social acceptance or demand. The disarray evidenced in his mediational activities is commensurate with that found frequently among those suffering from some major disorder.

It seems likely that many of his unusual or distorted translations are prompted by some enduring sets or preoccupations that should be evident as his ideational features are studied in detail.

IDEATION

Case 13.   Ideation Variables for a 25-Year-Old Male.

L	= 0.14	OBS	= No	HVI	= Yes	Critical Special Scores			
						DV	= 0	DV2	= 0
EB	= 5:3.0	EBPer	= 1.7	a:p	= 3:8	INC	= 0	INC2	= 0
				Ma:Mp	= 2:3	DR	= 3	DR2	= 0
eb	= 6:2	[FM = 3 m = 3]				FAB	= 2	FAB2	= 0
				M−	= 3	ALOG	= 1	CON	= 0
Intell Indx	= 4	MOR	= 5	Mnone	= 0	Sum6	= 6	WSum6	= 22
							(R = 16)		

M Response Features

IV   7. Do Ma− Hd,Hx AG,PHR
VI   9. W+ Mp.C'F.mpo Art,Hd,Sc 2.5 AG,MOR,PER,PHR
VII 11. W+ Mpo 2 H,Hh P 2.5 COP,GHR
VIII 14. D+ Mp.FC.FD− Hd,Cg,Sx 3.0 AG,PHR
X   16. Wv/+ Ma.mp− H,Hx,Bt,Sc 5.5 AB,AG,MOR,DR,PHR

The *EB* (5:3.0) indicates that he is an ideational person who tends to rely considerably on his conceptual thinking when addressing problems or making decisions. In most situations, he prefers to keep his feelings at a peripheral level and think things through before forming a decision or initiating behaviors. The value for *EBPer* (1.7) suggests that this is not an inflexible coping style. In some instances, his feelings will become more influential in forming decisions and behaviors, and there may be trial-and-error activity in some situations. This style of decision making can be effective if thinking is clear and logical, but if it is not, decisions and behaviors that are inappropriate for the situation are likely to occur. The findings concerning his mediational problems suggest that this may be the case here.

The *a*:*p* ratio (3:8) reveals that the right side value is nearly three times that of the left side value. This suggests that his ideational sets and values are well fixed and difficult to alter. This is an especially important finding if his thinking is disordered because disturbed thought often includes obsessional or delusional features that tend to be well fixed and difficult to challenge.

A very important finding concerning his thinking is the positive HVI. It signals the presence of a traitlike feature that often influences his conceptual thinking. It involves an anticipatory or hyperalert state of preparedness that relates to a negative or mistrusting attitude toward the environment. This breeds a sense of insecurity and feelings of vulnerability. This set is likely to cause his conceptual thinking to become less clear and somewhat inflexible, and if his thinking is seriously disordered, it will very likely promote paranoid-like characteristics.

Another factor that has a significant impact on his conceptual thinking is indicated by the five MOR responses. It denotes a very pessimistic set that orients him to conceptualize his relationship to the world with a sense of doubt, discouragement, and the anticipation of unwanted outcomes regardless of his efforts. This kind of set often produces narrow and concrete thinking, and if his thinking is disturbed, it will exacerbate his disorganization.

The left side *eb* value (6) implies that his experiences of peripheral or preconscious ideation are not greater than usually expected for an adult. However, the value includes three *m* determinants, indicating that the current level of his peripheral or subconscious thought has apparently increased because of situationally related stress. This could have a noticeable effect on his attention and concentration. Probably more important is the finding regarding the *Ma*:*Mp* ratio (2:3). It suggests that he is prone to defensively substitute fantasy for reality. While this is not uncommon among many people, it becomes a liability if thinking is disturbed because delusional systems usually evolve from elaborate fantasies.

Technically, the Intellectualization Index value (4) is meaningful, suggesting that he is more prone than most people to intellectualize feelings in order to deny or neutralize their impact. However, this is an equivocal finding. Response 16, "Somebody taking revenge . . . it has a message," is coded AB, apparently because in the inquiry he notes, "like a quick glimpse of what will happen on judgment day, that's what it represents. . . ." Although the coding is legitimate, it is unclear whether he is perceiving something that is symbolic or an abstract representation. Conversely, two of his answers (responses 7 & 16) contain *Hx* codings, which also connote that he attempts to contend with self-image issues in an intellectual manner. Thus, the likelihood that this process is employed more broadly than indicated by the value of four seems substantial.

The findings concerning *Sum6* (6) and *WSum6* (22) are much more ominous. To have six critical special scores is somewhat unusual in an average-length protocol, and especially so in a brief record. Moreover, the *WSum6* value of 22 is much higher than expected, and even more so because only 16 answers were given. These findings signify that he has serious problems in conceptualizing, which in turn, are likely to limit his reality testing rather markedly.

A subjective evaluation of the answers containing critical special scores illustrates some of the looseness and bizarreness that occur frequently in his thinking. The first (Card I, response 1, coded ALOG) is, "a queen crow . . . a special crow . . . the size of it lets the other crows know that she is majestic." It is a fantasy response in which judgment is sorely lacking. The second is a *FABCOM* (Card III, response 4), "the pelvis . . . and the kidney is in the middle of the pelvis." It is a less serious cognitive slip than response 1, but also ignores reality. The third (Card IV, response 6) is also a *FABCOM,* "A gorilla wearing lumberjack boots," is a more childlike bending of reality.

The fourth answer (Card V, response 8), "It didn't break cause it wasn't dry enough so nobody will get a wish," also connotes his concrete judgment. The fifth (Card VI, response 10) seems to illustrate the intensity of his preoccupations and their impact on his stream of thought, "like somebody wanted to make a point, to show that if you do wrong they'll really get you and cut you up and cut off your head and leave you hanging like this." The last (Card X, response 16) is also intriguing in a similar context, "Somebody is taking revenge . . . it has a message . . . it's all being ripped apart and scattered, like a quick glimpse of what will happen on judgment day . . . it's people and the world all disintegrating in the picture." It is remarkable for the intensity conveyed and the manner in which his preoccupations manifest.

Three of his five *M* responses are coded as having minus form quality, which also affirms the presence of peculiar or disturbed thinking. They include (response 7), "a face, too, like an evil-looking guy," (response 14) "somebody mooning . . . she's doing it on purpose, like to shock people," and (response 16) "Somebody is taking revenge." Any or all could be judged as Level 2 distortions. They are unique and reflect patterns of thinking that tend to disregard reality. None of the five *M* answers are primitive or juvenile. The remaining two are (Card VI, response 9), "A high speed photo of a fist smashing through something," and (Card VII response 11), "two little girls who have a secret." The latter is somewhat commonplace, but the remaining four are relatively sophisticated even though they are all somewhat bizarre.

Overall, the notion that his thinking is markedly disturbed cannot be avoided. Often his thoughts are not well organized, his judgment seems flawed and concrete, and his conceptualizations seem to be strongly influenced by preoccupations and delusions that ignore reality. Unfortunately, he is an ideationally oriented person whose attitudes and values are relatively well fixed. This reduces the likelihood that challenges to his way of thinking might be effective. Three other features compound this problem: a notably guarded and probably paranoid-like mistrust of the world, a chronically pessimistic set concerning his relationship with the world, and a tendency to take defensive flight into fantasy when the realities of a situation appear to be threatening. The collective of findings about his ideation connote substantial impairment. The pattern of dysfunction in his thinking appears to be consistent with that found among those with psychotic disturbances, and especially those who have a schizophrenic spectrum disorder.

CONTROLS

Case 13.   Control-Related Variables for a 25-Year-Old Male.

EB = 5:3.0	EA = 8.0		D = 0	CDI = 2
eb = 6:2	es = 8	Adj es = 6	AdjD = 0	L = 0.14
FM = 3 m = 3	SumC′ = 2	SumT = 0	SumV = 0	SumY = 0

The Adj D Score (0) and CDI (2) offer no reason to question his capacity for control. The *EA* value (8.0) falls in the average range and suggests that he probably has as much accessibility to resources as most adults. Neither side of the *EB* (5:3.0) contain zero values, and the composite of the *EA* and *EB* findings support the notion that the Adj D Score provides a valid indication that his capacity for control and tolerance for stress is very much like that of most adults. The reliability of the Adj D Score also appears to be confirmed by the *es* (8) and Adj *es* (6) data. In fact, when the components of the *eb* are examined, there is no evidence of any unusual demand experiences except for a slight elevation in peripheral ideation (*m* = 3) created by situationally related stress.

In effect, no problems are evidenced in the area of controls and stress tolerance. His capacity for control is like that of most adults. He appears to have about as much resource available to draw on in forming decisions and implementing behaviors as is expected for one of his age. There are no unusual internal demand experiences, although situational stress appears to have increased the presence of peripheral ideational activity, a finding that seems easily understood in light of his present circumstances.

AFFECT

Case 13.   Affect-Related Data for a 25-Year-Old Male.

EB	= 5:3.0			EBPer	= 1.7	**Blends**	
eb	= 6:2	L	= 0.14	FC:CF+C	= 4:1	M.C'F.m	= 1
DEPI	= 5		CDI = 2	Pure C	= 0	M.FC.FD	= 1
						M.m	= 1
SumC' = 2	SumT = 0			SumC':WSumC	= 2:3.0		
SumV = 0	SumY = 0			Afr	= 0.33		
Intellect	= 4	CP	= 0	S = 5 (S to I,II,III	= 2)		
Blends:R	= 3:16			Col-Shad Bl	= 0		
m + y Bl	= 1			Shading Bl	= 0		

The DEPI value (5) is positive. This indicates that his psychological organization is marked by features that give rise to frequent experiences of emotional disruption, such as depression, moodiness, tension, or anxiety. This is not uncommon among schizophrenic spectrum disturbances and hints that serious affective symptoms may have existed in his history, especially if psychotic episodes have occurred.

His predisposition to affective disruption is important in light of the previously discussed finding that the *EB* indicates he usually prefers to keep his feelings apart from his thinking during decision making. However, as also noted, the finding for *EBPer* (1.7) suggests that some flexibility exists in his ideational coping style. Thus, some circumstances may occur in which his feelings become influential during decision making or coping operations and possibly exacerbate his already disordered thinking.

The right side *eb* value (2) is not elevated, but of interest because it consists of two achromatic color answers (responses 9 and 12). This suggests that he experiences irritation because of a tendency to constrain emotional expression by internalizing feelings. However, the data for the *SumC':WSumC* ratio (2:3.0) offers no implication that this is done to excess. On the other hand, the *Afr* value (.33) is very low, signifying that he has a marked tendency to avoid emotional stimulation as much as possible. In a similar context, the previously noted Intellectualization Index (4) implies that he is prone to deny or neutralize emotions by dealing with them on an ideational level. An issue was raised about the accuracy of the Index because of the equivocal coding of AB for response 16. When considered in light of the *SumC'* responses and the low *Afr*, it probably reflects a true indication that he is prone to intellectualize excessively.

The notion that he tries to avoid or minimize the impact of emotion is also indicated by the values in the *FC:CF+C* ratio (4:1). They suggest that he attempts to exert stringent controls over his own emotional displays. This collective of findings connotes that he is prone to be very uncomfortable in emotionally arousing situations. This discomfort is likely to exacerbate his sense of mistrust and vulnerability and provoke concern about losing the tight controls that he has imposed on his feelings. When considered in light of his disturbed thinking and his very guarded and mistrusting attitude toward the world, it seems reasonable to speculate that he is withdrawn and socially isolated.

The value for *S* (5) is striking. It suggests that he harbors a negative, angry attitude toward the environment. It seems logical to speculate that a fear of being unable to deal with this anger has contributed to the stringent controls that he attempts to place on his emotional displays and his marked avoidance of emotional stimulation. This anger probably has also contributed significantly to the instigation of the violent acts to which he has confessed.

The number of blends (3) implies that, ordinarily, he is not a very complex person. However, two of his three blends contain three determinants, and the third (*M.m*) is apparently situationally related, suggesting that even though the current level of complexity is modest, it may be even greater than usual because of current stresses.

Overall, these findings raise interesting questions, especially when considered with other results that concern his disordered thinking and impaired reality testing. It seems clear that he tries to avoid involvement with his feelings and with emotionally loaded situations in general. His negative and angry attitude toward the environment seems likely to contribute much to this avoidance, but some awareness that his thinking is not always clear or logical may also contribute. If he has experienced psychotic episodes, and that is speculative, they may easily have been marked by a noticeable release of pent-up feelings that, if merged with disordered thought, could lead to emotionally intense and potentially violent behaviors.

SELF-PERCEPTION

Case 13.   Self-Perception Related Data for a 25-Year-Old Male.

R	= 16	OBS	= No	HVI = Yes	**Human Content, Hx, An & Xy Responses**
					III 4. DS+ FCu An 4.5 FAB
Fr+rF	= 0	3r+(2)/R	= 0.19		IV 7. Do Ma– Hd,Hx AG,PHR
					V 8. Wo F– An 1.0 MOR,DR
FD	= 1	SumV	= 0		VI 9. W+ Mp.C'F.mpu Art,Hd,Sc 2.5 AG,MOR,PER,PHR
					VI 10. W+ mp– Hd,Id MOR,DR,PHR
An+Xy	= 2	MOR	= 5		VII 11. W+ Mpo 2 H,Hh P 2.5 COP,GHR
					VII 12. WS+ FC'u Art,Hd,Cg 4.0 PHR
H:(H)+Hd+(Hd) = 2:6					VIII 13. WSo FCu (Hd) 4.5 PER,GHR
[EB = 5:3.0]					VIII 14. D+ Mp.FC.FD– Hd,Cg,Sx 3.0 AG,PHR
					X 16. Wv/+ Ma.mp– H,Hx,Bt,Sc 5.5 AB,AG,MOR,DR,PHR

The positive HVI has been emphasized earlier but warrants added consideration in the context of self-image. It denotes that he is preoccupied with a sense of vulnerability, and this is likely to be a core feature in his self-concept. The very low Egocentricity Index (0.19) is likely to be related to this, indicating that he is prone to judge himself much less favorably when comparing himself with others. There is one *FD* in the record, implying that he engages in some self-examination, but some or much of this probably occurs in the context of his flawed thinking and negative self-value.

There are two *An* responses is this brief protocol, strongly hinting at some unusual somatic concern. As noted, there are five MOR answers in this 16-response record. They not only reflect the pessimism that marks his thinking but also signal that his self-image is marked by many negative attributions in which he tends to perceive himself as damaged or distorted. Eight (50%) of his 16 responses contain human content, which is a substantial proportion even for an introversive person, but not necessarily for a hypervigilant individual.

Only two of the eight human content answers are Pure *H,* suggesting that his self-image is based largely on imaginary impressions or distortions of real experience. Typically, this creates a less mature and unrealistic impression of oneself. This is also suggested by the codings for his human content answers. Four of the eight (responses 7, 10, 14, & 16) have a minus form quality, denoting confused or distorted notions about self-image. Three (7, 9, & 14) contain *AG* special scores, and two (responses 7 & 16) include *Hx* codings. As noted, the latter usually signifies that issues of self-image are often intellectualized in ways that ignore reality. It can also connote ideational impulse control problems that can easily result in gross distortions of the self-concept.

The negative aspects of his self impressions are well illustrated by the projected material in eight responses that involve his minus and MOR answers. Seven of the eight are minus answers and include four of his five MOR contents. This group of eight responses also includes three of his five *M*s, one of his three *FM*s, and all three of his *m*s. The minus answers are: (response 2) "A face of a frog . . . frogs always have very big eyes if they're open"; (response 3) "A torn-up body . . . there's half on each side like somebody tore some animal apart"; (response 7) "a face, too, like an evil-looking guy . . . he's a mean person . . . he's really mad at something"; (response 8) "a chicken bone . . . a wishbone that has been pulled, it's still connected but it's partly broken . . . so nobody will get a wish"; (response 10) "somebody was crucified and they cut off his head and legs . . . if you do wrong they'll really get you and cut you up . . . and leave you hanging there"; (response 14) "somebody mooning . . . the pink is her drawers and the rest is her ass and her privates, she's doing it on purpose, like to shock people, make fun of them"; and (response 16) "Somebody is taking revenge, . . . everything is being ripped apart . . . it's all disintegrating . . . some force is causing everything to be scattered, it's not very nice to look at." The eighth answer, containing the fifth MOR is a fourth *M* (response 9), "A high speed photo of a fist smashing through something . . . you can get the force of the action by this stuff spatting out by the arm."

Two of these eight responses, the face of a frog with the big eyes, and the face of an evil-looking guy who is mad at something, presumably relate to his hypervigilant state. The remaining six responses are all intense and dramatic. Response 14 (mooning) is especially interesting because he retained the undergarments and jewelry of his three victims. Five of the six include violence or the products of violence. As a collective, these eight answers seem to convey a confused, damaged, and volatile sense of self.

Three of the other eight responses in the record contain his remaining three movement determinants. The first (response 1) is an *FM* answer, "A bird taking off, maybe it's a queen crow . . . the size lets other crows know that she is majestic." This hints at the possibility of a delusion of grandiosity. The second (response 6) is also an *FM*, "A gorilla wearing lumberjack boots . . . a big hulk . . . with a little head and scrawny arms . . . he's got these boots on. . . . I've seen lots of them." Gorillas do not have little heads or scrawny arms, and his main emphasis seems to be on the boots, which may represent some status for him. The third (response 11) is his fifth *M*, "Two little girls who have a secret . . . between them, little girls do that you know" is probably the most favorable response in his protocol, yet it also conveys his guardedness.

The other five answers in the group of eight also provide some insights about his self-impressions. The first (response 4) is, "like the pelvis and the kidney, too." It is an exposed, and somewhat confused response that may represent his sense of vulnerability. The remaining four all have concealment features (response 5) "like witches' shoes," (response 12) ". . . a negative of a woman wearing a big hat or scarf . . . you can't see the features," (response 13) "A *Star Wars* mask . . . the white slit is for the eyes," and (response 15) "a mask, too, probably from New Orleans or Venice when they have those celebrations . . . little holes out here for the eyes . . . just something to hide behind."

There seems to be little question that this man is tormented by an extremely negative and distasteful self-image, which is probably based largely on imagination or distortions of experience. However, when considered in the context of his disturbed thinking, his guardedness and mistrust of the world, his pessimistic set and his sense of damage, his current perceptions of himself may be realistic. He is in chaos and probably has some awareness of his situation. Regardless of whether that is true, he cannot be expected to function effectively in the world. He feels that it is important to conceal his negative features and may, on a speculative level, harbor some delusions about power and aggression that help to defend him from the unwanted realities of his self-image. In a similar context, it seems logical to assume that many of his behaviors have been formulated to maintain some semblance of personal integrity.

INTERPERSONAL PERCEPTION

Case 13.   Interpersonal Perception Data for a 25-Year-Old Male.

R = 16	CDI = 2	HVI = Yes	**COP & AG Responses**
a:p = 3:8	SumT= 0	Fd = 0	IV 7. Do Ma– Hd,Hx AG,PHR
	[eb = 6:6]		VI 9. W+ Mp.C'Fmpu Art,Hd,Sc 2.5 AG,MOR,PER,PHR
Sum Human Contents = 8		H = 2	VII 11. W+ Mpo 2 H,Hh P 2.5 COP,GHR
[Style = introversive]			VIII 14. D+ Mp.FC.FD– Hd,Cg,Sx 3.0 AG,PHR
GHR:PHR = 2:6			X 16. Wv/+ Ma.mp– H,Hx,Bt,Sc 5.5 AB,AG,MOR,DR,PHR
COP = 1	AG = 4	PER = 4	
Isolation Indx = 0.13			

As emphasized earlier, the positive HVI finding is important to any understanding of his psychology. It not only indicates a chronic pattern of hyperalertness, but also signals an orientation toward the interpersonal world that is characterized by mistrust, skepticism, excessive suspiciousness, and a failure to experience needs for closeness in ways that are common among people. In fact, he probably becomes more guarded and mistrusting when friendly gestures of closeness occur, mainly because they are so unexpected and difficult for him to comprehend.

His hypervigilance, combined with his strange and unrealistic thinking, creates a paranoid-like state that causes him to expend considerable energy in maintaining a defensive psychological posture when dealing with others. He is likely to be overly concerned with issues of personal space and may become alarmed easily when he perceives others being intrusive, either physically or emotionally. He is also prone to keep his interpersonal relations casual and superficial and will often misread gestures by others. He probably functions adequately in safe, reasonably isolated environments over which he feels a sense of control. Freelance photography fits this requirement very well.

It is not surprising that the $a:p$ ratio (3:8) reveals a marked tendency toward interpersonal passivity. Avoidance of social responsibility is an easy way to avoid emotional involvement and closeness with others. It also provides a convenient excuse whenever things do not go well. The datum for the sum of human contents (8) indicates that he is very interested in people, but this is not unusual for a hypervigilant person. In this case, it probably reflects his defensive concerns about others. The fact that only two of the eight are Pure H strongly implies that he does not understand people very well. Likewise, the GHR:PHR ratio (2:6) signifies that his interpersonal behaviors are not very effective and often may be regarded unfavorably by others.

The single COP response seems favorable but, as noted, it also conveys his guardedness. Much more important is the significant elevation in AG answers (4). It indicates that he perceives everyday interpersonal relations as naturally including contentious and belligerent behaviors and that he has incorporated these features into his own conceptualizations about interpersonal activity. Ordinarily, this finding might lead to the postulate that his behaviors have included considerable aggressive behavior that could be documented easily. In this case, however, the pronounced commitment to passivity suggests that most of his aggressiveness has manifested less directly, probably in the form of passive-aggressive behaviors. Nonetheless, the magnitude of AG answers in this brief protocol seems to ensure that his behavior patterns include aggressive activity on a regular basis. When this feature is considered together with his long-standing anger toward the world, couched in the context of his strange and illogical thought processes, and viewed in terms of his guarded and mistrusting view of others, the violence in which he has engaged is not surprising.

The elevated value for PER (4) connotes that he often adopts an inflexible, authoritarian approach in order to avoid the intrusions and manipulations of others, keeping them at a distance. Surprisingly, the Isolation Index (.13) is not positive, which may indicate the fact that he does interact regularly, but superficially, with clients. There is only one movement answer containing a pair. It is on Card VII (response 11), "Two little girls who have a secret . . . just sitting there looking at each other." Speculatively, it may imply that meaningful interactions are based on some intellectual sharing that involves no contact.

A postulate suggesting that his interpersonal world is impoverished is probably an understatement. He is very interested in people, but not because of his need to be close or has an interest in developing enduring relationships. On the contrary, he perceives people negatively and regards them as a potential risk to his security. He is easily threatened by the natural friendliness of others and works hard to keep his own feelings on a more intellectual, easily controlled level. Apparently, he has found a passive interpersonal role to be the safest and most productive in terms of his own needs, but he also has an unusual preoccupation with aggressiveness as a routine in exchanges between people. It is likely that his history is marked by many behaviors that would be regarded as passive-aggressive acts, and it also seems likely that his perception of aggressiveness has somehow combined with his distorted thinking and his intense anger to promote the violent actions to which he has confessed.

SUMMARY

This man presents a picture of psychological organization and functioning that closely approximates a paranoid schizophrenic condition. His thinking is often strange, somewhat disorganized, and frequently is bizarre. He is an ideationally oriented person who prefers to think things through before forming decisions or initiating behaviors, but his thinking is often influenced significantly by strong, well-fixed preoccupations, some of which probably have delusional features. These preoccupations have apparently evolved from a strong and persistent guarded and mistrusting view of the world, which in turn, has caused him to develop a marked sense of vulnerability. This ideational set has a substantial influence on many of his psychological functions and often contributes to his strange thinking.

Although he makes a strong effort to process information effectively, he does not perceive the world accurately or conventionally. In some instances, his translations of stimuli are not distortions, but simply products of his more personal sets and preoccupations. In other instances, his preoccupations lead to serious perceptual inaccuracies that promote gross distortions of reality. Ordinarily he has enough resources to ensure adequate control over his behavior. His tolerance for stress is like that of most adults, and there is no unusual magnitude of internal demands pressing on him. There is some evidence that current stresses have increased the complexity of his ideation, but not beyond tolerable limits.

He is not comfortable with emotion and works hard to keep his feelings well controlled. He apparently goes to considerable lengths to avoid emotionally arousing situations, including the frequent use of an apparently elaborate fantasy life into which he often takes flight to replace the harshness or stresses of reality. He also tries to defend against unwanted feelings by dealing with them on an intellectual level. His concerns about his emotions are likely to stem from the fact that he harbors considerable anger, which he probably has difficulty acknowledging and controlling. His problems in contending effectively with his feelings seem to predispose him to episodes of significant emotional distress that may manifest as tension or anxiety, but in some instances may cause experiences of depression.

While some of his anger appears related to his guarded and mistrusting view of the world, some also seems related to his negative and distasteful self-image, which appears to have evolved from a composite of imagination and distortions of experience, but which may also include some awareness of his own strangeness. This negative self-image has given rise to a strong sense of pessimism. He does not expect things to go well and probably becomes distraught often because of his plight. He regards himself poorly compared with others and has adopted an interpersonal approach that is mainly guarded, distant, and passive. However, he also perceives aggression to be a natural component of interpersonal life and it is likely that many of his own behaviors have included passive-aggressive features. He is defensively preoccupied with people, and he feels the necessity to be continually alert against the intrusions or manipulations of others. His fearfulness of emotion, when combined with his strange thinking and mistrust of people, often causes him to become easily threatened by others. In these threat situations, his judgment is usually faulty and concrete, and this can produce inappropriate patterns of decision making and behavior. Most of the time, his reaction to threats is likely to take the form of passive withdrawal, but the composite of disturbed thinking and perceptual distortion increases the potential for other forms of behavior, including the violent actions to which he has confessed.

RECOMMENDATIONS

Most competency laws include two issues: (1) Is the person able to comprehend the nature of the charges, and (2) is the person able to participate meaningfully in the preparation and conduct of his or her defense? If both issues are applicable in this case, Rorschach findings are consistent with the suggestion that he be found incompetent with regard to the second. It is likely that he can understand the charges, even though he may interpret them in his own idiosyncratic way. However, it is unlikely that he can participate meaningfully in his own defense. His problems in thinking and dealing with reality are likely to promote frequent distortions of information and events. In addition, his enduring mistrust of others, plus his tendency to be passive, are likely to breed activities in relation to his attorney and the court that could be significantly detrimental to his cause.

If he is brought to trial or judgment, the etiological basis for his actions can be speculatively explained elaborately by drawing inferences from the test findings, and it would not be unreasonable to support a contention of insanity under some statutes. On the other hand, issues such as his adequate controls, ability to formulate and implement behaviors (premeditation), intense anger, and tendencies toward aggressive behaviors, together with his reasonably consistent work history, can all be used as the basis for arguments that are detrimental to him.

EPILOGUE

A three-judge panel rejected a motion to declare him incompetent to stand trial. Subsequently, the defense attorney filed a plea of not guilty by reason of insanity. During the trial, the subject did not testify. The state law concerning insanity that was applied in this case reflects a composite of the *M'Naghten* (laboring under a defective reason from the disease of the mind as to not know the nature and quality of the act he was doing; or, if he did not know it, he did not know he was doing what was wrong) and *Durham* (insanity is considered the product of a mental disease or defect) decisions. He was found guilty on two counts of first-degree homicide. The death penalty was recommended in a separate sentencing trial. The last of three appeals caused the verdict to be set aside and a retrial ordered. In the new trial, he was found guilty of one count of first-degree homicide and a second count of second-degree homicide, but the sentencing trial yielded a recommendation of life imprisonment without the possibility of parole.

REFERENCES

Cruise, K. R., & Rogers, R. (1998). An analysis of competency to stand trial: An integration of case law and clinical knowledge. *Behavioral Sciences and the Law, 16*(1), 35–50.

Dusky v. United States, 362 U.S. 402 (1960).

Morse, S. J. (1999). Craziness and criminal responsibility. *Behavioral Sciences and the Law, 17*(2), 147–164.

Rogers, R. (1984). *Rogers Criminal Responsibility Assessment Scales (R-CRAS) and test manual.* Odessa, FL: Psychological Assessment Resources.

Rogers, R., Jackson, R. L., Sewell, K. W., & Harrison, K. S. (2004). An examination of the ECST-R as a screen for feigned incompetency to stand trial. *Psychological Assessment, 16*(2), 139–145.

Rogers, R., & Sewell, K. W. (1999). The R-CRAS and insanity evaluations: A re-examination of construct validity. *Behavioral Sciences and the Law, 17*(2), 181–194.

Rogers, R., Tillbrook, C. E., & Sewell, K. W. (1998). *Evaluation of Competency to Stand Trial-Revised (ECST-R).* Unpublished test. University of North Texas, Denton.

Rogers, R., Tillbrook, C. E., & Sewell, K. W. (2004). *Evaluation of Competency to Stand Trial-Revised (ECST-R).* Odessa, FL: Psychological Assessment Resources.

CHAPTER 16

Pain Problems in Personal Injury Litigation

C A S E   1 4

This 31-year-old woman was evaluated on behalf of an insurance company, under an agreement with her attorney, in conjunction with a pending lawsuit. Approximately six months ago, she was a passenger in a small car that was stopped at a red light when a bakery truck whose brakes failed struck it from behind. She and the driver of the car, a female friend, sustained whiplash injuries. Both were treated in the emergency room of a local hospital, and although the driver of the car was released, the woman in this case study was hospitalized overnight for further observation because she complained of severe neck and back pain. Physical and neurological examinations proved negative, and she was released with a neck brace and referred to an outpatient clinic specializing in bone and joint problems.

Three days after her first visit to the outpatient clinic, she began to experience sharp pains in her lower back and underwent further examinations including X-rays, an MRI, and a CT Scan. In the opinion of the attending physician, although the patient was in obvious discomfort, she probably tended to exaggerate the severity of the pain. She was prescribed medication for pain, told to rest, and appointments were made for her to begin physical therapy.

She wore the neck brace for approximately three weeks and was treated with physical therapy, involving exercise plus whirlpool and heat treatments, twice per week. According to reports from the physical therapist, she appeared to make satisfactory progress and voluntarily terminated her visits at the end of the third week. She denies this, stating that the physical therapy exacerbated her discomfort, and she decided to seek a second opinion from an orthopedic surgeon. After a second complete examination, the orthopedic surgeon concluded that she might have a compressed disk and prescribed anti-inflammatory and pain medication. He continued to see her at two-week intervals for three months and, at the end of that time, suggested cortisone injections to relieve the pain about which she continued to complain.

In the interim, she was contacted by the insurance company responsible for the bakery truck and offered a settlement that included all medical costs plus an additional "inconvenience payment" of $4,000. The driver of the car in which she had been a passenger accepted such a settlement, which also included replacement of the vehicle, but the subject declined to do so because of her persistent discomfort.

She claims that she is unable to pursue her activities as a homemaker and has been forced to engage temporary employment for both housecleaning and some cooking. She states that she is immobile much of the time. She says that the cortisone injections were of little use and has been referred to a second orthopedic surgeon who reports the possibility of a minor rupture to two disks. He believes that they may heal without intervention, but he also suggests that some form of surgery may be required.

In the context of her continuing discomfort, she has sought legal advice concerning her mounting expenses, and a letter of intent has been filed by her attorney calling for reimbursement for all medical and household expenses plus psychic injury damages in the amount of $300,000. After that letter was filed, the insurance company arranged for an orthopedic specialist and a neurologist to examine her independently. Both have reported negative findings, and the neurological consultant suggests the presence of a hysterical conversion reaction. Both physicians point out that if, in fact, a disk problem exists, it is extremely unlikely that the auto accident was the cause.

She is an only child. Her parents are both high school graduates. Her father, age 56, is the co-owner of a landscaping firm. Her mother, age 54, works as a housewife but held several waitressing jobs when the subject was in high school. She graduated from high school at age 18, and then completed three semesters at a local community college in a liberal arts curriculum. She withdrew to take employment as a salesperson in a large department store. She worked in that position for three years, at the end of which she was laid off because of a series of personnel cuts. She remained unemployed for approximately eight months and then accepted a position as a receptionist in a law firm. She worked at that job for approximately one year, leaving by mutual agreement. She has not been employed since that time.

She began dating her husband while employed at the law firm. He is an operator of a welding unit in a manufacturing production line specializing in large equipment. They were engaged for approximately six months and married shortly after her twenty-fourth birthday. She states that they did not want children "for awhile" but decided to begin a family when she was age 27. She has had two miscarriages, one at age 28 and the second at age 30, approximately six months prior to her accident. She states that she is not certain of their future plans concerning a family because of her current medical problems. She says that her husband has been very supportive throughout her period of distress but notes, "My depression has got on his nerves, too." She reports that she feels lethargic and that her continuing pain has sometimes caused their relationship to become more "distant."

The evaluation included the administration of the Halstead-Reitan Neuropsychological Battery, the MMPI-2, and the Rorschach. Her performance on all the Halstead-Reitan tests was within normal limits and the WAIS yielded a full-scale IQ of 111 (Verbal IQ = 113; Performance IQ = 108). The MMPI-2 Validity and Clinical scales show the following T-scores: Vrin (46), Trin (58), F (50), L (76), K (37), Hs (84), D (81), Hy (75), *Pd* (58), Mf (45), Pa (70), Pt (61), Sc (72), Ma (45), and Si (71). On the Content scales she has T-scores greater than 65 for anxiety (79), health concerns (81), cynicism (69), social discomfort (68), and work interference (82). The three-point code type is 1,2,3, which is sometimes referred to as a neurotic triad.

Assessment issues are: (1) Is it likely that the reported continuing pain is a product of a hysterical reaction or pain disorder? (2) How serious is the depression that she reports? (3) Are the data consistent with claims of a posttraumatic syndrome or other forms of psychic injury?

CASE FORMULATION AND RELEVANT LITERATURE

This woman reports continuing pain and increasing immobility in the six months that have passed since an automobile accident. She is moving toward a chronic pain syndrome, pain persisting continuously for more than six months and resulting in the need for long-term care (Miller & Kraus, 1990). Medical evaluations have been equivocal, but several physicians have suggested that her symptoms are more disabling than would be expected on the basis of physical findings. She has sought legal advice after refusing a settlement offered by the other driver's insurance company, and this evaluation is being done at the insurance company's request.

A comprehensive multimethod approach is indicated to respond to the referral questions, and the Rorschach can play a part in that process. Chapter 3 (Case 1) contains a general review of the Rorschach literature on somatic problems. Additionally, a review of the literature specific to pain syndromes will be helpful as the psychologist prepares a consultation.

Assessment of Pain Syndromes

Acklin and Alexander (1988) suggested that a core issue in psychosomatic difficulties is constrictedness and the inability to put emotions into words. They used Sifneos' (1973) concept of alexithymia to describe a trait syndrome that includes difficulty identifying and communicating emotions, confusion between emotional and somatic sensations, and difficulty moving beyond concrete, present-oriented cognitive operations. They tested psychosomatic patients with low back pain, gastrointestinal, dermatological, and headache complaints and found that, although all four groups differed significantly from nonpatients on a cluster of seven Rorschach constrictedness variables, there was considerable heterogeneity among the groups, with the low back pain patients composing the "benchmark alexithymic group" (p. 349). The seven Rorschach variables included low *R*, low *M*, low *WSumC*, low *FC*, low Blends, high *Lambda*, and low *EA*. These findings are similar to those of Leavitt and Garron (1982), who compared organic and functional low back pain patients and reported lower *SumC* and higher frequency of pure form (*F*) percepts in the functional group. Acklin and Alexander (1988) note that as constrictedness increases, pragmatic skill-oriented approaches that teach stress management and effective coping are most likely to be helpful.

In a related earlier study, Acklin and Bernat (1987) tested 33 chronic low back pain patients (length of complaints ranged from seven months to eight years) who had minimal or no demonstrable organic pathology. Approximately half of the patients were either receiving compensation or were planning litigation. Patients reporting head or neck pain were excluded from the study. The mean MMPI profile for the group fit in the 1-3 or "conversion V" code type, described by Graham (2000) as consistent with somatoform disorder diagnoses and characterized by a preference for medical explanations and minimal psychological insight.

Acklin and Bernat (1987) compared these low back pain patients with depressed inpatients and with a mixed personality disorder outpatient group. The low back pain patients were significantly lower on the Depression Index (DEPI) and all but one (Egocentricity Index) of its components, most constricted on the Rorschach alexithymia variables described earlier, and similar to the mixed personality-disordered outpatients on several *Comprehensive System* summary variables. The authors concluded that the low back pain patients could be distinguished from depressives and were actually more similar to the mixed personality disorder group.

Carlsson et al. (1993) studied patients with long-term patellofemoral (knee and thigh) pain syndrome and did not find the hypothesized Rorschach alexithymic characteristics. Carlsson (1987) compared 32 adult chronic pain patients with 20 nonpatient controls and found lower levels of emotional and intellectual control, lower ability to form positive interpersonal relationships, and higher levels of hostility in the pain patients. She speculated that these difficulties could impair ability to differentiate levels of pain intensity.

It is important to consider issues of response bias when evaluating self-reported pain syndromes in a forensic context. A multimethod approach that includes the MMPI-2 brings in data that can be specifically helpful in assessing potential malingering. Arbisi and Butcher (2004) note that the *DSM-IV* sets up a distinction between malingering, which is described as the intentional production of false or grossly exaggerated symptoms, and somatoform, conversion, and factitious disorders, which are not consciously intentional or motivated by external gain. The authors suggest that the ". . . dichotomy between intentional and unintentional production of symptoms and external versus internal incentive assumes that the conditions are mutually exclusive and sets up a false dichotomy that is unlikely to reflect clinical realities" (p. 384). Instead, as opposed to the oversimplistic malingered versus nonmalingered dichotomy, they suggest that psychological assessment can place individuals on a continuum that describes ". . . to what degree the individual is engaging in impression management and to what extent this is affecting the accuracy of the clinical presentation and self-report" (p. 384).

Arbisi and Butcher (2004) suggest first looking to see whether VRIN or TRIN are elevated beyond a T-Score of 80 as possibly suggesting lack of cooperation and then checking elevations on L, K, or S as representing overly virtuous self-presentation that deliberately omits potentially relevant information about psychological difficulties. They also describe a series of studies suggesting that ". . . factors tapped by an individual's response to the items on the Hysteria scale are associated with becoming disabled as a result of a work-related injury and remaining disabled after treatment" (p. 386).

Card	Response	Inquiry
I	1. It ll sthg dead, mayb lik a bird	**E:** (Rpts Ss response) **S:** Well it doesn't look lik its all there & its got holes in it **E:** Help me to c it lik u r **S:** Thes r wgs & a body but its all black & the holes & the wgs ll prts hav been torn off
	2. It cb an x-ray too, lik of the pelvis	**E:** (Rpts Ss response) **S:** I've had alot of em taken, thy hav ths shape & xys r all dark lik ths, some prts r grey & othrs r darkr, ur pelvis has wg lik thgs on it lik this & it has some holes lik ths too
II	3. It ll a cpl of dogs fighting, thy ll thyr both injured	**E:** (Rpts Ss response) **S:** Well u c thyr lik littl dogs, thy hav their noses togethr lik biting & ths red down here ll some bld, there's some on their coats too **E:** I'm not sur I'm seeg all of it lik u **S:** Don't count ths top red, just the bottm & their legs, & c thy hav splotches of red on their coats & here is where thry tryg to bite eo **E:** U said splotches of red on their coats **S:** C these red spots (points to red in D1)
	4. If u thk of the white in the cntr is lika rocket, ths red cb the flame lik when thy go up	**E:** (Rpts Ss response) **S:** Well it sorta ll those space ships, thy go off fr Fla., its lik pointed up lik it is taking off & this is the flame comg out of the back
	v5. Ths red here rem me of lungs	**E:** (Rpts Ss response) **S:** Thyr just tht shape & thyr all red, lik lungs r, thyr pink colord cuz thy hav bld in thm, tht makes thm pink lik ths
III	6. Ths ll an ad of ss, prob for men's formal wear	**E:** (Rpts Ss response) **S:** Well it ll the 2 guys r dressed in formal clothes, & thyr kinda leaning ovr ths thg in the middl c their arms & legs & the red decorations in the bckgrnd sort of to giv mor emphasis to the black tux's thyv got on, it's lik an ad for some rental place where u go to rent a tux
	7. Ths thgs up here (D2) ll sk of littl A's, just born, lik littl rats or mice	**E:** (Rpts Ss response) **S:** Thyr lik newborn rats or mice, thyr still all red lik when thy don't hav any hair & thy still hav the cord part attachd to thm, c the head & the littl body, thy look pretty helpless just layg there, I sur kno tht feeling
IV	8. It ll some big hairy monster lik he's sittg on a stool	**E:** (Rpts Ss response) **S:** Well he's got big legs & a littl head & he's got his arms just kinda hangin there, lik he's just sittg there takin a rest **E:** U said he is hairy? **S:** Oh yeah, c all thes lines in here r lik hair or fur (rubs card), it's lik one of thos creatures fr a science fict movies, mayb the big guy in Star Wars, Chabuka or smthg lik tht
	v9. Ths way it ll an eagle	**E:** (Rpts Ss response) **S:** Well its wgs r out lik eagles do when thy fly, spread out wide, I saw a thg on TV about thm when I was in the hospital, thy look so strong & thy can fly for a long time, just riding up & dwn on the currents & nothin bothrs thm, I wish I cb lik tht som day, nothin bothring me
V	10. Tht ll a bird too, he's got his wgs out too, lik he's flying	**E:** (Rpts Ss response) **S:** Well, its not lik the eagle but som othr bird, the wgs out here (points) & the body

(continued)

Card	Response	Inquiry
v11. Ths way it ll a bone of ss		E: (Rpts Ss response) S: I'm not sur wht kind, mayb the bones in your arm or leg, I thk I'v seen smthg lik ths in one of my xy's, yeah, now tht I thk of it mayb it's part of the pelvis E: I'm not clear wht makes it ll tht S: Well, it has tht arch to it & thes pointd parts (D9)
VI 12. Mayb its a cat tht got run ovr		E:(Rpts Ss response) S: It just ll one, the head & the whiskers & the legs out here, just spread out lik it was run ovr, there r black marks on the fur too, c his back is all furry (rubs) & it it has & it has these black markings (points to several dark areas in D1) lik from the tire prints or smthg
13. Ths top part is lik a flash of sharp pain		E: (Rpts Ss response) S: Well it ll wht u c in a cartoon to illustrate the presence of a sharp pain happening, with tht spiked part E: I'm not sur how ur seeing it S: Its just the way that pain is illustrated in cartoons, the spiked parts, lik in this instance it ll smbody's wrist or arm is in pain, when I look at it I almost feel lik I do sometimes when my back gets turned, real sharp pain, all the jagged parts
VII 14. Ths ll 2 littl girls sittg on a rock, lookg at eo		E: (Rpts Ss response) S: Its lik thyr squattg or sittg, lik mayb thv been playg & now thyr resting on some big rock, thy both hav pony tails & littl cute faces
<15. When I look ths way it ll a dog sniffg smthg, its the same on the othr side too		E: (Rpts Ss response) S: Well, thy hav a long tail & the ear & littl legs, a flat nose & it ll thyr sniffing smthg here (Dd23) I dk what it is, mayb a bush, dogs r always sniffing bushes
VIII 16. Tht re me of an MRI, u kno when thy put dye in u so thy can c ur organs & bones		E: (Rpts Ss response) S: It comes out all diff colors lik ths so thy can c where ur injured and thgs, altho thy don't always show everythg, I kno thy don't in mine E: I'm not quite sur how u'r seeg it S: Well, each color repres som prt or some bone, it really doesn't ll much, just insides
<17. When I look ths way I c an A lik a wolf, stepping on som stones, its all reflected down here		E: (Rpts Ss response) S: Well here he is, lik a wolf, c the head & legs & tail & he's stepping over these rocks & here is the wter, its blue & everythg is the same dwn here lik its reflected, he's going toward ths big green bush up here
v18. When I look ths way the red & orange parts ll jello		E: (Rpts Ss response) S: Ths prt with all the bright red & orange in it, it just rem me of jello E:I'm not sur wht maks it ll tht? S: Well its not just one color, there r several shades of red & orange, lik smbody mixed 2 kinds of jello togethr
IX 19. Ths ll a mask to me, one lik for halloween or a costume party		E: (Rpts Ss response) S: Well, it has the orange ears & big green cheeks, puffed out & ths pink dwn here is where the mouth is & there r little white slits for the eyes, I don't thk u cld c too well out of it

Card	Response	Inquiry
X	20. Thts lik anothr MRI, u can c the pelvic structure in ths one	**E:** (Rpts Ss response) **S:** It's sort of like the othr one, all diff colors to repres diff bones & organs & stuff, in ths one the top of the pelvic structure is here (D11) & it goes down along the pink areas, I dk wht the othr parts r, just nerves or organs
	v21. Ths way the blu prts ll crabs	**E:** (Rpts Ss response) **S:** Just a lot of legs, lik crabs hav
	v22. Thes yellow prts cb b canary birds	**E:** (Rpts Ss response) **S:** Thy hav the shape of birds & thyr yellow, lik a canary
	v23. Thes green parts ll seahorses but thy ll thyr connected at the bttm	**E:** (Rpts Ss response) **S:** Well, thy really do ll seahorses, thyr shaped lik tht but thyr connected, sort of lik siamese twin seahorses, ha,ha
	v24. Ths littl brown thg ll a seed, lik the one's tht come dwn fr a tree when the leaves die off	**E:** (Rpts Ss response) **S:** I dk wht kind of tree, oak I guess, thy hav ths shape to thm & I thk thyr brown too, thy r part of the dead leaf, lik dropping off & some take root & make a new tree

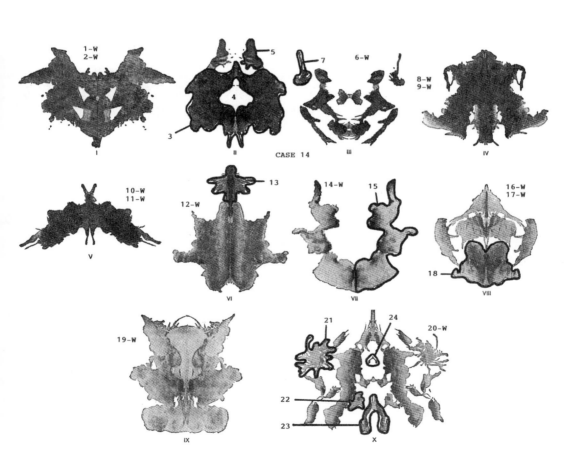

CASE 14

329

Case 14.   Sequence of Scores.

Card	No.	Loc.	No.	Determinant(s)	(2)	Content(s)	Pop	Z	Special Scores
I	1	WSo	1	FC'o		Ad		3.5	MOR
	2	WSo	1	FYo		Xy		3.5	PER
II	3	D+	6	FMa.CFo	2	A,Bl	P	3.0	AG,MOR,PHR
	4	DS+	5	ma.CFo		Sc,Fi		4.5	
	5	Do	2	FC–		An			
III	6	W+	1	Mp.C.FD.FC'o	2	Art,H,Cg,Id	P	5.5	GHR
	7	Do	2	FC.FMpo	2	A			INC
IV	8	W+	1	FT.Mpo		(H),Hh	P	4.0	GHR
	9	Wo	1	FMau		A		2.0	PER,DR
V	10	Wo	1	FMao		A		1.0	
	11	Wo	1	Fo		An		1.0	PER
VI	12	Wo	1	FT.FC'o		A	P	2.5	MOR
	13	D+	3	Mpu		Art,Hd,Hx		2.5	MOR,AB,PHR
VII	14	W+	1	Mpo	2	H,Ls	P	2.5	GHR
	15	W+	1	FMpo	2	A,Bt		2.5	
VIII	16	Wv	1	CFo		Xy			PER
	17	W+	1	FMa.Fr.CFo		A,Na	P	4.5	
	18	Dv	2	C.Y		Fd			
IX	19	WSo	1	FCo		(Hd)		5.5	GHR
X	20	Wo	1	CF–		An		5.5	
	21	Do	1	Fo	2	A	P		
	22	Do	2	FCu	2	A			
	23	D+	10	Fo	2	A		4.0	FAB
	24	Do	3	FCo		Bt			MOR

Case 14. Structural Summary.

Location Features	Determinants — Blends	Determinants — Single	Contents	S-Constellation
				NO . . .FV+VF+V+FD>2
			H = 2	YES . .Col-Shd Bl>0
Zf = 17	FM.CF	M = 2	(H) = 1	YES . .Ego<.31,>.44
ZSum = 57.5	m.CF	FM = 3	Hd = 1	YES . .MOR > 3
ZEst = 56.0	M.C.FD.FC′	m = 0	(Hd) = 1	NO . . .Zd > +− 3.5
	FC.FM	FC = 4	Hx = 1	NO . . .es > EA
W = 14	FT.M	CF = 2	A = 10	YES . .CF+C > FC
D = 10	FT.FC′	C = 0	(A) = 0	NO . . .X+% < .70
W+D = 24	FM.Fr.CF	Cn = 0	Ad = 1	YES . .S > 3
Dd = 0	C.Y	FC′ = 1	(Ad) = 0	NO . . .P < 3 or > 8
S = 4		C′F = 0	An = 3	YES . .Pure H < 2
		C′ = 0	Art = 2	NO . . .R < 17
		FT = 0	Ay = 0	6 . . . .TOTAL
DQ		TF = 0	Bl = 1	**Special Scores**
+ = 9		T = 0	Bt = 2		Lvl	Lv2
o = 13		FV = 0	Cg = 1	DV = 0x1	0x2
v/+ = 0		VF = 0	Cl = 0	INC = 1x2	0x4
v = 2		V = 0	Ex = 0	DR = 1x3	0x6
		FY = 1	Fd = 1	FAB = 1x4	0x7
		YF = 0	Fi = 1	ALOG = 0x5	
		Y = 0	Ge = 0	CON = 0x7	
Form Quality		Fr = 0	Hh = 1	Raw Sum6 = 3	
		rF = 0	Ls = 1	Wgtd Sum6 = 0	

	FQx	MQual	W+D				
+	= 0	= 0	= 0	Na = 1			
o	= 18	= 3	= 18	Sc = 1	AB = 1	GHR = 4	
u	= 3	= 1	= 3	Sx = 0	AG = 1	PHR = 2	
−	= 2	= 0	= 2	Xy = 2	COP = 0	MOR = 5	
none	= 1	= 0	= 1	Id = 1	CP = 0	PER = 4	
			(2) = 8			PSV = 0	

Ratios, Percentages, and Derivations

R = 24	L = 0.14			FC:CF+C = 5:7	COP = 0 AG = 1	
				Pure C = 2	GHR:PHR = 4:2	
EB = 4:10.5	EA = 14.5	EBPer = 2.6		SumC′:WSumC = 3:10.5	a:p = 5:6	
eb = 7:7	es = 14	D = 0		Afr = 0.60	Food = 1	
	Adj es = 13	Adj D = 0		S = 4	SumT = 2	
				Blends:R = 8:24	Hum Con = 5	
FM = 6	C′ = 3	T = 2		CP = 0	Pure H = 2	
m = 1	V = 0	Y = 2			PER = 4	
					Iso Indx = 0.21	

a:p = 5:6	Sum6 = 3	XA% = 0.88	Zf = 17.0	3r+(2)/R = 0.46
Ma:Mp = 0:4	Lv2 = 0	WDA% = 0.88	W:D:Dd = 14:10:0	Fr+rF = 1
2AB+Art+Ay = 4	WSum6 = 9	X−% = 0.08	W:M = 14:4	SumV = 0
MOR = 5	M− = 0	S− = 0	Zd = +1.5	FD = 1
	Mnone = 0	P = 7	PSV = 0	An+Xy = 5
		X+% = 0.75	DQ+ = 9	MOR = 5
		Xu% = 0.13	DQv = 2	H:(H)Hd(Hd) = 2:3

PTI = 0	DEPI = 4	CDI = 2	S-CON = 6	HVI = No	OBS = No

S-CON AND KEY VARIABLES

The S-CON (6) offers no meaningful finding. The first positive Key variable is a reflection response, indicating that the interpretation should begin with a study of data concerning self-perception, interpersonal perception, and controls. The remaining order for the interpretive routine, affect, processing, mediation, and ideation, is suggested by the second positive Key variable, the *EB*, which indicates an extratensive coping style.

SELF-PERCEPTION

Case 14.   Self-Perception Related Data for a 31-Year-Old Female.

R	= 24	OBS	= No	HVI = No	Human Content, Hx, An & Xy Responses
					I 2. WSo FYo Xy 3.5 PER
Fr+rF	= 1	3r+(2)/R	= 0.46		II 5. Do FC– An
					III 6. W+ Mp.C.FD.FC'o 2 Art,H,Hh,Id P 5.5 GHR
FD	= 1	SumV	= 0		IV 8. W+ FT.Mpo (H),Hh P 4.0 GHR
					V 11. Wo Fo An 1.0 PER
An+Xy	= 5	MOR	= 5		VI 13. D+ Mpu Art,Hd,Hx 2.5 MOR,AB,PHR
					VII 14. W+ Mpo 2 H,Ls P 2.5 GHR
H:(H)+Hd+(Hd) = 2:3					VIII 16. Wv CFó Xy PER
[EB = 4:10.5]					IX 19. WSo FCo (Hd) 5.5 GHR
					X 20. Wo CF– An 5.5

The presence of a reflection answer indicates an exaggerated self-involvement and an inflated sense of personal worth. This is a traitlike feature that often prompts an excessive use of defenses to protect personal integrity. One of the most prominent of these is externalization or rationalization of causes for unwanted or unwelcome events. The Egocentricity Index (.46) is slightly above average, which is also commensurate with considerable self-involvement. On a more positive note, there is an *FD* response in her protocol, intimating that she probably engages in self-inspecting behaviors routinely.

The presence of five *An+Xy* contents is striking and connotes a marked body concern. This is not surprising in light of her physical complaints. Similarly, the presence of five MOR answers is not unexpected. It implies that her self-image includes some negative attributions and a sense of fragility or damage. These findings may seem somewhat contrary to her previously noted inflated notion of personal worth, but that is not necessarily true. They could simply represent state-related preoccupations associated with the pain and trauma about which she complains. On the other hand, they might also reflect a more persistent psychological set to exaggerate any miseries that she experiences. In either event, they emphasize an injury or insult to her high self-regard.

The fact that only two of her five human content answers are pure *H* implies that her self-image includes many features based on imagination or distortions of real experiences. This suggests that her self-awareness may be limited or naive. In a related context, her record contains an *Hx* answer (response 13, *D+ Mpu Art, Hd, Hx 2.5*, MOR, *AB, PHR*). Usually, *Hx* responses, especially those that include an AB special score, signify tendencies to contend with issues of self-image or self-regard in an overly intellectualized manner that ignores or distorts reality. The codings for her other four human content responses are more favorable. Even though one is a color shading blend (response 6, *W+ Mp.C.FD.FC'o 2 Art, H, Cg, Id P 5.5, GHR*), all include appropriate form quality and none have negative special scores.

Both of her *FQ* minus responses involve anatomy (Card II, response 5), "lungs . . . pink colored cause they have blood in them," and (Card X, response 20), "another MRI, you can see the pelvic structure . . . all different colors to represent different bones and organs." They signify that her preoccupation can promote some distortions of reality. Her five MOR responses all involve death or injury. The first (Card I, response 1) is, "something dead, maybe like a bird . . . it's got holes in it . . . the wings look like parts have been torn off." The second (Card II, response 3) is, "dogs fighting, they look like they are both injured . . . they have splotches of red in their coats and here is where they are trying to bite each other." The third (Card VI, response 12) is, "a cat that got run over . . . just spread out like it was run over, there are black markings on the fur, too . . . like from tire prints or something."

The fourth is the most idiographic of the five MOR answers (Card VI, response 13), "a flash of sharp pain . . . what you see in a cartoon to illustrate the presence of sharp pain happening . . . when I look at it I almost feel like I do sometimes when my back gets turned, real sharp pain." It is an unusually dramatic self-representation that emphasizes her reported misery, but it also may reflect a set to simulate or exaggerate that condition.

The final MOR (Card X, response 24) is, "a seed, like the ones that come down from a tree when the leaves die off . . . they are part of the dead leaf . . . and some take root and make a new tree." It is the most optimistic of the MOR answers, raising the possibility of "a new tree."

Four of her five human content responses contain *M.* One of the four (flash of sharp pain) has been reviewed. The remaining three are far less dramatic, but notable for the passivity that each conveys. The first (Card III, response 6) is, "an ad some sort, probably for men's formal wear . . . two guys are dressed in formal clothes . . . leaning over this thing in the middle . . . the red decorations in the background sort of to give more emphasis to the black tux's they've got on . . . like an ad for some rental place." It is commensurate with her high sense of personal worth. The second (Card IV, response 8) is, "some big hairy monster like he's sitting on a stool . . . a little head and he's got his arms just hanging there, like he's sitting taking a rest." The third (Card VII, response 14) is, "little girls sitting on a rock, looking at each other . . . maybe they've been playing and now they are resting . . . both have pony tails and cute little faces." Her remaining human content answer (Card IX, response 19) is, "a mask, like one for Halloween or a costume party . . . little white slits for the eyes, I don't think you could see too well out of it." It is a concealment answer made more interesting because of the limited vision aspect.

The first of her six *FM* answers (dogs fighting) has already been reviewed. The remaining five includes an interesting mix of verbiage and contents. The second (Card III, response 7) is, "little animals, just born, like little rats or mice . . . they're still all red like when they don't have any hair and they still have the cord attached to them . . . they look pretty helpless just laying there, I sure know that feeling." It conveys immaturity and emphasizes a sense of helplessness. The third (Card IV, response 9) is, "an eagle . . . its wings are out like eagles do when they fly . . . they look so strong . . . just riding up and down the currents and nothing bothers them, I wish I could be like that some day, nothing bothering me." In this answer, she indirectly uses a high status bird to emphasize her own difficulties.

Her fourth *FM* answer is more benign (Card V, response 10), "a bird, too, he's got his wings out too, like he's flying . . . it's not an eagle but some other bird." The fifth (Card VII, response 15) seems to imply caution, "a dog sniffing something . . . I don't know what it is, maybe a bush, dogs are always sniffing bushes." The last (Card VIII, response 17) is her reflection response, "an animal like a wolf, stepping on some stones, it's all reflected down here." Her single *m* response (Card II, response 4) is, "a rocket, this red could be the flame like when they go up." It is a common response and does not contain any obvious projected features.

Seven responses have not been reviewed. The first three of these are *An* and *Xy* answers, and all convey vulnerability as well as give emphasis to her physical problems. The first (Card I, response 2) is, "an X-ray, like of the pelvis. . . . I've had a lot of them taken, they have this shape . . . your pelvis has wing things on it like this and it has some holes like this too." The second (Card V, response 11) is, "a bone of some sort. . . . I've seen something like this one in my X-rays, yeah, now that I think of it maybe its part of the pelvis." The third (Card VIII, response 16) is, "an MRI, you know when they put dye in you so they can see your organs and bones . . . all different colors like this so they can see where you're injured and things, although they don't always show everything, I know they don't in mine." The redundant self-reference in each appears to represent a set to emphasize her difficulties.

The other four answers are more benign for clear projections. The first (Card VIII, response 18) is probably the most intriguing: "The red and orange parts look like Jell-O . . . like somebody mixed two kinds of Jell-O together." It is a color shading blend that is void of form requirements and may suggest a sense of diffuseness regarding the self. The next two (Card X, responses 21 & 22) are "the blue parts look like crabs," and "yellow parts could be canary birds." Both seem to be straightforward descriptions of the distal elements of the figure. The fourth (Card X, response 23) is "seahorses, but they are connected at the bottom . . . sort of like Siamese twin seahorses, ha, ha." It is a concrete response that, in the inquiry, she contends with in a defensively playful manner.

The composite of findings does not present a clear picture of her self-concept. On the one hand, she seems to be self-involved and regards herself very favorably. There is also some evidence suggesting that she deals with her self-image in an intellectually defensive manner that permits her to avoid that her self-awareness may be limited or naive. On the other hand, she also conveys a marked body concern and a distinct sense of fragility, vulnerability, and damage. These features may be state-related preoccupations, associated with the pain and trauma about which she complains. However, she may have emphasized or exaggerated her problems and concerns, consciously or unconsciously, as a way of calling attention to the failure of others to acknowledge and correct the insult she has experienced.

INTERPERSONAL PERCEPTION

Case 14.   Interpersonal Perception Data for a 31-Year-Old Female.

R	= 24	CDI	= 2	HVI	= No	**COP & AG Responses**
a:p	= 5:6	SumT	= 2	Fd	= 1	II 3. D+ FMa.CFo 2 A,Bl P 3.0 AG,MOR,PHR
		[eb	= 7:7]			
Sum Human Contents = 5				H	= 2	
[Style = Extratensive]						
GHR:PHR = 4:2						
COP = 0		AG	= 1	PER	= 4	
Isolation Indx = 0.21						

The $a:p$ ratio (5:6) is marginal. It hints at, but is not clearly indicative of passivity. However, other data tend to support that notion. For instance, during the review of the self-perception data, it was noted that all four of her M responses are passive. This is unusual and typically occurs only when a marked interpersonally passive style is present. A second datum that supports the likelihood of passivity is the food response. It implies that she is likely to exhibit more dependency behaviors than usually is expected for an adult and suggests that she is inclined to rely on others for direction and support. Persons who hold themselves in high regard, and who also have passive-dependent features, typically expect others to acknowledge and be tolerant of their needs and demands and to take action in accord with those needs and demands.

Her protocol includes two texture answers, signaling substantial needs for emotional closeness. A finding such as this is usually related to a recent emotional loss, but there is no clear indication of this in the history. She states that her husband has been very supportive, but notes, "My depression has got on his nerves, too," adding that her pain has caused their relationship to become, "more distant." This may hint at problems that could breed loneliness. However, it is also likely that her strong needs for closeness may be chronic and related to her dependent style and her self-centeredness.

The five human contents suggest that she is interested in people, but only two of these are pure H indicating that she may not understand them very well. On the other hand, the GHR:PHR ratio (4:2) connotes that most of her interpersonal behaviors are likely to be adaptive for the situation. A more negative finding is the absence of COP responses, implying that she may not anticipate interactions that are routinely positive. If this is true, she may feel less comfortable in social situations than might be expected, and may be perceived by others to be distant or aloof.

The four PER answers provide some support for this postulate. They intimate that she tends to lack confidence in social situations and defends herself against these concerns by a form of intellectualizing that may cause others to perceive her as narrow minded. However, three of the four PER answers involve An or Xy contents and could be by-products of her previously noted tendency to emphasize her difficulties. Thus, it seems improbable that she is intellectually forceful with others. In fact, four of her five M and FM responses that contain pairs are passive (an ad for men's formal wear; little animals just born; little girls sitting; a dog sniffing). They also tend to support the notion that she is rather passive in her social interactions.

Overall, it seems probable that her interpersonal world is noticeably marked by passive and dependent behaviors that are probably adaptive, but that may also be somewhat superficial. Although she is interested in people, she does not seem to understand them very well. Her tendency to be overly concerned with herself and her passive dependent orientation are likely to limit the extent to which she can develop enduring relationships with others, except those who will be directly supportive for her.

CONTROLS

Case 14.   **Control-Related Variables for a 31-Year-Old Female.**

EB = 4:10.5	EA = 14.5		D = 0	CDI = 2
eb = 7:7	es = 14	Adj es = 13	AdjD = 0	L = 0.14
FM = 6 m = 1	SumC$'$ = 3	SumT = 2	SumV = 0	SumY = 2

The Adj D Score is zero and the CDI value is two. This indicates that her capacity of control and tolerance for stress is similar to that of most other adults. There is no obvious reason to challenge this assumption. The *EA* (14.5) is above average and derived from an *EB* (4:10.5) that has no zero values.

The Adj *es* (13) is higher than usually expected, mainly because of elevations in *FM* (6), *SumC'* (3), and *SumT* (2). At least two of these, *FM* and *SumT,* represent an atypical level of neediness and loneliness that may have a situational cause. Assuming that may be true, it seems reasonable to speculate that, under different circumstances, the Adj *es* could be significantly lower. If so, the Adj D Score would likely fall into the plus range and indicate a sturdier capacity for control and tolerance for stress than is currently indicated by the Adj D Score of zero.

AFFECT

Case 14.   Affect-Related Data for a 31-Year-Old Female.

								Blends	
EB	= 4:10.5			EBPer	= 2.6				
eb	= 7:7	L	= 0.14	FC:CF+C	= 5:7			M.C.FD.FC'	= 1
DEPI	= 4	CDI	= 2	Pure C	= 2			FM.Fr.CF	= 1
								FM.CF	= 1
SumC' = 3	SumT = 2			SumC':WSumC	= 3:10.5			FC.FM	= 1
SumV = 0	SumY = 2			Afr	= 0.60			m.CF	= 1
								C.Y	= 1
Intellect	= 4	CP	= 0	S = 4 (S to I,II,III	= 3)			FT.M	= 1
Blends:R	= 8:24			Col-Shad Bl	= 2			FT.FC'	= 1
m + y Bl	= 2			Shading Bl	= 1				

The *EB* (4:10.5) indicates that emotions play a significant role in her decision making. In effect, she has an intuitive coping style in which her feelings merge with and exert a noticeable influence on her thinking. She is likely to use trial-and-error tactics to test out her assumptions or decisions and is prone to display her feelings openly much of the time. Usually, there is no reason to suspect that this approach to coping may not be successful. However, the value for *EBPer* (2.6) signifies that she tends to persist in this approach, even where it is apparent that some delay and thoughtfulness might be more effective. This lack of flexibility in her approach to coping and making decisions can be a liability for her at times.

The DEPI value (4) offers no definitive evidence of affective disarray. However, the right side value of the *eb* (7) is substantial and is likely related to some of the distress and depression that she reports. It consists of noticeable elevations in *SumT* (2) and *SumC'* (3), plus two answers that contain diffuse shading. As noted, the texture responses are associated with irritating feelings caused by emotional neediness or loneliness. The diffuse shading responses are likely to be situationally provoked and indicative of feelings arising from a sense of helplessness.

The achromatic color responses are the most surprising of this group as they convey negative feelings caused by the constraint or suppression of feelings. This is somewhat contrary to her pervasive extratensive coping style, in which the release or display of feelings is customary. Apparently, she is experiencing some emotions that she is unwilling or unable to share openly. There is no reason to believe that she uses this tactic to excess as the *SumC'* : *SumC* ratio (3:10.5) provides no indications of unusual emotional constraint. However, the finding is interesting and should not be neglected as other interpretive postulates are formed.

The *Afr* value (.60) falls within the expected range for an extratensive person and intimates that she is as willing as most others to process and become involved with emotional stimuli. However, that willingness may be more selective than implied. The Intellectualization Index (4) is slightly elevated, and suggests that she is prone to neutralize or deny the impact of some unwanted emotions or emotional situations by dealing with them on an intellectual rather than an affective level. Her protocol also contains an *Hx* response, which connotes a tendency to deal with matters of self-image in an overly intellectualized manner that often disregards or distorts reality. These findings support the conclusion that intellectualization is an important defensive tactic for her. This finding has importance because an issue has been raised about the possibility of a hysterical reaction. It does not confirm that assumption, but an excessive use of intellectualization, as a major defense, is common among those with hysteroid features.

Interestingly, the *FC:CF+C* ratio (5:7) indicates that she is prone to be obvious or intense when displaying her emotions. This is not unusual for a pervasively extratensive person. However, the presence of two Pure *C* determinants denotes that she may be overly lax at times about modulating her emotional displays. This might convey the impression of immaturity or impulsiveness to others, but that seems unlikely as both of her Pure *C* responses (red decorations, Jell-O mixed together) have more of an intellectual than uncontrolled or primitive quality.

Her protocol also includes four *S* responses, implying that she is disposed to be somewhat more negative or oppositional about her environment than might be expected. This may have a relation to her current situation and could account for the previously noted tendency to constrain or suppress her feelings at times. On the other hand, it may reflect a persistent dissatisfaction with her life in general and could relate to her tendency to intellectualize excessively.

Her record includes eight blend responses (33%), which is not unusual for an extratensive person, and indicates that she is no more psychologically complex than might be expected. Two of these (*m.CF* and *C.Y*) appear to be situationally related, connoting that her current level of complexity is somewhat greater than usual. However, there are three blends that deserve special attention. Two of these are color shading blends (*Mp.C.FD.FC'* and *C.Y*), suggesting that she may often be confused by her feelings, and this may create difficulties for her in bringing closure to emotional situations. The third is a shading blend (*FT.FC'*) and indicates very painful emotions. One of the two determinants in this shading blend is texture, and may indicate that her emotional neediness or loneliness is very irritating and disruptive. It raises a question about her relationship with her husband, which she has described as "distant," while noting that her depression has been troublesome for him.

The findings concerning her affect reveal that she is quite involved with her feelings, and they influence her routinely in making decisions. Although this intuitive approach to coping can be effective, her lack of flexibility concerning its applications can become a liability. Typically, she displays her feelings openly, and often may convey an impression that she is less mature than is the case. However, she also has an unexpected tendency to intellectualize emotions and sometimes constrain or suppress her feelings. She probably uses these tactics to avoid some of the more confusing and painful experiences of distress that she experiences, and they may also relate to a sense of irritation or anger that she may have about her environment. There is no clear evidence of depression, but her distress, which seems related mainly to a sense of emotional neediness or loneliness, is considerable.

PROCESSING

Case 14.   Processing Variables for a 31-Year-Old Female.

EB	= 4:10.5	Zf	= 17	Zd	= +1.5	DQ+	= 9
L	= 0.14	W:D:Dd	= 14:10:0	PSV	= 0	DQv/+	= 0
HVI	= No	W:M	= 14:4			DQv	= 2
OBS	= No						

Location & DQ Sequencing

I: WSo.WSo	VI: Wo.D+
II: D+.DS+.Do	VII: W+.W+
III: W+.Do	VIII: Wv.W+.Dv
IV: W+.Wo	IX: WSo
V: Wo.Wo	X: Wo.Do.Do.D+.Do

The Zf (17) and $W:D:Dd$ ratio (14:10:0) indicate that she makes a considerable effort to process information. The location sequence is consistent, and reveals that she gave W answers as first responses to 9 of the 10 figures. The $W:M$ ratio (14:4) is somewhat disproportionate and implies that she may sometimes strive to accomplish more than may be realistic in light of her functional capabilities. The Zd of +1.5 is in the expected range and connotes that her scanning activities are similar to those of most people.

Nine of her 24 responses are synthesized, indicating that the quality of her processing is usually good and often complex. However, two of her answers are coded as DQv. This is unexpected, and indicates that her processing may become flawed at times. These DQv answers were given as the first and third responses to Card VIII, raising the possibility that her processing quality is most likely to falter under conditions in which she has difficulties dealing with emotional stimulation. Added support for that premise is that only two of the nine responses given to the fully chromatic figures, VIII, IX, and X, were synthesized; whereas there were seven $DQ+$ answers among the 15 responses given to the first seven figures. Although this problem may reduce the quality of her processing at times, it does not appear to cause marked impairment and, generally, her processing activities are respectable.

MEDIATION

Case 14.   Mediation Variables for a 31-Year-Old Female.

R = 24		L = 0.14		OBS = No	**Minus & NoForm Features**
FQx+	= 0		XA%	= .88	II 5. Do FC– An
FQxo	= 18		WDA%	= .88	VIII 18. Dv C.Y Fd
FQxu	= 3		X–%	= .08	X 20. Wo CF– An 5.5
FQx–	= 2		S–	= 0	
FQxnone	= 1				
(W+D	= 24)		P	= 7	
WD+	= 0		X+%	= .75	
WDo	= 18		Xu%	= .13	
WDu	= 3				
WD–	= 2				
WDnone	= 1				

The *XA%* (.88) and *WDA%* (.88) are both well within the expected range and denote that her translations of information are usually appropriate for the situation. This finding implies that her reality testing can be expected to be adequate most of the time. However, there is one NoForm answer (*C.Y.* Jell-O) in the record, suggesting that processing may be impeded at times by unusually strong emotions, especially those related to her dependency needs.

In a related context, there are two minus answers, both of which include chromatic color, that yield a modest *X−%* of .08. Usually this would be no cause for concern, but both are *An* answers (lungs & an MRI of the pelvic structure and other organs). Neither of these are severe distortions, but they suggest that her current somatic preoccupations may also promote some disregard for or create distortions of reality.

A more positive finding is the presence of seven Popular answers, signifying that expected or acceptable behaviors are likely to occur when the cues for those behaviors are obvious. Similarly, the value for the *X+%* (.75) is substantial, whereas the value for the *Xu%* (.13) is relatively modest. These data support the premise that she has a noticeable proclivity to formulate behaviors in accord with social expectations or demands.

Overall, the mediational findings are favorable. They suggest that her reality testing usually is adequate. There are indications that she may disregard or distort reality occasionally, when under substantial emotional provocation, or when her body concerns become overly influential in her conceptual thinking. However, these events do not appear to occur frequently and probably have only a limited impact on the potential effectiveness of her behaviors.

IDEATION

Case 14. Ideation Variables for a 31-Year-Old Female.

L	= 0.14	OBS	= No	HVI	= No	**Critical Special Scores**			
						DV	= 0	DV2	= 0
EB	= 4:10.5	EBPer	= 2.6	a:p	= 5:6	INC	= 1	INC2	= 0
				Ma:Mp	= 0:4	DR	= 1	DR2	= 0
eb	= 7:7	[FM = 6 m = 1]				FAB	= 1	FAB2	= 0
				M−	= 0	ALOG	= 0	CON	= 0
Intell Indx	= 4	MOR	= 5	Mnone	= 0	Sum6	= 3	WSum6	= 9
							(R = 24)		

M Response Features

III   6. W+ Mp.C.FD.FC′o 2 Art,H,Cg,Id P 5.5 GHR
IV   8. W+ FT.Mpo (H),Hh P 4.0 GHR
VI 13. D+ Mpu Art,Hd,Hx 2.5 MOR,AB,PHR
VII 14. W+ Mpo H,Ls 2.5 GHR

As noted, the *EB* (4:10.5) indicates that her emotions influence her thinking considerably, and her decision making will usually be marked by intuitive judgments. The *EBPer* (2.6) suggests that this is a pervasive inflexible coping approach. She typically employs a trial-and-error method of solving problems and relies on external feedback to evaluate her judgments. Even though somewhat inflexible, this form of coping can be effective if her thinking is not impaired and her emotions are not overly intense.

A more negative characteristic of her thinking is signified by the five MOR responses in her protocol. They have been discussed with regard to her self-image but also have considerable importance here. They denote the presence of a pessimistic set that prompts her to conceptualize her relationship to the environment in cynical ways, anticipating unfavorable or unwanted outcomes regardless of her own efforts. This set reflects a sense of discouragement that may be situationally related or may be a chronic characteristic in her psychology. In either event, it can lead to narrow or concrete judgments that reduce the quality of her thinking considerably.

Another relevant finding in this data set is the slightly elevated left side *eb* (7). It represents six *FM* answers and one *m*. The latter is of no special concern, but the former suggests the presence of more internal need states than is typical. They are probably causing excess peripheral mental activity, and this increases the possibility of some interference with her attention and concentration activities. This finding is not necessarily detrimental but, when considered in tandem with her pessimistic set, it may reduce the overall quality of her thinking.

Another negative finding concerning her thinking is the *Ma:Mp* ratio (0:4). It indicates that she has a marked tendency to use flights into fantasy as a routine way to deal with unpleasantness. In doing so, she avoids responsibilities and the necessity to make decisions, substituting a self-imposed form of passiveness that only serves to increase her dependence on others. As noted, the elevated Intellectualization Index (4) plus the presence of an *Hx* answer indicate an excessive use of intellectualization to contend with unwanted emotions or to defend the integrity of her self-image.

This impressive composite of defenses strongly suggests that she often tends to bend, ignore, or defy reality. This may seem to contradict the findings concerning mediation indicating that she is a reality-oriented person, but that is not really true. Her defenses usually come into play when she is confronted by threatening or unwanted events. In those instances, these defenses divert her attention from the threats and substitute something more positive and manageable. When threats to her integrity do not occur, she is likely to use her thinking more directly to deal with the events in her everyday life.

Actually, her thinking seems to be reasonably clear. Her record contains only three critical special scores, and none represent serious cognitive slips. The first (Card III, response 7) is coded INCOM because she attributes the presence of a cord to newborn rats or mice. The second (Card IV, response 9) is coded *DR* because of her detachment from the task, "I wish I could be like that someday, nothing bothering me." The last (Card X, response 23) is coded *FABCOM* for her report of seahorses connected, "like Siamese twin seahorses, ha, ha." The *WSum6* of 9 signals more faulty thinking than expected of an adult. However, although the coded components of answers represent inappropriate thinking, they seem to connote immaturity rather than a noticeable thinking problem.

All of her *M* responses include the appropriate use of form, supporting the notion that her thinking is reasonably clear. In addition, the quality of those answers ranges from the commonplace (hairy monster sitting on a stool; little girls sitting on a rock) to a more sophisticated level (an ad for men's formal wear; a flash of sharp pain . . . like somebody's wrist or arm is in pain).

That her thinking seems clear can be an asset for her, but aspects of it do not work to her advantage. The most distinctive of these is a marked pessimism that tends to breed doubt, discouragement, and the anticipation that her actions will have little influence on the outcome of events. This set may be situationally related, but more likely represents a persistent kind of thinking that has been exacerbated by recent events.

The underpinnings of this set seem to have been created by her passiveness and tendency to be dependent on others for decisions and direction. These behaviors provide a safe haven in many circumstances, but because they are not fully protective or rewarding, she has developed a rather elaborate system of defense. It involves an abusive use of fantasy and an excessive tendency to deal with emotions intellectually. Both of these tactics require her to divert her thinking from real world issues far too much and, as a result, her level of conceptual thought has tended to remain less mature than probably could be the case.

SUMMARY

This woman presents a psychological picture that is made somewhat more complex than might usually be the case because of her noticeable preoccupation with her physical well-being or lack thereof. Basically, she is a very self-centered person who tends to hold herself in high regard. However, she also feels fragile, vulnerable, and in considerable distress, and it is difficult to distinguish whether most of this relates to her current physical complaints or to long-standing issues.

She seems to be a very passive and dependent person who is inclined to rely on others for support and reassurance and expects them to be tolerant and accepting of her. Although her social behaviors are likely to be adaptive, her relationships also are likely to be superficial except with those who are very supportive. Ordinarily, she has adequate capacities for control and can tolerate stress well. Her feelings are quite influential on her thinking, and this orients her to a decision-making style in which intuition plays a significant role. She is not flexible about this coping approach, and at times, it can be less effective than she might desire. She is prone to express many of her emotions openly and often intensely, which may sometimes convey the impression that she is immature or impulsive, but neither of those assumptions is correct.

She is a very defensive person who works hard to avoid or deny unpleasant feelings much of the time. She does this mainly by using either of two defensive tactics. The first is intellectualization, which permits her to deny the presence of unwanted feelings, or deal with them in a manner that reduces their intensity. The second involves flights into fantasy during which she replaces the real world situation with ones that are more favorable and easily managed. At the same time, she is also quite concerned with behaving in socially acceptable or appropriate ways, and when her primary defenses seem inappropriate or ineffective in dealing with unwanted emotions, she will often constrain or suppress them. This seems most likely to occur when she experiences irritation or anger concerning her environment.

She is a needy and probably lonely person, but it is unclear whether this is a long-standing issue or has evolved because of her physical problems. In either event, these negative feelings compound her sense of fragility and vulnerability, and contribute to a markedly pessimistic set that she now has about herself. This set has a substantial influence on her thinking and breeds doubt and discouragement. Nonetheless, her thinking is reasonably clear and her overall cognitive operations are intact. She works hard to process information and usually does so effectively, and despite her defensiveness, her reality testing seems appropriate.

There is no question that she is in considerable distress, which she attributes to her physical difficulties. Some of this may be related directly to her purported injuries and the failures of others to contend effectively with them. The latter can be particularly irritating for a person who holds herself in high regard and is accustomed to relying on others for support and reassurance. On the other hand, many of the basic ingredients that are contributing to her distress may have existed for a much longer time.

For instance, the elaborate defenses that she has developed to deal with unwanted feelings may not be working well in her current situation and it is unlikely that she has developed a very broad social network on which to rely. She does not understand people well and is prone to be aloof or distant from most people, except those on whom she can depend for support. If those supports have wavered or are perceived by her to be insufficient, her discomfort will have increased considerably.

RECOMMENDATIONS

Legal consultations can be intricate depending on the objectives. In this instance, an insurance company representative has requested the referral with the obvious objective of avoiding a large settlement. A basic question raised concerns the possibility of a hysterical reaction or pain disorder. From a psychological perspective, either is possible. She has several hysteroid-like features. The most obvious of these are her tendencies to deny or ignore unwanted feelings, her seemingly rich fantasy world, her proneness to be overly intense in displaying her feelings, and her distinctive passive and dependent features. It is not surprising to find that her MMPI-2 yielded a 1-2-3 neurotic triad code type that includes substantial T-scores for each of the three scales (1 = 84; 2 = 81; 3 = 75). This configuration is often found among those who have a long-standing hypersensitivity to even minor physical dysfunctions and are likely to discount any relationship between physical and psychological problems (Greene, 2000). However, this composite of features identified from the Rorschach and MMPI-2 is not necessarily sufficient to firmly conclude that a hysterical reaction or pain disorder truly exists. Even if such a claim were to be put forth, it could also be argued that the trauma she has experienced has exacerbated some preexisting frailties.

Questions were also asked about the severity of her depression and about whether the findings seem consistent with a posttraumatic stress disorder or psychic injury. Although she does not have a major depressive disorder, she seems to be in considerable distress, which can easily breed the experience of depression. The components of her distress appear to include a marked sense of fragility and pessimism, feelings of neediness and loneliness, and general discouragement, all of which may exist in a posttraumatic stress disorder or psychic injury.

An issue that was not raised in the referral concerns the possibility that she may be feigning some or all of her physical problems. It seems clear that she emphasized, or possibly exaggerated those problems while taking the Rorschach. However, it is impossible to determine if this was done so deliberately or was simply the product of a less conscious set to convey the frustration and discouragement that she experiences. The latter is supported to some extent by some of the MMPI-2 findings, which include a substantial elevation on the L Scale ($T = 76$), plus the previously noted elevations on Scales 1 (Hs) and 3 (Hy). This combination is often noted among those who are naively histrionic and rely extensively on denial.

Thus, although many suspicions can be raised from the findings, none are sufficient to disregard the miseries that she claims. Under optimal circumstances and after any litigation has been resolved, some recommendation to her concerning intervention might be put forth, even though it seems likely that she would reject such a recommendation.

EPILOGUE

About one month after the psychological and neuropsychological evaluations were completed, a third neurological assessment was completed. The findings were essentially negative, although the consulting neurologist noted the possibility of two disk problems. Subsequently, an out-of-court settlement was reached that covered payment for her medical expenses and reimbursement in the amount of $90,000 for pain and suffering. No additional information is available.

REFERENCES

Acklin, M. W., & Alexander, G. (1988). Alexithymia and somatization: A Rorschach study of four psycho-somatic groups. *Journal of Nervous and Mental Diseases, 176*(6), 343–350.

Acklin, M. W., & Bernat, E. (1987). Depression, alexithymia, and pain prone disorder: A Rorschach study. *Journal of Personality Assessment, 51*(3), 462–479.

Arbisi, P. A., & Butcher, J. N. (2004). Psychometric perspectives on malingering of pain: Use of the Minnesota Multiphasic Personality Inventory-2. *Clinical Journal of Pain, 20*(6), 383–391.

Carlsson, A. M. (1987). Personality analysis using the Rorschach test in patients with chronic, non-malignant pain. *British Journal of Projective Psychology, 32*(2), 34–52.

Carlsson, A. M., Werner, S., Mattlar, C. E., Edman, G., Puukka, P., & Eriksson, E. (1993). Personality in patients with long-term patellofemoral pain syndrome. *Knee Surgery and Sports Traumatology and Arthroscopy, 1*(3/4), 178–183.

Graham, J. R. (2000). *MMPI-2: Assessing personality and psychopathology.* New York: Oxford University Press.

Greene, R. L. (2000). *The MMPI-2: An interpretive manual.* Needham Heights, MA: Allyn & Bacon.

Leavitt, F., & Garron, D. C. (1982). Rorschach and pain characteristics of patients with low back pain and "conversion V" MMPI profiles. *Journal of Personality Assessment, 46*(1), 18–25.

Miller, T. W., & Kraus, R. F. (1990). An overview of chronic pain. *Hospital and Community Psychiatry, 41,* 433–440.

Sifneos, P. E. (1973). The prevalence of "alexithymic" characteristics in psychosomatic patients. *Psychotherapy and Psychosomatics, 22,* 255–263.

PART FOUR

Using the Rorschach with Children and Adolescents

CHAPTER 17

An Issue of Deteriorating Academic Performance

————————————————— C A S E 1 5 —————————————————

This 9-year, 1-month-old female is within three months of finishing the third grade. She was described as an attractive youngster who looks her age, dressed neatly in a blouse and slacks. She was evaluated for two reasons: (1) her work performance has fluctuated enormously during the school year, ranging from exceptional in both reading and math to substandard in both of those subjects as well as other areas, and (2) during the past three months she has had several crying episodes that usually follow instances of being corrected for common mistakes in reading or math assignments.

The fluctuating academic performance is incongruous with her usually outstanding work in the first and second grades. She was in the highest math and reading groups and began the third grade similarly assigned. She excelled in those groups for about the first three months, but then her performance deteriorated. The teacher felt that she might be experiencing pressure to achieve and changed her to groups at the next level. For the next two months she excelled in those groups, but again her performance began to deteriorate. About that same time, the first crying episodes occurred. By parental request, she was administered cognitive and achievement testing and also had a complete physical examination. No medical problems were documented. Testing performance yielded: WISC-R Verbal IQ = 124, Performance IQ = 118, Full Scale = 124; WRAT reading = 112 standard score, spelling = 100 standard score, arithmetic = 126 standard score; Peabody achievement math = 121 standard score, reading recog = 119 standard score, reading comp = 114 standard score. All of the WRAT scores were commensurate with fifth-grade achievement.

Her third-grade teacher says that she seems to apply pressure to herself to perform well and suspects that the crying episodes follow some sense of failure even though it has not occurred. She notes that as the school year has progressed, she has been more reluctant to offer ideas, seems more anxious than other students, and does not have very good or persistent peer relations. The teacher notes that other children often appear to avoid playing with her, and some appear to dislike her, but for no obvious reasons.

The mother reports a normal developmental history. The child is the older of two children. Her brother, age 7, is in the first grade and doing above-average work. Her father, age 35, is an office equipment repairman and the mother, age 31, works mornings as a medical recording secretary. There is no psychiatric history in the immediate family. The parents deny any problems in the home and emphasize that they encourage good school performance, but not to excess. The family attends church weekly and the children are regular participants in Sunday

School. The parents express pride in reporting that a weekday routine exists whereby both children have a snack after school and then devote about 30 minutes to reading books of their choice before they are allowed to play. They report that punishment is infrequent and usually involves the denial of television privileges. The mother says that her daughter sometimes plays with two neighbor children after school, but usually prefers to watch television or cut out paper dolls and designs from newspapers. There is no computer in the home, although both children have asked for one.

The parents report that, after the medical examination, she began complaining of stomachaches and sore throats, and she has vomited several times after dinner. Two weeks prior to this evaluation, she was examined by a neurologist (including EEG and CT Scan) and all findings were negative. Neuropsychology screening done in this evaluation yielded: WISC Verbal IQ = 119, Performance IQ = 117, Full Scale IQ = 119; Categories = 34 errors, TPT rt = 4'11", lft = 2'3", both = 2'02" (memory = 6, local = 4), sensory-percept = 0 errors, trails A = 43", trails B = 56", speech sounds = 7 errors. She was anxious and reluctant during the evaluation. She refused to guess on WISC items as they became more difficult and wanted to give up during speech sounds. On the other hand, she responded quickly to the Rorschach blots.

Prior to the testing she indicated that she has many friends at school with whom she likes to play. This is contrary to the teacher's report about her peer relations. She spoke positively about both parents and her brother. She says that she likes school, especially arithmetic, but has difficulty with reading, "It's something that I don't do very well, I make too many mistakes." She notes that sometimes other children can be mean but, "I don't want to be mean to anybody." When asked to elaborate on her statement that other children can be mean, she stated, "Sometimes they are nasty and pick on people, but I don't do that." When she was asked about her health she said, "Not very good, I've had a lot of flu this year."

CASE FORMULATION AND RELEVANT LITERATURE

In contrast to her consistently good academic performance in first and second grades, the downward trajectory of this girl's work during her third grade year is cause for significant concern. Crying episodes on being corrected in school are unusual for third-graders, raising questions about the fragility of her self-concept. Even though she is reading two years above her grade level, her assessment is, "It's something I don't do very well. I make too many mistakes." The teacher notes that other children frequently ostracize her, leaving her isolated interpersonally and feeling victimized and different: "Sometimes they are nasty and pick on people, but I don't do that." She is beginning to display somatic symptoms and feels that her health is "Not very good."

The constellation of problems this girl shows is consistent with Quay's (1986) description of an anxious-withdrawn-dysphoric syndrome, characterized by fearful worry, frequent crying, interpersonal shyness, and poor, easily threatened self-esteem. Similarly, Ollendick and King (1994) describe a group of clinically related and factor-analytically associated internalizing disorders that include anxiety, fear, shyness, low self-esteem, sadness, and depression. Achenbach and McConaughy (1992) have identified four specific internalizing presentations in clinic-referred children and adolescents: anxious-depressed, schizoid, somatic, and withdrawn. All these authors note that symptoms of anxiety and depression frequently co-occur, and Costello, Mustillo, Erkanli, Keeler, and Angold (2003) found highly significant comorbidity between anxiety and depression in a longitudinal study of 1,420 children aged 9 to 16. The literature on assessing anxiety and depression in adults was reviewed in Chapters 3 and 4 (Cases 1 and 2), but it will be helpful to survey the child and adolescent literature as well.

Assessment of Anxiety and Depression in Children and Adolescents

Spigelman, Spigelman, and Englesson (1991) tested a nonclinical sample of 108 boys and girls aged 10 to 12, half of whose parents were divorced. Their review of the literature suggested that the following Rorschach content categories indicated anxiety: clouds, fire, smoke, maps, weird or bizarre concepts, unpleasant or dysphoric percepts, geometrical figures, and X-rays. They also used Elizur's (1949) approach to the Rorschach assessment of anxiety, which codes answers containing expressions of anxious emotions such as fear or horror, answers whose content has a fearful connotation (e.g., snakes or demons), and answers with an apprehensive quality, such as storm clouds foreboding disaster. They found significantly higher scores on both anxiety measures for children in the divorce group.

In a related study, Spigelman and Spigelman (1991) investigated Depression Index (DEPI) findings for the two groups of children previously described. Children in the divorce group were significantly higher on the DEPI, with more MOR answers, more color-shading blends, and more vista and achromatic color determinants.

In general, however, the DEPI as an index does not appear to be strongly related to observations of manifest depressive features in children and adolescents. Ball, Archer, Gordon, and French (1991) tested 67 outpatient children and adolescents ages 5 to 15 and 99 inpatient adolescents ages 12 through 18. They found no relationship between the DEPI and parent ratings of depressive features for the outpatients or treatment team diagnoses of dysthymic or major depressive disorder for the inpatient group.

Lipovsky, Finch, and Belter (1989) studied 60 adolescent inpatients, 35 of whom had been diagnosed by a multidisciplinary treatment team as meeting the *DSM-III* criteria for major depressive disorder, dysthymic disorder, or adjustment disorder with depressed mood. The 25 adolescents in the nondepressed group had a variety of diagnoses including conduct disorder and adjustment disorder with mixed emotional features. The DEPI did not discriminate between the two groups.

Carter and Dacey (1996) reviewed test data for 118 adolescents who had been hospitalized on an inpatient psychiatric unit. Using *DSM-III-R* criteria, a multidisciplinary treatment team had diagnosed 66 participants as depressed (depressive disorder not otherwise specified, major depression, dysthymic disorder, adjustment disorder with depressed mood) and 52 as nondepressed (conduct disorder, attention deficit disorder, adjustment disorder with disturbance of conduct, oppositional defiant disorder, impulse control disorder). All participants had taken the MMPI, Beck Depression Inventory (BDI; Beck, Ward, Mendelson, Mock, & Erbaugh, 1961), and the Rorschach. The depressed and nondepressed groups differed significantly on the MMPI Depression (D) scale but were not significantly different from each other on the DEPI. Although scores on the MMPI D scale and the BDI correlated significantly with each other, neither showed a significant correlation with the DEPI.

All these findings indicate that the DEPI as an index is unrelated to the observable behaviors that result in *DSM* depressive diagnoses for children and adolescents. Viglione, Brager, and Haller

(1988) and Viglione (1999) have emphasized the importance of taking the person's problem-solving style into account and suggested that the DEPI might have better discriminative ability for extratensive individuals as measured by the *EB*. However, a study by Krishnamurthy and Archer (2001) found that the DEPI had no greater ability to discriminate *DSM-III-R* depressed extratensive adolescents from extratensive adolescents with other diagnoses than it did for the introversive and ambitent patients in their sample.

There is some possibility that variables within the DEPI may have specific relationships to aspects of depressive function. Although Lipovsky et al. (1989) found that the DEPI did not discriminate between depressed and nondepressed adolescent inpatients, their results revealed moderate correlations ($r = .33$ and $.31$) between the number of Morbid contents on the Rorschach and two self-report measures, the MMPI D scale and the Children's Depression Inventory (CDI; Kovacs & Beck, 1977). The MMPI D scale was also significantly related to the number of shading (diffuse shading, texture, and vista) determinants, leading the authors to suggest, ". . . it is important to consider the presence of Shading responses as potential indicators of a painful affective experience associated with depression" (p. 455).

Case 15. A 9-Year-Old Female.

Card	Response	Inquiry
I	1. A black bird	**E:** (Rpts Ss resp) **S:** Not thes things here (Dd34), it has wgs & littl feet (D1) and a tail
	2. A burnt leaf	**E:** (Rpts Ss resp) **S:** Its missing some pieces here (spaces) & some othr pieces fell off (points to tiny exterior dots) **E:** U said it was burnt? **S:** It's black, blackish all over
II	3. A man's face	**E:** (Rpts Ss resp) **S:** Here's his eyes (space), nose (space), beard (D3) & his cheeks **E:** Help me c the beard **S:** Here (D3) its pointy lik whiskers, lik the shape at the edge ll a beard to me
	4. A little red flower up here	**E:** (Rpts Ss resp) **S:** C, up here (points) it's just a littl red flower, small lik really tiny, just there
	5. Mayb these r leaves	**E:** (Rpts Ss resp) **S:** Well thyr red lik in autumn but thyr not all the same color **E:** Not all the same color? **S:** Well there's dark red & lite red too, lik they change
III	6. A person's face	**E:** (Rpts Ss resp) **S:** Some color got put on his head, red paint just over his eyes, on his middle head **E:** I don't thk I c it yet help me **S:** Here's the color (D3) on his middle head & his eyes & nose (space) and mouth (space), c (outlines D1)
	7. A cat's face too	**E:** (Rpts Ss resp) **S:** It's not the same, it's here (outlines), these r the eyes (D3) & the nose & the mouth, he has a white nose & u can c teeth in his mouth (parts of D7)
IV	8. A tree	**E:** (Rpts Ss resp) **S:** The branches r here, & the top **E:** What makes it ll branches? **S:** Just the edges, thyr lik branches, c thy stick out here
V	9. A bug	**E:** (Rpts Ss resp) **S:** The W thg just ll a bug, it has feelers on its head
	10. A bf too	**E:** (Rpts Ss resp) **S:** It has wgs & it's got feelers on it too
VI	11. A wall hanging w a flower	**E:** (Rpts Ss resp) **S:** The flower is up on top & the rest is a board, lik a piece of wood w a design **E:** A design? **S:** It has bumps, down deep lik thy cut with a knife to make a design lik flower petals or sthg, mostly in the middl of the wood lik thy cut bumps in it
	12. A crab down here, a littl one	**E:** (Rpts Ss resp) **S:** It has littl bumps for eyes & clipper things (outlines), **E:** U said a littl one? **S:** It's so small here it must be a littl one

(continued)

351

Card	Response	Inquiry
VII	13. A picture frame but it doesn't hav a top	**E:** (Rpts Ss resp) **S:** Not for a wall but lik u'd put on a desk & put a picture in it but smbody took the top off **E:** I don't thk I c it, help me **S:** The picture goes in the middle (space) & all the rest is lik the frame
VIII	14. A flower	**E:** (Rpts Ss resp) **S:** It just has a lot of colors lik a flower, don't ask me what kind cuz I dkno
	15. A green tree	**E:** (Rpts Ss resp) **S:** Up here, it just ll a tree, the edges, & it's green lik trees r supposed to b green
IX	16. A flower too	**E:** (Rpts Ss resp) **S:** It has a lot of different colors lik a flower but I dkno what kind, just a pretty one
	17. A green bush	**E:** (Rpts Ss resp) **S:** Just here, it's got edges lik a bush & it's all green
	18. A face lik a horse	**E:** (Rpts Ss resp) **S:** U can c the eyes (space) & the nose (outlines), it ll a horse face or a cow face or some A face, prob a horse face
X	19. A rainbow	**E:** (Rpts Ss resp) **S:** It's got all the colors so it must be a rainbow, rainbows got all these colors, haven't u ever seen one? **E:** Yes
	20. A person's face, a peace person	**E:** (Rpts Ss resp) **S:** It's a man, w yellow eyes & a green mustache (outlines) & pink hair **E:** U said a peace person **S:** Sur, he's got pink hair, tht's why thy call them pinko's, peace people are pinko's

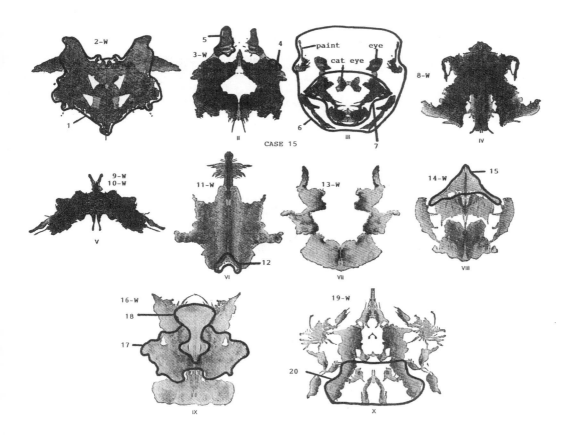

Case 15. Sequence of Scores.

Card	No.	Loc.	No.	Determinant(s)	(2)	Content(s)	Pop	Z	Special Scores
I	1	Ddo	99	FC'o		A			
	2	WSv	1	C'Fo		Bt			MOR
II	3	WSo	1	F–		Hd		4.5	DV,PHR
	4	Ddv	99	CFu		Bt			
	5	Dv	2	CF.YF–	2	Bt			
III	6	DdS+	99	CF–		Hd,Art		4.5	DV,PHR
	7	DdSo	99	FC'–		Ad		4.5	
IV	8	Wo	1	Fo		Bt		2.0	
V	9	Wo	1	F–		A		1.0	
	10	Wo	1	Fo		A	P	1.0	
VI	11	W+	1	FVu		Art,Bt		2.5	
	12	Ddo	33	F–		A			DV,ALOG
VII	13	WSo	1	F–		Art		4.0	MOR
VIII	14	Wv	1	C		Bt			
	15	Do	4	FCu		Bt			
IX	16	Wv	1	C		Bt			
	17	Do	11	CFo		Bt			
	18	DSo	8	F–		Ad		5.0	
X	19	Wv	1	C		Na			ALOG
	20	DdSo	99	FC–		Hd			ALOG,PHR

Case 15.   Structural Summary.

Location Features	Determinants Blends	Single	Contents	S-Constellation
				. . . . .FV+VF+V+FD>2
			H =	. . . . .Col-Shd Bl>0
Zf = 9	CF.YF	M = 0	(H) = 0	. . . . .Ego<.31,>.44
ZSum = 29.0		FM = 0	Hd = 3	. . . . .MOR > 3
ZEst = 27.5		m = 0	(Hd) = 0	. . . . .Zd > +− 3.5
		FC = 2	Hx = 0	. . . . .es > EA
W = 10		CF = 4	A = 4	. . . . .CF+C > FC
D = 4		C = 2	(A) = 0	. . . . .X+% < .70
W+D = 14		Cn = 0	Ad = 2	. . . . .S > 3
Dd = 6		FC′ = 2	(Ad) = 0	. . . . .P < 3 or > 8
S = 7		C′F = 1	An = 0	. . . . .Pure H < 2
		C′ = 0	Art = 2	. . . . .R < 17
		FT = 0	Ay = 0	x . . . .TOTAL

DQ		Single	Contents	**Special Scores**
		TF = 0	Bl = 0	Lv1 Lv2
+ = 2		T = 0	Bt = 9	DV = 3x1 0x2
o = 12		FV = 1	Cg = 0	INC = 0x2 0x4
v/+ = 0		VF = 0	Cl = 0	DR = 0x3 0x6
v = 6		V = 0	Ex = 0	FAB = 0x4 0x7
		FY = 0	Fd = 0	ALOG = 3x5
		YF = 0	Fi = 0	CON = 0x7
		Y = 0	Ge = 0	Raw Sum6 = 6
	Form Quality	Fr = 0	Hh = 0	Wgtd Sum6 = 18

	FQx	MQual	W+D	Contents	Special Scores
			rF = 0	Ls = 0	
+	= 0	= 0	= 0	Na = 1	
o	= 6	= 0	= 5	Sc = 0	AB = 0 GHR = 0
u	= 3	= 0	= 2	Sx = 0	AG = 0 PHR = 3
−	= 9	= 0	= 5	Xy = 0	COP = 0 MOR = 2
none	= 2	= 0	= 2	Id = 1	CP = 0 PER = 0
					PSV = 0

Single column: FD = 0, F = 7, (2) = 1

Ratios, Percentages, and Derivations

R = 20	L = 0.54		FC:CF+C = 2:7	COP = 0 AG = 0
			Pure C = 2	GHR:PHR = 0:3
EB = 0:9.0	EA = 9.0	EBPer = 9.0	SumC′:WSumC = 3:9.0	a:p = 0:0
eb = 0:5	es = 5	D = +1	Afr = 0.54	Food = 0
	Adj es = 5	Adj D = +1	S = 7	SumT = 0
			Blends:R = 1:20	Hum Con = 3
FM = 0	C′ = 3	T = 0	CP = 0	Pure H = 0
m = 0	V = 1	Y = 1		PER = 0
				Iso Indx = 0.55

a:p = 0:0	Sum6 = 6	XA% = 0.45	Zf = 9.0	3r+(2)/R = 0.05
Ma:Mp = 0:0	Lv2 = 0	WDA% = 0.50	W:D:Dd = 10:4:6	Fr+rF = 0
2AB+Art+Ay = 2	WSum6 = 18	X−% = 0.45	W:M = 10:0	SumV = 1
MOR = 2	M− = 0	S− = 6	Zd = +1.5	FD = 0
	Mnone = 0	P = 1	PSV = 0	An+Xy = 0
		X+% = 0.30	DQ+ = 2	MOR = 2
		Xu% = 0.15	DQv = 6	H:(H)Hd(Hd) = 0:3

PTI = 3	DEPI = 6*	CDI = 4*	S-CON = N/A	HVI = No	OBS = No

S-CON AND KEY VARIABLE

The S-CON was developed using an adult sample and, although it can be used with clients who are between the ages of 15 and 17, it has no demonstrated usefulness for younger persons. The first positive Key variable is that the DEPI is greater than five (6) *and* the CDI value (4) greater than three. This signals that the cluster interpretation should begin with a review of the data concerning interpersonal perception and self-perception and proceed to a study of information regarding controls and affect. The process will conclude with a review of the three data clusters that make up the cognitive triad.

INTERPERSONAL PERCEPTION

Case 15.   Interpersonal Perception Data for a 9-Year-Old Female.

R = 20	CDI = 4	HVI = No	**COP & AG Responses**	
a:p = 0:0	SumT = 0	Fd = 0	None Present	
	[eb = 0:5]			
Sum Human Contents = 3		H = 0		
[Style = Extratensive]				
GHR:PHR = 0:3				
COP = 0	AG = 0	PER = 0		
Isolation Indx = 0.55				

The positive CDI value (4) is not uncommon among younger children and usually indicates a continuing struggle with issues of identity and peer relations. It signals the likelihood that her dealings with others are rather inept and her relationships are typically superficial and not enduring. Children like this often are unsure and insecure about interacting with others and tend to shy away from social relations, settling instead for a more isolated existence. It is not surprising that the teacher reports her relations with other children are few, and often more negative than positive.

The absence of texture in her record, although other grey-black and shading answers were given, is probably related to her social situation. It implies that she is more cautious or conservative than others about expressing her needs for closeness, especially those involving tactile exchange. Likewise, there are only three human content responses in her protocol, none of which are Pure *H*. All three of these responses involve faces. This implies that her interests in people are quite modest, but more important, it suggests that she does not understand people very well and frequently misinterprets social gestures. Her comments about other children being mean and nasty are of interest in this context.

Each of her three human content answers is coded *PHR* (GHR:PHR = 0:3), connoting a substantial probability that her interpersonal behaviors are ineffective or maladaptive. Similarly, the absence of COP or *AG* answers hints that she is likely to feel somewhat uncomfortable in interpersonal situations and may be regarded by others as distant. A similar conclusion is indicated by the substantial value for the Isolation Index (0.55), which strongly suggests that she has difficulty creating meaningful relations with others and probably finds herself void of rewarding interactions. This composite of findings is unusual for a 9-year-old. Children of this age are typically very peer involved. However, she seems to be confused about people and rather ineffective in dealing with them. As a result, she has become somewhat insecure about, and isolated from, the routine social interactions that would be expected for her age. An obvious question that requires special attention as the interpretation proceeds is whether she has somehow aligned herself with a hypothetical model of conduct that runs contrary to that usually expected, or accepted, for a child of her age.

SELF-PERCEPTION

Case 15.   Self-Perception Related Data for a 9-Year-Old Female.

				Human Content, Hx, An & Xy Responses
R	= 20	OBS	= No	HVI = No	
					II 3. WSo F Hd 4.5 PHR
Fr+rF	= 0	3r+(2)/R	= 0.05		III 6. DdS+ Mao H,Art 4.5 DV,PHR
					X 20. DdSo FC– Hd ALOG,PHR
FD	= 0	SumV	= 1		
An+Xy	= 0	MOR	= 2		
H:(H)+Hd+(Hd) = 0:3					
[EB = 0:9.5]					

The Egocentricity Index (0.05) is extraordinarily low for anyone, and especially so for a child. It denotes a markedly low estimate of personal worth and indicates that she tends to judge herself very unfavorably when in comparison with others. Such a set about oneself creates a significant potential for sadness, moodiness, and feelings of helplessness. In a related context, there is a vista response in her record. It denotes an introspective rumination about self-image features that she regards negatively. It could reflect a sense of guilt concerning her recent school difficulties but, when considered in light of the very low Egocentricity Index, it probably has a more chronic origin. In either event, it is a process that tends to yield discomforting feelings and this preoccupation is extremely unusual for a 9-year-old.

She also gave two MOR responses, implying that her self-concept includes some negative features that tend to give rise to a pessimistic set about herself. This is not uncommon among children, especially those who tend to feel unsure or insecure about themselves. However, in this instance, the finding adds one more bit of information supporting the notion that she has a very disapproving set about herself. As noted during the review of data concerning interpersonal perception, she gave three human content answers, but none involve Pure *H*. All are *Hd*, and all have a minus form quality. This strongly suggests that her self-image is probably confused and distorted, and likely based mainly on imaginary impressions or faulty conclusions that have resulted from her experiences.

There are nine minus responses in her protocol. Several are somewhat homogeneous for features and substance, although none is especially rich for projected material. Six of the nine (responses 3, 6, 7, 13, 18, & 20) include the use of white space, and five of those six are face responses. An excessive emphasis on faces or facial parts, especially when it involves the use of space, usually connotes an unusual guardedness related to a sense of insecurity or alienation. As implied earlier, much of the verbiage in her minus answers focuses on identifying the location of various parts of the object and includes little or no obvious projected material. Her first two minus answers (Card II, response 3), "A man's face," and (Card II, response 5), "Maybe these are leaves . . . red like in autumn . . . dark red and light red, like they change," fall in this group.

Her third minus answer (Card III, response 6), "A person's face . . . some color got put on his head, red paint . . . on his middle head" is slightly more elaborate and concrete, but the implications regarding the color "on his head" are not very clear. The fourth minus (Card III, response 7), "A cat's face, too . . . he has a white nose and you can see the teeth in his mouth," is also seemingly void of clear projected material. The same is true for the fifth minus answer (Card V, response 9), "A bug . . . it's got feelers on its head." The sixth minus (Card VI, response 12) includes a hint that she may feel inferior or insecure, "A crab down here, a little one . . . it has little bumps for eyes . . . it's so small here it must be little."

The seventh minus (Card VII, response 13) is one of her MOR responses, "A picture frame but it doesn't have a top . . . like you'd put on a desk . . . but somebody took the top off." It suggests a sense of damage or incompleteness. The eighth minus (Card IX, response 18), "A face like a horse," includes only location-oriented information. The last minus (Card X, response 20) is more distinctive, "A person's face, a peace person . . . a man with yellow eyes and a green mustache and pink hair . . . that's why they call them pinko's, peace people are pinko's." The concreteness is striking, but the substance, a peace person, may be of greater significance. The history notes that she is shunned or disliked by others, and she reports that other children are nasty at times.

Her other MOR answer (Card I, response 2) probably includes the most projected material of any of her responses, "A burnt leaf . . . it's missing some pieces here and some other pieces fell off . . . it's blackish all over." It is a negative response that clearly implies a sense of fragility, damage, and incompleteness. None of her other answers include meaningful embellishments. In fact, the entire protocol is seemingly defensive and many of her answers are unexpectedly concrete.

The overall picture regarding her self-concept appears to be bleak, at best. She appears to view herself negatively and pessimistically and feels fragile and insecure. It is a kind of psychological set that breeds discomforting and disruptive emotions, and it clearly limits the extent to which she may be able to develop rewarding interactions with others.

CONTROLS

Case 15. Control-Related Variables for a 9-Year-Old Female.

EB = 0:9.0	EA = 9.0		D = +1	CDI = 4
eb = 0:5	es = 5	Adj es = 5	AdjD = +1	L = 0.54
FM = 0 m = 0	SumC' = 3	SumT = 0	SumV = 1	SumY = 1

The Adj D Score (+1) implies a substantial capacity for the volitional control of her behaviors and a rather sturdy tolerance for stress. However, other findings raise a question about whether such a conclusion is valid. One such finding is the positive CDI (4). It signals that she is socially immature, and her limited social skills make her vulnerable to difficulties when coping with the requirements of everyday living. As social failures accumulate, a sense of dissatisfaction with and confusion about the environment tends to build, which can impact negatively on her capacity for control, especially in complex social situations.

A second, and much more important finding that raises a question about her capacity for volitional control is that the left side *EB* value is zero while the right side value is substantial (9.0). This indicates that she is being overwhelmed or flooded by affect. It connotes intense and disruptive feelings that create a form of lability in which her emotions tend to provoke and direct her behaviors. Emotional flooding has a major impact on thinking, and especially on the ability to invoke forms of delay in ideational activity that are prerequisite for the attention and concentration functions necessary during decision making. As a result, thinking is often concrete, disconnected, and rushed, and the likelihood of behavioral impulsiveness or inappropriateness increases substantially.

The fact that the *eb* (0:5) contains a zero value, yielding an Adj *es* (5) that consists only of variables related to irritating forms of affect, is also disconcerting. This finding intimates a considerable likelihood that her intense emotions include many that can easily create a dysphoric mood, and this increases the probability of inappropriate behaviors.

Overall, her capacity for adequate volitional control of her behaviors is, at best, fragile and easily disrupted. It is surprising that the history only includes reports of occasional crying, as she seems readily vulnerable to much more disorganization that would be obvious to the casual observer.

AFFECT

Case 15.   Affect-Related Data for a 9-Year-Old Female.

EB	= 0:9.0			EBPer	= 9.0	**Blends**		
eb	= 0:5	L	= 0.54	FC:CF+C	= 2:7	CF.YF		= 1
DEPI	= 6	CDI	= 4	Pure C	= 3			
SumC' = 3	SumT = 0			SumC':WSumC	= 3:9.5			
SumV = 1	SumY = 1			Afr	= 0.54			
Intellect	= 3	CP	= 0	S = 7 (S to I,II,III	= 4)			
Blends:R	= 1:20			Col-Shad Bl	= 1			
m + y Bl	= 1			Shading Bl	= 0			

Usually, when both the DEPI (6) and CDI (4) are positive, difficulties in the interpersonal sphere have led to episodes of disappointment and distress and, gradually, significant affective problems evolve that add to difficulties in social adaptability. However, there are instances, especially in younger clients, when the reverse can be true. That is, a persistent affective problem can interfere significantly with social development and adaptiveness.

Typically, the distinction between cause and consequence can be detected from the social history but, in some cases, that differentiation is not readily identifiable. This appears to be such a case. The available social history, prior to her current grade, offers no hints of social difficulties, but neither are there suggestions of good social adaptability. Regardless of whether the affective or interpersonal issue is causal, it is important to approach the interpretation of the high DEPI (6) value cautiously. This is because two variables, COP < 2; Isolation Index > .24, both of which are positive in her CDI, also contribute one point to the DEPI value. In other words, the DEPI may be exaggerating the intensity and probable chronicity of the affective problem.

This caution does not minimize the likelihood that she is in distress, and possibly even depressed, but it reduces the probability of a chronic, major affective disturbance. There is no question about the presence of a serious affective problem. This has already been discovered in the review of the *EB* data (0:9.0) as they pertain to controls. She is emotionally labile and likely to have frequent episodes in which her emotions become overwhelming and provoke behaviors that otherwise would not occur. This finding also necessitates approaching almost all the data concerning affect conservatively and in context. This is because her intense emotions may tend to exaggerate or distort data that usually convey information about traitlike features.

The *EB* (0:9.0) and *EBPer* (9.0) data indicate that she has a markedly inflexible extratensive coping style in which her emotions play a major role in her thinking and decision making. This is a valid finding regarding her current state, but it is highly unlikely that this has been a persistent feature. She may have an extratensive coping style, and it may have existed for some time. This is common among young children. However, if it were as markedly inflexible as currently indicated, the probability of her being able to achieve a superior academic performance during the first and second grades, and at times during the third grade, would be remote. The same would be true regarding the likelihood of her being able to perform at well-above-average levels on intelligence and achievement testing.

As with the *EB,* the right side *eb* value (5) is probably a valid indicator of her current state. In that it is higher than the left side value (0), it signifies distress, but there is no way of knowing for how long the right side value has been higher. Had she been tested prior to the onset of the emotional flooding, it is likely some responses contributing to a left side *eb* value greater than zero would have been given. The slight elevation in *SumC'* (3), reflecting a tendency to inhibit or suppress feelings, may well be long standing, especially because the *Afr* (.54) is slightly lower than expected for one of her age, indicating a proneness to avoid emotionally provoking situations. However, the presence of a vista response could represent either a situational or a long-standing feature. In other words, the distress feature may be more reactive than longstanding.

In a similar context, the *FC:CF+C* ratio (2:7), which includes three Pure *C* responses, denotes a significant laxness in the modulation of her emotional displays. Most are likely to be intense, and some will be characterized by impulsive-like behaviors. Such findings are not uncommon among very young children, but are much less frequent among 9-year-olds. This finding also seems contrary to the reported history, which does not include any reports of overly intense or impulsive-like expressions of affect, except for her recent crying episodes. Thus, it is probable that the finding represents her current state rather than a persistent laxness in handling emotions.

Added support for this postulate is found in a review of her three Pure *C* responses. They occur as first answers to each of the last three cards. They are vague, evasive, concrete answers that are more like responses typically given by a 6- or 7-year-old than by an intelligent 9-year-old. They could represent a form of defensiveness on her part, but it is equally plausible to assume that they reflect more of a cognitive impairment that is being created by the intensity of her feelings.

One of the most important findings among the affect-related data is the presence of seven space responses. As noted during the review of self-perception data, six of these have a minus form quality, and five of the six are face responses. When *S* appears with such a high frequency, it usually signals considerable anger, often generated by a marked sense of insecurity or alienation. This could be a key element in the emotional flooding that she is experiencing. Typically, anger of this magnitude is reflected in behaviors. Often, it is direct and obvious but, in some instances, it is expressed in subtle and indirect forms. The deterioration in her recent academic performance could well be such an instance.

There is only one blend in her protocol (*CF.YF*). This is surprising, as much more complexity might be expected in light of her emotional turmoil. However, the absence of complexity is not uncommon where immaturity is a significant factor, which seems likely in light of the positive CDI. Also, less complexity is expected when emotions interfere substantially with basic cognitive functioning.

Overall, it seems clear that she is experiencing a significant affective problem. The roots of the problem appear to be interpersonal, and related to her limited and inadequate social skills, but other elements appear to be contributing. She seems cautious and unsure about emotions and has become prone to avoid or suppress them when possible. She has not yet learned how to deal with her feelings very directly or adaptively and, as a result, has become vulnerable to becoming easily overwhelmed by them. This composite appears to have led to feelings of insecurity and alienation that have crystallized into considerable anger, which is expressed subtly and indirectly in her behaviors. A major issue yet to be addressed is how this turmoil impacts on her cognitive functioning. The PTI value (3) already hints that there are notable difficulties in some of those operations.

PROCESSING

Case 15.   Processing Variables for a 9-Year-Old Female.

EB	= 0:9.0	Zf	= 9	Zd	= +1.5	DQ+	= 2
L	= 0.54	W:D:Dd	= 10:4:6	PSV	= 0	DQv/+	= 0
HVI	= NO	W:M	= 10:0			DQv	= 6
OBS	= NO						

Location & DQ Sequencing

I:	Ddo.WSv	VI: W+.Ddo
II:	WSo.Ddv.Dv	VII: WSo
III:	DdS+.DdSo	VIII: Wv.Do
IV:	Wo	IX: Wv.Do.DSo
V:	Wo.Wo	X: Wv.DdSo

The value for *Zf* (9) implies that her processing effort is similar to most people, but other information in the cluster raises questions about the accuracy of that statement. For instance, the $W:D:Dd$ ratio (10:4:6) suggests the possibility of a greater effort than is typical, as there are more *W* than *D* locations and a considerable number of *Dd* locations. This also seems supported by the $W:M$ ratio (10:0). However, an inspection of the location sequence, the *DQ* distribution, and the *DQ* sequence appears to indicate that neither statement is true.

The location sequence reveals that she gives *W* answers as a first response to eight of the 10 cards, but three of those eight *W* answers are coded *DQv*, as is a fourth *W* answer. In fact, 6 of her 20 responses are coded *DQv*. This signals a very casual and/or defensive approach to processing. In a similar context, five of her nine *Z* responses involve the use of *S*, as do three of her six *Dd* responses. This indicates an unusual form of processing, probably influenced by a negative set that is most common among those in considerable emotional disarray.

Although the *Zd* score (+1.5) connotes appropriate scanning activity, such a conclusion is highly suspect because the five higher than usual *Z* values are created by *S* responses. If those answers are hypothetically disregarded, the remaining four answers involving *Z* would produce a *ZSum* of 6.5, which is considerably lower than the *Zest* (10) for a *Zf* of 4, yielding an underincorporative *Zd* (−3.5). Whether she is haphazard in scanning is speculative; however, only 2 of her 20 answers are *DQ+* responses, which is an incongruous finding for an intelligent 9-year-old. Neither of those two *DQ+* responses—(response 6), "A person's face . . . red paint just over his eyes"; (response 11), "A wall hanging with a flower . . . on top and the rest is the board, like a piece of wood with a design"—is very well developed.

It is difficult to form definitive conclusions about her processing habits. It does seem clear that her current processing activities are far less sophisticated than would be expected in light of her intellectual talents and achievements. Much of her processing activity appears to be concrete and not very efficient. It is probable that some of her processing behaviors are constricted because of a defensive set. However, it is equally likely that they are noticeably influenced by a negative set that has an integral relationship to the emotional disarray discussed earlier. Possibly, the findings concerning mediation and ideation will provide some added clarification regarding her processing limitations.

MEDIATION

Case 15.   Mediation Variables for a 9-Year-Old Female.

R = 20	L = 0.54		OBS = No	**Minus & NoForm Features**
FQx+	= 0	XA%	= .40	II 3. WSo F– Hd 4.5 DV,PHR
FQxo	= 5	WDA%	= .43	II 5. Dv CF.YF– 2 Bt
FQxu	= 3	X–%	= .45	III 6. DdS+ CF– Hd,Art 4.5 DV,PHR
FQx–	= 9	S–	= 6	III 7. DdSo FC'– Ad 4.5
FQxnone	= 3			V 9. Wo F– A 1.0
(W+D	= 14)	P	= 1	VI 12. Ddo33 F– A DV,ALOG
WD+	= 0	X+%	= .25	VII 13. WSo F– Art 4.0 MOR
WDo	= 4	Xu%	= .15	VIII 14. Wv C Bt
WDu	= 2			IX 16. Wv C Bt
WD–	= 5			IX 18. DSo F– Ad 5.0
WDnone	= 3			X 19. Wv C Na ALOG
				X 20. DdSo FC– Hd ALOG,PHR

The $XA\%$ (.40) and $WDA\%$ (.43) are very low and connote a significant mediational impairment. In addition, the $X-\%$ (.45) is very high. When considered, independent of other findings, these data signify that the impairment is severe and impacting very negatively on reality testing. They also raise a question about the possibility of a prodromal thought disturbance. However, three findings in the cluster review tend to discount that likelihood.

The first finding is the presence of three NoForm responses, all of which are Pure C, as alluded to earlier. They lower the $XA\%$ by 7 percentage points and, because all are W answers, lower the $WDA\%$ by more than 20 percentage points. Taken alone, the NoForm answers do not rule out the implication that the impairment is severe or the possibility of a serious thinking problem. However, when considered in concert with other findings, the picture does not appear to be quite so bleak.

The second finding concerns the high $X-\%$ (.45), which connotes considerable dysfunction. The datum cannot be discounted, but when interpreted in context, it seems to overestimate the broad array of dysfunction that it implies. As noted, six of her nine minus answers are S responses, three of which are to Dd areas. Five of the six are faces, and they were given to chromatically colored cards (II, III, IX, and X). This sort of homogeneity indicates that the dysfunction is likely to be a product of an affective problem that probably has as its core considerable negativism or anger.

The third finding relevant to the issues of reality testing and the possibility of a thought disturbance concerns the distortion levels of her minus answers. All include some features that are congruent with the distal properties of the field. Thus, while all are accurately coded as minus, none represent markedly spoiled answers or severe distortions of the stimuli.

Collectively, these three findings seem to negate the possibility of a serious thought disorder. They do not discount that her reality testing is impaired or that she has a severe affective problem. In fact, they tend to highlight the latter and suggest that it is, in essence psychologically immobilizing her. This notion gains added support when other data in the cluster are reviewed. Her protocol contains only one Popular answer (Card V, a butterfly). It intimates that her behaviors are likely to be less conventional, even when the cues for conventional behaviors are simple and rather precisely defined. This conclusion coincides with one derived from her very low $X+\%$ (.25). It implies that her behaviors are likely to be atypical and unconventional more often than not. If the findings regarding Populars and the $X+\%$ are considered in light of the $X-\%$, they connote a significant increase in the likelihood of atypical and inappropriate behaviors.

Overall, the findings indicate that her mediational functioning is somewhat limited and ineffectual and impairs her ability to deal with reality. Apparently, this impairment is being created by a reasonably intense affective problem. This problem seems to have evolved from a very strong sense of negativism or alienation that gives rise to considerable anger. It tends to shape her view of reality and leads her into situations where she ignores even obvious cues relevant to her decisions and behaviors. Her limited and ineffective mediational functioning tends to parallel the findings regarding her limited processing activities. Both are consistent with the notion that she is experiencing considerable cognitive impairment.

IDEATION

Case 15.   Ideation Variables for a 9-Year-Old Female.

L	= 0.54	OBS	= No	HVI	= No	**Critical Special Scores**				
						DV	= 3	DV2	= 0	
EB	= 0:9.0	EBPer	= 9.0	a:p	= 0:0	INC	= 0	INC2	= 0	
				Ma:Mp	= 0:0	DR	= 0	DR2	= 0	
eb	= 0:5	[FM = 0 m = 0]				FAB	= 0	FAB2	= 0	
				M−	= 0	ALOG	= 3	CON	= 0	
Intell Indx	= 3	MOR	= 2	Mnone	= 0	Sum6	= 6	WSum6	= 18	
								(R = 20)		

M Response Features
No M responses appear in this protocol

As discussed during the review of findings concerning affect, the *EB* (0:9.0) and *EBPer* (9.0) indicate a markedly intuitive style in which her emotions are very influential on her thinking and decision making. This tends to breed imprecise and ambiguous logic systems, as well as a proneness to rely on external feedback for reassurance. Because of the emotional flooding, however, it is impossible to determine with any certainty if this has been a persistent style for her. Data regarding her previous academic achievements suggest that this is very unlikely. Nonetheless, the findings reflect her current state.

When emotions play such a dominating role in the psychology of a person, especially a child, the impact on thinking often can be quite detrimental. As the tactics of delay and thoughtfulness are reduced in frequency, ideation easily becomes strained and concrete, and conclusions and decisions are often reached prematurely. Evidence that her thinking is like this seems fairly clear, even though the overall data concerning ideation are sparse because of the absence of any movement answers. She has five responses that include six special scores related to her thinking, yielding a *WSum6* of 18. It signals the likelihood that episodes of faulty conceptualization cloud her thinking and promote more instances of flawed judgment than are common for her age.

Three of her six special scores are simple *DV* forms of slippage (response 3, pointy like whiskers; response 6, his middle head; response 12, clipper things). None are serious, and all might be expected from a young child. On the other hand, three responses are coded as ALOG (response 12, it's so small it must be a little one; response 19, it's got all the colors so it must be a rainbow; response 20, he's got pink hair, that's why they call them pinko's). These are very concrete judgments. They do not reflect disorganization or bizarreness, but they indicate that her conceptualizations tend to be flawed and immature. The concreteness in them is similar to the concreteness reflected in her Pure *C* answers.

Typically, when faulty judgments of this kind mark thinking, the significant impact on reality testing becomes generalized to other cognitive functions, especially processing and mediation. That is probably the case in this instance. The end product is a sort of cognitive functioning that falls well short of that reflected in her past academic performance or the cognitive capacity implied by her performance on intelligence testing.

SUMMARY

This youngster is in serious trouble. Her emotions appear to be overwhelming her. She is in considerable distress and probably experiences episodes of sadness or depression much more often than readily meets the eye. In this state, her capacity to control and direct her thinking and behavior is quite fragile, and she is highly vulnerable to instances in which her feelings dominate and direct her decisions and behaviors with little regard for the realities of a situation.

At least in part, many of the strong emotions that are now so disruptive appear related to a strong sense of alienation and anger that has a significant role in her psychology. These feelings have probably developed over a considerable time period in which her social naiveté and immaturity have placed significant limits on the extent to which she has been able to create or maintain rewarding relations among her peers. According to the history, she has become somewhat distant from them and may have experienced rejection. She is confused about people and feels insecure around them, and it appears as if, gradually, she has become socially isolated.

Her self-image is much more negative than positive. She feels fragile, insecure, pessimistic, and disapproving about herself. It seems likely that her conceptualization of herself is based largely on her confused notions about people, her imagination, and some probable misinterpretations of her own experiences. All of this has undoubtedly been reinforced by the accumulation of social failures in her young life. This negative self-concept increases her sense of fragility and provokes negative feelings. She seems to mistrust her emotions and is cautious about sharing or displaying them.

As the intensity of her emotions has increased, they have had a negative impact on many of her psychological features and operations. She has become less able to contain and direct her feelings effectively, and they have become disruptive to her basic cognitive functioning. Her processing of new information is somewhat casual, constricted, and often ineffectual, and her translations of new data tend to disregard reality. Her thinking is much more simplistic than should be the case and is frequently marked by noticeably faulty judgments. These cognitive impairments are at least partially responsible for the marked deterioration in her recent academic performance.

In many ways this child is like an emotional time bomb waiting to explode. Her emotions are intense and seemingly filled with anger and confusion. No doubt, she is plagued by doubts and fears and feels helpless. She is struggling hard to maintain some sort of psychological equilibrium but is in jeopardy of losing the battle. Her recent crying episodes probably reflect a seepage of her smoldering feelings, which otherwise, remain concealed, but this state cannot be sustained for very long. The overall picture resembles that of a child who has been psychologically abused in some way and who is floundering badly. It has been noted that her increasingly poor academic performance has some relation to the cognitive impairments that she suffers. However, the fact that she remains able to perform quite adequately in intelligence testing and neuropsychological screening raises a speculative question of whether her poor perfomance may reflect or include a silent cry for help.

RECOMMENDATIONS

Several important unanswered questions concerning this case have a direct bearing on most specific recommendations. The first is whether there is any evidence of unreported abuse in the home. This question must be addressed cautiously, but thoroughly. It should not be restricted to matters of physical abuse but expanded to consider psychological abuse possibilities such as disparagements, affective shunning, forced isolation, and the general tenor of interactions within the family. In a related context, the parental achievement expectations should also be reviewed more thoroughly. The parents admit that they make efforts to encourage a good academic performance, but they deny doing this to excess. Encouragement by adults is sometimes perceived as demands by children.

A third area that requires more thorough investigation concerns her social activities while in the first and second grades, during which her performance was outstanding. The specific question is whether other children avoided her during this time or whether her relationships were more typical. It would also be useful to learn more about her relationship with her brother and with the neighbor children with whom she plays occasionally.

Regardless of how the information concerning the preceding issues develops, it is obvious she is in dire need of frequent, supportive, and reassuring treatment. Among the first objectives for the intervention will be providing opportunities for emotional ventilation while structuring the treatment in a way that invokes thoughtful delay. The obvious goal of the latter is to aid in reconstituting her cognitive functioning to a higher level. Ultimately, the treatment plan should focus on the development of social skills, but that probably cannot happen until the more basic affective issues are addressed. Consideration of other treatment options should be deferred until more information unfolds regarding the home environment and her earlier social activities.

EPILOGUE

Her parents responded to feedback with obvious reservations, and they were not forthcoming with additional information about interactions within the family. They were adamant in rejecting the possibility of pharmacological intervention even before the matter was broached. They did agree to a recommendation for individual treatment for a minimum three-month period. They rejected the suggestion that she participate weekly in a play group of youngsters her own age.

The individual therapy was a semistructured model involving play and task completion. The therapist noted that, although she was very timid at first, she became much more active by the third session and was very critical in speaking about the object, doll, or task with which she might be involved. In speaking with the therapist about home and school, she often emphasized the importance of avoiding mistakes and being correct. At the end of the second month, the therapist arranged for two 40-minute sessions involving the whole family, during which the parents were instructed to direct and assist their children in the completion of three tasks. One consisted of adding numbers, the second concerned solving a puzzle, and the third required organizing 10 photos to create a story.

It was noted that both parents, and especially the mother, frequently chided the children for errors in addition or for creating nonsensical photo stories. The parents were counseled about their negative tactics and it was suggested that participation in group therapy for parents might be of use to them. They discussed the recommendation with their minister, who encouraged them to do so, and they began meeting weekly with the group. At the end of the school year, the teacher reported that crying episodes had ceased after the second month of treatment and her academic performance improved considerably. She also noted that a few of the children also seemed friendlier to the patient than had been the case previously. No further information is available.

REFERENCES

Achenbach, T. M., & McConaughy, S. H. (1992). Taxonomy of internalizing disorders of childhood and adolescence. In W. M. Reynold (Ed.), *Internalizing disorders in childhood and adolescence* (pp. 19–60). New York: Wiley.

Ball, J. D., Archer, R. P., Gordon, R. A., & French, J. (1991). Rorschach Depression indices with children and adolescents: Concurrent validity findings. *Journal of Personality Assessment, 57*(3), 465–476.

Beck, A., Ward, C., Mendelson, M., Mock, J., & Erbaugh, J. (1961). An inventory for measuring depression. *Archives of General Psychiatry, 4,* 53–63.

Carter, C. L., & Dacey, C. M. (1996). Validity of the Beck Depression Inventory, MMPI, and Rorschach in assessing adolescent depression. *Journal of Adolescence, 19*(3), 223–231.

Costello, E. J., Mustillo, S., Erkanli, A., Keeler, G., & Angold, A. (2003). Prevalence and development of psychiatric disorders in childhood and adolescence. *Archives of General Psychiatry, 60,* 837–844.

Elizur, A. (1949). Content analysis of the Rorschach with regard to anxiety and hostility. *Rorschach Research Exchange, 13,* 247–284.

Kovacs, M., & Beck, A. T. (1977). An empirical-clinical approach toward a definition of childhood depression. In J. G. Schulterbrandt & A. Raskin (Eds.), *Depression in childhood: Diagnosis, treatment, and conceptual models.* New York: Raven.

Krishnamurthy, R., & Archer, R. P. (2001). An evaluation of the effects of Rorschach EB style on the diagnostic utility of the Depression Index. *Assessment, 8*(1), 105–109.

Lipovsky, J. A., Finch, A. J., & Belter, R. W. (1989). Assessment of depression in adolescents: Objective and projective measures. *Journal of Personality Assessment, 53*(3), 449–458.

Ollendick, T. H., & King, N. J. (1994). Diagnosis, assessment, and treatment of internalizing problems in children: The role of longitudinal data. *Journal of Consulting and Clinical Psychology, 62*(5), 918–927.

Quay, H. C. (1986). Classification. In H. C. Quay & J. S. Werry (Eds.), *Psychopathological disorders of childhood* (3rd ed., pp. 1–34). New York: Wiley.

Spigelman, A., & Spigelman, G. (1991). Indications of depression and distress in divorce and nondivorce children reflected by the Rorschach test. *Journal of Personality Assessment, 57*(1), 120–129.

Spigelman, G., Spigelman, A., & Englesson, I. (1991). Hostility, aggression, and anxiety levels of divorce and nondivorce children as manifested in their responses to projective tests. *Journal of Personality Assessment, 56*(3), 438–452.

Viglione, D. J. (1999). A review of recent research addressing the utility of the Rorschach. *Psychological Assessment, 11*(3), 251–265.

Viglione, D. J., Brager, R. C., & Haller, N. (1988). Usefulness of structural Rorschach data in identifying inpatients with depressive symptoms: A preliminary study. *Journal of Personality Assessment, 52*(3), 524–529.

CHAPTER 18

A Problem with Aggressiveness

— CASE 16 —

This 10-year-old boy was evaluated because of a high frequency of apparently unwarranted aggressive actions in school. He has completed four months in the fifth grade, during which time he has been subject to disciplinary action seven times for aggressive acts, the last of which occurred in the cafeteria when he hit another boy with a tray, causing lacerations about the head.

He is the younger of two children whose parents were divorced when he was age three. His older sister, age 13, is currently in the seventh grade. His mother, age 34, is a registered nurse. She works in an obstetrics-gynecology clinic four and one half days each week. She has legal custody of the children. She has agreed to limited visitation privileges for the father, age 35, who is a senior partner in a real estate sales firm. He spends two weekends per month with the children, and he and his wife usually take them on vacation for two or three weeks each summer.

The mother reports that her son developed normally and has had no unusual illnesses. She states that she, her daughter, and her son are close and that he is rarely difficult at home: "I have to watch over him sometimes about his homework but that's the only problem." She says that the divorce was bitter and both parents sought custody of the children. She filed for the divorce after her husband left the home and began living with another woman, whom he later married. The father continues to contribute $1,500 per month for the support of the children. She stated that she has not considered marrying again, although she dates frequently. She expresses the belief that the school may be exaggerating the aggressiveness of her son and was defensive about the current evaluation. She says that he is never aggressive at home, and she has never observed him to be aggressive while playing with neighborhood children.

In a separate interview, the father expressed surprise about the reports of aggressiveness. He pointed to his son's success in playing baseball and football as evidence that he gets along well with other children. He conceded that his son is "a very active guy when he's with us, a little hard to manage sometimes, especially when we're on vacations. I've always figured that it was probably because she [the mother] was hard on him at home and he sees vacation as a time he can let off some steam." When this issue was pursued, the father noted, "He just gets too excited about some things and you have to calm him down."

He is slightly taller and huskier than most 10-year-old boys and might easily be judged as being a year or two older. He admits to fighting frequently in school but is avid in his claim that he never initiates these actions. This is contrary to the report of his fifth-grade teacher; she regards him as "a young man with a chip on his shoulder," who seems to look for trouble much of the time. The teacher reports that he frequently tries to verbally or physically dominate other children and has observed that most try to avoid him whenever possible. She notes that, when the class is involved in small group projects, the group that he is assigned to is often disrupted because he is argumentative or threatening. She also believes that he has taken various articles from other children, but has not confirmed this suspicion. She noted that a ballpoint pen was taken from her desk, and she was "almost certain" that he took it. She did discover chalk and an eraser in his desk, but he claimed that someone else put it there to get him in trouble.

The teacher reports that his academic performance is generally adequate and that he is often eager to answer questions or express his opinions. She believes that much of his aggressiveness is an attention-getting tactic and has shared this postulate with his mother, but found her to be unresponsive to the idea. The teacher also reported that she has asked the physical education teacher to give some special attention to the boy during gym classes. He has done so and reported that the boy does well in most of the games and exercises, but has observed several instances in which he is overly aggressive with the other boys and notes that a few are very submissive to him. Much of the time his aggressiveness is verbal, but in some instances it includes physical contacts, such as punching on the arm, kicking, or scuffling.

The boy claims that he has many close friendships and points with some pride that he is the third baseman on a Little League baseball team and plays fullback for a Pee Wee football team. He speaks fondly of his father, "We do a lot of neat things with him," and says that he and his sister both get along well with their mother, "She always takes good care of us." He states that he and his sister usually get along well. He concedes that they sometimes argue about the computer that they share, "She wants to be online too much," or about television programs to watch. He says that the only time he has any trouble at home is if he does not do his homework, or if his mother is called to the school because of his aggressiveness, "She gets pretty upset and sometimes I have to be in my room a lot or sometimes she won't let me watch TV." He says that he would like to be an explorer or an astronaut when he grows up. He expresses regret for the recent injury of the other student and concedes, "I just lost my temper because he was being so dumb."

The school psychologist conducting the evaluation reports that he was cooperative. His performance on the WISC-R yielded a full scale IQ of 111 (Verbal IQ = 107; Performance IQ = 116). There was no substantial scatter among the subtests with the exception of Block Design on which he obtained a scaled score of 16, which is four points higher than any other subtest score.

The school psychologist has requested a consultation from a colleague regarding the test data, with specific focus on several issues: (1) Is there evidence of emotional disturbance? (2) Should a special class for behavioral management be considered? (3) What advice can be given to his teacher and his physical education instructor concerning management issues? (4) Is any form of psychological treatment needed at this time? (5) How best to formulate feedback to the parents and specific recommendations to the mother?

CASE FORMULATION AND RELEVANT LITERATURE

This fifth-grade boy's behavior has been consistently and increasingly aggressive over the past four months. Although his most recent aggressive act injured another youngster, his divorced parents are surprised and defensive about the school's concern, which they tend to minimize. Contrary to his teacher's report, this boy insists that he never starts fights, instead externalizing blame for problems: "I just lost my temper because he was being so dumb." When his teacher found some school materials in his desk, he claimed that other students had put them there to get him into trouble. He is taller and huskier than most of his classmates, and his teachers note that he frequently intimidates other children either verbally or physically. Although he says that he has many close friendships, his teachers report that his classmates either avoid him or, in a few cases, become submissive to him.

His academic achievement is generally adequate. WISC-R Performance IQ (116) is somewhat higher than his Verbal IQ of 107, and he did particularly well on Block Design (Scale Score of 16). His teacher sees him as a "young man with a chip on his shoulder," but wonders if his aggressive behavior is a way to ensure attention for himself. After testing this boy, the school psychologist has requested a consultation to evaluate for the presence of emotional disturbance and develop an intervention strategy.

In many U.S. school districts, a finding of emotional disturbance as opposed to social maladjustment has significant implications for the availability of special education services. The federal Individuals with Disabilities Education Act (1997) delineates specific criteria for emotional disturbance and requires that it be differentiated from social maladjustment. Although there has been significant controversy as to whether emotional disturbance and social maladjustment are distinct categories (Hughes & Bray, 2004), the Act currently excludes children from special education services if their only difficulties involve social maladjustment, which is, at least initially, how this boy's presenting problems would be characterized. Making this differentiation poses ongoing challenges for school psychologists (Olympia et al., 2004) and assessment consultants.

The Rorschach literature on aggression was surveyed in Case 12 (Chapter 14), and there are only a few studies in this literature specifically about aggression in children. However, other parts of the child psychopathology literature on conduct disorder and bullying can be helpful in alerting the psychologist to alternative hypotheses for consideration when reviewing this boy's Rorschach and the behavioral picture he presents.

Assessment of Aggressive and Antisocial Behavior in Children

The *DSM-IV-TR* (American Psychiatric Association, 2000, p. 93) defines Conduct Disorder as ". . . a repetitive and persistent pattern of behavior in which the basic rights of others or major age-appropriate societal norms or rules are violated." Frick (2004) has suggested that there are several somewhat distinct pathways through which children reach this diagnosis. His delineation provides a helpful way of working through data from history, observation, and psychological testing to develop comprehensive and individualized interventions.

An important variable in assessing conduct disorders involves age of onset. Frick (2004) notes that the childhood-onset pattern often begins with mild problems that increase in frequency and severity as the child moves into adolescence. The adolescent-onset group does not exhibit conduct difficulties until later, and these more normative difficulties are less likely to continue into adulthood. Another variable Frick (2004) identifies focuses on callous and unemotional traits, defined as the absence of empathy or remorse. Children with conduct problems who also manifest these callous/unemotional traits show a more severely aggressive pattern, a preference for dangerous activities, less reaction to threatening and emotionally upsetting stimuli, and less sensitivity to punishment, particularly when seeking rewards. As Frick (2004) notes, "This reward-oriented response set may make this group of children less responsive to many behavior management plans used in schools that emphasize punishments for misbehavior, rather than incentives for more appropriate behaviors" (p. 827). Frick (2004) further suggests that the presence of callous/unemotional traits and low sensitivity to punishment can impair the development of empathy, anxiety, and guilt about misbehavior. Although there are no Rorschach studies currently available, one can speculate that findings such as COP, texture, diffuse shading, and vista would tend to mitigate against this callous/unemotional style.

In substantial contrast, Frick (2004) notes that children in the childhood-onset group who do not manifest callous/unemotional traits are less proactively aggressive, often with histories that involve poor parenting and verbal intelligence deficits. The pattern for this group appears to be one of difficulties with emotional regulation, and these children show greater empathy, more emotional distress, and greater sensitivity to negative experiences (Frick, Lilienfeld, Ellis, Loney, & Silverthorn, 1999; Loney, Frick, Clements, Ellis, & Kerlin, 2003; Pardini, Lochman, & Frick, 2003).

Frick (2004) suggests that interventions that focus on the development of empathy may be most specifically appropriate for children whose conduct disorders involve callous/unemotional traits, while approaches that emphasize impulse control may be most relevant for conduct-disordered children without those traits. He stresses the importance of thorough assessment in planning individualized intervention.

There are currently no Rorschach studies specifically contrasting conduct-disordered children with and without callous/unemotional traits. The most extensive Rorschach survey of conduct-disordered children comes from Gacono and Meloy (1994), who accumulated a sample of 60 mostly male inpatients between ages 5 and 12, who were hospitalized with diagnoses of conduct disorder. Children with comorbid diagnoses were not included in the sample. Because the sample size was not large enough to allow meaningful descriptive statistics on a year-by-year basis, the authors analyzed all 60 cases as a single group. Although the resulting descriptive statistics present averages for variables such as the Egocentricity Index, which change significantly over the developmental years, it is possible to note some trends that would not be expected at any point in the 5-to-12 age range.

Gacono and Meloy (1994) found that 65% of their sample had *Lambda* greater than .99, and 47% of the sample were ambitents. These findings suggest a simplifying approach that is likely to become increasingly ineffective in the face of greater complexity. From an interpersonal standpoint, 60% of the children had no COP in their Rorschachs and only 12% had a texture determinant. In general, the group viewed themselves negatively in comparison with others, with 72% having Egocentricity Index findings below .33. Even when presented with high-information, low-ambiguity data, these children were relatively unconventional; 50% produced fewer than four Popular answers in their protocols.

As in this case, aggression and intimidation are frequent referral issues for school psychologists. It will be useful to review the literature on bullying to understand the function it serves for this boy and to plan the most appropriate intervention. Elinoff, Chafouleas, and Sassu (2004) define bullying as ". . . a form of aggression that is hostile and proactive, and involves both direct and indirect behaviors that are repeatedly targeted at an individual or group perceived as weaker" (p. 888). They go on to write, "The key to defining a bullying situation is the existence of a power imbalance among those involved" (p. 889).

Coolidge, DenBoer, and Segal (2004) gathered parent report data on 41 middle school students, ages 11 to 15, who had received three or more disciplinary office referrals during the school year and compared them with parent reports for a matched group of students with no office referrals. Ratings on the Coolidge Personality and Neuropsychological Inventory (CPNI; Coolidge, 1998) for mild neurocognitive deficits, general neuropsychological dysfunction, and executive function deficits were significantly and clinically elevated for the disciplinary group. The Depressive Disorder scale was also significantly and clinically elevated for the disciplinary group, with two of the top four items that discriminated between the groups describing feelings of sadness and low self-esteem.

A study by McConville and Cornell (2003) suggests that attitude about aggression is another important assessment focus when aggressive behavior is part of a child's presenting problem. They measured 403 middle school students' attitudes toward peer aggression at the beginning of a school year and correlated their findings with self-reports of aggressive and bullying behavior, peer nomination of students as bullies, teacher nominations of students as bullies, and office referrals for discipline infractions. Students with more positive attitudes about the acceptability of aggression were more likely to report engaging in bullying or physical aggression. Aggressive attitudes correlated positively with both peer and teacher nominations for bullying, with self-reported aggressive behavior seven months later, and with total disciplinary office referrals, total detentions, and total school suspensions. The authors comment that, although no single variable can serve as an accurate predictor of future aggressive behavior, the assessment of attitudes toward peer aggression is an important part of comprehensive assessment. This case provides an example of how the Rorschach can help in determining the level of conflict that surrounds the person's view of aggression.

In summary, when aggression toward peers is part of the referral, several questions are important to consider. The assessment should begin with a careful review of the youngster's history to determine the age of onset and the course the behavior has taken. Cognitive/neuropsychological testing can furnish data about higher-level executive function. Assessment for the presence of affect dysregulation, callous/unemotional traits, and attitude toward the acceptability of aggression can provide greater understanding of the function this behavior serves for the individual. As this case illustrates, Rorschach variables can help in responding to these questions and developing more precise intervention recommendations.

Case 16. A 10-Year-Old Male.

Card	Response	Inquiry
I	1. A bat I thk, I'm not sur, yeah a bat	**E:** (Rpts Ss resp) **S:** I dk, it's got wgs, c how thyr shaped & it's got a tail in the back **E:** Tak ur tim, look som more, I thk u'll find smthg else too
	2. A littl question mark	**E:** (Rpts Ss resp) **S:** Rite ovr here, c it, it's shaped just lik a question mark
II	3. A cat tht got paint on it	**E:** (Rpts Ss resp) **S:** It's just lik a cat, c his ears up here, thy got red paint on em & he's got his mouth open here (DS5) & he's got paint on his whiskers dwn here (D3) **E:** Whiskers? **S:** Sur, thy all pointy lik whiskers but he got in som paint so thyr red
	4. Two weird guys, thyr lookg at eo	**E:** (Rpts Ss resp) **S:** Up here where the ears r, it ll a man facing a man, just the faces, u can c an eye & a nose & a mouth, thyr just lookg at e.o.
III	5. A red bowtie	**E:** (Rpts Ss resp) **S:** It just ll tht **E:** I kno it does but help me c it too **S:** It has the littl ball in the cntr & on the outside it's shaped lik fishtails, it's lik Mr (principal) wears, he wears one everyday **E:** U said it ll a ball in the cntr? **S:** Yeah u kno when u mak a knot it's a ball, lik a bulge, it bulges out
	6. Two peopl w deer legs	**E:** (Rpts Ss resp) **S:** Thyr bending ovr tryg to pick up ths thg **E:** Wht is there tht maks them ll people **S:** The head, the nose sticks out & the body & thes r deer legs, c the hoof **E:** U said thyr tryg to pick up ths thg? **S:** Yeah, I dk wht, som big barrel, ths round thg (D7)
IV	v7. A spider	**E:** (Rpts Ss resp) **S:** It has legs, 6 legs, no 8 legs, & an antenna & littl teeth **E:** Show me the legs & the teeth **S:** Sur, 2 here, 2 here, 2 here, 2 here & thes r littl teeth
	8. A gorilla, sittg on smthg	**E:** (Rpts Ss resp) **S:** Lik King Kong, a big gorilla, he's got big feet & his head's all scrunched down lik thy don't hav a neck, all furry, he's sitting on a stump or smthg, he's sur got big feet **E:** U said it's all furry? **S:** Yeah, he looks all furry (rubs blot)
V	9. A bat, he's flyg	**E:** (Rpts Ss resp) **S:** The big wgs & the legs r hangg out, he's got big pointed thgs comg out of his head, c up here (points), lik big feelers
	10. Two alligators	**E:** (Rpts Ss resp) **S:** The head, one ovr here too, thyv both got their mouth open lik thyr gonna bite on smthg, my friend used to hav a baby alligator, it ll ths, u had to put gloves on to feed it
VI	11. A skin of sk, kind of lik the fur of an A	**E:** (Rpts Ss resp) **S:** It's all dark & lite, lik the fur of an animal, u can c the legs too, it's all raggedy around the edge lik after u cut the skin off it's not even

Case 16. Continued.

Card	Response	Inquiry
	12. Ths prt up here ll a fly	**E:** (Rpts Ss resp) **S:** It has a littl body & the wgs, lik a fly
VII	13. Two rabbits tht r gettg ready to fight	**E:** (Rpts Ss resp) **S:** Thyr squattg dwn on ths rock, c their ears and tail **E:** U said thyr gettg ready to fite? **S:** Yep, thyr ready to jump at e.o., tht's why thy hav their ears up, I saw how thy fite in a movie about rabbits, thy jump at e.o.
	v14. Ths way it ll a big bird	**E:** (Rpts Ss resp) **S:** Just the top part, it has big wgs, lik thos birds in the mts, not eagles, bigger than eagles
VIII	15. A blue bird, lik the last one	**E:** (Rpts Ss resp) **S:** In the middl, it's got big wgs too, I don't rem the name but thyr really big, thy can even pick up a dog, I saw em on TV, thy live in the mts
	v16. Ths bottm is lik a boomerang	**E:** (Rpts Ss resp) **S:** Thyr shaped lik ths, if u saw Crocodile Dundee, well ths is lik thy had, thos Aborine guys, u can knock smbody dwn w em but if u miss thy com back to u
	17. Two tigers grabbing ths thg up here, some A, prob a jungle A	**E:** (Rpts Ss resp) **S:** Thyv crept up on it & now thyr grabbing it so thy hav somthg to eat, it's up in ths bush & thyr standg on thes orange rocks dwn here so thy can reach it **E:** I'm not sur I c it right **S:** Look, here r the tigers, c their heads & legs & thyr grabbg ths A up here (D4), c thyv got it's legs, it's up on ths bush or smthg (D5) & dwn here r lik rocks thyr standg on to get it
IX	18. It ll a fire	**E:** (Rpts Ss resp) **S:** The orange flames shootg up here at the top mak it ll a fire, lik ths green stuff is burning up, lik paper or smthg & the white in the cntr is lik the smoke going up **E:** U say the white in the cntr is lik smoke? **S:** Yeah, it's hazy lookg lik smoke, not just white but darkr white too, lik smoke
	v19. Some jewels	**E:** (Rpts Ss resp) **S:** Thyr red, 4 of em, thy ll som jewels **E:** I'm not sur I c them lik u **S:** Here (D6), there's 4 circles, lik 4 red jewels, thes 2 on the outside (D4) r sort of in front of the othr 2 cuz u can't c all of them, thy just ll jewels
	20. Two ghost, lik in cartoons	**E:** (Rpts Ss resp) **S:** Thes littl white things, thy ll ghosts, c one here & here **E:** I'm not sur why thy ll ghosts **S:** Thyr white, lik ghosts in cartoons
X	21. Two guys r tryg to push ths thg ovr	**E:** (Rpts Ss resp) **S:** Thy'r not real guys, just made up one's, lik in cartoons or smthg, c thyv got littl feet & thos funny thgs on their heads & thyr pushg on ths thg, tryg to knock it ovr lik a big post

(continued)

Card Response	Inquiry
22. A littl seed, off a tree	**E:** (Rpts Ss resp) **S:** Thy ll tht, thy hav thes littl side thgs, thy fall off and twirl around, u kno, thyr brown lik ths
v23. Mayb a bird, w really big wgs, flyg toward u	**E:** (Rpts Ss resp) **S:** It's got big green wgs & a littl body, not a real bird fr now, but lik when the world was first made, he's lik flyg toward u **E:** Flyg toward u? **S:** Well, it's lik off in the distance, coming toward ths way, toward u

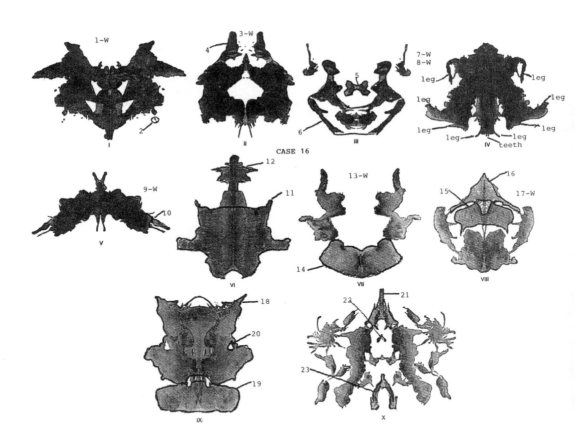

CASE 16

Case 16. Sequence of Scores.

Card	No.	Loc.	No.	Determinant(s)	(2)	Content(s)	Pop	Z	Special Scores
I	1	Wo	1	Fo		A	P	1.0	
	2	Ddo	99	Fu		Id			
II	3	WSo	1	CF.FMp−		Ad,Art		4.5	DV
	4	D+	2	Mp−	2	Hd		5.5	PHR
III	5	Do	3	FC.FDo		Cg			PER
	6	D+	1	Mao	2	H,Hh	P	3.0	COP,INC2,PHR
IV	7	Wo	1	F−		A		2.0	
	8	W+	1	FMp.FTo		A,Bt		4.0	
V	9	Wo	1	FMao		A	P	1.0	INC
	10	Do	10	FMao	2	Ad			AG,PER,PHR
VI	11	Do	1	TFo		Ad	P		
	12	Do	3	Fu		A			
VII	13	W+	1	FMao	2	A,Ls		2.5	AG,ALOG,PER,PHR
	14	Do	4	Fo		A			
VIII	15	Do	5	FCu		A			PER
	16	Do	4	Fu		Id			PER,DV
	17	W+	1	FMa.CFo	2	A,Ls	P	4.5	AG,GHR
IX	18	DSv/+	2	ma.CF.YFo		Fi,Sc		2.5	MOR,AG
	19	D+	6	CF.FDu	2	Art		2.5	
	20	DdSo	29	FC'o	2	(H)			GHR
X	21	D+	11	Mau	2	(H),Sc		4.0	AG,COP,PHR
	22	Do	3	FCo		Bt			
	23	Do	10	FMa.FD.FCu		(A)			

Case 16. Structural Summary.

Location Features	Determinants Blends	Single	Contents	S-Constellation
				. . . . .FV+VF+V+FD>2
			H = 1	. . . . .Col-Shd Bl>0
Zf = 12	CF.FM	M = 3	(H) = 2	. . . . .Ego<.31,>.44
ZSum = 37.0	FC.FD	FM = 3	Hd = 1	. . . . .MOR > 3
ZEst = 38.0	FM.FT	m = 0	(Hd) = 0	. . . . .Zd > +– 3.5
	FM.CF	FC = 2	Hx = 0	. . . . .es > EA
W = 7	m.CF.YF	CF = 0	A = 9	. . . . .CF+C > FC
D = 14	CF.FD	C = 0	(A) = 1	. . . . .X+% < .70
W+D = 21	FM.FD.FC	Cn = 0	Ad = 3	. . . . .S > 3
Dd = 2		FC' = 1	(Ad) = 0	. . . . .P < 3 or > 8
S = 3		C'F = 0	An = 0	. . . . .Pure H < 2
		C' = 0	Art = 2	. . . . .R < 17
		FT = 0	Ay = 0	x . . . .TOTAL

		Single	Contents	Special Scores
DQ		TF = 1	Bl = 0	Lv1 Lv2
+ = 7		T = 0	Bt = 2	DV = 2x1 0x2
o = 15		FV = 0	Cg = 1	INC = 1x2 1x4
v/+ = 1		VF = 0	Cl = 0	DR = 0x3 0x6
v = 0		V = 0	Ex = 0	FAB = 0x4 0x7
		FY = 0	Fd = 0	ALOG = 1x5
		YF = 0	Fi = 1	CON = 0x7
		Y = 0	Ge = 0	Raw Sum6 = 5
Form Quality		Fr = 0	Hh = 1	Wgtd Sum6 = 13

	FQx	MQual	W+D	Single	Contents		
+	= 0	= 0	= 0	rF = 0	Ls = 2		
o	= 13	= 1	= 12	FD = 0	Na = 0	AB = 0	GHR = 2
u	= 7	= 1	= 6	F = 6	Sc = 2	AG = 5	PHR = 5
–	= 3	= 1	= 3		Sx = 0	COP = 2	MOR = 1
none	= 0	= 0	= 0		Xy = 0	CP = 0	PER = 5
				(2) = 8	Id = 2		PSV = 0

Ratios, Percentages, and Derivations

R = 23	L	= 0.35		FC:CF+C = 4:4	COP = 2 AG = 5
				Pure C = 0	GHR:PHR = 2:5
EB = 3:6.0	EA	= 9.0	EBPer = 2.0	SumC':WSumC = 1:6.0	a:p = 8:3
eb = 8:4	es	= 12	D = –1	Afr = 0.64	Food = 0
	Adj es	= 12	Adj D = –1	S = 3	SumT = 2
				Blends:R = 7:23	Hum Con = 4
FM = 7	C'	= 1	T = 2	CP = 0	Pure H = 1
m = 1	V	= 0	Y = 1		PER = 5
					Iso Indx = 0.17

a:p	= 8:3	Sum6 = 5	XA% = 0.87	Zf = 12.0	3r+(2)/R = 0.35
Ma:Mp	= 2:1	Lv2 = 1	WDA% = 0.86	W:D:Dd = 7:14:2	Fr+rF = 0
2AB+Art+Ay	= 2	WSum6 = 13	X–% = 0.13	W:M = 7:3	SumV = 0
MOR	= 1	M– = 1	S– = 1	Zd = –1.0	FD = 3
		Mnone = 0	P = 5	PSV = 0	An+Xy = 0
			X+% = 0.57	DQ+ = 7	MOR = 1
			Xu% = 0.30	DQv = 0	H:(H)Hd(Hd) = 1:3

PTI = 0	DEPI = 3	CDI = 3	S-CON = N/A	HVI = No	OBS = No

376

S-CON AND KEY VARIABLES

The S-CON is not applicable for children of this age. The first positive Key variable is the Adj D Score that is in the minus range. It indicates that the interpretation should begin with a review of data regarding controls but does not suggest an order for addressing the remaining data clusters. That decision is guided by the second positive Key variable, the *EB* (3:6.0), which reveals an extratensive coping style. This denotes that the interpretive routine should move next to the information concerning affect and then proceed to the clusters regarding self-perception and interpersonal perception. The last segment of the interpretation will involve a review of the three data groups that comprise the cognitive triad: processing, mediation, and ideation.

CONTROLS

Case 16.   Control-Related Variables for a 10-Year-Old Male.

EB = 3:6.0	EA = 9.0		D = −1	CDI = 3
eb = 8:4	es = 12	Adj es = 12	AdjD = −1	L = 0.35
FM = 7 m = 1	SumC′ = 1	SumT = 2	SumV = 0	SumY = 1

The ADj D Score of −1 indicates that he is in a persistent state of stimulus overload. This limits his capacity for control and creates a susceptibility for some disorganization and impulsiveness to occur under stressful circumstances. Although an overload of this magnitude increases vulnerability, it does not automatically impair functioning, especially if the challenges and demands of the environment are routine and predictable. It is not necessarily an unusual finding for a 10-year-old, but when it exists, limited resources are usually the cause. That does not appear to be true in this case. The *EA* (9.0) is well within the average range for his age and the *EB* (3:6.0) contains no zero values. This implies that his resource availability should be adequate to contend with most circumstances.

The origins of his overload are revealed by the Adj *es* value (12), which is substantially higher than expected for most people, especially children. It intimates considerable internal stimulus demands that tend to exceed his capacity to deal with all of them in a consistent and effective manner. The *eb* (8:4) provides some information about these demands.

The left side *eb* value (8) is higher than expected and is mainly comprised of seven *FM* answers. They signal the probability that he is experiencing more seemingly random patterns of peripheral thinking than is usual. They are likely to be related to ungratified need states. These provoke mental activity that tends to intrude on his deliberate thinking and can often distract his attention and concentration. In addition, the right side value of the *eb* (4) is slightly elevated because of two texture answers. Their presence suggests some strong feelings of emotional neediness or loneliness.

Overall, his capacity for control and tolerance for stress are somewhat limited because of much internal stimulation that he does not contend with satisfactorily. These limitations create a vulnerability to disorganization and increase the likelihood for impulsive thoughts or behaviors to occur when he is confronted with environmental demands or expectations that are substantially different from those to which he is accustomed.

AFFECT

Case 16.   Affect-Related Data for a 10-Year-Old Male.

EB	= 3:6.0			EBPer	= 2.0	**Blends**		
eb	= 8:4	L	= 0.35	FC:CF+C	= 4:4	FM.FD.FC	= 1	
DEPI	= 3	CDI	= 3	Pure C	= 0	FM.CF	= 1	
						FM.FT	= 1	
SumC' = 1	SumT = 2			SumC':WSumC	= 1:6.0	m.CF.YF	= 1	
SumV = 0	SumY = 1			Afr	= 0.64	CF.FM	= 1	
						CF.FD	= 1	
Intellect	= 2	CP	= 0	S = 3 (S to I,II,III = 1)		FC.FD	= 1	
Blends:R	= 7:23			Col-Shad Bl	= 1			
m + y Bl	= 1			Shading Bl	= 0			

The *EB* (3:6.0) indicates that his feelings usually are quite influential on his thinking and promote an intuitive approach to making decisions. This mode of coping is rather common among children and typically involves testing out postulates and assumptions through trial-and-error behaviors. The value for *EBPer* (2.0) suggests that he is probably flexible about the use of this coping approach and, at times, will push feelings aside in favor of a more ideational strategy.

As noted, the right side value in the *eb* is slightly elevated because of two texture answers. In that there are no indications of a recent emotional loss, they appear to signal persistent feelings of loneliness or emotional neediness. However, no other evidence in this data set suggests strong feelings of emotional irritation or distress. The DEPI value (3) is not significant. The left side value of the *eb* (8) is much higher than the right side, and the other variables that contribute to the right side *eb* value (*SumC'*, *SumV*, and *SumY*) are all modest.

The *Afr* (.64) is well within the expected range and implies that he is as willing as most others of his age to process and become involved with emotionally toned stimuli. The *FC:CF+C* ratio (4:4) and the absence of a Pure *C* response indicate that he is somewhat more conservative about modulating his emotional displays than are most children of his age. Typically, the right side value in this ratio will be higher than that of the left side for most 10-year-olds, and Pure *C* answers are not uncommon.

The *FC:CF+C* finding is surprising in light of the reports concerning his aggressiveness and his previously noted vulnerability to a loss of control. It supports the notion that his aggressive acts are not simply manifestations of loosely controlled emotions. His protocol includes three space responses, implying that he is disposed to be negative or oppositional toward his environment. However, this is not necessarily a liability. It may impede the development of harmonious social relations, but it does not really provide a basis from which to explain his aggressive behaviors.

His record contains seven blended answers, one of which appears to be situationally related (*m.CF.YF*) and is his only color shading blend. Five of the six remaining blends contain two variables. This finding is generally consistent with that expected of an extratensive person and does not indicate any unusual psychological complexity.

Most of the findings concerning his emotions are much more favorable than might be expected in light of the history. He is reasonably consistent in his approach to making decisions and, like many of his age, emotions play a significant role in that process. He seems open to emotional exchange and, surprisingly, appears to modulate or control the display of his feelings more stringently than do most 10-year-olds. He seems to be emotionally needy or lonely, and he is also some-what negative or oppositional about his environment. These elements may contribute to his aggressive behaviors, but there is no evidence to suggest that his aggressiveness is a direct consequence of them or related to any significant emotional disturbance.

SELF-PERCEPTION

Case 16.   Self-Perception Related Data for a 10-Year-Old Male.

R	= 23	OBS	= No	HVI = No	**Human Content, Hx, An & Xy Responses**
					II 4. D+ Mp– 2 Hd 5.5 PHR
Fr+rF	= 0	3r+(2)/R	= 0.35		III 6. D+ Mao 2 H,Hh P 3.0 COP,INC2,PHR
					IX 20. DdSo FC'o 2 (H) GHR
FD	= 3	SumV	= 0		X 21. D+ Mau 2 (H),Sc 4.0 AG,COP,PHR
An+Xy = 0		MOR	= 1		

H:(H)+Hd+(Hd) = 1:3
   [EB = 3:6.0]

The Egocentricity Index (.35) is considerably lower than expected for a 10-year-old. It indicates that he tends to judge himself less favorably when compared with others and that his estimate of self-worth is negative. In addition, his protocol includes three *FD* responses, which is unusual for a child. They signify that he is involved in considerable rumination about himself. Although this may represent a striving for self-betterment, it is more likely that this introspective process focuses on personal faults and, as such, simply reinforces his unfavorable view of himself.

His record contains four human content answers, but only one is pure *H*. This implies that his self-image tends to be formulated largely from imaginary impressions or distortions of real experiences. This is not necessarily unusual for a youngster but, typically, the result is unrealistically positive. If the yield from these impressions is more negative than positive, it creates a potential for both intrapsychic and interpersonal difficulties. The latter seems likely in this case when the codings for his human content responses are considered.

The codings for all four of his human content answers include some sort of undesirable feature in the coding. The first (response 4) is an *M–* answer. The second (response 6) is a Popular response to Card III but also contains an INC2. The third (response 20) is a *DdS* response involving achromatic color, and the fourth (response 21) is a parenthesized human content answer that includes both aggressive and cooperative movement.

His three minus responses are not especially rich for projected material. The first (Card II, response 3) is, "A cat that got paint on it . . . his ears up here, they got red paint on them and he's got his mouth open and he's got paint on his whiskers." It is concrete, but not necessarily unusual for a child. The second (Card II, response 4) is a bit more revealing, "Two weird guys, they are looking at each other . . . a man facing a man, just the faces . . . they're just looking at each other." The fact that they are "weird" may imply something about his self-image, and his emphasis on "just looking" may convey a sense of deliberate constraint. The third minus (Card IV, response 7) is, "A spider . . . it has six legs, no eight legs and an antenna and little teeth." It has an ominous and threatening quality.

The substance of his single MOR response (Card IX, response 18) is not uncommon but has some unique features and includes aggressiveness. It is, "a fire . . . flames shooting up at the top, this green stuff is burning up, like paper or something . . . the smoke going up . . . not just white but darker white too." A unique feature is that it is paper that is burning and not the more commonly identified forest. This may imply fragility. A second uncommon feature is his differentiation of coloring in the white area, which may emphasize a sense of helplessness that he is experiencing.

The first of his three *M* answers, "weird guys looking at each other," has been reviewed. The second (Card III, response 6) is, "Two people with deer legs . . . bending over trying to pick up this thing." He seems to have included the incongruous feature very casually while giving this Popular answer and makes no effort to alter or comment about it when given the opportunity in the inquiry. It may have some similarity to his earlier answer about "weird guys," but that is speculative. However, his third *M* (Card X, response 21) is also analogous. It is one of his five aggressive answers, "Two guys are trying to push this thing over . . . not real guys just made up ones like in cartoons . . . they've got little feet and those funny things on their heads." The humans or human-like characters in each of these answers have something strange about them, implying that he may experience himself in this way. The fourth human content response (Card IX, response 20) is also unreal, "Two ghosts, like in cartoons."

The first of his seven *FM* answers, "A cat that got paint on it," has been reviewed. The next two *FM* answers contain references to strange features (Card IV, response 8) "A gorilla, sitting on something . . . like King Kong . . . his head's all scrunched down like they don't have a neck, all furry," and (Card V, response 9), "A bat, he's flying . . . he's got big pointed things coming out of his head . . . like big feelers." The next three *FM* responses all include some form of aggressiveness. The first (Card V, response 10) is "Two alligators . . . both got their mouth open like they're gonna bite something." The second (Card VII, response 13) is "Two rabbits getting ready to fight . . . ready to jump at each other, that's why they have their ears up," and the third (Card VIII, response 17) is "Two tigers grabbing this thing up here, some animal . . . they've crept up on it and now they're grabbing it so they have something to eat." The final *FM* (Card X, response 23) also emphasizes strangeness, "a big bird, with really big wings, flying toward you . . . big green wings and a little body, not a real bird from now, but like when the world was first made."

Two of the remaining 10 responses also have some features that seem worth noting. Both are Card VIII responses. Response 15, is "A blue bird . . . it's got big wings . . . they can even pick up a dog," and response 16 is, "a boomerang . . . you can knock somebody down with them but if you miss they come back to you." The aggressive potential in each seems obvious.

The remaining seven answers are predominantly descriptions of distal features of the areas used. They include response 1 (a bat); response 2 (a little question mark); response 5 (a red bowtie); response 11 (a skin of some kind); response 12 (a fly); response 14 (a big bird); response 19 (some jewels); and response 22 (a little seed off a tree).

The projected material that is included in 15 of his 23 answers tends to emphasize strangeness or aggressiveness. None contain ordinary human figures and none have verbiage or content that can easily be described as positive. Typically, children of this age are still seeking identities. Although their self-images are not yet fully developed in the context of reality, they usually include more positive than negative features. That does not appear to be the case with this youngster. He does not regard himself favorably and seems to ruminate a great deal about himself.

It is likely that he feels out of step with his peers and perceives himself as being more strange than common. Possibly, his size has some relevance to this impression. He has a very distinct preoccupation with aggression. This is probably related to his limited sense of self-worth and the notion that he is atypical. Children with these features often find aggressiveness to be an effective way of protecting their integrity and concealing their insecurities.

A more basic issue concerns his identification. His self-image is diffuse and fragile. This raises an important question about the sources from which his identity has developed, and his relationship to those sources. According to his report, his relationship with both parents is positive and satisfying, but this seems inconsistent with his diffuse and negative sense of self and his strong feelings of neediness or loneliness. On a speculative level, it seems as if he has no firm role model with whom to identify and, as a result, has tended to flounder in his quest for self-knowledge and his search for an appropriate role in a world that he perceives as threatening and ungiving.

INTERPERSONAL PERCEPTION

Case 16.   Interpersonal Perception Data for a 10-Year-Old Male.

				COP & AG Responses
R = 23	CDI = 3	HVI = No		III 3. D+ Mao 2 H,Hh P 3.0 COP,INC2,PHR
a:p = 8:3	SumT = 2	Fd = 0		V 10. Do FMao 2 Ad AG,PER,PHR
	[eb = 8:4]			VII 13. W+ FMao 2 A,Ls 2.5 AG,ALOG,PER,PHR
Sum Human Contents = 4		H = 1		VIII 17. W+ FMa.CFo 2 A,Ls P 4.5 AG,GHR
[Style = Extratensive]				IX 18. DSv/+ ma.CF.YFo Fi,Sc 2.5 MOR,AG
GHR:PHR = 2:5				X 21. D+ Mau 2 (H),Sc 4.0 AG,COP,PHR
COP = 2	AG = 5	PER = 5		
Isolation Indx = 0.17				

None of the data for the CDI, HVI, or $a:p$ ratio (8:3) have interpretive relevance. The first significant datum in this group has been mentioned previously. It is the two texture responses, intimating that he has substantial feelings of emotional neediness or loneliness. As there is no evidence of a recent emotional loss, it seems likely that this is a chronic state with origins in events where his emotional needs have been neglected and unsatisfied. Such incidents usually accumulate and gradually breed a sense of longing, loneliness, or even abandonment. When this experience persists, it can have a negative influence on self-esteem and self-image.

As noted during the study of data concerning self-perception, his four human content responses include only one Pure *H*. The implication is that he is reasonably interested in people but does not understand them very well. This lack of understanding can easily lead to a misinterpretation of social cues that, in turn, creates a potential for behaviors that may alienate others. The GHR:PHR ratio (2:5) supports the premise that his interpersonal behaviors are often ineffective or maladaptive. It denotes a lack of awareness about social amenities. This can easily lead to patterns of behavior that can cause others to shun or reject him.

Although his record contains two COP responses, it also includes five *AG* responses. This denotes that he is prone to perceive aggressiveness as a natural element in social relationships and is likely to be noticeably forceful or aggressive in his everyday behaviors. This is not surprising in light of the history, but it raises a question about whether these behaviors are a way of contending with a sense of personal and social insecurity or simply represent learned ways of interacting with people. The findings concerning self-perception suggest that the former is likely to be true. This premise is also supported by the five PER responses, many more than expected. Substantial elevations in PER signify a marked habit of using bits of knowledge to fend off perceived challenges to one's integrity in social situations.

He has six *M* and *FM* answers that include pairs. Four of these are *AG* responses. A fifth has a minus form quality and the sixth includes a serious incongruity (INC2), which reinforces the notion that his interpersonal world is probably threatening to him and his responses to it are likely to be inappropriate.

The overall interpersonal picture is not favorable, and less so when considered in light of findings about self-perception. He seems confused by the social world and insecure in it. This insecurity is likely to be exacerbated by his unfavorable self-regard. He seems to have found forcefulness and aggressiveness to be convenient ways of maintaining a superficial sense of personal integrity and warding off threats from others. However, beneath his aggressive facade is a needy and lonely youngster who feels vulnerable.

PROCESSING

Case 16.   Processing Variables for a 10-Year-Old Male.

EB	= 3:6.0	Zf	= 12	Zd	= –1.0	DQ+	= 7
L	= 0.35	W:D:Dd	= 7:14:2	PSV	= 0	DQv/+	= 1
HVI	= No	W:M	= 7:3			DQv	= 0
OBS	= No						

Location & DQ Sequencing

I:	Wo.Ddo	VI:	Do.Do
II:	WSo.D+	VII:	W+.Do
III:	Do.D+	VIII:	Do.Do.W+
IV:	Wo.W+	IX:	DSv/+.D+.DdSo
V:	Wo.Do	X:	D+.Do.Do

The *Zf* (12) is within the average range and suggests a processing effort similar to most children of his age. However, the *W:D:Dd* ratio (7:14:2) indicates that he is conservative about how he applies this effort. This is confirmed by the location sequence. Five of his seven *W* answers were given to the first five cards, four of which were to the more solid figures, I, IV, and V. Only one *W* answer was included in the nine responses given to the last three cards. This economical approach is also implied by the *W:M* ratio (7:3), which is average for adult extratensives, but more conservative than expected for a 10-year-old. The *Zd* score (–1.0) denotes that his scanning efficiency is similar to children his age, and the presence of seven *DQ+* responses and the absence of *DQv* answers signify that the quality of his processing is usually quite adequate. The fact that five of his seven *DQ+* responses are not first answers implies that he often perseveres when processing, to ensure that he considers all aspects of new information. The overall findings regarding his processing activities are generally favorable. They indicate that he is somewhat conservative when dealing with new information, but this should not be viewed as a problem.

MEDIATION

Case 16.   Mediation Variables for a 10-Year-Old Male.

R = 23		L = 0.35 ·			OBS = No	**Minus & NoForm Features**
FQx+	= 0		XA%	= .87		II 3. WSo CF.FMp– Ad,Art 4.5 DV
FQxo	= 13		WDA%	= .86		II 4. D+ Mp– 2 Hd 5.5 PHR
FQxu	= 7		X–%	= .13		IV 7. Wo F– A 2.0
FQx–	= 3		S–	= 1		
FQxnone	= 0					
(W+D	= 24)		P	= 5		
WD+	= 0		X+%	= .57		
WDo	= 12		Xu%	= .30		
WDu	= 6					
WD–	= 3					
WDnone	= 0					

The *XA%* (.87) and *WDA%* (.86) are both substantial and indicate that his translations of information are usually appropriate for the situation. The *X–%* (.13), representing three minus answers, is not substantial and indicates that events of mediational dysfunction occur no more frequently than is customary for most people. There is no obvious homogeneity among his three minus answers. One is the face of a cat with paint on it. The second is two weird guys looking at each other, and the third is a spider with eight legs and little teeth. None of these involve serious distortions of the distal features. This composite of findings confirms that the basic ingredient for adequate reality testing is intact.

His protocol includes five Popular answers, which is within the expected range for someone his age. This suggests that he will usually make conventional responses when the cues for expected or acceptable behaviors are obvious. On the other hand, the *X+%* (.57) and *Xu%* (.30) denote that he may often disregard social demands or expectations and decide on less conventional patterns of behavior. Sometimes this can be a healthy form of individualism. In this case, however, it probably reflects the concerns that he has with protecting his integrity and seems likely to account for his frequent willingness to substitute aggressive behaviors for those that might be more acceptable to others. Thus, even though his reality testing appears to be quite adequate, his tendency to be less concerned about social conventions or expectations seems to be an important issue that should be weighed carefully when treatment planning is considered.

IDEATION

Case 16.   Ideation Variables for a 10-Year-Old Male.

L	= 0.35	OBS	= No	HVI	= No	**Critical Special Scores**	

						DV = 2	DV2 = 0
EB	= 3:6.0	EBPer	= 2.0	a:p	= 8:3	INC = 1	INC2 = 1
				Ma:Mp	= 2:1	DR = 0	DR2 = 0
eb	= 8:4	[FM = 7 m = 1]				FAB = 0	FAB2 = 0
				M–	= 1	ALOG = 1	CON = 0
Intell Indx	= 2	MOR	= 1	Mnone	= 0	Sum6 = 5	WSum6 = 13
						(R = 23)	

M Response Features

II   4. D+ Mp– 2 Hd 5.5 PHR
III   6. D+ Mao 2 H,Hh P 3.0 COP,INC2,PHR
X 21. D+ Mau 2 (H),Sc 4.0 AG,COP,PHR

As noted, the *EB* (3:6.0) indicates that he is prone to merge emotions with his thinking and approach decisions in an intuitive way. His thinking is not less consistent or more illogical because of this, but it can often be made more complex because of the intermingling of feelings. However, the *EBPer* (2.0) provides no basis for believing that he is inflexible about using this approach to make decisions. This is an asset worth considering when planning treatment. On the other hand, the values in the *a:p* ratio (8:3) are disparate, with the left side value being more than two and one half times that of the right side. This indicates that his ideational sets and values are reasonably well fixed and probably difficult to alter.

The left side *eb* value (8) also raises some concerns. The presence of seven *FM* responses signals that internal needs states are causing him to experience substantial peripheral or subconscious mental activity. During the review of data regarding controls, it was noted that this is contributing significantly to his persistent overload. This sort of mental activity not only adds to internal stimulus demands, but often also leaks into conscious ideation and interrupts directed patterns of thinking. The resulting loss of concentration can be frustrating, especially for a child, and it also reduces the probability that decisions will be well thought through.

The *WSum6* (13) is a bit higher than expected for a 10-year-old. It suggests that his ideational activity is marked by more cognitive slippage or flawed judgment than is typical for most children his age. It does not necessarily reflect a thinking problem but it signifies that his thinking is sometimes less clear or less sophisticated than might be desired.

Five of his responses have critical special scores. Two of these are relatively insignificant *DV* answers. One (response 3) is coded for the use of the word "pointy," and in the second (response 16) he substituted the word "Aborine" for Aborigine. Another answer (response 10) is coded INCOM because he included "big pointed things coming out of his head . . . like big feelers" when describing a bat. It is a naive description but, as with the *DV* responses, does not represent a serious problem.

The other two answers that are coded for critical special scores are of more concern. The first (response 6), "Two people with deer legs," is coded INCOM2. It is a concrete and somewhat bizarre incongruity. When afforded the opportunity to clarify the answer in the inquiry, he simply reaffirms the discrepancy rather than commenting on its strangeness or changing the description as do most children. This emphasizes the notion that his judgment is sometimes seriously flawed. This is also suggested in the second of these two answers (response 13) which is coded ALOG. In this response when asked about the rabbits getting ready to fight, he replies, "they're ready to jump at each other, that's why they have their ears up." It is not as seriously unrealistic as the people with deer legs, but it is naively simplistic and concrete. These sorts of cognitive slip are not necessarily unusual for one his age, but they illustrate potential areas of concern when considering various approaches to treatment.

Although it is evident that his thinking is not sophisticated, there is no evidence of a pervasive thought disturbance. His conceptualizations and judgments are sometimes naive, concrete, and oversimplistic, but this is not unusual for a 10-year-old. Like many of his age, he is intuitive in his approach to making decisions and this can be effective for him. However, his attitudes and values seem to be well fixed and this can limit his consideration of options when he is confronted with making a decision. This limitation is likely to be increased because his thinking is frequently distracted by the intrusion of peripheral or subconscious thoughts prompted by a substantial level of unfulfilled needs. These interruptions to his concentration are probably frustrating for him, and because he has problems with controls, there is an increased likelihood that some of his decisions may be formed more impulsively.

SUMMARY

This is a very insecure youngster who is burdened by many unfulfilled needs that tend to create substantial irritation for him. He is unable to deal with these needs easily or effectively, and as a result, he is in an ongoing state of stimulus overload. This limits his capacity for control and his tolerance for stress and increases the likelihood that his thinking and behavior will be marked by impulsiveness.

Although some of these needs are natural human experiences, two interrelated elements appear to have increased them. The first is a low sense of self-esteem or personal worth. He does not regard himself as favorably as others and tends to view himself as having strange or undesirable features. He works hard to conceal these impressions, and he seems to have found aggressiveness to be a useful defense for this purpose. The second is a noticeable sense of emotional neediness or loneliness, which can be quite irritating. Apparently, he has not been able to develop emotional attachments that are sufficiently gratifying for him. Some of his loneliness is probably an indirect result of his aggressiveness. It causes peers to avoid him and limits the possibilities for close friendships, but the source of his neediness probably goes well beyond the lack of rewarding social relations. His low self-esteem suggests that he is lacking a consistent source of identification and also lacking emotional support and reassurance. The history fails to include any noticeably positive comments about him from his parents. His father describes him as active and hard to manage at times, and his mother believes that his aggressiveness is being exaggerated by the school. It is difficult to avoid raising a question about his parental relations and the apparent absence of adequate role models in his life.

It seems obvious that his interpersonal world is impoverished. In part, this is because of his aggressiveness, but it is also apparent that he is naive about socially adaptive behaviors. He seems confused by his social world and apparently is able to connect with it in a rewarding manner only through his athletic accomplishments.

On a more positive note, his basic cognitive operations are intact. His approach to processing new information is conservative but adequate. He usually translates information in the context of reality, and his thinking is usually clear even though sometimes marked by simplistic and naive judgments.

There is no evidence of pathology or a serious emotional disturbance, but he is somewhat less mature and more naive than should be the case. He is very unsure of himself and feels quite vulnerable. He has learned to conceal this and defend himself with aggression, and because he has limited controls, his aggressiveness is likely to manifest more routinely and impulsively under unfamiliar circumstances or conditions that he perceives to be stressful.

It is important to emphasize that his aggressiveness is not the product of meanness or anger. It is a routine defensive tactic that disguises his neediness, loneliness, and insecurity. Unfortunately, he invokes this tactic too frequently, and it only serves to distance him more from the social and emotional attachments that could be rewarding for him.

RECOMMENDATIONS

The consultation request includes five issues. The first raises a question about a possible emotional disturbance. Although he is needy, lonely, and immature, there is no evidence from which to conclude that an emotional disturbance is present. A second issue concerns the possibility of placement in a special class for behavior management. This would be counterproductive. It would reinforce his sense of low self-value and strangeness and probably lead to a higher frequency of aggressive behaviors because it would increase the necessity to defend himself.

A third issue concerns advice to his teacher and his physical education instructor. His teacher's suggestion that his aggressiveness may be an attention-getting tactic has merit and is partially true. However, it does not account for much of his unwanted behavior, and it would be unrealistic to suggest that most of his difficulties can be resolved mainly in the school. Nonetheless, it would be worthwhile to assist them in developing a listing of possible reactions, both positive and negative, that they could use to respond to his various behaviors. If both teachers are consistent in their responses to his favorable and unfavorable behaviors, some reduction in unwanted behavior might occur, especially if positive reinforcements are used wisely. However, the issues of neediness, loneliness, and diffuse identity generally require much more than this.

The last two issues concern possible forms of intervention and feedback to the parents. It seems obvious that some form of intervention should be formulated, but it is impractical to make specific treatment recommendations without first obtaining much more information about the family members, their perceptions of him, and interactions with him. The parents should be informed of this while providing feedback to them regarding his low self-esteem and his use of aggressiveness as a defensive and possible attention-getting tactic. Their reactions to this should provide some guidelines about how best to address his neediness, loneliness, and lack of adequate role models as this information is likely to pose some threat to one or both of them that can be counterproductive.

A well-structured cognitive intervention seems appropriate for him, but the possibility of family intervention should also be considered as additional information about his history becomes available. In addition, earlier school records should be reviewed to determine the onset of his excessive use of aggressiveness. This may be a long-standing characteristic and, if so, would suggest a somewhat different intervention strategy than if it has appeared recently. Ultimately, the matter of identity will be an important focal point in the intervention and the relation between the parents and their accessibility, either individually or together, should also provide some guidance regarding identification models and their usefulness in the intervention process.

EPILOGUE

Feedback concerning the evaluation was provided jointly to his parents. His mother expressed some skepticism about the causes for his aggressiveness but agreed to enter the boy in individual treatment that would focus on behavior management and social skill development. She also agreed to permit the boy to spend two additional days per month with his father, and the father volunteered to interact closely with the therapist to develop a schedule of positive reactions that he might use to reward favorable behaviors. His teacher admitted that she would prefer special class placement but acquiesced to the suggestion that she try out a systematic routine of rewards for desirable behaviors.

The teacher reported that, during the next three months, no additional episodes of physically aggressive behaviors were observed but also noted that she did not perceive much of a decrease in verbal aggressiveness. She conceded that his academic performance showed "general improvement" and noted that other children tended to respond more favorably to him. No additional information is available.

REFERENCES

American Psychiatric Association. (2000). *Diagnostic and statistical manual of mental disorders* (4th ed., text rev.). Washington, DC: Author.

Coolidge, F. (1998). *Coolidge Personality and Neuropsychological inventory for children.* Colorado Springs, CO: Author.

Coolidge, F., DenBoer, J., & Segal, D. (2004). Personality and neuropsychological correlates of bullying behavior. *Personality and Individual Differences, 36,* 1559–1569.

Elinoff, M., Chafouleas, S., & Sassu, K. (2004). Bullying: Considerations for defining and intervening in school settings. *Psychology in the Schools, 41*(8), 887–897.

Frick, P. (2004). Developmental pathways to conduct disorder: Implications for serving youth who show severe aggressive and antisocial behavior. *Psychology in the Schools, 41*(8), 823–834.

Frick, P., Lilienfeld, S., Ellis, M., Loney, B., & Silverthorn, P. (1999). The association between anxiety and psychopathy dimensions in children. *Journal of Abnormal Child Psychology, 27,* 381–390.

Gacono, C. B., & Meloy, J. R. (1994). *The Rorschach assessment of aggressive and psychopathic personalities.* Hillsdale, NJ: Erlbaum.

Hughes, T., & Bray, M. (2004). Differentiation of emotional disturbance and social maladjustment: Introduction to the special issue. *Psychology in the Schools, 41*(8), 819–821.

Individuals with Disabilities Education Act (IDEA), 20 U.S.C. 1400 (1997).

Loney, B., Frick, P., Clements, C., Ellis, M., & Kerlin, K. (2003). Callous-unemotional traits, impulsivity, and emotional processing in antisocial adolescents. *Journal of Clinical Child and Adolescent Psychology, 32,* 139–152.

McConville, D., & Cornell, D. (2003). Aggressive attitudes predict aggressive behavior in middle school students. *Journal of Emotional and Behavioral Disorders, 11*(3), 179–187.

Olympia, D., Farley, M., Christiansen, E., Petterson, H., Jenson, W., & Clark, E. (2004). Social maladjustment and students with behavioral and emotional disorders: Revisiting basic assumptions and assessment issue. *Psychology in the Schools, 41*(8), 835–847.

Pardini, D., Lochman, J., & Frick, P. (2003). Callous/Unemotional traits and social cognitive processes in adjudicated youth. *Journal of the American Academy of Child and Adolescent Psychiatry, 42,* 364–371.

CHAPTER 19

Drug Overdose in an Adolescent

―――――――――――――――――――― C A S E 1 7 ――――――――――――――――――――

This 14-year-old boy was evaluated on the eleventh day as an inpatient in a psychiatric unit and after a total of 14 days of hospitalization. He was initially admitted to a general medical facility in a comatose state. Apparently, he had overdosed on cocaine, and his breathing was very shallow when he was discovered in his mother's automobile, in the garage of the family's home. He remained comatose for about four hours, but gradually revived. When he regained consciousness, he was in a disoriented and disorganized state. Although he improved slightly during the next 24 hours, he was transferred to the psychiatric unit for further observation.

By the fourth day, he seemed in reasonably good contact, but he remained confused for time and place. He admitted to smoking a cocaine derivative and stated that he had done this several times in his mother's or father's car in the garage. He also noted that he had smoked this substance several times with friends, but refused, or was not able, to identify any of them.

He is the younger of two children. His father, age 39, is a corporate attorney. His mother, age 37, is a middle management executive for an advertising firm. He has an older sister, age 16, who is in her third year of high school. He is currently in his first year of high school and most of his grades are above average. Group intelligence test data provided by the school indicate an estimated IQ of 118. Although neither parent has a psychiatric history, the mother's brother has been hospitalized twice with a diagnosis of schizophrenia.

Both parents expressed shock and dismay regarding their son's situation, although they admit that they found marijuana in his room when he was in the seventh grade. They claim that they counseled him extensively concerning drug abuse, but there is reason to believe, based on some of the mother's statements, that both parents have used marijuana routinely for several years. They state that, other than the marijuana episode, he has never been a problem. His mother describes him as, "always somewhat quiet. He liked to play by himself even though we encouraged him to play with other children." His father suspects that other children have "picked on him, but I thought that had passed as he got older." The father also expresses regret that "I didn't have more time to spend with him the last few years."

A review of academic records indicates that he was an above-average student in grades five through eight. Most of his teachers do not know him well because he has attended his present school for only four months. According to their records, his academic performance is average or above. Some anecdotes recorded by his seventh- and eighth-grade teachers indicate that he seemed detached from his peers, but none of the teachers considered this to be a major problem. He says that he likes school and has several friends. He expresses regret that he is not very athletic, "If you're good at a sport, a lot of people like you."

He claims that his drug involvement has been experimental. He says that he knew that drug use was not acceptable but remained curious about why so many people use drugs and felt that he could only learn the answer by trying them. He says that he usually purchases drugs from an older student at school, whom he refuses to identify. He is somewhat disorganized in explaining how often he smoked marijuana or used other drugs, but he claims that this was something he could control easily until he got "some bad stuff."

His sister reports that she and her brother have only limited contact with their parents because both work. She says that when her brother comes home from school, he usually spends most of his time in his room doing homework or playing games on a computer. Although he claims to have many friends, his sister says that this is not true, "He's by himself a lot." She notes that she has occasionally seen him with two boys who have bad reputations because of drug abuse. She states that she has known about his drug use for some time and has warned him about this, but that he "always says one thing and then does another." She says that she did not tell their parents about this because "it would have betrayed him," but now she regrets withholding information from them. She also notes that she and her brother are aware that their parents smoke marijuana.

During the 10 days that he has been hospitalized in the psychiatric unit, he has been interviewed seven times by each of two psychiatrists and a psychologist. All three note that his thinking is somewhat disorganized and that he tends to ramble when sensitive issues such as his relationship to his parents, peer friendships, or drug use are broached. All three professionals suspect that there may be a prodromal schizophreniform condition and speculate that his drug abuse may have been a form of self-medication. Hospital staff report that he is generally cooperative but reclusive, although two nurses and one attendant report that he is easily engaged in one-to-one conversations and note that they have observed no characteristics of a psychotic state. One nurse reports that he spends much of his time watching television and has frequently asked for permission to have his computer brought to the hospital. A drug screen, completed two days prior to this evaluation, was essentially negative although some trace elements of cocaine were detected.

There are two main assessment issues: (1) Is there a serious underlying psychiatric condition or is the current disorganization related mainly to the drug episode? (2) What recommendations concerning discharge and possible postdischarge treatment planning seem appropriate?

CASE FORMULATION AND RELEVANT LITERATURE

This young man presents a complex challenge for the assessing psychologist. His hospitalization resulted from a cocaine overdose, and he reports relatively extensive drug involvement. Now, two weeks past the overdose episode and with an essentially negative drug screen, his thinking continues to be mildly disorganized when he discusses sensitive issues. The psychologist and psychiatrists working with him wonder if he is experiencing the onset of a schizophrenic spectrum disorder, and they suggest that his drug usage may represent an attempt at self-medication in the face of increasing disorganization. On the other hand, ward staff members find him easy to engage in casual conversation, with no indication of psychotic decompensation, and his school performance has been above average.

Although the typical age of onset for psychotic disorders is in the early 20s, onset during adolescence is not uncommon (Hafner & Nowotny, 1995; Remschmidt, Schulz, Martin, & Warnke, 1994), and this young man has a second-degree relative (an uncle) with a schizophrenic diagnosis. A review of the literature on thought disorder in adolescence will be helpful for the psychologist in providing consultation about this case.

Assessment of Thought Disorder in Adolescence

Anna Freud, noting that adolescence ". . . constitutes by definition an interruption of peaceful growth which resembles in appearance a variety of other emotional upsets and structural upheavals," (1958, p. 267) wondered whether it was possible to differentiate "adolescent upsets" from true pathology. Bilett, Jones, and Whitaker (1982) addressed this question in a study in which they presented Rorschach, WAIS, and Whitaker Index of Schizophrenic Thinking (WIST; Whitaker, 1973) data from four adolescent hospitalized schizophrenics, four adolescent psychiatrically hospitalized nonschizophrenics, and four adolescent controls to 10 experienced doctoral-level clinical psychologists. Interestingly, all 10 of the judges were able to identify the Rorschachs of two of the schizophrenic adolescents, none identified the Rorschach of the third schizophrenic adolescent, and only 3 of the 10 judges identified the fourth schizophrenic protocol. Although the overall correct classification rate was significantly greater than chance, there is no way to know the specific Rorschach variables each judge used for making determinations.

Armstrong, Silberg, and Parente (1986) moved beyond the global approach taken by Bilett et al. (1982) by anchoring Rorschach and Wechsler data to observable behavior. They placed 138 psychiatrically hospitalized adolescents, ages 12 through 18, into four groups, based on high versus low thought disorder findings derived from Wechsler (WISC-R, WAIS, or WAIS-R) data rated using the Thought Disorder Index (TDI; Johnston & Holzman, 1979) and from the Rorschach Schizophrenia Index (SCZI). The TDI classifies verbalizations along a continuum of thought disorder ranging from mild difficulties such as clang associations to serious indicators such as incoherence and bizarre neologisms. Observable patient symptoms in 21 areas were rated from hospital charts using the Psychiatric Evaluation Form (PEF; Endicott & Spitzer, 1972).

Armstrong et al. (1986) found that 10 of the 21 PEF symptom variables were differentially distributed among the four groups. Adolescents who showed significant thought disorder in both their Wechsler and Rorschach results were characterized by hallucinations, suspicion/persecution, and daily routine impairment. Both groups with high Rorschach thought disorder findings showed hallucinations, disorientation, and memory confusion or impairment, inappropriate affect, and blunted affect or psychomotor retardation. Psychotic disorder diagnoses (schizophrenia, schizophreniform disorder, schizoaffective disorder, atypical psychosis, and major depression with psychotic features) were also more common in the two high Rorschach thought disorder groups, as were longer hospital stays and the use of medication. The patients with high Wechsler and low Rorschach thought disorder findings appeared to be socially isolated individuals with essentially no observable psychotic symptoms.

The Armstrong et al. (1986) findings highlight the importance of multimethod approaches to the assessment of thought disorder in adolescence. Combinations of findings from multiple instruments allow increasingly fine-grained descriptions. The authors hypothesize, "It may be that pathologies are differentially sensitive to the various test conditions, so that the content in which a thought disorder appears would be crucial to understanding the nature of the disturbance" (p. 454).

In a similar study, Skelton, Boik, and Madero (1995) investigated thought disorder measured by the TDI in the WAIS/WAIS-R and Rorschach findings of four groups of hospitalized adolescents, ages 16 to 18. The schizophreniform disorder group had high thought disorder scores on both the WAIS/WAIS-R and the Rorschach. Adolescents diagnosed with *DSM-III-R* identity disorder had high thought disorder scores on the Rorschach, produced significantly less thought disorder on the more structured WAIS/WAIS-R, and showed the greatest difference between the two tests. Adolescents diagnosed with conduct disorder or oppositional defiant disorder had relatively low thought disorder findings on both tests.

A common theme in both of these studies (Armstrong et al., 1986; Skelton et al., 1995) is that, as thought disorder becomes more severe, it emerges on structured cognitive measures in addition to less structured instruments like the Rorschach. A study by Brickman et al. (2004) provides more detailed support for this finding. The authors compared neuropsychological battery performance for 29 unmedicated adolescent patients experiencing a first psychotic episode with that of 17 age- and sex-matched normal volunteers. The patients performed significantly less well than the normal controls throughout, with particular difficulties on the parts of the battery that assessed attention, memory, and executive function. They had less significant deficits in tests of motor speed, language, and perceptual-motor function. The younger male patients showed greater deficits than the older male patients, leading the authors to speculate, ". . . younger male patients may represent a unique psychosis subtype with a neurodevelopmental etiology and therefore manifest greater neuropsychological deficits" (p. 621).

Conversely, several studies have emphasized the importance of taking very high intellectual ability into account when using the Rorschach to assess thought disorder in adolescents. Gallucci (1989) found significantly more *DV* and *DR* special scores, more *Dd* locations, and higher *X*−% in adolescents with IQs higher than 135 in comparison with an average IQ control group. However, the superior intelligence group did not produce more serious special scores (ALOG and *CONTAM*) than the average IQ control group.

Franklin and Cornell (1997) studied a group of 43 adolescent girls, ages 12 to 17, who were selected for early college entrance on the basis of high intelligence, academic aptitude, and excellent adjustment. In comparison with a group of gifted girls who had not pursued early college entrance, the girls in the accelerated group were significantly higher on the SCZI. Fourteen of the 43 had SCZI scores of four or more compared with only two of the 19 nonaccelerated students. Interestingly, the SCZI was *positively* correlated with two self-report measures that assessed for emotional and social adjustment, autonomous thinking, and positive self-concept. Examination of the variables making up the SCZI indicated that, as opposed to the relatively frequent finding of low form quality, only one participant in either group gave more than one Level 2 special score. The authors suggest that the presence of Level 2 special scores ". . . might be particularly important to consider in judging whether Rorschach responses indicate creativity or pathology" (p. 194).

Within pathological adolescent groups, Rorschach variables indicating thought disorder appear to have high test-retest reliability. As part of a broader longitudinal study of Rorschach changes over the developmental years, Exner, Thomas, and Mason (1985) studied the stability of variables associated with reality testing and cognitive slippage in seriously disturbed adolescents. They retested 29 schizophrenic adolescents, ages 12 to 15, who had been assessed 11 to 14 months earlier as first admission inpatients. At the time of the second testing, 18 had been discharged to parental custody or residential schools and 11 remained in the inpatient facility. There were no statistically significant mean or median differences between the two test administrations for

$X+\%$, $X-\%$, $M-$, or the sum or weighted sum of five special scores (*DV,* INCOM, *FABCOM,* ALOG, and *FABCOM*), with retest correlations ranging from .72 to .87. The authors suggest that their findings ". . . are supportive of the common hypothesis that the major operations affected by schizophrenia do not change readily, if at all" (p. 18). They speculate, ". . . the magnitude of the disarray is apparently sufficient to thwart many changes that might otherwise occur as a function of development" (p. 19).

Several studies have investigated the Rorschach's relationship to observable symptoms of thought disorder. Archer and Gordon (1988) studied 134 adolescent inpatients, ages 12 to 17, who had taken Rorschachs and MMPIs within five days of admission. The participants were divided into five diagnostic categories (schizophrenia/schizophreniform, major depression, dysthymic disorder, personality disorder, and conduct disorder) based on *DSM-III* treatment team discharge diagnoses. The mean $X+\%$ for the schizophrenia group was significantly lower than mean values for the conduct and dysthymic disorder groups, and the mean $X-\%$ for the schizophrenia group was higher than findings for all other groups except personality disorders. Human movement minus ($M-$) answers occurred more frequently in the schizophrenia and major depression groups than in any of the other diagnostic categories.

A study by Smith, Baity, Knowles, and Hilsenroth (2001) also found that $M-$ may be a particularly sensitive indicator of thought disorder in children and adolescents. They studied the relation of Rorschach variables (SCZI, PTI, $M-$, and $X-\%$) to behavior ratings and self-reports of thought disorder in 42 inpatient children and adolescents, ages 8 to 18. Behavior ratings came from the Atypicality and Withdrawal scales of the Basic Assessment System for Children-Parent Rating Form (BASC-PRF; Reynolds & Kamphaus, 1992). Self-report data came from the Reality Distortion Composite, Hallucinations and Delusions, Feelings of Alienation, and Social Withdrawal Composite scales of the Personality Inventory for Youth (PIY; Lachar & Gruber, 1995).

Smith et al. (2001) found no significant correlations between the SCZI or PTI and any of the parent rating or self-report scales. However, $M-$ correlated positively with BASC Atypicality and PIY Reality Distortion, Hallucinations and Delusions, and Feelings of Alienation. When a cutoff of >2 was used for the five-item PTI, patients with positive PTI values had significantly higher scores on BASC Atypicality and all of the PIY scales. The same pattern emerged in a categorical comparison of patients with one or more $M-$ determinant versus those with no $M-$ answers.

In summary, assessment of thought disorder in adolescents should involve a multimethod approach that includes both cognitive/neuropsychological and personality instruments. When thought disorder findings occur on both types of instruments, they may signal more pervasive psychopathology, particularly in the context of early onset. Within the Rorschach, $M-$ and Level 2 special scores are of particular note.

Card		Response	Inquiry
I	1.	A forest w trees, it's very peaceful	**E:** Rpts Ss resp **S:** It's the diff shapes here, it all ll trees blowg in the wind, lik if u were lookg at a forest & the trees were in frnt of u **E:** U say it ll theyr blowg in the wind? **S:** The way thy r shaped maks it ll thyr movg, just a peaceful place **E:** U said thyr in frnt of u? **S:** Lik ur in a distance lookg at the forest **E:** Tak ur time and u'll prob c smthg else
	2.	Mayb a skull	**E:** Rpts Ss resp **S:** Lik an A skull, mayb a bull cuz its got the big horns, c the eyes & the mouth **E:** I'm not sur why it ll a skull **S:** I'm not either, I just thot of tht, I guess bec it has the eye slots, no eyes, just holes
II	3.	It ll a bridge on a road going some where, ovr a big canyon or valley & mts all around it	**E:** Rpts Ss resp **S:** Here is a bridge at the top of the white going ovr ths valley lik u can hardly c it, & the white spot is a deep canyon & there's a tree behind the bridge & mts all around, don't count the red prts **E:** I'm not sur about the mts **S:** Well, thyr just all big & dark lik mts wld b if u look fr far away, the bridge is going fr one mt to another mt ovr the canyon, if u didn't hav the bridge u couldn't get fr one to the othr
III	4.	It ll 2 ppl tht r leang on the table havg an argument	**E:** Rpts Ss resp **S:** The shape, nose, legs, it ll thy r bendg ovr, ths favors a table, sk of strang lookg table **E:** U said it ll thyr havg an argument? **S:** The way thy r leang & the facial expressions, thy look grim, lik neithr one likes the othr one, its som personal argument about their friendship or their friendships w othr people, thyr pretty intense about it
IV	5.	It ll a big mtn tht big birds build their nests on	**E:** Rpts Ss resp **S:** It ll the mtns & trees, at the top is where thy lay their eggs **E:** I'm not sur I am seeg it rite **S:** The way its shaped, its lik a mt & thy lay eggs on the top, only really big birds can fly up there **E:** U said it ll there r trees? **S:** It ll trees, all the dark spots r groups of huge big trees, lik if u lookd at it fr far off, ths is what it ll, but u can't c the birds, thyr hiding smwhere up at the top, guarding their nests
	6.	Mayb a map of som secret island w buried treasure	**E:** Rpts Ss resp **S:** Just down here, lik if the rest wasn't there it wb an island, the white prt around it wb the water **E:** U said w buried treasure? **S:** U can tell by the the lite & dark coloring of it & the way its shaped, islands tht hav treasure r colord tht way & r always long in their shape
V	7.	It ll a bird of sk, the way he's flyg ll he's flyg south for the winter, its too cold up there	**E:** Rpts Ss resp **S:** Well, he's got big wgs & the body, lik flyg **E:** U said he's flyg south for the winter **S:** When thy spread their wgs ths big thyr flyg fast & thy only do tht when thyr in a hurry, lik when thy want to get out of the cold & go south

Card	Response	Inquiry
	8. Thr is littl rivers in betwn 2 penninsulas	**E:** Rpts Ss resp **S:** Its the white in here, lik the mouth of a littl river tht runs betwn thes 2 pieces of land, lik 2 peninsulas, lik ur seeg it fr an airplane w all the trees **E:** All the trees? **S:** Just on the big one, it has coloring, lik diff heights of trees, the othr is just sand I guess cuz it doesn't hav changg coloring to it
VI	9. It ll a lake, w Jesus ovr it	**E:** Rpts Ss resp **S:** Jesus is at the top, w his arms out lik he's lookg out ovr ths lak, he's got his arms out lik he wants evrybody to kno he's concernd about the environment **E:** I'm not sur I c it rite **S:** The lake is all the green prt dwn here (D1), he's standg way dwn at the far end, the top of the lake where the grey starts, c his body & his arms r out, he's tryg to get people to notice him & quit polluting the lake **E:** U say its green? **S:** Well, greenish grey, lik polluted, it should just be pur green
	<10. Ths is a dog head lik swimming	**E:** Rpts Ss resp **S:** The way its shaped ll when a dog sticks its head out of the water when it swims, all of ths wld b water & he's swimming but u just c his head **E:** I'm not sur why it ll water **S:** It has to b, wht else wld he swim in
VII	11. It ll a littl island, the water comes in here	**E:** Rpts Ss resp **S:** C the way its shaped, lik an island, w the water in the middl, the white is all water, & there's a river dividg the island, ths gap ll it's a river **E:** I'm not sur about the river **S:** It looks lik its dwn in a gorge, c it's darkr, lik a river & it wld cut thru the island, dividing it
	v12. Mayb its 2 dogs tht got hung by their chins to a board	**E:** Rpts Ss resp **S:** There's one on each side, lik dogs or sm A tht got hung up by their chins to this thg, I guess a board, its weird, why wld somone do tht **E:** Show me the dogs **S:** Here & here (D2), the tail & legs & head & their chin is on ths board, lik thyr hangg on it, lik somone hung thm up lik tht to hurt thm
VIII	13. Tht ll tht cb a flowr garden w a stream	**E:** Rpts Ss resp **S:** All the diff colors ll flowers & there's a stream running rite thru the middl **E:** What makes it ll a stream? **S:** It just does, it narrows off in the middle into little pools of water, these white parts, but it runs rite up to the top too, it keeps the garden watered **E:** & u say the diff colors ll flowrs? **S:** Yes, each color is a diff flower or plant lik u'd c by a stream
	<14. Oh, ths way it ll an A walkg ovr som colord rocks	**E:** Rpts Ss resp **S:** I dk wht kind, not a dog, mayb a cat or a fox, he has his legs & head & tail & he's walkg ovr thes thgs, lik rocks, thyr all diff colors

(continued)

Card	Response	Inquiry
IX 15.	A face, lik a clown, all painted up	**E:** Rpts Ss resp **S:** He's got orange ears & green cheeks & a white nose & a pink collar, lik a clown in the circus, it looks lik he's laughing **E:** Laughing? **S:** Yes, the way his cheeks go out, u kno, clowns laugh all the time
16.	Dwn here's anothr face but not a clown, a ghost	**E:** Rpts Ss resp **S:** He's pink but he's got white eyes & a big nose, not a real ghost, but lik one u c on the TV, its lik he's got a white beard too
<17.	A whale in the water	**E:** Rpts Ss resp **S:** The shape of it ll a humpback whale, there's one on the othr side too, lik he's floatg in the water, just takin it easy, thy do tht smtimes, I saw a film about thm **E:** I'm not sur why it ll tht **S:** Just the shape, curvy, lik the top of a whale lik when its just restg in the water, c the littl hump there, thts why thy call 'em humpbacks
X v18.	Ths cb a bf	**E:** Rpts Ss resp **S:** It ll wgs, lik its flyg toward u, c the littl body & the wgs r out
v19.	The face of a guy who's squinting	**E:** Rpts Ss resp **S:** His eyebrows (D10) r tilted, lik when u squint, or get mad or smthg, thes r his eyes (D2) & nose (D6) & mouth (D3) & he's got a grey beard, he looks lik he's pretty mad to me
20.	Ths ll 2 guys smokg a pipe	**E:** Rpts Ss resp **S:** Weird, thyr pink, thy must hav som strong stuff tht maks them pink, it's just ths top part (of D9), c their faces, their nose & eyes & thyv each got a pipe tht thyr touchg togethr in the middl

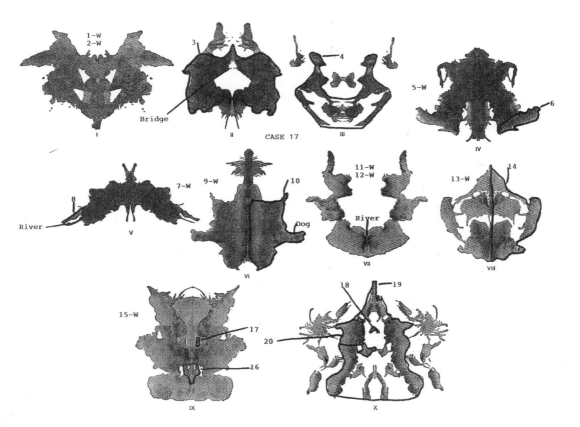

Case 17. Sequence of Scores.

Card	No.	Loc.	No.	Determinant(s)	(2)	Content(s)	Pop	Z	Special Scores
I	1	Wv	1	mp.FD–		Ls			DV
	2	WSo	1	Fo		An		3.5	
II	3	DS+	6	FD.FC'u		Sc,Ls		4.5	DR
III	4	D+	1	Mao	2	H,Hh,Hx	P	3.0	AG,GHR
IV	5	Wv/+	1	FVu		Ls		4.0	DR2
	6	DdS+	99	FY–		Ge		5.0	ALOG
V	7	Wo	1	FMao		A		1.0	ALOG
	8	DS+	10	FVu		Na		4.0	
VI	9	W+	1	Mp.FD.FYo		H,Na		2.5	FAB2,CP,MOR,PHR
	10	D+	4	FMau		Ad,Na		2.5	
VII	11	WS+	1	FVo		Na		4.0	
	12	W+	1	FMpo	2	A,Id		2.5	MOR,FAB2
VIII	13	WS+	1	CF.mau		Na		4.5	
	14	D+	1	FMa.CFo		A,Ls	P	3.0	
IX	15	WSo	1	FC.FC'.Mau		(Hd),Cg		5.5	DR,PHR
	16	DdSo	99	FC.FC'–		(Hd)		5.0	PER,PHR
	17	DdS+	23	FMp–	2	A,Na		5.0	PER
X	18	Do	3	FMa.FD–		A			
	19	DdSo	22	Ma.FC'–		Hd,Hx			PHR
	20	Dd+	99	Mp.FCu	2	Hd,Sc		4.0	ALOG,PHR

Case 17. Structural Summary.

Location Features	Determinants Blends	Single	Contents	S-Constellation
				.....FV+VF+V+FD>2
			H = 2	.....Col-Shd Bl>0
Zf = 17	m.FD	M = 1	(H) = 0	.....Ego<.31,>.44
ZSum = 63.5	FD.FC′	FM = 4	Hd = 2	.....MOR > 3
ZEst = 56.0	M.FD.YF	m = 0	(Hd) = 2	.....Zd > +– 3.5
	CF.m	FC = 0	Hx = 2	.....es > EA
W = 9	FM.CF	CF = 0	A = 5	.....CF+C > FC
D = 6	FC.FC′.M	C = 0	(A) = 0	.....X+% < .70
W+D = 15	FC.FC′	Cn = 0	Ad = 1	.....S > 3
Dd = 5	FM.FD	FC′ = 0	(Ad) = 0	.....P < 3 or > 8
S = 10	M.FC′	C′F = 0	An = 1	.....Pure H < 2
	M.FC	C′ = 0	Art = 0	.....R < 17
		FT = 0	Ay = 0	x ....TOTAL
DQ		TF = 0	Bl = 0	**Special Scores**
		T = 0	Bt = 0	Lv1 Lv2
+ = 12		FV = 3	Cg = 1	DV = 1x1 0x2
o = 6		VF = 0	Cl = 0	INC = 0x2 0x4
v/+ = 1		V = 0	Ex = 0	DR = 2x3 1x6
v = 1		FY = 1	Fd = 0	FAB = 0x4 2x7
		YF = 0	Fi = 0	ALOG = 3x5
		Y = 0	Ge = 1	CON = 0x7
		Fr = 0	Hh = 1	Raw Sum6 = 9
Form Quality		rF = 0	Ls = 4	Wgtd Sum6 = 42
FQx MQual W+D		FD = 0	Na = 6	
+ = 0 = 0 = 0		F = 1	Sc = 2	AB = 0 GHR = 1
o = 7 = 2 = 7			Sx = 0	AG = 1 PHR = 5
u = 7 = 2 = 6			Xy = 0	COP = 0 MOR = 2
– = 6 = 1 = 2			Id = 1	CP = 1 PER = 2
none = 0 = 0 = 0				PSV = 0
		(2) = 4		

Ratios, Percentages, and Derivations

R = 20	L = 0.05		FC:CF+C = 3:2	COP = 0 AG = 1
			Pure C = 0	GHR:PHR = 1:5
EB = 5:3.5	EA = 8.5	EBPer = N/A	SumC′:WSumC = 4:3.5	a:p = 7:6
eb = 8:9	es = 17	D = –3	Afr = 0.67	Food = 0
	Adj es = 15	Adj D = –2	S = 10	SumT = 0
			Blends:R = 10:20	Hum Con = 6
FM = 6	C′ = 4	T = 0	CP = 1	Pure H = 2
m = 2	V = 3	Y = 2		PER = 2
				Iso Indx = 0.85

a:p = 7:6	Sum6 = 9	XA% = 0.70	Zf = 17.0	3r+(2)/R = 0.20			
Ma:Mp = 2:3	Lv2 = 3	WDA% = 0.87	W:D:Dd = 9:6:5	Fr+rF = 0			
2AB+Art+Ay = 0	WSum6 = 42	X–% = 0.30	W:M = 9:5	SumV = 3			
MOR = 2	M– = 1	S– = 4	Zd = +7.5	FD = 4			
	Mnone = 0	P = 2	PSV = 0	An+Xy = 1			
		X+% = 0.35	DQ+ = 12	MOR = 2			
		Xu% = 0.35	DQv = 1	H:(H)Hd(Hd) = 2:4			

PTI = 3	DEPI = 5*	CDI = 3	S-CON = N/A	HVI = YES	OBS = No

S-CON AND KEY VARIABLE

The S-CON is not applicable for a 14-year-old. However, the possibility that the drug overdose may have represented a form of suicide gesture should not be neglected. The first positive Key variable is that the D Score (−3) is less than the Adj D Score (−2), signaling that the interpretation should begin with a review of data concerning controls and situationally related stress. The remainder of the interpretive routine is decided on the basis of the next positive Key variable. In this instance, it is that the Adj D Score is less than zero but, like the first Key variable, it only calls for a review of data concerning controls. The third positive Key variable (HVI is positive) resolves the issue. Thus, after findings for controls and stress have been studied, the review will proceed to the data concerning ideation, processing, and mediation. It will then move to the information regarding self-perception and interpersonal perception, and end with the data concerning affect.

CONTROLS

Case 17.   Control-Related Variables for a 14-Year-Old Male.

EB = 5:3.5	EA = 8.5		D = −3	CDI = 3
eb = 8:9	es = 17	Adj es = 15	AdjD = −2	L = 0.05
FM = 6 m = 2	SumC′ = 4	SumT = 0	SumV = 3	SumY = 2

The Adj D Score (−2) intimates that he is highly vulnerable to difficulties with control and is susceptible to disorganization under stress. The *EA* (8.5) is in the average range and the *EB* (5:3.5) contains no zero values. They suggest that there is no reason to suspect that the Adj D Score is misleading. It implies that controls are a problem because he experiences more internal stimulus demands than he can contend with effectively, resulting in a persistent overload state.

The internal features causing the overload appear to consist mainly of more peripheral, subconscious, need related, mental activity than is typical (*FM* = 6), plus considerable emotional irritation that stems from the suppression of feelings (*SumC′* = 4), and negative emotions generated by self-degrading rumination (*SumV* = 3). The latter raises a question about whether the Adj D Score might be exaggerated by situationally related factors. Usually, vista responses represent a traitlike ruminative process but, in some instances, situationally related feelings of guilt or remorse also give rise to this process. Other data confirm that he is experiencing some noticeable stress that is situationally related, and thus it seems best to address this question in the context of those data.

SITUATIONALLY RELATED STRESS

Case 17.   Situational Stress Data for a 14-Year-Old Male.

EB	= 5:3.5	EA = 8.5	D = −3	**Blends**
eb	= 8:9	es = 17 Adj es = 15	AdjD = −2	M.FD.YF = 1
				M.FC = 1
FM	= 6 m = 2	C′ = 4 T = 0 V = 3 Y = 2		M.FC′ = 1
		(3r+(2)/R) = .20		FC.FC′.M = 1
				FC.FC′ = 1
Pure C = 0 M− = 1	MQnone = 0		Blends = 10	CF.m = 1
				FM.CF = 1
				FM.FD = 1
				m.FD = 1
				FD.FC′ = 1

The D Score (−3) is a point less than the Adj D Score (−2), indicating situationally related factors are causing added control problems and increasing his vulnerability to disorganization. This is not surprising in light of his recent drug overdose experience and the fact that he now finds himself in a psychiatric facility. The one point difference between the two D Scores suggests that the impact of the stress is moderate, but the resulting experience of helplessness is increasing both his peripheral ideation activity ($m = 2$) and his experience of discomforting feelings ($SumY = 2$).

A question was raised earlier about whether the three vista answers might also have some situational basis and whether they might have caused the Adj D Score to be exaggerated. If the vista answers are situationally related and might not exist otherwise, the Adj *es* would be reduced to 12, yielding an Adj D Score of −1. It would still signify an overload state, but a less substantial vulnerability to problems in control or potentials for disorganization. The Egocentricity Index is relevant to this issue.

The Egocentricity Index is quite low (.20), connoting a negative appraisal of self-worth. Vista answers are not uncommon when there are problems concerning self-value. Thus, it seems unlikely that his self-degrading rumination can be attributed entirely to recent events. Certainly, the process may have been exacerbated by recent events, but not so much as to alter the interpretation of the Adj D Score or D Score findings. The persistence of his overload state should be considered as serious and the potential for disorganization as substantial. These factors should be given careful consideration when treatment options are considered.

IDEATION

Case 17.   Ideation Variables for a 14-Year-Old Male.

L	= 0.05	OBS	= No	HVI	= Yes	**Critical Special Scores**				
						DV	= 1	DV2	= 0	
EB	= 5:3.5	EBPer	= NA	a:p	= 8:5	INC	= 0	INC2	= 0	
				Ma:Mp	= 3:2	DR	= 2	DR2	= 1	
eb	= 8:9	[FM = 6 m = 2]				FAB	= 0	FAB2	= 2	
				M–	= 1	ALOG	= 3	CON	= 0	
Intell Indx	= 0	MOR	= 2	Mnone	= 0	Sum6	= 9	WSum6	= 42	
							(R = 20)			

M Response Features

III   4. D+ Mao 2 H,Hh,Hx P 3.0 AG,GHR
VI   9. W+ Mp.FD.YFo H,Na 2.5 FAB2,CP,MOR,PHR
IX   15. WSo FC.FC′.Mau (Hd),Cg 5.5 DR,PHR
X   19. DdSo Ma.FC′– Hd,Hx PHR
X   19. Dd+ Mp.FCu 2 Hd,Sc 4.0 ALOG,PHR

The *EB* (5:3.5) indicates that his patterns of thinking are not very consistent when he approaches coping issues and decision making. At times, he may delay decisions and think through alternative possibilities while keeping his feelings at bay. In other instances, his decisions are much more intuitively formed and markedly influenced by his feelings. This lack of a consistent coping style is not unusual among youngsters at one time or another during their developmental years. However, it is less efficient, and his inconsistency in how he forms decisions creates a potential for errors in judgment.

A much more important finding is the positive HVI. This is a traitlike feature that is quite influential on his conceptual thinking. Its basic feature is a guarded and mistrusting attitude toward the environment that has developed over time. Apparently, events have accumulated in which he has found himself unable to be confident about predicting the responses of significant others concerning his behaviors, especially his emotional behaviors. As a result, he tends to feel insecure and vulnerable, and maintains a state of hyperalertness in the anticipation of unwanted events. His mistrusting attitude about people creates an ideational set that can easily lead to unclear or even illogical thinking. This sort of thinking is not necessarily pathological, but if the hypervigilant state is exacerbated, thinking often takes on paranoid-like features.

The left side *eb* value (8) comprises six *FM* and two *m* answers and denotes a considerable level of peripheral or subconscious mental activity. Much of this is provoked by internal need states, and because it is substantial, it is likely that his attention and concentration are easily impaired. When that occurs, his sense of insecurity increases and his hypervigilant set tends to intensify.

A much more negative finding is indicated by the *WSum6* value (42). It signifies that his thinking is probably seriously impaired. It intimates that his ideation is likely to be disorganized, inconsistent, and frequently illogical. When conceptualization is impaired to this extent, reality testing becomes marginal, at best. An important issue concerning this assumption is the extent to which each of the responses, coded for critical special scores and contributing to the high *WSum6* value, truly reflect seriously impaired thought.

Nine answers are involved. The codings for three of them are justifiable, but represent instances where the cognitive slippage or inappropriateness is, at best, mild. The first is (Card I, response 1), "A forest with trees," a mild redundancy, coded *DV*. The second is (Card II, response 3), "a bridge on a road going somewhere, going over a canyon or valley . . . if you didn't have the bridge you couldn't get from one to the other." It is coded *DR* because it is concrete and unnecessary, but represents only a mild lapse in judgment, very common among adolescents. The third is (Card IX, response 15), "A face like a clown . . . like he's laughing . . . clowns laugh all the time." It is also coded *DR* because of the inappropriate concreteness, but it provides no clear evidence of disturbed thought.

The remaining six answers represent a more serious problem. The first of these (Card IV, response 5, *DR2*) is "a big mountain that big birds build their nests on . . . only really big birds can fly up there . . . you can't see the birds, they're hiding somewhere up at the top, guarding their nests." It is a strange and somewhat illogical answer. A similar kind of strained logic is reflected in the next response (Card IV, response 6, ALOG), "a map of some secret island with buried treasure . . . islands that have treasure are colored that way and are always long in their shape." It is the type of extremely concrete and unrealistic response that might be expected from a 6-year-old, but not a 14-year-old. Some of the guarded or suspicious features of his thinking seem reflected in both answers. The birds are hiding, guarding their nests, and the island is secret.

The third of these six answers (Card V, response 7, ALOG) is, "A bird of some kind, the way he's flying looks like he's flying south for the winter, it's too cold up there . . . when they spread their wings this big they're flying fast and they only do that when they're in a hurry, like when they want to get out of the cold and go south." Again, his logic is strained. The fourth of these responses (Card VI, response 9, FAB2) is "a lake with Jesus over it . . . he's got his arms out like he wants everybody to know he's concerned about the environment . . . he's trying to get people to notice him and quit polluting the lake." It is a bizarre answer that does not distort the distal properties of the figure, but involves considerable projection that disregards reality. The fifth of these six answers (Card VII, response 12, FAB2) is "two dogs that got hung up by their chins to a board . . . it's weird, why would someone do that . . . their chin is on this board, like they're hanging on it . . . someone hung them up like that to hurt them." It is also a response in which the stimulus features are not distorted, but the substance of his conceptualization is concrete and illogical. The same is true of the sixth answer in this group (Card X, response 20, ALOG), his last response in the test, "two guys smoking a pipe . . . they're pink, they must have some strong stuff that makes them pink."

It seems clear that much of his ideation, although often sophisticated, is clouded by very flawed judgments. When they occur, his thinking becomes concrete, and he forms conceptualizations that tend to defy reality. The breadth and magnitude of these serious forms of cognitive slippage seem to reflect a more persistent pathology instead of products of a recent toxic episode. Findings about his processing and mediational activities may provide additional information to clarify this issue.

PROCESSING

Case 17.   Processing Variables for a 14-Year-Old Male.

EB	= 5:3.5	Zf	= 17	Zd	= +7.5	DQ+	= 12
L	= 0.05	W:D:Dd	= 9:6:5	PSV	= 0	DQv/+	= 1
HVI	= Yes	W:M	= 9:5			DQv	= 1
OBS	= No						

Location & DQ Sequencing

I: Wv.WSo	VI: W+.D+
II: DS+	VII: WS+.W+
III: D+	VIII: WS+.D+
IV: Wv/+.DdS+	IX: WSo.DdSo.DdS+
V: Wo.DS+	X: Do.DdSo.Dd+

The Zf (17) implies that he invests considerable effort when processing new information. This notion is also supported by the $W:D:Dd$ ratio (9:6:5), which includes a greater number of W than D responses, and a substantial number of Dd location selections. This is not surprising in light of his hypervigilance, which usually includes concerns that new information be surveyed very carefully. His location sequencing is reasonably consistent. Seven of his nine W answers are first responses, and are given to solid or semibroken figures (I, IV, V, VI, VII, VIII, & IX). His five Dd selections are less consistently distributed. All are second or last responses, but four of the five were given to Cards IX and X.

A substantial processing effort is also signified by the Zd score (+7.5), which indicates an over-incorporative style. It connotes a striving to avoid neglecting the details of new information that prompts a marked scanning effort. This can be an asset, but it may also contribute to some of his strained thinking because it can promote vacillation in decision making if pathology is present. The distribution of DQ scores is of interest in this context. He gave 12 $DQ+$ responses, a finding greater than expected for one his age. It implies that his processing habits are usually quite good and often complex.

However, he also gave one DQv answer and one $DQv/+$ response. This is unusual when an abundance of $DQ+$ responses appear and hints that, at times, his processing may be flawed or less mature than expected. Such an unusual mix often signals some sort of psychological disarray. This seems confirmed by the fact that five of his 12 synthesized answers are also marked by forms of serious cognitive slippage. This suggests that, although his processing habits are usually good, the composite of his hypervigilance and his impaired thinking sometimes promotes inefficiency in his processing activities. The data concerning mediation should aid in understanding the cognitive disarray that seems to be present.

MEDIATION

Case 17.   Mediation Variables for a 14-Year-Old Male.

R = 20		L = 0.05		OBS = No	**Minus & NoForm Features**
FQx+	= 0		XA%	= .70	I 1. Wv mp.FD– Ls DV
FQxo	= 7		WDA%	= .87	IV 6. DdS+ FY– Ge 5.0 ALOG
FQxu	= 7		X–%	= .30	IX 16. DdSo FC.FC′– (Hd) 5.0 PER,PHR
FQx–	= 6		S–	= 4	IX 17. DdS+ FMp– 2 A,Na 5.0 PER
FQxnone	= 0				X 18. Do FMa.FD– A
(W+D	= 15)		P	= 2	X 19. DdSo Ma.FC′– Hd,Hx PHR
WD+	= 0		X+%	= .35	
WDo	= 7		Xu%	= .35	
WDu	= 6				
WD–	= 2				
WDnone	= 0				

The combination of his *XA%* (.70) and *WDA%* (.87) signifies that his mediational translations are generally appropriate in obvious situations, but become less so when cues are less distinctive. The considerable difference between the two values is created because of his six *Dd* responses, of which four involve distortions or misidentifications. They represent two thirds of the six minus answers that cause his *X–%* (.30) to be substantial.

Ordinarily, an *X–%* of this magnitude denotes a serious mediational impairment, which in turn usually connotes a widespread reality testing problem, possibly with serious consequences. In this case, however, that issue is not as clear as expected because four of his six minus answers, all to *Dd* areas, include the use of white space. This suggests that much of his mediational dysfunction is related to an affective problem having to do with negativism, alienation, and anger. In a related context, four of his six minus answers, including three *DdS* responses, were given to the last two cards. This is not to suggest that the mediational problem is less impairing, or less important, but it seems possible that it may be less widespread than implied.

Some of the impairment may be the result of an exacerbation of his hypervigilant style in which a preoccupation with issues of mistrust and feelings of alienation are prompting him to bend and distort reality more than should be the case. It seems interesting to note that three of his six minus answers convey a sort of isolation theme (A forest, it's very peaceful; a secret island; a whale in the water, just taking it easy).

A more positive finding is that none of his minus responses involve severe distortions. There are, however, only two Popular answers in the protocol and the *X+%* (.35) is low, whereas the value for the *Xu%* (.35) is substantial. This suggests that his translations of events, and his behaviors, are likely to disregard convention, even when the cues for conventional translations and behaviors are rather obvious. In part, this is because of his reality testing problem, but it also occurs because social demands or expectations do not influence him very much.

When the composite of findings concerning his mediational activities and his thinking is considered, it seems obvious that he is in a state of serious cognitive disarray. His thinking often is flawed and unrealistic and his translations of information are often marked by considerable distortion. A question was raised in the referral about whether this might be the result of his recent toxicity or represent a more persistent problem. Many of his distortions appear to have an affective basis, and much of his impaired thinking involves concrete judgments. This sort of mix is more likely to occur in a chronic problem than as the aftermath of a toxic state.

As issues regarding affect are important to understanding his situation, it seems appropriate to alter the order by which the remaining clusters are addressed. Thus, the data concerning affect will be studied before reviewing those segments of the protocols that deal with self-perception and interpersonal perception.

AFFECT

Case 17.   Affect-Related Data for a 14-Year-Old Male.

EB	= 5:3.5			EBPer	= NA	**Blends**	
eb	= 8:9	L	= 0.05	FC:CF+C	= 3:2	M.FD.YF	= 1
DEPI	= 5	CDI	= 3	Pure C	= 0	FC.FC'.M	= 1
						M.FC	= 1
SumC' = 4	SumT = 0			SumC':WSumC	= 4:3.5	M.FC'	= 1
SumV = 3	SumY = 2			Afr	= 0.67	FM.CF	= 1
						FM.FD	= 1
Intellect	= 0	CP	= 0	S = 10 (S to I,II,III= 2)		CF.m	= 1
Blends:R	= 10:20			Col-Shad Bl	= 2	FC.FC'	= 1
m + y Bl	= 2			Shading Bl	= 0	FD.FC'	= 1
						m.FD	= 1

The DEPI value (5) suggests that his psychology is currently organized in a way that creates a potential for experiences of affective disruption. This is not necessarily surprising in light of his cognitive difficulties and the problems that they create for him. As noted, he is not very consistent in the way that he uses his emotions in relation to his thinking and decision making ($EB = 5:3.5$). Sometimes, they play an important role and prompt an intuitive approach to decision making. In other instances, he pushes his feelings aside and tries to approach decisions more logically and carefully.

This inefficient lack of consistency in decision-making habits is not unusual for an adolescent and, ordinarily, is not seriously detrimental. However, it becomes more serious when cognitive disarray is present. Regardless of the process that leads to decisions, faulty reality testing increases the likelihood of unrewarding outcomes. Such events usually breed negative emotional reactions and this often promotes a confusion about feelings and a tendency to be more constrained about their use. That may well be the case here.

His higher right side eb (8:9) signals some distress or emotional discomfort. The main elements contributing to the substantial right side value are four achromatic color answers plus three vista responses. The former represents negative feelings created by a marked tendency to contain or suppress feelings, while the latter reflects the presence of irritating emotions resulting from a self-degrading ruminative process. As mentioned, recent events might have increased some of this self-degrading rumination but the process is likely to be long standing. Regardless, he is suffering considerable irritation that he is unable to handle satisfactorily. In fact, the WSumC':WSumC ratio (4:3.5) implies that he is inhibiting or constraining the release of his feelings much more often than should be the case, and is experiencing considerable discomfort as a result.

Interestingly, the *Afr* value (.67) implies that he is as willing as most others to be involved with emotionally toned situations, but that finding may be misleading. His record includes a color projection answer (response 9). These are rare answers and connote that he often denies the presence of irritating or unwanted feelings by substituting an inappropriately positive emotional value to the situation. It is a naive and immature defense that requires a considerable bending of reality to avoid dealing directly with feelings.

Moreover, his 20-response protocol includes 10 *S* responses. This is a very striking finding that signals a great deal of negativism, alienation, and probably anger. Five of his *S* answers were included among the eight responses that he gave to the last three cards. All four of his achromatic color determinants appear in responses that include space. It seems logical to speculate that much of his effort to constrain or suppress feelings is related to the intense feelings of negativism or anger that he harbors. In a similar context, the *FC:CF+C* ratio (3:2) suggests that he usually modulates his emotional displays as much as most adults. However, this is an unusual finding for a child or young adolescent and implies that he exerts more stringent control over his emotional displays than is customary for one of his age.

Ten of his 20 answers are blends, indicating that his psychological functioning is much more complex than is typical for a 14-year-old. Two of these blends appear to be related to his current situation (*CF.m, m.FD*), but even if only eight were present, it would still signal an unusual level of complexity. Two of those eight are color shading blends (*FC.FC'.M, FC.FC'*), suggesting that he is often confused by feelings and probably experiences them more intensely than do most of his age.

There seems to be no doubt that he is in considerable emotional disarray, and this matter is made worse because he is not accustomed to dealing with his emotions in a consistent manner. Apparently, he is unable to express his turmoil very directly and, instead, works reasonably hard to constrain or deny his feelings. This simply creates more irritation for him and increases his turmoil. Much of his irritation appears to manifest psychologically as alienation or anger, and it is not unreasonable to suspect that he is burdened by a hidden rage that is very confusing for him. Some of this is likely the result of his cognitive difficulties, which he probably does not understand very well and which easily promote more emotional disruption for him.

It was noted in the history that those who have evaluated him during his hospitalization have speculated that his drug abuse may be a form of self-medication as a way of dealing with his problems. In light of the findings related to his cognitive and emotional processes, such a speculation seems reasonable, but it seems equally plausible to speculate that his drug involvement is a way of escaping from both himself and the environment.

SELF-PERCEPTION

Case 17.   Self-Perception Related Data for a 14-Year-Old Male.

R	= 20	OBS	= No	HVI = Yes	**Human Content, Hx, An & Xy Responses**
					I 2. WSo Fo An 3.5
Fr+rF	= 0	3r+(2)/R	= 0.20		III 4. DS+ Mao 2 H,Hh,Hx P 3.0 AG,GHR
					VI 9. W+ Mp.FD.YFo H,Na FAB2,CP,MOR,PHR
FD	= 4	SumV	= 3		IX 15. WSo FC.FC'.Mau (Hd),Cg 5.5 DR,PHR
					IX 16. DdSo FC.FC'− (Hd) 5.0 PER,PHR
An+Xy	= 1	MOR	= 2		X 19. DdSo Ma.FC'− Hd,Hx PHR
					X 20. Dd+ Mp.FCu 2 Hd,Sc 4.0 ALOG,PHR
H:(H)+Hd+(Hd) = 2:4					
[EB = 5:3.5]					

As noted, his hypervigilance includes a significant preoccupation with a sense of vulnerability. He is often uncertain about the actions or reactions of others, and he strives to try to ensure that his own behaviors are appropriate to avoid the risk of being degraded. It is difficult to sustain this form of guardedness and still not be judged as odd by others, especially if thinking is not reasonably clear. This is because externalizations (rationalizations) of blame are often used to justify decisions or behaviors that have unwanted results ("It's not my fault because . . .").

If thinking is not clear, the faulty logic underlying the externalization tactic becomes transparent to others and ineffective as a defense of the self. When this occurs, the impact on self-image and self-value can be quite negative, and negative judgments regarding the self-conflict with the premise that is the psychological linchpin for hypervigilance (it is the world that is bad). There is some evidence that he is involved in this sort of conflict. The Egocentricity Index (.20) is very low, connoting a more negative than positive estimate of self-worth. When he compares himself with others, the result is usually unfavorable for him.

Likewise, the presence of four *FD* answers and three vista responses indicates a very ruminative involvement with self-examining behavior. Apparently, much of this is focusing on perceived features of himself that he regards negatively, and this is causing painful feelings. In addition, there are two MOR answers in the protocol, suggesting that there are some features of his self-concept that he judges to be unfavorable, and this tends to promote a pessimistic view of himself. He gave six human content responses, but only two are Pure *H*. This intimates that his self-image is based largely on imaginary impressions or distortions of his real experiences. This is not necessarily unusual for a young person whose self-image is still developing, but in this case, the codings for his human content answers connote far more negative features than should be the case. Two of the six contain his color shading blends. Three include the use of *S*. Three are to *Dd* areas. Three include achromatic color determinants. Four involve *Hd* or *(Hd)* contents, and three are coded for critical special scores, including one FAB2 and one ALOG. As a collective, these elements imply much more confusion about his self-concept than should be expected.

The substance of his responses appears to include numerous projected self-representations. As noted, three of his six minus answers convey an isolation theme: Card I, response 1, "A forest with trees, it's very peaceful"; Card IV, response 6, "a map of some secret island with buried treasure"; Card IX, response 17, "A whale . . . like he's floating in the water, just taking it easy." Two of the remaining three minus responses involve faces. The first is to Card IX, response 16, "another face, but not a clown, a ghost . . . pink but he's got white eyes . . . not a real ghost but one you see on the TV." It may reflect his more diffuse and insecure sense of self. The second is to Card X, response 19, "The face of a guy who's squinting . . . he looks like he's pretty mad to me." It appears to be a direct representation of his intense feelings discussed earlier. The remaining minus, Card X, response 18, is "a butterfly . . . flying toward you, see the little body." It also seems to convey the notion of insecurity.

His two MOR responses have also been mentioned earlier. The first, Card VI, response 9 is, "a lake with Jesus over it . . . he wants everybody to know he's concerned about the environment . . . he's trying to get people to notice him and quit polluting the lake." It is his color projection answer (greenish grey) in which he appears to be suggesting that the disregard of others is leading to an environment in which he cannot live. The second MOR, Card VII, response 12, denotes a sense of being damaged by others, "two dogs that got hung by their chins to a board . . . like someone hung them up like that to hurt them." In each of these responses, others are to blame.

Two of his five *M* answers, a lake with Jesus over it and the face of a guy squinting, have been reviewed. The remaining three also contain important projected material. The first, to Card III, response 4, is "two people . . . having an argument . . . they look grim, like neither one likes the other one, it's a personal argument about their friendship or their friendships with other people, they are pretty intense about it." It is an angry response that could reflect an internal conflict as well as interpersonal difficulties. The second is to Card IX, response 15, "a clown, all painted up . . . like he's laughing . . . clowns laugh all the time." It is a concealment response in which any notions of unpleasantness are nonexistent. The last, Card X, response 20, is, "two guys smoking a pipe . . . they must have some strong stuff that makes them pink." It is an illogical response that may convey something about the personal importance of his substance abuse; that is, it holds the potential for making one more attractive.

Three of his six *FM* answers have also been reviewed earlier (dogs hung by their chin, a whale taking it easy, a butterfly with the small body). The first of the remaining three, Card V, response 7, is "a bird of some kind, the way he's flying he's flying south for the winter, it's too cold up there . . . in a hurry like when they want to get out of the cold." It is an escape response that conveys his dissatisfaction with the environment . The second, Card VI, response 10, is "a dog head like swimming." It has no obvious connotations but some speculation about keeping one's head above water might be made. The remaining *FM* answer, Card VIII, response 14, is "an animal walking over some colored rocks." It also has no obvious connotations.

One of his two *m* answers has been reviewed earlier (a forest with trees, it's very peaceful). The second is also somewhat of an isolation answer, Card VIII, response 13, "a flower garden with a stream . . . running right through the middle." Similarly, four of the five answers that have not been studied thus far appear to convey an isolation theme. They include: Card II, response 3, "a bridge on a road going somewhere, over a big canyon or valley"; Card IV, response 5, "a big mountain that big birds build their nests on . . . you can't see the birds, they are hiding somewhere"; Card V, response 8, "little rivers in between two peninsulas"; and Card VII, response 11, "a little island, the water comes in here." Interestingly, three of the four include the use of white space as does the fifth answer in this group, Card I, response 2, "a skull . . . maybe a bull because it's got big horns . . . it has the eye slots, no eyes just holes." Collectively they seem to imply a clear relationship between his anger and his apparent isolation.

Overall, he seems to regard himself much more negatively than is customary for a young adolescent. His self-image appears to include concerns about insecurity, uncertainty, the need for guardedness, and a sense of isolation. It is much more diffuse and frail than expected for a youngster of his age. He seems lost in his world and tends to perceive himself as being victimized by an unkind and ungiving environment.

INTERPERSONAL PERCEPTION

Case 17.   Interpersonal Perception Data for a 14-Year-Old Male.

R = 20	CDI = 3	HVI = Yes	**COP & AG Responses**
a:p = 8:5	SumT = 0	Fd = 0	III 4. D+ Mao 2 H,Hh,Hx P 3.0 AG,GHR
	[eb = 8:8]		
Sum Human Contents = 6		H = 2	
[Style = Ambitent]			
GHR:PHR = 1:5			
COP = 0	AG = 1	PER = 2	
Isolation Indx = 0.85			

When hypervigilance is present, it does not bode well for close or effective interpersonal relations, because the underpinning sense of vulnerability breeds excessive guardedness when dealing with others. Typically, hypervigilant people do not expect to be close to others, and they usually sustain relationships only in circumstances where they experience no sense of threat and feel able to easily maintain control of the situation. These features seem to characterize this young fellow with reasonable accuracy.

The absence of texture answers, which is the linchpin variable in the HVI, suggests that he does not acknowledge or express needs for closeness openly and is cautious about creating emotional ties with others. The presence of six human content answers, of which only two are Pure *H,* intimates that he is interested in people but does not understand them very well. In addition, neither of the Pure *H* answers are especially positive when considered in regard to interpersonal perceptions or behaviors. The first (response 4) is two people having an argument, while the second involves Jesus trying to get people to notice him and stop polluting a lake. In a related context, the GHR:PHR ratio (1:5) implies that he often engages in forms of social behavior that are unlikely to be adaptive for the situation.

The absence of COP responses signifies that he feels somewhat uncomfortable in interpersonal situations and may be regarded by others as distant or aloof, and the two PER answers suggest that he may be more defensive in social situations than are most children his age. The Isolation Index (.85) is very high and supports the notion that he is socially isolated and finds it difficult to create or sustain smooth and rewarding relations with people.

Four *M* or *FM* responses contain pairs. The *M*s involve people arguing and two guys smoking a pipe, with some strong stuff that makes them pink. The *FM*s include dogs that got hung by their chins to a board and a whale taking it easy. None provide a basis from which to speculate that his interpersonal behaviors may be effective.

Generally, he appears to be a very guarded and defensive person who tends to mistrust others. He is probably cautious and aloof in his relationships and may well engage in social behaviors that are far less adaptive than should be the case. He does not understand people very well and seems prone to isolate himself in an attempt to maintain a sense of security and personal integrity.

SUMMARY

There is little doubt that this young man is in considerable disarray. Although his thinking can be reasonably sophisticated at times, it varies substantially in consistency and clarity. Even though he makes a concerted effort to process new information, and does so reasonably well, his thoughts are often confused and his logic becomes extremely flawed. When this occurs, he tends to bend or distort reality. Much of his thinking is influenced by a strong sense of mistrust about his world and those in it, and this has a far-reaching impact on much of his psychology.

He seems uncertain about his ability to predict how others will respond to him and his behaviors, and he tends to anticipate unfavorable outcomes. This causes him to be excessively cautious and guarded about his interactions with people and, as a result, he has become socially isolated. His situation is frustrating for him, and as he has attempted to deal with it, his thinking has become more confused and his emotions have become disruptive.

Psychologically, he is complex, and much of that complexity is prompted by a composite of neediness and irritating or confusing feelings. As a result, he often experiences episodes of distress or discomfort that add to his sense of frustration. He has not learned how to deal with his emotions in a consistent or effective manner and usually works hard to constrain, suppress, or deny unwanted feelings. Although these defensive tactics may be effective for brief intervals, they also increase his turmoil over longer periods because he has not contended with the emotions effectively.

He has developed marked feelings of alienation and anger that he is unable to express directly, and this also serves to increase his confusion. His emotional turmoil has bred a persistent state of psychological overload that has been increased by the stresses he is experiencing as a result of recent events. However, even without this increase, the composite of his persistent overload plus his serious cognitive problems makes him highly vulnerable to disorganization and sharply limits his ability to maintain control of his thoughts and behaviors.

He is very introspective and struggling to understand himself, but the result of this process is not favorable. His self-image is negative and includes concerns about insecurity, uncertainty, and a sense of isolation. It is much more diffuse and frail than should be the case for one of his age. In effect, he seems lost in a confusing and threatening world and tends to regard himself as being victimized. He does not understand people well and is uncomfortable in interpersonal situations. His social behaviors are likely to be marked by aloofness and defensiveness and are generally ineffective. In that social failures add to his misery, he appears to have isolated himself from the world as much as possible in an attempt to maintain some sense of personal integrity.

Overall, this is a youngster who is in much disarray and has considerable difficulty maintaining adequate contact with reality. His thinking is often seriously impaired. His emotions are intense and perplexing for him, and his relationships with others are, at best, superficial and unrewarding. It is a picture that conveys the notion of decompensation. Although there is no evidence of hallucinatory experiences, this composite of features is not unlike those present in prodromal schizophreniform conditions.

RECOMMENDATIONS

It seems appropriate to recommend continued inpatient status and careful observation. Any residual effects of the drug overdose should dissipate within the next 5 to 10 days, during which continued evaluations of his seemingly impaired thinking can occur. If possible, pharmacological intervention should be avoided. Support and reassurance are critically important during this period to provide an atmosphere that minimizes his sense of mistrust. Intervention tactics should be designed to provide some opportunities for him to describe his drug episodes as well as his family and peer relationships. When possible, avenues should be offered through which he can express some of his feelings.

He has assets with which to work. He processes new information carefully and thoroughly, and he has been able to maintain above-average grades in school. His feelings of helplessness and distress should make him amenable to a support system, provided that it is not threatening to him. His discharge from hospitalization should be contingent on a well-devised plan for outpatient care that should include considerations for pharmacological as well as psychotherapeutic intervention, depending on the results of his overall evaluation while an inpatient. If decompensation is occurring, a well-developed outpatient care format could minimize some of the risks and aid him to achieve a much more effective level of adjustment than has been the case. Ultimately, consideration of family intervention to create a broader basis of support for him seems important.

EPILOGUE

He remained hospitalized for an additional eight days during which he continued to be cooperative with staff and participated agreeably in structured group activities. However, his participation in group therapy, which focused on postdischarge planning, was limited and he tended to avoid much interaction with other patients. His attending psychiatrist noted that his thinking seemed to remain disorganized at times, especially when family issues were broached. He recommended a combination of individual and family therapy after discharge and also suggested that a trial of antipsychotic medication might be appropriate if obvious thinking problems persisted.

During the first two postdischarge months, he was seen twice weekly by a psychiatrist for 30-minute sessions and the family engaged in a 90-minute session weekly with a different therapist. His sister proved to be an active participant in the family treatment, and on three occasions her comments about her parents' marijuana use caused him to become agitated and hostile and he rambled considerably about the faults of other family members.

After the third incident, the treatment regimen was changed. His individual sessions were lengthened to approximately one hour each; he was permitted to discontinue participation in the family sessions; and he was placed on a moderate dosage level of an antipsychotic that was discontinued after three months with no noticeable effects, although his thinking remained "strained" at times. His mother, father, and sister continued in family treatment for another two months but he refused to participate. He was able to complete his first year of high school without incident and with above-average grades. He also attended a computer science camp for six weeks during the following summer. At the end of the eighth month of treatment, the therapist noted that there was no evidence of drug abuse and some progress was evident in peer relationships. His thinking continued to be strange at times, but these incidents did not interfere noticeably with his overall behavior.

REFERENCES

Archer, R. P., & Gordon, R. A. (1988). MMPI and Rorschach indices of schizophrenic and depressive diagnoses among adolescent inpatients. *Journal of Personality Assessment, 52*(2), 276–287.

Armstrong, J., Silberg, J. L., & Parente, F. J. (1986). Patterns of thought disorder on psychological testing: Implications for adolescent psychopathology. *Journal of Nervous and Mental Diseases, 174*(8), 448–456.

Bilett, J. L., Jones, N. F., & Whitaker, L. C. (1982). Exploring schizophrenic thinking in older adolescents with the WAIS, Rorschach and WIST. *Journal of Clinical Psychology, 38*(2), 232–243.

Brickman, A., Buchsbaum, M., Bloom, R., Bokhoven, P., Reshmi, P., Haznedar, M., et al. (2004). Neuropsychological functioning in first-break never-medicated adolescents with psychosis. *Journal of Nervous and Mental Diseases, 192*(9), 615–622.

Endicott, J., & Spitzer, R. L. (1972). What! Another rating scale? The Psychiatric Evaluation Form. *Journal of Nervous and Mental Diseases, 154,* 88–104.

Exner, J. E., Thomas, E. A., & Mason, B. J. (1985). Children's Rorschachs: Description and prediction. *Journal of Personality Assessment, 49*(1), 13–20.

Franklin, K. W., & Cornell, D. G. (1997). Rorschach interpretation with high-ability adolescent females: Psychopathology or creative thinking? *Journal of Personality Assessment, 68*(1), 184–196.

Freud, A. (1958). Adolescence. *Psychoanalytic Study of the Child, 13,* 255.

Gallucci, N. T. (1989). Personality assessment with children of superior intelligence.*Journal of Personality Assessment, 53*(4), 749–760.

Hafner, H., & Nowotny, B. (1995). Epidemiology of early-onset schizophrenia. *European Archives of Psychiatry and Clinical Neuroscience, 245*(2), 80–92.

Johnston, M., & Holzman, P. (1979). *Assessing schizophrenic thinking.* San Francisco: Jossey-Bass.

Lachar, D., & Gruber, C. P. (1995). *Personality Inventory for Youth: Technical guide.* Los Angeles: Western Psychological Services.

Remschmidt, H., Schulz, E., Martin, M., & Warnke, A. (1994). Childhood-onset schizophrenia: History of the concept and recent studies. *Schizophrenia Bulletin, 20*(4), 727–745.

Reynolds, C. R., & Kamphaus, R. W. (1992). *Behavior assessment system for children.* Circle Pines, MN: American Guidance Service.

Skelton, M. D., Boik, R. J., & Madero, J. N. (1995). Thought disorder on the WAIS-R relative to the Rorschach: Assessing identity-disordered adolescents. *Journal of Personality Assessment, 65*(3), 533–549.

Smith, S. R., Baity, M. R., Knowles, E. S., & Hilsenroth, M. J. (2001). Assessment of disordered thinking in children and adolescents: The Rorschach Perceptual-Thinking Index. *Journal of Personality Assessment, 77*(3), 447–463.

Whitaker, L. (1973). *Manual for the Whitaker Index of schizophrenic thinking.* Los Angeles: Western Psychological Services.

PART FIVE

The Rorschach and Issues of Impression Management

CHAPTER 20

Issues of Malingering

In an ideal world, a person's test findings would always provide a perfectly reliable and valid description of his or her psychological makeup. In the real world, however, the multiple sources of random and systematic error variance that are an inevitable component of assessment ensure that there will always be a gap between test findings and psychological "truth." This is never more the case than in situations that motivate the person to present himself or herself in a particular light. At those times, as Meyer and Deitsch (1995) put it, "Malingering is often more understandable by the evident incentives and circumstances of the situation, rather than by the person's individual psychology" (p. 234).

The two chapters in this section focus on Rorschach assessment when impression management—an attempt to portray oneself positively or negatively—makes up a significant part of the error variance that stands between test findings and accurate description. This chapter discusses malingering to fake serious psychological disturbance. The next chapter focuses on simulating positive adjustment to portray oneself as competent and free of emotional difficulties. Because part of the error variance created by impression management is systematic, the literature can provide at least some guidance for interpreting test findings when the person stands to benefit by modifying his or her presentation.

ASSESSMENT OF MALINGERING

At the most basic level, there is little doubt that direct sets can produce some alterations in a Rorschach record. Hutt, Gibby, Milton, and Pottharst (1950) demonstrated that increases in the frequencies for location types, movement, color, and form occur when participants are specifically instructed to give those kinds of responses. Gibby (1951) found that participants can increase *W* locations or *A* content if instructed to produce those types of answer.

Fosberg (1938, 1941, 1943) was the first to test the potential for impression management by using a counterbalanced retest design. He concluded that the test data were not easily alterable and that, regardless of instructions, the basic features of personality would continue to emerge in the structural features of the test. Carp and Shavzin (1950), who also used a retest counterbalanced design with instructions to give *good* and *bad* impressions, concluded that individuals can produce a different personality picture under different sets. Easton and Feigenbaum (1967) used a similar design but with a control group tested twice under standard instructions. They detected a decrease in *R, D, H, A, Ad,* and *P* as a result of instructions to malinger.

Negative impression management is too broad a category to treat generically. The question that must be addressed is not simply whether an effort at malingering has occurred but, more specifically, what kind of pathology the person has attempted to approximate. For that reason, the literature on malingering of psychosis or schizophrenia will be reviewed first, followed by an illustrative case of a man indicted for second-degree homicide. Then the literature on the malingering of distress or depression will be reviewed, followed by a case of a man requesting continuation of insurance benefits.

Malingering Psychosis or Schizophrenia

A study by Albert, Fox, and Kahn (1980) provides an early example of the multicell designs that have characterized much of the research on the malingering of psychosis and schizophrenia. These researchers tested 24 participants: 6 nonpatient controls, 6 paranoid schizophrenics, and 12 nonpatients who were asked to approximate a schizophrenic condition in their Rorschachs. Six of the 12 nonpatients (uninformed fakers) were asked to simulate schizophrenia with no information about the syndrome while the remaining 6 (informed fakers) listened to an audio recording containing information about paranoid schizophrenia. The authors then sent packets containing one protocol from each of the four conditions to expert judges (Fellows of the Society for Personality Assessment). They found that the judges diagnosed the uninformed fakers psychotic as frequently as the actual schizophrenics and that they diagnosed the informed fakers psychotic more often than the actual schizophrenics. The authors concluded that expert clinical judgments about the Rorschach are susceptible to the malingering of a serious disturbance.

This multicell design was confounded by several implementation errors. A single examiner administered all the tests and in doing so may have been influenced in the inquiry by hypothesis-related biases. This error was made more complex because none of the records were scored before they were sent to the judges. In addition, the authors obtained no information from the 46 judges concerning their experience with the test or the approach that they used in their evaluations.

Mittman (1983) attempted to correct for the methodological errors that occurred in the Albert et al. (1980) study. She used 12 naive examiners to collect 30 protocols. Eighteen of the 30 were taken from nonpatient adults recruited to participate in a standardization study. All were workers in a manufacturing plant. Six were administered the test with the standard instructions. The other 12 were asked to simulate a schizophrenic protocol, with 6 given no syndrome-specific information and the other 6 asked to listen to the Albert et al. (1980) audio recording about paranoid schizophrenia before taking the test. The remaining 12 records were collected from 6 inpatient schizophrenics and 6 inpatient depressives, all of whom were first admission patients who took the test as a part of the admission routine. The 30 records were all scored and Structural Summaries were calculated. Schizophrenia Index and Depression Index data were not included, as the research concerning their development had not been completed at the time.

Each of 110 experienced judges received a randomly selected packet of four protocols, one from each condition. The packet also contained a questionnaire for each protocol with a listing of 12 possible diagnostic categories, including normal and malingered classifications. Ninety judges responded, yielding a range of between 81 and 99 judgments per record. Of the 89 judgments made for the six schizophrenic protocols, only 51 (57%) correctly identified the presence of that condition. Twelve (13%) of the remaining 38 judgments for the schizophrenic records did identify serious pathology (endogenous depression, manic depression, borderline personality with psychotic features), but the remaining 26 (29%) assigned less serious diagnoses from the listing of 12 provided in the questionnaire. None of the records were identified as normal, but one judgment of malingered was assigned.

Five (5%) of 91 judgments for the six records of uninformed fakers identified the presence of schizophrenia. Interestingly, four of the five were assigned to the same record. Twenty-three (25%) of the remaining 86 judgments identified a major affective disturbance, while an additional 44 (48%) assigned one of five personality disorder categories. Eighteen (20%) judgments used the normal classification, and only one (1%) identified a record as being malingered.

Sixteen (18%) of 90 judgments for the six records of informed fakers identified the presence of schizophrenia. Thirteen of the 16 schizophrenia decisions were assigned to two of the six records. Fifteen (16%) other judgments concerning this group of six records identified a major affective problem and, interestingly, 10 of the 15 were assigned to the same two records that had been identified as schizophrenic 13 times. Fifty-four (59%) of the additional judgments concerning this group of records used one of the five personality disorders categories, while only four (4%) used the normal classification and 1 (1%) identified a malingered record.

None of the six nonpatient control records were judged to be schizophrenic, although 12 (12%) of the 99 judgments used a major affective disorders classification. Twenty-three (23%) of the remaining 87 judgments used a category of reactive depression, and 43 (43%) others used one of the five personality disorder categories. Only 19 (19%) of the judgments identified the records as being normal, and 2 (2%) assigned the malingered classification.

Two important findings emerged from the Mittman (1983) study. First, 3 of the 12 subjects asked to malinger schizophrenia, two from the informed group and one from the uninformed group, were able to do so with considerable success. Actually, 17 of 35 judgments concerning those three protocols identified them as being schizophrenic while 14 of the remaining 18 judgments identified them as major affective disturbances. These findings tend to support the conclusions of Albert et al. (1980) that Rorschachs evaluated by expert judges are susceptible to malingering, especially if participants have some awareness of the type of condition they are trying to approximate.

Second, the 90 judges who rendered a total of 450 judgments concerning the 30 protocols were disposed to find pathology or psychological liabilities. Approximately 45% of all the judgments used one of the five personality disorders categories. It is true that when major pathology was present, the majority of judgments were in that direction (about 70% of the decisions made for the six schizophrenic records and about 60% of the judgments made concerning the depressive protocols), but when major pathology was not obvious, as in the two malingered groups and the nonpatient group, slightly more than 50% of all judgments used the personality disorders classifications.

Several studies using multicell designs have moved away from involving expert judges and instead have asked volunteer participants to malinger schizophrenia and then compared their Rorschach structural findings with various control or pathological groups. Perry and Kinder (1992) gave a brief description of the symptoms of schizophrenia to undergraduates in an experimental group and compared their findings with a control group of undergraduates who took the Rorschach after receiving standard instructions. Students in the experimental group had elevations on the Schizophrenia Index, the *WSum6*, the *X−%*, and *M−*, and showed decreased Populars and *X+%*.

Netter and Viglione (1994) assigned 40 nonpatient volunteers to either a control or a malingering group and compared their test-taking approach with that of 20 chronic inpatients who met the *DSM-III-R* criteria for schizophrenia. The participants in the malingering group read a nontechnical description of the symptoms of schizophrenia based on the *DSM-III-R* criteria and were instructed to attempt to convince the Rorschach examiner that they were schizophrenic. They found that the informed fakers were more likely to create a dramatic story about their percepts, pretend that the percept was alive, and spoil Popular responses.

A study by Ganellen, Wasyliw, Haywood, and Grossman (1996) is unique in that it involved actual malingerers instead of volunteers asked to fake a psychotic condition. They studied archival data for 48 defendants accused of crimes that carried either long potential prison sentences or the death penalty. The defendants had taken Rorschachs and MMPIs as part of evaluations to assess either fitness to stand trial or sanity.

Using an MMPI *F*-scale *T*-score cutoff of 90 to separate the defendants into honest and malingered groups, Ganellen et al. (1996) compared Rorschach data for the two groups. The only significant difference occurred on a composite measure of dramatic contents and Special Scores (Blood, Sex, Fire, Explosions, Morbid, and Aggressive), which was higher for the malingered group. The authors concluded that their findings ". . . suggest that real-life criminal defendants attempting to feign psychosis may produce unusual Rorschach responses, but have difficulty looking 'psychotic' on the Rorschach," (p. 74), and that ". . . this deliberate dramatization did not have an effect on Rorschach Structural Summary scores in the actual forensic situations we examined" (p. 75). They suggest that a pattern of extreme elevations on MMPI scales *F,* Paranoia (*Pa*), and Schizophrenia (*Sc*) coupled with low scores on MMPI scales *L* and *K,* few structural Rorschach indicators of psychosis, and overly dramatic Rorschach content may constitute a combination associated with intentional malingering of psychosis.

Several MMPI scales are useful in assessing malingered psychosis. Berry, Baer, and Harris (1991) performed a meta-analysis of MMPI variables thought to assess malingering and found that scale *F* had the highest effect size. Although they did not suggest a specific cutoff score, the authors reported high correct classification rates when a *T*-score greater than 88 was used to discriminate malingering from honest responders.

Gough (1950) suggested that the raw score difference between scales *F* and *K* (*F-K* Index) was useful in identifying attempts to minimize or maximize psychological difficulties. An *F-K* finding greater than +13 provides a conservative indicator of likely overreporting of symptoms.

Arbisi and Ben-Porath (1995) developed the Infrequency-Psychopathology [*F(p)*] scale to identify infrequent responding among even very pathological individuals. They identified a set of 27 MMPI-2 items answered infrequently by both psychiatric inpatients and individuals in the normative sample. Although they do not suggest a specific cutoff point, they note that a *T*-score greater than 100 on *F(p)* is a likely indicator of malingering.

CASE 18: ASSESSMENT OF PSYCHOSIS IN A HOMICIDE CASE

This 26-year-old man has been indicted for second-degree homicide in the death of his live-in girlfriend. He was evaluated on the referral of his attorney, who is questioning whether competency or sanity issues should play a part in his defense. He has been incarcerated for 46 days, having been arrested 12 days after a duck hunter found the victim's body in a marshland.

The girlfriend had been reported missing by the office manager at the automobile dealership where she had been employed as a secretary for the past four years. When she did not report for work for two consecutive days, the office manager called some of her friends, none of whom were able to provide any information about her disappearance. When she called the defendant, he claimed that she had moved out of their apartment a week earlier. However, neighbors reported to police investigators that she had been living with the defendant until the time of her disappearance.

In his first interview with investigators, the defendant reaffirmed his claim that his girlfriend had moved out a week prior to her disappearance. In the second interview, however, he changed his story and indicated that her departure had been only two or three days before she began missing work. He claimed that she had met another man and decided to go off with him. A search of the apartment revealed that all her clothes were still there, as well as her cosmetics and several personal items. The defendant was described as visibly anxious and sullen during questioning, saying that he and his girlfriend had "not been getting along very well" lately and that he had not been surprised when she decided to move out.

Neighbors reported several loud arguments between the two during the weeks before her disappearance. The defendant admitted to frequent arguments but denied ever having physically assaulted his girlfriend. He said they argued mostly about her desire to go out to dance clubs at night. He noted that he was usually too tired and that sometimes she would become angry and go out by herself. He claimed that on at least two occasions she had not come home and that this led to their disputes. He also claimed that she would often be "high" when she returned home. He admitted that they both used cocaine "sometimes but not much."

According to the coroner's report, the victim was stabbed 18 times. Two knives matching the general description of the weapon used were taken from the defendant's kitchen, and although both had been washed thoroughly, one had blood stains that were confirmed as a match for the victim. A search of the defendant's car yielded a blanket with stains that also matched her blood type.

When confronted with the forensic evidence, the defendant first argued that she probably had cut herself while cooking. He later said that he sometimes had "blackout spells" during which he was unsure of his activities. He claimed that these usually happened after he had "a beer or two." Nonetheless, he insisted, "I never would have hurt her, even though I knew she was a slut."

The defendant is the older of two children. His sister, age 20, is a firefighter, his father, age 56, is a truck driver, and his mother, age 54, is a housewife. He graduated from high school at age 18 and attended a technical school studying auto mechanics for approximately one year. He has been employed as a mechanic for a trucking firm for the past five years. He also has taken three night courses in English and history at a local community college and says that he has been saving money to return to college and obtain a degree. His employer describes him as a quiet but capable and conscientious worker.

He has been sullen and uncooperative since his incarceration. His court-appointed attorney says the defendant seems distant and that his speech has been rambling and incoherent. He continues to insist that he did not commit the crime, but concedes that, if he did, it was during one of his blackouts.

The defendant's performance on the WAIS-R yielded a Full Scale IQ of 99 (Verbal IQ = 102; Performance IQ = 96). The scaled scores on the Verbal subtests ranged from 9 (Digit Span and Vocabulary) to 12 (Similarities). His scaled scores on the Performance subtests ranged from 6 (Picture Arrangement) to 10 (Block Design).

The basic assessment question is whether there is any evidence to support a claim of incompetency to stand trial and whether there is evidence of a pervasive psychotic condition that could serve as a basis for an insanity defense.

Case 18.   A 26-Year-Old Male.

Card	Response	Inquiry
I	1. It's sk of air photo of 2 continents w a wm standg in there betwn thm, its lik a German photo	**E:** (Rpts Ss response) **S:** Its continents alrite, a comparison of the 2, I can tell caus I'v travld a lot, it mite b the middle line tht wb st lik the Germans wld do, lik ths w ths wm w no head & all the drkness of the continents arnd her **E:** I'm not sur I c it lik u do, help me **S:** I'm lik undergrnd lookg up, it all a pattern, lik it represents a sign, lik the TV or st evil lik tht **E:** ak ur time & look som mor, I thk u'll find st else **S:** I don't c at else
II	2. Ths is lik the Catholics, I'd rather not talk abt it, It's Christ, he's pierced & dying, thers bld all ovr	**E:** (Rpts Ss response) **S:** It must b anothr wrld, he's dying & bloody, rite here (D4) & the drk is all smoke & the red is all blood, c the smok & bld (points)
	3. An A image, lik a stingray	**E:** (Rpts Ss response) **S:** Dwn here (D3), it ll a stingray, lik a death instrument, its strange & powerful, its bad, evil, it can kill u, lik eels & serpents can kill, c the stingers, its lurking, waiting to kill
	4. There's emptiness here too	**E:** (Rpts Ss response) **S:** Rite here (DS5), its all empty, j nothing, just empty lik after evil triumphs, ths is the feeling thts left, just lik a hole in the soul
III	5. Ths repres 2 figs, thyr human lik a young boy & a young girl, just young, thy hav sheep faces, its not good	**E:** (Rpts Ss response) **S:** The color bothrs me, I'm not lookg at it, c here's the boy (left side) & the girl (rite side), thyr lik twins, thyr afraid of st, the way thyr standg, lookg arnd, waitg for some evil to come
	6. The head of a fly too	**E:** (Rpts Ss response) **S:** It has big eyes, bulging out, lookg for st to eat, its just his ugly head (D7) **E:** I'm not sur abt the bulging out **S:** Thyr drkr, fuller, lik bulging eyes
IV	7. A pair of feet here	**E:** (Rpts Ss response) **S:** C, rite here, a pr of feet, one on e side, lik smbodys feet, thy hav big toes
	8. A flower up here on the top	**E:** (Rpts Ss response) **S:** Yes, it ll a flower, its opened up lik w the petals, it looks soft **E:** Soft? **S:** The petals, thy look lik velvet, soft to the touch
	9. There r faces inside of ths	**E:** (Rpts Ss response) **S:** All kinds of faces, w lites on their helmets, it's prob evil, its not good, sort of a master plan, eb's lookg around for the plan, its lik a stage of civilization, thyr all undergrnd & its drk arnd them, its all black & grey
V	10. It cld only b a bat	**E:** (Rpts Ss response) **S:** Its shaped lik a bat w feelers & feet & wgs & ths (lower midline) is the point of entry, its lik a doubl take or split personality, lik sane & insane at the same time, it ll some decay there too, its drkr at the split view

Card	Response	Inquiry
VI	11. Ths is interestg, its lik som insides w a brain, u can c the passageway fr the insides to the brain	**E:** (Rpts Ss response) **S:** The brain is the important prt, no one has ever seen anythg lik it befor, its all drk, blk, the insides & passagewy & brain, it gets greyer lik a big brain, its a process in action
	12. It cb a totem pole too	**E:** (Rpts Ss response) **S:** J the top prt, it ll som great mysterious god lik totem tht all com to worship, its beautiful and so neatly carved to keep evryones attention
VII	13. Its 2 figs rep the peopl of diff nations, thy c eo but ther is a dividg line to show how thyr aprt. Thyr supp to b togthr but thyr held apart	**E:** (Rpts Ss response) **S:** Thyr peopl of diff classes lookg at eo, it cb a form of suicide but ther is really no way out, its diff classes waitg for st to happen, its a stage of advancement, a foreign race, mayb an asiatic mind & a chinese hand stretchd out & the line divides thm, life fr death, its evil & full of death because its so drk & gloomy
VIII	14. Ths repr rats devourg human flesh, female insides, its lik a cycle movg thru a stage	**E:** (Rpts Ss response) **S:** Yes 2 rats, on e side, thyr devourg a menu, it repres food, human food, its an oriental death, all the middl repres female prts, it repres the season whn ths happns, a chain betwn man & nature, lik childbirth, the red is all the bld, & its being eaten by rats, its a cycle
	15. A coat of arms too, lik a doubl cross	**E:** (Rpts Ss response) **S:** It rep wm against man, the homosxual struggl to b free of everythg, the insides of the coat of arms show all their colors, to show the fabulus thgs in people but ther is ugliness too, on the outside, the 2 thgs r pulling apart to show their rejection of eo & a preference for their own, no children will be left
IX	16. Its a trick, ths is nothg except a a womb, its not nice to c it ths way, all spread, but the baby is gone, its a premature birth	**E:** (Rpts Ss response) **S:** I don't lik ths one, its a lousy abortion, all bloody & oozing by som whore who didn't want her own & scrapped her gut to rid it off, but its mark will always b there & the chord, its in the middl, will nevr go away & it will pain her in the ass too bec she did ths lousy messy bloody thg, the lower is a red mess, she deserves it
X	17. Ther r insects at som functnal stage of how insects develop, thyr developing thgs at the top	**E:** (Rpts Ss response) **S:** Thr performg ss of operation on ths pole, lik eatg it up or changg it, thyr evil & thyr conferrg abt how to finish the job, thyr monsters, an evil race of ss
	18. Ths lousy pink is lik an unborn child & all thes thgs arnd it r tryg to poison it, thyr waitg 2 devour it & the ovaries in the middl, lik poisond amoebae & thy r ready to get at it	**E:** (Rpts Ss response) **S:** He's all red, his mothrs's blood is on him, the head is formed so far but he's still attachd to thos damned ovaries & thes germs r going to eat him up. Thyr discussg how to get to him for themselvs, its some master plan at work & its evil & the ovaries will b eaten so tht the evil can survive
	19. The seed of life is there too	**E:** (Rpts Ss response) **S:** Its floatg in the cntr, not being seen by anyone, but its there in all its richness & life giving power. If u get it & swallow it u becom indestructible & no one can harm u, but no one knows where it is, thy can't c it so it floats until it can b found

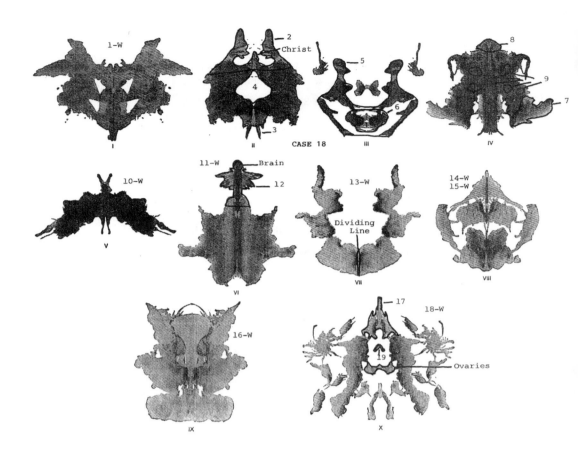

Case 18. Sequence of Scores.

Card	No.	Loc.	No.	Determinant(s)	(2)	Content(s)	Pop	Z	Special Scores
I	1	W+	1	FD.Mp.YFu	2	Art,Ge,Hd		4.0	AB,FAB2,PER,PHR
II	2	Dd+	99	Mp.Y.C–		H,Ay,Bl,Fi		3.0	DR2,MOR,PHR
	3	Do	3	Mau		A			AG,DR,PHR
	4	DSv	5	Mpo		Hx			DR2,MOR,AB,PHR
III	5	Do	9	Mpo		H,Hx			INC2,DR,PHR
	6	Do	7	FMp.FV–		Ad			AG,PHR
IV	7	Do	2	Fo	2	Hd			PHR
	8	Do	3	FTo		Bt			
	9	Dd+	99	Mp.C'F–		Hd,Cg,Ls		3.5	FAB2,PHR
V	10	Wo	1	FYo		A	P	1.0	DR2,MOR
VI	11	Wo	1	FC'.Mp–		An		2.5	DR2,PHR
	12	Do	8	Fo		Ay			DR
VII	13	W+	1	Mp.YFo		H	P	2.5	AB,MOR,DR2,PHR
VIII	14	W+	1	FMa.Mp.CFo	2	A,An,Bl	P	4.5	AB,AG,MOR,DR2,PHR
	15	W+	1	Ma.CFo	2	Art		4.5	AB,AG,DR2,PHR
IX	16	W+	1	Mp.CF–		Hd,Sx,Bl		5.5	MOR,DR2,PHR
X	17	D+	11	Mao	2	(A),Sc		4.0	FAB2,COP,AG,PHR
	18	W+	1	Ma.CF–	2	(H),An,A,Bl		5.5	FAB2,COP,AG,MOR,PHR
	19	Dv	3	Mpo		Id			DR2,PHR

Case 18.   Structural Summary.

Location Features	Determinants Blends	Single	Contents	S-Constellation
				NO . . .FV+VF+V+FD>2
		H = 3		YES . .Col-Shd Bl>0
Zf = 11	FD.M.YF	M = 5	(H) = 1	NO . . .Ego<.31,>.44
ZSum = 40.5	M.Y.C	FM = 0	Hd = 4	YES . .MOR > 3
ZEst = 34.5	FM.FV	m = 0	(Hd) = 0	YES . .Zd > +– 3.5
	M.C'F	FC = 0	Hx = 2	NO . . .es > EA
W = 8	FC'.M	CF = 0	A = 4	YES . .CF+C > FC
D = 9	M.YF	C = 0	(A) = 1	YES . .X+% < .70
W+D = 17	FM.M.CF	Cn = 0	Ad = 1	NO . . .S > 3
Dd = 2	M.CF	FC' = 0	(Ad) = 0	NO . . .P < 3 or > 8
S = 1	M.CF	C'F = 0	An = 3	NO . . .Pure H < 2
	M.CF	C' = 0	Art = 2	NO . . .R < 17
		FT = 1	Ay = 2	5 . . . .TOTAL

DQ		Single	Contents	Special Scores
		TF = 0	Bl = 4	Lv1 Lv2
+ = 9		T = 0	Bt = 1	DV = 0x1 0x2
o = 8		FV = 0	Cg = 1	INC = 0x2 1x4
v/+ = 0		VF = 0	Cl = 0	DR = 3x3 9x6
v = 2		V = 0	Ex = 0	FAB = 0x4 4x7
		FY = 1	Fd = 0	ALOG = 0x5
		YF = 0	Fi = 1	CON = 0x7
		Y = 0	Ge = 1	Raw Sum6 = 17
Form Quality		Fr = 0	Hh = 0	Wgtd Sum6 = 95

	FQx	MQual	W+D	Single	Contents		
				rF = 0	Ls = 1		
+	= 0	= 0	= 0	FD = 0	Na = 0		
o	= 11	= 7	= 11	F = 2	Sc = 1	AB = 5	GHR = 0
u	= 2	= 2	= 2		Sx = 1	AG = 6	PHR =16
–	= 6	= 5	= 4		Xy = 0	COP = 2	MOR = 7
none	= 0	= 0	= 0		Id = 1	CP = 0	PER = 1
				(2) = 6			PSV = 0

Ratios, Percentages, and Derivations

R = 19	L = 0.12			FC:CF+C = 0:5	COP = 2 AG = 6	
				Pure C = 1	GHR:PHR = 0:16	
EB = 14:5.5	EA = 19.5	EBPer = 2.5		SumC':WSumC = 2:5.5	a:p = 5:11	
eb = 2:8	es = 10	D = +3		Afr = 0.46	Food = 0	
	Adj es = 7	Adj D = +4		S = 1	SumT = 1	
				Blends:R = 10:19	Hum Con = 8	
FM = 2	C' = 2	T = 1		CP = 0	Pure H = 3	
m = 0	V = 1	Y = 4			PER = 1	
					Iso Indx = 0.16	

a:p = 5:11	Sum6 = 17	XA% = 0.68	Zf = 11.0	3r+(2)/R = 0.32
Ma:Mp = 4:10	Lv2 = 14	WDA% = 0.76	W:D:Dd = 8:9:2	Fr+rF = 0
2AB+Art+Ay = 14	WSum6 = 95	X–% = 0.32	W:M = 8:14	SumV = 1
MOR = 7	M– = 5	S– = 0	Zd = +6.0	FD = 1
	Mnone = 0	P = 3	PSV = 0	An+Xy = 3
		X+% = 0.58	DQ+ = 9	MOR = 7
		Xu% = 0.11	DQv = 2	H:(H)Hd(Hd) = 3:5

PTI = 4*	DEPI = 5*	CDI = 1	S-CON = 5	HVI = No	OBS = No

Case 18

MMPI-2 Validity and Clinical Scales Profile

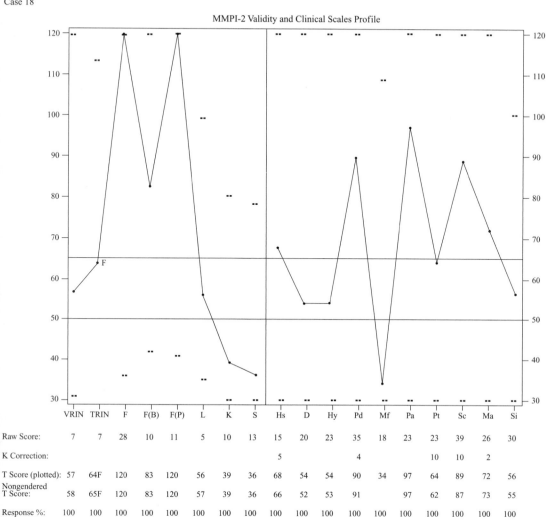

	VRIN	TRIN	F	F(B)	F(P)	L	K	S	Hs	D	Hy	Pd	Mf	Pa	Pt	Sc	Ma	Si
Raw Score:	7	7	28	10	11	5	10	13	15	20	23	35	18	23	23	39	26	30
K Correction:							5					4			10	10	2	
T Score (plotted):	57	64F	120	83	120	56	39	36	68	54	54	90	34	97	64	89	72	56
Nongendered T Score:	58	65F	120	83	120	57	39	36	66	52	53	91		97	62	87	73	55
Response %:	100	100	100	100	100	100	100	100	100	100	100	100	100	100	100	100	100	100

Cannot Say (Raw):   0   Percent True: 51

F-K (Raw):   18   Percent False: 49

Welsh Code: 64*8"9'1+7-023/:5# F***'"+-L/:K#   Profile Elevation: 73.5

Note: The highest and lowest T scores possible on each scale are indicated by a "--".

Case 18

MMPI-2 Content Scales Profile

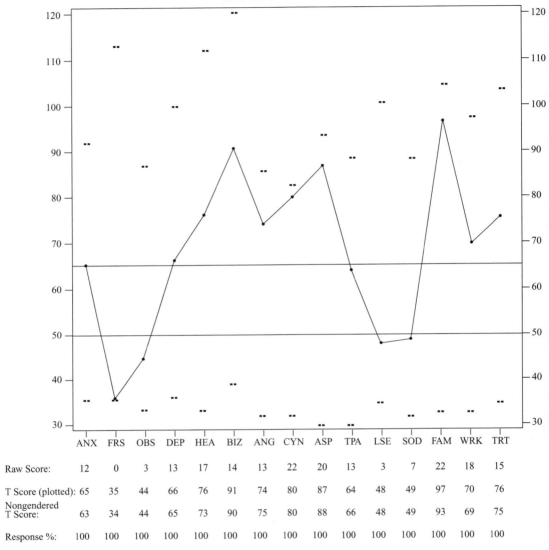

	ANX	FRS	OBS	DEP	HEA	BIZ	ANG	CYN	ASP	TPA	LSE	SOD	FAM	WRK	TRT
Raw Score:	12	0	3	13	17	14	13	22	20	13	3	7	22	18	15
T Score (plotted):	65	35	44	66	76	91	74	80	87	64	48	49	97	70	76
Nongendered T Score:	63	34	44	65	73	90	75	80	88	66	48	49	93	69	75
Response %:	100	100	100	100	100	100	100	100	100	100	100	100	100	100	100

Note: The highest and lowest Uniform T scores possible on each scale are indicated by a "--".

Case 18

MMPI-2 Supplementary Scales Profile

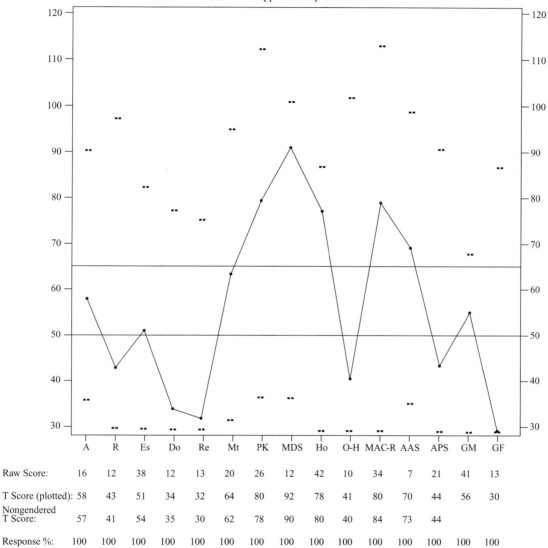

	A	R	Es	Do	Re	Mt	PK	MDS	Ho	O-H	MAC-R	AAS	APS	GM	GF
Raw Score:	16	12	38	12	13	20	26	12	42	10	34	7	21	41	13
T Score (plotted):	58	43	51	34	32	64	80	92	78	41	80	70	44	56	30
Nongendered T Score:	57	41	54	35	30	62	78	90	80	40	84	73	44		
Response %:	100	100	100	100	100	100	100	100	100	100	100	100	100	100	100

Note: The highest and lowest T scores possible on each scale are indicated by a "--".

CASE 18: OVERVIEW

Although this man has a significant value on the Perceptual Thinking Index (PTI = 4), suggesting the likelihood of substantial cognitive disarray, his Rorschach findings are characterized by such extreme findings as to create suspicion about the genuineness of his psychopathology. His *WSum6* of 95, the presence of 14 Level 2 special scores, and five *M*− in a 19-response record are especially noteworthy. They tend to signify serious reality testing problems and yet, while the value for the *X*−% (.32) is substantial, only 4 of the 17 responses given to *W* and *D* areas are minus (*WDA%* = .76). In fact, nine of his Level 2 special scores occurred in answers with appropriate form quality (responses 1, 4, 5, 10, 13, 14, 15, 17, and 19), including two that are Popular responses. This is atypical for someone with a noticeably active psychotic process. Most of his answers that include critical cognitive special scores are inappropriately dramatic, raising a question about whether someone with this magnitude of cognitive dysfunction could actually complete the Rorschach. Interestingly, his score of 19 on the composite of Dramatic contents (Blood, Sex, Fire, Explosions, Morbid, and Aggressive) identified by Ganellen et al. (1996) is markedly higher than the mean of 6.92 for the malingering defendants in that study.

His MMPI-2 findings are consistent with the malingering stance suggested by the Rorschach. His *T*-score of 120 on scale *F* suggests that he is much more likely to be a malingerer than an honest responder. His *F*-*K* Index of +18 indicates significant overreporting of symptoms, and his *T*-score of 120 on *F(p)* indicates that he has endorsed many items that are rarely selected by seriously disturbed inpatients.

EPILOGUE

A consulting psychiatrist, having no knowledge of the results of the psychological evaluation, interviewed him twice for 90 minutes each time. He questioned the possibility of feigning disturbance but left open the possibility that the crime might have been committed during a brief dissociative experience. The attorney decided against employing a competency or insanity defense. Ultimately, a plea bargain was reached and a sentence of 15 to 30 years was rendered.

Malingering Distress or Depression

The number of investigations concerning efforts to malinger or approximate depression are far fewer than those that focus on schizophrenia. The findings are sparse and somewhat equivocal, but they tend to suggest that malingered depression may be less easily detected than attempts to approximate schizophrenia.

In the study by Mittman (1983) described previously, judges were inconsistent in identifying the records of the six inpatient depressives. Thirty-eight of the 81 judgments (47%) concerning this group of six records correctly identified a major affective disturbance. Twelve (15%) judgments assigned the schizophrenia category. Thirty (37%) judgments identified the records as those from personality disorder subjects and one assigned the malingering category. None of the records were identified as normal.

Meisner (1988) used five experienced examiners, blind to the experimental condition of the study, to administer Rorschachs to 58 nondepressed university students. Immediately before taking the Rorschach, half of the students were given a description of depression based on the *DSM-III*, instructed to appear severely depressed, and offered a $50 cash reward for the most convincing test approximation of depression. The remaining 29 were administered the test under standard instructions. Meisner found that when subjects attempted to fake depression, their protocols showed a reduction in *R* and an increase in blood content and MOR Special Scores. No determinants were significantly affected by attempts to fake depression. Meisner concluded that the susceptibility of the Rorschach indices of depression to faking is markedly limited.

Frueh and Kinder (1994) tested 40 male undergraduates, randomly assigned either to a control or a syndrome-informed malingerer group, and compared their Rorschach, MMPI, and Mississippi Scale for Combat Related PTSD (Keane, Caddell, & Taylor, 1988) findings with those of Vietnam veterans diagnosed with posttraumatic stress disorder (PTSD). The malingerer and PTSD patient groups did not differ significantly from each other and both were significantly higher than the control group on the Mississippi scale, a face-valid self-report measure derived from the *DSM-III* criteria for PTSD. MMPI scale *F* and the *F-K* Index significantly differentiated the three groups, with controls lowest, PTSD patients higher, and malingerers highest on both these measures.

Frueh and Kinder (1994) found that the malingerers were significantly higher than either controls or PTSD patients on a composite measure of Rorschach dramatic contents, ". . . calculated as the sum of responses that included themes of depression, sex, blood, gore, confusion, mutilation, hatred, fighting, decapitation, negative emotion, or evil" (p. 288). They were also higher on *SumC, CF+C* and *X−%*. The PTSD patient group was significantly higher on *Lambda* than both the controls and the malingerers.

Exner and Ros i Plana (1997) studied the malingering of depression on both the Rorschach and MMPI with 24 nonpatient adults and 16 adult patients (8 inpatients and 8 outpatients) who met the *DSM-III* criteria for major depressive disorder or dysthymic disorder. The 24 nonpatients were randomized into three groups. One group was administered the Rorschach and MMPI using standard instructions; a second group was asked to take the tests as if they were seriously depressed but were given no information about the syndrome; and the third group listened to an audio cassette that described the *DSM-III* depression criteria and included a statement by a seriously depressed person and were then asked to take the tests with the intent of approximating serious depression.

Exner and Ros i Plana (1997) found that 6 of the 16 malingering subjects gave protocols in which the DEPI value was 5 or higher, with 4 of the 6 from the informed malingering group. Interestingly, however, all six of the nonpatient fakers who malingered depression successfully on the DEPI had MMPI *F-K* findings of +12 or greater, suggesting overreporting of symptoms. Seven of the 16 patients were positive on the DEPI, a finding that did not significantly differentiate them from the four out of eight positive DEPIs in the informed faker group. Additionally, the two malingering groups gave as many MOR, *C′*, and *vista* responses as did the patients. The Coping Deficit Index (CDI) was more effective in discriminating malingerers from depressed patients. Eleven of the 16 patients had a CDI value greater than 3, while only 3 of the 16 malingerers had this finding.

One of the conclusions from the Exner and Ros i Plana (1997) study can be generalized as a guideline whenever psychological tests are used to evaluate malingering. The authors write that their findings ". . . suggest that the simulation of depression is possible on either the Rorschach or MMPI, but it seems reasonable to suggest that the simulation is far less likely to be present in a seemingly valid manner when both tests are used to evaluate the findings from each other"

(p. 37). This is similar to the comment made by Ganellen et al. (1996): "Our data suggest that the combination of the MMPI and the Rorschach *Comprehensive System* provide a powerful psychometric technique for detecting deliberate malingering of a psychotic disorder" (p. 78). Multi-method approaches consistently produce more accurate data and, when impression management is likely, their use becomes mandatory.

CASE 19: EVALUATION FOR A DISABILITY CLAIM

This 51-year-old man was referred by his disability insurance carrier for an independent medical evaluation. He was self-employed as president and owner of a financial planning service but has been out of work due to depression for a year and a half.

He was born into a family of modest means and received an athletic scholarship to attend college. He completed college in four years and then went on to get an advanced degree while awaiting placement with the U.S. navy as a pilot. He completed pilot training and flew for the navy for approximately six years, although he never went overseas or flew during combat. He was carrier-rated, including night carrier landings.

He has been married for over 30 years and has two daughters, both of whom graduated from college, live independently, and are doing well. After leaving the navy, he worked in management for another company before starting his own organization. He indicates that the business went well for a long time, but his clients became increasingly upset as the stock market began to fail. This seemed to affect him greatly, and approximately 18 months prior to the evaluation, he became unable to work.

He is in generally good health with no significant medical problems, having been an avid exerciser until fairly recently. He is on two antidepressant medications and a low dose of one of the atypical antipsychotics. He sees a psychologist for therapy once a month. Generally they talk about "flying, the weather, and how the stock market is doing."

He has no history of substance abuse, does not smoke, and rarely consumes alcohol. He reports a significant decrease in libido from his predepression days. He indicates that he would like to have a more active sexual life with his wife but worries that it may not happen. His previous outdoor activities included hunting, fishing, and jogging, but he is not currently participating in any of these and has gained some weight.

He states that his personal investments have done relatively well, although he currently has a cash flow problem. He reports no other significant losses or other problems and attributes his depression to the demands his clients were making on him. He says, "I'm tired of having to explain to people what's going on and having to pacify them."

Because this depressive episode has gone on for a year and a half with no indication of progress or resolution, the insurance company is asking whether malingering is involved or whether something other than depression is occurring.

Case 19.   A 51-Year-Old Male.

Card	Response	Inquiry
I	1. Spider...(handed card to **E**)	**E:** (Rpts Ss response) **S:** Ths is mouth & here is 2 of the littl legs & tentacles & here is the tail **E:** Most ppl c more thn 1 thng **S:** Ok...look at it this way or other way? **E:** Up to u
	2. St lik Halloween...monstr or st (handed card to **E**)	**E:** (Rpts Ss response) **S:** Ll eyes & mayb mouth going ovr here & ths is ears
II	3. Spider...tht's been steppd on & smashd & som of the bl comg out of it (handed card to **E**) **E:** Take u'r time	**E:** (Rpts Ss response) **S:** Blood is red of course, black portion is spider. I can't tell u wht is the head or tail **E:** Black part? **S:** J overall shape of it I mean
	4. A set of lungs (handed card to **E**)	**E:**(Rpts Ss response) **S:** Overall shape of black I mean. It's got the same shape of lungs even though not symmetrical, smooth on edges
III	v5. Tht's definitely a spider...I guess u want me to come up w st else...ll a spider w 2 broken legs off (handed card to **E**)	**E:** (Rpts Ss response) **S:** Here's tentacles, legs comg out & there r som other ones he used to hav. He is lookg at u head on. Here is 2 eyes here & here. Two of frnt legs holdg up in the air & walkg on other 2 legs **E:** Broken? **S:** Yes, possibly
IV	v6. A bat...a smashed on bat, but tht has been smashed, steppd on, rolled ovr, flattend	**E:** (Rpts Ss response) **S:** Yes, j a bat, a flat out bat. It's black & it has 2 littl eyes here & here. I think this here but ll from the top, is a top view **E:** Smashed? **S:** Looks flat, of course its a picture. It is I c no depth to it at all, really ll its been rolld ovr
V	v7. I have no idea... (**E:** J tak u'r time) If I guess at it, I'd say a leaf... a burnt leaf if u wanted to say	**E:** (Rpts Ss response) **S:** Yes, u know it doesn't really hav the shape of a leaf tht much, best I could come up wth it, darkness of it & som littl veins u can c it som here **E:** Veins? **S:** Rite here, a littl liter.
VI	8. A skin & hide of a dead A... tht's been made into a taptestry on the wall	**E:** (Rpts Ss response) **S:** Well...ths would hav been the tail, ths would hav been front legs out to one side, ths would hav been rear legs, mounted head. Obviously, rest of it is furry, som ko A tht has characteristic of stripe dwn its back **E:** Furry? **S:** Som...I dk, not smooth but ll som change in definition of the surface **E:** Stripe? **S:** Its drkr has mor definition of wher it begins & ends
VII	v9. A crab	**E:** (Rpts Ss response) **S:** 2 legs ovr here & here & I mean rest of it. Whiteness in the middle would b back or back mayb comg frm bottom. Only thng I came up wth was crab

(continued)

431

Case 19.   Continued.

Card	Response	Inquiry
v10.	I'll call it a spider again too but about only thng I can come up with	**E:** (Rpts Ss response) **S:** Only other thng tht comes to mind was spider & tht's only bec of legs again
VIII 11.	Two wild A's eatg anothr dead A, tearg it apart	**E:** (Rpts Ss response) **S:** Here is A & here is A, whatevr thng in the middle I dk actually. Ll mayb it ll paw of A & pullg ths one pullg on one of legs & tht one pullg on one of legs. Ths is I dk mayb a rock & also ll mirror image of one anthr, didn't c tht at first **E:** Rock? **S:** J roughness of it
IX v12.	Diffrnt compositions of algae	**E:** (Rpts Ss response) **S:** Nothng has any shape, form, or fashion. Nothng to tht at all. I c nothng in here **E:** Algae? **S:** No, I j...no, it j, I dk, it j ll som ko slime which is algae I guess, I believe
X 13.	A bunch of trash	**E:** (Rpts Ss response) **S:** All ovr, I mean no identity of anythng at all to me. Can't really place anythng **E:** Trash? **S:** All jumbled up
14.	And I also c it as a bunch of germs undr a microscope in a organ of the body.	**E:** (Rpts Ss response) **S:** In this, yes as far as shape of it, not as far as color bec I don't thnk germs hav color, growth or certain germs or cancer, I dk, but cancer is gonna b black I know that

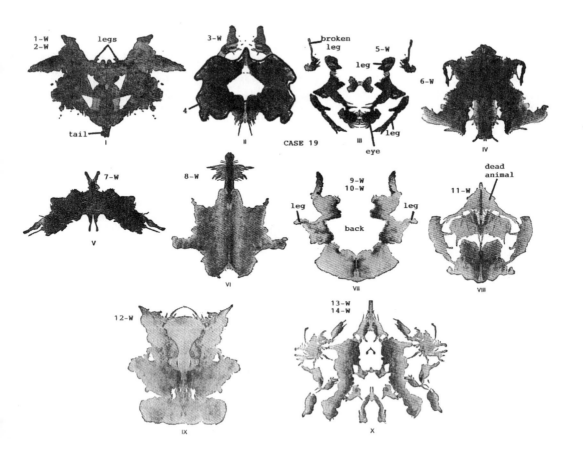

Case 19. Sequence of Scores.

Card	No.	Loc.	No.	Determinant(s)	(2)	Content(s)	Pop	Z	Special Scores
I	1	Wo	1	F–		A		1.0	INC
	2	WSo	1	Fo		(Hd)		3.5	GHR
II	3	W+	1	mp.CF–		A,Bl		4.5	MOR,INC
	4	Do	6	F–		An			
III	5	W+	1	FMa–		Ad		5.5	MOR,INC,DR
IV	6	Wo	1	FC'o		A		2.0	MOR
V	7	Wo	1	FYu		Bt		1.0	MOR
VI	8	Wo	1	FT.FYo		Ad	P	2.5	MOR
VII	9	WSo	1	F–		A		4.0	
	10	WSo	1	F–		A		4.0	PSV
VIII	11	W+	1	FMa–	2	A,Ad,Ls	P	4.5	MOR,AG,PHR
IX	12	Wv	1	Fu		Bt			
X	13	Wv	1	Fu		Id			
	14	Wv	1	Fu		Id			PSV

Case 19. Structural Summary.

Location Features	Determinants Blends	Single	Contents	S-Constellation
				NO . . .FV+VF+V+FD>2
			H = 0	NO . . .Col-Shd Bl>0
Zf = 10	m.CF	M = 0	(H) = 0	YES . Ego<.31,>.44
ZSum = 32.5	FT.FY	FM = 2	Hd = 0	YES . .MOR > 3
ZEst = 31.0		m = 0	(Hd) = 1	NO . . .Zd > +− 3.5
		FC = 0	Hx = 0	YES . .es > EA
W = 13		CF = 0	A = 6	YES . .CF+C > FC
D = 1		C = 0	(A) = 0	YES . .X+% < .70
W+D = 14		Cn = 0	Ad = 3	NO . . .S > 3
Dd = 0		FC′ = 1	(Ad) = 0	YES . .P < 3 or > 8
S = 3		C′F = 0	An = 1	YES . .Pure H < 2
		C′ = 0	Art = 0	YES . .R < 17
		FT = 0	Ay = 0	8 . . . .TOTAL
DQ		TF = 0	Bl = 1	**Special Scores**
+ = 3		T = 0	Bt = 2	Lv1 Lv2
o = 8		FV = 0	Cg = 0	DV = 0x1 0x2
v/+ = 0		VF = 0	Cl = 0	INC = 3x2 0x4
v = 3		V = 0	Ex = 0	DR = 1x3 0x6
		FY = 1	Fd = 0	FAB = 0x4 0x7
		YF = 0	Fi = 0	ALOG = 0x5
		Y = 0	Ge = 0	CON = 0x7
Form Quality		Fr = 0	Hh = 0	Raw Sum6 = 4
		rF = 0	Ls = 1	Wgtd Sum6 = 9
	FQx	MQual	W+D	FD = 0	Na = 0	
+ = 0	= 0	= 0	F = 8	Sc = 0	AB = 0 GHR = 1
o = 3	= 0	= 3		Sx = 0	AG = 1 PHR = 1
u = 4	= 0	= 4		Xy = 0	COP = 0 MOR = 6
− = 7	= 0	= 7		Id = 2	CP = 0 PER = 0
none = 0	= 0	= 0			PSV = 2
		(2) = 1		

Ratios, Percentages, and Derivations

R = 14	L = 1.33		FC:CF+C = 0:1	COP = 0 AG = 1
			Pure C = 0	GHR:PHR = 1:1
EB = 0:1.0	EA = 1.0	EBPer = N/A	SumC′:WSumC = 1:1.0	a:p = 2:1
eb = 3:4	es = 7	D = −2	Afr = 0.40	Food = 0
	Adj es = 6	Adj D = −1	S = 3	SumT = 1
			Blends:R = 2:14	Hum Con = 1
FM = 2	C′ = 1	T = 1	CP = 0	Pure H = 0
m = 1	V = 0	Y = 2		PER = 0
				Iso Indx = 0.21

a:p	= 2:1	Sum6 = 4	XA% = 0.50	Zf = 10.0	3r+(2)/R	= 0.07
Ma:Mp	= 0:0	Lv2 = 0	WDA% = 0.50	W:D:Dd = 13:1:0	Fr+rF	= 0
2AB+Art+Ay	= 0	WSum6 = 9	X−% = 0.50	W:M = 13:0	SumV	= 0
MOR	= 6	M− = 0	S− = 2	Zd = +1.5	FD	= 0
		Mnone = 0	P = 2	PSV = 2	An+Xy	= 1
			X+% = 0.21	DQ+ = 3	MOR	= 6
			Xu% = 0.29	DQv = 3	H:(H)Hd(Hd)	= 0:1

PTI = 3	DEPI = 6*	CDI = 4*	S-CON = 8*	HVI = No	OBS = No

Case 19

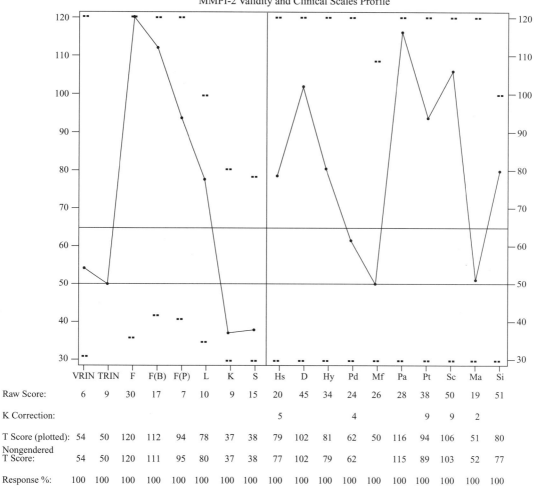

MMPI-2 Validity and Clinical Scales Profile

	VRIN	TRIN	F	F(B)	F(P)	L	K	S	Hs	D	Hy	Pd	Mf	Pa	Pt	Sc	Ma	Si
Raw Score:	6	9	30	17	7	10	9	15	20	45	34	24	26	28	38	50	19	51
K Correction:									5			4		9	9	2		
T Score (plotted):	54	50	120	112	94	78	37	38	79	102	81	62	50	116	94	106	51	80
Nongendered T Score:	54	50	120	111	95	80	37	38	77	102	79	62		115	89	103	52	77
Response %:	100	100	100	100	100	100	100	100	100	100	100	100	100	100	100	100	100	100

Cannot Say (Raw): 0   Percent True: 55

F-K (Raw): 21   Percent False: 45

Welsh Code: 682**7*30"1'+4-95/ F***"L'+-/:K#   Profile Elevation: 86.4

Note: The highest and lowest T scores possible on each scale are indicated by a "--".

435

Case 19

MMPI-2 Content Scales Profile

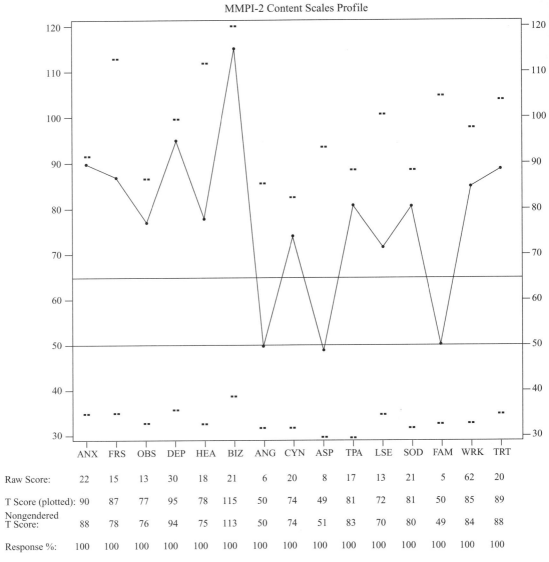

	ANX	FRS	OBS	DEP	HEA	BIZ	ANG	CYN	ASP	TPA	LSE	SOD	FAM	WRK	TRT
Raw Score:	22	15	13	30	18	21	6	20	8	17	13	21	5	62	20
T Score (plotted):	90	87	77	95	78	115	50	74	49	81	72	81	50	85	89
Nongendered T Score:	88	78	76	94	75	113	50	74	51	83	70	80	49	84	88
Response %:	100	100	100	100	100	100	100	100	100	100	100	100	100	100	100

Note: The highest and lowest Uniform T scores possible on each scale are indicated by a "--".

Case 19

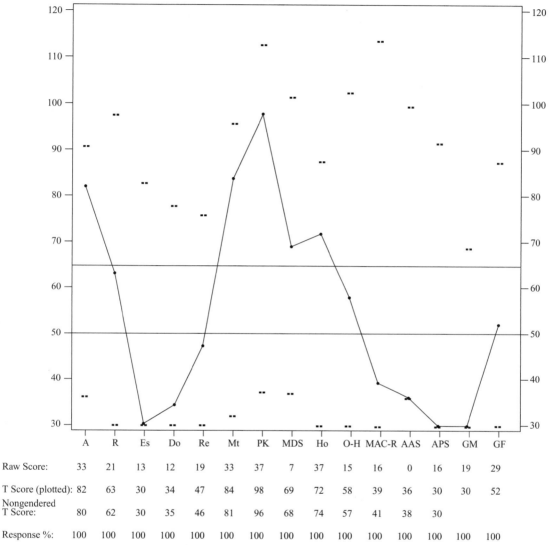

MMPI-2 Supplementary Scales Profile

	A	R	Es	Do	Re	Mt	PK	MDS	Ho	O-H	MAC-R	AAS	APS	GM	GF
Raw Score:	33	21	13	12	19	33	37	7	37	15	16	0	16	19	29
T Score (plotted):	82	63	30	34	47	84	98	69	72	58	39	36	30	30	52
Nongendered T Score:	80	62	30	35	46	81	96	68	74	57	41	38	30		
Response %:	100	100	100	100	100	100	100	100	100	100	100	100	100	100	100

Note: The highest and lowest T scores possible on each scale are indicated by a "--".

437

CASE 19: OVERVIEW

This man is positive on the DEPI (6), CDI (4), and S-CON (8). Although his protocol is brief, 14 responses, much of the structural data and the content are consistent with the premise that a serious affective disarray exists and there is a possibility of a suicidal preoccupation. The D Score (-2) suggests that he is in considerable overload and vulnerable to impulsiveness, and the absence of M responses ($EB = 0:1.0$) raises a question about affective flooding. In a related context, the $XA\%$, $WDA\%$, and $X-\%$ each have values of .50, implying that his mediational processes are noticeably impaired and marked difficulties in reality testing are likely to exist.

In effect, much of the record is not unlike one that might be given by a first admission patient who is seriously disorganized. However, there are some variables that may raise questions about the veracity of his Rorschach protocol. He has a high *Lambda* value (1.33), which is incongruous with the other data and the notion that he is seriously disorganized. In addition, the low number of responses and substantial elevation on MOR (6) are similar to the findings Meisner (1988) reported with his group of informed fakers. Also, throughout the Rorschach there is a sort of thematic perseveration about damage ("a spider that's been stepped on and smashed," "a spider with two broken legs off," "a bat that has been smashed, stepped on, rolled over, flattened," "two wild animals eating another dead animal, tearing it apart") that may suggest a conscious decision to emphasize that theme. These elements do not discount the presumption of a serious affective disarray, but they raise some cautions that require further exploration using other data sources.

The history indicates that his depressive episode has existed for about 18 months with no indication of progress or resolution. It also indicates that he sees a therapist only once per month and that "generally, they talk about flying, the weather, and how the stock market is doing." Whereas the Rorschach appears to indicate severe disorganization and distress, the history offers no such indications.

His MMPI-2 provides some important data regarding these apparent discrepant findings. The MMPI-2 data suggest that he is maximizing his reporting of difficulties, with scale F at a T-score of 120, $F(b)$ at 112, and the F-K Index at +21. Moreover, the very high T-scores on the clinical scales 6 (116), 8 (106), and 2 (102) suggest severe emotional distress likely to be characterized by dysphoria and agitation plus considerable fearfulness, apprehension, and inappropriate affect, none of which are mentioned concerning his recent history. However, it should be noted that a meta-analysis (Rogers, Sewell, Martin, & Vitacco, 2003) indicates that genuinely depressed psychiatric patients can produce extreme validity scale elevations, especially on F and $F(b)$.

Thus, while the Rorschach and the MMPI-2 contain indications that he may be a likely candidate for hospitalization, they also contain significant suggestions of malingering. Consequently, additional assessment resources should be employed. They should include a comprehensive interview with him, as well as the collection of additional information about him from some of the important people in his life, especially his wife and his therapist.

EPILOGUE

An extensive interview with him by an independent psychiatrist yielded no indications of serious disorganization or suicidal ideation but some evidence of a pervasively moderate depression was noted. No further information is available.

REFERENCES

Albert, S., Fox, H., & Kahn, M. (1980). Faking psychosis on the Rorschach. *Journal of Personality Assessment, 44,* 115–119.

Arbisi, P. A., & Ben-Porath, Y. S. (1995). An MMPI-2 infrequent response scale for use with psychopathological populations: The Infrequency-Psychopathology Scale, *F(p)*. *Psychological Assessment, 7*(4), 424–431.

Berry, D. T., Baer, R. A., & Harris, M. J. (1991). Detection of malingering on the MMPI: A meta-analysis. *Clinical Psychology Review, 11,* 585–598.

Carp, A. L., & Shavzin, A. R. (1950). The susceptibility to falsification of the Rorschach psychodiagnostic technique. *Journal of Consulting Psychology, 14,* 230–233.

Easton, K., & Feigenbaum, K. (1967). An examination of an experimental set to fake the Rorschach test. *Perceptual and Motor Skills, 24,* 871–874.

Exner, J. E., & Ros i Plana, M. (1997). Rorschach and MMPI simulation of depression. *British Journal of Projective Psychology, 42*(1), 27–38.

Fosberg, I. A. (1938). Rorschach reactions under varied instructions. *Rorschach Research Exchange, 3,* 12–30.

Fosberg, I. A. (1941). An experimental study of the reliability of the Rorschach psychodiagnostic technique. *Rorschach Research Exchange, 5,* 72–84.

Fosberg, I. A. (1943). How do subjects attempt to fake results on the Rorschach test? *Rorschach Research Exchange, 7,* 119–121.

Frueh, B. C., & Kinder, B. N. (1994). The susceptibility of the Rorschach Inkblot Test to malingering of combat-related PTSD. *Journal of Personality Assessment, 62*(2), 280–298.

Ganellen, R. J., Wasyliw, O. E., Haywood, T. W., & Grossman, L. S. (1996). Can psychosis be malingered on the Rorschach? An empirical study. *Journal of Personality Assessment, 66*(1), 65–80.

Gibby, R. G. (1951). The stability of certain Rorschach variables under conditions of experimentally induced sets: The intellectual variables. *Journal of Projective Techniques, 15,* 3–25.

Gough, H. G. (1950). The F minus K dissimulation index for the MMPI. *Journal of Consulting Psychology, 13,* 408–413.

Hutt, M., Gibby, R. G., Milton, E. O., & Pottharst, K. (1950). The effect of varied experimental "sets" upon Rorschach test performance. *Journal of Projective Techniques, 14,* 181–187.

Keane, T. M., Caddell, J. M., & Taylor, K. L. (1988). Mississippi scale for combat-related posttraumatic stress disorder: Three studies in reliability and validity. *Journal of Consulting and Clinical Psychology, 56,* 85–90.

Meisner, S. (1988). Susceptibility of Rorschach distress correlates to malingering. *Journal of Personality Assessment, 52*(3), 564–571.

Meyer, R. G., & Deitsch, S. M. (1995). The assessment of malingering in psychodiagnostic evaluations: Research-based concepts and methods for consultants. *Consulting Psychology Journal: Practice and Research, 47*(4), 234–245.

Mittman, B. L. (1983). Judges' ability to diagnose schizophrenia on the Rorschach: The effect of malingering (Doctoral dissertation, Long Island University, 1983). *Dissertation Abstracts International, 44,* 1248B.

Netter, B. E., & Viglione, D. J. (1994). An empirical study of malingering schizophrenia on the Rorschach. *Journal of Personality Assessment, 62*(1), 45–57.

Perry, G. G., & Kinder, B. N. (1992). Susceptibility of the Rorschach to malingering: A schizophrenia analogue. In C. D. Spielberger & J. N. Butcher (Eds.), *Advances in personality assessment* (Vol. 9, pp. 127–140). Hillsdale, NJ: Erlbaum.

Rogers, R., Sewell, K. W., Martin, M. A., & Vitacco, M. J. (2003). Detection of feigned mental disorders: A meta-analysis of the MMPI-2 and malingering. *Assessment, 10*(2), 160–177.

CHAPTER 21

Simulation of Good Adjustment

There are many circumstances in which it is to the person's advantage to be seen in the best light possible. Divorcing parents in custody evaluations are typically motivated to appear well adjusted and free of psychological difficulties that could compromise their parenting capacity. Individuals applying for a well-paying job have a substantial incentive to depict themselves as competent, interpersonally skilled, and robust in their ability to handle stress. In such situations, methods to identify the underreporting of psychological difficulties and the simulation of unrealistically positive adjustment become an important part of a comprehensive psychological assessment.

Paulhus (1984) has proposed a two-factor model that allows a finer-grained understanding of assessment data when socially desirable responding is likely. Other-deception—positive impression management or faking good—involves a conscious attempt to fool the assessing psychologist by unrealistically portraying oneself as problem-free. Self-deception, on the other hand, involves a positive presentation that the individual genuinely believes to be accurate. Within the commonly used MMPI validity scales, Nichols and Greene (1988) found that the L scale loads significantly on the other-deception factor. At present, there are no Rorschach studies that focus specifically on the differentiation of other- versus self-deception.

As noted, a multimethod approach is important when assessing validity issues. However, for both the Rorschach and the MMPI (Bagby et al., 1997), studies on positive impression management are fewer and less powerful than the more extensive research that has accumulated on the malingering of psychopathology. Nonetheless, a survey of the available literature and two cases—one involving a custody evaluation and the other a work-related situation—will illustrate the challenges the psychologist faces when socially desirable responding is involved.

ASSESSMENT OF POSITIVE SIMULATION

The Rorschach literature concerning attempts to simulate or approximate a positive or desirable state is, at best, sparse. Fosberg (1938, 1943) was the first to test whether the Rorschach was susceptible to impression management by using a counterbalanced retest design with instructions to give *good* or *bad* impressions. He found that the basic structural features of the test data were not altered, and many of the variables that he studied showed retest reliabilities exceeding .80. Carp and Shavzin (1950) also used a counterbalanced retest design with 20 participants instructed to give *good* or *bad* impressions. They found differences between the groups but could not predict the direction in which the data were altered using the instructional set as the basis for the prediction.

Phares, Stewart, and Foster (1960) used standard instructions with one group of participants but informed a second group that there were specific right and wrong answers. They did not find significant differences between the groups and concluded that the effects of the instructional set were negligible.

Seamons, Howell, Carlisle, and Roe (1981) tested 48 individuals with varying degrees of pathology in a counterbalanced retest design. The participants were asked to respond as if they were normal and well adjusted in one testing and as if they were seriously mentally ill in the second. They found that when instructed to approximate normality, participants gave significantly more Popular responses and significantly fewer answers containing *es* related variables, inappropriate combinations, and dramatic contents.

It seems likely that individuals involved in custody disputes would be motivated to simulate good adjustment. In that context, the protocols of 25 pairs of nonpatient men and women tested in conjunction with custody litigation were reviewed and compared with equal size random samples drawn from a nonpatient sample (Exner, 1991). Essentially, the distribution of scores for the 50 custody litigants differed very little from the nonpatient group, although some differences were found when the groups were compared by sex. The 25 males averaged nearly 25 responses, slightly higher than nonpatient males. Conversely, the 25 females averaged only 19 responses, which is slightly lower than nonpatient females. The males had an average *EA* of 10.5 (median = 9), which is slightly higher than the control sample, and none of the men gave Pure *C* responses. The average *Zf* for males was 15.4, which is significantly higher than the control sample or the female group. None of the 50 individuals in the custody litigation group had a positive CDI, and only two, one male and one female, were positive on the DEPI. One male was also positive on the OBS. Some frequency data for the sample are shown in Table 21.1.

The absence of baseline records taken prior to litigation makes it impossible to use these data for more than speculation. Nonetheless, the findings suggest that, if attempts at simulation were commonplace for this group of custody litigants, the results were often less than favorable. The frequency data in Table 21.1 indicate that 10% of the group have Adj D Scores less than zero; 12% have values of *CF+C* that are considerably greater than the *FC* value; 40% have an *X+%* that is less than 70%; 16% have an *X−%* greater than 15%; 12% are underincorporators; 20% have more passive than active human movement; 18% give at least one *M−* response; 22% have more than four Critical Special Scores; 18% are *T-less*; 18% gave at least one reflection answer; and 46% have Egocentricity Indices that fall outside the average range.

An inspection of the 50 records reveals that all contained at least one characteristic that usually would be viewed as a liability when compared with an optimal standard, and 41 of the 50 included at least three such characteristics. The presence of some liabilities in the protocols of nonpatients is common, but if someone were successful at simulating exceptional adjustment, it seems doubtful that any would appear.

Possibly the most intriguing findings for both the male and female custody litigants concern the Intellectualization Index, the PER special score, and the number of Popular responses. More than half the individuals in both groups have an Intellectualization Index that is interpretively significant, and 52% of the total group gave more than two PER answers. These substantial frequencies seem to reflect efforts to appear mature or sophisticated when confronted with the demands of the test. The frequencies are so much greater than the normative data that it seems reasonable to assume that these elevations were driven by the situational motive to put the best face forward. Similarly, 36% of the group gave more than seven Popular answers, which is quite different from the

Table 21.1   Some Frequency Data for 25 Nonpatient Male–Female Pairs Involved in Custody Litigation.

Variable	Female N	Female %	Male N	Male %	Total N	Total %
Ambitent	6	24	8	32	14	28
D Score > 0	3	12	6	24	9	18
D Score < 0	4	16	4	16	8	16
Adjusted D Score > 0	3	12	6	24	9	18
Adjusted D Score < 0	2	8	3	12	5	10
FC > (CF+C)+2	2	8	5	20	4	8
FC > (CF+C)+1	9	36	8	32	17	34
CF+C > FC+1	8	32	6	24	14	28
CF+C > FC+2	3	12	3	12	6	12
X+% > .89	2	8	4	16	6	12
X+% < .70	11	44	9	36	20	40
Xu% > .20	12	48	10	40	22	44
X–% > .15	5	20	3	12	8	16
Popular < 4	3	12	2	8	5	10
Popular > 7	8	32	10	40	18	36
Lambda > 0.99	1	4	2	8	3	6
Zd > +3.0	5	20	8	32	13	26
Zd < –3.0	4	16	2	8	6	12
Mp > Ma	6	24	4	16	10	20
M– >0	5	20	4	16	9	18
Sum 6 Spec Scores > 4	5	20	6	24	11	22
Intellectual Index > 3	16	64	14	56	30	60
Intellectual Index > 5	12	48	7	28	19	38
COP > 1	15	60	12	48	27	54
COP > 2	10	40	9	36	19	38
AG > 1	6	24	7	28	13	26
AG > 2	3	12	5	20	8	16
PER > 2	15	60	11	44	26	52
T = 0	5	20	4	16	9	18
T > 1	6	24	3	12	9	18
Pure H < 2	7	28	7	28	14	28
Pure H > 2	9	36	7	28	16	32
All human content > 6	8	32	9	36	17	34
Egocentricity Index < .33	5	20	4	16	9	18
Egocentricity Index > .44	8	32	6	24	14	28
Fr+Rf > 0	5	20	4	16	9	18

nonpatient sample. These findings coincide with those of Seamons et al. (1981) and support the notion that people attempting to do well tend to respond to obvious cues and give more conventional answers.

Overall, Rorschach research concerning simulation of good adjustment is spotty and incomplete. The composite of data suggests that it is probably difficult to simulate psychological health unless some elements of good adjustment already exist, and even then, any liabilities of substance are likely to be conveyed in the data.

Several MMPI scales and indexes are relevant in the assessment of positive simulation. Traditionally, the Lie (*L*) and Correction (*K*) scales are thought to measure defensive minimizing of difficulties, at naive and somewhat more subtle levels respectively. The *F-K* Index (Gough, 1950) has also been used to assess both over- and underreporting of symptoms.

Butcher and Han (1995) developed the Superlative (*S*) scale to assess the tendency to describe oneself in an extremely positive light. The authors identified the 50 items that make up the scale by comparing male airplane pilot applicants with men in the MMPI-2 normative sample. They suggest that *S* scale elevations may be associated with unrealistic reporting of positive adjustment and with denial of irritability, anger, and moral flaws. However, as with the Rorschach, problems in adjustment emerge on the MMPI-2 even in the context of attempts to present oneself positively. Bagby, Nicholson, Buis, Radovanovic, and Fidler (1999) tested 58 female and 57 male custody litigants and found that 40% had clinically significant ($T > 64$) scores on at least one clinical scale. Paranoia (*Pa*) and Psychopathic Deviancy (*Pd*) were the two most frequently elevated scales, at 19% and 16% respectively.

CASE 20: A CUSTODY EVALUATION

This 36-year-old woman is being evaluated as part of a disputed custody action in which both she and her ex-husband are requesting full custody of their 8-year-old son. She completed two years of college in business administration and has held jobs in hospital and social service settings. Her current position is as an administrative director in a social service agency.

This woman's parents divorced when she was 12, and she has had little contact with her father since that time. Both of her parents have histories of alcoholism, and her mother received psychiatric treatment for manic-depressive difficulties. A younger sister made a suicide attempt during early adolescence, spent most of her teens in a residential facility, and has not remained in contact.

She indicates that both her parents were physically and emotionally abusive, describing spankings with switches and belts by her father and alcoholic binges by her mother. She maintains some contact with her mother, who subsequently remarried, and she feels that their relationship has improved.

This woman's first marriage was at age 21. She gave birth to a son within a year and ended the marriage shortly thereafter, saying that her first husband "wanted to be in control of everything." She retained custody of the child from that marriage. He is now age 14. She married the man with whom she is currently involved in custody litigation five years later and gave birth to a second son. That marriage ended after seven years with both parties agreeing to a joint custody arrangement.

She says that her ex-husband was abusive and had significant alcohol problems, and she recounts several incidents in which she had to involve the police because of threats he made. There were some difficult periods toward the end of their marriage, and he pleaded guilty to at least one charge of spousal abuse and was also found guilty of several counts of unemployment fraud. He describes his ex-wife as irresponsible, leaving without arranging for child care and using credit cards inappropriately. Her own legal history has involved two guilty findings for writing bad checks and a conviction for driving while intoxicated.

She married for the third time shortly after the divorce was finalized and describes this marriage to a 43-year-old man in very positive terms. She is seeking full custody of her second son, arguing that her current living situation would be the better alternative for everyone in that it would create a blended two-parent family with her two sons and the two daughters (ages 10 and 12) of her current husband. She says that her ex-husband is less well equipped, both emotionally and financially, to care for their 8-year-old son.

Card	Response	Inquiry
I	1. Angels dancg	**E:** (Rpts Ss response)
		S: Thy r angels lik cupids, c there is wngs, heads, & littl round bodies
	E: Most ppl c mor thn 1 thng	**E:** Heads?
		S: Nose, eyes, wngs, littl baby bodies, arms, arms, & legs
	2. I c a cat's face, ko scary lik a Halloween cat	**E:** (Rpts Ss response)
		S: There is ears, eyes, nose, mouth, c feline shape of th head
	3. I c a moth	**E:** (Rpts Ss response)
		S: Here is littl . . . I dk moth anatomy but I guess littl moth antennae. These r th wngs & these r th markgs
	4. I c 2 ppl standg togthr w their arms raisd in greetg. Is tht enough? **(E:** Up to u)	**E:** (Rpts Ss response)
		S: Here r their heads, thy r wearg robes or dresses. C th line divides their legs. C these r th arms lik ths (demo)
II	5. Hmmm . . . ok, ths time I c 2 rabbits facg ech othr w, I guess . . . rabbits hav paws, hands up	**E:** (Rpts Ss response)
		S: Ths is rabbit. Ths is rabbit. Rabbits ears don't stick up, thy lay back. There r their ears so here r their ears, their heads, these r th paws frnt at top. These r the ones thy r standg on
	6. I c a man's face w lik lambchop sideburns & a beard. I thnk I'm done	**E:** (Rpts Ss response)
		S: There r eyes, nose, & here is th big sideburns growg into th beard in a way lik a Victorian man. Ths is bottom of nose & ths is his mouth
III	7. Its 2 um . . . um . . . I j c th 2 wm, thy r really prominant	**E:** (Rpts Ss response)
		S: Couldn't c anythng else. Obviously their heads, their profiles. These r breasts, arms, sway of back, bodies bent, knees, hi-heel shoes, hand & hand. She is th same, ko ll African American folk art, u kno th figures
		E: African American folk art?
		S: Th long narrow shape of th body, exaggerated curves w breasts too, th rounded head, close croppd hair & of course, thy r dark
IV	8. Th back of a racoon (laughs)	**E:** (Rpts Ss response)
		S: Look at aerially, c ll a racoon head w his whiskers. U can c white markgs th way it would come up I guess if this is top of head. Ths is bdy & ths is his tail
		E: Aerially?
		S: Bec if u look dwn at it, ths is top of head & ths almst ll a spine endg in a tail
	9. Cowboy boots	**E:** (Rpts Ss response)
		S: Big furry spurs, no not rite . . . chaps & here's pointd toe. Pointd heel ko kickg out.
		E: Furry?
		S: Its wide & uneven edges & mottled colors. I guess it ll fur to me. Tht's why I said racoon too
	10. Ko an aerial view of a cow	**E:** (Rpts Ss response)
		S: Reverse from racoon, ths ll cow skull tht u c in artifact shops or where u c landscape or scenery in movies of America deserts u c bleachd skull. Although ths doesn't ll a skull bec it has a lot of definition but it j remnds u. Thes r ears, eyes, & bovine side of head & there is eyelids. Th reason I say bovine & not equine is bec th snout is wide & not narrow
		E: Help me to c it lik u do
		S: Head caught my attitude. These would b legs & these. Ths remnds me of spine. I saw tht in beaver too & I'm seeing it again

(continued)

Card	Response	Inquiry
V	11 Ths is a bat	**E:** (Rpts Ss response) **S:** Here r 2 littl legs, here r long bat wngs & head. Ths is back of bat & bat ears. Those big narrow ears for radar.
VI	12. Here is a man's face w a long beard	**E:** (Rpts Ss response) **S:** Eyes u c'em, here is beard. C eyes ko ll shadowg in Shroud of Turin if u saw tht documentary. **E:** Shadowing? **S:** Its gray & black in middle. Black forms eyes, nose, & there's beard. I kno u c his face.
	13. Bearskin rug	**E:** (Rpts Ss response) **S:** Ths ll a bearskin rug j laid out on a wall **E:** Wht makes it ll tht? **S:** Th shape of it, head would hav been here & th fur **E:** Fur? **S:** Well, shadg again, diffrnt colors, uneven edges
	14. Indian totem	**E:** (Rpts Ss response) **S:** Rite here, c here's totem pole. Again, here is face. There is feathr & wooden arms outstretchd & here is feathrd cape or painted on or real dependg on wht u'r lookg at **E:** Feathers? **S:** Ths is feathrs, arms lik littl bird wngs. Can c lines tht define them
	15 Stingray	**E:** (Rpts Ss response) **S:** Ths is stingray, mouth, or whtevr thy hav. Shape of bdy is lik stingray w long narrow tail, wide. These cusps, I dk if thy'r called feelers or horns but I seem to rem thy hav these littl cusps
VII	16. Two littl girls w ponytails facg ech othr. Thts all I can c	**E:** (Rpts Ss response) **S:** U know profiles or old fashioned charm bracelets. Here is forehead, her bangs, hair, & here is ponytail almst lik jumpg, caught up in wind. Littl snub nose, chin, & body torso, hands, waist. There's their skirts
VIII	17. Ok, these r 2 A's, mayb wolves, st lik tht	**E:** (Rpts Ss response) **S:** Rite here c'em, here is head, paw, paw or leg, excuse me, leg, leg, leg, leg, & head ridges thts why I said wolf or st. It ll ridged fur **E:** Ridged fur? **S:** Do u c how it appears to stand up lik a dog or st
	18. Ko ll a print or a souvenir blanket	**E:** (Rpts Ss response) **S:** U know SW souvenir blankets. Its those type of colors associatd w SW design motif. Ths ko turquoise, coral, orange & blue gray & of course, bec I c wolves thts all I associate w tht. Uneven stripes or layers & I'm thinkg of fabric so I say stripes **E:** Layers? **S:** Rows of colors, I'm sorry.
	19. Oh there's a man here...face lik w th big headdress & a robe	**E:** (Rpts Ss response) **S:** SW Indian all ovr this. Here r his eyes, nose, how it comes dwn to become curve. There is lines, here is mouth, so there's his face & there r his shouldrs. Face is long & descends into his torso ko a Warlord. Here r shouldrs & this is his robe. It falls on shouldr, if u were to draw fabric th shadg u can c where it falls. Here's head, eyes & nose & ths becomes headdress, not hair, he is wearg st

Card	Response	Inquiry
	20. Here is a bf	**E:** (Rpts Ss response) **S:** Here is his sectioned wngs & here's his head, orange & coral area & legs, whatevr thy hav, & colors. Th colors r pretty
IX	21. Skull	**E:** (Rpts Ss response) **S:** Round top of skull, got a big forehead & comes dwn to I guess, this is forehead. Here is eye sockets, here & here **E:** U said eye sockets? **S:** Thy r holes & outside shadg makes 'em look 3D, ths line here
	22. Um, heart & lungs	**E:** (Rpts Ss response) **S:** This ll a heart, the chambers 1, 2, 3, 4. J remnds me of a picture of a heart & lungs in school. Ths is prob lungs. I saw ths as heart & lungs. I saw a heart, th chambers, these, & lungs
	23. Ko lik a big skull w fire comg out of it. Remnds me of my son's video games, my 14 yr old's computr video games	**E:** (Rpts Ss response) **S:** Dk name of it. Here's big skull again & here's fi comg out of it, th flames, th orange flames **E:** Skull? **S:** So, if these r eyes, I guess flames r comg out of his head not lik he is on fire here lik he is wearg 'em **E:** Eyes? **S:** Not on this skull, I guess flames r comg out of eyes lik big eyes. Ths is nose, nose holes, nostrils. Flames r lik shootg out of his eyes, not lik he is on fi, it is lik he is doing tht.
X	24. Ok, well I c a man's face w a handlebar mustache, sunglasses, red hair	**E:** (Rpts Ss response) **S:** Here's red hair, here is sunglasses meetg in th middl & go behnd into his hair. Here is his nose & handlbar mustache.
	25. I c bells	**E:** (Rpts Ss response) **S:** Rite here, c ths is a bell, c bell shape, here's handle, c them
	26. I c crabs (D7)	**E:** (Rpts Ss response) **S:** These r crabs. Thy'r th color of a sandcrab & thy r th shape, crab shape & have long legs comg outside exactly where long legs would come out of
	27. I c beavers. Ther is a cartoon show my childrn watch w angry beavers. Thy r here.	**E:** (Rpts Ss response) **S:** These r littl beavers, this is littl beaver head & there's fur tails, arms, angry beavers hav arms, thy r upright & fur legs **E:** U said angry beavers? **S:** No, hey thy don't look angry at all, j bec th show is abt 2 beavers who walk upright, thy r not angry.

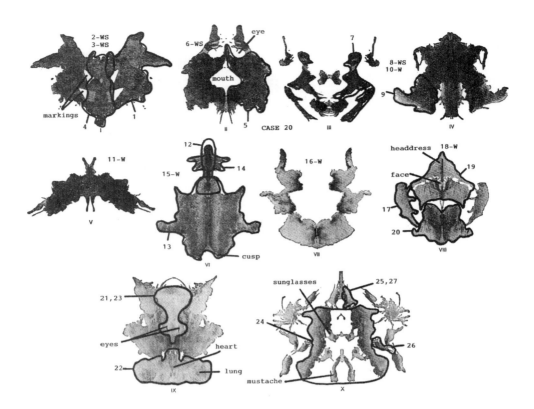

Case 20. Sequence of Scores.

Card	No.	Loc.	No.	Determinant(s)	(2)	Content(s)	Pop	Z	Special Scores
I	1	Dd+	99	Mao	2	(H)		6.0	COP,GHR
	2	WSo	1	Fo		(Ad)		3.5	
	3	WSo	1	Fo		A		3.5	
	4	D+	4	Mao	2	H,Cg		4.0	COP,GHR
II	5	D+	1	FMpo	2	A		3.0	INC
	6	WSo	1	F–		Hd		4.5	PHR
III	7	D+	9	FC'+	2	H,Cg,Art	P	3.0	GHR
IV	8	Wo	1	FD.FC'o		A		2.0	
	9	Do	6	FTo		Cg			
	10	Wo	1	FD–		A		2.0	
V	11	Wo	1	Fo		A	P	1.0	
VI	12	Ddo	99	FY–		Hd			PER,PHR
	13	Do	1	FTo		Ad,Hh	P		
	14	Do	8	FYo		Ay			
	15	Wo	1	Fu		A		2.5	
VII	16	W+	1	Ma.mpo	2	H,Cg	P	2.5	GHR
VIII	17	Do	1	Fo	2	A	P		
	18	Wo	1	CFo	2	Art,A	P	4.5	
	19	DS+	8	mp.FY–		Hd,Ay,Cg		4.0	PHR
	20	Do	2	FCo	2	A			
IX	21	DSo	8	FV–		An		5.0	
	22	Do	6	F–		An			PER
	23	DS+	8	ma.CF–		(Hd),Fi		5.0	PER,PHR
X	24	DdS+	99	FC–		Hd,Sc		6.0	PHR
	25	Do	8	F–	2	Id			
	26	Do	7	FCo	2	A			
	27	Do	8	Mpu	2	(A)			PER,GHR

Case 20. Structural Summary.

Location Features	Determinants Blends	Single	Contents	S-Constellation
				YES . .FV+VF+V+FD>2
		H = 3		NO . . .Col-Shd Bl>0
Zf = 17	FD.FC′	M = 3	(H) = 1	NO . . .Ego<.31,>.44
ZSum = 62.0	M.m	FM = 1	Hd = 4	NO . . .MOR > 3
ZEst = 56.0	m.FY	m = 0	(Hd) = 1	YES..Zd > +− 3.5
	m.CF	FC = 3	Hx = 0	YES . .es > EA
W = 9		CF = 1	A = 10	NO . . .CF+C > FC
D = 15		C = 0	(A) = 1	YES . .X+% < .70
W+D = 24		Cn = 0	Ad = 1	YES . .S > 3
Dd = 3		FC′ = 1	(Ad) = 1	NO . . .P < 3 or > 8
S = 7		C′F = 0	An = 2	NO . . .Pure H < 2
		C′ = 0	Art = 2	NO . . .R < 17
		FT = 2	Ay = 2	5 . . . .TOTAL

DQ

		Single	Contents	Special Scores
+ = 8		T = 0	Bt = 0		Lv1	Lv2
o = 19		FV = 1	Cg = 5	DV = 0x1 0x2
v/+ = 0		VF = 0	Cl = 0	INC = 1x2 0x4
v = 0		V = 0	Ex = 0	DR = 0x3 0x6
		FY = 2	Fd = 0	FAB = 0x4 0x7
		YF = 0	Fi = 1	ALOG = 0x5
		Y = 0	Ge = 0	CON = 0x7
		Fr = 0	Hh = 1	Raw Sum6 = 1

Form Quality

	FQx	MQual	W+D
+	= 1	= 0	= 1
o	= 15	= 3	= 14
u	= 2	= 1	= 2
−	= 9	= 0	= 7
none	= 0	= 0	= 0

Single	Contents
rF = 0	Ls = 0
FD = 1	Na = 0
F = 8	Sc = 1
	Sx = 0
	Xy = 0
	Id = 1
(2) = 11	

Wgtd Sum6 = 2

AB = 0		GHR = 5
AG = 0		PHR = 5
COP = 2		MOR = 0
CP = 0		PER = 4
		PSV = 0

Ratios, Percentages, and Derivations

R = 27	L = 0.42		FC:CF+C = 3:2	COP = 2 AG = 0
			Pure C = 0	GHR:PHR = 5:5
EB = 4:3.5	EA = 7.5	EBPer = N/A	SumC′:WSumC = 2:3.5	a:p = 4:4
eb = 4:8	es = 12	D = −1	Afr = 0.69	Food = 0
	Adj es = 8	Adj D = 0	S = 7	SumT = 2
			Blends:R = 4:27	Hum Con = 9
FM = 1	C′ = 2	T = 2	CP = 0	Pure H = 3
m = 3	V = 1	Y = 3		PER = 4
				Iso Indx = 0.00

a:p = 4:4	Sum6 = 1	XA% = 0.67	Zf = 17.0	3r+(2)/R = 0.41
Ma:Mp = 3:1	Lv2 = 0	WDA% = 0.71	W:D:Dd = 9:15:3	Fr+rF = 0
2AB+Art+Ay = 4	WSum6 = 2	X−% = 0.33	W:M = 9:4	SumV = 1
MOR = 0	M− = 0	S− = 5	Zd = +6.0	FD = 2
	Mnone = 0	P = 6	PSV = 0	An+Xy = 2
		X+% = 0.59	DQ+ = 8	MOR = 0
		Xu% = 0.07	DQv = 0	H:(H)Hd(Hd) = 3:6

PTI = 2	DEPI = 4	CDI = 1	S-CON = 5	HVI = No	OBS = No

Case 20

MMPI-2 Validity and Clinical Scales Profile

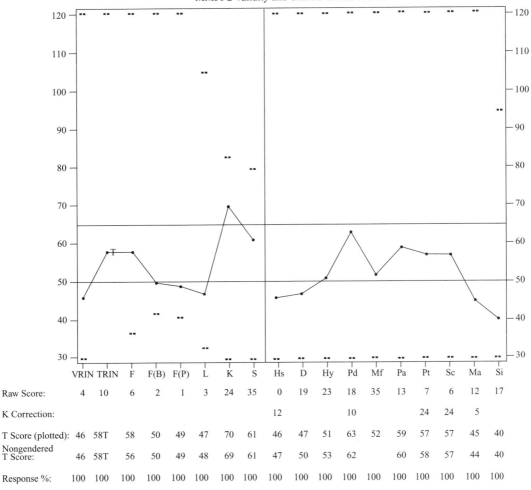

	VRIN	TRIN	F	F(B)	F(P)	L	K	S	Hs	D	Hy	Pd	Mf	Pa	Pt	Sc	Ma	Si
Raw Score:	4	10	6	2	1	3	24	35	0	19	23	18	35	13	7	6	12	17
K Correction:									12			10			24	24	5	
T Score (plotted):	46	58T	58	50	49	47	70	61	46	47	51	63	52	59	57	57	45	40
Nongendered T Score:	46	58T	56	50	49	48	69	61	47	50	53	62		60	58	57	44	40
Response %:	100	100	100	100	100	100	100	100	100	100	100	100	100	100	100	100	100	100

Cannot Say (Raw): 0

F-K (Raw): -18

Welsh Code: 4-678 53/2190: K'+-F/L:

Percent True: 32

Percent False: 68

Profile Elevation: 53.1

Note: The highest and lowest T scores possible on each scale are indicated by a "--".

450

Case 20

MMPI-2 Content Scales Profile

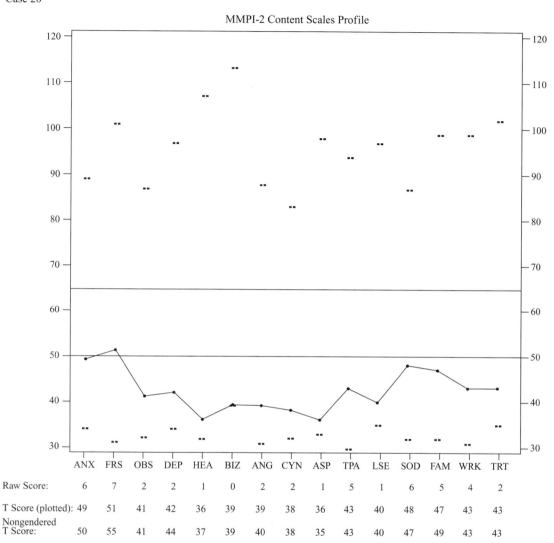

	ANX	FRS	OBS	DEP	HEA	BIZ	ANG	CYN	ASP	TPA	LSE	SOD	FAM	WRK	TRT
Raw Score:	6	7	2	2	1	0	2	2	1	5	1	6	5	4	2
T Score (plotted):	49	51	41	42	36	39	39	38	36	43	40	48	47	43	43
Nongendered T Score:	50	55	41	44	37	39	40	38	35	43	40	47	49	43	43
Response %:	100	100	100	100	100	100	100	100	100	100	100	100	100	100	100

Note: The highest and lowest Uniform T scores possible on each scale are indicated by a "--".

Case 20

MMPI-2 Supplementary Scales Profile

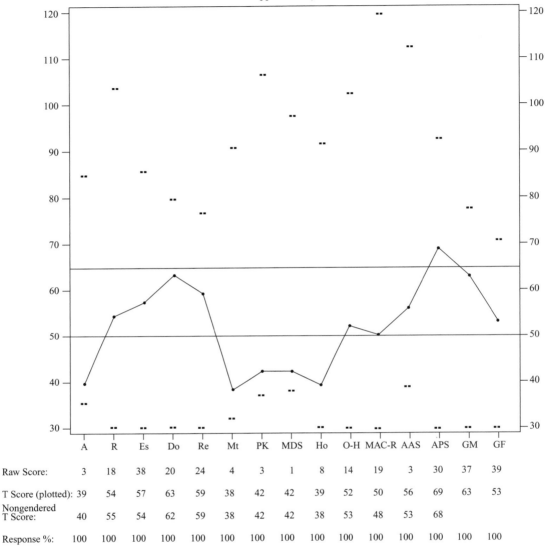

	A	R	Es	Do	Re	Mt	PK	MDS	Ho	O-H	MAC-R	AAS	APS	GM	GF
Raw Score:	3	18	38	20	24	4	3	1	8	14	19	3	30	37	39
T Score (plotted):	39	54	57	63	59	38	42	42	39	52	50	56	69	63	53
Nongendered T Score:	40	55	54	62	59	38	42	42	38	53	48	53	68		
Response %:	100	100	100	100	100	100	100	100	100	100	100	100	100	100	100

Note: The highest and lowest T scores possible on each scale are indicated by a "--".

CASE 20: OVERVIEW

Data from both the Rorschach and the MMPI-2 suggest that this woman's approach to presenting herself in a positive light is a sophisticated one. Her Rorschach Intellectualization Index is four and she has four PER, two COP, and no *AG,* suggesting an attempt to depict herself as a mature, knowledgeable, and collaborative person. Her findings on MMPI scales *L, K,* and *S* are somewhat different than the mean scores reported by Bagby et al. (1999) in a sample of 58 women tested during custody evaluations. She is lower on *L* and higher on *K,* suggesting a less naive and possibly more ego-syntonic presentation of herself as well adjusted.

For this woman, it is her Rorschach that is most clearly suggestive of some potential difficulties. She has seven space responses, of which four occur after Card II and five involve minus form quality. It is likely that anger and a sense of alienation can become disorienting for her, even though she works hard to minimize these issues. In the Inquiry for response 27 (Card X), when asked about cartoon beavers she had described as "angry," she modified her answer to say "No, they don't look angry at all, just because the show is about two beavers that walk upright, they are not angry." Her very low score (*T* = 39) on the MMPI Anger (*ANG*) content scale is consistent with this sort of denial. Her feelings of angry alienation may conflict with the interpersonal neediness reflected by the elevation of Texture on her Rorschach and of *Hy2* (Need for Affection) on her MMPI. It is likely that she could become upset in situations in which she did not feel well supported interpersonally, a potential liability for someone about to undertake the parenting of four children moving into their teens.

EPILOGUE

A settlement was reached by which the ex-husband retained joint custody rights but agreed that the son should live with his mother. A trial schedule of visitation privileges for 24 weekends per year plus two full weeks during the summer was agreed on with the stipulation that this arrangement be reevaluated after 18 months.

CASE 21: A WORK-RELATED QUESTION

This 32-year-old divorced woman is being evaluated in conjunction with a licensing board action. She is a registered nurse who has been working full time in the intensive care unit of a metropolitan hospital. Although there are no reports of problems in her work with patients, a series of interpersonal difficulties has brought her to the attention of the licensing board.

She has given birth to four children, the first at age 17, born out of wedlock, and three when she was 26, 28, and 30 during her recently ended marriage. At age 26, following the birth of her second child, she experienced a serious postpartum depression and was briefly hospitalized. A combination of weekly outpatient psychotherapy sessions and medication was helpful in resolving the depression. During this period, however, she developed a strong attraction toward the psychiatrist who was treating her and began driving by his home frequently. She carried a knife to his office during their last several sessions and ultimately wrote him a threatening note, for which she was arrested on charges of harassment and convicted for "terrorizing" behavior. She has been on probation for the past five years with the condition that her conviction will be reduced from a felony to a misdemeanor if no further difficulties occur.

She reports that her depression did not interfere with her care of patients or her other professional obligations. After her conviction, she continued in treatment with a different psychiatrist for an additional six months. Sometime during that period, her psychiatric difficulties were reported to the state licensing board (she suspects that her former psychiatrist did this), and her licensure status was categorized as "special" for the length of her probation.

Approximately one year ago, she became emotionally involved with a coworker, but after several months, the relationship deteriorated to frequent arguments and finally to an incident in which she struck him at work. He reported this to her supervisor, who was aware of her psychiatric history and her special license status. The supervisor was concerned about the possibility of a relapse and suspended her while meeting with representatives of the hospital personnel department and the licensing board. The supervisor also reported that she has had difficulties with this woman, whom she finds intrusive and harassing. Consequently, the nursing board requested an evaluation to determine whether her license should be revoked, suspended, or continued in its current status.

This woman is the fifth of five children, four girls and one boy. She reports that her father was very strict with all the children and used physical punishment, most extensively with her and the sister closest to her in age. She says that her mother never intervened and was typically quite passive. Her brother is age 43 and operates a small farm. One sister has a congenital heart disease and has remained single. A second sister is married and has two children. Her oldest sister is divorced and works as a secretary. There is no significant psychiatric history in the immediate family, although a paternal aunt was hospitalized several years ago, probably with schizophrenia.

She graduated from high school at age 18 with grades that were well above average, even though she became pregnant at age 16. At that time, her family sent her to a boarding home for pregnant women. She placed the baby, born when she was 17, for adoption. She says that she was depressed for about four months after that delivery and for a brief period contemplated suicide. She hopes to meet that child at some time in the future.

Following graduation from high school, she entered a nursing program and completed her training at age 21. She has been employed full time continuously, and her work history is reported to be excellent. At age 24, she married a man who was two years older, but soon found that he did not show much affection and did not help with responsibilities in the home. He worked in sales and traveled much of the time. She began to feel that she did not love him but persisted in the marriage until shortly after the birth of her youngest child. She describes her ex-husband as a "nice person," who shares responsibility in raising the children and in other financial matters. She is currently dating a 37-year-old bachelor she met approximately two months ago.

She says that she loves her work as an ICU nurse: "I'm very good at it. I like to think that I do things well and I get along well with other nurses. Sometimes my expectations of myself and others get me into trouble because they are too high." She says that she has several close friends, mainly coworkers. She continues to feel ambivalent about her parents but visits them frequently.

Although she was irritated by the necessity for this evaluation, she was cooperative and forthcoming in describing her history, feelings, values, attitudes, and experiences. She says she has difficulty trusting people and may be overly suspicious of those who have authority over her. She describes herself as having little tolerance for ambiguity in relationships, especially with supervisors, and she admits that she has high expectations of people in general, particularly those with whom she works.

Case 21. A 32-Year-Old Female.

Card	Response	Inquiry
I	1. I'd prob say a bug	**E:** (Rpts Ss response) **S:** In the middl (D4), it's not a real bug more lik an x-ray of one **E:** An x-ray? **S:** It has the shape of one w the littl feelrs at the top but is all dark lik an x-ray wb
	Tak ur tim & look som mor, I thk u'll find smthg else too	
	2. Smthg else? Well I suppos it cb a bird but it ll more lik a bug	**E:** (Rpts Ss response) **S:** I supp u cld say thes r wgs & the cntr wb the body, lik a bird
II	3. Thts 2 animals puttg thr paws against eo	**E:** (Rpts Ss response) **S:** It's all of it, there's one on each side, the feet dwn hre (D3), paws hre (D4) & their heads up here (D2), big animals **E:** U said puttg their paws against eo? **S:** Lik tryg to push eo over, fitg lik, mayb 2 bears fiting
	4. Thy really ll more lik 2 weird A's, lik the body of a bear & the head of a duck	**E:** (Rpts Ss response) **S:** Well, I said bears first, but thy really ll 2 weird A's, the shape of ths part (D1) ll the body of a bear but up here it ll the heads of ducks
III	5. (lafs) Obviously thts 2 ppl, 2 females w thr breasts hangg out, thr hands r on a bucket	**E:** (Rpts Ss response) **S:** See thr chest, heels or shoes hre, thy hav slendr builds, j th shape of a woman, lik thy r doing smthg, mayb pickg up ths bucket dwn here, yeah it's prob a bucket & thyr pickg it up
IV	6. Lik u'r lkg up at th backside of smthg, I thk ur stndg on the ground lkg at th backside of a creature, hres the bottm of his feet, smthg ud c aftr a bad weekend (lafs)	**E:** (Rpts Ss response) **S:** All of it, lik standg on th grnd lkg up at a creature, the spine is hre, th color chnges as it goes up, here's his tail, th changes in color ll ll its furry, he's got littl arms & ths is the bk of his head, it's a weird thg
V	7. Thts a bf	**E:** (Rpts Ss response) **S:** Wings hre, antenae, th thgs hre in th back r feet, it just ll a bf
VI	8. Ur lkg dwn, hres a cat kinda spread out	**E:** (Rpts Ss response) **S:** The cats head up here (D3), whiskers hre & the legs spread out lik it's just layg there in a strang position w its legs out, the colors on its back give a furry impression
	9. Also ths cntr prt ll a spine	**E:** (Rpts Ss response) **S:** Rite dwn the middl, the darkr part ll a spine to me, lik an x-ray of it **E:** X-ray? **S:** It's dark lik an x-ray, the dark colors chang
VII	10. Ths ll 2 girls w ponytails makg kissy faces	**E:** (Rpts Ss response) **S:** Girls w pony tails, thy ll thyr turning thr backs, lik lookg arnd, makg kissy faces, c their lip r stuck out **E:** I'm not sur I'm seeg thm rite, u say theyr turning their backs? **S:** No I didn't say tht, I said turning their heads, their backs r to eo & thyv turnd their heads arnd makg faces lik sayg goodbye
	v11. Ths white prt ll lampshade	**E:** (Rpts Ss response) **S:** Here in the middl, it has the shape of one

(continued)

455

Card Response	Inquiry
VIII <12. Tht one is kinda neat thts a . . . som type of animal walkg ovr rocks, its reflected	**E:** (Rpts Ss response) **S:** A reflection in water, th shape of th A, th color of th rocks, th reflection is suggested by th flip flop of th picture **E:** I'm not sur I c all of it rite **S:** Ths is the A (D1), c the head & legs, & ths stuff is the rocks (half of D4 & D2), c thy r diff colors & the blue is the water & its all the same dwn here, lik a reflection
13. Ths littl prt ll a rib cage	**E:** (Rpts Ss response) **S:** It has tht shape, c the spaces between the ribs
IX <14. I c sb on a motorcycl going up a hill, its being reflectd in the water here	**E:** (Rpts Ss response) **S:** Th pink is lik exhaust coming out, here's the person & the cycle (D1), u can mak out the shape of wheels, th orange dirt hill, & it's all reflectd dwn here, it has tht shape to it & its pretty colorful **E:** U said reflectd in the water? **S:** Yep, ths line (centerlin) wb the water
X 15. Ths is a bunch of bugs, all diff colors	**E:** (Rpts Ss response) **S:** Two black bugs at the top, two green grashopers dwn here, some spiders here (D1), here r yellow bugs (D2) & pink worms (D9) & som othr green bugs up here (D12) just a lot of colrful bugs
v16. Also I c a face whn u lk at it upside down	**E:** (Rpts Ss response) **S:** The eyebrows hre r archd, he has a mean look the way thyr shaped, here r the eyes (D2), the eyebrows (D10) mouth (D3) & a beard (D11), he's lookg very mean the way so lifts their eyebrows when thyr angry, don't count this stuff out here on the sides, just here (outlines DdS22)

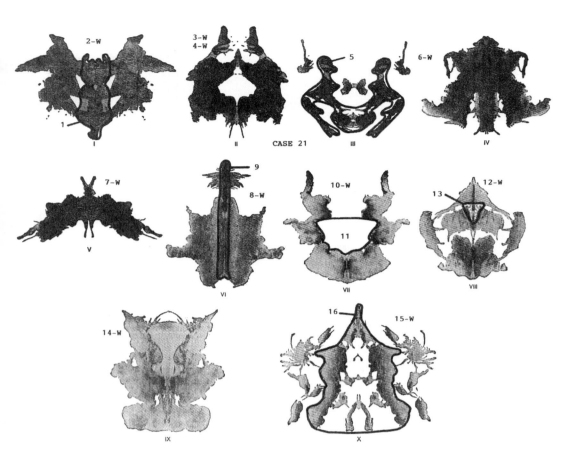

CASE 21

Case 21. Sequence of Scores.

Card	No.	Loc.	No.	Determinant(s)	(2)	Content(s)	Pop	Z	Special Scores
I	1	Do	4	FYo		A,Xy			
	2	Wo	1	Fo		A		1.0	
II	3	W+	1	FMao	2	A		4.5	AG,PHR
	4	Wo	1	Fu	2	A		4.5	INC2
III	5	D+	1	Mao	2	H,Cg,Hh	P	3.0	COP,GHR
IV	6	Wo	1	FD.FTo		(A)		2.0	
V	7	Wo	1	Fo		A	P	1.0	
VI	8	Wo	1	FD.FMp.FTu		A		2.5	
	9	Do	5	FYo		Xy			
VII	10	W+	1	Mpo	2	H	P	2.5	GHR
	11	DSo	10	Fo		Hh			
VIII	12	W+	1	FMa.CF.Fro		A,Na	P	4.5	
	13	DSo	3	Fo		An			
IX	14	W+	1	Ma.Fr.CF.mao		H,Na,Sc		5.5	GHR
X	15	Wo	1	CF.C'Fo	2	A	P	5.5	
	16	DdSo	22	Mp–		Hd,Hx			AG,PHR

Case 21. Structural Summary.

Location Features	Determinants Blends	Single	Contents	S-Constellation
				NO . . .FV+VF+V+FD>2
		H = 3		YES . .Col-Shd Bl>0
Zf = 11	FD.FT	M = 3	(H) = 0	YES . .Ego<.31,>.44
ZSum = 36.5	FD.FM.FT	FM = 1	Hd = 1	NO . . .MOR > 3
ZEst = 34.5	FM.CF.Fr	m = 0	(Hd) = 0	NO . . .Zd > +− 3.5
	M.Fr.CF.m	FC = 0	Hx = 1	YES . .es > EA
W = 10	CF.C'F	CF = 0	A = 8	YES . .CF+C > FC
D = 5		C = 0	(A) = 1	NO . . .X+% < .70
W+D = 15		Cn = 0	Ad = 0	NO . . .S > 3
Dd = 1		FC' = 0	(Ad) = 0	NO . . .P < 3 or > 8
S = 3		C'F = 0	An = 1	NO . . .Pure H < 2
		C' = 0	Art = 0	YES . .R < 17
		FT = 0	Ay = 0	5 . . . .TOTAL

DQ

		Single	Contents	Special Scores
		TF = 0	Bl = 0		Lv1	Lv2
+ = 5		T = 0	Bt = 0	DV = 0x1	0x2
o = 11		FV = 0	Cg = 1	INC = 0x2	1x4
v/+ = 0		VF = 0	Cl = 0	DR = 0x3	0x6
v = 0		V = 0	Ex = 0	FAB = 0x4	0x7
		FY = 2	Fd = 0	ALOG = 0x5	
		YF = 0	Fi = 0	CON = 0x7	
		Y = 0	Ge = 0	Raw Sum6 = 1	

Form Quality

	FQx	MQual	W+D	Single	Contents	Special Scores
				Fr = 0	Hh = 2	Wgtd Sum6 = 4
+	= 0	= 0	= 0	rF = 0	Ls = 0	
o	= 13	= 3	= 13	FD = 0	Na = 2	AB = 0	GHR = 3
u	= 2	= 0	= 2	F = 5	Sc = 1	AG = 2	PHR = 2
−	= 1	= 1	= 0		Sx = 0	COP = 1	MOR = 0
none	= 0	= 0	= 0		Xy = 2	CP = 0	PER = 0
				(2) = 5	Id = 0		PSV = 0

Ratios, Percentages, and Derivations

R = 16	L = 0.45		FC:CF+C = 0:3	COP = 1 AG = 2
			Pure C = 0	GHR:PHR = 3:2
EB = 4:3.0	EA = 7.0	EBPer = N/A	SumC':WSumC = 1:3.0	a:p = 5:3
eb = 4:5	es = 9	D = 0	Afr = 0.45	Food = 0
	Adj es = 8	Adj D = 0	S = 3	SumT = 2
			Blends:R = 5:16	Hum Con = 4
FM = 3	C' = 1	T = 2	CP = 0	Pure H = 3
m = 1	V = 0	Y = 2		PER = 0
				Iso Indx = 0.25

a:p = 5:3	Sum6 = 1	XA% = 0.94	Zf = 11.0	3r+(2)/R = 0.69
Ma:Mp = 2:2	Lv2 = 1	WDA% = 1.00	W:D:Dd = 10:5:1	Fr+rF = 2
2AB+Art+Ay = 0	WSum6 = 4	X−% = 0.06	W:M = 10:4	SumV = 0
MOR = 0	M− = 1	S− = 1	Zd = +2.0	FD = 2
	Mnone = 0	P = 5	PSV = 0	An+Xy = 3
		X+% = 0.81	DQ+ = 5	MOR = 0
		Xu% = 0.13	DQv = 0	H:(H)Hd(Hd) = 3:1

| PTI = 0 | DEPI = 4 | CDI = 2 | S-CON = 5 | HVI = No | OBS = No |

Case 21

MMPI-2 Validity and Clinical Scales Profile

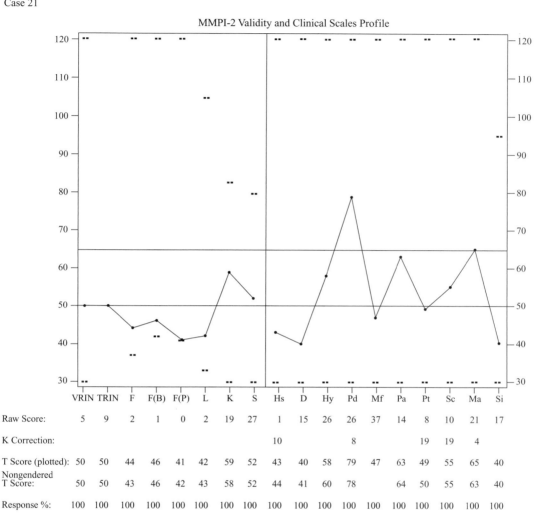

	VRIN	TRIN	F	F(B)	F(P)	L	K	S	Hs	D	Hy	Pd	Mf	Pa	Pt	Sc	Ma	Si
Raw Score:	5	9	2	1	0	2	19	27	1	15	26	26	37	14	8	10	21	17
K Correction:									10		8			19	19	4		
T Score (plotted):	50	50	44	46	41	42	59	52	43	40	58	79	47	63	49	55	65	40
Nongendered T Score:	50	50	43	46	42	43	58	52	44	41	60	78		64	50	55	63	40
Response %:	100	100	100	100	100	100	100	100	100	100	100	100	100	100	100	100	100	100

Cannot Say (Raw):   0

F-K (Raw):   -17

Welsh Code: 4'9+6-38/75120: K/FL:

Percent True: 35

Percent False: 65

Profile Elevation: 56.5

Note: The highest and lowest T scores possible on each scale are indicated by a "--".

459

Case 21

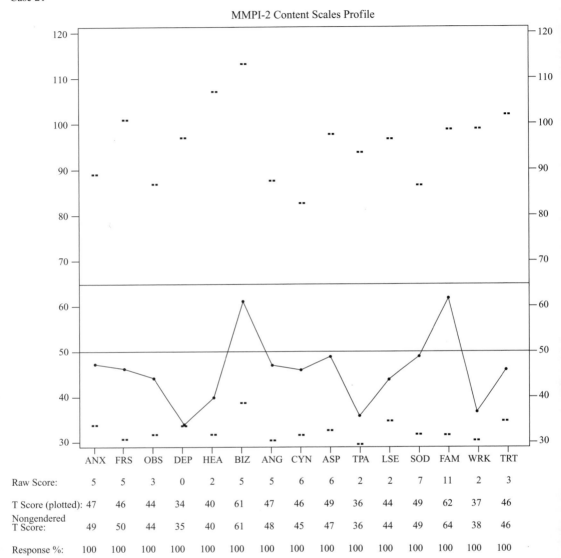

MMPI-2 Content Scales Profile

	ANX	FRS	OBS	DEP	HEA	BIZ	ANG	CYN	ASP	TPA	LSE	SOD	FAM	WRK	TRT
Raw Score:	5	5	3	0	2	5	5	6	6	2	2	7	11	2	3
T Score (plotted):	47	46	44	34	40	61	47	46	49	36	44	49	62	37	46
Nongendered T Score:	49	50	44	35	40	61	48	45	47	36	44	49	64	38	46
Response %:	100	100	100	100	100	100	100	100	100	100	100	100	100	100	100

Note: The highest and lowest Uniform T scores possible on each scale are indicated by a "--".

Case 21

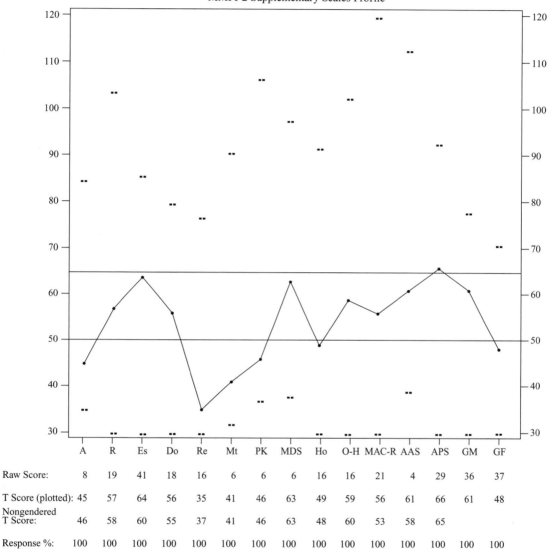

MMPI-2 Supplementary Scales Profile

	A	R	Es	Do	Re	Mt	PK	MDS	Ho	O-H	MAC-R	AAS	APS	GM	GF
Raw Score:	8	19	41	18	16	6	6	6	16	16	21	4	29	36	37
T Score (plotted):	45	57	64	56	35	41	46	63	49	59	56	61	66	61	48
Nongendered T Score:	46	58	60	55	37	41	46	63	48	60	53	58	65		
Response %:	100	100	100	100	100	100	100	100	100	100	100	100	100	100	100

Note: The highest and lowest T scores possible on each scale are indicated by a "--".

CASE 21: OVERVIEW

For this woman, it is her MMPI profile that most clearly suggests a defensive need to minimize difficulties (*F-K* Index = −17). Nonetheless, her *T*-score of 79 on *Pd* suggests that conflicts with authority are an ongoing problem for her. Some Rorschach data that may relate to that postulate are noted by the three Space responses, none of which occurred for the first two cards, plus the presence of two *AG* answers as contrasted with one COP response. Although she tries to stay away from affectively provocative situations (*Afr* = .45), her *FC:CF+C* ratio of 0:3 suggests that her emotional displays may be poorly modulated when she feels angry or oppositional, especially when her personal integrity is challenged, as two of her three *CF* responses also include reflections. Their presence connotes that she is self-centered and this increases the likelihood that she will externalize responsibility for any seemingly out-of-control incidents, just as she tended to minimize problems on the MMPI.

However, the majority of findings from both the Rorschach and MMPI-2 are more positive than negative. Her defensive approach to the MMPI-2, with the exception of the high *T*-score on *Pd*, produced *T*-scores on most scales that tend to imply reasonably good adjustment or, at least, the absence of significant problems. Likewise, the Rorschach findings suggest no noticeable problems in control, adequate processing habits, reasonable concerns for reality when translating inputs, clarity of thinking much of the time, and adequate or appropriate social perceptions and behaviors. Her main problems seem to stem from her self-centeredness, difficulties with authority, a probable sense of alienation, and a likely failure to handle her emotions effectively in stressful situations.

In light of the test findings and her history, it seems reasonable to suggest that she re-enter psychotherapy with the specific objective of focusing on anger management and social sensitivity. This form of intervention, if even for a brief interval, is likely to reduce the possibilities for a recurrence of incidents such as the one that occurred with her coworker.

EPILOGUE

Her temporary suspension was revoked and she was returned to a special licensing status with the stipulation that it be continued for the remainder of her probationary period (32 months). She accepted a recommendation to reenter an intervention program with focus on anger management. No further incidents were reported during the next nine months.

REFERENCES

Bagby, R. M., Nicholson, R. R., Buis, T., Radovanovic, H., & Fidler, B. (1999). Defensive responding on the MMPI-2 in family custody and access evaluations. *Psychological Assessment, 11*(1), 24–28.

Bagby, R. M., Rogers, R., Nicholson, R., Buis, T., Seeman, M., & Rector, N. (1997). Effectiveness of the MMPI-2 validity indicators in the detection of defensive responding in clinical and nonclinical samples. *Psychological Assessment, 9*(4), 406–413.

Butcher, J. N., & Han, K. (1995). Development of an MMPI-2 scale to assess the presentation of self in a superlative manner: The S scale. In J. N. Butcher & C. D. Spielberger (Eds.), *Advances in personality assessment* (Vol. 10, pp. 25–50). Hillsdale, NJ: Erlbaum.

Carp, A. L., & Shavzin, A. R. (1950). The susceptibility to falsification of the Rorschach psychodiagnostic technique. *Journal of Consulting Psychology, 14,* 230–233.

Exner, J. E. (1991). *The Rorschach: A Comprehensive System: Vol. 2. Interpretation* (2nd ed.). New York: Wiley.

Fosberg, I. A. (1938). Rorschach reactions under varied instructions. *Rorschach Research Exchange, 3,* 12–30.

Fosberg, I. A. (1943). How do subjects attempt fake results on the Rorschach test? *Rorschach Research Exchange, 7,* 119–121.

Gough, H. G. (1950). The F minus K dissimulation index for the MMPI. *Journal of Consulting Psychology, 14,* 408–413.

Nichols, D. S., & Greene, R. L. (1988, March). *Adaptive or defensive: An evaluation of Paulhus' two-factor model of social desirability responding in the MMPI with non-college samples.* Paper presented at the 23rd Annual Symposium on Recent Developments in the Use of the MMPI. St. Petersburg, FL.

Paulhus, D. L. (1984). Two-component models of socially desirable responding. *Journal of Personality and Social Psychology, 46,* 598–609.

Phares, E. J., Stewart, L. M., & Foster, J. M. (1960). Instruction variation and Rorschach performance. *Journal of Projective Techniques, 24,* 28–31.

Seamons, D. T., Howell, R. J., Carlisle, A. L., & Roe, A. V. (1981). Rorschach simulation of mental illness and normality by psychotic and non-psychotic legal offenders. *Journal of Personality Assessment, 45,* 130–135.

PART SIX

Some New
Nonpatient Data

CHAPTER 22

Progress in Building a New Nonpatient Sample

An appreciation of the response rates for the various features of answers and the relationship of those response rates to the structural features of the test usually enhance an understanding of the Rorschach. The codes assigned to responses form the base for developing this array of data. They identify the features of responses for which there is some empirical linkage to interpretation. In turn, the frequencies for the coded features create the platform for deriving the structural data that form the interpretive core of the test.

Ordinarily, normative (nonpatient) data that have been established for the test provide the source from which this information is gleaned. They provide descriptive information about groups and offer reference points against which individual scores can be compared. Possibly most important is the basis that they provide for developing some general interpretive postulates, using the *deviation principle,* that focuses on findings that are different than expected.

Almost any normative samples will have limitations, and those formed to create tables for use with the *Comprehensive System* are no exceptions. The nonpatient records used to create those samples were collected over approximately 13 years, from 1973 to 1986. The first published nonpatient sample consisted of only 200 protocols that had been collected mainly from the greater New York City metropolitan area (Exner, 1974). Between 1976 and 1986, the number of available records accumulated to slightly more than 1,100. During that period, the tables were revised twice as attempts to stratify the samples ensued to make them more representative (Exner, 1985; Exner, Weiner, & Schuyler, 1976). Stratification criteria included age, sex, geographic area, and socioeconomic level. The 1985 sample was increased in size to include 600 protocols with equal numbers of males and females and stratified for six age ranges, five geographic areas, and three broad socioeconomic levels.

Although the 1985 sample appeared to be satisfactory, a third major revision was required in 1990 because of findings indicating that brief records (those containing less than 14 answers) are likely to be invalid (Exner, 1988). A search of the total pool of nonpatient protocols revealed that more than 200 records contained fewer than 14 answers, including 74 of the 600 protocols that made up the 1985 published sample. All those records were discarded and a revised sample of 700 was selected using the stratification criteria of sex, geographic area, and socioeconomic level (Exner, 1990).

When the sample of 700 was selected using the stratification criteria, more than 200 duplicate records were inadvertently included. They were discovered in 1999 and removed from the sample. It was impossible to replace all the duplicates without significantly altering some of the demographic features that had been used in the stratification. Thus, the revision reduced the sample size to include the protocols of 600 adult nonpatients (Exner, 2001). This fourth revision represents 300 males and 300 females, and includes 120 subjects from each of five geographic areas, Northeast, South, Midwest, Southwest, and West. The sample is partially stratified for socioeconomic level. Attempts were made to equalize the number of males and females from each region but that was not always possible. Thus, the number of males and females are nearly equal for four regions, but the Southwest group includes 72 females and 48 males, whereas the Midwest group contains 74 males and 46 females.

THE GENERAL DESIGN FOR COLLECTING NONPATIENT DATA

The 600 protocols represented by the 2001 nonpatient sample were collected by 42 examiners working within the constraints of problems created by subject recruitment and sample sizes. No examiner contributed more than 25 protocols to this sample. All the subjects are, in one sense or another, volunteers. None had special reasons to be examined, and none have any significant psychiatric history. About 17% (101) of the subjects gave histories that included having eight or fewer contacts (the maximum permitted for inclusion) in their past with psychologists or educational counselors. Sixty-nine did so for purposes of academic or vocational counseling. Nineteen had been involved in brief marital counseling, and 13 had received brief supportive treatment following the loss of a family member or friend.

Volunteers were recruited by letters, distributed at workplaces or through cooperating organizations. The letters discounted any possibility of feedback concerning results and identified the project as one involving the standardization of the test. The 600 subjects in the 2001 sample include 409 who volunteered through their places of work, usually under conditions of encouragement by supervisors or union leaders, and typically were provided with time away from work for the testing. An additional 153 persons volunteered through social or interest organizations to which they belonged, such as the PTA, Audubon groups, bowling leagues, and so on, and the remaining 38 were recruited through the assistance of social service agencies. None were financially reimbursed for their participation, although all received greeting cards of appreciation.

THE REPRESENTATIVENESS OF THE SAMPLE

Among the issues that confront those who use normative data as a guide for interpretation is the extent to which the data are truly representative of nonpatients, and whether the sample has been cross validated. Shaffer, Erdberg, and Haroian (1999) used graduate students to test 123 volunteer nonpatients. Many of their findings are similar to those in the published sample of 600 nonpatients. However, there are also some striking differences. The mean for R is 20.83, with a median of 18 and a mode of 14, as contrasted with a mean R of 22.32, with a median of 22 and a mode of 23 for the sample of 600. *Lambda* values greater than 0.99 occurred for 51 (41%) of the persons in the Shaffer et el. sample compared with 58 (10%) in the sample of 600. Some other substantial differences between the two samples include means of .48 versus .67 for the *Afr;* .78 versus .92 for the *XA%*, and .82 versus .94 for the *WDA%*.

The differences between the samples for the *XA%* and *WDA%* reflect differences for the other variables related to form use. The means are .51 versus .77 for the *X+%*; .28 versus .15 for the *Xu%*; and .21 versus .07 for the *X−%*. Only 44 (36%) of persons in the Shaffer et al. sample gave at least one texture answer, while 490 (82%) of those in the larger sample did so. Nearly 30% of the persons in the Shaffer et al. sample gave at least one reflection response as contrasted with only 8% in the sample of 600. In addition, the means for *WSumC, EA,* and *es* in the Shaffer et al. sample are about two points lower than those for the sample of 600. Interestingly, when the Shaffer et al. sample was increased to include 283 nonpatients (Shaffer & Erdberg, 2001), only modest changes in the values for these variables were noted.

The differences noted between the Shaffer et al. data and those in the 2001 *Comprehensive System* sample of 600, plus the fact that most of the protocols included in the 2001 sample were collected more than 20 years ago, prompted the Research Council of Rorschach Workshops[1] to recommend the collection of a new nonpatient sample to ascertain the utility of the sample published in 2001.

BUILDING THE NEW SAMPLE

The project to collect a new nonpatient sample was initiated during the fall of 1999, using essentially the same design and exclusionary criteria as for the 1973 to 1986 project. There are three differences in the current model. About 75% of the nonpatients tested between 1973 and 1981 were recruited by persons employed primarily to solicit subjects for various investigations. In the current project, examiners recruit their own subjects through organizations and businesses, using essentially the same procedures previously used by recruiters, including a slightly modified version of the original solicitation letter (Exner, 2002). A second difference concerns prescribed medications or illegal drug use. Questions concerning these issues were not asked of persons tested between 1973 and 1986. However, both seem more important at this time. *Anyone* volunteering to participate in the project is tested, but the records of those having a prolonged or significant history involving prescribed psychotropics ($N = 7$), or admitting to regular use of illegal drugs ($N = 4$), are excluded from the sample. A third difference concerns the financial structure. Persons tested in the original project were not paid. In the current project, volunteers also are not paid, but as an enticement, a $25 donation is paid, in the name of the subject, to any recognized charity that the person selects.

More than 10 years were required to develop the original pool of more than 1,100 nonpatient records from which the various samples were drawn. The current project is proceeding at about the same pace. During the approximately six years since the project was initiated, nearly 500 subjects, from 22 states,[2] have been tested by 29 experienced examiners, most having collected between 12

---

[1] Research Council membership at the time of the recommendation included Thomas Boll, Philip Erdberg, John Exner, Mark Hilsenroth, Gregory Meyer, William Perry, and Donald Viglione.

[2] States represented in the current sample include Alaska, Arizona, California, Connecticut, Delaware, Florida, Georgia, Iowa, Kentucky, Maryland, Massachusetts, Minnesota, Missouri, New Hampshire, New Jersey, New York, North Carolina, Tennessee, Texas, Virginia, Vermont, and West Virginia.

and 25 protocols each. Each examiner codes the records that he or she has collected, and the coding is reviewed for errors in the central office of Rorschach Workshops when it is computer entered. Data concerning errors are used to provide feedback to examiners when relevant.

In addition, approximately one sixth of the protocols have been recoded by the Director of Rorschach Workshops and percentages of correct agreement are recorded as a tactic to review scoring accuracy. Percentages of correct agreement, calculated for 70 records, yield findings ranging from 95% to 99% for *W, D, S, Dd, DQ+, DQo, M,* active and passive movement, *SumT, SumV,* pairs, reflections, *P, Zf* and the special scores INC, FAB, and COP. Correct agreement levels from 89% to 94% include *DQv/+, DQv,* Pure *F, FM, m, FC, FD,* the form quality codes for ordinary, unusual, and minus, and the special scores *AG, DV,* and MOR. Agreement levels between 83% and 88% are noted for *CF,* Pure *C, SumY, SumC',* the special scores AB and *DR,* and the form quality coding of plus.

CURRENT FINDINGS FROM THE NEW SAMPLE

Descriptive statistics for the codings and some calculated variables for the first 450 persons included in this project are shown in Table 22.1. Table 22.2 includes some demography information concerning the group, plus frequency data for cutoff points related to some general interpretive principles.

SOME COMPARISONS OF THE TWO SAMPLES

The data for most of the variables in Table 22.1 for the new sample of 450 nonpatients are similar to those published for the 2001 sample of 600 nonpatients. However, some differences between the two groups warrant consideration. There are 14 items identified by an *L* or *H* in Table 22.2 as having proportional frequencies that differ by more than 7% from those for the 2001 sample of 600. They are related to eight ratios, frequencies, and proportions that are reviewed routinely in the interpretive process (form quality, chromatic color use, developmental quality, white space, *Affective Ratio,* Populars, Cooperative Movement, active and passive human movement).

Table 22.3 includes data for 17 variables from the sample of 600 nonpatients and those for the 450 records from the current project. Most of these are related to the items identified in Table 22.2 for which proportional differences are greater than 7%. Some, plus *R* and *Lambda,* also relate to variables described earlier for which there were noticeably discrepant findings between the Shaffer et al. (1999) sample and the 2001 sample of 600 subjects.

The sizes of the samples yield very large *degrees of freedom* when *t* tests are used to study differences between the means, and resulting *p* values can be misleading or misinterpreted. Thus, it is more appropriate to evaluate the differences by using the values for Cohen's *d* and Pearson correlations to provide information about effect sizes (Cohen, 1992). These are also included in Table 22.3.

The first 10 items shown in Table 22.3 (*R, S, FC, CF, SumT, SumY, Ma, Mp, EA,* and *es*) are all frequency variables. The means for these variables for the two samples are reasonably similar for all 10. Cohen (1992) has provided some benchmarks for use in judging effect sizes when *d* scores

Table 22.1 Descriptive Statistics for 450 Nonpatient Adults.

Variable	Mean	SD	Min	Max	Freq	Median	Mode	SK	KU
AGE	34.90	13.42	19.00	86.00	450	31.00	27.00	1.20	1.24
Years Education	14.00	1.99	8.00	21.00	450	14.00	12.00	0.91	0.89
R	23.36	5.68	14.00	59.00	450	23.00	22.00	1.89	6.75
W	9.10	3.70	2.00	37.00	450	8.00	8.00	2.12	9.48
D	12.66	4.75	0.00	36.00	448	13.00	14.00	0.29	1.92
Dd	1.60	[2.06]	0.00	21.00	317	1.00	1.00	3.77	24.48
S	2.37	[1.97]	0.00	17.00	407	2.00	1.00	2.27	9.69
DQ+	8.43	3.07	1.00	21.00	450	8.00	9.00	0.64	1.47
DQo	14.29	4.66	4.00	40.00	450	14.00	14.00	1.30	4.26
DQv	0.37	[0.72]	0.00	4.00	119	0.00	0.00	2.34	6.36
DQv/+	0.27	[0.61]	0.00	6.00	97	0.00	0.00	3.46	19.76
FQx+	0.54	[0.93]	0.00	7.00	153	0.00	0.00	2.32	7.87
FQxo	15.09	3.22	6.00	29.00	450	15.00	16.00	0.02	0.87
FQxu	4.85	2.93	0.00	24.00	448	4.00	4.00	1.99	7.10
FQx-	2.73	2.01	0.00	18.00	425	2.00	2.00	2.21	9.86
FQxNone	0.15	[0.41]	0.00	3.00	57	0.00	0.00	3.09	10.65
MQ+	0.42	[0.72]	0.00	4.00	136	0.00	0.00	1.71	2.54
MQo	3.74	1.79	0.00	9.00	443	4.00	3.00	0.29	-0.35
MQu	0.44	0.81	0.00	5.00	139	0.00	0.00	2.65	9.45
MQ-	0.23	[0.57]	0.00	5.00	81	0.00	0.00	3.48	17.58
MQNone	0.01	[0.08]	0.00	1.00	3	0.00	0.00	12.16	146.64
SQual-	0.58	[0.89]	0.00	6.00	182	0.00	0.00	2.13	6.33
M	4.83	2.18	0.00	12.00	449	5.00	4.00	0.44	0.18
FM	4.04	1.90	0.00	10.00	441	4.00	4.00	0.33	0.36
m	1.57	1.34	0.00	10.00	361	1.00	1.00	1.57	5.33
FC	2.97	1.78	0.00	11.00	416	3.00	2.00	0.59	0.71
CF	2.80	1.64	0.00	12.00	426	3.00	2.00	0.99	3.42
C	0.17	[0.45]	0.00	3.00	64	0.00	0.00	3.02	10.37
Cn	0.00	[0.07]	0.00	1.00	2	0.00	0.00	14.95	222.48
Sum Color	5.95	2.47	0.00	14.00	448	6.00	5.00	0.38	0.16
WSumC	4.54	1.98	0.00	15.00	448	4.50	4.00	0.74	2.06
Sum C'	1.60	[1.33]	0.00	9.00	371	1.00	1.00	1.58	4.62
Sum T	1.01	[0.69]	0.00	4.00	364	1.00	1.00	0.76	1.86
Sum V	0.35	[0.77]	0.00	5.00	106	0.00	0.00	2.88	9.92
Sum Y	0.97	[1.20]	0.00	9.00	261	1.00	0.00	2.27	8.62
Sum Shading	3.94	2.45	0.00	21.00	445	3.00	3.00	2.24	8.97
Fr+rF	0.20	[0.67]	0.00	7.00	54	0.00	0.00	5.08	34.50
FD	1.43	[1.15]	0.00	8.00	360	1.00	1.00	1.21	3.10
F	7.91	3.70	0.00	32.00	449	7.00	7.00	1.56	6.00
(2)	8.82	3.08	2.00	30.00	450	9.00	8.00	1.54	7.18
3r+(2)/R	0.40	0.10	0.12	0.87	450	0.39	0.38	0.77	2.23
Lambda	0.58	0.37	0.00	2.33	449	0.47	0.50	1.56	2.82
FM+m	5.61	2.51	0.00	20.00	449	5.00	5.00	1.06	4.02
EA	9.37	3.00	2.00	24.00	450	9.50	8.00	0.51	1.64
es	9.55	4.01	2.00	34.00	450	9.00	8.00	1.91	8.12
D Score	-0.12	0.99	-7.00	3.00	142	0.00	0.00	-1.84	9.39
AdjD	0.19	0.83	-3.00	3.00	167	0.00	0.00	-0.19	3.07
a (active)	6.76	2.87	0.00	19.00	447	7.00	7.00	0.29	0.84
p (passive)	3.73	2.34	0.00	17.00	430	3.00	3.00	1.41	4.48
Ma	2.93	1.67	0.00	10.00	423	3.00	3.00	0.59	0.84
Mp	1.93	1.37	0.00	10.00	395	2.00	1.00	1.17	3.43
Intellect	2.17	2.15	0.00	15.00	360	2.00	1.00	1.78	4.82
Zf	13.45	4.22	2.00	41.00	450	13.00	14.00	1.81	6.72
Zd	0.25	3.71	-13.50	12.00	420	0.00	-2.00	0.06	0.79
Blends	5.56	2.55	0.00	20.00	446	5.00	5.00	0.77	2.88
Blends/R	0.24	0.10	0.00	0.71	446	0.24	0.17	0.43	1.03
Col-Shd Blends	0.67	[0.93]	0.00	6.00	207	0.00	0.00	2.02	6.35
Afr	0.61	0.17	0.18	1.42	450	0.60	0.50	0.45	1.22

(continued)

Table 22.1   Continued.

Variable	Mean	SD	Min	Max	Freq	Median	Mode	SK	KU
Populars	6.28	1.53	1.00	12.00	450	6.00	7.00	0.02	0.69
XA%	0.88	0.07	0.57	1.00	450	0.89	0.88	−0.71	0.77
WDA%	0.91	0.06	0.69	1.00	450	0.91	0.95	−0.66	0.47
X+%	0.68	0.11	0.33	0.95	450	0.70	0.67	−0.58	0.20
X-%	0.11	0.07	0.00	0.38	425	0.11	0.10	0.72	0.73
Xu%	0.20	0.09	0.00	0.49	448	0.19	0.17	0.42	−0.01
Isolate/R	0.19	0.09	0.00	0.60	440	0.18	0.14	0.55	0.92
H	3.18	1.70	0.00	10.00	432	3.00	3.00	0.43	0.30
(H)	1.35	1.12	0.00	8.00	348	1.00	1.00	1.19	3.11
Hd	1.14	[1.26]	0.00	11.00	293	1.00	1.00	2.16	9.83
(Hd)	0.62	0.87	0.00	5.00	191	0.00	0.00	1.64	3.11
Hx	0.15	[0.50]	0.00	4.00	47	0.00	0.00	4.45	23.71
H+(H)+Hd+(Hd)	6.29	2.66	0.00	20.00	449	6.00	5.00	0.93	2.32
A	8.18	2.56	2.00	25.00	450	8.00	7.00	1.08	3.79
(A)	0.42	[0.69]	0.00	5.00	151	0.00	0.00	2.02	5.81
Ad	2.90	[1.65]	0.00	15.00	438	3.00	2.00	1.60	7.20
(Ad)	0.13	[0.38]	0.00	2.00	53	0.00	0.00	2.92	8.36
An	0.88	[1.05]	0.00	7.00	258	1.00	0.00	1.87	5.53
Art	1.19	1.42	0.00	14.00	282	1.00	0.00	2.60	15.24
Ay	0.56	[0.69]	0.00	4.00	211	0.00	0.00	1.23	1.98
Bl	0.24	[0.51]	0.00	3.00	93	0.00	0.00	2.25	5.40
Bt	2.22	1.52	0.00	7.00	388	2.00	2.00	0.47	−0.18
Cg	2.16	1.57	0.00	9.00	391	2.00	2.00	0.98	1.64
Cl	0.16	[0.41]	0.00	2.00	61	0.00	0.00	2.71	6.99
Ex	0.21	[0.47]	0.00	4.00	87	0.00	0.00	2.65	10.68
Fi	0.81	[0.84]	0.00	4.00	264	1.00	0.00	1.01	1.08
Food	0.26	[0.55]	0.00	3.00	99	0.00	0.00	2.21	5.16
Ge	0.14	[0.45]	0.00	3.00	45	0.00	0.00	3.81	15.82
Hh	1.24	1.06	0.00	5.00	327	1.00	1.00	0.69	0.10
Ls	0.93	1.04	0.00	9.00	275	1.00	1.00	2.11	9.71
Na	0.45	[0.81]	0.00	6.00	144	0.00	0.00	2.74	11.51
Sc	1.64	[1.41]	0.00	13.00	360	1.00	1.00	1.87	9.44
Sx	0.19	[0.53]	0.00	4.00	67	0.00	0.00	3.62	16.81
Xy	0.08	[0.28]	0.00	2.00	32	0.00	0.00	3.81	14.87
Idiographic	0.34	[0.65]	0.00	6.00	121	0.00	0.00	2.87	14.37
DV	0.34	[0.67]	0.00	5.00	117	0.00	0.00	2.84	12.10
INCOM	0.71	[0.93]	0.00	5.00	212	0.00	0.00	1.47	2.30
DR	0.85	[1.01]	0.00	7.00	251	1.00	0.00	1.89	6.82
FABCOM	0.45	[0.77]	0.00	6.00	147	0.00	0.00	2.39	9.13
DV2	0.00	[0.07]	0.00	1.00	2	0.00	0.00	14.95	222.48
INC2	0.06	[0.25]	0.00	2.00	23	0.00	0.00	4.74	24.02
DR2	0.03	[0.18]	0.00	1.00	15	0.00	0.00	5.21	25.33
FAB2	0.05	[0.24]	0.00	2.00	23	0.00	0.00	4.49	20.83
ALOG	0.04	[0.21]	0.00	1.00	20	0.00	0.00	4.43	17.76
CONTAM	0.00	[0.00]	0.00	0.00	0	—.—	0.00	—.—	—.—
Sum 6 Sp Sc	2.54	1.90	0.00	14.00	394	2.00	2.00	1.25	3.67
Lvl 2 Sp Sc	0.15	[0.39]	0.00	2.00	60	0.00	0.00	2.65	6.69
WSum6	7.12	5.74	0.00	38.00	394	6.00	0.00	1.49	3.99
AB	0.21	[0.56]	0.00	4.00	69	0.00	0.00	3.25	12.09
AG	0.89	1.02	0.00	7.00	254	1.00	0.00	1.46	3.34
COP	2.07	1.30	0.00	6.00	401	2.00	2.00	0.36	−0.24
CP	0.01	[0.11]	0.00	1.00	5	0.00	0.00	9.35	85.98
GOODHR	5.06	2.09	0.00	13.00	444	5.00	5.00	0.21	0.29
POORHR	2.12	1.81	0.00	15.00	380	2.00	1.00	1.71	6.43
MOR	0.93	[1.01]	0.00	6.00	267	1.00	0.00	1.35	2.85
PER	0.99	[1.10]	0.00	8.00	274	1.00	0.00	1.76	6.04
PSV	0.12	[0.38]	0.00	2.00	43	0.00	0.00	3.45	11.91

Table 22.2 Demography Data and Frequencies for 36 Variables for 450 Nonpatient Adults.

DEMOGRAPHY VARIABLES

MARITAL STATUS			AGE			RACE		
Single	145	32%	18-25	119	26%	White	374	83%
Lives w/S.O	20	4%	26-35	158	35%	Black	39	9%
Married	210	47%	36-45	85	19%	Hispanic	30	7%
Separated	13	3%	46-55	45	10%	Asian	7	2%
Divorced	53	12%	56-65	26	6%	Other	0	0%
Widowed	9	2%	OVER 65	17	4%			

				EDUCATION	
SEX			UNDER 12	8	2%
Male	220	49%	12 Years	117	26%
Female	230	51%	13-15 Yrs	216	48%
			16+ Yrs	109	24%

RATIOS, PERCENTAGES AND SPECIAL INDICES

STYLES			FORM QUALITY DEVIATIONS		
Introversive	173	38%	XA% > .89	203	45%L
Pervasive Introversive	27	6%	XA% < .70	4	1%
Ambitent	80	18%	WDA% < .85	72	16%H
Extratensive	138	31%	WDA% < .75	7	2%
Pervasive Extratensive	20	4%	X+% < .55	55	12%H
Avoidant	59	13%	Xu% > .20	202	45%H
. . . .			X–% > .20	46	10%
D-SCORES			X–% > .30	4	1%
D Score > 0	64	14%			
D Score = 0	308	68%	FC:CF+C RATIO		
D Score < 0	78	17%	FC > (CF+C) + 2	68	15%L
D Score < -1	28	6%	FC > (CF+C) + 1	118	26%L
			(CF+C) > FC+1	117	26%H
Adj D Score > 0	122	27%	(CF+C) > FC+2	62	14%H
Adj D Score = 0	283	63%			
Adj D Score < 0	45	10%			
Adj D Score < -1	14	3%	S-Constellation Positive	11	2%
			HVI Positive	20	4%
Zd > +3.0 (Overincorp)	89	20%	OBS Positive	3	1%
Zd < -3.0 (Underincorp)	64	14%			

PTI = 5	0	0%	DEPI = 7	2	0%	CDI = 5	9	2%
PTI = 4	1	0%	DEPI = 6	16	4%	CDI = 4	30	7%
PTI = 3	1	0%	DEPI = 5	44	10%			

MISCELLANEOUS VARIABLES

R < 17	26	6%	(2AB+Art+Ay) > 5	35	8%
R > 27	65	14%	Populars < 4	16	4%
DQv > 2	8	2%L	Populars > 7	81	18%L
S > 2	169	38%H	COP = 0	49	11%L
Sum T = 0	86	19%	COP > 2	164	36%
Sum T > 1	77	17%	AG = 0	196	44%
3r+(2)/R < .33	89	20%	AG > 2	32	7%
3r+(2)/R > .44	134	30%	MOR > 2	30	7%
Fr + rF > 0	54	12%	Level 2 Sp.Sc. > 0	60	13%
PureC > 0	64	14%	GHR > PHR	384	85%
PureC > 1	10	2%	Pure H < 2	76	17%
Afr < .40	41	9%	Pure H = 0	18	4%
Afr < .50	107	24%H	p > a+1	44	10%
(FM+m) < Sum Shading	81	18%	Mp > Ma	103	23%H

H or L = Differs by more than 7% from sample of 600: (H = higher; L = lower)

473

Table 22.3   A Comparison of Data for 17 Variables from the 2001 Sample of 600 Nonpatients and 450 Nonpatients from the Current Project.

Variable	Mean	SD	Range	Freq	Median	Mode	Sk	Ku	d	r
R (600)	22.32	4.40	14–43	600	22	23	0.86	1.90		
R (450)	23.36	5.68	14–59	450	23	22	1.89	6.75	−.16	.08
Space (600)	1.57	1.28	0–10	514	1.00	1.00	4.00	24.01		
Space (450)	2.37	1.97	0–17	407	2.00	1.00	2.27	9.69	−.41	.20
FC (600)	3.56	1.88	0–9	580	3.00	3.00	0.38	−0.24		
FC (450)	2.97	1.78	0–11	416	3.00	2.00	0.59	0.71	.36	.18
CF (600)	2.41	1.31	0–7	564	2.00	3.00	0.29	−0.17		
CF (450)	2.80	1.64	0–12	426	3.00	2.00	0.99	3.42	−.26	.13
SumT (600)	0.95	0.61	0–4	490	1.00	1.00	0.83	3.33		
SumT (450)	1.01	0.69	0–4	364	1.00	1.00	0.76	1.86	−.04	.02
SumY (600)	0.61	0.96	0–10	262	0.00	0.00	3.53	23.46		
SumY (450)	0.97	1.20	0–9	261	1.00	0.00	2.27	8.62	−.25	.13
Mactive (600)	2.90	1.57	0–8	583	3.00	2.00	0.52	−0.26		
Mactive (450)	2.93	1.67	0–10	423	3.00	3.00	0.59	0.84	.00	.00
Mpassive (600)	1.42	1.03	0–5	493	1.00	1.00	0.53	−0.13		
Mpassive (450)	1.93	1.37	0–10	395	2.00	1.00	1.17	3.43	−.35	.18
EA (600)	8.66	2.38	2–18	600	9.00	9.50	−0.04	0.42		
EA (450)	9.37	3.00	2–24	450	9.50	8.00	0.51	1.64	−.20	.10
es (600)	8.34	2.99	3–31	600	8.00	7.00	1.43	6.58		
es (175)	9.55	4.01	2–34	450	9.00	8.00	1.91	8.12	−.22	.13
Lambda (600)	0.60	0.31	0.11–2.33	600	0.53	0.50	2.27	8.01		
Lambda (450)	0.58	0.37	0.00–2.33	450	0.47	0.50	1.56	2.82	.00	−.001
Afr (600)	0.67	0.16	0.23–1.29	600	0.67	0.67	0.35	0.65		
Afr (450)	0.61	0.17	0.18–1.42	450	0.60	0.50	0.45	1.22	.37	−.18
XA% (600)	0.92	0.06	0.57–1.00	600	0.94	0.96	−1.34	3.68		
XA% (450)	0.88	0.07	0.57–1.00	450	0.89	0.88	−0.71	0.77	.63	.30
WDA% (600)	0.94	0.06	0.54–1.00	600	0.95	1.00	−1.42	4.93		
WDA% (450)	0.91	0.06	0.69–1.00	450	0.91	0.95	−0.66	0.47	.47	.23
X+% (600)	0.77	0.09	0.35–1.00	600	0.78	0.80	−0.86	2.33		
X+% (450)	0.68	0.11	0.33–0.95	450	0.70	0.67	−0.58	0.20	−.82	.38
Xu% (600)	0.15	0.07	0.00–0.45	600	0.15	0.13	0.54	0.86		
Xu% (450)	0.20	0.09	0.00–0.49	448	0.19	0.17	0.42	−0.01	−.56	.27
X−% (600)	0.07	0.05	0.00–0.43	513	0.05	0.04	1.41	4.56		
X−% (450)	0.11	0.07	0.00–0.38	425	0.11	0.10	0.72	0.73	−.65	.31

or Pearson correlations are used. In Cohen's categorization, *d* values of .20, .50, and .80 represent small, medium, and large effect sizes respectively, as do *r*s of .10, .30, and .50.[3] Three of these 10 variables (*R, SumT,* and *Ma*) have *d* scores less than .20 and *r*s of less than .10, and four others (*CF, SumY, EA, es*) have *d* scores falling between .20 and .26. and *r*s between .10 and .13. In essence, these findings tend to confirm that the differences between the two groups for these seven variables are small and probably inconsequential. The remaining three variables in this group (*Space,*

[3] Cohen's benchmarks should be thought of as operationally defined reference points that serve as guidelines from which to judge the effect sizes from scores that are higher or lower than the benchmark on a continuous scale that ranges upward from zero. Cohen avoids identifying fixed ranges for small, medium, and large effect sizes because specific reference points may vary depending on sample sizes and variances within the samples.

FC, Mp) have *d* scores of .41, .36, and .35 respectively, with *r* values of .20, .18, and .18. They signify medium effect sizes and relate to some of the differences between the samples that are highlighted in Table 22.2.

For example, the *d* score of .36 and *r* of .18 for *FC* is related to the data shown in Table 22.2 concerning the *FC:CF+C* ratio. The mean *FC* in the new sample is more than a half point lower than in the sample of 600. This, plus the modest increase in the mean for *CF,* accounts for the fact that only 41% of persons in the new sample have *FC* values that are greater than the total of *CF+C* responses as contrasted with 67% of those represented in the sample of 600 (*d* = .41, *r* = .20). This finding is of interest, but provides no basis from which to suggest that the interpretive guidelines concerning the *FC:CF+C* ratio should be altered. Likewise, the *d* score of .35 and *r* of .18 for *Mp,* suggesting a medium effect size, are related to the Table 22.2 data indicating that 23% of the persons in the new sample have *Ma:Mp* ratios in which *Mp* is the larger value. This contrasts with only 15% in the sample of 600 but, as with the *FC:CF+C* ratio, the difference is not a sufficient basis to warrant an alteration of the current interpretive guidelines.

The data for the use of white space are more compelling in the context of interpretation. The mean value for *S* in the 2001 sample (1.57) is nearly one point less than in the new sample (2.37), and this is reflected in the *d* score of −.41 and *r* of .20, which seem to represent a medium effect size. The difference is created mainly by a greater frequency of *WS* responses to Card I (animal face or mask) and *DS5* responses to Card II (rocket or spaceship) by persons in the new sample. The current interpretive guidelines suggest that if a protocol contains three *S* responses, it should be surmised that the person may be disposed to be more negativistic or oppositional toward the environment (Exner, 2000, 2003). The finding from the new sample suggests that postulate should be considered applicable only when the value for *S* is four rather than three, *or* if the presence of three *S* answers does not include the common animal face or mask answers to Card I and the rocket or spaceship response to Card II.

The remaining seven items in Table 22.3 (*Lambda, Afr, XA%, WDA%, X+%, Xu%,* and *X−%*) are all proportional variables and the differences between the samples vary. One of these seven, *Lambda,* has a *d* score and *r* value of zero, signifying that there is essentially no difference between the groups. A second, *Afr,* shows a *d* score of .37 and *r* of −.18, suggesting a medium effect size. This reflects the .06 difference in the means for the two groups and the fact that the modal value for the new group is .50 as contrasted with .67 for the sample of 600. It seems likely that the differences for *Afr* are created largely because the new sample includes a slightly greater proportion of persons with an introversive style than in the group of 600 (38% versus 35%), and substantially fewer persons with an extratensive style (31% versus 38%).

The data for the remaining five variables are more distinctive. All relate to form quality. The *WDA%* and *XA%* have mean and median values that range from .03 to .05 lower in the new sample than in the group of 600. There are also marked reductions in the kurtosis values concerning the distributions of these variables in the new sample compared with the larger group. This relates to the fact that 71% of the persons in the sample of 600 had *XA%*s greater than .89 compared with only 45% in the new group. The *d* scores of .47 and .63, with *r*s of .23 and .30, indicating medium effect sizes, reflect these several differences. However, the differences are not large enough to revise the interpretive guidelines for these two variables.

Data for the three remaining variables, *X+%, Xu%,* and *X−%,* are more discrepant. The greatest disparity occurs for the *X+%.* It has a mean value (.68) in the sample of 450, which is .09 lower than the sample of 600. The sample also has an *X+%* modal value of .67, which is .13 lower than the larger group. The *d* score of −.82 and *r* of .38 indicate a large effect size. When the *X+%* is lowered, there is usually a corresponding increase in the $Xu\%$ and/or $X-\%$. This is depicted by an $Xu\%$ mean that is .06 higher and an $X-\%$ mean that is .04 higher in the group of 450 compared with the sample of 600. The d score ($-.56$) and r (.27) for the $Xu\%$ indicate a medium effect size, while d score ($-.65$) and r (.31) for the $X-\%$ tend to hover between a medium and large effect size.

It seems likely that the findings concerning form use represent true differences between the two samples. However, as Meyer (2001) has noted, the differences in pre- and post-1990 data sets for form quality scores may simply reflect the revisions and expansions of the form quality table during the 15-year period after the first version of the table was published. Regardless of the sources for the differences between the two groups concerning form use, some are of a magnitude that suggest a review of the interpretive principles related to them.

As noted, the differences between the groups for the core form quality variables, $XA\%$ and $WDA\%$, are modest and do not suggest the need to alter the basic rules of interpretation for those two variables. On the other hand, the data for the $X+\%$ and $Xu\%$ are compelling. Assuming that the new sample is the more representative, some revision of two guidelines for interpreting findings for the $X+\%$ and $Xu\%$ seems in order.

One current interpretive principle suggests that if the $X+\%$ falls between .70 and .85 and the $Xu\%$ is between .10 and .20, it indicates that the person has a substantial proclivity to formulate behaviors that are in accord with social expectations (Exner, 2000, 2003). Using the data from the new sample as a basis, the range for the $X+\%$ should be narrowed upward to: "falls between .75 and .85." A new statement should also be added: "If the $X+\%$ falls between .63 and .74 and the $Xu\%$ is .17 or greater, a reasonable concern for social expectations exists and often influences the person when mediational decisions are formulated."

A second current interpretive principle states, "When the $X+\%$ is between .55 and .69 and the $Xu\%$ is .20 or greater, it can be assumed that the person makes more mediational decisions that disregard social demands or expectations than do most people" (Exner, 2000, 2003). Data from the new sample suggest that the range for the $X+\%$ should be narrowed downward to: "is between .55 and .62," and the designated value for the $Xu\%$ should be increased to ".25 or greater."

The issue of whether the differences between the data for the $X-\%$ in the new sample and the sample of 600 encourage an alteration of the interpretive guidelines for this variable is more equivocal. The mean for the $X-\%$ (.11) in the new sample is .04 greater than in the sample of 600, and the median (.11) and modal (.10) values are both .05 higher. As noted, the d ($-.65$) and r (.31) values denote a medium effect size and may denote a large effect size. One element contributing to the substantial d and r values is a change in the proportion of records that have no minus answers. In the sample of 600, this occurred in 15% of the protocols compared with only 6% of the records in the new sample. This probably accounts to some extent for the fact that the kurtosis value for the $X-\%$ distribution in the new sample is nearly four points lower than in the sample of 600. Although the differences between the groups regarding the $X-\%$ data are of considerable interest, they do not seem to warrant alterations of the current interpretive guidelines regarding this variable.

SOME TENTATIVE CONCLUSIONS ABOUT THE TWO SAMPLES

The new sample is not yet comparable in size to the larger group and does not have the more precise stratification for geographic distribution or SES that is represented in the larger group. Nonetheless, it is contemporary and holds an advantage in that context. Probably the most important overall finding is the striking similarities between the two groups for nearly all variables except some related to form use. This tends to support the notion that both samples are reasonably representative. As such, both provide a rational basis from which to gain some understanding of the response rates. They also provide sources to identify the proportions of nonpatients that can be expected to fall within, or outside, established parameters for various ratios and other indices that form the core of structural data from which numerous interpretive principles have been developed.

The data for the new sample have evolved from a project that began six years ago and is ongoing. It is not yet quite large enough or sufficiently stratified to prompt a decision to replace the sample of 600 as the standard nonpatient reference group for the *Comprehensive System*. However, that will occur when the size and demographic objectives for the project are achieved. Nonetheless, as illustrated, the data for the new group already have considerable usefulness.

REFERENCES

Cohen, J. (1992). A power primer. *Psychological Bulletin, 112,* 155–159.

Exner, J. E. (1974). *The Rorschach: A Comprehensive System.* New York: Wiley.

Exner, J. E. (1985). *A Rorschach workbook for the Comprehensive System* (2nd ed.). Bayville, NY: Rorschach Workshops.

Exner, J. E. (1988). Problems with brief Rorschach protocols. *Journal of Personality Assessment, 52*(4), 640–647.

Exner, J. E. (1990). *A Rorschach workbook for the Comprehensive System* (3rd ed.). Asheville, NC: Rorschach Workshops.

Exner, J. E. (2000). *A primer for Rorschach interpretation.* Asheville, NC: Rorschach Workshops.

Exner, J. E. (2001). *A Rorschach workbook for the Comprehensive System* (5th ed.). Asheville, NC: Rorschach Workshops.

Exner, J. E. (2002). A new nonpatient sample for the Rorschach Comprehensive System: A progress report. *Journal of Personality Assessment, 78,* 391–404.

Exner, J. E. (2003). *The Rorschach: A Comprehensive System: Vol. 1. Basic foundations and principles of interpretation* (4th ed.). New York: Wiley.

Exner, J. E., Weiner, I. B., & Schuyler, W. (1976). *A Rorschach workbook for the Comprehensive System.* Bayville, NY: Rorschach Workshops.

Meyer, G. J. (2001). Evidence to correct misperceptions about Rorschach norms. *Clinical Psychology: Science and Practice, 8,* 389–396.

Shaffer, T. W., & Erdberg, P. (2001, March). *An international symposium on Rorschach nonpatient data: Worldwide findings.* Annual meeting, Society of Personality Assessment, Philadelphia.

Shaffer, T. W., Erdberg, P., & Haroian, J. (1999). Current nonpatient data for the Rorschach, WAIS-R, and MMPI-2. *Journal of Personality Assessment, 73,* 305–316.

CHAPTER 23

Frequency Data by Card and Location

In the review and analysis of the new nonpatient sample for differences from the 2001 sample of 600 nonpatients, some comparisons have been made of the two groups for frequency of responses to specific cards and specific locations. These comparisons have often provided more precise information about apparent differences between the two groups. For instance, as noted in Chapter 22, the increase in the mean value for *S* responses in the new sample is created largely by a greater frequency of *WS* responses to Card I and *DS5* responses to Card II.

While frequency data sets by card and location are useful in comparing groups, they have much greater importance in providing a clear picture of the potency or valence of some of the distal features in each of the 10 figures. The issue of the stimulus potency of the Rorschach figures has often been discussed, either directly or indirectly, with regard to propositions put forth about the response process. For instance, Frank's (1939) formulation of the *projective hypothesis* was based largely on the assumption that all the figures are ambiguous and, because of the ambiguity, projection becomes a major element in the process that ensues when a person is asked to give responses.

Beck (1933, 1945) was among the first to put forth the notion that the Rorschach figures are not of equal difficulty levels. He cautioned that, because of this, the interpretation of *W* or *M* responses to one card might be quite different than the interpretation of *W* or *M* answers to a different card. It was his research concerning this postulate that led him to develop the table of *Z* score weights that continues to be used in differentiating organizational activity.

Numerous investigators used reaction times as a crude indicator of stimulus complexity or difficulty levels of the various cards. One of the most intricate of these studies was done by Meer (1955), who also added two dependent variables, form level ratings of responses, and subjective judgments by participants in the study regarding card difficulty. Meer's results, derived from studying the protocols of 50 undergraduate students at the University of Pennsylvania, clearly support the notion that the cards vary for difficulty levels, especially when studied for the ease or difficulty of creating *W* versus *D* responses. Meer noted that Card III is one of the easiest figures to respond to, but the most difficult to create answers that integrate the entire figure. He noted a similar pattern of findings for Card VIII. Meer concluded that Cards I and V are probably the least ambiguous of the figures and the easiest for creating *W* answers. He deduced that Cards II, VI, VII, and IX are fairly difficult to integrate as *W* answers, mainly because each contains at least one relatively nonambiguous detail area, and identified Card X as being the most difficult "despite the fact that it contains several relatively non-ambiguous forms."

Several investigators have manipulated stimulus features of the Rorschach figures, such as color and shading, in attempts to understand the influence of those features on response productivity or response content (Baughman, 1959; Dubrovner, VonLackum, & Jost, 1950; Exner, 1959,

1961; Grayson, 1956; Perlman, 1951; Silva, 2002). Exner (1989) also used that approach to differentiate answers that contain projected features from those that simply identify distal features of the figures.

Some authors have discussed the potencies of the distal features of the Rorschach figures in the context of "card pull." This concept was first put forth in 1950 by Ranzoni, Grant, and Ives, who defined it as "those properties of the ink-blot that seem to predispose the subject to use certain aspects of the blot." They used a sample of 194 adolescents who were retested at regular intervals between the ages of 11 and 18 to obtain response frequency data and reported the proportions for location selections, determinant use, and the presence of human and animal contents. They found the largest proportion of *W* answers was usually given to Cards I, V, and VI and the largest proportion of *D* answers were usually given to Cards VIII, IX, and X. Peterson and Schilling (1983) cautioned that card pull is often neglected by those who stress ambiguous or unstructured stimuli as a prerequisite to projection. They correctly point out that projection may occur regardless of the extent to which a stimulus field is structured.

Weiner (1998) has used the concepts of overt and covert card pull as basic premises relevant to interpretation. He defines overt card pull as those numerous stimulus features of the inkblot figures to which subjects respond directly when forming and giving answers and suggests that these baseline features are useful in detecting deviations in response patterns. He identifies covert card pull as the characteristics of the figures that subjects seldom mention, either because of a lack of conscious awareness or because of censorship, but which do influence how they respond. He proposes that these features include what the various blots are likely to signify, and notes that an awareness of this is a source from which information about a subject's personality dynamics can be gleaned.

Exner (1996) has studied issues of potency of the distal features of the Rorschach figures in the context of the perceptual theory of critical bits (Attneave, 1954; Hochberg, 1988; Hochberg and McAlister, 1953). They are the stimulus features that define or restrict the parameters of judgments or identifications concerning a distal environment. He has demonstrated how the critical stimulus bits in the figures, such as the contour areas on Cards I and V, the color features on Cards II and III, and the color and white space relationship on Card II, promote or discourage certain classes of response. He has also established how mental sets can also serve as critical bits that influence translations of the distal environment of the Rorschach figures.

Exner (2003) has postulated that Rorschach probably became aware of the importance of critical bits in the inkblot figures as his investigation proceeded between 1917 and 1919. At some point during that time, Rorschach used his considerable artistic skill to draw more precise versions of some of the inkblots that he had created and attempted to use for several months. He often added or modified colors in creating more precise versions of the figures, but most of his drawings included the addition of many more contours than had appeared in the original blots. He did this to ensure that each figure included numerous distinctive features that could easily be identified as being similar to objects stored in the memory traces of the individual. In a sense, Rorschach sought to create a kind of embedded figures test, assuming that the manner in which persons identified features of the figures or parts of them would relate to elements of personality or pathology.

Almost all of the relatively few investigations that have been published concerning the distal features of the Rorschach figures have involved modest size samples, and/or have included analyses that focus on a limited number of variables. Although all of them have contributed useful and reasonably consistent information about difficulty levels of the cards or information about the potency of stimulus elements, none have provided information concerning the total array of features for which the test is usually scored or coded. The main reason for this was that the mechanics involved in tallying and analyzing data for large numbers of protocols were unwieldy or often impossible to manage. Fortunately, rapid advances in computer technology since the 1980s have simplified those tasks enormously, and as a result, large data sets can be stored and easily analyzed.

Most of the remainder of this chapter consists of pairs of tables that include frequency data. One table in the pair reflects data derived from the new sample of 450 nonpatients. The second table in the pair represents data for the combination of the new nonpatient group plus the 2001 sample of 600 nonpatients. The pairs of tables are presented in four general segments. The first segment, consisting of Tables 23.1 and 23.2, includes frequencies and proportions of responses, by card, for each of the six types of location selection. The second segment comprises Tables 23.3 through 23.6, showing frequencies and proportions of responses, by card, for developmental quality and form quality codings; and Tables 23.7 through 23.26, which include frequency data for developmental quality and form quality coding, plus the number of blends, by card number and location areas.

The third segment consists of Tables 23.27 and 23.28 which are summaries, by card, of the frequencies and proportions by which the various determinants were coded in each of the samples, plus Tables 23.29 to 23.48 which show the frequencies for each of the determinant codings, by card number and location areas. The final segment includes Tables 23.49 and 23.50 in which summary frequencies for the two samples, by card, are shown for each of the 27 content codings, plus Tables 23.51 to 23.70 in which the frequencies for each content coding, by card number and location areas are presented for each of the samples. Percentages are not included for the content data in Tables 23.49 and 23.50 because a substantial number of answers (more than 30%), contain multiple contents, and proportional data can be very misleading. As a collective, the data in these tables have considerable usefulness in identifying some of the more potent distal features in each of the 10 figures and providing additional guidelines that can be used to identify deviant or unique responses.

LOCATION FREQUENCIES BY CARD

Table 23.1   Frequencies for Location Selections by Card for 450 Nonpatients.

		Location Selection						
		W	WS	D	DS	DD	DDS	Total
Card Number	1	521 47.8%	221 20.3%	273 25.0%	1 .1%	47 4.3%	27 2.5%	1090 100.0%
	2	218 20.4%	60 5.6%	558 52.1%	199 18.6%	20 1.9%	15 1.4%	1070 100.0%
	3	56 6.0%	16 1.7%	764 82.4%	31 3.3%	27 2.9%	33 3.6%	927 100.0%
	4	551 62.8%	12 1.4%	251 28.6%	5 .6%	56 6.4%	2 .2%	877 100.0%
	5	622 77.5%	0 .0%	138 17.2%	0 .0%	39 4.9%	4 .5%	803 100.0%
	6	313 35.1%	0 .0%	490 55.0%	0 .0%	85 9.5%	3 .3%	891 100.0%
	7	376 40.3%	51 5.5%	417 44.6%	53 5.7%	29 3.1%	8 .9%	934 100.0%
	8	431 40.2%	17 1.6%	513 47.8%	47 4.4%	53 4.9%	12 1.1%	1073 100.0%
	9	285 26.2%	20 1.8%	587 54.1%	67 6.2%	80 7.4%	47 4.3%	1086 100.0%
	10	308 17.5%	15 .9%	1293 73.4%	12 .7%	46 2.6%	87 4.9%	1761 100.0%
Total		3681 35.0%	412 3.9%	5284 50.3%	415 3.9%	482 4.6%	238 2.3%	10512 100.0%

Table 23.2   Frequencies for Location Selections by Card for 1050 Nonpatients.

		Location Selection						
		W	WS	D	DS	DD	DDS	Total
Card	1	1250	375	653	2	99	58	2437
Number		51.3%	15.4%	26.8%	.1%	4.1%	2.4%	100.0%
	2	463	92	1296	399	55	39	2344
		19.8%	3.9%	55.3%	17.0%	2.3%	1.7%	100.0%
	3	203	29	1614	46	40	66	1998
		10.2%	1.5%	80.8%	2.3%	2.0%	3.3%	100.0%
	4	1212	13	609	8	103	3	1948
		62.2%	.7%	31.3%	.4%	5.3%	.2%	100.0%
	5	1433	1	310	1	109	5	1859
		77.1%	.1%	16.7%	.1%	5.9%	.3%	100.0%
	6	658	0	1237	0	177	5	2077
		31.7%	.0%	59.6%	.0%	8.5%	.2%	100.0%
	7	763	132	1022	90	73	13	2093
		36.5%	6.3%	48.8%	4.3%	3.5%	.6%	100.0%
	8	1053	21	1197	101	92	31	2495
		42.2%	.8%	48.0%	4.0%	3.7%	1.2%	100.0%
	9	703	39	1295	185	152	90	2464
		28.5%	1.6%	52.6%	7.5%	6.2%	3.7%	100.0%
	10	727	37	3297	20	77	169	4327
		16.8%	.9%	76.2%	.5%	1.8%	3.9%	100.0%
Total		8465	739	12530	852	977	479	24042
		35.2%	3.1%	52.1%	3.5%	4.1%	2.0%	100.0%

LOCATION SELECTIONS

The proportions of the six location selections are similar in both data sets and generally consistent with those for *W* and *D* areas reported by Meer (1955). *W* or *WS* answers appear in more than 75% of the responses given to Card V and more than 60% of the answers given to Cards I and IV. These are the only figures for which more than half of the responses involve the use of the whole distal field. Card III is at the other extreme. Only 8% of the responses to this card from the sample of 450 and 12% of the answers from the combined sample involve the whole field, while close to 85% of the answers to Card III in each sample are to *D* areas.

The findings for these two samples are also similar to those reported by Meer (1955) for Card X. Only about 18% of the answers to this figure include the entire field, whereas about 75% are *D* responses. The data are considerably different from those noted by Meer for Card VIII. *W* answers to Card VIII appeared in his sample with a very low frequency. In contrast, about 42% of the responses to Card VIII in the samples shown in Tables 23.1 and 23.2 are *W* or *WS* answers, and both show that about 52% of the answers given are to *D* areas. The other figures that have relatively low proportions of *W* or *WS* responses are Cards II, VI, and IX, with each sample including about one-third or fewer answers involving the whole field. Interestingly, Cards VI and IX have the highest proportions of *Dd* or *DdS* answers, about 10% in each sample.

DEVELOPMENTAL QUALITY BY CARD

Table 23.3 Frequencies and Percentages for DQ Codes by Card for 450 Nonpatients.

		Developmental Quality Codes				
		DQ+	DQo	DQv	DQv/+	Total
Card Number	1	217 19.9%	866 79.4%	5 .5%	2 .2%	1090 100.0%
	2	607 56.7%	428 40.0%	27 2.5%	8 .7%	1070 100.0%
	3	523 56.4%	391 42.2%	13 1.4%	0 .0%	927 100.0%
	4	178 20.3%	685 78.1%	10 1.1%	4 .5%	877 100.0%
	5	102 12.7%	696 86.7%	3 .4%	2 .2%	803 100.0%
	6	144 16.2%	742 83.3%	2 .2%	3 .3%	891 100.0%
	7	510 54.6%	379 40.6%	16 1.7%	29 3.1%	934 100.0%
	8	458 42.7%	573 53.4%	32 3.0%	10 .9%	1073 100.0%
	9	477 43.9%	537 49.4%	26 2.4%	46 4.2%	1086 100.0%
	10	577 32.8%	1133 64.3%	32 1.8%	19 1.1%	1761 100.0%
Total		3793 36.1%	6430 61.2%	166 1.6%	123 1.2%	10512 100.0%

Table 23.4   Frequencies and Percentages for DQ Codes by Card for 1050 Nonpatients.

		Developmental Quality Codes				
		DQ+	DQo	DQv	DQv/+	Total
Card Number	1	440 18.1%	1983 81.4%	11 .5%	3 .1%	2437 100.0%
	2	1350 57.6%	895 38.2%	87 3.7%	12 .5%	2344 100.0%
	3	1160 58.1%	793 39.7%	45 2.3%	0 .0%	1998 100.0%
	4	386 19.8%	1442 74.0%	108 5.5%	12 .6%	1948 100.0%
	5	202 10.9%	1651 88.8%	3 .2%	3 .2%	1859 100.0%
	6	324 15.6%	1738 83.7%	12 .6%	3 .1%	2077 100.0%
	7	1100 52.6%	848 40.5%	31 1.5%	114 5.4%	2093 100.0%
	8	991 39.7%	1287 51.6%	205 8.2%	12 .5%	2495 100.0%
	9	1060 43.0%	1203 48.8%	120 4.9%	81 3.3%	2464 100.0%
	10	1323 30.6%	2773 64.1%	122 2.8%	109 2.5%	4327 100.0%
Total		8336 34.7%	14613 60.8%	744 3.1%	349 1.5%	24042 100.0%

DEVELOPMENTAL QUALITY

The proportions of synthesis (*DQ+*) versus single object (*DQo*) answers to some of the areas of each card provide a basis for understanding the features of various areas. An examination of Tables 23.3 and 23.4 indicates that a large proportion of *W* responses to Cards I, IV, V, and VI are *DQo* answers, indicating that the distal properties of the whole figure are amenable to identifying it as a single object. Conversely, the majority of *W* answers to Cards II, III, VII, VIII, IX, and X are synthesized, indicating that these fields do not have features commensurate with single objects, and it is likely that more processing and conceptualizing effort is required to generate a response that will incorporate the entire field.

FORM QUALITY BY CARD

Table 23.5   Frequencies and Percentages for Form Quality Codes for 450 Nonpatients.

		\multicolumn{5}{c}{Form Quality Codes}					Total
		FQno	FQ–	FQu	FQo	FQ+	Total
Card Number	1	1 .1%	71 6.5%	117 10.7%	881 80.8%	20 1.8%	1090 100.0%
	2	19 1.8%	96 9.0%	185 17.3%	729 68.1%	41 3.8%	1070 100.0%
	3	5 .5%	159 17.2%	113 12.2%	573 61.8%	77 8.3%	927 100.0%
	4	1 .1%	112 12.8%	196 22.3%	561 64.0%	7 .8%	877 100.0%
	5	1 .1%	64 8.0%	101 12.6%	629 78.3%	8 1.0%	803 100.0%
	6	0 .0%	81 9.1%	206 23.1%	596 66.9%	8 .9%	891 100.0%
	7	0 .0%	108 11.6%	191 20.4%	599 64.1%	36 3.9%	934 100.0%
	8	12 1.1%	136 12.7%	278 25.9%	625 58.2%	22 2.1%	1073 100.0%
	9	12 1.1%	169 15.6%	302 27.8%	591 54.4%	12 1.1%	1086 100.0%
	10	15 .9%	233 13.2%	494 28.1%	1007 57.2%	12 .7%	1761 100.0%
Total		66 .6%	1229 11.7%	2183 20.8%	6791 64.6%	243 2.3%	10512 100.0%

Table 23.6   Frequencies and Percentages for Form Quality Codes for 1050 Nonpatients.

		Form Quality Codes					
		FQno	FQ–	FQu	FQo	FQ+	Total
Card Number	1	1	114	198	2078	46	2437
		.0%	4.7%	8.1%	85.3%	1.9%	100.0%
	2	37	153	306	1744	104	2344
		1.6%	6.5%	13.1%	74.4%	4.4%	100.0%
	3	18	355	217	1230	178	1998
		.9%	17.8%	10.9%	61.6%	8.9%	100.0%
	4	1	180	423	1306	38	1948
		.1%	9.2%	21.7%	67.0%	2.0%	100.0%
	5	1	120	242	1481	15	1859
		.1%	6.5%	13.0%	79.7%	.8%	100.0%
	6	1	146	413	1491	26	2077
		.0%	7.0%	19.9%	71.8%	1.3%	100.0%
	7	0	214	393	1427	59	2093
		.0%	10.2%	18.8%	68.2%	2.8%	100.0%
	8	24	260	637	1505	69	2495
		1.0%	10.4%	25.5%	60.3%	2.8%	100.0%
	9	23	291	501	1600	49	2464
		.9%	11.8%	20.3%	64.9%	2.0%	100.0%
	10	32	408	1015	2774	98	4327
		.7%	9.4%	23.5%	64.1%	2.3%	100.0%
Total		138	2241	4345	16636	682	24042
		.6%	9.3%	18.1%	69.2%	2.8%	100.0%

FORM QUALITY

Notable differences between the samples of 450 and 600 nonpatients for the means and distributions for the five form quality summary scores (XA%, WDA%, X+%, Xu%, and X–%) were discussed in Chapter 22. The data in Tables 23.5 and 23.6 provide some added clarification regarding those differences. A comparison of the proportions of + and o responses for the combined sample with those for the group of 450 reveal higher percentages in the combined group, ranging from 2% to 8% for seven cards (I, IV, V, VI, VII, VIII, and X) and a 12% differential for Card IX. The proportions are essentially the same only for Card III. Likewise, a comparison of the two samples indicates that there are greater proportions of minus answers, ranging from 1% to 4% higher, for 9 of the 10 cards in the group of 450. Again, the proportions are essentially the same only for Card III.

While the proportions differ for the two samples, the general trends are similar. In each sample, the highest proportions of + and o responses were given to Cards I, V, and II in that order, whereas the lowest proportions of + and o answers appear for Cards VIII, IX, and X. Similarly, the greatest proportions of minus answers appear in Cards III and IX, whereas the lowest proportion of minus responses occurs to Card I.

DQ, FQ, AND BLENDS BY CARD AND LOCATION

Table 23.7   Card I Frequencies for DQ, FQ, and Blends for 450 Nonpatients (R = 1090).

Loc		Developmental Quality				Form Quality					
		DQ+	DQo	DQv	DQv/+	FQno	FQ–	FQu	FQo	FQ+	Blends
Loc	W	127	609	4	2		23	61	641	17	91
	1	5	13				2	1	15		1
	2	11	49				2	14	44		1
	3		20				3	2	15		
	4	67	90				8	3	143	3	26
	7		19				1	7	11		
	21	1	3	1		1	2	1	1		
	22		1					1			
	23		1				1				
	24		5					1	4		
	25		1					1			
	26		1						1		
	28	3	2				3	2			
	29		1					1			
	30		2						2		
	31		1				1				
	35		1					1			
	99	3	47				25	21	4		

Table 23.8   Card I Frequencies for DQ, FQ, and Blends for 1050 Nonpatients (R = 2437).

Loc		Developmental Quality				Form Quality					
		DQ+	DQo	DQv	DQv/+	FQno	FQ–	FQu	FQo	FQ+	Blends
Loc	W	289	1323	10	3		34	97	1451	43	226
	1	6	19				3	1	21		1
	2	16	143				6	23	130		2
	3		72				3	5	64		
	4	115	228				26	9	305	3	47
	7		56				1	10	45		
	21	1	4	1		1	3	1	1		
	22		2					2			
	23		2				2				
	24		15					2	13		
	25		1					1			
	26		18					2	16		
	28	5	4				3	5	1		
	29		14					3	11		
	30		4						4		
	31	1	4				2	3			
	35		1					1			
	99	7	73				31	33	16		2

Table 23.9 Card II Frequencies for DQ, FQ, and Blends for 450 Nonpatients (R = 1070).

Loc		Developmental Quality				Form Quality					Blends
		DQ+	DQo	DQv	DQv/+	FQno	FQ–	FQu	FQo	FQ+	
Loc	W	215	50	9	4	6	41	50	144	37	202
	1	111	44				5	4	144	2	42
	2	15	60	11		9	16	44	17		16
	3		158	6	1	4	11	35	115		19
	4	6	17				1	16	6		3
	5	124	52		1		3	5	169		124
	6	124	23	1	2		6	17	125	2	42
	7		1						1		1
	22	1	3				1	3			
	24	1						1			
	30		1					1			
	31		1				1				
	99	10	18				11	9	8		3

Table 23.10 Card II Frequencies for DQ, FQ, and Blends for 1050 Nonpatients (R = 2344).

Loc		Developmental Quality				Form Quality					Blends
		DQ+	DQo	DQv	DQv/+	FQno	FQ–	FQu	FQo	FQ+	
Loc	W	439	100	11	5	6	65	66	368	50	419
	1	428	57				6	8	423	48	201
	2	31	145	26		24	25	67	86		49
	3	4	348	43	1	6	23	67	300		39
	4	8	28				3	23	10		4
	5	221	142	5	1	1	3	10	355		231
	6	167	32	2	4		7	26	166	6	66
	7		2						2		2
	22	19	4				1	22			
	24	1	1					1	1		
	30		1					1			
	31		1				1				
	99	32	34		1		19	15	33		22

Table 23.11 Card III Frequencies for DQ, FQ, and Blends for 450 Nonpatients (R = 927).

		Developmental Quality			Form Quality					
		DQ+	DQo	DQv	FQno	FQ–	FQu	FQo	FQ+	Blends
Loc	W	60	12			21	8	28	15	46
	1	360	40			33	29	283	55	83
	2	10	66	12	5	19	32	32		13
	3	1	165			15	7	144		9
	5	1	14				9	6		2
	7	3	41	1		36	7	2		1
	8		3			3				
	9	64	14			1	2	68	7	9
	22		1					1		
	23	2	1				3			
	24	1	2			1	2			
	29	1	1			2				1
	31	1	4			1	2	2		
	32	1	6			2	2	3		
	33		1				1			
	34	2	1				1	2		
	35	1					1			
	99	15	19			25	7	2		6

Table 23.12 Card III Frequencies for DQ, FQ, and Blends for 1050 Nonpatients (R = 1998).

		Developmental Quality			Form Quality					
		DQ+	DQo	DQv	FQno	FQ–	FQu	FQo	FQ+	Blends
Loc	W	209	23			36	12	95	89	190
	1	782	53			45	36	674	80	161
	2	14	161	42	16	67	84	50		21
	3	5	331			36	18	282		16
	5	4	26			1	18	11		5
	7	4	92	1		84	11	2		3
	8		33			33				
	9	92	20			1	3	99	9	16
	22		2					2		
	23	2	2				3	1		
	24	2	2			2	2			
	29	1	1			2				1
	31	2	6			2	4	2		
	32	2	8			2	3	5		
	33		1				1			
	34	7	1				5	3		3
	35	2	1			1	2			
	99	32	30	2	2	43	15	4		12

Table 23.13 Card IV Frequencies for DQ, FQ, and Blends for 450 Nonpatients (R = 877).

		Developmental Quality				Form Quality					
		DQ+	DQo	DQv	DQv/+	FQno	FQ–	FQu	FQo	FQ+	Blends
Loc	W	145	407	8	3	1	29	102	425	6	240
	1	5	60				25	28	12		5
	2	2	22	1			2	8	15		
	3	2	38				15	18	7		1
	4	9	35				1	10	33		2
	5	1	8		1		3	4	3		3
	6	3	19				2	6	14		2
	7	2	48					3	46	1	11
	21		1					1			
	29	1					1				
	30		3					3			1
	32		4				1	3			
	33		1					1			
	99	8	39	1			33	9	6		6

Table 23.14 Card IV Frequencies for DQ, FQ, and Blends for 1050 Nonpatients (R = 1948).

		Developmental Quality				Form Quality					
		DQ+	DQo	DQv	DQv/+	FQno	FQ–	FQu	FQo	FQ+	Blends
Loc	W	309	813	92	11	1	50	194	943	37	514
	1	10	175				50	74	61		10
	2	2	57	1			3	13	44		
	3	2	111	13			22	64	40		1
	4	14	58	1			2	21	50		5
	5	1	14		1		3	5	8		4
	6	30	33				2	11	50		6
	7	3	83				1	6	78	1	21
	10		8					5	3		
	21		4					1	3		
	22		1					1			
	26		1					1			
	29	1					1				
	30		6					6			1
	32		8				2	5	1		
	33		2					1	1		
	99	14	68	1			44	15	24		10

Table 23.15 Card V Frequencies for DQ, FQ, and Blends for 450 Nonpatients (R = 803).

Loc		Developmental Quality				Form Quality					Blends
		DQ+	DQo	DQv	DQv/+	FQno	FQ−	FQu	FQo	FQ+	
Loc	W	86	531	3	2	1	16	36	562	7	79
	1	4	7				2	3	6		2
	4	6	35				6	14	20	1	2
	6		5				1	4			
	7	2	36				11	18	9		
	9		4				3	1			
	10	1	38				5	13	21		1
	29	1	1				2				
	30		1				1				
	34		3				2	1			
	35		11				2	1	8		1
	99	2	24				13	10	3		3

Table 23.16 Card V Frequencies for DQ, FQ, and Blends for 1050 Nonpatients (R = 1859).

Loc		Developmental Quality				Form Quality					Blends
		DQ+	DQo	DQv	DQv/+	FQno	FQ−	FQu	FQo	FQ+	
Loc	W	175	1253	3	3	1	25	86	1308	14	167
	1	9	16				2	5	18		4
	4	8	85				10	51	31	1	3
	6		15				9	6			
	7	2	85				17	31	39		
	9		4				3	1			
	10	3	84				10	35	42		4
	29	1	1				2				
	30		2				2				
	32		10					2	8		
	34		6				2	4			
	35		32				4	2	26		1
	99	4	58				34	19	9		6

Table 23.17   Card VI Frequencies for DQ, FQ, and Blends for 450 Nonpatients (R = 891).

Loc	W	DQ+	DQo	DQv	DQv/+	FQ−	FQu	FQo	FQ+	Blends
		Developmental Quality				Form Quality				
Loc	W	78	231	1	3	13	85	210	5	62
	1	6	212	1		13	11	195		11
	2	2	5			1	2	4		1
	3	16	179			7	42	146		4
	4	12	17			3	9	15	2	5
	5	3	6			3	5	1		2
	6	4					3	1		3
	8	14	5				4	14	1	5
	12	1	7				5	3		1
	21		2				1	1		
	22		2				1	1		
	23		4			1	3			
	24		15			5	8	2		1
	25		1				1			
	26		1				1			
	27		2			2				
	29		5			3	2			
	31		1				1			
	32		6			5	1			
	33	1	11			5	7			2
	99	7	30			20	14	3		3

Table 23.18   Card VI Frequencies for DQ, FQ, and Blends for 1050 Nonpatients (R = 2077).

Loc	W	DQ+	DQo	DQv	DQv/+	FQno	FQ−	FQu	FQo	FQ+	Blends
		Developmental Quality				Form Quality					
Loc	W	156	489	10	3	1	31	176	442	8	106
	1	8	596	2			17	16	573		19
	2	2	25				11	7	9		1
	3	34	361				12	76	306	1	7
	4	42	56				4	16	62	16	33
	5	4	8				3	8	1		3
	6	6	2					6	2		4
	8	52	11					8	54	1	12
	12	1	27				1	10	17		2
	21		3					1	2		
	22		2					1	1		
	23	2	5				1	6			
	24		22				10	10	2		1
	25	1	11					12			
	26		2					2			
	27		4				2	2			
	29		7				4	3			
	31		6					3	3		
	32		18				9	9			
	33	1	15				6	10			2
	99	15	68				35	31	17		4

Table 23.19   Card VII Frequencies for DQ, FQ, and Blends for 450 Nonpatients (R = 934).

		Developmental Quality				Form Quality				Blends
		DQ+	DQo	DQv	DQv/+	FQ−	FQu	FQo	FQ+	
Loc	W	339	47	14	27	18	41	335	33	97
	1	59	23		1	6	9	67	1	8
	2	88	74	1		13	17	131	2	12
	3	6	84			18	44	28		5
	4	2	50	1		18	21	14		2
	5		6			1	5			1
	6	1	14			5	7	3		2
	7	1	41			3	26	13		
	8	2	5					7		1
	9	3	3			2	1	3		
	10		5			1	1	3		
	21		3			1	2			
	22	3	4		1	4	3	1		
	23	1	5			5	1			
	25		2			1	1			
	28		2			1	1			
	99	5	11			11	4	1		2

Table 23.20   Card VII Frequencies for DQ, FQ, and Blends for 1050 Nonpatients (R = 2093).

		Developmental Quality				Form Quality				Blends
		DQ+	DQo	DQv	DQv/+	FQ−	FQu	FQo	FQ+	
Loc	W	687	75	24	109	38	98	704	55	238
	1	95	48		2	9	17	118	1	14
	2	277	240	1		22	34	459	3	41
	3	11	152			29	71	63		9
	4	3	113	5	2	30	66	27		8
	5	2	12			1	13			1
	6	1	44			31	11	3		3
	7	1	76			5	36	36		
	8	4	8				11	1		2
	9	4	5			2	2	5		
	10		6			1	1	4		
	21		17	1		3	13	2		
	22	3	4		1	4	3	1		
	23	1	6			5	2			
	25		2			1	1			
	28		4			2	2			
	99	11	36			31	12	4		7

Table 23.21 Card VIII Frequencies for DQ, FQ, and Blends for 450 Nonpatients (R = 1073).

Loc		Developmental Quality				Form Quality					
		DQ+	DQo	DQv	DQv/+	FQno	FQ–	FQu	FQo	FQ+	Blends
Loc	W	358	73	11	6	9	27	42	350	20	302
	1	54	78				3	9	119	1	32
	2	5	135	13	1	2	29	80	42	1	23
	3	1	48				3	5	41		
	4	7	89	1			25	51	21		13
	5	18	46	6	2	1	3	36	32		22
	6	3	22	1			11	7	8		3
	7		14				2	9	3		1
	8	1	13		1		7	7	1		2
	11		1						1		
	21	1	4					4	1		
	22	4	1					4	1		1
	24	1	2				1	2			
	25		2					2			
	29		3				1	2			
	30		2					2			
	32		4					2	2		
	33		11				1	9	1		
	99	5	25				23	5	2		5

Table 23.22 Card VIII Frequencies for DQ, FQ, and Blends for 1050 Nonpatients (R = 2495).

Loc		Developmental Quality				Form Quality					
		DQ+	DQo	DQv	DQv/+	FQno	FQ–	FQu	FQo	FQ+	Blends
Loc	W	793	183	91	7	19	42	117	833	63	621
	1	80	208				10	13	263	2	59
	2	6	346	78	1	3	88	201	137	2	41
	3	1	85	22			3	32	73		1
	4	12	148	3			39	85	39		22
	5	74	73	10	3	2	3	73	82		47
	6	3	28	1			14	8	10		4
	7		96				10	46	40		1
	8	2	15		1		7	9	2		3
	11		2						2		
	21	1	4					4	1		
	22	5	4					5	4		1
	24	1	3				1	3			
	25		4					4			
	26		1						1		
	29		6				1	5			
	30	4	5				3	6			1
	32		11				2	3	6		1
	33		16				1	14	1		
	99	9	49				36	9	11	2	9

Table 23.23 Card IX Frequencies for DQ, FQ, and Blends for 450 Nonpatients (R = 1086).

Loc		Developmental Quality				Form Quality					Blends
		DQ+	DQo	DQv	DQv/+	FQno	FQ–	FQu	FQo	FQ+	
Loc	W	186	62	18	39	9	28	63	204	1	142
	1	103	68	1	1	1	24	29	112	7	14
	2	10	32	1	3		2	14	29	1	12
	3	107	57		1		6	25	133	1	72
	4		30				3	8	19		2
	5		7				3	3	1		1
	6	32	32	3		2	17	21	27		30
	8	10	89		1		22	46	32		19
	9	3	29	1			3	17	13		1
	11	1	19	1			13	6	2		1
	12	8	4				1	8	3		5
	21		7				1	1	5		1
	22	4	17				8	9	4		5
	23		5	1				4	2		
	24		4				1	3			
	25		3				1	2			
	26		2				1	1			
	28		1				1				
	29		2					2			
	30	1						1			1
	31		5					5			
	32	1	3					4			2
	33		10				1	6	3		
	34		4					4			
	35		2					2			
	99	11	43		1		33	18	2	2	12

Table 23.24 Card IX Frequencies for DQ, FQ, and Blends for 1050 Nonpatients (R = 2464).

Loc		Developmental Quality				Form Quality					Blends
		DQ+	DQo	DQv	DQv/+	FQno	FQ–	FQu	FQo	FQ+	
Loc	W	439	154	78	71	15	50	89	585	3	314
	1	238	116	2	2	1	31	50	265	11	23
	2	13	41	1	4		2	17	39	1	16
	3	235	224	6	1	3	14	62	382	5	166
	4		77	2			5	15	59		3
	5		11				4	5	2		1
	6	46	53	6		4	23	38	40		41
	8	13	245		1		36	81	142		68
	9	4	55	1			22	23	15		6
	11	2	27	18			34	10	3		3
	12	29	7				2	11	6	17	25
	21		15				2	3	10		1
	22	5	39				14	16	14		6
	23		9	1				7	3		
	24		4				1	3			
	25		5	2			1	4	2		
	26		2				1	1			
	28		1				1				
	29		3					3			
	30	1	3					4			1
	31		8					6	2		
	32	1	3					4			2
	33		21					8	12		
	34		8				1	6	1		
	35		5					5			
	99	34	67	3	2		46	30	18	12	36

Table 23.25 Card X Frequencies for DQ, FQ, and Blends for 450 Nonpatients (R = 1761).

Loc	W	DQ+	DQo	DQv	DQv/+	FQno	FQ−	FQu	FQo	FQ+	Blends
Loc	W	255	33	17	18	11	22	53	226	11	209
	1	16	159	5	1		6	33	142		18
	2	1	149	1			12	16	123		17
	3		102				7	19	76		4
	4	2	82				6	8	70		4
	5	1	32					1	32		1
	6	27	10	1		1	5	9	23		13
	7	4	114				14	24	80		21
	8	14	82				9	66	21		6
	9	57	100	6		2	34	91	36		51
	10	23	21				1	21	22		17
	11	102	40				13	83	45	1	34
	12	1	18	1			3	9	8		1
	13	1	47				8	29	11		8
	14		7				3	3	1		
	15	23	55				2	9	67		12
	21	2	6				3	1	4		
	22	22	30				49	3			15
	25	9	2						11		4
	28	1							1		1
	29	2	7				1	3	5		1
	30	1	1				2				
	33		4				1	2	1		
	34		1				1				
	99	13	31	1		1	31	10	3		10

Table 23.26 Card X Frequencies for DQ, FQ, and Blends for 1050 Nonpatients (R = 4327).

Loc	W	DQ+	DQo	DQv	DQv/+	FQno	FQ−	FQu	FQo	FQ+	Blends
Loc	W	536	54	66	108	21	34	92	540	77	465
	1	30	539	9	1	4	8	45	521	1	31
	2	6	433	4			27	40	374	2	87
	3		325				13	89	223		7
	4	3	162				8	13	144		7
	5	2	57				2	4	53		4
	6	98	25	2		2	8	22	93		28
	7	17	318				19	38	278		91
	8	21	165				17	140	29		8
	9	166	190	15		3	67	150	136	15	162
	10	30	38				1	30	37		24
	11	291	69	1			18	199	142	2	99
	12	1	29	2			9	13	10		1
	13	1	112				13	67	33		32
	14		15	16			12	18	1		
	15	33	87	4			4	14	106		17
	21	2	11				5	1	7		
	22	28	37				62	3			17
	25	12	2						14		4
	28	1						1			1
	29	3	13				1	4	10	1	2
	30	3	2				2	3			
	31	2		1			1		2		
	33		6				1	3	2		
	34		2				2				
	99	37	82	2		2	74	26	19		13

DEVELOPMENTAL QUALITY

The frequencies of answers to *D* areas vary considerably. In 9 of the 10 figures, however, there are some *D* areas that seem to promote the identification of single objects (*DQo*) with notably high frequencies. This is probably because the areas are relatively discrete and obvious for critical distal features. These 19 areas include *D4* in Card I; *D3* in Card II; *D3* in Card III; *D1* and *D7* in Card IV; *D1* and *D3* in Card VI; *D2, D3,* and *D4* in Card VII; *D1, D2,* and *D4* in Card VIII; *D3* and *D8* in Card IX; and *D1, D2, D3,* and *D7* in Card X. There are 13 *D* areas that seem to have distal properties that encourage synthesis (*DQ+*) answers. Four of these, *D4* in Card I, *D2* in Card VII, *D1* in Card VIII, and *D3* in Card IX also have high frequencies of *DQo* responses, but the remaining nine do not. They include *DS5, D1,* and *D6* in Card II; *D1* and *D9* in Card III; *D1* in Card VII; *D1* in Card IX; and *D9* and *D11* in Card X. Collectively, these 28 areas account for a large proportion of the *D* responses that are given.

FORM QUALITY

An examination of the data by card (Tables 23.7 to 23.26) reveals that minus responses tended to occur to nearly all areas of each figure but somewhat greater frequencies of minus answers were given to specific distal areas in at least 8 of the 10 figures.

Noticeably higher frequencies of minus responses occurred to the *D4* area of Card I, the *D2* and *D3* areas of Card II, the *D7* area of Card III, the *D1* and *D3* areas of Card IV, the *D7* area of Card V, the *D3* and *D4* areas of Card VII, the *D2* and *D4* areas of Card VIII, and the *D9* and *DdS22* areas of Card X. One reason that higher frequencies of minus answers may occur to these areas is that the distal properties of the areas are generally distinctive and/or semidiscrete within the total field and, as such, are likely to provoke added scanning when processing occurs. However, additional scanning does not explain why these areas seem to be easily misidentified. A closer study of the distal features in each of the areas, with regard to the classes of minus answers given to them, is warranted.

BLENDS

The proportions of blends, by card, are not shown in the summary tables in this segment. The frequencies of blend answers, by card and location areas, are shown in Tables 23.7 to 23.26. As might be suspected, the largest proportion of blends in each sample were given mainly to the figures that include color features (Card II = 44%; Card VIII = 33%; Card IX = 29%; Card X = 26%; and Card III = 21%) plus one achromatic figure, Card IV (29%). The responses to the remaining achromatic figures included much lower proportions of blended responses (Card I = 11%; Card V = 14%; Card VI = 9%; and Card VII = 15%).

FREQUENCIES OF DETERMINANTS BY CARD

Table 23.27 Frequencies and Percentages for Determinant Codes for 450 Nonpatients.

Card	F	Human Movement			Animal Movement			Inanimate Movement			Color Codes			Achromatic Color	Texture	Vista	Diffuse Shading	FD	Reflection
		Ma	Mp	Ma-p	FMa	FMp	FMa-p	ma	mp	ma-p	FC	CF	C						
1	587 53.9%	121 11.1%	112 10.3%	13 1.2%	124 11.4%	48 4.4%	0 .0%	4 .4%	12 1.1%	0 .0%	0 .0%	0 .0%	0 .0%	122 11.2%	0 .0%	22 2.0%	37 3.4%	13 1.2%	6 .6%
2	227 21.2%	132 12.3%	94 8.8%	1 .1%	164 15.3%	81 7.6%	0 .0%	156 14.6%	23 2.1%	1 .1%	189 17.7%	294 27.5%	20 1.9%	124 11.6%	11 1.0%	14 1.3%	44 4.1%	59 5.5%	12 1.1%
3	219 23.6%	385 41.5%	88 9.5%	2 .2%	28 3.0%	27 2.9%	1 .1%	5 .5%	29 3.1%	0 .0%	147 15.9%	46 5.0%	17 1.8%	95 10.2%	1 .1%	7 .8%	12 1.3%	29 3.1%	2 .2%
4	334 38.1%	59 6.7%	147 16.8%	0 .0%	55 6.3%	55 6.3%	0 .0%	4 .5%	28 3.2%	0 .0%	0 .0%	0 .0%	0 .0%	58 6.6%	102 11.6%	39 4.4%	63 7.2%	244 27.8%	6 .7%
5	412 51.3%	24 3.0%	37 4.6%	0 .0%	205 25.5%	37 4.6%	0 .0%	0 .0%	7 .9%	0 .0%	0 .0%	0 .0%	0 .0%	116 14.4%	6 .7%	1 .1%	21 2.6%	21 2.6%	6 .7%
6	359 40.3%	11 1.2%	31 3.5%	0 .0%	21 2.4%	16 1.8%	0 .0%	27 3.0%	57 6.4%	0 .0%	0 .0%	0 .0%	0 .0%	27 3.0%	302 33.9%	15 1.7%	82 9.2%	43 4.8%	8 .9%
7	314 33.6%	288 30.8%	183 19.6%	0 .0%	14 1.5%	10 1.1%	0 .0%	13 1.4%	87 9.3%	0 .0%	0 .0%	0 .0%	0 .0%	37 4.0%	4 .4%	16 1.7%	52 5.6%	45 4.8%	11 1.2%
8	241 22.5%	13 1.2%	6 .6%	0 .0%	401 37.4%	43 4.0%	0 .0%	25 2.3%	21 2.0%	1 .1%	291 27.1%	325 30.3%	11 1.0%	39 3.6%	12 1.1%	11 1.0%	37 3.4%	21 2.0%	26 2.4%
9	273 25.1%	171 15.7%	61 5.6%	0 .0%	34 3.1%	28 2.6%	0 .0%	93 8.6%	49 4.5%	1 .1%	240 22.1%	301 27.7%	12 1.1%	30 2.8%	10 .9%	26 2.4%	59 5.4%	86 7.9%	9 .8%
10	593 33.7%	100 5.7%	95 5.4%	0 .0%	311 17.7%	112 6.4%	2 .1%	30 1.7%	34 1.9%	0 .0%	469 26.6%	296 16.8%	16 .9%	74 4.2%	8 .5%	8 .5%	28 1.6%	84 4.8%	4 .2%
Total	3559 33.9%	1304 12.4%	854 8.1%	16 .2%	1357 12.9%	457 4.3%	3 .0%	357 3.4%	347 3.3%	3 .0%	1336 12.7%	1262 12.0%	76 .7%	722 6.9%	456 4.3%	159 1.5%	435 4.1%	645 6.1%	90 .9%

Table 23.28 Frequencies and Percentages for Determinant Codes for 1050 Nonpatients.

		Human Movement				Animal Movement			Inanimate Movement			Color Codes			Achromatic Color	Texture	Vista	Diffuse Shading	FD	Reflection
		F	Ma	Mp	Ma-p	FMa	FMp	FMa-p	ma	mp	ma-p	FC	CF	C						
Card	1	1331 54.6%	309 12.7%	189 7.8%	29 1.2%	277 11.4%	135 5.5%	0 .0%	5 .2%	22 .9%	0 .0%	0 .0%	0 .0%	0 .0%	281 11.5%	0 .0%	50 2.1%	71 2.9%	31 1.3%	13 .5%
	2	437 18.6%	362 15.4%	157 6.7%	1 .0%	410 17.5%	172 7.3%	0 .0%	368 15.7%	46 2.0%	1 .0%	471 20.1%	627 26.7%	37 1.6%	258 11.0%	24 1.0%	25 1.1%	86 3.7%	82 3.5%	21 .9%
	3	477 23.9%	893 44.7%	179 9.0%	3 .2%	50 2.5%	47 2.4%	2 .1%	11 .6%	47 2.4%	0 .0%	317 15.9%	164 8.2%	39 2.0%	186 9.3%	1 .1%	12 .6%	19 1.0%	58 2.9%	9 .5%
	4	872 44.8%	129 6.6%	311 16.0%	0 .0%	108 5.5%	107 5.5%	0 .0%	8 .4%	72 3.7%	0 .0%	0 .0%	0 .0%	0 .0%	144 7.4%	159 8.2%	74 3.8%	119 6.1%	489 25.1%	14 .7%
	5	918 49.4%	47 2.5%	99 5.3%	0 .0%	517 27.8%	110 5.9%	0 .0%	0 .0%	9 .5%	0 .0%	0 .0%	0 .0%	0 .0%	245 13.2%	9 .5%	3 .2%	45 2.4%	35 1.9%	11 .6%
	6	828 39.9%	24 1.2%	55 2.6%	0 .0%	49 2.4%	23 1.1%	0 .0%	64 3.1%	108 5.2%	0 .0%	0 .0%	0 .0%	0 .0%	58 2.8%	779 37.5%	33 1.6%	146 7.0%	111 5.3%	13 .6%
	7	719 34.4%	576 27.5%	430 20.5%	0 .0%	37 1.8%	23 1.1%	0 .0%	30 1.4%	156 7.5%	0 .0%	0 .0%	0 .0%	0 .0%	170 8.1%	29 1.4%	74 3.5%	86 4.1%	90 4.3%	20 1.0%
	8	513 20.6%	23 .9%	8 .3%	0 .0%	791 31.7%	101 4.0%	0 .0%	41 1.6%	46 1.8%	1 .0%	839 33.6%	721 28.9%	23 .9%	97 3.9%	18 .7%	19 .8%	61 2.4%	38 1.5%	50 2.0%
	9	583 23.7%	421 17.1%	126 5.1%	0 .0%	46 1.9%	48 1.9%	0 .0%	205 8.3%	79 3.2%	2 .1%	784 31.8%	567 23.0%	20 .8%	64 2.6%	15 .6%	45 1.8%	143 5.8%	149 6.0%	13 .5%
	10	1594 36.8%	263 6.1%	182 4.2%	0 .0%	742 17.1%	286 6.6%	2 .0%	88 2.0%	58 1.3%	0 .0%	1103 25.5%	635 14.7%	31 .7%	143 3.3%	12 .3%	11 .3%	71 1.6%	292 6.7%	5 .1%
Total		8272 34.4%	3047 12.7%	1736 7.2%	33 .1%	3027 12.6%	1052 4.4%	4 .0%	820 3.4%	643 2.7%	4 .0%	3514 14.6%	2714 11.3%	150 .6%	1646 6.8%	1046 4.4%	346 1.4%	847 3.5%	1375 5.7%	169 .7%

DETERMINANTS

The data presented in Tables 23.27 and 23.28 reveal that Cards I and V are the only figures for which about half of the answers given involve Pure *F*. Interestingly, the lowest proportions of Pure *F* answers were given to Cards II and VIII. Human movement answers appear among responses to each of the 10 figures but occurred with distinctly higher proportions among the responses to Cards III and VII. Interestingly, Card IV is the only figure to which the greater proportion of human movement answers given are *passive*. Animal movement answers also appear among those given to each figure. They appear with the greatest proportions in the responses given to Cards VIII, V, II, and X and least often to Cards VII, III, and IX, in that order. Inanimate movement answers also appear among those given to every figure but the largest proportion of *m* answers appear among those given to Cards II and IX.

Chromatic color answers appear with a considerable frequency among the responses given to each of the five figures that include those distal features. More than half of the answers given to Cards VIII and IX include chromatic color use as do more than 40% of the answers given to Cards II and X. On the other hand, only about one-fourth of the responses given to Card III include chromatic color use. This is probably because of the distal potency of the grey-black *D9* or *D1* areas, which are easily identified as human figures without involving the chromatic areas of the figure. Achromatic color responses also appear among those given to each figure, but most occurred in answers to Cards I, II, III, and V.

The texture determinant was given in more than one-third of the responses to Card VI and more than 10% of the answers to Card IV. It was also given with low frequencies to six of the remaining eight figures, but only once to Card III, and it does not appear at all in the answers given to Card I. The vista determinant appears among responses to all 10 cards, but with notably higher frequencies to Cards IV, VI, VII, and IX, and a very low frequency to Card V. Likewise, determinants representing diffuse shading appear in some responses to all 10 figures, with the greatest proportions among the answers given to Cards IV, VI, and IX, but also with notable frequencies to Cards II and VII. All three types of shading responses, texture, vista, and diffuse, appear with the highest proportions to Cards IV and VI. This suggests that the distal properties of those fields have the greatest variations in saturation levels of any of the 10 figures.

Form dimension answers appear among the responses to each of the 10 cards but with a clearly greater proportion, about one in four, in the answers given to Card IV. Reflection answers also appear among the answers to each of the 10 figures but, generally, with very low frequencies. The highest frequency is to Card VIII, representing about 2% of the responses given to that figure.

FREQUENCIES OF DETERMINANTS BY CARD AND LOCATION

Table 23.29 Card I Determinant Frequencies for 450 Nonpatients (R = 1090).

| Loc | F | Human Movement | | | Animal Movement | | Inanimate Movement | | Achromatic Color | | Vista | | Diffuse Shading | | | Reflection |
		Ma	Mp	Ma-p	FMa	FMp	ma	mp	FC'	C'F	FV	VF	FY	YF	FD	Fr
W	403	58	40	13	118	34	3	11	109	6	7	1	16	11	11	4
1	4	5	4			5		1			1					1
2	42	8			4	5										
3	19					1										
4	41	49	65		1	1	1		2	1	13		6	1	2	
7	17					1			1							
21	3		1			1										
22	1															
23	1															
24	5															
25	1															
26	1															
28	3	1											1			
29	1															
30									2							
31	1		1													
35			1													
99	44				1				1				2			1

502

Table 23.30 Card I Determinant Frequencies for 1050 Nonpatients (R = 2437).

Loc	F	Human Movement			Animal Movement		Inanimate Movement		Achromatic Color		Vista		Diffuse Shading		FD	Reflection	
		Ma	Mp	Ma-p	FMa	FMp	ma	mp	FC'	C'F	FV	VF	FY	YF		Fr	rF
W	843	162	66	29	265	113	4	19	234	33	19	2	29	22	28	7	1
1	8	6	4			7					1					2	
2	130	12	1		6	8		2									
3	71					1											
4	98	126	115		3	2	1	1	3	2	27		12	1	3		
7	53					1			1								
21	4																
22	2																
23	2																
24	15																
25	1																
26	17	1							1								
28	7												1				
29	14																
30	4								4								
31			1														
35			1														1
99	62	2			3	2			3		1		6			2	

Table 23.31 Card II Determinant Frequencies for 450 Nonpatients (R = 1070).

| Loc | F | Human Movement | | | Animal Movement | | Inanimate Movement | | | Color | | | Achromatic Color | | | Texture | Vista | | Diffuse Shading | | | FD | Reflection |
		Ma	Mp	Ma-p	FMa	FMp	ma	mp	ma-p	FC	CF	C	FC'	C'F	C'	FT	FV	VF	FY	YF	Y	FD	Fr
W	20	87	69	1	33	7	17	7	1	80	110	7	61	16	5	5	2	3	4	8		27	8
1	37	16	5		60	32		1		9	21		9	1		3	2		2		1	3	2
2	29	4	6		8	4	3	5		17	9	9					2		3	1		2	
3	66				1	5	5	4		69	20	4					3		4	2		1	
4	10	2	3				1						1	1			1		1			6	
5	37	2	1		62	31	128	1		1	117		3	9					6	2		9	
6	18	12	4				2	4		11	14		14	3		3	1	2	1	3		11	1
7								1															1
22	1	1																					
24	1	2																					
30	1																						
31	1																						
99	6	6	6			2				2	3		1						6				

504

Table 23.32 Card II Determinant Frequencies for 1050 Nonpatients (R = 2344).

Loc	F	Human Movement			Animal Movement		Inanimate Movement			Color			Achromatic Color			Texture	Vista			Diffuse Shading			FD	Reflection
		Ma	Mp	Ma-p	FMa	FMp	ma	mp	ma-p	FC	CF	C	FC'	CF'	C'	FT	FV	VF	V	FY	YF	Y	FD	Fr
W	28	224	94	1	73	12	29	11	1	223	183	7	121	28	5	8	3	5		7	13		39	13
1	46	59	34		228	106		1		78	95	24	24	1		11				7	1	2	4	5
2	51	12	9		17	6	31	5		26	59	6					2			5	3		2	
3	185		1		7	6	16	21		120	47			9		1	4			8			1	
4	19	2	4				1						2	1			2			1			8	
5	68	11	2				274	1		1	211		5	19			2		1	8	13		10	
6	24	19	6		83	37	6	6		17	25		20	6		4	3	3		1	5		17	1
7		2						1																2
22	2	20									1													
24	1																							
30	1																							
31	1																							
99	11	13	7		2	5	11			6	6		5	12						11	1		1	

505

Table 23.33 Card III Determinant Frequencies for 450 Nonpatients (R = 927).

Loc	F	Human Movement			Animal Movement			Inanimate Movement		Color			Achromatic Color		Texture	Vista	Diffuse Shading		FD	Reflection
		Ma	Mp	Ma-p	FMa	FMp	FMa-p	ma	mp	FC	CF	C	FC'	C'F	FT	FV	FY	YF	FD	Fr
W	5	35	15	2	1	4			8	13	17	11	11	1	1	2	4		14	
1	25	305	38		7	6	1	2	4	19	10	1	59	3		2	4	1	12	1
2	39	9	3		7	11			13	9	12	5				1			2	
3	60				7	1			1	101	2									
5	11				2			2			2									
7	34		2			1			1				4			1	1	1	1	
8	2																			
9	11	35	22		5	3		1	2				7			1	1			1
22	1												1							
23	3																			
24					2															
29			2								1									
31	4												1							
32	6		1																	
33	1																			
34			2		1															
35	1																			
99	16	1	3		3	1				5	2		5	3		1				

Table 23.34 Card III Determinant Frequencies for 1050 Nonpatients (R = 1998).

Loc	F	Human Movement			Animal Movement			Inanimate Movement		Color			Achromatic Color		Texture	Vista	Diffuse Shading				Reflection	
		Ma	Mp	Ma-p	FMa	FMp	FMa-p	ma	mp	FC	CF	C	FC'	C'F	FT	FV	FY	YF	Y	FD	Fr	rF
W	9	144	52	3	4	6		1	12	46	115	22	27	1	1	3	4			25	1	1
1	33	684	73		10	13	2	4	5	37	13	2	110	6		4	6	1	1	21	3	
2	118	10	5			19			21	27	22	15									1	
3	125				12	2			2	196	6					2						
5	18				2			5		5	5									7		
7	78		2		4	1		1	1				8				2	1		2		
8	32															1	1					
9	15	50	30		8	5		1	3				14								2	
22	1												2									
23	4																					
24					3																	
29			2								1											
31	7												1									
32	7		2														1					
33	1								3													
34			7		1																	
35	3																					
99	26	5	6		6	1				6	2		10	7		2			2	3	1	

507

Table 23.35 Card IV Determinant Frequencies for 450 Nonpatients (R = 877).

Loc	F	Human Movement		Animal Movement		Inanimate Movement		Achromatic Color		Texture		Vista		Diffuse Shading			FD	Reflection	
		Ma	Mp	FMa	FMp	ma	mp	FC'	C'F	FT	TF	FV	VF	FY	YF	Y		Fr	rF
W	152	53	127	43	34	3	14	35	4	86	5	28	1	23	10	1	222	2	2
1	50	2		2	2			6				1		4			3		
2	15			2	3			2		1		2							
3	30			1	1	1		3	1			1		5	1		1		
4	22		2	1	6		8	2						2	1				
5	3			1	1		1	1						4			1		
6	15		1	1	1		1	1				2		3			1		
7	16	4	15	3	1		1	1		7		2					16		
21	1																		
29	1																		
30	2				1					1									
32	3		1																
33	1																		
99	23		1	2	6		4	1	1	2		4		9				2	

508

Table 23.36 Card IV Determinant Frequencies for 1050 Nonpatients (R = 1948).

		Human Movement		Animal Movement		Inanimate Movement		Achromatic Color		Texture		Vista		Diffuse Shading				Reflection	
Loc	F	Ma	Mp	FMa	FMp	ma	mp	FC'	C'F	FT	TF	FV	VF	FY	YF	Y	FD	Fr	rF
W	401	104	276	83	66	7	52	90	6	133	9	54	2	54	22	1	450	6	5
1	149	2		7	15			8				2		5			7		
2	43			2	4			4				4		2					
3	100				1			18		1		1		6			1		
4	38		5	1	7	1	13	3	2					4	1		2		
5	6			1	1			2				2		6	2		2		
6	27	17	1	8	3		1	5		9		1		4			2		
7	35	6	23	4	2		1	4									25		
10	8																		
21	3		1																
22	1																		
26	1																		
29	1																		
30	5				1					1									
32	6		2																
33	2																		
99	46		3	2	7		5	1	1	3	3	8		12				3	

509

Table 23.37 Card V Determinant Frequencies for 450 Nonpatients (R = 803).

		Human Movement		Animal Movement		Inanimate Movement	Achromatic Color			Texture		Vista	Diffuse Shading			Reflection
Loc	F	Ma	Mp	FMa	FMp	mp	FC'	C'F	C'	FT	TF	FV	FY	YF	FD	Fr
W	291	22	25	182	27	5	107	2	1	3	1		14	2	14	6
1	4	2	3											1	4	
4	28		4	2	2	1	1						2		2	
6	5															
7	31		1		5											
9	3		1													
10	21			17	1										1	
29	1			1												
30			1													
34	2		1										1			
35	10						1									
99	16		1	2	2	1	2	2		2		1		1		

510

Table 23.38 Card V Determinant Frequencies for 1050 Nonpatients (R = 1859).

Loc	F	Human Movement		Animal Movement		Inanimate Movement	Achromatic Color			Texture		Vista	Diffuse Shading		FD	Reflection
		Ma	Mp	FMa	FMp	mp	FC'	C'F	C'	FT	TF	FV	FY	YF	FD	Fr
W	611	44	75	487	92	7	208	4	2	4	2	1	32	2	21	11
1	12	3	6												8	
4	74		7	2	2	1	4						2	1	3	
6	15															
7	71		5	1	9								1			
9	3		1													
10	60			23	4		1								3	
29	1			1												
30			2													
32	10															
34	3		1				1						2			
35	31						5						1			
99	27		2	3	3	1	5	20		3		2	1	3		

Table 23.39 Card VI Determinant Frequencies for 450 Nonpatients (R = 891).

Loc	F	Human Movement		Animal Movement		Inanimate Movement		Achromatic Color		Texture		Vista		Diffuse Shading		FD	Reflection
		Ma	Mp	FMa	FMp	ma	mp	FC'	C'F	FT	TF	FV	VF	FY	YF		Fr
W	96	2	9	8	4	17	39	6	6	125	5	2	1	26	7	22	7
1	28	2	1	2	2	1	11	1	1	166	4			5	6		
2	5					1								1	1		
3	153	1	5	7	1	3	2	4				1		19		3	1
4	14	1	4	1	2	2	3	2		1				2	1	1	
5	4			1				1						2	1		
6			1			2		1				2		1		2	
8	4		5		1	1								1		12	
12							1	1				7					
21	2																
22	2																
23	2	2															
24	9		1	2	4			1									
25	1																
26	1																
27	1				1												
29	4															1	
31	1																
32	5		1	1	1			3						1		1	
33	7		4		1								1	7		1	
99	21	3	4				1				1	1			1		

Table 23.40 Card VI Determinant Frequencies for 1050 Nonpatients (R = 2077).

| Loc | F | Human Movement | | Animal Movement | | Inanimate Movement | | Achromatic Color | | Texture | | Vista | | Diffuse Shading | | FD | Reflection |
		Ma	Mp	FMa	FMp	ma	mp	FC'	C'F	FT	TF	FV	VF	FY	YF		Fr
W	236	5	18	11	6	25	68	11	7	266	8	3	2	42	9	53	10
1	78	2	1	4	2	1	18	1	2	486	15			9	6		
2	23	1				1								2	1		
3	305	2	8	14	1	13	2	16		1		4		32			
4	49	1	5	1	2	20	16	3	2	1				3	24	5	3
5	5						1	3						2	1	2	
6	1		2			2		2						1			
8	17		12		2	1		2				2		1		4	
12	6					1	1	3				20				42	
21	3																
22	2																
23	2	3			2												
24	14			4	4												
25			2	10				1									
26	2																
27	1			3													
29	5																
31	6				1											2	
32	17		1		1			3						1			
33	10		6		2			2		1				10		2	
99	46	10		2			2			1	2	1	1		2	1	

Table 23.41   Card VII Determinant Frequencies for 450 Nonpatients (R = 934).

		Human Movement		Animal Movement		Inanimate Movement		Achromatic Color		Texture	Vista		Diffuse Shading			Reflection
Loc	F	Ma	Mp	FMa	FMp	ma	mp	FC'	C'F	FT	FV	VF	FY	YF	FD	Fr
W	45	229	71	5		8	73	6	15	1	5	3	13	16	36	6
1	18	14	43	1	2	1	5	4		1	1		3			2
2	61	40	51	2	4	2	3	6		1	1		4			3
3	59	2	10	3	4		2	3			1		6	1	1	
4	44	1	2	1		1					1			1	1	
5	3			1			2							1		
6	10					1		2			3		2		1	
7	39							1							1	
8	1		2												4	
9	4		2													
10	5															
21	3															
22	5	1	1	1									1			
23	3		1													
25	2															
28	2															
99	10	1					1			1	1		3	1	1	

514

Table 23.42 Card VII Determinant Frequencies for 1050 Nonpatients (R = 2093).

Loc	F	Human Movement		Animal Movement		Inanimate Movement		Achromatic Color		Texture		Vista		Diffuse Shading			Reflection
		Ma	Mp	FMa	FMp	ma	mp	FC'	C'F	FT	TF	FV	VF	FY	YF	FD	Fr
W	80	409	188	15	5	24	131	63	54	2	12	30	7	23	26	76	8
1	42	20	70	2	3	2	8		11	1		2		4		1	4
2	211	136	145	4	11	2	7	8		10		2		6			8
3	115	4	14	4	4		3	13				2		8	3	2	
4	81	2	2	3		1	1	11		2		22			5	1	
5	5			5			3	1							1		
6	34			1		1		1				5		5		1	
7	70							5								2	
8	2		4					2								6	
9	6		3														
10	6																
21	18																
22	5	1	1				1							1			
23	4		1	1													
25	2																
28	4																
99	34	4	2	2			2	1		2		4		3	1	1	

Table 23.43   Card VIII Determinant Frequencies for 450 Nonpatients (R = 1073).

Loc	F	Human Movement		Animal Movement		Inanimate Movement			Color			Achromatic Color			Texture		Vista		Diffuse Shading			FD	Reflection
		Ma	Mp	FMa	FMp	ma	mp	ma-p	FC	CF	C	FC'	C'F	C'	FT	TF	FV	VF	FY	YF	Y	FD	Fr
W	15	5	3	286	30	3	7	1	158	202	7	3	9	1	4	1	2	2	4	5	2	13	26
1	43			75	5				25	13		1	1		1	1	3	2	2	7		1	
2	36		1		4		1		45	68	2				3	1	3	2	7	7			
3	38											10											
4	45	2		27	1	4	1		12	3	1	6	1		1		1		2	1		1	
5	16	1		4	3	16	10		20	20	1	2								1		2	
6	6			2			1		10	7		1			1				1	1		1	
7	2								11	1													
8	6						1		3	4		1							1	1			
11	1																						
21	2	3		1		2																	
22	1	1																				1	
24	1		1																			1	
25	2								2														
29	2											1											
30	2																						
32	2								2	4		2											
33	5								3	3									2				
99	18	1	1	6													1		2			1	

516

Table 23.44 Card VIII Determinant Frequencies for 1050 Nonpatients (R = 2495).

		Human Movement		Animal Movement		Inanimate Movement			Color			Achromatic Color			Texture		Vista		Diffuse Shading				Reflection
Loc	F	Ma	Mp	FMa	FMp	ma	mp	ma-p	FC	CF	C	FC'	C'F	C'	FT	TF	FV	VF	FY	YF	Y	FD	Fr
W	24	6	4	616	76	3	10	1	454	429	14	6	22	2	7	1	2	2	6	8	4	18	50
1	147			115	10				44	22	2	1	1		2		2	2	5			2	
2	77		1		5		1		169	179	3				3	2	4	8	12	11			
3	68								2			36			1				1			1	
4	73	6		40	4	6	4		18	7	2	11	1		1		2		2	1		7	
5	27	2		4	4	26	28		61	49	2	2								1		2	
6	7			3			1		12	9		2								1			
7	19								65	10					1				1				
8	7				2		2		3	5		1							2	1			
11	2																						
21	2					2																1	
22	3	5	2	1																		1	
24	1	1																					
25						4			4														
26	1																						
29	5											1											
30	5											1											
32	8			1					2	6		3											
33	8								5	5													
99	29	3	1	11								6					1		5			5	

517

Table 23.45 Card IX Determinant Frequencies for 450 Nonpatients (R = 1086).

Loc	F	Human Movement		Animal Movement		Inanimate Movement			Color			Achromatic Color		Texture			Vista			Diffuse Shading			FD	Reflection	
		Ma	Mp	FMa	FMp	ma	mp	ma-p	FC	CF	C	FC'	C'F	FT	TF	T	FV	VF	V	FY	YF	Y	FD	Fr	rF
W	11	8	10	10	11	68	24	1	84	177	9	1	2		1	1	7	2	1	8	20	1	30	3	1
1	50	73	27	5	4		3		9	6	1	1		1						1			5	1	1
2	2	2				6	3		14	26											4		3	1	
3	35	84	6	10	4	14	8		49	29		1		2						3	1		4		
4	13	1	1						7	8										1			2		
5	4						1		2														1		
6	10			2			6		23	26	2			2	1		3	2		1	4		23	1	
8	39		2		2	1			21	5		21					9	1		9			3		
9	24				1	1			4	3										1			1		
11	14		1						4	2										1			1		
12	1	2	1	2					5	5					1								1		
21	5			2					1																
22	13		4						1	2		2											6		
23	1		2										1					1					1		
24	4																								
25	3																								
26	2																								
28	1																								
29	1			1																					
30									1	1													1		
31	4								1																
32							3		1	2															
33	9																								
34	4																								
35	1									1															
99	22	1	6	2	4	3	1		13	8		1		1							4		4	1	

Table 23.46 Card IX Determinant Frequencies for 1050 Nonpatients (R = 2464).

Loc	F	Human Movement		Animal Movement		Inanimate Movement			Color			Achromatic Color		Texture			Vista			Diffuse Shading			FD	Reflection	
		Ma	Mp	FMa	FMp	ma	mp	ma-p	FC	CF	C	FC'	C'F	FT	TF	T	FV	VF	V	FY	YF	Y		Fr	rF
W	16	14	15	15	15	161	49	2	339	336	14	6	4		2	2	13	4	1	21	33	2	74	4	1
1	94	189	41	7	8	1	3		13	11	1	1		1				1		1			7	2	2
2	2					7	4		22	30			1								6		4	1	
3	123	187	31	13	5	27	8		172	59	3	1	1	3						3	6		7		
4	40	1	1						16	19			2							1			2		
5	6						1		3										1	1			2		
6	13		2	3	4	1			34	44	2			2	1	2	5	3		2			29	2	
8	115		2		2	2	8		86	6		39					10	1		52	4		4		
9	29				6	1			10	19										1			2		
11	17		2		1				14	15										1			2		
12	2		1	2					25	7					1						1		1		
21	11	22	2	2					1																
22	34	2	5				2		1	3		3											7		
23	1		2										2					1					2		
24	4																								
25	7																								
26	2																								
28	1			2																					
29	1									1															
30	3								3														1		
31	5								1																
32							3		9	2															
33	12																								
34	8																2								
35	2									1							3								
99	35	2	24	2	7	5	1		35	14		4		1						2	5	1	5	1	

519

Table 23.47 Card X Determinant Frequencies for 450 Nonpatients (R = 1761).

Loc	F	Human Movement		Animal Movement			Inanimate Movement		Color			Achromatic Color			Texture		Vista	Diffuse Shading			FD	Reflection	
		Ma	Mp	FMa	FMp	FMa-p	ma	mp	FC	CF	C	FC'	C'F	C'	FT	T	FV	FY	YF	Y	FD	Fr	rF
W	11	28	9	133	7	2	21	9	115	156	12	5		1	2		3	3	2	1	52	1	1
1	130	3		16	8		1	6	17	15			1		2		1						
2	51			3	46			1	39	21								3	4				
3	86						2		5									1			12		
4	27			6	4				48	3		1											
5	16	2	10						5														
6	8	19	7	1	1			2	2		1								1		13		
7	45	5	2	47	6		1		38	2		1			1				1		1		
8	64	16	29	8	10		1	1	2			12						3				2	
9	34	6	12	8	2			3	78	29	2	7				1	1	2	1	1			
10	9	12	1	1	7			1	15	6		7					1	1	1		1		
11	30			79			3		3			33	2				1		2		3		
12	11			1	12			1	8	1					1								
13	17			1					17	6								1			1		
14	6																1						
15	2	1		3	6		1	4	28	46													
21	3	1		1					4														
22	16	2	10					3	23	8		5	2		1				1		1		
25	4		5					1	3														
28			1		1				1														
29	3		4									2											
30	1		1						1														
33	1	1																					
34	1																	1					
99	17	5	4	3	2			2	17	3	1	2							1				

520

Table 23.48 Card X Determinant Frequencies for 1050 Nonpatients (R = 4327).

Loc	F	Human Movement		Animal Movement			Inanimate Movement		Color			Achromatic Color			Texture		Vista	Diffuse Shading			FD	Reflection	
		Ma	Mp	FMa	FMp	FMa-p	ma	mp	FC	CF	C	FC'	C'F	C'	FT	T	FV	FY	YF	Y	FD	Fr	rF
W	17	43	15	191	13	2	54	17	269	407	20	8		1	4		5	3	3	2	220	1	1
1	459	4		64	9		2	10	27	26	4	1	2		2		1						
2	169	2	4	16	134			2	159	34					1			3	6				
3	262						3		27	2								2			34		
4	79			11	2				68	6													
5	25	5	15	3	8			2	11									3					
6	16	85	13	176	4		1	3	10		2	2									21		
7	117	7	3	16	8		2	3	118			1							2		1		
8	133			13			2		3			19			1			5					
9	61	59	84	1	36		5	2	195	63	3						2	4	4	1		3	
10	20	9	16		2			3	22	6		11	1			2	1	4	1		2		
11	54	18	1	236	14		20	2	5	1		81	2				1	1	19		9		
12	21			1					10	1								1					
13	33			2	44			2	49	13					1								
14	27								3								1	1			1		
15	3			5	9		1	6	56	60													
21	4	1		1					8														
22	22	3	11					3	27	9		5	2		1			2			2		
25	6		5					1	3														
28			1																				
29	7		7		1				1			3											
30	4								1												1		
31	2	1	1						1														
33	2									1								2					
34	2																						
99	49	26	6	6	2			2	30	4	2	4						4	2		1		

521

FREQUENCIES FOR CONTENTS BY CARD

Table 23.49 Frequencies for Content Selections by Card for 450 Nonpatients.

Card	H	(H)	Hd	(Hd)	Hx	A	(A)	Ad	(Ad)	An	Art	Ay	Bl	Bt	Cg	Cl	Ex	Fi	Food	Geo	Hh	Idio	Ls	Na	Sc	Sx	Xy
1	208	65	31	102	2	508	18	92	28	23	21	3		14	133	5		11	1	1		7	4	5	18	5	1
2	138	36	58	21	12	296	8	199	6	38	34	14		9	165	17	6	186	2	5	3	12	17	18	202	22	3
3	446	16	28	20	10	196	11	53	3	74	46	4	84	5	239			24	3		222	43	39	2	40	15	7
4	31	240	17	8	6	156	96	182	3	17	15	7	15	152	68	2	2	4	1	4	14	5	16	10	23	3	5
5	49	9	40	4		602		58	1	9	19	3		13	46			1	1	1	4	1	6	3	12	2	5
6	26	13	29	5	1	126	5	399		12	39	176	1	15	22	4	4	6	4	4	27	6	37	16	94	11	1
7	314	31	152	29	6	122	6	72	4	23	85	20		4	68	33		5	5	14	110	8	58	32	75	11	1
8	7	4	18	17	4	614	2	56	1	95	95	15	1	259	67			5	11	3	17	19	167	49	34	3	4
9	123	113	55	42	2	96	13	136	8	36	57	3	1	174	103	2	66	99	56	10	138	15	31	45	126	5	4
10	88	81	86	29	23	967	32	56	4	68	126	8	6	354	61	8	16	22	35	19	13	36	43	22	115	9	3

Table 23.50 Frequencies for Content Selections by Card for 1050 Nonpatients.

Card	H	(H)	Hd	(Hd)	Hx	A	(A)	Ad	(Ad)	An	Art	Ay	Bl	Bt	Cg	Cl	Ex	Fi	Food	Geo	Hh	Idio	Ls	Na	Sc	Sx	Xy
1	478	108	102	133	3	1259	33	182	50	36	45	3		33	261	10		18	2	3	11	22	6	9	57	9	1
2	366	68	87	26	18	738	16	345	11	71	67	20		14	361	30	12	341	3	7	29	61	27	63	414	43	8
3	1025	26	42	33	13	352	34	135	5	132	97	6	167	32	401		2	63	16		429	119	94	2	66	24	13
4	50	541	33	11	9	321	155	448	7	24	44	9	35	350	158	2	2	9	3	6	43	16	26	17	35	3	10
5	119	27	85	9		1384	2	85	1	13	26	4		75	74	1		2	15	1	5	20	13	7	23	3	8
6	43	39	70	8	2	283	10	902	2	23	72	386	1	29	43	5	10	19	7	6	50	19	111	53	250	22	3
7	717	49	327	52	8	289	12	167	9	60	157	27		6	98	98			12	15	198	79	183	69	108	24	5
8	12	8	31	24	6	1375	5	134	4	220	300	20	7	582	161	1	2	8	17	16	29	74	324	93	58	4	6
9	302	348	107	96	6	157	39	208	18	71	102	5	2	439	189	12	154	182	96	16	390	28	76	86	191	12	7
10	277	159	147	42	30	2368	48	112	10	106	237	15	11	879	159	11	32	56	90	29	21	190	97	45	306	13	3

CONTENTS

As noted, percentages have not been included in Tables 23.49 and 23.50 because nearly one-third of all answers include multiple contents, and proportional data are misleading. Another clarification about the content tables is also necessary. Although the revised sample of 600 nonpatients was published in 2001, most of the protocols included in the sample were collected between 1973 and 1983. During that period, the content codings of *Hx* and *Sc* were not used and most *Sc* answers would have been coded *Idio*. In 1989, about 300 of those records were recoded for *Sc* responses in conjunction with another investigation but approximately 300 were not. Likewise, in 1991 about 150 protocols in that sample were recoded for *Hx*, but all were not. As a consequence, the frequency data in the combined sample for the categories *Hx* and *Sc* are underrepresented and the frequencies for *Idio* are overrepresented. The frequency distributions for these three content categories in the new sample of 450 nonpatients are probably much more representative.

Human contents, except *Hx*, appear among the responses to all 10 cards but the proportions vary considerably. Cards III and VII generate the highest number of human content answers while they appear least frequently to Cards VIII, VI, and V. Anatomy (*An*) responses appear among those given to every figure but occur most often to Cards III and VIII. Blood (*Bl*) responses were given exclusively, with one exception, to the chromatically colored figures and most frequently to Card II. Cloud (*Cl*) content appears among answers given to eight of the cards, most often to Card VII, but never to Cards I and V. Explosion (*Ex*) responses were given to only six cards and most often to Card IX. Fire (*Fi*) responses were given to every card but most often to Cards II and IX. Likewise, Food (*Fd*) answers appear among those given to every card, but much more frequently to Card IX.

FREQUENCIES OF CONTENTS BY CARD AND LOCATION

Table 23.51 Card I Content Frequencies for 450 Nonpatients (R = 1090).

Loc	H	(H)	Hd	(Hd)	Hx	A	(A)	Ad	(Ad)	An	Art	Ay	Bt	Cg	Cl	Fi	Food	Geo	Hh	Idio	Ls	Na	Sc	Sx	Xy
W	69	54	3	86	1	415	13	63	26	16	16	2	9	59	5	9	1		2	6	3	4	10		1
1	2		7			2		5					1	4							1				
2	2	7		2		37	5	5				1	2	4				1	1						
3			12			4		2					1											2	
4	135		3			19					2			64		2									
7						11		7																	
21				1	1	4																			
22			1																						
23											1													1	
24								1															5		
25																									
26		1																							
28			1	1									1												
29								3						2											
30		2																					1		
31																				1					
35			1																						
99		1	3	12		16		6	2	7	2											1	2	2	

Table 23.52 Card I Content Frequencies for 1050 Nonpatients (R = 2437).

Loc	H	(H)	Hd	(Hd)	Hx	A	(A)	Ad	(Ad)	An	Art	Ay	Bt	Cg	Cl	Fi	Food	Geo	Hh	Idio	Ls	Na	Sc	Sx	Xy
W	190	90	8	111	2	1006	25	137	47	27	33	2	24	122	10	16	2		10	14	5	6	16		1
1	2		8			3		8					2	6							1				
2	4	11		2		114	8	11			4	1	4	7											
3			62			5		3					1					3	1						
4	281		14			49		9			3			121		2								2	
7						46																			
21						5																			
22			2																						
23				1	1						2													2	
24																				2			13		
25								1																	
26		2												1						5		1	9		
28			2	2				5					1	4											
29																							14		
30		4																							
31								1					1							1					
35			1																						
99	1	1	5	17		29		7	3	9	3											2	5	5	

Table 23.53 Card II Content Frequencies for 450 Nonpatients (R = 1070).

Loc	H	(H)	Hd	(Hd)	Hx	A	(A)	Ad	(Ad)	An	Art	Ay	Bl	Bt	Cg	Cl	Ex	Fi	Food	Geo	Hh	Idio	Ls	Na	Sc	Sx	Xy
W	112	29	21	12	8	51	1	12	3	15	18	2	33	2	123	6		58	1		6	5	2	11	21	6	1
1	12				2	63	3	75		1			18		16			5		3				2			
2		4	8	6		9	3	32	3	1	3	1	13	3	3	1	4	5		2		4	1		1	1	
3			6	1		125		3		8	5	1	13		1		1	4				1				5	
4	1		7							1		5			1						1		2		9	5	
5	1		2		1	1					2	4			3	7					3	1	2	4	163	1	
6	7	1	2			43	1	71		9	3	1	7	3	16	3	1	111	1			1	8	1	6	2	1
7					1	1												3									
22	1		2	1						1	1												1				
24			1								1															1	
30				1																							
31								1						1													
99	4	2	9			3		5		2	1			1	2						1		1		2	1	1

Table 23.54 Card II Content Frequencies for 1050 Nonpatients (R = 2344).

Loc	H	(H)	Hd	(Hd)	Hx	A	(A)	Ad	(Ad)	An	Art	Ay	Bl	Bt	Cg	Cl	Ex	Fi	Food	Geo	Hh	Idio	Ls	Na	Sc	Sx	Xy
W	248	46	34	15	11	132	3	16	3	23	32	2	49	2	259	9		77	1		12	6	2	23	34	14	2
1	79	2			4	218	6	173	2	2	1		56		58			9		3	4	34		2	10	1	3
2		13	12	8		18	5	48	6	5	4	1	31	5	8	1	7	52		4		4	2	16	2	1	
3			10	1		287		4		21	16	2	17		1		1	14			1	2	3		2	12	
4	2		9							2	1	9			2						2	1			11	7	
5	1	1	2		1	2					4	4			3	14	4	183			8	11	4	18	328	3	
6	11	3	2			54	2	91		14	4	2	12	5	24	6		6	2			2	13	2	12	2	1
7					2	2																					
22	19		2	1		18		1		1	1												1				
24			1								1															2	
30				1																							
31								1																			
99	6	3	15			7		11		3	3		2	2	6						2	1	2	2	15	1	2

Table 23.55 Card III Content Frequencies for 450 Nonpatients (R = 927).

Loc	H	(H)	Hd	(Hd)	Hx	A	(A)	Ad	(Ad)	An	Art	Ay	Bl	Bt	Cg	Fi	Food	Hh	Idio	Ls	Na	Sc	Sx	Xy
W	43	5	10	2	4	9	2	5	2	5	19	3	4		25	10	1	22	1	3		4	5	
1	334	6	4	3	2	32	6	14		8	13	1	10	3	120	11		188	39	36	1	14	6	
2	8	1	2	2	1	31	1	8		10	6		1		2			1				10		
3			1		1	83	1	1		24	2			1	52	2						3	2	
5						8																5		
7			3	8		1		8		21	1				2									6
8								2																1
9	57	3			2	17	1			1	3				27	1	1	7	2			4	1	
22						1																		
23						3											1							
24										1	1										1			
29	1									1	1													
31			2	1				5							3									
32			1																					
33										1														
34	1			1		1									1			1	1					
35	1																							
99	1	1	5	3		10		9	1	2				1	7			3					1	

528

Table 23.56 Card III Content Frequencies for 1050 Nonpatients (R = 1998).

Loc	H	(H)	Hd	(Hd)	Hx	A	(A)	Ad	(Ad)	An	Art	Ay	Bl	Bt	Cg	Ex	Fi	Food	Hh	Idio	Ls	Na	Sc	Sx	Xy
W	182	7	16	6	6	20	2	6		8	60	5	8		53		43	9	54	33	5		9	7	
1	743	8	4	4	3	50	7	21	3	11	17	1	25	8	164		13	4	353	68	88	1	20	8	
2	11	1	4	4	1	88	1	12		22	9		2	17	6		1		2	8	1		17	3	
3			1		1	128	22	2		50	4			3	125								6		
5						13		3						1									9		
7			3	9		1		41		32	2				3		5			4					10
8								32																	1
9	79	5			2	26	2			1	3				35		1	2	12	2			5	4	
22						2																			
23						4												1							
24										2	1											1			
29	1									1	1														
31			2	2				6							4					2					
32			2																						
33						1				2					1										
34	2	3		2															2	2					
35	2		1																						
99	5	2	9	6		19		12	2	3				3	10	2			6					2	2

Table 23.57   Card IV Content Frequencies for 450 Nonpatients (R = 877).

Loc	H	(H)	Hd	(Hd)	Hx	A	(A)	Ad	(Ad)	An	Art	Ay	Bt	Cg	Cl	Ex	Fi	Food	Geo	Hh	Idio	Ls	Na	Sc	Sx	Xy
W	23	207		5	5	107	88	59	3	6	11	3	131	33	2		2	1		11	3	5	7	12	1	2
1		1	2			11		36		6	1	2	4	1							2	2		2	1	
2						6		7					1	10					1			2				
3			2		1	3	1	24		3		1	5	2		1						1				
4	1		2			5		31			1	1	5							1		2	1	5		2
5						5		2		1			1									1		1		
6		1		1		1		3					1	13					2	1		1	1	1		
7	5	30				5	7	2						4												2
21			1																							
29			1											1												
30			2					1			1															
32			1					3																		
33																								1		
99	1	1	6	2		13		14		1	1		4	4		1	2		1	1		2	1	1	1	1

Table 23.58 Card IV Content Frequencies for 1050 Nonpatients (R = 1948).

Loc	H	(H)	Hd	(Hd)	Hx	A	(A)	Ad	(Ad)	An	Art	Ay	Bt	Cg	Cl	Ex	Fi	Food	Geo	Hh	Idio	Ls	Na	Sc	Sx	Xy
W	36	467		7	7	226	139	110	5	8	37	4	312	73	2		6	2		17	3	7	11	18	1	4
1	2	1	3			42		117	1	6	1	2	9	1						3	12	2		3	1	
2						6		10					1	40					2	1		2				
3						4		103	1	4			8	3		1		1				1				
4	2	2	2		2	7	1	46			2	1	8	1						1		4	1	9		
5			6			5		3		2		2	3									2		1		
6		18		2		5	2	7					3	26					3	17	1	4	4	1		4
7	9	52				8	13	3						7						1						
10								8																		
21			4																							
22														1										1		
26			1																							
29			1							1	1															
30			3					3																		
32			2					6																		
33										1														1		
99	1	1	11	2		18		32		2	3		6	6		1	3		1	3		4	1	1	1	2

Table 23.59 Card V Content Frequencies for 450 Nonpatients (**R** = 803).

Loc	H	(H)	Hd	(Hd)	A	Ad	(Ad)	An	Art	Ay	Bt	Cg	Fi	Food	Geo	Hh	Idio	Ls	Na	Sc	Sx	Xy
W	46	7	1		545	6		7	10	3	2	42	1	1	1	3		1	3	3		4
1			7			2					5									1		
4	2	1	14	4	4	11	1		8		1					1		4				
6					2															3		
7	1	1			33	1		1	1			2								1		
9			2			1						1								2		
10					4	30					3						1					
29					2																1	
30			1																			
34			1			1																
35			9			2														1		
99			5		12	4		1			2	1						1			1	1

Table 23.60   Card V Content Frequencies for 1050 Nonpatients (R = 1859).

Loc	H	(H)	Hd	(Hd)	A	(A)	Ad	(Ad)	An	Art	Ay	Bt	Cg	Cl	Fi	Food	Geo	Hh	Idio	Ls	Na	Sc	Sx	Xy
W	112	14	1		1269		10		10	11	4	4	70	1	2	2	1	3	1	3	6	8		6
1			17				4					11				1		1	12	7	1	1		
4	4	1	22	9	4		18	1		13		2	2			12			4			2		
6					4		18					1							4			6		
7	2	12	2		67	2	2		1	2		1	2									1		
9			1				1						1									1	1	
10			1		8		41					35							3	1		2		
29					2																			
30			2																					
32					10							2										2		
34			1				1																	
35			30				2					20										2	2	2
99	1		9		20		6		2			20	1					1		2			2	2

533

Table 23.61 Card VI Content Frequencies for 450 Nonpatients (R = 891).

Loc	H	(H)	Hd	(Hd)	Hx	A	(A)	Ad	(Ad)	An	Art	Ay	Bl	Bt	Cg	Cl	Ex	Fi	Food	Geo	Hh	Idio	Ls	Na	Sc	Sx	Xy
W	12	3	2		1	55	5	155	1	2	25	33	1	4	10	3	2	3	1		11	1	13	10	62		
1	1	1	1			10		193		3	2			3					1	3	9	1		1	1	2	1
2						1					1										3			1	3	2	
3	3	3	2	1		33		21			4	126		5	6	1					1				8	2	
4	3		7	2		2		5		2	2			1	3		2	2				1	1		11		
5						3				2	1			1								1	1	1	2		
6	1											1			1							1	2		2		
8	3	2	4			4					3	12			1						1		11	1	1	4	
12											1							1					2				
21			2					2																			
22			3					2																			
23								2														1	2				
24						4		5		5																	
25		1																									
26																											
27			1					1															1				
29			2	2				1																			
31						1																					
32	1					1								1	1				2	1	2		2	1	2	1	
33			1			3		2															2	1	2	2	
99	2	3	4			9		10				4															

Table 23.62 Card VI Content Frequencies for 1050 Nonpatients (R = 2077).

Loc	H	(H)	Hd	(Hd)	Hx	A	(A)	Ad	(Ad)	An	Art	Ay	Bl	Bt	Cg	Cl	Ex	Fi	Food	Geo	Hh	Idio	Ls	Na	Sc	Sx	Xy
W	19	8	2		2	176	10	220	1	3	41	60	1	11	19	3	3	7	2		19	7	36	16	159	2	1
1	1	1	1			16		571		3	3			4	1	1			1	4	10	1		1	1	2	
2						4		2			1			1							6	1		1	10	3	
3	8	8	3	2		43		34	1	1	6	269		8	12	1	7	11			10	2	1		14	3	
4	4		34	4		4		7			11			1	3							1		29	46		
5						3				3	3			2									1	1	3		
6	2		6			6					5	2			2			1			1	2	4		2		
8	4	11				5		1		1	2	50			4						2		48	1	1	6	
12																							12				
21								3																			
22								2																			
23			3					4																			
24			4			4		9						1	1					1		1	2				
25		2						10																			
26								2		12																	
27			1	2				3																			
29			3																				2				
31	1		2			3						5													2	1	
32						1																3	3	2	3	2	
33			2			3		2													2		2	2	9	3	
99	4	9	9			15		32						1	1				4	1							2

535

Table 23.63 Card VII Content Frequencies for 450 Nonpatients (R = 934).

Loc	H	(H)	Hd	(Hd)	Hx	A	(A)	Ad	(Ad)	An	Art	Ay	Bt	Cg	Cl	Fi	Food	Geo	Hh	Idio	Ls	Na	Sc	Sx	Xy
W	265	21	11	7	5	10	1	1		8	43	2	2	42	29	4	4	9	84	6	46	25	65	1	1
1	8	1	55	4	1	8		5		1	22	1		4	1				1	1	1		1	1	
2	32	5	55	7		50	3	10	1		11	2		6	1			1	1		1				
3	1	1	11	9		16	1	45	3	1	2			3	1			1	1			1			
4	2		2	1		27	1	4		8			1	4	1					1	2	3	4	3	
5								2		1			1									1			
6		2	3			1				3						1			1	1	1	3		4	
7			4			1		1			2	15		5					16		3	1	3		
8	2																								
9			2	1							1							2	1						
10		1	1							1	1								3					1	
21			2			2								1							1				
22	2		1			3		2			1			2			1	1			2				
23			1			1																			
25			1			1																			
28			1																					1	
99	2		5			2		2			2			1				1	3		1	1	2	1	

Table 23.64 Card VII Content Frequencies for 1050 Nonpatients (R = 2093).

Loc	H	(H)	Hd	(Hd)	Hx	A	(A)	Ad	(Ad)	An	Art	Ay	Bt	Cg	Cl	Fi	Food	Geo	Hh	Idio	Ls	Na	Sc	Sx	Xy
W	546	32	19	11	6	20	5	14		13	93	3	2	56	79	6	11	10	131	67	134	57	93	2	1
1	18	3	90	7	2	13		13		1	28	1		7	2					1	2		1		
2	137	9	160	16		157	5	29			22	3		13	12				2	2	5				
3	1	2	17	14		24	1	84	5	2	4			5	3			1	12						
4	3		2	2		50	1	9	4	10				7	2	1				7	25	3	7	3	3
5						3		4		1															
6		2	10			2		1					2						2	1	1	3		14	1
7			8			2		1		21	2	20	1	5					41			2			
8	4			2		1							1								5	2	3		
9			3							1	2							2	2						
10			2			2		1		1	2								3					1	
21			6			3								1				1			7		1		
22	2	1	6			1		3			2			2			1				2				
23			1			1																			
25			1			1																		1	
28			1																					1	
99	6		7			9		8		10	2			2				1	5	1	2	2	3	2	

537

Table 23.65 Card VIII Content Frequencies for 450 Nonpatients (R = 1073).

Loc	H	(H)	Hd	(Hd)	Hx	A	(A)	Ad	(Ad)	An	Art	Ay	Bl	Bt	Cg	Cl	Ex	Fi	Food	Geo	Hh	Idio	Ls	Na	Sc	Sx	Xy
W	4	3	4	11	4	335	2	7		21	68	7		192	6	1	2	4	5	1	4	7	107	45	6	1	3
1			1			132		1						32	32				1		1	4	10	1			
2		1	1	2		27		21		7	9		1	18					3	2	1	1	33	1	1	1	
3			1			2				44		1										1					
4	1		1			59		6	1	5	2	1		4	4			1	1		9	1	7		10		
5			1			20		1		1	8	3			15						1	5	1		13		1
6			1			6		1		6	6			8	4				1		1		2				
7						9		4															1				
8			1			2		1		5		2		1	1						1		2	1		1	1
11										1																	
21										2																	
22			4			2		1						1									1		2		
24	1		1					1																			
25								2																			
29			1																						2		
30						2																					
32						4																					
33			3			3		5		1	1			3									1	1			
99	1		3	4		11		4		2	1	1			5								2				

538

Table 23.66 Card VIII Content Frequencies for 1050 Nonpatients (R = 2495).

Loc	H	(H)	Hd	(Hd)	Hx	A	(A)	Ad	(Ad)	An	Art	Ay	Bl	Bt	Cg	Cl	Ex	Fi	Food	Geo	Hh	Idio	Ls	Na	Sc	Sx	Xy
W	7	4	6	16	6	770	4	9	2	81	243	10	4	453	9	1	2	6	8	2	8	22	214	66	8	2	3
1						288		1						49					1		2	5	11	1			
2		1	3			96	1	46		9	16		3	56	91				5	14	1	1	69	22	6	1	
3			1	2		2		5		100		1										1					
4	2	3	1			92		9	1	5	3	3		7	8			2	1		15	6	16		13		
5						27		1		2	27	3			27							39	1		22		
6			1			7		1		9	8			9	4				1		1		2			1	1
7						44		35						2	13								2				
8			1			2		1		5		2		1	1						1		2				
11										2														2			2
21										2				1									1		2		
22			7			4		1						1													
24	1		2					1																			
25								4																			
26								1																			
29			1																1		1						
30						2		3																1	4		
32						10		1		1	2			4											3		
33						5		8			1												1	1			
99	2		8	6		26		7		4		1			8								5				

Table 23.67 Card IX Content Frequencies for 450 Nonpatients (R = 1086).

Loc	H	(H)	Hd	(Hd)	Hx	A	(A)	Ad	(Ad)	An	Art	Ay	Bl	Bt	Cg	Cl	Ex	Fi	Food	Geo	Hh	Idio	Ls	Na	Sc	Sx	Xy
W	5	7	5	15	1	15	4	7	3	9	38	3	1	113	18	7	62	56	7	3	43	6	20	26	11		2
1	98	3	5		1	19		39	1	3	1			3	17				2	4	36	1	1	1	47		
2		2	1	4		4					4			22	1		1	6	1			1	3	5			
3	15	84		5		18	6	18	3	1	4			2	50		2	30	6		1	4	1	1	30		
4	1		11					5		1	1			2					10						1		
5		11				2	1			1	1							1					1		1		
6			7			7		4		5	2			11	5			1	24		5	1			4	2	
8			1	2		5		23		5	1			5	6			3			38	1	1	2	10		
9						2		1		3	2			6							6				16		
11			2			11				4				1	2	1	1			1				1	1		
12	1	1				2	2				1			2	1			2	3				2	1			
21			2	12				4																			
22			3	1				6						2							2				1		
23			1					1														1					
24			1			1		3											1								
25								2																			
26			1																								
28			1																								
29						1									1								1		1		
30	1			1				1			1																
31																									1		
32			3					8																4			
33								4																			
34			1			1																					
35			2																							2	
99	2	5	8	2		8		10	1	4	1			5	2				2	2	7		1	4	2	1	2

Table 23.68 Card IX Content Frequencies for 1050 Nonpatients (R = 2464).

Loc	H	(H)	Hd	(Hd)	Hx	A	(A)	Ad	(Ad)	An	Art	Ay	Bl	Bt	Cg	Cl	Ex	Fi	Food	Geo	Hh	Idio	Ls	Na	Sc	Sx	Xy
W	6	13	14	29	5	23	9	12	4	15	75	5	2	337	27	10	148	104	11	6	75	8	40	50	12		4
1	228	3	10		1	38	7	57	4	3	1			6	25			1	2	6	137	2	1	2	66		
2		4	1			5									1		1	8	1		1	1	3	7			
3	23	301		5		34	18	24	4	2	4			30	71		3	60	8		2	11	2	1	64		
4			37	22				7	1	1	8			5					20						1		
5	2					2				3	1			12									2		1		
6	1	17	10			10	1	6	1	8	2			15	7	1	1	1	42		8	1	1	3	6	2	
8			1	4		7		31	1	5	2			6	33						146	2			13	1	1
9						3		6		18	2			8		1	1	4			7				20		
11			3			15				7	2			2	14				5	2				2	1		
12	21	1				3	4				2			2	2			2	3				21	1			
21			7					7																			
22			3	32				8	1					3													
23			1	1				1		2												1			2		
24			1					3															2				
25						1		4							1												
26			1																						1		
28			1																							3	
29						2		2						2					2								
30	1			1							1												1		1		
31			3																								
32								19																4			
33			1			1		7																			
34			1																								
35			2											1												4	
99	20	9	10	2		13		14	2	7	2			10	8			1	2	2	12	2	3	16	3	2	2

Table 23.69 Card X Content Frequencies for 450 Nonpatients (R = 1761).

Loc	H	(H)	Hd	(Hd)	Hx	A	(A)	Ad	(Ad)	An	Art	Ay	Bl	Bt	Cg	Ex	Fi	Food	Geo	Hh	Idio	Ls	Na	Sc	Sx	Xy
W	10	8	6	9	10	184	16	4	1	2	64	2	1	156	10	15	11	3		4	3	18	6	16		2
1				1		165	1	1			3			10	1	1		2			1	1	8			
2				1		120	2	1	2	3	1			4	1			15					2	6		
3		1						3		14	6			33						1	3			37		
4			1			6	1	2		1				1										1		
5	15	2				78		15						1	2											
6	25	1	2			1	2		1	3	1	1			6		1	1		1		16	1	1	3	
7	2		1			3								3	1								1			
8		7		2	1	109	4	2		3	1			1							1	1		1	1	1
9	12	41	3	2	2	81	2	5		20	2	3	5	4	31			8	13	2	9	4	3	3	1	
10	16	4	4			52	2	7		1	8			3	1					1	1	1		9		
11		8	1	1		90	2	3		16	9	3		58							13			29		
12						15		1						4							1					
13						25		1						13												
14										1	1							4	5	3	1	2		6		
15						16								56			10							2		
21			1			1		3				1		4	1					1				1	1	
22	3	1	38	7	3					2	22				2					1				1		
25			7	4	1						3							1	1		1					
28				1																						
29	1	6	1			1		1		1	3	1			1									1		
30			1											2				1								
33			1		1													1								
34										3														1		
99	4	2	19	1	5	10		7		3	3			1	4						2		1		3	

Table 23.70 Card X Content Frequencies for 1050 Nonpatients (R = 4327).

Loc	H	(H)	Hd	(Hd)	Hx	A	(A)	Ad	(Ad)	An	Art	Ay	Bl	Bt	Cg	Ex	Fi	Food	Geo	Hh	Idio	Ls	Na	Sc	Sx	Xy
W	19	12	12	14	16	309	23	5	1	4	152	5	2	393	14	31	37	5		5	73	22	14	29		2
1						547		3		1	3			25		1		3			2	1	16			
2	4		2	1		357	2	2		4	1			8	3			49			3		4	13		
3		2		1		19	2	3	2	19	8			101	1			6		1	33			137		
4			3			153		4		1				1				1						1		
5	25	2				2	2	23	5						4											
6	96	3	5			7				4	3	2		2	23		1	2		2	1	62	2	2	2	
7	3		1		1	318	5		2	1				16	2			1					2		4	
8	82	10		3	3	164	5	4		32	3	1	9	2										2		
9	23	86	6	2		89	3	28		1	9			8	88		5	14	19	3	25	4	5	4	2	
10		6	10			15	2	8						6	1					1	2	1		15	1	
11		14	1	1		254	4	4		26	13	3		179							33			74		1
12						25		2						5							1					
13						66		2						28				5	9		2					
14	1					2				2		2					13			5	3	4				
15		1				25					1			91							2			20		
21			2	7	3	1				4		1		7	1				1					3	1	
22	5		47	5	1						27				4			2		2	1			1		
25			9	1							4													1		
28		11										1														
29	2		1	1		1					6				1			2		2				2		
30														3												
31			1											3										2		
33			2		1																					
34																										
99	17	12	44	6	5	14		18		6	7			1	17						8	1	2	3	3	

SUMMARY

The model used to present these data sets is fairly general and leaves many questions unanswered about specific types of responses to specific areas of the various cards. Nonetheless, the data seem to have usefulness as presented in that they highlight some of the most distinctive features, or critical distal bits, in each of the figures. Many of the findings among the several data sets are not surprising, especially those involving high frequencies or percentages. The low frequency data are also intriguing as they tend to identify characteristics of more unusual answers that are given to each of the cards.

Obviously, the data are amenable to much more precise forms of analysis. A study of first responses to each of the cards in the context of location plus determinant(s) and content(s) should contribute more information regarding the potency of the distal features in each of the figures. Likewise, a more systematic review of minus and unusual answers in a similar context of locations plus determinants and contents may contribute information that can enhance or refine interpretive guidelines concerning those types of answer. Optimally, such analyses will be accomplished as the size of the new nonpatient sample becomes sufficient to use as the baseline group in addressing such issues more directly and to undertake comparisons of nonpatient responses with those of patients from various groups.

REFERENCES

Attneave, F. (1954). Some informational aspects of visual perception. *Psychological Review, 61,* 183–193.

Baughman, E. E. (1959). An experimental analysis of the relationship between stimulus structure and behavior in the Rorschach. *Journal of Projective Techniques, 23,* 134–183.

Beck, S. J. (1933). Configurational tendencies in Rorschach responses. *American Journal of Psychology, 45,* 433–443.

Beck, S. J. (1945). *Rorschach's Test: Vol. 2. A variety of personality pictures.* New York: Grune & Stratton.

Dubrovner, R. J., VonLackum, W. J., & Jost, H. (1950). A study of the effect of color on productivity and reaction time in the Rorschach Test. *Journal of Clinical Psychology, 6,* 331–336.

Exner, J. E. (1959). The influence of chromatic and achromatic color in the Rorschach. *Journal of Projective Techniques, 23,* 418–425.

Exner, J. E. (1961). Achromatic color in Cards IV and VI of the Rorschach. *Journal of Projective Techniques, 25,* 38–40.

Exner, J. E. (1989). Searching for projection in the Rorschach. *Journal of Personality Assessment, 53,* 520–536.

Exner, J. E. (1996). Critical bits and the Rorschach response process. *Journal of Personality Assessment, 67,* 464–477.

Exner, J. E. (2003). *The Rorschach: A Comprehensive System: Vol. 1. Basic foundations and principles of interpretation* (4th ed.). Hoboken, NJ: Wiley.

Frank, L. K. (1939). Projective methods for the study of personality. *Journal of Psychology, 8,* 389–413.

Grayson, H. M. (1956). Rorschach productivity and card preferences as influenced by experimental variation of color and shading. *Journal of Projective Techniques, 20,* 288–296.

Hochberg, J. (1988). Visual perception. In R. C. Atkinson, R. J. Herrnstein, G. Lindzey, & R. D. Luce (Eds.), *Stevens' handbook of experimental psychology* (2nd ed., Vol. 1, pp. 195–276). New York: Wiley.

Hochberg, J., & McAlister, E. (1953). A quantitative approach to figural "goodness." *Journal of Experimental Psychology, 46,* 361–364.

Meer, B. (1955). The relative difficulty of the Rorschach cards. *Journal of Projective Techniques, 19,* 43–53.

Perlman, J. A. (1951). Color and the validity of the Rorschach 8-9-10 percent. *Journal of Consulting Psychology, 15,* 122–126.

Peterson, C. A., & Schilling, K. M. (1983). Card pull in projective testing. *Journal of Personality Assessment, 47,* 265–275.

Ranzoni, J. H., Grant, M. Q., & Ives, V. (1950). Rorschach "card pull" in a normal adolescent population. *Journal of Projective Techniques, 14,* 107–133.

Silva, D. (2002). The effect of color on the productivity in Card X of the Rorschach. *Rorschachiana, 25,* 123–138.

Weiner, I. B. (1998). *Principles of Rorschach interpretation.* Mahwah, NJ: Erlbaum.

Author Index

Achenbach, T. M., 348, 365
Ackerman, S. J., 194, 212
Acklin, M. W., 33, 34, 51, 325, 343
Adrian, C., 173, 190
Ainsworth, M. D., 19, 26, 30, 52
Albert, S., 416, 417, 439
Alexander, G., 33, 34, 51, 325, 343
Allison, R. B., 126, 147
Alperin, R. J., 283, 302
Alpher, V. S., 193, 194, 212, 259, 277
Alterman, A. I., 194, 212, 213
American Psychiatric Association, 20, 25, 82,
    99, 125, 147, 172, 190, 283, 301, 369, 387
American Psychological Association, 19, 25
Andersen, R., 82, 99
Andersen, T. J., 59, 79
Andronikof-Sanglade, A., 13, 17
Angold, A., 349, 365
Appelbaum, S. A., 57, 58, 78
Arbisi, P. A., 326, 343, 418, 439
Arceneaux, J. M., 20, 21, 26
Archer, R. P., 12, 17, 23, 26, 59, 79, 349, 350,
    365, 393, 411
Armstrong, J. G., 126, 147, 391, 392, 411
Aron, L., 32, 52
Attneave, F., 480, 544
Auerbach, S. N., 32, 52
Auslander, L. A., 103, 121

Baekeland, F., 193, 212
Baer, R. A., 418, 439
Bagby, R. M., 33, 34, 52, 53, 441, 447, 453, 462
Baity, M. R., 5, 18, 23, 26, 283, 284, 301, 393,
    412
Ball, J. D., 349, 365
Barach, P., 126, 127, 128, 147
Barison, F., 217, 235
Bash, K. W., 33, 52

Baughman, E. E., 479, 544
Bauman, G., 217, 234
Beck, A., 349, 365
Beck, A. T., 58, 78, 350, 365
Beck, S. J., 3, 19, 25, 30, 52, 479, 544
Belter, R. W., 349, 366
Belyi, B. I., 103, 121
Benjamin, L. S., 217, 234, 284, 301
Benn, A. F., 285, 302
Ben-Porath, Y. S., 418, 439
Beres, D., 172, 190
Berg, M., 58, 79
Berger, D., 31, 52
Bernat, E., 325, 343
Bernstein, E. M., 127, 147
Berry, D. T., 418, 439
Bihlar, B., 24, 26
Bilett, J. L., 391, 411
Binder, H., 30, 52
Bitter, E. J., 283, 302
Blais, M. A., 23, 26
Blake, S. E., 217, 218, 234
Blanchard, W. H., 217, 234
Blatt, S. J., 34, 52, 57, 78
Blondheim, S. H., 285, 302
Bloom, R., 412
Boik, R. J., 392, 412
Bokhoven, P., 412
Braff, D., 103, 121, 172, 190
Brager, R. C., 349, 366
Braun, B. G., 126, 147
Bray, M., 369, 387
Brickman, A., 392, 412
Bridges, M. R., 285, 302
Buchsbaum, M., 412
Buis, T., 447, 462
Burke, W. F., 217, 234
Burns, B., 5, 17, 34, 52

Butcher, J. N., 284, 301, 326, 343, 447, 462
Butler, S., 193, 213

Caddell, J. M., 429, 439
Cadenhead, K., 172, 190
Caldwell, A. B., 24, 26
Carlisle, A. L., 442, 463
Carlson, C. F., 59, 78
Carlson, E. B., 127, 147
Carlsson, A. M., 24, 26, 168, 325, 343
Carp, A. L., 415, 439, 441, 462
Carpenter, W., 171, 190
Carter, C. L., 349, 365
Castlebury, F. D., 23, 26, 195, 213
Chafouleas, S., 370, 387
Christiansen, E., 387
Cipolli, C., 193, 213
Clark, E., 387
Clemence, A. J., 194, 212
Clements, C., 370, 387
Cleveland, S. E., 205, 213
Cohen, J., 470, 474, 477
Cohen, L., 82, 99
Colson, D. B., 57, 58, 78
Coolidge, F., 371, 387
Coonerty, S., 194, 213
Coons, P., 147
Cornell, D. G., 371, 387, 392, 412
Costello, E. J., 348, 365
Cruise, K. R., 305, 321

Dacey, C. M., 349, 365
Dahlstrom, W., 284, 301
Dam, H., 59, 79
Darby, J., 240, 255
Davis, P., 33, 52
de Almeida, M. M., 168
de Carvalho, L. B., 151, 168
DeCato, C. M., 194, 212
Deitsch, S. M., 415, 439
DenBoer, J., 371, 387
de Ruiter, C., 82, 99
Diamond, D., 194, 213
Dies, R. R., 26
Dill, P., 147
Docherty, J., 171, 190
Dougherty, R. J., 193, 213
Drob, S. L., 127, 147
Dubrovner, R. J., 479, 544
Dusky v. United States, 304, 321

Eagle, P., 127, 147
Easton, K., 415, 439

Ebner, D. L., 240, 255
Eddy, S., 57, 79
Edman, G., 343
Elinoff, M., 370, 387
Elizur, A., 30, 32, 52, 349, 365
Ellis, M., 387
Emery, G., 58, 78
Endicott, J., 391, 412
Engelman, D. H., 23, 26
Englesson, I., 349, 366
Erbaugh, J., 349, 365
Erdberg, P., 468, 469, 477
Eriksson, E., 343
Erkanli, A., 348, 365
Exner, J. E., 5, 8, 12, 13, 17, 18, 24, 26, 32, 35,
    52, 53, 57, 59, 78, 79, 103, 121, 283, 302,
    392, 412, 429, 439, 442, 463, 467, 468, 469,
    475, 476, 477, 479, 480, 544
Eyde, L., 26

Farley, M., 387
Feigenbaum, K., 415, 439
Feldman, L., 217, 234
Ferruzza, E., 217, 235
Fidler, B., 447, 462
Finch, A. J., 349, 366
Fink, A. D., 31, 52
Finn, S. E., 23, 26
Finney, B. C., 282, 283, 302
First, M. B., 20, 26
Fischer, C. T., 23, 26
Fisher, S., 57, 79, 205, 213
Flett, G. L., 151, 168
Fosberg, I. A., 415, 439, 441, 463
Foster, J. M., 442, 463
Fowler, J. C., 12, 17, 23, 26, 57, 58, 79, 194, 212
Fox, H., 416, 439
Frank, L. K., 479, 544
Frankel, S. A., 23, 26
Franklin, K. W., 392, 412
French, J., 349, 365
Freud, A., 391, 412
Frick, P., 369, 370, 387
Fridkin, K., 31, 53
Friedman, G., 217, 234
Frost, R. O., 151, 168
Frueh, B. C., 429, 439
Fukui, K., 213
Fukui, Y., 213

Gacono, C. B., 283, 285, 302, 370, 387
Galina, H., 31, 52
Galliani, I., 193, 213

Gallucci, N. T., 392, 412
Ganellen, R. J., 418, 428, 430, 439
Gardner, R., 241, 255
Garron, D. C., 33, 52 , 325, 343
Garssen, B., 82, 99
Gellens, H. K., 194, 213
Gibbon, M., 20, 26
Gibby, R. G., 415, 439
Gill, H., 241, 255
Gill, M. M., 20, 26, 30, 33, 52, 82, 99, 103, 121
Golding, E. R., 21, 26
Goldman, G. D., 239, 255
Gordon, M., 240, 255
Gordon, R. A., 349, 365, 393, 411
Gorlitz, P., 217, 234
Gottheil, E., 194, 213
Gough, H. G., 418, 439, 447, 463
Graham, J. R., 239, 255, 284, 301, 325, 343
Grant, M. Q., 480, 545
Grayson, H. M., 480, 544
Greene, R. L., 342, 343, 441, 463
Greenwald, D. F., 59, 79
Greenway, A. P., 59, 79
Greenway, P., 33, 52
Grossman, L. S., 285, 302, 418, 439
Gruber, C. P., 5, 17, 393, 412
Gruden, D., 58, 79
Gyoerkoe, K. L., 285

Hafner, H., 391, 412
Haller, N., 349, 366
Hamann, M. S., 83, 99
Hammond, K. R., 193, 213
Han, K., 447, 462
Handler, L., 194, 217, 218, 234
Haroian, J., 468, 477
Harris, M. J. 418, 439
Harrison, K. S., 304, 322
Hartmann, E., 58, 59, 79
Havel, J. A., 151, 168
Hayakawa, S., 213
Haywood, T. W., 418, 439
Haznedar, M., 412
Healy, B. J., 34, 53
Heath, D. H., 151, 168
Heise, M. R. 126, 147
Henry, W. P., 193, 212, 259, 277
Hertz, M. R., 3, 57, 79
Hewitt, P. L., 151, 168
Hilsenroth, M. J., 5, 12, 17, 18, 23, 26, 57, 58,
    79, 194, 195, 212, 213, 283, 284, 301, 393,
    412
Hochberg, J., 480, 544

Hofman, K. 240, 255
Holdwick, D. J., 12, 17, 23, 26, 57, 79, 195, 213
Holland, M., 31, 53
Holt, R. R., 19, 26, 30, 52, 151, 168, 283, 302
Holzman, P., 391, 412
Horner, M. S., 194, 213
Howell, R. J., 442, 463
Hughes, T., 369, 387
Humphrey, L. L., 217, 234
Huprich, S. K., 285, 302
Hutt, M., 415, 439
Hyams, J. S., 33, 52
Hyler, S. E., 83, 99
Hynan, L. S., 240, 255
Hyyppä, M. T., 168

Ihanus, J., 33, 52
Ives, V., 480, 545

Jackson, R. L., 304, 322
Jansak, D., 5, 18, 35, 53
Jenson, W., 387
Jeste, D. V., 103, 121
Johnson, J., 31, 52
Johnston, M., 391, 412
Jones, N. F., 391, 411
Jorgensen, K., 59, 79
Jost, H., 479, 543

Kaemmer, B., 284, 301
Kahn, M., 416, 439
Kamphaus, R. W., 5, 17, 393, 412
Kaser-Boyd, N., 173, 190
Katz, M., 24, 26
Kay, G. G., 26
Keane, T. M., 429, 439
Keeler, G., 348, 365
Kerlin, K., 370, 387
Khouri, S., 59, 79
Kinder, B. N., 417, 429, 439
King, N. J., 348, 366
Kleiger, J. H., 103, 121
Klett, C. J., 26
Klopfer, B., 3, 19, 20, 26, 30, 52
Klopfer, W. G., 26, 30, 52
Knauss, J., 193, 213
Knowles, E. S., 5, 18, 393, 412
Kobayashi, T., 193, 213
Koga, E., 213
Kotkov, B., 193, 213
Kovacs, M., 350, 365
Kraaimaat, F., 82, 99
Krall, V., 33, 52

Krauss, R. F., 325, 343
Krishnamurthy, R., 350, 365
Kronholm, E., 168
Kula, M. L., 59, 78

Labott, S. M., 126, 127, 128, 140, 145, 147
Lachar, D., 5, 17, 393, 412
Lahart, C., 151, 168
Lang, E., 57, 79
Leavitt, F., 33, 52, 126, 127, 145, 147, 325, 343
Lerner, H., 34, 52
Lesswing, N. J., 193, 213
Levander, S., 171, 172, 190
Levine, M., 240, 255
Levy, S., 171, 190
Lilienfeld, S., 370, 387
Lipovsky, J. A., 349, 350, 365
Litwin, D., 241, 255
Lochman, J., 370, 387
Loewenstein, R. J., 126, 147
Loney, B., 370, 387
Lopes, E. A., 168
Lorr, M., 24, 26
Loveland, N., 217, 235
Lundwall, L., 193, 213
Lyerly, S., 24, 26
Lynn, S. J., 127, 147

Madero, J. N., 392, 412
Magni, G., 217, 235
Marten, P., 151, 168
Martin, L. S., 12, 17
Martin, M., 391, 412
Martin, M. A., 438, 439
Masling, J., 285, 302
Mason, B. J., 12, 17, 392, 412
Mattlar, C.-E., 151, 168, 343
Mavissakalian, M., 83, 99
Mayman, M., 34, 52
McAlister, E., 480, 544
McConaughy, S. H., 348, 365
McConville, D., 371, 387
McCown, W., 31, 52
McDaniel, P. S., 283, 301
McDougall, A., 172, 190
McGlashan, T., 171, 190
McNair, D., 26
Meadow, A., 193, 213
Meer, B., 479, 481, 544
Meisner, S., 428, 429, 438, 439
Melnick, B., 240, 255
Meloy, J. R., 283, 285, 302, 370, 387
Meltzoff, J., 239, 241, 255

Mendelson, M., 349, 365
Meyer, G. J., 5, 12, 17, 18, 22, 23, 26, 34, 35, 52, 53, 59, 79, 190, 476, 477
Meyer, R. G., 415, 439
Mihura, J. L., 283, 284, 302
Miller, T. W., 325, 343
Milne, L. C., 33, 52
Milton, E. O., 415, 439
Minassian, A., 172, 190
Mittman, B. L., 416, 417, 428, 439
Mock, J., 249, 365
Modestin, J., 58, 79
Moreland, K. L., 26
Morey, L. C., 284, 302
Morse, S. J., 305, 321
Mortimer, R. L., 21, 26
Murillo, L. G., 13, 17, 24, 26
Murray, H. A., 194, 213
Mustillo, S., 348, 365

Nakamura, N., 217, 235
Nakamura, S., 217, 235
Nathan-Montano, E., 283, 284, 302
Netter, B. E., 417, 439
Neves, A. C., 168
Nichols, D. S., 441, 463
Nicholson, R. R., 447, 462
Nowotny, B., 391, 412
Nygren, M., 258, 259, 277

Oberholzer, E., 30, 52
Oleichik, I. V., 59, 79
Ollendick, T. H., 348, 366
Olympia, D., 369, 387
Ono, I., 213

Padawer, J. R., 12, 17, 23, 26, 57, 79, 194
Pantle, M. L., 240, 255
Pardini, D., 370, 387
Parente, F. J., 391, 411
Parker, J. D., 33, 34, 52, 53
Paulhus, D. L., 441, 463
Perfetto, G. A., 193, 212, 259, 277
Perlman, J. A., 480, 544
Perry, G. G., 417, 439
Perry, W., 5, 17, 18, 34, 35, 52, 53, 103, 121, 172, 173, 190
Peterson, C. A., 480, 544
Petterson, H., 387
Phares, E. J., 442, 463
Piers, C., 12, 17, 23, 26, 57, 58, 79
Piotrowski, Z. A., 3, 19, 26, 31, 52, 151, 168
Porcelli, P., 34, 52

Pottharst, K., 415, 439
Putnam, F. W., 127, 147
Puukaa, P., 343

Quay, H. C., 348, 366

Rabie, L., 285, 302
Radovanovic, H., 447, 462
Ranzoni, J. H., 480, 545
Rapaport, D., 3, 20, 26, 30, 33, 52, 82, 99, 103, 121
Rector, N., 46
Remschmidt, H., 391, 412
Reshmi, P., 412
Reynolds, C. R., 5, 17, 393, 412
Rider, S. O., 83, 99
Rierdan, J., 57, 79
Rijken, H., 82, 99
Ritsher, J. B., 5, 17, 59, 79
Ritzler, B. A., 57, 78
Rock, M. R., 151, 168
Roe, A. V., 463
Rogers, L. S., 193, 213
Rogers, R., 304, 305, 322, 438, 439, 462
Roman, M., 217, 234
Rorschach, H., 19, 26, 30, 52, 239, 255, 480
Rose, D., 283, 302
Rosenberg, N. K., 82, 99
Rosenblate, R., 151, 168
Ros i Plana, M., 429, 439
Ross, C. A., 147
Rozensky, R. H., 31, 53
Rubin, N. I., 20, 21, 26
Rush, A. J., 58, 78
Rybakow, T., 19, 26
Rytöhonka, R., 168

Sachs, R. G., 126, 147
Saether, L., 58, 79
Sandberg, D. A., 127, 147
Santasalo, H., 168
Sassu, K., 370, 387
Schafer, R., 3, 20, 26, 30, 33, 52, 82, 99, 103, 121
Schilling, K. M., 480, 545
Schneider, R. B., 285, 302
Schulz, E., 391, 412
Schuyler, W., 467, 477
Scroppo, J. C., 127, 128, 145, 147
Seamons, D. T., 442, 443, 463
Seeman, M., 462
Segal, D., 371, 387
Sewell, K. W., 304, 322, 438, 439

Shaffer, T. W., 468, 469, 470, 477
Shalit, B., 31, 53
Shavzin, A. R., 415, 439, 441, 462
Shaw, B. F., 58, 78
Sifneos, P. E., 33, 53, 325, 343
Silberg, J. L., 391, 411
Silva, D., 480, 545
Silva, L., 168
Silva, T. A., 168
Silverthorn, P., 370, 387
Singer, J. L., 239, 240, 255
Singer, M., 217, 235
Siris, S., 171, 190
Skelton, M. D., 392, 412
Slap-Shelton, L., 194, 212
Slivko-Kolchik, E. B., 59, 79
Smith, S. R., 5, 18, 393, 412
Smith, W. H., 21, 26
Spielberger, C. D., 32, 52
Spielmann, D., 58, 79
Spigelman, A., 349, 366
Spigelman, G., 349, 366
Spitzer, R. L., 20, 26, 83, 99, 391, 412
Spivack, G., 240, 255
Spohn, H. E., 239, 240, 255
Sprock, J., 172, 190
St. Laurent, C. M., 59, 78
Steiner, M. E., 151, 168
Stewart, L. M., 442, 463
Stewart, T. D., 21, 26
Stiles, P. G., 31, 53
Stricker, G., 34, 53
Strupp, H. H., 193, 212, 213, 259, 277
Szajnberg, N. M., 33, 52

Taylor, G. J., 33, 34, 52, 53
Taylor, K. L., 429, 439
Tellegen, A., 284, 301
Thackrey, M., 193, 213
Thomas, E. A., 392, 412
Thornton, C. C., 194, 213
Tillbrook, C. E., 322
Toman, K. M., 194, 213
Tonsager, M. E., 23, 26
Torem, M., 126, 147
Tovian, S. M., 31, 53
Treem, W. P., 33, 52

Urist, J., 194, 213, 283, 302

Viglione, D. J., 5, 17, 18, 34, 35, 52, 53, 103, 121, 172, 173, 188, 190, 349, 350, 366, 417, 439

Vincent, N. K., 151, 168
Vitacco, M. J., 438, 439
VonLackum, W. J., 479, 543

Wagner, C. F., 147
Wagner, E. E., 126, 127, 145, 147
Walker, J. R., 151, 168
Wallach, H. R., 128, 147
Wang, C. E., 58, 79
Ward, C., 349, 365
Warnke, A., 391, 412
Wasyliw, O. E., 285, 302, 418, 439

Weatherill, R., 194, 212
Weinberger, J. L., 127, 147
Weiner, I. B., 13, 18, 467, 477, 480, 545
Werbart, A., 171, 172, 190
Werner, S., 343
Whipple, G. M., 19, 26
Whitaker, L. C., 391, 412
Wight, B., 240, 255
Willi, J., 217, 235
Williams, J. B., 20, 26
Wylie, J., 12, 17, 57
Wynne, L., 217, 235

Subject Index

Adjusted D Score (*AdjD*), 13, 32–33
  minus values, 40, 69, 223, 290, 377, 399
Adjusted experienced stimulation (*Adj es*) high
  values, 40, 336
Affect:
  Case 1, 45–46
  Case 2, 71–72
  Case 3, 92–93
  Case 4, 108–109
  Case 5, 134–136
  Case 6, 164–165
  Case 7, 179–180
  Case 8, 206–207
  Case 9, 227–228
  Case 10, 249–250
  Case 11, 270–272
  Case 12, 295–296
  Case 13, 315–316
  Case 14, 336–337
  Case 15, 358–360
  Case 16, 378–379
  Case 17, 405–406
Affective ratio (*Afr*), low values, 33, 71–72, 92,
  109, 135, 296, 316
Aggression, 300
  assessment of, 282–285, 369–371
Alexithymia, 33–34, 325
Ambitent. *See* Response styles
Anatomy content, 33
Antisocial behavior, assessment of, 369–371
Anxiety:
  assessment of, 30–33, 349–350
  state versus trait, 32
Assessment:
  integrating findings, 24–25
  psychological, 21–25
Avoidant. *See* Response styles

Beck Depression Inventory (*BDI*), 58–59,
  349
Blends, frequency data, 485, 487–488

Children and adolescents:
  depression, 349–350
  literature/studies, 5, 369–371, 391–393
Clusters:
  analyses within, 15–17
  organizing, 6–7
  search order, 8
Cocaine addiction, assessment of, 193
Cognition, 294–295
  impairment, 363–364, 392
Color-shading blends:
  literature/studies, 57–58
  related to suicide risk, 57–58
Competency to stand trial, assessment of,
  304–305
Conduct disorders. See Antisocial behavior
Consensus protocols, 217–218
Consultation, 22, 24–25
Contents, frequency data, 522–543
Controls:
  Case 1, 40
  Case 2, 69
  Case 3, 88
  Case 4, 109–110
  Case 5, 136
  Case 6, 160–161
  Case 7, 180–181
  Case 8, 201
  Case 9, 223
  Case 10, 246
  Case 11, 269–270
  Case 12, 290
  Case 13, 314–315

Controls *(Continued)*
  Case 14, 335–336
  Case 15, 357–358
  Case 16, 377
  Case 17, 399
Coping Deficit Index *(CDI)*, 12–13, 35
  positive values, 40–41, 71, 223–224, 246–247,
    355, 357, 359, 438
Coping styles. *See* Response styles
Couples, assessment of, 217–218
Criminal responsibility, assessment of, 305
Custody evaluations, 441–453

D Score, 32–33
  minus, 70, 136–137, 202, 399–400
DSM-IV, 82, 125, 172, 283–284, 326, 369
Delusional thinking, assessment of, 103
Depression:
  assessment of, 58–59
  children and adolescents, 349–350
  endogenous versus reactive, 58, 72
  malingering, 428–430
  variables related to, 58–59
Depression Index *(DEPI)*, 12
  literature/studies, 12, 59, 325, 349–350
  positive values, 65, 71, 108, 134, 315, 338, 438
Determinants, frequency data, 499–521
Developmental quality *(DQ)*, frequency data,
  484–485, 488–498
Dissociation:
  assessment of, 126–128
  disorders, 125, 145
  malingering, 125, 128

Egocentricity Index (3r+(2)/R):
  high values, 42, 66–67, 138, 265
  low values, 296, 317, 356, 379, 400, 407
Ego Impairment Index *(EII)*, 172–173
Epilogues:
  Case 1, 53
  Case 2, 78
  Case 3, 98–99
  Case 4, 121
  Case 5, 146–147
  Case 6, 167–168
  Case 7, 189–190
  Case 8, 212
  Case 9, 234
  Case 10, 255
  Case 11, 276–277
  Case 12, 301
  Case 13, 321

  Case 14, 343
  Case 15, 365
  Case 16, 387
  Case 17, 411
  Case 18, 428
  Case 19, 438
  Case 20, 453
  Case 21, 462
Erlebnistypus style *(EB)*, 14–15
Experience base *(eb)*, higher right side values,
  45, 71, 336, 359, 405
Extratensive. *See* Response styles

Form quality *(FQ)*, frequency data, 486–498
Formulation and relevant literature, 21–22
  Case 1, 30–33
  Case 2, 57–59
  Case 3, 82–83
  Case 4, 103
  Case 5, 125
  Case 6, 150
  Case 7, 171
  Case 8, 192–193
  Case 9, 216–217
  Case 10, 239
  Case 11, 258
  Case 12, 282
  Case 13, 304
  Case 14, 324–325
  Case 15, 348–349
  Case 16, 369
  Case 17, 390–391
Frequency data, 479–544
  blends, 488–498
  Card I, 488, 502–503, 524–525
  Card II, 489, 504–505, 526–527
  Card III, 490, 506–507, 528–529
  Card IV, 491, 508–509, 530–531
  Card V, 492, 510–511, 532–533
  Card VI, 493, 512–513, 534–535
  Card VII, 494, 514–515, 536–537
  Card VIII, 495, 516–517, 538–539
  Card IX, 496, 518–519, 540–541
  Card X, 498, 520–521, 542–543
  contents, 522–543
  determinants, 499–521
  developmental quality, 484–485, 488–498
  form quality, 486–498
  location selections, 482–483
  summary, 544

Good Human Representation *(GHR)*, 5–6

Human Representational Variable (*HRV*):
  good (*GHR*), 5–6
  literature/studies, 5–6, 34–35
  poor (*PHR*), 5–6
Hypervigilance Index (*HVI*), 103
  positive, 15, 65–67, 310, 313, 317–319, 399, 401

Ideation:
  Case 1, 48–49
  Case 2, 74–75
  Case 3, 89–90
  Case 4, 116–118
  Case 5, 143–144
  Case 6, 161–162
  Case 7, 187–188
  Case 8, 209–210
  Case 9, 230–231
  Case 10, 252
  Case 11, 272–273
  Case 12, 291–292
  Case 13, 312–314
  Case 14, 339–341
  Case 15, 362–363
  Case 16, 384–385
  Case 17, 401–402
Illustrations:
  Case 1: (stress management), 29–51
  Case 2: (depression/suicide risk), 55–78
  Case 3: (panic attacks), 81–99
  Case 4: (delusional thinking), 101–120
  Case 5: (dissociation), 123–147
  Case 6: (anxiety and sleep problems), 149–168
  Case 7: (acute psychotic episode), 169–190
  Case 8: (substance abuse), 191–212
  Case 9: (substance abuse), 215–234
  Case 10: (impulse control), 237–255
  Case 11: (interpersonal problems), 257–277
  Case 12: (danger to self/others), 281–301
  Case 13: (sanity and competency), 303–321
  Case 14: (personal injury litigation), 323–343
  Case 15: (academic performance), 347–365
  Case 16: (aggressiveness), 367–387
  Case 17: (adolescent drug overdose), 389–411
  Case 18: (psychosis in homicide case), 418–428
  Case 19: (disability claim), 430–438
  Case 20: (custody evaluation), 444–453
  Case 21: (work-related question), 453–462
Impulse control, assessment of, 239–241
Interpersonal competence, assessment of, 34–35

Interpersonal perception:
  Case 1, 41
  Case 2, 65–66
  Case 3, 95–96
  Case 4, 113–114
  Case 5, 140–141
  Case 6, 159–160
  Case 7, 184–185
  Case 8, 204–206
  Case 9, 224–225
  Case 10, 247
  Case 11, 268–269
  Case 12, 299
  Case 13, 318–320
  Case 14, 334–335
  Case 15, 355–356
  Case 16, 381–382
  Case 17, 409
Interpretation:
  search sequence, 10–11
  strategies, 8–11
Introversive. *See* Response styles
Isolation Index, high values, 41, 247, 409

Key variables, 9–11. *See also* Suicide Constellation

Lambda, 13–14
  high values, 33, 246, 249, 259, 370, 438
  low values, 310
Literature review, 21–23
  aggression, 282–285, 369–371
  antisocial behavior, 369–371
  anxiety, 30–33, 349–350
  cocaine addiction, 193
  competency to stand trial, 304–305
  criminal responsibility, 305
  couples, 217–218
  delusional thinking, 103
  depression, 58–59, 349–350, 428–430
  dissociation, 126–128
  impulse control, 239–241
  malingering, 415–418, 428–430, 441–444
  pain syndromes, 325–326
  panic disorders, 82–83
  positive simulation, 441–444
  psychodynamic capacity, 258–259
  psychotic disorganization, 172–173
  recovery style, 171–172
  sexual acting out, 285
  sleep difficulties, 151
  stress, 30–33

Literature review *(Continued)*
 suicide risk, 57–58
 thought disorders, 391–393
 treatment capacity, 193–195
 vocational adaptation, 151
Location selections, frequency data, 482–483

Malingering:
 assessment of, 415–418, 428–430,
  441–444
 depression, 428–429
 dissociative disorder, 125, 128, 145
 distress or depression, 428–430
 psychosis or schizophrenia, 416–418
Mediation:
 Case 1, 47–48
 Case 2, 73–74
 Case 3, 91
 Case 4, 115–116
 Case 5, 142
 Case 6, 163
 Case 7,186–187
 Case 8, 208–209
 Case 9, 229–230
 Case 10, 251–252
 Case 11, 274–275
 Case 12, 294
 Case 13, 311–312
 Case 14, 338–339
 Case 15, 361–362
 Case 16, 383
 Case 17, 404–405
MMPI-2:
 profiles, 239, 342
  Case 18, 425–427
  Case 19, 435–438
  Case 20, 450–453
  Case 21, 459–462
 studies, 23, 59, 284–285, 305, 325–326,
  349–350, 418, 429–430, 443–444
Movement:
 high *FM* values, 40, 336, 377, 384
 inanimate (*m*), 30–33
 literature/studies, 31–32, 239–241
Mutuality of Autonomy (*MOA*), 194–195

Narcissism, 42, 138, 144, 165, 202–203,
  210–211, 265–266
Nonpatient sample, 467–469
 collection of, 469–470
 comparisons, 470–476, 479, 481
 conclusions, 476–477

 design, 468
 findings, 470–476
 representativeness, 468–469
 summary, 498

Obsessive style index (*OBS*), positive, 42, 48–49,
  157
Overincorporation. *See* Processing

Pain syndromes, assessment of, 325–326
Panic disorders, assessment of, 82–83
Paranoid. *See* Delusional thinking
Passivity, 15, 44, 50, 96–97, 319, 335, 341
Perceptual-Thinking Index (*PTI*), 4–5, 12
 positive, 310, 428
Personality Assessment Inventory (*PAI*), 284
Pervasive. *See* Response styles
Poor Human Representation (*PHR*), 5–6
Positive simulation, assessment of,
  441–444
Processing:
 Case 1, 47
 Case 2, 72–73
 Case 3, 90–91
 Case 4, 114–115
 Case 5, 141–142
 Case 6, 162–163
 Case 7, 185–186
 Case 8, 207–208
 Case 9, 228–229
 Case 10, 250–251
 Case 11, 273–274
 Case 12, 293
 Case 13, 310–311
 Case 14, 338
 Case 15, 360–361
 Case 16, 382–383
 Case 17, 402–403
 overincorporation, 47, 185–186, 229, 403
 underincorporation, 73, 251
Psychoanalytic Rorschach Profile (*PRP*), 217
Psychodynamic capacity, assessment of,
  258–259
Psychotic disorganization, 314–315
 assessment of, 172–173

Recovery style, assessment of, 171–172
Response styles:
 ambient, 90, 108, 249, 370, 401
 avoidant, 13–14, 251–252
 extratensive, 14–15, 65, 71–72, 171, 179, 201,
  332, 337, 358–359

introversive, 14, 40, 45, 157, 171, 296, 310
  pervasive, 14, 339
Rorschach:
  consultation model, 19–25
  structure, 19
  systems, 3, 19–20
Rorschach Oral Dependency scale (*ROD*), 285

Schizophrenia:
  Index (*SCZI*), 4–5, 391–392
  studies, 103, 173, 239–240, 391–392
Self-destructive behavior. *See* Suicide risk
Self-perception:
  Case 1, 42–45
  Case 2, 66–69
  Case 3, 93–95
  Case 4, 110–113
  Case 5, 137–140
  Case 6, 157–159
  Case 7, 181–184
  Case 8, 202–204
  Case 9, 225–227
  Case 10, 248–249
  Case 11, 265–268
  Case 12, 296–298
  Case 13, 316–318
  Case 14, 332–334
  Case 15, 356–357
  Case 16, 379–381
  Case 17, 406–408
Sexual acting out, assessment of, 285
Shading:
  diffuse (*FY, YF, Y*), 30–33
  literature/studies, 30–32
Sleep difficulties, assessment of, 151
Snow White Syndrome, 231
Somatic issues, assessment of, 33–34
Stress:
  AdjD score, 13
  assessment of, 30–33
  controllable and uncontrollable, 31
  situationally-related;
    Case 2, 70–71
    Case 3, 88–89
    Case 5, 136–137
    Case 8, 201–202
    Case 17, 400
  tolerance, 32
Suicide Constellation (*S-Con*), 12
  and key variables:
    Case 1, 40
    Case 2, 65

Case 3, 88
Case 4, 108
Case 5, 134
Case 6, 157
Case 7, 179
Case 8, 201
Case 9, 223
Case 10, 246
Case 11, 265
Case 12, 290
Case 13, 310
Case 14, 332
Case 15, 355
Case 16, 377
Case 17, 399
  literature/studies, 12, 23, 57–58
  positive values, 65, 135, 438
  related to suicide risk, 57–58
Suicide risk:
  literature/studies, 57–58
  related to color-shading blends, 57–58
  related to S-CON, 57–58
SumC', high values, 40, 223, 270, 336
Summaries:
  Case 1, 49–50
  Case 2, 76–77
  Case 3, 96–97
  Case 4, 118–119
  Case 5, 144–145
  Case 6, 165–166
  Case 7, 188–189
  Case 8, 210–211
  Case 9, 232–233
  Case 10, 253–254
  Case 11, 275–276
  Case 12, 299–300
  Case 13, 320–321
  Case 14, 341–342
  Case 15, 363–364
  Case 16, 385–386
  Case 17, 409–410
  Case 18, 428
  Case 19, 438
  Case 20, 453–454
  Case 21, 463
  frequency data, 544
SumT, high values, 40, 201–202, 270, 336

Tertiary variables, 10–11
Thematic Apperception Test (*TAT*), 194
Thought disorders, assessment of, 391–393
Treatment capacity, assessment of, 193–195

Treatment planning, 24–25
Treatment recommendations:
  Case 1, 50
  Case 2, 77
  Case 3, 97–98
  Case 4, 119–120
  Case 5, 145–146
  Case 6, 166–167
  Case 7, 189
  Case 8, 211–212
  Case 9, 233–234
  Case 10, 254–255
  Case 11, 276
  Case 12, 300–301
  Case 13, 321
  Case 14, 342
  Case 15, 364–365
  Case 16, 386
  Case 17, 410–411

Underincorporation. *See* Processing

Validity, 23, 441
  related to *S-Con*, 57–58
  studies, 31, 57–58, 173
Variables:
  new, 4–6
  summary, 32
Vocational adaptation, assessment of, 151

WDA%, 4
  high values, 74, 163, 208, 383
  low values, 311, 361
WSum6, high values, 117, 291, 313–314,
    384, 401

XA%, 4
  high values, 74, 163, 208, 383
  low values, 311, 361
X-%, high values, 361–362, 404